BANK AND CUSTOMER LAW IN CANADA

Other books in the *Essentials of Canadian Law Series*

Statutory Interpretation
Intellectual Property Law
Income Tax Law
Immigration Law
International Trade Law
Family Law
Copyright Law
Remedies: The Law of Damages
Individual Employment Law
The Law of Equitable Remedies
Administrative Law
Ethics and Canadian Criminal Law
Public International Law
Environmental Law 2/e
Securities Law
Youth Criminal Justice Law
Computer Law 2/e
The Law of Partnerships and Corporations 2/e
The Law of Torts 2/e
Media Law 2/e
Maritime Law
Criminal Law 3/e
Insurance Law
International Human Rights Law
Legal Research and Writing 2/e
The Law of Evidence 4/e
The Law of Trusts 2/e
Franchise Law
The Charter of Rights and Freedoms 3/e
Personal Property Security Law
The Law of Contracts
Pension Law
Constitutional Law 3/e
Legal Ethics and Professional Responsibility 2/e
Refugee Law
Mergers, Acquisitions, and Other Changes of Corporate Control

ESSENTIALS OF CANADIAN LAW

BANK AND CUSTOMER LAW IN CANADA

M.H. OGILVIE

LSM, B.A., LL.B., M.A., D.Phil., D.D., F.R.S.C.
Of the Bars of Ontario and Nova Scotia
Chancellor's Professor and Professor of Law,
Carleton University

Bank and Customer Law in Canada
© Irwin Law Inc., 2007

All rights reserved. No part of this publication may be reproduced, stored in a retrieval system, or transmitted, in any form or by any means, without the prior written permission of the publisher or, in the case of photocopying or other reprographic copying, a licence from Access Copyright (Canadian Copyright Licensing Agency), 1 Yonge Street, Suite 800, Toronto, ON, M5E 1E5.

Published in 2007 by

Irwin Law Inc.
14 Duncan Street
Suite 206
Toronto, ON
M5H 3G8

www.irwinlaw.com

ISBN-13: 978-1-55221-136-6

Library and Archives Canada Cataloguing in Publication

Ogilvie, M. H.
    Bank and customer law in Canada / M.H. Ogilvie.

(Essentials of Canadian law)
Includes bibliographical references and index.
ISBN 978-1-55221-136-6

1. Banking law—Canada. I. Title. II. Series.

KE999.O448 2007   346.71'082   C2007-902516-1
KF974.O448 2007

The publisher acknowledges the financial support of the Government of Canada through the Book Publishing Industry Development Program (BPIDP) for its publishing activities.

We acknowledge the assistance of the OMDC Book Fund, an initiative of Ontario Media Development Corporation.

Printed and bound in Canada.

1 2 3 4 5   11 10 09 08 07

SUMMARY TABLE OF CONTENTS

PREFACE *xv*

CHAPTER 1: Banks and Banking Defined *1*

CHAPTER 2: The Domestic and International Framework of Canadian Banking Law *24*

CHAPTER 3: The Regulation of Banks and Banking in Canada *37*

CHAPTER 4: Banks as Business Corporations *83*

CHAPTER 5: Banking Business *148*

CHAPTER 6: Bank and Customer Relationships *175*

CHAPTER 7: Bank Accounts *226*

CHAPTER 8: Bank Account Operation *253*

CHAPTER 9: Electronic Funds Transfer Systems *315*

CHAPTER 10: Electronic Payments *345*

CHAPTER 11: Credit Cards and Other Payment Mechanisms *370*

CHAPTER 12: Safekeeping *395*

CHAPTER 13: Bank and Customer Dispute Resolution *402*

TABLE OF CASES *413*

INDEX *449*

ABOUT THE AUTHOR *479*

DETAILED TABLE OF CONTENTS

PREFACE xv

CHAPTER 1:
BANKS AND BANKING DEFINED 1

A. Introduction 1
B. Jurisdiction over Banking 6
C. Defining Banking 10
    1) Defining Banking from an Institutional Perspective 11
    2) Defining Banking from an Activities Perspective 14
D. Defining Banking at Common Law 19

CHAPTER 2:
THE DOMESTIC AND INTERNATIONAL FRAMEWORK OF CANADIAN BANKING LAW 24

A. Introduction 24
B. Application to the "Chartered" Banks 25
C. Interpretation of the *Bank Act* 26
D. *Bank Act* Reform 27
E. Financial Institutions Regulation Generally 32
F. International Regulation 34

CHAPTER 3:
THE REGULATION OF BANKS AND BANKING IN CANADA 37

A. Introduction 37
B. Bank of Canada 38
C. Office of the Superintendent of Financial Institutions 44
D. The Canadian Bankers Association 52
E. The Canadian Payments Association 53
F. The Canada Deposit Insurance Corporation 58
G. The Financial Consumer Agency of Canada 69
H. The Ombudsman for Banking Services and Investments 74
I. The Financial Transactions and Reports Analysis Centre of Canada 78
J. Conclusion 81

CHAPTER 4:
BANKS AS BUSINESS CORPORATIONS 83

A. Introduction 83
B. Incorporation 84
C. Status and Powers 87
D. Starting Business 90
E. Directors and Officers 91
   1) Role 91
   2) Statutory Requirements for Directors 92
   3) Statutory Powers and Activities of Directors 94
   4) Directors' Standards of Care 98
   5) Directors' Liabilities and Indemnification 101
F. Shareholders 103
   1) Shareholders' Meetings 103
   2) Access to Records 109
   3) Shareholders' Auditors 111
   4) Pre-emptive Rights 114
   5) Approval and Remedial Rights 115
   6) Shareholder Liability 117
G. Capital Structure 117
   1) Equity Financing 118

Detailed Table of Contents   ix

    2) Debt Financing *122*
    3) Prospectus Requirements *124*
    4) Insider Trading *125*

H. Financial Statements *126*

I. Amendments, Amalgamation, and Transferring Business *127*

J. Ownership *128*

K. Bank Holding Companies *132*

L. Foreign Banks *136*

M. Liquidation and Dissolution *139*

N. Conclusion *146*

CHAPTER 5:
BANKING BUSINESS *148*

A. Introduction *148*

B. Permitted Business *150*
    1) Operating Branches *150*
    2) Borrowing and Dealing in Money *152*
    3) Lending *152*
    4) Providing Guarantees *155*
    5) Acting as a Financial Agent *155*
    6) Selling Tax Deferral Plans *156*
    7) Providing Investment Counselling and Portfolio Management *156*
    8) Providing Payment, Credit, and Charge Cards *156*
    9) Dealing with Real Property *156*
    10) Providing Information Processing Services *157*
    11) Promoting Merchandise and Services *157*
    12) Keeping Property *157*
    13) Acting as Receiver or Liquidator *157*
    14) Networking *158*
    15) Lending to Receivers or Liquidators *158*
    16) Selling Securities *158*
    17) Lending on Hydrocarbons and Minerals *158*

C. "Special Security" *160*

D. Permitted Investments *165*

E. Permitted Self-Dealing *167*

F. Prohibited Business *169*
    1) Dealing in Goods, Wares, and Merchandise *170*
    2) Fiduciary Activities *170*

- 3) Taking Deposits 171
- 4) Dealing in Securities 171
- 5) Dealing in Insurance 172
- 6) Leasing 173
- 7) Creating Security Interests 173
- 8) Receivers 174
- 9) Entering Partnerships 174

G. Conclusion 174

CHAPTER 6:
BANK AND CUSTOMER RELATIONSHIPS 175

A. Introduction 175

B. The "Customer" 176

C. The Bank and Customer Relationship 178

D. The Contract 180
- 1) Statutory Requirements 181
- 2) Express Terms 184
- 3) Implied Terms 186

E. Contract Modification 188

F. Proper Law of the Contract 190

G. Termination of the Contract 190

H. The Fiduciary and Tortious Relationships 193
- 1) Fiduciary Obligation 194
- 2) Undue Influence 197
- 3) Unconscionability 205
- 4) Unequal Bargaining Power 207
- 5) Misrepresentation 207
- 6) Fiduciary and Tortious Relationships in Banking Practice 209
  - a) Giving Advice 210
  - b) Taking Security 212
  - c) Giving References 214

I. Constructive Trustee 217

J. Duty to Life Insure Mortgages 224

K. Conclusion 225

CHAPTER 7:
BANK ACCOUNTS 226

A. Introduction 226

B. The Legal Nature of a Bank Deposit 227

C. Overdrafts 230

D. Limitation of Actions 232

E. Deposit Receipts and Passbooks 233

F. Joint Accounts 235

G. Trust Accounts 242

H. Garnishment of Deposits 244

I. Appropriation of Payments 244

J. Set-off and Account Combination 247

K. Bankers' Liens 251

L. Conclusion 252

CHAPTER 8:
BANK ACCOUNT OPERATION 253

A. Introduction 253

B. General Background 255

C. The Paying Bank 257

   1) Requirements for Payment 257
   2) Postdated Cheques 264
   3) Certified Cheques 265
   4) Wrongful Dishonour of Cheques 271
   5) Termination of the Duty to Pay and Countermand of Cheques 273
   6) Wrongful Payment by a Paying Bank 279
   7) Recovery of Money Paid by Mistake 284

D. The Collecting Bank 288

   1) Requirements for Collection 288
   2) Statutory Protection of the Collecting Bank 292

E. Rendering Statements of Account 296

F. Maintaining Confidentiality 303

   1) General Considerations 303
   2) *Tournier* 305
   3) *Tournier* Qualifications 306

G. Conclusion 314

CHAPTER 9:
ELECTRONIC FUNDS TRANSFER SYSTEMS 315

A. Introduction 315
B. The Regulation of Payment Systems 317
C. The Automated Clearing and Settlement System (ACSS) 320
D. The United States Bulk Exchange System (USBES) 329
E. The Large Value Transfer System (LVTS) 330
F. Legal Significance for Customers 333
G. International Clearing and Settlement 334
H. The Legal Nature of Electronic Funds Transfer (EFT) 337
I. Conclusion 344

CHAPTER 10:
ELECTRONIC PAYMENTS 345

A. Introduction 345
B. The Evolution of Plastic Cards 346
C. Debit Cards 350
D. Electronic Money 356
E. Prepaid Cards 361
F. Third Party Payment Systems (3PPS) 363
G. Conclusion 369

CHAPTER 11:
CREDIT CARDS AND OTHER PAYMENT MECHANISMS 370

A. Introduction 370
B. Credit Cards 371
   1) Legal Nature 371
   2) The Cardissuer and Cardholder Agreement 375
   3) The Cardissuer and Merchant Agreement 380
   4) The Cardholder and Merchant Agreement 381
   5) Clearing and Settlement 382
C. Travellers' Cheques 383
D. Money Orders 388

E. Bankers' Drafts 390
F. Letters of Credit 392
G. Conclusion 393

CHAPTER 12:
SAFEKEEPING 395

A. Introduction 395
B. Safekeeping 396
C. Safety Deposit Boxes 398
D. Night Safe Depositories 400
E. Conclusion 401

CHAPTER 13:
BANK AND CUSTOMER DISPUTE RESOLUTION 402

A. Introduction 402
B. The Evolution of ADR in the Banking Sector 403
C. The Ombudsman for Banking Services and Investments (OBSI) 406
D. How OBSI Works 407
E. Conclusion 411

TABLE OF CASES 413

INDEX 449

ABOUT THE AUTHOR 479

PREFACE

When Jeffrey Miller of Irwin Law suggested that it was possible to write a book of not more than 400 pages on banking law for the Essentials of Canadian Law series, I was skeptical. After all, big institutions and big bodies of law require big books, and typical banking law texts are closer to 1,000 pages, if not considerably more. However, here is that little book about banking law of about 400 pages.

To achieve this target, I kept continuously in mind the introductory student and the consumer for whom this book was written. The needs of this audience explain the topics chosen for inclusion and those omitted, as well as the degree of detail in which the topics included are discussed. Certain parts of the *Bank Act*, including the 2007 amendments, for example, are included in some detail, in particular, those setting out the corporate governance structure for banks and the types of activities in which banks are permitted to engage in Canada. Considerably less is included about foreign banks, bank subsidiaries, and bank holding companies, partly because much of the Act relating to these mirrors the parts relating to banks, but also because they are of considerably less relevance to a consumer's everyday banking concerns. Again, a number of the more esoteric regulations and guidelines are also omitted since their content is largely of interest to bank regulators. On the common law side, the focus is on bank account operation, including paper and electronic payment orders, but virtually nothing is said about letters of credit, international banking and trade law, or complex lending and securitization issues.

A special challenge posed for any writer on banking law today is the fast-changing nature of electronic banking and the challenges posed by non-bank third party payment providers to traditional banking and banks. Essentially, there is no law and no regulation to discuss, so that

I was reduced to describing some of the current practices in the full knowledge that this will be quickly outdated. However, I believe there is enough information provided here, especially directions to relevant websites, for the interested reader to use this book as a base from which to update as time goes on.

I have incurred several debts in the preparation of this volume. I am grateful to the Law Foundation of the Canadian Bar Association for financial support. I am grateful to my student, Carolyn Popp, for research assistance, and to my secretary at Carleton University, Barb Higgins, for ensuring that the manuscript is publisher-ready. Most of all, however, I am deeply grateful to Marion Armstrong, who word processed the entire manuscript from my virtually illegible handwriting with speed, accuracy and grace. I am truly grateful.

Finally, although he played no role in the production of this volume, my husband David Conn provided cheerful companionship throughout and my dedication of this little book to him reflects my eternal thankfulness to him.

M.H. Ogilvie
12 August 2006
Ottawa

For David

CHAPTER 1

BANKS AND BANKING DEFINED

A. INTRODUCTION

Banking is a method of financial intermediation whereby surplus funds are transmitted from savers to borrowers, and banks are the institutions which effect that transmission.[1] The funds that banks lend are funds deposited by customers whose reward, if any, is the amount of interest promised to them by the bank for their deposits. Historically, the primary economic function of banks in any economy is to hold funds deposited with them, to manage those funds on behalf of the depositors, and to make the funds available at a cost to borrowers, that is, to be the primary source for money in an economy. Lending at a profit provides banks with the incentive to engage in deposit taking in the first place and compensates for the cost of safekeeping savers' deposits and permitting access to them through payment instructions such as cheques or electronic funds transfers.

Although banks are the oldest financial intermediaries in the West,[2] in the past two centuries, other financial institutions, such as

---

1   This definition is adapted from Benjamin Geva, *Bank Collections and Payment Transactions: Comparative Study of Legal Aspects* (Oxford: Oxford University Press, 2001) at 7.
2   See generally E. Victor Morgan, *The Theory and Practice of Central Banking 1797–1913* (New York: A.M. Kelley, 1943); James Milnes Holden, *The History of Negotiable Instruments in English Law* (London: Athlone Press, 1995); George

trust and loan companies, cooperatives, and credit unions, have offered this same financial service to savers, in addition to their respective and unique roles in the economy. Many consumers commonly refer to these institutions as "banks" and, broadly speaking, when they are carrying on deposit-taking activities, they are subject to a legal and regulatory framework similar to that of banks, as well as to the laws and regulations relating to their distinctive activities. But as discussed later,[3] they are not, legally speaking, banks, and therefore they are largely excluded from the scope of this text, which is about banks and banking law.

Deposit taking and lending, together with payment instruction facilities to effect fund transmission, are at the heart of banking, and their interrelationship is the reason for the economic efficiencies in banking. Banks retain only adequate reserves to meet reasonable customer cash withdrawal requirements and they lend the rest, thereby reducing safekeeping costs for customers and increasing profits from borrowers. By developing interbank transfer facilities with other banks, it becomes possible to transfer funds throughout the economy by transferring credit, thereby reducing the need for interbank cash deliveries. Multilateral clearing and settlement among banks is made more efficient through final settlement among bank accounts kept by each bank at a central bank, such as the Bank of Canada, so that the physical transfer of money is unnecessary; both bank notes and deposits held at the central bank are of equal value and are obligations of the central bank. These features are found in the early modern precursors of the

---

Tucker, *The Theory of Money and Banks Investigated* (New York: A.M. Kelley, 1964); Richard D. Richards, *The Early History of Banking in England* (New York: A.M. Kelley, 1965); Raymond Bogaert, *Les origines antiques de la banque de dépôt* (Leyde: A.W. Sijthoff, 1966); Edward Nevin and E.M. Davis, *The London Clearing Banks* (London: Elek Books, 1970); J. Kirschner, ed., *Business, Banking and Economic Thought in Late Medieval and Early Modern Europe: Selected Studies of Raymond de Roover* (Chicago: University of Chicago Press, 1974); Frank T. Melton, *Sir Robert Clayton on the Origins of English Deposit Banking 1658–1685* (Cambridge: Cambridge University Press, 1986); Benjamin Geva, "From Commodity to Currency in Ancient History: On Commerce, Tyranny and the Modern Law of Money" (1987) 25 Osgoode Hall L.J. 115; Edwin Green, *Banking: An Illustrated History* (New York: Rizzoli, 1989); Glyn Davies, *A History of Money from Ancient Times to the Present Day* (Cardiff: University of Wales Press, 1994); David Mitchell, ed., *Goldsmiths, Silversmiths and Bankers: Innovation and the Transfer of Skill, 1550 to 1750* (Stroud, Gloucestershire: Allan Sutton, 1995); Richard Roberts & David Kynaston, eds., *The Bank of England: Money, Power and Influence 1694–1944* (Oxford: Clarendon Press, 1995).

3 See Section C, below in this chapter, for more about trust companies, cooperatives, and credit unions.

contemporary Canadian banking system, so stable, practical, and efficient have these key ingredients been over the centuries.

In the West, banking evolved from early medieval money changing. Money changers specialized in transmitting funds between parties at a distance, first by physically transporting coinage to geographical locations at which fairs were held and later by developing the early bill of exchange, because of the notorious dangers of transporting money about. By the twelfth century, to pay for goods purchased at a distance, the purchaser would deliver the price to a money changer at the purchaser's place of residence. The money changer would issue a bill payable by a money changer at the vendor's place in the vendor's currency. The indebtedness between the two money changers would be settled as one of many transactions between them, and any outstanding balance would be paid *in specie* at a future fair. Coinage in large amounts no longer needed to be transported about, only the bills.

By the turn of the thirteenth century, money changers in Venice began to receive funds for long-term safekeeping and to lend them out for a fee, operating as embryonic private banks. In 1587, the establishment of the State Bank of Venice marked a move from private to public banks which enjoyed sufficient credibility that merchants settled claims through transfers on their banks. The state bank concept mushroomed across Western Europe, and the Bank of Amsterdam (founded in 1609) emerged as one of the most innovative. The Bank of Venice operated until 1797, when the French revolutionary army invaded the city and destroyed many of its institutions; the Bank of Amsterdam operated until 1814, when it became clear that it could not repay depositors' funds foolishly lent to the Dutch East India Company.

However, in the course of the seventeenth century, the English banking system also developed rapidly and in distinctive ways. English banking originated in goldsmith banking during the Protectorate of Oliver Cromwell (1651–59). Until the English Civil War, merchants had deposited funds in the Royal Mint in the Tower of London for safekeeping. However, after Charles I extracted a forced loan from those funds in 1640, merchants began to entrust funds to various London goldsmiths, who issued receipts for them. The goldsmith's note contained a promise to pay their bearer and evolved into promissory notes. Goldsmiths also permitted depositors to withdraw funds up to the amount of the deposit and to direct payment of those funds to a payee through a demand written on paper. This document evolved into the cheque.

Goldsmiths' notes and cheques facilitated the transmission of credit so that the physical movement of coins was no longer required for commercial transactions. The reliability of payment came to be understood to rest on the credibility of the goldsmiths who issued these notes as having sufficient funds at their disposal to support the promises to pay. During the later seventeenth century, goldsmiths developed a network among themselves permitting interbank payments based on trust and on mutual credit monitoring. Effectively, an informal clearing system came into being.

In 1694, with the establishment of the Bank of England, the final element for a modern banking system was put in place, whereby a network of banks can be linked to each other through a central bank. Initially, the Bank of England operated alongside the goldsmith banks, but because it acted as the banker for the government, its political power added greater credibility to its notes so that over time Bank of England notes overtook goldsmiths' notes as the preferred means of transferring credit. Only in the nineteenth century did it assume the full role of a central bank as the lender of last resort and as a guarantor or curator of the banking system. By the late nineteenth century, clearing and final settlement on the books of the central bank became the standard practice so that the architecture of the modern banking system was in place.

At the beginning of the nineteenth century, no viable means of exchange existed in the Canadian colonies.[4] English coinage was used, but insufficient amounts were available, so that in addition to a barter economy, other forms of payment were created. Merchants in Lower Canada issued their own paper notes, which could be redeemed in goods from their issuer, and these were also exchanged among merchants and their suppliers. In 1819, nine merchants in Montreal entered articles of association to conduct banking activities among themselves, and in 1822 this association obtained a charter from the Crown to operate as the Bank of Montreal. By virtue of this charter, the Bank of Montreal acquired a public status, which added credibility and stability to its operations.

The Bank of Montreal modelled its activities on the second Bank of the United States, founded in 1817 and immediately operated as a bank

---

4 The following account is drawn from Muharem Kianieff, "Private Banknotes in Canada from 1867 (and Before) to 1950" (2004) 30 Queen's L.J. 400. See also Roeliff M. Breckenridge, *The Canadian Banking System 1817–1890* (Baltimore: Guggenheimer, Weil, 1895); James Holladay, *The Canadian Banking System* (Boston: Bankers Publishing, 1938); R. Craig McIvor, *Canadian Monetary, Banking and Fiscal Development* (Toronto: MacMillan, 1958); E.P. Neufeld, ed., *Money and Banking in Canada* (Toronto: McClelland and Stewart, 1964); Adam Shortt, *Adam Shortt's History of Canadian Currency and Banking 1660–1880* (Toronto: Canadian Bankers Association, 1986).

of deposit and issued its own notes. The practice of incorporating new banks by charter brought security for the public into Canadian banking from the outset because a charter meant state regulation of banking in Canada. The success of the Bank of Montreal led to the establishment by charter of other banks and to the acceptance of bank notes in place of merchant's notes as the means of exchange.

Canadian banks adopted the practices of interbank clearing and settlement of value developed by British banks in the nineteenth century and also, in contrast to the American banking system, created a national branch bank system which was believed to diversify risk and enhance stability by making loans in different geographical regions and conditions. The branch network facilitated the transfer of funds around the country and was also believed to be a better means of promoting economic growth.

After Confederation, when the federal government acquired central authority over banking and currency, it began to issue its own Dominion notes backed by gold, which were required to be held as cash reserves by the chartered banks. Periodic economic and political crises exposed the inability of this dual system of Dominion notes and private banknotes to provide for and encourage credit, especially during the First World War and the Depression, with the result that a central bank, the Bank of Canada, was created in 1935. By 1950, private banknotes had been phased out in favour of Bank of Canada notes, and the Bank of Canada assumed the role of a central bank, similar to that of the Bank of England.

The provision of interbank clearing and settlement remained within the banking community's own network until 1983. One of the original functions of the Canadian Bankers Association (CBA), first established in 1891 as a voluntary association, was to develop interbank clearing through clearing houses in major Canadian cities from the 1890s onward. The CBA operated pursuant to a statutory monopoly it received in 1900 and lasting until 1983. At that time, the Canadian Payments Association, which was incorporated in 1980, fully assumed the function of operating a clearing and settlement system, which ultimately settles through interbank transfers in accounts at the Bank of Canada.

The English banking system developed three distinctive features that were carried over into the Canadian banking system: close correspondent relationships among banks, which provided mutual support to one another; the development of a national interbank payment system by the extension of credit between banks; and the presence of a central bank as a source of liquidity and as a site for multilateral settlements through reserve accounts at the central bank.[5] These features constitute the fundamental structure for banking and payment systems worldwide.

B. JURISDICTION OVER BANKING

In Canada, banking has been a highly regulated activity since Confederation. The definition of "banking" as a legal activity itself has been entangled by constitutional considerations unknown to the common law which relied on judicial definitions. The most famous of these was a definition by Lord Denning M.R. in *United Dominions Trust Ltd. v. Kirkwood*:

> There are, therefore, two characteristics usually found in bankers today: (i) They accept money from, and collect cheques for, their customers and place them to their credit; (ii) They honour cheques or orders drawn on them by their customers when presented for payment and debit their customers accordingly. These two characteristics carry with them also a third, namely: (iii) They keep current accounts, or something of that nature, in their books in which the credits and debits are entered.[6]

Even before the decline in the use of cheques on which this definition hinges, this definition was far from comprehensive, as demonstrated by comparison with that of Isaacs J. in *Commissioners of the State Savings Bank of Victoria v. Permewan, Wright & Co. Ltd.*:

> The essential characteristics of the business of banking are ... the collection of money by receiving deposits upon loan, repayable when and as expressly or impliedly agreed upon, and the utilization of the money so collected by lending it again in such sums as are required. These are the essential functions of a bank as an instrument of society. It is, in effect, a financial reservoir receiving streams of currency in every direction, and from which there issue outflowing streams where and as required to sustain and fructify or assist commercial, industrial or other enterprises or adventures ... The methods by which the functions of a bank are effected—as by current account, deposit account at call, fixed deposit account, orders, cheques, secured loans, discounting bills, note issue, letters of credit, telegraphic transfers, and any other modes that may be developed by the necessities of

---

5   Geva, above note 1 at 13.
6   [1966] 1 All E.R. 968 at 975 (C.A.) [*United Dominions Trust*].

business—are merely accidental and auxiliary circumstances, any of which may or may not exist in any particular case.[7]

Definitions of "banking" as a legal activity are contextual. The content of any given definition depends largely on the circumstances in which it is proposed. The older common law definitions came from case law dealing with traditional services such as deposit taking and account operation and may not reflect current banking practices. In most Western countries, the recent trend toward statutory definitions of banking means that for legal purposes, banking is defined by legislation, and the common law supplements ambiguities and gaps in that legislation. Statutory approaches differ. At one end of the spectrum is legislation defining a "bank" as any institution recognized as such by the state and "banking" as the activities carried on by those institutions. At the other end of the spectrum is legislation that expressly lists certain activities only as banking, so that for legal definitional purposes, only those institutions that carry on only those activities are banks engaged in banking. Variations are found between these two points.

The former approach bestows great power on the state to shape the financial institutions sector and the economy. The latter approach is unduly restrictive and fails to accommodate the dynamic nature of that sector and the economy. The Canadian approach is located closer to the former than the latter end of the spectrum: "banks" and "banking" for legal purposes are defined by the state, but the statutory formulation contains a dynamic element within which the common law may occasionally operate.[8] In Canada, as in other federal states, the question of what banking is, is preceded by the question of which part of the state, federal or provincial, has the constitutional authority to define banking for legal purposes. Thus, issues of legal definition and constitutional jurisdiction are enmeshed.

The *Constitution Act, 1867*,[9] grants Parliament legislative authority in relation to "Banking, Incorporation of Banks, and the Issue of Paper Money." No definition of "banking" is provided, so the courts have had to look elsewhere to define concurrently what banking is and what is the extent and nature of federal authority over banking. At the outset,

---

7 (1914), 19 C.L.R. 457 at 470–71 (H.C.A.).
8 For further discussion of U.K. and E.U. approaches to definition, see Ross Cranston, *Principles of Banking Law*, 2d ed. (Oxford: Oxford University Press, 2002) at 4–9 and E.P. Ellinger, Eva Lomnicka, & Richard J.A. Hooley, *Modern Banking Law*, 3d ed. (Oxford: Oxford University Press, 2002) c. 3.
9 Enacted as the *British North America Act, 1867* (U.K.) 1867, 30 & 31 Vict., c. 3, reprinted in R.S.C. 1985, App. II, No. 5.

it is evident that banking for the purpose of legislation and banking as a dynamic market activity need not be identical, as Beetz J. has observed:

> the concept of banking as a business and the meaning of the word 'banking' in section 91(15), are not necessarily coextensive; the meaning of 'banking' in the section might very well be wider than the concept of banking as a business.[10]

Section 91(15) is one component of a section of the *Constitution Act, 1867*, the original intention of which was to ensure strong federal jurisdiction over the national economy. The other subsections reinforce this: "The Regulation of Trade and Commerce" (s. 91(2)); "Currency and Coinage" (s. 91(14)); "Savings Banks" (s. 91(16)); "Bills of Exchange and Promissory Notes" (s. 91(18)); "Interest" (s. 91(19)); and "Legal Tender" (s. 91(20)). Conversely, not only does section 92 (which sets out provincial jurisdiction) make no mention of banking, but the other subsections that are tangentially relevant are few: "The Incorporation of Companies with Provincial Objects" (s. 92(11)); "Property and Civil Rights in the Province" (s. 92(13)); and "Generally all Matters of a Merely Local or Private Nature in the Province" (s. 92(16)).

Other internal evidence from the *Constitution Act, 1867*, for the position that federal jurisdiction over banking is extensive include the following: (i) the residual power of Parliament to make laws for the "Peace and Order and good Government" of Canada set out in the preamble; (ii) the exclusive and exhaustive nature of the division of powers between the federal and provincial governments as set out in the opening provisions in section 91 and section 92, respectively; and (iii) the exclusion of section 91 matters from s. 92(16) jurisdiction.

Before considering how the courts have interpreted these provisions, three reminders are in order. First, in the mid-nineteenth century, banking was not necessarily regarded as a significant instrument of state monetary and economic policy.[11] Banking was still largely a private activity, although legislative charters were the usual means of creating banks, starting in 1822, when the Bank of Montreal was incorporated and there was a lively appreciation of the use of the charter

---

10   *Canadian Pioneer Management Ltd. v. Saskatchewan Labour Relations Board* (1980), 107 D.L.R. (3d) 1 at 25 (S.C.C.) [*Canadian Pioneer Management*]. See also *Commonwealth of Australia v. Bank of New South Wales* (1948), 76 C.L.R. 1 at 195 (H.C.A.), Latham C.J., aff'd [1950] A.C. 235 (P.C.).

11   Emilio Binavince & H. Scott Fairley, "Banking and the Constitution: Untested Limits of Federal Jurisdiction" (1986) 65 Can. Bar Rev. 328 at 328–37.

to control banks. The late-nineteenth-century evolution of the branch network highlighted the potential for banks to be engines of economic development. Secondly, the meaning of banking was not and could not be settled by the *Constitution Act, 1867*. Section 91(15) defines a subject for legislation, not a definite object,[12] and those subjects are regarded by the courts as dynamic in nature, and not frozen in 1867.[13]

Thirdly, from before Confederation and after, federal and provincial governments have incorporated and regulated other financial institutions that have offered core banking services such as deposit taking, although the *Constitution Act, 1867*, contains no references to these. As with other enterprises and activities for which no constitutional provision is made, these are considered to be shared jurisdictions, and Parliament has never attempted to use section 91(15) as a means for asserting plenary authority over the entire financial institutions sector in Canada. Instead, section 91(15) has been considered to apply strictly to "banks" defined by a core function of deposit taking. Since the first permanent *Bank Act* in 1871,[14] only federally chartered banks can use that name, and those banks have been denied power to act as trustees and insurers. Conversely, other financial institutions have been permitted by their legislation to offer "banking" services, although they cannot call themselves "banks."[15] From the *Bank Act, 1980*,[16] financial institutions legislation has moved toward great assimilation of the historic "four pillars" (banks, insurance companies, trust companies and brokerages) but significant differences among them remain in law.[17]

---

12 William R. Lederman, *The Courts and the Canadian Constitution* (Toronto: McClelland and Stewart, 1964) at 183.
13 *Attorney-General of Alberta v. Attorney-General of Canada*, [1947] A.C. 503 at 516, [1947] 4 D.L.R. 1 (P.C.), Viscount Simon [*A.G. Alta. v. A.G. Canada*]. See also the use of the "banking" analogy in *EGALE Canada Inc. v. Canada (Attorney General)*, [2001] 11 W.W.R. 685 at 707–11 (B.C.S.C.), Pitfield J. and the dismissal of the "frozen concept" approach in *Reference re Same-Sex Marriage* (2004), 246 D.L.R. (4th) 193 at 204–6 (S.C.C.), *per curiam*.
14 *An Act Relating to Banks and Banking*, S.C. 1871, c. 5. For earlier temporary Acts, see S.C. 1867–68, c. 11; S.C. 1869, c. 49; S.C. 1870, c. 11.
15 *Trust and Loan Companies Act*, S.C. 1991, c. 45 as am.; *Insurance Companies Act*, S.C. 1991, c. 47 as am. For the prohibition of the use of the name "bank," see *Bank Act*, S.C. 1991, c. 46 as am., s. 983.
16 *Banks and Banking Law Revision Act, 1980*, S.C. 1980-81-82-83, c. 40, [*Bank Act, 1980*]. The current *Bank Act* is R.S.C. 1985, c. B-1.
17 See Chapter 2.

C. DEFINING BANKING

To define banking is to face immediately the challenge of characterizing the essential nature of the changing bundle of activities carried on by banks over time. Banking is both so complex and dynamic that there may well be no essential core for a court to identify and ascribe to section 91(15). Judicial attempts to define the nature and scope of constitutional jurisdiction appear to be ultimately impossible.

Since the clearest approach would be to permit Parliament to define the content of section 91(15) through legislation, the courts have the option of either accepting that definition or attempting to qualify, annul, or constrain it. Notwithstanding the complex and comprehensive legislation in relation to banking, Parliament has left room for the courts to operate when specific issues of jurisdiction and definition arise, so that the content of both jurisdiction over banking and the legal definition of banking remain matters of ongoing dialogue between Parliament and the courts. From the earliest to the latest cases, the courts have considered both concurrently, yet the outcome remains, as it was in 1867, that Parliament has jurisdiction over banking, whatever that is.

The earliest case, *Tennant v. Union Bank of Canada*[18] is still the leading case. In *Tennant*, the issue was whether a bank that had taken warehouse receipts as security pursuant to the federal *Bank Act* had an enforceable security. The plaintiff argued that provincial legislation applied pursuant to section 92(13) "Property and Civil Rights in the Province," and that Parliament had no jurisdiction in security matters. The Privy Council agreed that provincial powers extended to legislation about warehouse receipts under section 92(13), but once Parliament chose to legislate on the matter in relation to banking, Parliament had "paramount authority,"[19] although it would be practically impossible to so legislate without affecting provincial jurisdiction.[20] The Board upheld the validity of the warehouse receipts and the federal *Bank Act* and concluded:

> The legislative authority conferred by [section 91(15)] is not confined to the mere constitution of corporate bodies with the privilege of carrying on the business of bankers.... It also comprehends "banking," an expression which is wide enough to embrace every transaction coming within the legitimate business of a banker.[21]

---

18 [1894] A.C. 31 (P.C.).
19 *Ibid.* at 45, Lord Watson.
20 *Ibid.*
21 *Ibid.* at 46.

Tennant is, undoubtedly, ambiguous. Yet several firm conclusions may be drawn: (i) Parliament has exclusive jurisdiction over banking under section 91(15); (ii) Parliament's jurisdiction is paramount when overlap occurs with section 92(13); (iii) Parliament enjoys exclusive authority over the incorporation of banks; and (iv) "banking" is an expansive concept. Other matters remain less certain, including: (i) the distinction between banking and other forms of financial intermediation or institutions; (ii) the content of legitimate banking business; and (iii) the question of which branch of government has authority to decide what is legitimate banking business, either Parliament through legislation or the courts through giving content to "banking" in section 91(15). If it is the latter, then the banking community may well have the final power to determine "banking" simply through expansion into enterprises not expressly prohibited by Parliament and subsequent ratification by the courts.

Subsequent case law has explored the scope and meaning of Parliament's jurisdiction over banking in two groups of cases: (i) cases about the incorporation of other financial institutions both provincially and federally and (ii) cases about provincial legislation that appears to infringe on the federal banking power. The former group explores the scope of banking from an institutional perspective, while the latter group does so from an activities perspective: what "banks" are and what "banks" do.

1) Defining Banking from an Institutional Perspective

As in other Western countries, a variety of financial institutions operate in Canada, not all of which are called banks or considered to be such, and this has been the case since the early nineteenth century. Parliament has never attempted to assert control over these through a comprehensive definition of "banking" in section 91(15). Instead, it has operated within the four-pillars framework (banks, insurance companies, trust companies, and brokerages) and the dual federal and provincial jurisdictions expressed in section 91(15) and sections 92(11) and 92(16), respectively. Parliament has enacted legislation pursuant to section 91(2) regarding its residual power to regulate other financial institutions such as trust and loan companies or insurance companies that operate across provincial boundaries, and the courts have consistently upheld the constitutional validity of provincial legislation in relation to provincial "near banks" pursuant to sections 92(11), (13), and (16).[22]

---

22 Daniel J. Baum, "The Near Banks: Trust Companies of Canada" (1970–71) 45 Tul. L. Rev. 546; Patrick M. MacDonald, "The *B.N.A. Act* and the Near Banks: A Case Study in Federalism" (1972) 10 Alb. L. Rev. 155.

Several cases have upheld provincial jurisdiction to incorporate and regulate trust companies operating within provincial boundaries. In *Re Dominion Trust Company and U.S. Fidelity Claim*,[23] a trust company incorporated pursuant to a B.C. companies act and authorized to receive money on deposit failed after transfer to federal jurisdiction by a private act of Parliament. The B.C. Supreme Court decided the incorporation was not *ultra vires* the province, that is, it was not a "bank." The trust company's practice of receiving funds in trust for investment and permitting payment orders in relation to these funds was unobjectionable. Since the company had not called itself a "bank" or referred to its activities as "banking," it had not violated federal jurisdiction and could operate legally.

Stronger support for the constitutional validity of provincially incorporated trust companies offering similar financial services to those offered by banks is found in *Re Bergethaler Waisenamt*,[24] which was concerned with a Manitoba trust company that had powers under provincial legislation to act as trustee for persons of unsound mind. In a winding-up, a dispute between trustee creditors and deposit creditors in relation to the assets led to the argument that the deposit creditors' claim was based on an *ultra vires* activity, "banking," and therefore should fail. To decide whether the company was engaged in "banking," the court adopted a common law approach by considering what is meant by "banking" in section 91(15). The court concluded that because the trust company did not honour cheques, although it offered many other "banking" services, it was not a bank because an essential characteristic of banking is the banker's obligation to honour cheques. Both trustee and depositor creditors' claims ranked equally. A provincially incorporated trust company may provide the same financial services as banks without being engaged in banking under section 91(15).

The strongest support for the concurrent role of trust companies in the financial services sector came from the Supreme Court of Canada in *Canadian Pioneer Management Ltd. v. Saskatchewan Labour Relations Board*.[25] A federally incorporated trust company, Pioneer Trust, argued that a provincial labour relations board lacked jurisdiction to certify an employee union or to regulate its employment relations, on the ground that its activities fell completely within federal jurisdiction, including the various "banking" services that it provided, which, effectively, made

---

23 [1918] 3 W.W.R. 1023 (B.C.S.C.).
24 [1948] 1 D.L.R. 761 (Man. K.B.), rev'd [1949] 1 D.L.R. 769 (Man. C.A.) [*Bergethaler*].
25 Above note 10.

it a bank. After an extensive discussion of what banking is under section 91(15), the Supreme Court of Canada decided that it was not a bank.

In an unanimous decision,[26] the Court proceeded along traditional common law lines of attempting to characterize the essential nature of banking. Beetz J. followed three approaches: (i) characterization of the nature of the bank and customer relationship; (ii) identification of the functions of banking; and (iii) discernment of formal or institutional means of identifying banks.[27] Neither the first nor the second approach yielded any unique essential feature of banking. However the institutional or formal approach did. Effectively, "banks" are simply those institutions authorized pursuant to the *Bank Act* to hold themselves out and call themselves banks, and "banking" simply describes the activities in which those institutions are permitted by Parliament to engage.[28] If "banks" and "banking" are simply such because they are carried out under the *Bank Act*, then Pioneer Trust and other near banks are not banks nor are they engaged in banking, notwithstanding the similarity of their services to those provided by banks.

Although not a bank as defined by the Supreme Court of Canada in *Canadian Pioneer Management*, Pioneer Trust's legal right to carry on business as a federally incorporated trust company in Canada was neither impugned nor even considered in the case, so secure is the distinctive legal existence of both federally and provincially incorporated trust companies in Canada.

The courts have also upheld the constitutional validity of provincially incorporated credit unions and provincially operated savings offices and treasury branches.[29] In *Caisse Populaire Notre Dame Ltée v. Moyen*,[30] Tucker J. decided that credit unions were not an intrusion into banking because their primary purpose was mutual self-help, although in pith and substance some of their activities were banking.[31] In *Prov-*

---

26   Laskin C.J.C. delivered a brief concurring judgment to that of Beetz J.
27   These are more fully discussed in Section D, below in this chapter.
28   Above note 10 at 27–28. See also *Transamerica Commercial Finance Corp., Canada v. Imperial T.V. & Stereo Ltd. (Receivership)*, [1994] 1 W.W.R. 506 (Alta. Q.B.), where this reasoning meant a finance company could not be a "banker" under a debenture.
29   The Province of Ontario Savings Office and Alberta Treasury Branches were established during the Depression as an alternative to the chartered banks. The former was sold to Desjardins Credit Union in 2003 and the latter continues to operate.
30   (1967), 61 D.L.R. (2d) 118 (Sask. Q.B.).
31   *Ibid.* at 145–46.

incial *Treasurer of Alberta v. Long*,[32] Milvain C.J.T.D. upheld the constitutional validity of the Alberta Treasury Branches on the ground that Parliament had not exercised its jurisdiction over banking to prohibit other corporations from carrying on banking activities.[33]

These decisions confirm the constitutional validity of the various types of financial institutions, whether federal or provincial, operating today. In theory, Parliament has jurisdiction to define banking so comprehensively as to occupy the entire financial institutions market, yet it has never done so. From 1867 it could have defined "banking" in successive Bank Acts so as to drive other financial institutions, including provincial corporations, out of operation. Instead, it has preferred to use its section 91(15) power to restrict banking by prohibiting banks from offering fiduciary, insurance, and other financial services, as banks do in other countries. The outcome is a multitude of financial institutions and jurisdictions eager to ensure continued restriction. On the other hand, the logic of judicial decisions upholding the constitutional validity of the near banks and of the services they offer, provided they do not use the word "bank" or "banking," easily spills over into an argument to permit reciprocity to the banks, so that if Parliament should continue the assimilation of the financial sector begun in 1980, the ultimate outcome could come close to Parliament fulfilling its constitutional destiny expressed in a comprehensive content for section 91(15).

2) Defining Banking from an Activities Perspective

Canadian Pioneer Management confirmed that "banks" only are "banks" because that is what Parliament has decreed and concurrently confirmed that other financial institutions are legally constituted, provided that they do not call themselves banks and provided that they operate according to their legislation. That decision amounted to an incursion into any plenary and comprehensive definition of the scope of section 91(15). But the courts have also considered other incursions in the form of provincial legislation that may impact on banking operations and therefore on the scope and legal definition of banking.

The earliest incursion occurred in *Bank of Toronto v. Lambe*[34] in relation to taxation pursuant to section 92(2), "Direct Taxation within the Province in order to the raising of a Revenue for Provincial Purposes."

---

32   (1973), 49 D.L.R. (3d) 695 (Alta. S.C.).
33   *Ibid.* at 700–1. This ambiguous position is also reflected in *Breckenridge Speedway Ltd. v. The Queen in Right of Alberta* (1967), 64 D.L.R. (2d) 488 (Alta. S.C.A.D.).
34   (1887), 12 App. Cas. 575 (P.C.).

The Privy Council found that Quebec legislation imposing a tax on the paid-up capital of banks, insurance companies, and certain other companies was valid because its pith and substance was taxation within the province. Conversely, in *Alberta Bank Taxation Reference (1938)*,[35] the Privy Council found Alberta legislation that imposed a special tax on banks alone was *ultra vires* the province because in pith and substance it was about banks as part of a larger legislative scheme to impose a new economic order on the province. Apparently, banks may be subject to provincial legislation when its purpose is to raise local direct taxes from corporations generally.

Secondly, provincial legislation in relation to bank deposits has also been considered by the courts. In *Royal Bank of Canada v. The King*,[36] Alberta government legislation to seize funds deposited in a bank account in Montreal relating to a project in Alberta was struck down on the ground that it was concerned with property and civil rights in another province. It may be surmised that the Privy Council might have concluded that it was also *ultra vires* because it infringed section 91(15). In the *Quebec Bank Deposits Case*,[37] however, the Privy Council struck down Quebec legislation that purported to appropriate deposits unclaimed for a thirty-year period in "credit institutions" on the ground that the pith and substance of the legislation was banking.

Thirdly, the courts have considered in two leading cases the extent to which provincial legislation may regulate security taking by banks. In *Tennant*,[38] the Privy Council upheld the validity of the bank's warehouse receipts taken as security for a loan pursuant to the *Bank Act* over provincial legislation relating to warehouse receipts and the paramountcy of section 91(15) over section 92(13). In *Bank of Montreal v. Hall*,[39] the Supreme Court of Canada sustained the position that bank security taking is to be regulated solely pursuant to the *Bank Act* and so falls solely under section 91(15). In *Hall*, the Court found that where the special security provisions[40] of the Act were silent about giving notice prior to seizure, provincial legislation relating to security taking with the province could not be used to fill in that silence. The *Bank Act* was considered to be a complete code on the matter. This does

---

35 *Attorney-General of Alberta v. Attorney-General of Canada*, [1939] A.C. 117 (P.C.) [*Alberta Bank Taxation Reference*].
36 (1913), 9 D.L.R. 337 (P.C.).
37 *Attorney-General of Canada v. Attorney-General of Quebec*, [1947] A.C. 33 (P.C.).
38 Above note 18.
39 (1990), 65 D.L.R. (4th) 361 (S.C.C.). See also M.H. Ogilvie, "Section 91(15) Revisited Again—and Again" (1991) 18 Can. Bus. L.J. 432.
40 Above note 16 at ss. 425–29.

not mean, however, that bank security taking is entirely exempt from provincial jurisdiction, rather it may be subject to provincial legislation in relation to incidental issues not encompassed within the pith and substance of banking, such as the levy of municipal taxes[41] and workers' compensation assessments.[42]

Fourthly, the courts have found that provincial legislation relating to evidence and civil procedure may be invoked for court orders to inspect and take copies of bank records in the course of litigation because such legislation is in pith and substance concerned with procedure in the courts of a province.[43] Fifthly, as federally incorporated institutions, banks may be subject to search warrants issued by the Canadian Human Rights Commission, although provincially incorporated life insurance companies are not.[44]

Sixthly, as banks have been permitted to offer certain types of insurance, the courts have considered whether they must comply with provincial insurance legislation. In *Bank of Nova Scotia v. British Columbia (Superintendent of Financial Institutions)*,[45] the agent of a bank to which the bank had outsourced the telemarketing of the bank's credit-card-balance insurance had done so without obtaining a licence to solicit insurance applications, although such a licence was required under provincial legislation. The B.C. Court of Appeal found that on construction of that legislation, the bank and its agent were exempt from its application. The court further found that the doctrine of interjurisdictional immunity applied; that is, a province cannot legislate so as to interfere with core aspects of a federal jurisdiction. Since Parliament had enacted legislation to permit banks to engage in this type of insurance, it was a core part of the business of banking and subject to interjurisdictional immunity; therefore, there was no overlap

---

41 *Re Electrical Fittings and Foundry Co. Ltd.*, [1926] 1 D.L.R. 752 (Ont. S.C. in Bkcy.); *Re P.W. Ellis Co. Ltd.* (1929), 36 O.W.N. 202 (H.C.J.); *Brantford v. Imperial Bank of Canada*, [1930] 4 D.L.R. 658 (Ont. S.C.A.D.); *Re Metal Studios Ltd.; Ex parte City of Hamilton*, [1934] O.W.N. 173 (S.C. in Bkcy.).

42 *Re Canadian Logging Co.*, [1927] 1 W.W.R. 406 (B.C.S.C. in Bkcy.); *Royal Bank of Canada v. Workmen's Compensation Board of Nova Scotia*, [1936] 4 D.L.R. 9 (S.C.C.). For paramountcy in relation to another federal statute, see *Re Swaan* (1980), 37 C.B.R. (N.S.) 1 (B.C.S.C.).

43 *Sommers v. Sturdy* (1957), 10 D.L.R. (2d) 269 (B.C.C.A.), leave to appeal to S.C.C. refused, [1957] S.C.R. x; *Astral Films Ltd. v. Sherman* (1978), 19 O.R. (2d) 206 (H.C.J.); *I.T.L. Industries Ltd. v. Winterbottom* (1979), 97 D.L.R. (3d) 553 (Ont. H.C.J.). See also *Bank Act*, ss. 238–39.

44 *Sun Life Assurance Co. of Canada v. Canada (Human Rights Commission)*, [1991] 3 S.C.R. 689.

45 (2003), 223 D.L.R. (4th) 126 (B.C.C.A.).

of jurisdiction and no conflict, so that the doctrine of paramountcy did not need to be considered at all. The court stated that marketing credit-card-balance insurance was a core part of banking and tied this assertion to its understanding of that insurance as a form of security for the loan inherent in using a credit card. The court further stated that taking security is a core banking business.

In *Canadian Western Bank v. Alberta*,[46] the seven largest domestic banks and the largest foreign bank sought to promote in Alberta various insurance products that they were permitted to promote by the *Bank Act* without obtaining a licence under provincial insurance legislation. The Alberta Queen's Bench began by assuming that it was for the court, rather than Parliament, to determine what banking is for the purposes of section 91(15) and further to find that the promotion of insurance is not a central part of banking, but rather a separate line of business entered into for its profitability. The court did not think insurance to be central to taking security for loans, but rather that it was a collateral matter, so it did not have to characterize insurance as part of a long-established core banking business.[47] Therefore, the court decided that the doctrine of interjurisdictional immunity did not apply to the facts as it found them. Rather, this was a case falling under the doctrine of paramountcy. However, the facts did not engage the paramountcy doctrine because the provincial legislation complemented, rather than overlapped or conflicted with, the empowerment by Parliament of banks to promote insurance. The banks were required to comply with the provincial legislation in order to promote insurance in Alberta.[48]

The approach of the Alberta Queen's Bench, upheld by the Alberta Court of Appeal, may be distinguished from that of the previous law in at least three significant ways: (i) the court did not defer to Parliament's determination of "banking" as expressed in section 91(15) or to the *Bank Act*; (ii) the court did not construe that Act's provisions[49] in relation to insurance as a complete code as the *Hall* case would have predicted; and (iii) the court took a narrow approach to security taking so that it did

---

46   (2003) 4 C.C.L.I. (4th) 59 (Alta. Q.B.) [*Canadian Western Bank*]. See also Terence D. Hall, "Bank Promotion of Insurance: Canadian Western Bank v. Alberta," (2003–04) 19 B.F.L.R. 457.
47   *Canadian Western Bank*, *ibid.* at 135, Slatter J.
48   *Ibid.* at 150–51. The Alberta Court of Appeal upheld this decision: *Canadian Western Bank v. Alberta* (2005), 249 D.L.R. (4th) 523 (Alta. C.A.).
49   Above note 15 at ss. 416(1)–(4) and Insurance Business (Banks and Bank Holding Companies) Regulations SOR/92-330 as am. SOR/95-171; SOR/2001-190; SOR/2002-269.

not have to consider the role of insurance in managing credit risk. *Canadian Western Bank* is the odd case out in the trajectory of constitutional law in relation to "banking."

Generally speaking, to determine the scope and content of section 91(15) where provincial legislation relates to banking, the courts begin with the *Bank Act*. Where the Act is not explicit but ambiguous, the courts characterize the provincial legislation to determine whether it falls more within section 91(15) or section 92, by virtue of its pith and substance. Where the provincial legislation affects a core area of banking as expressly set out in the Act, the doctrine of interjurisdictional immunity would apply and the provincial legislation would be *ultra vires*. Where the legislation overlaps, then the doctrine of paramountcy would apply, so that the provincial legislation, although *intra vires* the provinces, would not apply to banks. Where there is complementarity with the *Bank Act*, the court would permit the provincial legislation to apply to the extent of that complementarity.

The key issue in each of these instances is how a court characterizes banking, that is, what the court conceptualizes banking to be as a human activity. The case law shows that taking security for loans is the only activity clearly considered to be part of banking among the narrow range of fact situations considered by the courts to date. In the other cases, the courts have evaluated how closely the provincial regulation comes to core banking business without defining what that core might be in the context of that fact situation. Instead, the courts favour solutions that permit the complementary operation of dual federal and provincial legislation, rather than unnecessarily expanding the scope of banking to everything that banks do.

This approach is coherent with the fact that Parliament has never tried to define banking so as to preclude expressly provincial jurisdiction in all matters tangential to banking. Yet the logic of the cases would also suggest the outcome of driving provincial legislation from the field should Parliament ever determine to preclude such provincial jurisdiction by comprehensive legislation pursuant to section 91(15).

In addition to the areas discussed above, in which the courts have determined the scope and content of the banking power, a number of areas exist in which there is potential for jurisdictional conflict, depending on how future courts might view the relationship of provincial legislation to the *Bank Act*. These include securities, unfair trade practices, cost of borrowing disclosure and credit reporting, all of which are provincially regulated under sections 92(13) or (16). Notwithstanding considerable federal and provincial discussions over the past few decades, there remains considerable legal ambiguity in relation to each of these issues.

The ambiguity inherent in defining what banking is from a constitutional perspective is, finally, expressly built into the *Bank Act* itself. Section 409(1) permits banks to carry on the business of banking as defined by the Act, as well as "such business generally as appertains thereto." This phrase or a similar one has appeared in successive Bank Acts since the late nineteenth century, and *prima facie* appears to expand the business of banking as defined by the Act without providing further guidance as to the limits of its operation. In *Central Computer Services Ltd. v. Toronto-Dominion Bank*,[50] the Manitoba Court of Appeal concluded that the provision of computerized payroll services and small business accounting services to any person willing to pay for them was a permissible banking activity, although their purchasers were not "customers" as traditionally understood,[51] nor were these services traditionally associated with banking. The majority[52] thought that these services were ancillary to banking prior to the advent of computerized banking so that computerization made little difference. But the majority also appeared content to permit innovation by banks to be a guide to the meaning of pertaining to banking.[53] This effectively means that banks themselves may have a judicially approved part to play in the expansion of the definition of "banking" in section 91(15) simply by unilaterally moving into businesses incidental to banking, conditional on subsequent judicial approval.

D. DEFINING BANKING AT COMMON LAW

In the end, to define the scope and content of the federal banking power, either by giving content to section 91(15) or by interpreting the *Bank Act*, the courts must state what they think banking is as a human activity where the Act is silent or ambiguous. There is no escape from the common law. Lord Watson's statement in *Tennant v. Union Bank of Canada*[54] that banking embraces "every transaction coming within the legitimate business of a banker" remains both the starting point for judicial attempts to define banking and a summary of what those attempts have achieved. Definition there must be to determine the outcome in

---

50 (1979), 107 D.L.R. (3d) 88 (Man. C.A.) [*Central Computer Services*].
51 For the definition of "customer," see Chapter 6, Section B.
52 *Central Computer Services*, above note 50. Monnin and O'Sullivan JJ.A. were in the majority. Matas J.A. dissented.
53 *Ibid.*, Monnin J.A. at 90 and O'Sullivan J.A. at 105.
54 Above notes 18 and 21.

legislation, but a definitive statement seems impossible, as Monnin J.A. conceded in *Central Computer Services*: "There is no exact definition of a banker or a bank."[55] Or, as Lord Denning M.R. earlier remarked: "Like many other beings, a banker is easier to recognise than to define."[56]

To define banking at common law, the courts have consistently applied two general principles. First, they have taken a progressive approach to the meaning of "banking" in section 91(15) and by extension in the *Bank Act*. The meaning of banking is not frozen in 1867 but interpreted in light of the current Act.[57] Secondly, the common law has recognized the dynamic nature of banking as a commercial activity; as Salmon J. stated in *Woods v. Martins Bank*:[58] "[T]he limits of a banker's business cannot be laid down as a matter of law. The nature of such business must in each case be a matter of fact."[59]

The approach of the common law to defining banking set out above[60] by Lord Denning M.R. and Isaacs J. is reflected in Canadian law.[61] While the standard English definition established in *United Dominions Trust Ltd. v. Kirkwood*[62] emphasized account operation as the essential business of banking, instead Canadian attempts to capture the essential nature of banking preferred to emphasize dealing in credit.[63] The fullest discussions of banking at common law are found in *Bergethaler*[64] and *Canadian Pioneer Management*.[65] In the former case, the Manitoba Court of Appeal decided that the essential characteristic of banking is the obligation of the banker to honour cheques, after drawing up lists of what bankers did in the mid-twentieth century, in order to determine which activity was the core activity. Even so, the court still conceded that other financial institutions also provided this service,[66] making the task of defining banking murky. The predominance of electronic funds transfer today makes this definition even more problematical unless it is framed as an obligation to honour payment

---

55 Above note 50 at 89.
56 *United Dominions Trust*, above note 6 at 979.
57 *A.G. Alta. v. A.G. Canada*, above note 13 at 9 (cited to D.L.R.), Viscount Simon.
58 [1959] 1 Q.B. 55 (Leeds Assizes).
59 *Ibid.* at 70.
60 See Section B, above in this chapter.
61 See above note 8 for discussions of English approaches on which the Canadian approach is based.
62 Above note 6.
63 *Alberta Bank Taxation Reference*, above note 35 and *A.G. Alta. v. A.G. Canada*, above note 13.
64 Above note 24.
65 Above note 10.
66 Above note 24 at 778–79, Coyne J.A., and at 773–74, Richards J.A.

instructions. In the latter case, the Supreme Court of Canada concluded that the pursuit of a common law definition was futile once Parliament had spoken through the *Bank Act* but provided no assistance for those situations where the Act is silent or ambiguous.

In *Canadian Pioneer Management*, Beetz J. attempted to define the essential nature of banking by examining the nature of the bank and customer relationship; the economic and legal functions performed by banks within society; and the formal, or institutional, character of banks themselves. The extensive analysis required by this approach was dictated by the far-reaching argument of the intervener in the case, the Attorney General of Canada, that although Pioneer Trust was not a bank, its business was banking business at common law. Since there was no federal and provincial concurrent jurisdiction over banking, all institutions engaged in banking business should be federally regulated pursuant to section 91(15); provincial jurisdiction was non-existent; and all provincially incorporated financial institutions were operating illegally.

Beetz J.'s examination of the bank and customer relationship was inconclusive. He conceded that 99 percent of Pioneer Trust's business was identical to the business carried on by a bank, yet concluded, without explaining why, that its relationship with its customers was fiduciary, not one of debtor and creditor. Further, he rejected both functional approaches because neither the economic nor the legal functions performed by banks were exclusive to them. Other financial institutions engaged in financial intermediation in the economy and offered the services defined as banking at common law in the earlier cases. Finally, the Court decided that the institutional test was the best one to define "banks" and "banking" as an activity or group of activities. It rejected versions of an institutional test that focused on bankers holding themselves out as such or acquiring a reputation as such in favour of one based on the *Bank Act*. A bank is simply an institution authorized under the Act to call itself a bank, and banking denotes the activities carried on by such institutions.[67]

The definition of banking to mean those activities so defined by Parliament is only as comprehensive as the legislation defining banking. Where legislation is ambiguous or silent, the options are either to consider the *Bank Act* to be a complete code so that any other activities carried on by banks are not banking or to consider the possibility that the common law still defines activities outside the Act as banking for the very reason that banks engaged in them either by virtue of the fact

---

67 Above note 10 at 28.

that those activities pertained to banking pursuant to section 409(1) or by virtue of the common law itself, which continues to operate where legislation is silent or ambiguous. Some activities that the courts have upheld include entering isolated transactions to realize the amount of a legally constructed indebtedness,[68] carrying on the business of a debtor to enable it to be sold as a going concern,[69] and permitting bank lobbies to be used for the purposes of taking photographs of customers as a promotional scheme to increase their goodwill.[70]

Canadian Pioneer Management determined that where activities statutorily defined as banking are carried on by other financial institutions, they are not banking nor are those institutions banks, so any common law definition would not have the effect of converting them into banks. This argument of the Attorney General failed in *Canadian Pioneer Management*. Rather, the impact of the common law would be on banks alone—and the matter is not academic, as the decision in *Canadian Western Bank* shows, because that decision is based on the court's perception of what banking is apart from the Act. Since the Act is not a complete code, banking at common law remains to be discerned from time to time by means of the incremental approach implicit in the continuing provision in successive Bank Acts for business pertaining to banking to be included in banking. The characterization of banking with a single unique activity at its core in the traditional common law manner is, however, no longer possible. Banking is a bundle of activities dynamic in nature and denominated as such because Parliament has so legislated. As Beetz J. stated in *Canadian Pioneer Management*: "'Banking' involves a set of interrelated financial activities carried out by an institution that operates under the nomenclature and terms of incorporation which clearly identify it as having the distinctive institutional character of a bank."[71] The *Bank Act* identifies most of these activities, but the common law must still supplement that list with others.

By virtue of section 91(15), Parliament has plenary authority over banking, but by restricting its exercise to those institutions it chooses to call banks, Parliament has restricted its potential to declare jurisdiction over the entire financial institutions sector. Given the wide array of provincially incorporated financial institutions and the other fed-

---

68 *Ontario Bank v. McAllister* (1910), 43 S.C.R. 338; *Re Harris; Ex parte Union Bank* (1926), 29 O.W.N. 307 (S.C.).
69 *White v. Bank of Toronto*, [1953] O.R. 479 (C.A.).
70 *Laarakker v. Royal Bank of Canada* (1980), 118 D.L.R. (3d) 716 (Ont. H.C.J.).
71 Above note 10 at 24, adopting the wording from the factum of the Attorney-General of New Brunswick, another intervener.

erally incorporated financial institutions, it is politically unwise and unlikely that Parliament will ever assert the jurisdiction it was granted in 1867 by attempting to regulate all financial institutions as "banks." Furthermore, by declining to define "banking" comprehensively in successive Bank Acts, Parliament has also left room for the common law to continue to operate both by virtue of section 409(1) and by virtue of the silences and ambiguities in the Act. In the end, the common law will continue to play a role in defining banking. Albeit a role which is ultimately unable to yield a definitive definition. Insofar as Parliament has defined "bank" and "banking," their meanings are known, but where Parliament is silent or ambiguous, the meaning of "banking" may ultimately be determined by the common law.

CHAPTER 2

THE DOMESTIC AND INTERNATIONAL FRAMEWORK OF CANADIAN BANKING LAW

A. INTRODUCTION

Since 1867, Parliament has exercised its jurisdiction over banking pursuant to section 91(15) of the *Constitution Act, 1867*, primarily through successive Bank Acts dating from the first temporary Act passed during the session of 1867–68 to the current Act, which has been in force since 1991, with numerous subsequent amendments.[1] The importance of the *Bank Act* cannot be overstated. It is the charter of, and applies to, every bank, domestic or foreign, operating in Canada, and it reflects current government policy about the financial institutions sector generally and about the economy. The present Act is the outcome of a quarter-century of intensive public policy debate in Canada about the financial institutions sector and is one of four major pieces of legislation introduced in 1991,[2] under which the entire federally regulated financial institutions sector operates, together with a web of provincial legislation relating

---

1   The successive *Bank Acts* are as follows: S.C. 1867–8, c. 11; S.C. 1869, c. 49; S.C. 1870, c. 11; S.C. 1871, c. 5; R.S.C. 1886, c. 120; S.C. 1890, c. 31; R.S.C. 1906, c. 29; S.C. 1913, c. 9; S.C. 1923, c. 32; R.S.C. 1927, c. 12; S.C. 1934, c. 24; S.C. 1944–45, c. 30; R.S.C.1952, c. 12; S.C. 1953–54, c. 48; S.C. 1966–67, c. 87; S.C. 1980–81–82–83, c. 40; S.C. 1991, c. 46 as am.
2   *Bank Act*, S.C. 1991, c. 46 as am.; *Trust and Loan Companies Act*, S.C. 1991, c. 45 as am.; *Insurance Companies Act*, S.C. 1991, c. 47 as am.; and *Cooperative Credit Associations Act*, S.C. 1991, c. 48 as am.

to insurance companies, trust and loan companies, stock brokerages, credit unions, and *caisses populaires* that operate within a given province. The *Bank Act* is the centrepiece of this legislation.

Canadian banks are also part of an international network of banks providing cross-border payment and other services within the global economy. In addition to domestic legislation, Canadian banks comply with certain international banking standards to which Canada is a signatory, to ensure the efficiency, security, and solvency of cross-border payments systems. In this chapter, the regulatory framework, both domestic and foreign, for banks in Canada within the broad context of the financial institutions sector generally will be considered. In Chapter 3, the other legislation, regulating daily bank operations in particular, to ensure the safety and security of the banking industry as the key player within the Canadian economy, will be considered.

B. APPLICATION TO THE "CHARTERED" BANKS

The earliest banks in nineteenth-century Canada were incorporated under individual charters granted by the colonial legislatures.[3] Over the course of the second half of that century, federal banking legislation moved incrementally toward comprehensive legislation of general application to all banks, and in 1923[4] the *Bank Act* became the charter for all banks operating in Canada. The use of one comprehensive statute as the common charter for all banks doing business in Canada has been a distinctive feature of Canadian banking regulation since 1923.

Sections 13 and 14 of the *Bank Act* state that the Act is the charter of, and applies to, every bank in Canada, including domestic Canadian banks ("Schedule I banks"), foreign bank subsidiaries ("Schedule II banks"), and authorized foreign banks ("Schedule III banks").[5] Once incorporated, a bank will be listed in a schedule and chartered to do business in Canada for a period of five years from the coming into force of the Act, with two exceptions: (i) Parliament dissolves within a three-

---

3   For the legislative history of banking in Canada, see successive editions of the classic Canadian banking law text, Bradley Crawford, ed., *Falconbridge on Banking and Bills of Exchange*, 8th ed. (Toronto: Canada Law Book, 1986).
4   S.C. 1923, c. 32, s. 5.
5   See the three Schedules as amended from time to time for the lists of all banks operating in Canada. For the distinction between Schedule II and Schedule III banks, see Chapter 4, Section L.

month period prior to the day on which the *Bank Act* expires, so that banks may continue in business for 180 days after the first day of the first session of the next Parliament; and (ii) the Governor in Council may extend once by six months the period of time during which banks may carry on business.[6]

The concept of permitting banks to operate for fixed periods of time and then being subject to review is a peculiar feature of Canadian banking law. The reason is historical. After 1867, the chartered banks were unwilling to give up their powers to issue paper notes to the federal government, which responded from the 1871 *Bank Act*[7] onward by permitting banks to operate for ten-year periods subject to review of their operations generally. From 1881,[8] the decennial review concept became customary, so that Bank Acts were typically revised every ten years until 1991,[9] when the period was shortened to five years. Associated with the concept of periodic review and renewal of the charter was the practice of amending successive Bank Acts only at the review, so that typically[10] no amendments to the Act would be made between reviews. Since 1991, the *Bank Act*, like other legislation, has been subject to such frequent amendment as Parliament deems necessary. Amendment between reviews is anticipated to be the future practice.

C. INTERPRETATION OF THE *BANK ACT*

The *Bank Act* is subject to the ordinary rules of statutory interpretation,[11] including the federal *Interpretation Act*[12] but not provincial Interpretation Acts. The Act is to be applied uniformly across the country, including in Quebec.[13] Most interpretation cases have arisen in the context of constitutional division-of-power litigation concerning the relationship of the security provisions of the Act and provincial legislation about secured transactions pursuant to section 92(13), and these

---

6   Sections 21(1), (2), & (3).
7   S.C. 1871, c. 5. See also Muharem Kianieff, "Private Banknotes in Canada from 1867 (and Before) to 1950" (2004) 30 Queens L.J. 400 at 415–24.
8   R.S.C. 1886, c. 120.
9   S.C. 1991, c. 46, s. 12.
10 Some examples include S.C. 1877, c. 44; S.C. 1915, c. 1; S.C. 1924, c. 7; S.C. 1984, c. 30, c. 40.
11 See any standard legal textbook on statutory interpretation.
12 R.S.C. 1985, c. I-21 as am.
13 *Exchange Bank v. Fletcher* (1891), 19 S.C.R. 278 at 288–89, Patterson J.

cases show that the ordinary rules apply.[14] Extensive nineteenth-century case law about the meaning of particular sections of special bank charters no longer appears to have application.[15]

In addition to the ordinary rules of statutory interpretation, the Act itself contains intrinsic aids to interpretation, including sections 2 to 12, which comprise a comprehensive definition code for the entire Act, as well as various definitions and provisions scattered throughout the Act of particular application in the context in which they are found in the Act.[16] Since those provisions of the Act relating to the corporate governance of banks are modelled on equivalent provisions in the *Canada Business Corporations Act*,[17] it may be asserted that judicial interpretation of those provisions in the context of the *CBCA* would apply equally to the *Bank Act*.[18] Finally, the numerous government policy papers of the past quarter-century[19] discussing banking policy in Canada may also be used by the courts to discern the meaning and scope of the Act.[20]

D. *BANK ACT* REFORM

The current *Bank Act* is the outcome not only of almost 150 years of banking legislation in Canada but more especially of "a mound of research studies, discussion papers and committee reports"[21] of the past quarter-century, in which the policies underlying the legislation are debated. The modern starting point is the federal government's 1975 *White Paper on the Revision of Canadian Banking Legislation*,[22] on which the 1980 *Bank Act* was based. The 1980 Act is considered to be the first "modern" Act because it incorporated significant changes that have

---

14 *Rogerson Lumber Co. v. Four Seasons Chalet Ltd.* (1980), 113 D.L.R. (3d) 671 at 677 (Ont. C.A.), Arnup J.A.
15 For a complete list, see M.H. Ogilvie, *Canadian Banking Law*, 2d ed. (Toronto: Carswell, 1998) at 27, note 31.
16 These are typically found in the various parts of the Act and will be referred to where appropriate in this text.
17 R.S.C. 1985, c. C-44 as am. [*CBCA*].
18 Canada, Department of Finance, *White Paper on the Revision of Canadian Banking Legislation* (Ottawa: Department of Finance, 1976) at 41.
19 See Section D, below in this chapter.
20 *Canadian Western Bank v. Alberta* (2003), 4 C.C.L.I. (4th) 59 at 91–104 (Alta. Q.B.), Slatter J. [*Canadian Western Bank*].
21 *Ibid.* at 97.
22 Above note 18.

been developed in subsequent Acts, including expanding the scope of banking business beyond deposits and cheques to such activities as residential mortgages, credit cards, and computerized services; assimilating the corporate governance of banks with the corporate governance of business corporations in the *CBCA*; and permitting foreign banks, for the first time, to operate in Canada legally.

After 1980, a series of reports and studies[23] appeared in preparation for the next decennial review and in light of the significant changes taking place within the financial institutions sector domestically and internationally. One of the most important of these changes was the move toward universal banking, whereby a single financial institution would be permitted to offer banking, investment, and insurance services and products through a holding company and subsidiary network. The Second Banking Directive[24] permitted E.U. banks to move toward universal banking, which has operated successfully in Germany for several centuries, and in Canada the four pillars segregation of financial services was increasingly questioned by banks, trust companies, securities dealers, and insurers, each of which had their own versions of how a universal financial institutions sector might be shaped.

The outcome of a decade of study were the four acts[25] regulating the sector enacted as a package in 1991 and coming into force on 1 June 1992. The *Bank Act, 1991*, continued in the direction of the 1980 Act, including permitting banks to diversify financial services through financial institution subsidiaries such as trust and insurance subsidi-

---

23 Canada, Department of Finance, *The Regulation of Canadian Financial Institutions: Proposals for Discussion* (Ottawa: Department of Finance, 1985) ["the Green Paper"]; Canada, Department of Finance, *The Regulation of Financial Institutions: Proposals for Discussion, Technical Supplement* (Ottawa: Department of Finance, 1985); Canada, Department of Finance, *New Directions for the Financial Sector* (Ottawa: Department of Finance, 1986) ["the Blue Paper"]; Canada, Department of Finance, *Reform of Federal Financial Institutions Legislation: Overview of Legislative Proposals* (Ottawa: Department of Finance, 1990) ["the 1990 White Paper"]. In addition to the Department of Finance reports in which the government's policies were set out, the House of Commons Standing Committee on Finance, Trade and Economic Affairs and the Senate Standing Committee on Banking, Trade and Commerce issued various reports as well. See also the earlier studies: Stanley Goldstein, *Changing Times: Banking in the Electronic Age* (Ottawa: Government of Canada, 1979) ["the Goldstein Report"]; and Ontario, Electronic Funds Transfer Study Project, *The Challenge of EFT: Policy and Legislative Responses* (Toronto: The Project, 1978) ["the McLaren Report"].
24 Directive 89/646/EEC [1989] OJL386/1. See now Banking Consolidated Directive of 2000, Directive 2000/12/EC [2000] OJL126/1.
25 Above note 2.

aries; expanding bank in-house powers, such as extended lending powers, portfolio management, and giving investment advice; permitting banks to network services such as credit cards, Interac, or related goods and services; permitting banks to have limited ownership of shares in non-financial institutions; and reconfiguring how foreign banks may operate.[26]

While the 1991 Act recognized the new forces at work in the financial institutions sector, including the globalization of commerce, computerization, and the introduction of new banking services, it adopted a cautious approach, necessitating more study in preparation for the legislative review in five years. The conclusion of that review[27] was that the general framework established in 1980 and 1991 continued to work well, so that the 1997 Act[28] amendments were minor. These adjustments included fine-tuning the corporate governance provisions, strengthening consumer protection by such additions as privacy safeguards for consumer information, disclosure of the costs of banking services, and protection against abuses in tied selling; and easing of some regulatory burdens by permitting banks to provide services through subsidiaries, streamlining self-dealing provisions, and modifying the foreign banks' entry requirements.

The most important outcome of the financial services sector review prior to the 1997 amendments was the decision by the Minister of Finance to appoint a task force[29] to undertake a root-and-branch study of the entire sector in light of the substantial unresolved issues, including the possible collapse of the four pillars into universal "one-stop-shopping" financial institutions; permitting bank mergers to allow Canadian banks to acquire the bulk required to compete globally; permitting foreign banks to operate on a level playing field with Canadian banks;

---

26 *Ibid.* For a discussion of these changes, see James C. Baillie, Peter D. Maddaugh, & Stephen O. Marshall, "Federal Financial Institution Reform: The Current Proposals" (1991) 7 B.F.L.R. 1; M.H. Ogilvie, "Financial Institutions Reform in Canada" [1992] J. Bus. L. 615 and "What's Really New in the New Bank Act" (1993) 25 Ottawa L. Rev. 385.

27 Canada, Department of Finance, *1997 Review of Financial Sector Legislation: Proposals for Changes* (Ottawa: Department of Finance, 1996). See also A. Michael Andrews & Brent A. Sutton, "More Green Than White? Federal Proposals for Changes to Canada's Financial Sector Legislation" (1997) 12 B.F.L.R. 251.

28 S.C. 1997, c. 15.

29 Task Force on the Future of the Canadian Financial Services Sector, *Change, Challenge, Opportunity: The Future of the Canadian Financial Services Sector* (Ottawa: Department of Finance, 1998).

enforcing consumer protection; and reform and expansion of the payment and clearing system.

The Task Force on the Future of the Canadian Financial Services Sector (the "MacKay Task Force") released its report[30] in September 1998. The Report[31] is probably the most intensive and comprehensive study of the sector ever undertaken and consists of the Report itself, five background papers, and eighteen research studies prepared by some of the country's leading economics and business scholars. In response, the government released a policy paper[32] in which it stated how it would respond to the Task Force recommendations by identifying four general policy goals for the 2001 legislative review: (i) promotion of efficiency and growth in the financial institutions sector; (ii) fostering domestic competition; (iii) consumer protection and empowerment; and (iv) improving the regulatory environment.

To accomplish the first goal, the government proposed a bank holding company regime to provide greater flexibility while protecting deposits and assets; a transparent bank merger review process, including a formal mechanism for public input; and changes to the bank ownership rules to allow for strategic alliances. To accomplish the second goal, proposals included liberalizing bank ownership rules and lowering minimum capital requirements, to encourage the creation of new banks, some with regional or specialized-market service targets; permitting the numerous and widely scattered credit unions to form a national structure to facilitate their competition with the banks; expanding access to the payments system to provide additional competition from non-bank deposit takers; and allowing foreign banks to open branches directly without incorporating a subsidiary in Canada. Among the proposals to advance the third goal of consumer protection and empowerment were the creation of an agency with oversight over statutory consumer protection provisions; the creation of a national financial institutions ombudsman; improvement in low-income access

---

30 Ibid.
31 For discussions of the Report, see Jack L. Carr, "The MacKay Report: What Kinds of 'Change, Challenge and Opportunity'?" (1999) 31 Can. Bus. L.J. 235; James R. Savary, "The Consumer Implications of the MacKay Report" (1999) 31 Can. Bus. L.J. 248; David A. Brown, "Regulating Financial Services: Realigning Federal-Provincial Responsibilities" (1999) 31 Can. Bus. L.J. 258; Blair W. Keefe & Stephen Johnson, "Overview of Revisions to Financial Institution Legislation" (2001–2002) 17 B.F.L.R. 379; M.H. Ogilvie, "Change, Challenge, Opportunity: Canadian Banking Sector Restructured Again" [2003] J. Bus. L. 487.
32 Canada, Department of Finance, *Reforming Canada's Financial Services Sector: A Framework for the Future* (Ottawa: Department of Finance, 1999).

to banking services; and improved delivery of information about banking services. Finally, to improve the regulatory environment, streamlined regulatory requirements were suggested in relation to the Canada Deposit Insurance Corporation, the Office of the Superintendent of Financial Institutions, and the payments system.

The 2001 *Bank Act* amendments[33] codified most of these proposals, and since then, the government has turned to the question of large bank mergers in its 2003 response to reports on the matter from both the Senate and the House of Commons.[34] To date, however, public discussion about the financial institutions sector has not advanced to acceptance of widespread mergers, universal one-stop-shopping financial institutions, a completely level playing field for domestic and foreign banks, a comprehensive consumer protection code, or an electronic funds transfers code. This cautious approach is mirrored in the *White Paper* released by the government in 2006[35] as the background to the legislative changes proposed for the financial institutions sector in the 2007 legislation including the 2007 amendments to the *Bank Act*.[36]

The *White Paper* identified three key objectives for the 2007 amendments: (i) enhancing the interests of consumers; (ii) increasing legislative and regulatory efficiency; and (iii) adapting the existing framework to new developments. The first objective involves improving disclosure to consumers about deposit-type investment products such as guaranteed investment certificates (GICs) and term deposits, branch closure requirements, complaint-handling procedures, and cost of borrowing. The second objective involves simplifying the foreign bank entry requirements to increase competition, and streamlining various existing regulations which may impede market entry and competition. The final objective involves legislative changes to permit electronic cheque imaging and electronic transmission of cheque images for presentment and payment, changing the administration of the special security sys-

---

33 Found in legislation with the politically deceptive title *Financial Consumer Agency of Canada Act*, S.C. 2001, c. 9.
34 Canada, Department of Finance, *Response of the Government to Large Bank Mergers in Canada: Safeguarding the Public Interest for Canadians and Canadian Businesses and Competition in the Public Interest—Large Bank Mergers in Canada* (Ottawa: Department of Finance, 2003).
35 Canada, Department of Finance, *2006 Financial Institutions Legislation Review: Proposals for an Effective and Efficient Financial Services Framework* (Ottawa: Department of Finance, 2006) [*White Paper*].
36 Bill C-37, *An Act to amend the law governing financial institutions and to provide for related and consequential matters*, 1st Sess., 39th Parl., 2006 (Royal Assent 29 March 2007).

tem, and changes to bank ownership threshold regimes. Some of these objectives are reflected in the 2007 amendments to the *Bank Act* as discussed throughout the book.

E. FINANCIAL INSTITUTIONS REGULATION GENERALLY

The *Bank Act* is the centrepiece of financial institutions legislation in Canada because of the central role banks play in the national economy, as well as the psychological and symbolic presence they have in consumers' minds.[37] But it is only one part of a complex maze of financial sector legislation in Canada reflecting the numerous and complex varieties of financial institutions in the country. The *Constitution Act, 1867*, provided that the federal government should have sole authority over the banking sector (sections 91(15) and (16)), yet in 1867 other financial institutions operated pursuant to colonial legislation and continue to do so pursuant to federal and provincial legislation.

Each province through its provincial finance ministry regulates all non-bank financial institutions operating within that province, including trust and loan companies, cooperatives, *caisses populaires*, insurance companies, pension plans, and treasury branches, as well as securities commissions, to regulate the issue and trading of shares, money market instruments, bonds, and exchange-traded derivatives. Non-bank financial institutions that operate across provincial boundaries are regulated by Parliament pursuant to section 91(2) and have been since 1867. In addition, numerous federally regulated non-bank financial institutions, including trust companies, loan companies, insurance companies, *caisses populaires*, and pension plans, operate pursuant to legislation parallel to the *Bank Act*.

Since the 1871 Act, banks have been denied the power to act as trustees or fiduciaries on the ground that a bank might face a conflict of interest between acting for a customer in managing funds as a trustee and acting for itself as a bank in making a profit from deposited funds. During the final quarter of the nineteenth century, trust companies expanded their fiduciary role but were concurrently prohibited from taking deposits, underwriting securities, or promoting insurance products. In the early twentieth century, they were allowed to take de-

---

37 The *Insurance Companies Act*, above note 2, is the larger legislation, second only in length to the *Income Tax Act*, R.S.C. 1985, c. 1 (5th Supp.) as am.

posits and lend on mortgages and thus began to grow into near banks, offering many of the same services as banks, in addition to fiduciary services. Meanwhile, banks have continued to be denied direct expansion into fiduciary activities.

During this period, because banks were prohibited from offering residential mortgages, a market vacuum was created, and this permitted the parallel development of loan companies, which were licensed to take deposits and offer personal loans but could not act as fiduciaries. At the same time, legislation restricted insurance companies to offering insurance products, including life insurance and property and casualty insurance, and prohibited them from developing deposit taking and fiduciary products. By the beginning of the twentieth century, the financial institutions sector in Canada was characterized by discrete and segregated divisions, created largely by legislation undergirded by anti-bank populist sentiments and fear of bank monopolies. This division was heightened by the provincial regulation of brokerages from the outset and the regional nature of cooperatives, credit unions, and *caisses populaires* as local alternatives to the banks. While federal and provincial legislation permitted trust companies, loan companies, and cooperatives to offer "banking" services, in addition to their own unique services, banks were restricted to carrying out only the traditional core banking businesses.

In the 1970s trust and loan companies expanded rapidly after the introduction of deposit insurance made them "safer" institutions for consumers' deposits.[38] In the 1980s the trust companies expanded into commercial lending and residential mortgages, but the recession in the real estate sector in the late 1980s exposed solvency risks which the banks were able to use to their advantage after the 1991 *Bank Act* amendments permitted banks to own trust and loan companies through subsidiaries. The 1991 Act represented a significant move toward the assimilation of the four pillars (banks, insurance companies, trust companies, and brokerages), and throughout the 1990s the banks bought trust and loan companies and brokerages which they continued to operate as subsidiaries. This allowed them to become involved in the traditional specific activities of these companies. However, banks continue to be excluded from full participation in insurance,[39] and numerous insurance companies, trust and loan companies, cooperatives, and

---

38   Financed in large part by the greater premiums paid by the banks to sustain the CDIC insurance fund.
39   See Chapter 1, Section C. See also *Canadian Western Bank*, above note 20 at 91–104, Slatter J.

credit unions continue to operate independently, so that from a legislative perspective, discrete legislation is still required until universal financial institutions are permitted and the traditional four pillars are completely collapsed.

The move toward a bank holding company regime[40] in the 2001 amendments may indicate future developments, although various legal and economic issues remain to be clarified in relation to such matters as the solvency risks associated with continuing core banking with securities especially,[41] anti-competitive and anti-trust concerns resulting from the concentration of economic power, and the varieties of conflicts of interest created for which the present fiduciary law provides no clear solutions.[42] Comparison of the four federal statutes[43] in regulating the various financial institutions demonstrates such great uniformity in the corporate governance and regulation of each of the four pillars that if a future policy decision favours multifunctional, universal financial institutions through holding company structures, the legislative framework is largely in place.

F. INTERNATIONAL REGULATION

As a trading nation, Canada's financial system cannot be isolated from the global economy but must present a transparent, static, and secure financial sector if the economy and the country are to flourish. Therefore, although Parliament enjoys domestic sovereign authority over banks and banking, cooperation with other countries in relation to banking is necessary, and the main international body that coordinates financial institutions policy is the Bank for International Settlements (BIS),[44] based in Basel, Switzerland.

The BIS was originally founded in 1930 by several central banks to deal with German World War I reparations, but because of unsavoury connections with the Nazi regime in Germany, it remained relatively obscure until the third quarter of the twentieth century, effecting payments between central banks and arranging periodic meetings of central bankers. The BIS is a private bank incorporated in Switzerland

---

40 See Chapter 4, Section K.
41 This concern prompted the U.S. *Glass-Steagall Act* in 1933.
42 Ross Cranston, *Principles of Banking Law*, 2d ed. (Oxford: Oxford University Press, 2002) 21–24.
43 Above note 2.
44 For current information, see online: www.bis.org.

and is owned by various central banks, including the Bank of Canada. Its charter limits it to taking deposits from its member central banks and permits it to make loans only to its members. It is a central bank for central banks, and in addition to effecting payments between central banks, serves as a confidential forum for discussing monetary and regulatory policy on an international basis.

In 1975 the Basle Committee on Banking Supervision was established at the BIS, and it consists of the banking regulators of major financial countries, including Canada. The Committee's specific mandate is to address the reduction of risk posed to the global financial system by bank failures. It operates by encouraging dialogue and cooperation and suggesting agreed capital adequacy standards for domestic banks. While its suggestions have no formal legal status or authority, its recommendations ("soft law") are followed by banking regulators internationally. The Basle Committee has drawn up sets of principles from time to time, such as the 1975 Concordat,[45] the 1983 Concordat[46] together with the 1992 supplement to deal with the collapse of BCCI, the 1988 Capital Accord[47] amended in 1996, and the 2001 Core Principles.[48] All of these were concerned with various aspects of risk and solvency. As part of its regulation of banks and banking in Canada, the federal government applies the principles proposed from time to time by the Basle Committee.

Several other international bodies are often associated with the financial sector, so it is important to mention them here. However, it is more important to emphasize also that—unlike the BIS—they have no regulatory impact on banks or banking in Canada. The International Monetary Fund (IMF), together with the World Bank and the World Trade Organization (formerly the General Agreement on Tariffs and Trade (GATT)), was established after World War II to help member countries maintain fixed currency exchange rates when independent macroeconomic policies were being pursued by each country. After fixed exchange rates were abandoned in the 1970s, the IMF acquired

---

45 The 1975 Concordat was concerned with sharing information and with the division between home and host countries of regulatory responsibility for subsidiaries and branches.
46 The 1983 Concordat was concerned with consolidated supervision and assessing capital adequacy on a consolidated basis—that is, the worldwide capital adequacy of an international bank; not just its home-country adequacy.
47 The 1988 Capital Accord recommended a basis for calculating capital adequacy.
48 The 2001 Core Principles recommended a new capital adequacy framework based on minimum capital requirements, a supervisory review process, and use of market discipline. It also provided for systemic risks in payments system.

a new role of arranging short-term credit for countries facing liquidity problems as a lender of last resort. Most countries in the world are members and provide financial support on a subscription quota basis; the IMF operates entirely through the cooperation of governments and has no independent legal authority.

The World Trade Organization (WTO) came into existence in 1995 as a successor to GATT and as an international organization whose mandate was to set and police global rules of trade among nations, including trade in goods and services. Again, most countries in the world are members, and all members are required to submit trade disputes to a WTO panel and to abide by the panel's decision. The WTO agreement permits members to regulate financial institutions within their own jurisdictions, although the WTO frowns on discrimination against smaller financial institutions and favours international harmonization and free trade in financial services.

Finally, the World Bank is not a bank. Originally established to deal with the reconstruction of postwar Europe and to finance the development of pre-industrial economies, the World Bank consists of a group of agencies which act as finance companies for development projects internationally. It does not take deposits but gains funding for its projects by issuing publicly traded debt in capital markets and using these borrowed funds to make loans secured by sovereign guarantees from the country in which the project is being undertaken. In theory, the World Bank fills an alleged gap or market failure in the provision of credit by the private sector. In addition, it serves as a forum for the discussion of developmental strategies and produces various related studies. Both the World Bank and the IMF are smaller than a number of the largest international commercial banks. Again, as in the case of the IMF and the WTO, the World Bank plays no regulatory role in relation to banks and banking in Canada, but it is part of the larger world economy in which they operate.

CHAPTER 3

THE REGULATION OF BANKS AND BANKING IN CANADA

A. INTRODUCTION

Historically, the *Bank Act* has been the primary regulatory mechanism by which Parliament has exercised its jurisdiction under section 91(15) over banks and banking in Canada. However, since the mid-twentieth century, Parliament has expanded its governance of the banking sector as well as the federal financial institutions sector generally by enacting legislation regulating particular aspects of banking that relate either to the security and solvency of the national economy or to the safety and security of customers' deposits and other retail transactions. Oversight is exercised either directly through the Minister of Finance or indirectly through various corporations or arms length government agencies with statutory authority over specific aspects of banking business, which in turn report to Parliament through the Minister of Finance. When conducting their day-to-day business, consumers of banking services are generally not aware of the significant role these organizations play in ensuring the security of the financial services sector. Nevertheless, the nature of this oversight and the roles these organizations play ensure the safe, secure, and efficient completion of those millions of daily transactions.

B. BANK OF CANADA

The Bank of Canada came into existence as the central bank on 11 March 1935.[1] In contrast to other common law countries, the creation of a central bank was relatively late in Canadian economic history, probably because many central bank functions had been accommodated within the chartered banks over the course of the nineteenth century. The existence of national banks of significant commercial sophistication meant that one, the Bank of Montreal, could carry out some of the functions of a central bank, particularly the management of the federal government account. A national branch bank clearing system obviated the clearing problems experienced, for example, in the United States prior to the establishment of the Federal Reserve System and senior bankers advised and cooperated with the government. Such cooperation was evident during the First World War, when the Department of Finance was formed and relied on the banking community for advice when it performed some of the functions of a central bank such as holding reserves and supervising bank notes.

The economic boom of the 1920s and the economic bust of the early 1930s, together with the problem of settling balances between Canada and London once the United Kingdom abandoned the gold standard in 1931, prompted discussion of the need for a central bank to regulate monetary policy and settle international accounts. In 1933, the British Law Lord, Lord Macmillan, who had recently chaired a U.K. commission on financial matters, agreed to chair the Royal Commission on Banking and Currency in Canada which recommended the establishment of a central bank. The Bank of Canada began operations in March 1935.

The functions of the Bank of Canada are set out in the preamble to its Act:

> … to regulate credit and currency in the best interests of the economic life of the nation, to control and protect the external value of the national monetary unit and to mitigate by its influence fluctuations in the general level of production, trade, prices and employment, so far as may be possible within the scope of monetary action, and generally to promote the economic and financial welfare of Canada.[2]

---

1 For a history of early origins, see George S. Watts, *The Bank of Canada: Origins and Early History* (Ottawa: Carleton University Press, 1993), which incorporates articles published earlier in the *Bank of Canada Review* (May 1972) 14; (August 1972) 12; (November 1972) 6; (April 1973) 2; (November 1973) 2; (November 1974) 2; (January 1976) 2.

2 *Bank of Canada Act*, R.S.C. 1985, c. B-2 as am. For current information, see online: www.bankofcanada.ca.

The Bank of Canada is a corporation[3] established by legislation, not a Crown corporation, department, or agency of the federal government. Its head office is in Ottawa, but it may establish other branches and agencies within Canada and abroad.[4] It is managed by a board of directors composed of the Governor, a Deputy Governor and twelve directors, together with the Deputy Minister of Finance, who does not have the right to vote.[5]

The Governor and Deputy Governor of the Bank are appointed by the board with the approval of the Governor in Council[6] for renewable seven-year terms.[7] They are to have proven financial experience,[8] be Canadian citizens under seventy-five years of age, and not be employed by any other government agency or have associations with any other organization of a related nature.[9] Additional Deputy Governors may be appointed by the board.[10] The Governor is the chief executive officer of the Bank.[11]

The directors are appointed by the Minister of Finance with the approval of the Governor in Council for renewable three-year terms.[12] A director must be a Canadian citizen ordinarily resident in Canada, under seventy-five years of age, and not employed by any other government agency or have associations with any other organization of a related nature.[13] Directors are subject to statutory disclosure of conflict rules[14] and are entitled to directors' fees for attendance at directors' meetings.[15] The Governor is the chair of the board of directors.[16]

The Act provides that it is an offence for a Governor, Deputy Governor, or director to hold or continue in office knowing of his or her ineligibility. The penalties are on summary conviction a fine of not more

---

3 *Ibid.*, s. 3. *Bain v. Bank of Canada*, [1935] 4 D.L.R. 112 (B.C.C.A.); *Walsh Advertising Co. v. R.*, [1962] Ex. C.R. 115; *Kawneer Co. of Canada Ltd. v. Bank of Canada* (1975), 60 D.L.R. (3d) 636 (Ont. H.C.J.); *Bank of Canada v. Bank of Montreal* (1977), 76 D.L.R. (3d) 385 (S.C.C.).
4 *Ibid.*, ss. 4(1) & (2).
5 *Ibid.*, ss. 5(1) & (2).
6 *Ibid.*, s. 6(1).
7 *Ibid.*, s. 6(3).
8 *Ibid.*, s. 6(2).
9 *Ibid.*, s. 6(4). See s. 6(4) for particular details.
10 *Ibid.*, ss. 7(1) & (2).
11 *Ibid.*, s. 8.
12 *Ibid.*, s. 9.
13 *Ibid.*, s. 10. See s. 10 for particular details.
14 *Ibid.*, s. 10.1.
15 *Ibid.*, s. 11.
16 *Ibid.*, s. 12. For the executive committee of the board, see s. 13.

than $100,000 or imprisonment for not more than six months or both.[17] All directors, officers, and employees are required to take an oath or make a solemn affirmation of fidelity and secrecy.[18]

The Bank of Canada is required to have a minimum base capital of $5M divided into 100,000 shares at a par value of $50.00 each issued to the Minister of Finance to hold on behalf of the Crown in right of Canada.[19] The board may employ such officers and employees as the executive committee deems necessary and establish a pension fund for them.[20] The Bank is required to establish a reserve fund into which any annual surplus from the operations of the Bank is to be applied if the reserve fund is less than the paid-up capital until the reserve fund is five times the paid-up capital. Then the surplus shall form part of the Consolidated Revenue Fund.[21] The affairs of the Bank are to be audited annually by two firms of accountants appointed by the Governor in Council on the recommendation of the Minister of Finance.[22] The board is empowered to make by-laws relating to meetings, quorums, directors' fees, duties and conduct of the officers and employees, the form of the annual statement of accounts, and the management generally of the bank.[23] Insolvency and winding-up legislation does not apply to the Bank, as it can be wound up only by Parliament.[24] In short, the Bank of Canada as a body corporate operates in a relatively similar fashion to any other body corporate in Canada.

The business and powers of the Bank set it apart from other corporations for the specific functions it was incorporated to perform. The Act sets out numerous activities in which it may engage, such as buying and selling precious metals, foreign currencies, government securities guaranteed by the governments of Canada, the United States, Japan, or any European Union country, International Monetary Fund (IMF) special drawing rights, certain negotiable instruments, and any other securities in a severe and unusual stress to promote Canadian financial stability.[25] The Bank of Canada may also make loans to the Canadian

---

17   Ibid., s. 31.
18   Ibid., s. 16 and Sch. I.
19   Ibid., s. 17.
20   Ibid., s. 15.
21   Ibid., s. 27. See s. 27 for particular details and s. 27.1 for a special reserve fund to offset unrealized valuation losses resulting from fair value changes in the bank's investment portfolio.
22   Ibid., s. 28.
23   Ibid., s. 35.
24   Ibid., s. 34.
25   Ibid., ss. 18(a)–(g.1) and (k). See s. 18 for particular details and s. 19 for publication.

Payments Association or to the federal or provincial governments;[26] accept deposits from the federal or provincial governments, any bank or certain foreign banks, the central banks of other countries, the Bank for International Settlements (BIS), the IMF, or other international financial organizations;[27] open accounts in other central banks or in the BIS;[28] deal in real property;[29] and engage in any incidental or consequential business activity.[30]

In addition to these activities, which the Bank of Canada may carry out on its own in its own right, the Act also authorizes the Bank to act in relation to other financial institutions. First, the Bank may acquire from any bank or foreign bank any collateral securities held under Part VIII of the *Bank Act* and exercise all rights and remedies inherent in them.[31] Secondly, the Bank is the depository for unclaimed balances, which the *Bank Act* requires Canadian banks to remit to the central bank if unclaimed for a period of ten years,[32] and becomes liable for the balance to the customer or the customer's legal representative. However, the Bank of Canada is not liable if the unpaid balance was less than $1,000 and forty years have passed since the last transaction on the account or the last time a statement of account was requested or acknowledged by the customer.[33] The Bank is required to pay interest on these deposits.[34] Once the forty-year period has elapsed, the Bank is required to pay the amount it received, without interest, to the Receiver General of Canada, to form part of the Consolidated Revenue Fund, and the Bank may then destroy all records relating to the debt.[35]

Thirdly, the Bank may require the Superintendent of Financial Institutions to inspect any financial institution, and the Superintendent may in turn require the Bank to pay any extraordinary costs of the inspection.[36] Fourthly, the Bank acts as the fiscal agent of the Government

---

26   *Ibid.*, ss. 18(h)–(j). See s. 18 for particular details and s. 19 for publication.
27   *Ibid.*, ss. 18(l)–(m) and (o). See s. 18 for particular details and s. 19 for publication.
28   *Ibid.*, s. 18(m).
29   *Ibid.*, s. 18(n).
30   *Ibid.*, s. 18(p).
31   *Ibid.*, s. 20.
32   *Bank Act*, S.C. 1991, c. 46, ss. 438–39.
33   *Bank of Canada Act*, above note 2, s. 22(1). See s. 22(1.1) for negotiable instruments and s. 22(1.2) for liquidation claims in the winding-up of a federal financial institution.
34   *Ibid.*, s. 18(o).
35   *Ibid.*, ss. 22(3) & (4). The Bank of Canada is not liable when the financial institution has paid the creditor: s. 22(2).
36   *Ibid.*, s. 22.1.

of Canada, including management of the public debt at the request of the Minister of Finance.[37] Fifthly, the Bank of Canada has the sole right to issue banknotes.[38] These notes are a first charge on the assets of the Bank[39] and are not negotiable instruments within the *Bills of Exchange Act*.[40] The Bank remains responsible for the redemption of notes issued prior to 11 March 1935 that constituted a liability to Canada, as well as notes issued prior to 1 January 1950 by Canadian banks.[41]

The *Bank of Canada Act* also expressly provides that the Bank may not be involved in certain activities. It is not permitted to engage in or have a direct interest in any trade or business; use its own shares or the shares of any bank except the BIS as security; lend on the security of any real property except when any claims of the Bank, in the opinion of the board, are endangered; make unsecured loans; pay interest on money deposited with the Bank except for transferred unclaimed balances; or allow the renewal of negotiable instruments that come to the Bank except when the board authorizes one renewal only, in exceptional circumstances.[42]

Although the Bank of Canada is an arms length corporation, with independent statutory purposes as outlined in the preamble to its Act, the government retains significant supervisory control over its activities. First, the Governor, the Deputy Governor and the entire Board of Directors are effectively Ministerial appointees.[43] Secondly, the Governor and the Minister of Finance are required to consult regularly on monetary policy and on its relation to general economic policy, with the Minister of Finance having the final statutory authority to give the Bank binding directives concerning monetary policy.[44] Thirdly, all of the Bank's shares are vested in the Minister to hold on behalf of the Crown in right of Canada.[45] Fourthly, the Bank is required to publish its minimum interest rate for loans and advances.[46] Fifthly, the auditors of the Bank are appointed by the Governor in Council and make a report to the Minister of Finance at the same time as to the Bank.[47]

---

37   *Ibid.*, ss. 24 & 24.1.
38   *Ibid.*, s. 25.
39   *Ibid.*, s. 25(1).
40   *Ibid.*, s. 25(6).
41   *Ibid.*, s. 26.
42   *Ibid.*, s. 23.
43   *Ibid.*, ss. 6 and 9.
44   *Ibid.*, s. 14.
45   *Ibid.*, s. 17.
46   *Ibid.*, s. 21.
47   *Ibid.*, s. 28.

Sixthly, the Bank is required to transmit its balance sheet to the Minister every Wednesday as soon as practicable after the close of business on that day[48] and also to transmit its balance sheet every month as soon as practicable after the last business day of each month, setting out information about the Bank's investment in securities issued or guaranteed by the Government of Canada.[49] Each balance sheet is to be published in the next issue of the *Canada Gazette*.[50] Seventhly, the Bank is required to send its audited financial statements to the Minister of Finance within two months after the end of each financial year,[51] and the Minister is required to lay a copy, together with the accompanying Governor's report,[52] before Parliament on any of the first twenty-one days either House is sitting after the Minister receives it.[53]

Finally, the *Bank of Canada Act* creates a statutory immunity from liability for the Crown, the Minister, and any officer, employee, or director of the Bank or any agent of the Governor for acts and omissions done in good faith in the discharge of any powers or duties under the Act.[54] Further, it is an offence for any director, officer, or auditor of the Bank to verify any statement, account, or list required by the Minister under the Act resulting on summary conviction in a fine of not more than $100,000 or imprisonment for not more than six months or both.[55] The same penalties apply to any officer of the Bank or any other bank that fails to comply with the Act.[56]

This list demonstrates that while the Bank of Canada has primary responsibility for monetary policy, the Governor in Council has final control pursuant to section 14 of the Act. However, this power has never been used. The responsibilities of the Bank of Canada have recently been expanded beyond those in its own Act, through the *Payment Clearing and Settlement Act*,[57] which grants the Governor certain powers to ensure that the clearing and settlement system is not disrupted by "systemic risk."[58] Systemic risk is defined as the inability of a "participant"[59]

---

48   Ibid., s. 29(1). As well as post it on the Bank's website.
49   Ibid., s. 29(2).
50   Ibid., s. 29(3).
51   Ibid., ss. 30(1) & (2).
52   Ibid., ss. 30(2.1) & (2.2).
53   Ibid., s. 30(3).
54   Ibid., s. 30.1.
55   Ibid., s. 32.
56   Ibid., s. 33.
57   S.C. 1996, c.6, Sch. as am.
58   Ibid., s. 2 "systemic risk."
59   Ibid., "participant."

to meet its obligations as they become due so as to cause a ripple effect for the other participants, causing the system to collapse. These powers include guaranteeing settlement,[60] making liquidity loans to the "clearing house"[61] and to the "central counter-party"[62] of a designated system,[63] and acting as a central counter-party,[64] that is, the party in a clearing and settlement system through whom all other participants' obligations are netted.

The powers given to the Bank of Canada under the *Payment Clearing and Settlement Act* flesh out its powers under its own Act to be the settlement bank in the payments system[65] and to make loans to clearers in that system to avoid systemic risk.[66] This role for the Bank points to two other functions that it carries out in the financial institutions sector generally although they are not explicit in any legislation. First, the Bank of Canada is popularly referred to as the lender of last resort to the banks. This does not mean that it will guarantee the solvency of any financial institution, nor is it known how often it has done so,[67] but its role of ensuring the safety of the entire system means that it is there to act should action be absolutely necessary. The second informal function of the central bank is to use "moral suasion" within the banking sector to move it or individual banks in a prudent direction should such be necessary. How often the Bank of Canada has played either informal role is necessarily unknown but those roles are testimony to the unique and vital supervisory role of the Bank of Canada in the banking system.

C. OFFICE OF THE SUPERINTENDENT OF FINANCIAL INSTITUTIONS

The Office of the Superintendent of Financial Institutions (OSFI) was created by legislation in 1987[68] as a result of the amalgamation of the

---

60 *Ibid.*, s. 7(a). To date, the Governor has designated only the Large Value Transfer System (LVTS) under s. 4 as a system so guaranteed. For more details about LVTS, see Chapter 9, Section E.
61 *Ibid.*, s. 2 "clearing house" and s. 7(b).
62 *Ibid.*, s. 2 "central counter-party."
63 *Ibid.*, s. 7(b).
64 *Ibid.*, s. 7(c).
65 *Bank of Canada Act*, above note 2, s. 18(1.1).
66 *Ibid.*, s. 18(h).
67 One known example is that of the Northland Bank prior to its insolvency in 1985.
68 R.S.C. 1985, c. 18 (3d Supp.). For current information, see online: www.osfi-bsif.gc.ca.

Department of Insurance and the Office of the Inspector General of Banks. As their names suggest, the former had supervisory authority over insurance companies and the latter over banks. The Inspector General's office was established in 1924, after several bank failures and amid concerns about alleged corruption in the administration of banks. OSFI was created amid similar concerns about the financial institutions sector generally following the failures of a number of trust companies in the 1980s and of two banks in 1985, the Canadian Commercial Bank and the Northland Bank.[69] It was created as a single regulatory office with oversight over all federally incorporated financial institutions and federally regulated employer-sponsored pension plans.[70] Subsequently, OSFI has also taken on the roles of providing actuarial advice to the federal government[71] and of conducting reviews of certain provincially incorporated financial institutions by virtue of federal-provincial agreements or by virtue of agency agreements with the Canada Deposit Insurance Corporation (CDIC).[72]

The *OSFI Act* expressly provides that financial institutions and pension plans are to be regulated by the Government of Canada for the purpose of contributing to public confidence in the Canadian financial system.[73] The statutory objects of the office are: (i) to supervise financial institutions in order to determine whether they are in sound financial condition and comply with the law; (ii) to advise promptly a financial institution that is not in sound financial condition or legal compliance and to require its board and management to take corrective measures to deal with the situation expeditiously; (iii) to monitor how financial institutions control and manage risk; and (iv) to monitor the entire sector for issues that may have a negative impact on it.[74] The Act further provides that in pursuing these objects, OSFI is required: (i) to protect the rights and interests of depositors and creditors of banks,

---

[69] See Canada, Inquiry into the Collapse of the CCB and the Northland Report, *Report of the Inquiry into the Collapse of the CCB and the Northland Report* (Ottawa: Supply and Services, 1986) ["the Estey Report"].
[70] *Pension Benefits Standards Act*, R.S.C. 1985, c. 32 (2d Supp.).
[71] Through the Office of the Chief Actuary.
[72] For more about the relationship between OSFI and the CDIC, see Section F, below in this chapter.
[73] *Office of the Superintendent of Financial Institutions Act*, above note 68, s. 3.1. Although the Act refers to financial institutions and pension plans, the following discussion will focus on the provisions relating to banks, given that the subject of this book is banking law.
[74] *Ibid.*, s. 4(2). For a judicial discussion of prudent lending and investment policies in a provincial regulatory context, see *Fraser Valley Credit Union v. Canada (Superintendent of Financial Institutions)* (1999), 65 B.C.L.R. (3d) 85 (C.A.).

having due regard to the need for banks to compete effectively and take reasonable risks;[75] and (ii) to have regard to the responsibility of boards of directors for the management of banks that operate in a competitive environment, necessitating the management of risk in the context of the fact that financial difficulties can lead to failure.[76] The Office is expressly established as an office of the Government of Canada, and the Minister of Finance is to "preside" over it and be responsible for it.[77] The Governor in Council appoints a deputy head of the Office, who is called the Superintendent of Financial Institutions.[78] In contrast to the earlier Inspector General of Banks, OSFI is part of the Government of Canada and not independent of it, making the Government expressly responsible for the federal financial institutions sector generally.

The Superintendent is appointed for a seven-year renewable term[79] and holds office during good behaviour.[80] In the event of absence or incapacity, the Governor in Council may appoint a replacement for up to six months.[81] The Superintendent is responsible to the Minister of Finance for the administration of the *Bank Act*,[82] as well as for the duties assigned under the *OSFI Act*.[83]

To assist the Superintendent in carrying out the statutory duties assigned by these two Acts, the *OSFI Act* makes provision for the Office itself. The Superintendent may appoint Deputy Superintendents,[84] to whom the powers and duties of the Superintendent may be delegated,[85] as well as additional employees.[86]

The Act provides that the expenses of running the Office are to be defrayed from the Consolidated Revenue Fund,[87] supplemented by assessments authorized by the Act against each financial institution supervised.[88]

---

75 *Ibid.*, s. 4(3)(a).
76 *Ibid.*, s. 4(4).
77 *Ibid.*, s. 4(1).
78 *Ibid.*, s. 5(1).
79 *Ibid.*, ss. 5(2) and (4).
80 *Ibid.*, s. 5(3).
81 *Ibid.*, ss. 5(5) & (6).
82 *Ibid.*, s. 6(1). For exceptions, see s. 6(1), as well as other legislation governing financial institutions in Canada.
83 *Ibid.*, s. 6(1).
84 *Ibid.*, s. 8.
85 *Ibid.*, ss. 9 & 10.
86 *Ibid.*, s. 11. See also ss. 11–15 relating to employment standards for such employees.
87 *Ibid.*, ss. 16, 17(1) & (2).
88 *Ibid.*, ss. 23, 23.1, & 23.2. Annually, these assessments constitute almost the entire budget of the Office, meaning that the financial institutions sector pays for its own supervision.

However, the aggregate of expenditures from the Consolidated Revenue Fund is not permitted to exceed by more than $40 million the total of the assessments and revenues against the regulated institutions.[89] Treasury Board approval is required if the aggregate of expenditure from the Consolidated Revenue Fund exceeds the assessments and money appropriated by Parliament.[90]

The role of OSFI in the supervision of financial institutions is facilitated under the Act by a committee consisting of the Superintendent, the Commissioner of the Financial Consumer Agency of Canada,[91] the Governor of the Bank of Canada, the Chair of the Canada Deposit Insurance Corporation, and the Deputy Minister of Finance.[92] The purpose of this committee is to facilitate consultation and the exchange of information relating to this supervision,[93] and all committee members are entitled to any information relating directly to supervision.[94] Members of the committee are not permitted to own shares, directly or indirectly, in any financial institution or related institution[95] or to borrow money from them without informing the Minister in writing.[96] Nor is a committee member permitted to receive a grant or annuity from a financial institution or from any director, officer, or employee of such an institution.[97] The penalty for doing so is a fine of not more than $2,000 or imprisonment for not more than six months or both on summary conviction or $10,000 or five years or both on indictment.[98]

OSFI receives information of vital importance to the national economy from the institutions it regulates, and the Act makes provision for the confidentiality of that information.[99] The Superintendent is permitted to make disclosures to certain persons provided confidentiality will be maintained, including to any government body or other agency that regulates or supervises financial institutions, the CDIC, the Deputy Minister of Finance, or any other authorized officer of the Department of Finance, the Governor of the Bank of Canada, or any other authorized

---

89   Ibid., s. 17(3).
90   Ibid., s. 17(4).
91   See Section G, below in this chapter.
92   Ibid., s. 18(1). The committee is chaired by the Superintendent: s. 18(2).
93   Ibid., s. 18(3).
94   Ibid., ss. 18(4) & (5).
95   Ibid., s. 19.
96   Ibid., s. 20.
97   Ibid., s. 21(1).
98   Ibid., s. 21(2).
99   Ibid., s. 22(1).

Bank of Canada officer.[100] The terms of any disclosures may be regulated by the Governor in Council.[101] The Superintendent is also required to make such disclosures as authorized by the Minister of Finance of information obtained under the *Bank Act* for the purpose of analysis of the financial condition of a financial institution, as well as of any other information obtained by the Superintendent while conducting industry surveys.[102] Disclosures of customer information to the Minister are prohibited in the absence of contrary regulations.[103] Finally, the Superintendent must prepare a report concerning information disclosure by financial institutions, especially its enhancement, and this report must be included in the Minister's annual report to Parliament.[104]

The Act makes extensive provision for penalties when a financial institution does not comply with an order, direction, or prudential agreement with the Superintendent under any financial institutions legislation.[105] However, the Act also provides for a Crown exemption from liability for any act or omission in good faith in the discharge of any powers or duties under the Act by the Crown, the Minister of Finance, the Superintendent, or anyone acting under the direction of the Superintendent.[106]

As stated earlier, the duties of the Superintendent are set out in both the *OSFI Act* and especially in the *Bank Act*. The *OSFI Act* makes provision for only a few specific duties in addition to the general supervisory authority already discussed. First, the Superintendent may inquire into any dealing in securities by a financial institution or its officers or employees and report to the Minister.[107] Secondly, the Superintendent shall administer any regulations made by the Governor in Council in relation to dealing in securities,[108] with the discretion set out in any regulations.[109] Otherwise, the *OSFI Act* provides that the Superintendent shall be employed only as the Superintendent[110] and may not be rewarded for any other duties performed for the Crown.[111] These restrictions ensure

---

100 *Ibid.*, s. 22(2).
101 *Ibid.*, s. 22(2.1).
102 *Ibid.*, ss. 22(3) & (4).
103 *Ibid.*, s. 22(5).
104 *Ibid.*, ss. 22(6) and 40.
105 *Ibid.*, ss. 24–38.
106 *Ibid.*, s. 39.
107 *Ibid.*, ss. 6(2) and (5).
108 *Ibid.*, s. 6(3).
109 *Ibid.*, s. 6(4).
110 *Ibid.*, s. 7(1).
111 *Ibid.*, s. 7(2).

that there is no hint of conflict of interest, which might compromise the integrity of the Office.

For banks,[112] the supervisory duties of the Superintendent are set out in considerable detail in the *Bank Act*, which places on the Superintendent numerous duties in relation to the day-to-day supervision of banks from incorporation to winding-up. The Act requires banks to apply to OSFI for numerous types of approvals, consents, exemptions, and extensions.[113] But the most important role of OSFI is that of ensuring the solvency of each bank and the security of depositor and shareholder interests in the event of insolvency. Part XIII of the *Bank Act* is concerned with this matter.

First, the *Bank Act* requires a bank to provide to the Superintendent such information as the Superintendent requires at any time.[114] Secondly, banks are required to make annual reports to the Superintendent concerning balances[115] and bills of exchange[116] for which no transaction has taken place for a period of nine years or more, stating such information as names, addresses, amounts, and branches for each.[117] Thirdly, banks are required to make annual returns showing the names and other pertinent information of all directors and auditors.[118] Fourthly, banks are required to file by-laws with the Superintendent within thirty days of their coming into force.[119] Fifthly, the Superintendent is required to maintain a register of banks, including incorporating instruments and all other returned information.[120] This register shall be available to any persons[121] and the information admissible in evidence in all courts as *prima facie* proof of the facts contained therein.[122]

Sixthly, the Superintendent may require any person who controls a bank or any affiliated entity of a bank to provide such information as the Superintendent requires to ensure that the bank is in a sound financial condition and the *Bank Act* is being observed.[123]

---

112 For the other financial institutions, equivalent provisions are found in their Acts for the role of OSFI.
113 *Bank Act*, above note 32, s. 976. But see throughout the *Bank Act*.
114 *Ibid.*, s. 628(1).
115 *Ibid.*, s. 629. See Section 638 for publication in the *Canada Gazette*.
116 *Ibid.*, s. 630. See Section 638 for publication in the *Canada Gazette*.
117 *Ibid.*, s. 631 for calculation of the totals if a return under ss. 629–30 is omitted.
118 *Ibid.*, s. 632.
119 *Ibid.*, s. 633.
120 *Ibid.*, ss. 634(1) & (2).
121 *Ibid.*, s. 634(3).
122 *Ibid.*, s. 634(4).
123 *Ibid.*, s. 635.

Seventhly, the Superintendent is required to disclose information obtained under the Act at the instance of the Minister of Finance to analyze the financial condition of a bank.[124] Eighthly, although the information obtained by the Superintendent as a result of statutory disclosures to the Superintendent is to be treated as confidential,[125] the Superintendent may disclose that information to certain persons if satisfied that it will be treated as confidential, including any government or other agency or body that regulates financial institutions, the CDIC, the Deputy Minister of Finance or other authorized Department of Finance officer, or the Governor of the Bank of Canada or other authorized Bank of Canada officer.[126] The Governor in Council may make regulations relating to the disclosure of confidential information.[127] Ninthly, all banks are required to make public disclosure of information concerning compensation for their executives and relating to their business and affairs for the purpose of analysis of their financial condition as required by the Governor in Council.[128] Finally, the Superintendent must report annually to the Minister of Finance about bank disclosures and progress in enhancing disclosures in the financial services sector generally.[129]

In addition to the *Bank Act* provisions requiring banks to make these reports to the Superintendent, the Act further provides that the Superintendent shall make an examination of each bank at least annually, to ensure that the bank is in compliance with the *Bank Act* and in sound financial condition, and the results are to be reported to the Minister of Finance.[130] For this examination, the Superintendent has access to all records and persons associated with the bank[131] and all the powers of a commissioner under the *Inquiries Act*[132] for the purpose of obtaining evidence under oath.[133]

The *Bank Act* contains the statutory provisions pursuant to which the Superintendent acts when a bank is not in a sound condition. When the Superintendent is of that opinion, the bank may be directed to cease or refrain from the unsound conduct and do such acts as are necessary

---

124 *Ibid.*, s. 639. With the exception of customer information: s. 641.
125 *Ibid.*, s. 636(1).
126 *Ibid.*, s. 636(2).
127 *Ibid.*, s. 637.
128 *Ibid.*, s. 640(1). With the exception of customer information: s. 641.
129 *Ibid.*, s. 642.
130 *Ibid.*, s. 643(1).
131 *Ibid.*, s. 643(2).
132 R.S.C. 1985, c. I-11, as am.
133 *Bank Act*, above note 32, s. 644.

to remedy the situation.[134] The Superintendent may enter into a "prudential agreement" with the bank to implement any measure designed to ensure safety and soundness[135] and may obtain a court order to enforce the agreement against the bank and any other person.[136] When a bank has been notified by the Superintendent or has entered into a prudential agreement, the Superintendent has statutory authority to remove directors or senior officers from office who are disqualified on the basis of competence, business record, experience, conduct or character, or because of a contravention of the Act or of any order or condition imposed by the Superintendent.[137]

Finally, the Superintendent may take control of the bank for a period of sixteen days or indefinitely.[138] The Act contains an extensive list of situations in which control may be taken,[139] and the purpose of doing so must be to protect the interests of the depositors and creditors.[140] When the Superintendent takes control, the powers of the directors and officers are suspended[141] and the Superintendent manages the bank in their place.[142] Control expires on the day when the Superintendent notifies the directors and officers that the situation has been substantially rectified and the bank can resume control of its business and affairs.[143] On the other hand, the Superintendent may request the Attorney General of Canada to apply for a winding-up order under the *Winding-Up and Restructuring Act*.[144] The decision to retain control or wind up must be made within forty-two days of the Superintendent's taking control.[145]

The *Bank Act* also provides for reimbursement of the costs associated with taking control. The Superintendent may appoint a committee from among the banks that pay assessments under the *OSFI Act* to advise OSFI in relation to its duties and responsibilities in exercising control.[146] Since the only statutory condition for being on that committee is liability to assessment, it may be assumed that the costs associated with control will be

---

134 *Ibid.*, s. 645.
135 *Ibid.*, s. 644.1.
136 *Ibid.*, s. 646.
137 *Ibid.*, ss. 646.1, 647, & 647.1.
138 *Ibid.*, s. 648(1).
139 *Ibid.*, ss. 648(1.1) & (1.2).
140 *Ibid.*, s. 648(3).
141 *Ibid.*, s. 649(1).
142 *Ibid.*, ss. 649(2) and 648(3).
143 *Ibid.*, s. 650.
144 *Ibid.*, s. 651; R.S.C. 1985, c. W-11 as am.
145 *Bank Act*, above note 32, s. 652.
146 *Ibid.*, s. 653.

an issue for the committee. The *Bank Act* further provides that the Superintendent may direct the bank under control to be liable for all or part of the costs that would otherwise be borne by the other banks assessed by OSFI.[147] An assessment against the bank under control is a debt due to the Crown and recoverable in court[148] and ranks in priority after all other claims but prior to any claim in respect of shares of the bank.[149]

Under the general oversight of the Minister of Finance, OSFI carries on much of the work necessary to ensure the security and soundness of the Canadian banking system. Together with the Bank of Canada, it is a member of the Basle Committee on Banking Supervision and has taken a leading role in setting rules for banks in G-10 countries, as well as ensuring that the best rules apply to Canadian banks.

D. THE CANADIAN BANKERS ASSOCIATION

Although a non-governmental organization, rather than a government body or agency, the Canadian Bankers Association (CBA) has historically played an important role in banking in Canada and continues to do so. The CBA began as a voluntary association in 1891 to promote the common interests of the banking community by monitoring banking legislation, lobbying for legislation, organizing professional courses, and publishing journals and other materials of interest to bankers.[150] The CBA was incorporated in 1900 by Parliament.[151] From an external banking system perspective, the most important role of the CBA from its earliest days was the development of a national, paper-based clearing and settlement system. By 1897 clearing houses existed in Saint John, Halifax, Montreal, Toronto, Hamilton, and Winnipeg, and others were subsequently established as Canada spread westward. The CBA also administered the Bank Circulation Redemption Fund, established by the 1890 *Bank Act*, to redeem the banknotes of failed banks.

The *CBA Act* requires that all banks to which the *Bank Act* applies be members.[152] The Act also makes provision for bank officers to be

---

147 *Ibid.*, s. 654(1).
148 *Ibid.*, s. 654(2).
149 *Ibid.*, ss. 655 & 656.
150 See generally: J. Harvey Perry, "Origins of the Canadian Bankers' Association" (1967) 79 *Canadian Banker* 96 and s. 5 of the *Canadian Bankers Association Act*, S.C. 1900, c. 93 [*CBA Act*]. For current information, see online: www.cba.ca.
151 *CBA Act*, ibid.
152 *Ibid.*, s. 2(a).

"associates" for as long as they are bank officers.[153] The Act provides for the usual governance framework of such organizations, for officers,[154] annual general meetings,[155] an executive council,[156] voting,[157] by-laws,[158] and dues.[159] The 1900 Act also granted the CBA a monopoly to run a clearing system that any bank might voluntarily join or withdraw from at any time.[160] All banks had an equal voice in making the clearing rules, whether or not they joined the clearing system.[161] Prior to taking effect, the rules required Treasury Board approval.[162] This monopoly ended in 1980, when the Canadian Payments Association was incorporated for the purpose of running the national clearing and settlement system. The transition occurred in 1983, and since that time, the Canadian Payments Association has operated the national system.[163]

The CBA continues to be an important organization for Canadian banks and banking by sponsoring educational programs for bankers,[164] conducting research on banking matters generally, brokering agreements among banks for the introduction of new banking practices and services, representing Canadian banking interests internationally in organizations such as the United Nations Commission on International Trade Law (UNCITRAL) and the Society for Worldwide Interbank Financial Telecommunication (SWIFT), making representations to the government about desirable banking law reforms, and, of course, continuing to represent the unique perspectives of the banking sector to both government and the public.

E. THE CANADIAN PAYMENTS ASSOCIATION

The Canadian Payments Association (CPA) was created by Act of Parliament in 1980 for the purpose of establishing and operating a nation-

---

153 *Ibid.*, ss. 2(b), 3, & 4.
154 *Ibid.*, ss. 8, 9, & 10.
155 *Ibid.*, ss. 11 & 12. For subsections, see s. 6.
156 *Ibid.*, ss. 13 & 14.
157 *Ibid.*, s. 8.
158 *Ibid.*, ss. 8 and 16.
159 *Ibid.*, s. 15.
160 *Ibid.*, s. 7.
161 *Ibid.*, ss. 7(2) and 16(3).
162 *Ibid.*
163 *Banks and Banking Law Revision Act*, S.C. 1980–81–82–83, c. 40, s. 90(3) repealed s. 7 of the *CBA Act*, with effect from 1 June 1983.
164 Institute of Canadian Bankers, Toronto.

al clearing and settlement of payments system, and in 1983 it took over that function from the CBA. In the decade prior to the incorporation of the CPA, the demands of non-bank financial institutions to have direct access to the payments systems and the rapid development of costly electronic funds transfers, in addition to the traditional paper-based system, suggested the need for a national electronic transfer system accessible to all financial institutions directly.

The *Canadian Payments Act*[165] creates a unique corporation: a non-profit, non-share capital corporation,[166] which is not a government agency[167] and whose members are the Bank of Canada and various financial institutions that fund the corporation's activities, over which the Governor in Council, the Minister of Finance, and the Governor of the Bank of Canada exercise oversight. The CPA is truly *sui generis*, structured and funded like a private corporation but subject to public regulation of its activities.

The statutory objects of the CPA are the following: (i) to establish and operate national clearing and settlement of payments systems and other arrangements for the making or exchange of payments; (ii) to facilitate the interaction of its systems with other systems in the exchange, clearing, or settlement of payments; and (iii) to facilitate the development of new payment methods and technologies.[168] In fulfilling these objects, the CPA is also under a statutory duty to promote the efficiency, safety, and soundness of its systems and to take into account the interests of its users.[169]

The CPA fulfills the first object by running the Automated Clearing Settlement System (ACSS) and the Large Value Transfer System (LVTS), and it fulfills the second object insofar as subordinate systems such as Interac and the Debt Clearing Service of the Canadian Depository for Securities Ltd. (CDS) rely on the ACSS and LVTS to settle the payment obligations of their participants at the Bank of Canada.[170] However, other third party payment systems are not linked because of the ambiguity in relation to the third object, which permits the CPA to facilitate but not necessarily to operate and regulate new payment systems.

---

165 R.S.C. 1985, c. C-21 as am. For current information, see online: www.cdnpay.ca. See also Deborah Wilson and Isabelle Lepage, "The Canadian Payments System — Recent Legislative Changes" (2002–03) 18 B.F.L.R. 261.
166 *Canadian Payments Act, ibid.*, s. 3(1). Certain sections of the *Canada Business Corporations Act*, R.S.C. 1985, c. C-44 as am. apply, but the *Canada Corporations Act*, R.S.C. 1985, c. C-32 does not: *ibid.*, ss. 34(1) & (2).
167 *Ibid.*, s. 3(2).
168 *Ibid.*, s. 5(1).
169 *Ibid.*, s. 5(2).
170 See Chapter 9.

The *Canadian Payments Act* extends membership in the Canadian Payments Association beyond the banks. The members are the Bank of Canada, every bank operating in Canada,[171] and any other person entitled to be a member who applies for membership,[172] that is, a credit union central, a trust company or loan company that accepts deposits transferable by order to a third party, any province or agent that accepts deposits transferable by order to a third party, a life insurance company, a securities dealer, a cooperative credit association, the trustee of a qualified trust, and a qualified corporation on behalf of its money market mutual fund.[173] Non-bank members cease to be members if they cease to meet the requirement for membership or decide to cease to be members.[174]

The CPA is governed by a board of directors consisting of sixteen members, of whom the chair is appointed by the Bank of Canada,[175] three members are appointed by the Minister of Finance,[176] and the remaining twelve are elected by the members, who are divided into classes for the purpose of representation on the board.[177] With the exception of the Ministerial appointees, alternative directors may also be elected, and any one of these directors may act as a director when the director is absent or unable to act.[178] At least three quarters of the directors must be Canadian citizens ordinarily resident in Canada.[179] The board may be chaired by the alternate Bank of Canada appointee if the chair is absent or unable to act, and the chair enjoys a second vote in the event of a tie vote.[180]

The Act contains standard corporate governance provisions for a chief executive officer,[181] the duties and powers of the board to manage the affairs of the CPA,[182] by-laws,[183] committees,[184] budgets,[185] annual

---

171 *Ibid.*, ss. 4(1)(a)–(c).
172 *Ibid.*, s. 4(1)(d).
173 *Ibid.*, s. 4(2) and s. 2(1) for definitions.
174 *Ibid.*, ss. 4(5)–(7) and By-law No. 1, SOR/2003-174, ss. 72–110.
175 *Ibid.*, ss. 8 and 9(1).
176 *Ibid.*, ss. 9(1.1), (1.2), (1.3), (5), (6), & (7).
177 *Ibid.*, ss. 9(2), (3), & (4); 10, 11, 12, & 13.
178 *Ibid.*, ss. 9(1)(b) and 12.
179 *Ibid.*, s. 14.
180 *Ibid.*, s. 15.
181 *Ibid.*, s. 16.
182 *Ibid.*, ss. 6, 7, and 17.
183 *Ibid.*, s. 18. Also statements of principle and standards: s. 19.1. The by-laws currently in force are: By-Law No. 1—General, SOR/2003-174; By-Law No. 2—Finance, SOR/2003-175; By-Law No. 3—Payment Items and ACSS, SOR/2003-346; By-Law No. 6—Compliance, SOR/2003-347; By-Law No. 7—LVTS, SOR/2001-281.
184 *Ibid.*, ss. 20, 21, & 21.1.
185 *Ibid.*, ss. 22, 23, & 24.

meetings,[186] and the appointment of an auditor.[187] However, CPA affairs are also subject to government supervision in light of the systemic risks to the Canadian economy should its systems fail and payments can neither be made nor settled. This supervision includes the following: (i) the board chair must be a Bank of Canada appointee and three directors are Ministerial appointees; (ii) by-laws must be approved by the Minister of Finance;[188] (iii) rules relating to the payment and settlement system must be sent to the Minister of Finance within ten days after they have been made, and the Minister may disallow them in whole or in part;[189] (iv) the Minister of Finance may issue a directive to make, amend, or repeal any by-law, rule, or standard;[190] (v) the Minister may request any information or documents at any time;[191] (vi) the Minister shall be consulted about board appointments to the Stakeholder Advisory Council (SAC);[192] (vii) only Parliament may wind up the affairs of the CPA;[193] (viii) the Governor in Council may make regulations in relation to directors, committees, membership, voting, and any other matter connected with the Act;[194] and (ix) the Minister of Finance may designate a payment system to be of national importance and issue guidelines and directives for it.[195] The CPA is no ordinary corporation.

Two other types of accountability for the CPA are also provided by the Act. First, through the right to elect directors, the financial services sector generally has a means of shaping CPA affairs; secondly, the Act provides for the Stakeholder Advisory Council (SAC). The object of the SAC is to provide advice to the board on any matters relating to the CPA objects.[196] The SAC consists of twenty members,[197] of whom up to two are appointed from the board[198] and the remaining number are appointed by the board in consultation with the Minister of Finance.[199]

---

186 *Ibid.*, s. 25. For electronic meetings, see s. 28.
187 *Ibid.*, s. 26. For fiscal year, see s. 27.
188 *Ibid.*, s. 18.
189 *Ibid.*, ss. 19 and 19.2.
190 *Ibid.*, s. 19.3.
191 *Ibid.*, s. 19.4.
192 *Ibid.*, s. 21.2(4).
193 *Ibid.*, s. 32.
194 *Ibid.*, s. 35.
195 *Ibid.*, ss. 36–42.
196 *Ibid.*, s. 21.2(2).
197 *Ibid.*, ss. 21.2(1), (6), & (7).
198 *Ibid.*, s. 21.2(3).
199 *Ibid.*, s. 21.2(4).

The SAC members are broadly representative of users and service providers to the payment systems.[200]

To carry out its statutory objects, the CPA is empowered to employ various officers and employees[201] and to arrange for the exchange of payment items at such places within Canada as it deems appropriate.[202] Its operations are funded by its members, and the board establishes the amount of the dues.[203] The board is also permitted to establish its own modes of operation, subject to the various regulatory approvals.[204] All members have the right to present payment items and to participate in the payment system.[205]

The *Canadian Payments Act* also contains provisions permitting the Minister of Finance to designate a payment system, presumably including any payment system run by the CPA. Section 37(1) provides that the Minister may do so if of the opinion that: (i) it is in the public interest; (ii) the system is national or substantially national in its scope; and (iii) the system plays a major role in supporting transactions in the Canadian financial markets or the Canadian economy.[206] The Minister will consider the following in taking the decision: (i) the level of financial safety provided by the payment system; (ii) the efficiency and competitiveness of payment systems in Canada; and (iii) the best interests of the financial system in Canada.[207] The Minister shall also consult with the President and with participants in the payment system, as well as with interested parties prior to making the designation,[208] but the ultimate decision is made by the Minister alone.[209] Once a system is designated, the Minister is to be sent copies of the system's rules[210] and may issue directives and guidelines.[211]

No insolvency or winding-up legislation of general application applies to the CPA; it can be wound up only by Parliament.[212] Where a winding-up order has been made against a member, the Act makes provi-

---

200 *Ibid.*, s. 21.2(5).
201 *Ibid.*, ss. 6(1)(c) & (d).
202 *Ibid.*, s. 6(1)(a).
203 *Ibid.*, s. 6(1)(b).
204 *Ibid.*, ss. 6, 17, and 19.
205 *Ibid.*, s. 29.
206 *Ibid.*, s. 37(1).
207 *Ibid.*, s. 37(2).
208 *Ibid.*, ss. 37(3), 41, & 42.
209 *Ibid.*, s. 37(3). The Minister must also give notice of decision: ss. 37(4) & (5).
210 *Ibid.*, s. 38.
211 *Ibid.*, ss. 39 & 40.
212 *Ibid.*, s. 32.

sion for the protection of certain kinds of payment instruments, but the meaning of these provisions is unknown and untested in the courts.[213]

Finally, the *Canadian Payments Act* makes provision for the confidentiality of all information and documents obtained under the Act[214] and for various penalties for contravention of the Act, including fines of up to $500,000 by an entity and $100,000 for an individual, together with up to twelve months' imprisonment.[215] Where a person fails to comply with the Act or a directive under it issued by the Minister of Finance, the Minister may seek a court order directing compliance.[216] Neither the Crown nor the Minister nor anyone acting under the direction of the Minister is liable for acts or omissions, provided that those acts or omissions were done in good faith in the discharge of duties under the Act.[217]

With the exception of cash transactions, almost all other payments in Canada, whether paper or electronic, are made through the payment clearing and settlement systems operated by the CPA. It has been considered the "plumbing system" of the Canadian economy, but it may more properly be thought of as the organization that operates the circulation systems for the flow of economic value throughout the country.

F. THE CANADA DEPOSIT INSURANCE CORPORATION

The Canada Deposit Insurance Corporation (CDIC) was established in 1967 for the purpose of insuring the repayment of all or part of deposits in the event of the insolvency of a financial institution. Private deposit insurance had been available in Canada and the United Kingdom from the nineteenth century, the Federal Deposit Insurance Corporation had been established in the United States in 1933, and the Deposit Protection Fund in the United Kingdom was started in 1979. After 1967 various provinces also established provincial deposit insurance schemes for provincially regulated deposit-taking institutions. The CDIC provides insurance for all federally regulated deposit-taking institutions, whether or not they are banks.

---

213 *Ibid.*, s. 31.
214 *Ibid.*, s. 43.
215 *Ibid.*, s. 47.
216 *Ibid.*, ss. 45 & 46.
217 *Ibid.*, s. 44. Section 48 permits the Minister to delegate any powers, functions, or duties to any Minister of State appointed to assist the Minister.

Since 1967 the CDIC has been required to intervene in relation to a number of failed member institutions, largely trust and loan companies, but also in relation to two failed banks in 1985, the Canadian Commercial Bank and the Northland Bank. It has also intervened when individual financial institutions appear to be in difficulty and acts together with the Bank of Canada, OSFI, and the government when financial difficulties appear within the financial institutions sector generally. The last time a financial institution failed was in 1996, and the rate of loss from recent failures is approximately 17 cents on the dollar.[218]

The CDIC is established as a corporation that is an agent of the Crown in right of Canada for all purposes under the Act.[219] Its head office is in Ottawa,[220] and its affairs are directed by a board of directors consisting of the Chairperson, the Governor of the Bank of Canada, the Deputy Minister of Finance, the Superintendent of Financial Institutions, the Commissioner of the Financial Consumer Agency of Canada, an officer of OSFI appointed by the Minister of Finance, and not more than five other directors approved by the Governor in Council.[221] The Act further provides that a director may not hold any other public or publicly funded position or be a member of any federal or provincial legislature or a director, officer, or employee of any financial institution.[222] The Chairperson is to be appointed by the Governor in Council and holds office for a stipulated term during good behaviour.[223] In addition to the qualifications for directors, the Chairperson must also have proven financial ability[224] and be under seventy-five years of age.[225] The Governor in Council fixes the remuneration for the Chairperson.[226]

The board administers the affairs of the CDIC in all matters, and under the legislation has the usual powers of a board to enter into contracts and make by-laws, including by-laws relating to standards of sound business practices for financial institutions[227] and defining what is an insurable deposit.[228] The Act also grants to the board all powers

---

218 *CDIC 2004 Annual Report* (Ottawa: CDIC, 2004) at ii. For current information, see online: www.cdic.ca.
219 R.S.C. 1985, c. C-3 as am., s. 3 [*CDIC Act*]. For the scope of the Act, see s. 2.1.
220 *Ibid.*, s. 4(1). For other offices, see s. 4(2).
221 *Ibid.*, ss. 5(1) & (2).
222 *Ibid.*, s. 5(1.1). For vacancies, see ss. 5(3) & (4). For remuneration, see ss. 5(5) & (5.1).
223 *Ibid.*, s. 6(1). For meetings, see s. 6(4).
224 *Ibid.*, ss. 6(1) & (2).
225 *Ibid.*, s. 6(3).
226 *Ibid.*, s. 6(5).
227 *Ibid.*, ss. 11(1) and (2)(e).
228 *Ibid.*, ss. 11(1) and (2)(f).

under Part II of the *Inquiries Act*[229] when carrying out any inspection authorized by the *CDIC Act* or by a policy of deposit insurance.[230]

The Act further provides that the CDIC may enjoy many of the usual rights and powers associated with corporations, including maintaining bank accounts[231] and employing officers, agents, and employees.[232] All information obtained in the performance of its statutory duties is confidential,[233] and the CDIC, its directors, officers, and employees are exempted from liability to any member financial institution, a depositor, creditor, or shareholder for damages incurred by reason of anything done in good faith in the execution of any statutory powers and duties.[234] The auditor of the CDIC is the Auditor General of Canada,[235] and the corporation can be wound up only by Parliament and is not subject to any insolvency or winding-up legislation.[236]

The objects of the CDIC are: (i) to provide insurance against part or all of deposits; (ii) to be instrumental in the promotion of sound business and financial practices for member institutions and to promote and otherwise contribute to the stability of the financial system in Canada; and (iii) to pursue these objects for the benefit of depositors and so as to minimize the exposure of the CDIC to loss.[237] The CDIC is further authorized to do all things necessary or incidental to the objects of the corporation, including reducing risk or loss to the corporation; to enter into agreements with provincial governments relating to the insurance of provincially regulated deposits; to act as a liquidator, receiver, or inspector of a member institution; to assume the costs of winding up a member institution; to acquire various assets, including the assets of a member institution; and to inspect member institutions as authorized by the Act.[238] The CDIC may also request and the Minister of Finance may lend out of the Consolidated Revenue Fund money to the CDIC for its statutory purposes, provided the loan does not exceed $6 billion or any greater amount approved by Parliament.[239]

---

229 Above note 132.
230 *CDIC Act*, above note 219, s. 11(3).
231 *Ibid.*, s. 41.
232 *Ibid.*, ss. 44–45.
233 *Ibid.*, s. 45.2.
234 *Ibid.*, s. 45.1.
235 *Ibid.*, s. 43. For the CDIC's financial year, see s. 40.
236 *Ibid.*, s. 46.
237 *Ibid.*, s. 7.
238 *Ibid.*, s. 10.
239 *Ibid.*, s. 10.1.

The corporation is required to insure each deposit, with the following exceptions: (i) deposits that are not payable in Canada or in Canadian dollars; (ii) deposits for which the Crown in right of Canada is a preferred claimant; and (iii) so much of any deposit that exceeds $100,000.[240] A "deposit" is defined as the unpaid balance of the aggregate of moneys held by a financial institution[241] on behalf of any person in the usual course of deposit-taking business for which the institution is obligated to give credit to an account or has issued a receipt, certificate, instrument, draft, certified draft or cheque, traveller's cheque, prepaid letter of credit, money order, or other instrument and is obligated to repay on demand or on a fixed day, including interest.[242] A deposit also includes moneys held by an institution in respect of realty taxes on mortgaged property.[243] In situations where the money in dispute does not fit neatly into any of these categories, the courts have interpreted deposit as being commonly understood to mean funds deposited with a financial institution in the expectation of their return.[244]

In addition to the exceptions to the definition of insured deposits, the *Canada Deposit Insurance Corporation Act* (*CDIC Act*) qualifies the definition of deposit as follows: (i) moneys received on or after 17 April 1967 are not deposits unless the institution is obliged to repay those moneys within five years of the date of deposit and the institution was not CDIC insured when the moneys were received;[245] (ii) moneys deposited by a trust company in its own guaranteed trust fund on behalf of itself as trustee are deemed to be repayable to the same extent as if the moneys had been deposited by a trustee other than itself;[246] (iii) moneys received on or after 1 April 1977 for which the instrument evidencing the deposit does not record the person entitled to repayment are not a deposit unless the instrument records the person entitled to repayment, who shall be deemed to be the depositor unless the records show a more recent transferee and the entry of the transfer in the records is not made subsequent to the termination or cancellation of the deposit insurance policy;[247] and (iv) moneys received on or after 1 Janu-

---

240 *Ibid.*, s. 12.
241 *Ibid.*, ss. 8 & 9. This includes provincial institutions, where the CDIC has arranged to be the insurer: see ss. 37–39.
242 *Ibid.*, Sch., s. 2(1).
243 *Ibid.*, Sch., ss. 2(1.1) and 3(7).
244 *Saskatchewan Co-operative Credit Society Ltd. v. Wilson* (1990), 65 D.L.R. (4th) 437 (F.C.T.D.), aff'd (1991), 77 D.L.R. (4th) 186 (Fed. C.A.).
245 *CDIC Act*, above note 219, Sch., ss. 2(2), (2.1), & (2.2).
246 *Ibid.*, Sch., s. 2(3).
247 *Ibid.*, Sch., s. 2(5).

ary 1977 for which the instrument of indebtedness, other than a draft, certified draft or cheque, traveller's cheque, prepaid letter of credit or money order, is payable outside Canada or in a currency other than Canadian dollars do not constitute an insured deposit.[248]

The definition of an insured deposit is not limited to individual depositors on their own behalf but also extends to joint deposits,[249] trust deposits,[250] and deposits so defined within RRSPs[251] and RRIFs.[252] Thus, a single individual at a single institution may have insured deposits of $100,000 each in deposit accounts and joint accounts, in an RRSP/RRIF, and as a trustee for a beneficiary, and that individual may replicate that pattern of insured deposits at more than one financial institution.

The *CDIC Act* also protects insured deposits when financial institutions merge by deeming deposits in each of the amalgamating institutions to be separate for insurance purposes on the day of amalgamation.[253] A deposit made with an amalgamated institution after the day of amalgamation is insured up to the $100,000 limit with that amalgamated institution.[254] In addition, where a member institution assumes any deposit liabilities of another member institution, the two institutions are deemed to be amalgamating[255] and the deposit liabilities are deemed to be deposited with the institution that assumes them on the day they were assumed.[256]

Repayment of insured deposits to a depositor is to be made where a winding-up order has been given in respect of a member institution.[257] Once the order is made and the obligation to pay arises, payment may be made in one of two ways: in cash or by a transfer of the sum insured to another member institution.[258] The CDIC will normally make the payment where the member institution cannot, or the deposit insurance policy has terminated or is cancelled, or when the Governor in Council has ordered either the vesting of the institution's shares in the CDIC or the appointment of a receiver.[259]

---

248 *Ibid.*, Sch., s. 2(6).
249 *Ibid.*, Sch., ss. 2(3)(1) & (1.1).
250 *Ibid.*, Sch., ss. 2(3)(1), (2), (3), (3.01), (3.1), & (4).
251 *Ibid.*, Sch., s. 2(5).
252 *Ibid.*, Sch., s. 2(6).
253 *Ibid.*, s. 13(1).
254 *Ibid.*, s. 13(2).
255 *Ibid.*, s. 13(3).
256 *Ibid.*, s. 13(4).
257 *Ibid.*, s. 14(2).
258 *Ibid.*, s. 14(1).
259 *Ibid.*, s. 14(2.1).

Payment of the insured deposit includes payment of any interest accruing and payable up to the date of the commencement of the winding-up[260] and up to the $100,000 insured limit.[261] Prior to making the payment and with the approval of OSFI or the appropriate provincial supervisor if a provincial institution, the CDIC is permitted access to all records of the member institution relating to deposit liabilities and may make enquiries of directors, officers, auditors, or receivers in this regard,[262] with the costs of the examination to be paid by the member institution.[263]

Once payment of the insured deposit has been made, the CDIC is discharged from all further liability.[264] When a payment is made, the CDIC is subrogated to all the rights and interests of the depositor to the extent of the amount paid.[265] Where the CDIC has made a payment, it ranks equally with the depositor in respect of the deposit and interest payable with the deposit after the date of the winding-up order.[266] Thus, it has been held that where a liquidated financial institution has remaining assets, CDIC has both a statutory and a common law right to those assets up to the amount of the deposits and payable interest.[267]

The CDIC may withhold payment of any deposit until it has received a written assignment of all the rights and interests of the depositor in relation to the deposit.[268] And an action against the CDIC to enforce payment of an insured obligation must be commenced within ten years after the date of the commencement of the winding-up.[269] Finally, the CDIC may sell to the liquidator of any member institution any information gathered or produced at the expense of the CDIC if the expense is not otherwise recoverable,[270] and the amount paid for the information by the liquidator is a cost incurred in the winding-up.[271]

The funds used to pay insured deposits to customers in the event of the winding-up of a financial institution are drawn from the Deposit

---

260 *Ibid.*, ss. 14(2.3) and (2.9).
261 *Ibid.*, ss. 14(2.4) & (2.5). For interest calculation on index-linked deposits, see s. 14(2.51).
262 *Ibid.*, s. 14(2.7).
263 *Ibid.*, s. 14(2.8).
264 *Ibid.*, s. 14(3).
265 *Ibid.*, s. 14(4).
266 *Ibid.*, s. 14(4.1).
267 *Canada (Attorney General) v. Security Home Mortgage Corp.* (2003), 231 D.L.R. (4th) 353 (Alta. Q.B.).
268 *CDIC Act*, above note 219, s. 14(5).
269 *Ibid.*, ss. 14(6) & (7).
270 *Ibid.*, s. 14.1(1).
271 *Ibid.*, s. 14.1(2).

Insurance Fund into which premiums are paid by each member institution.[272] Each member pays an annual premium,[273] which is assessed in accordance with the premium by-laws established by the board[274] and based on returns required to be submitted to the CDIC.[275] The by-laws concerned with the premium calculation must be approved by the Minister of Finance.[276] An unpaid premium is a debt owing to the Crown in right of Canada.[277] All federal and provincial financial institutions are eligible to be members,[278] and banks as deposit-taking institutions are required to be members under the *Bank Act*.[279]

Each member institution is subject to an annual inspection by OSFI, as well as any other inspections the CDIC may require.[280] The purpose of these inspections is to provide a rating of the safety and soundness of the institution; to comment on the operations of the institution; and for provincial institutions, to comment on whether there is compliance with provincial legislation.[281] The CDIC is entitled to all the information gathered during the examination.[282] Any information that might materially affect the position of the CDIC as an insurer must be reported without delay.[283] The CDIC may specifically request that the examination review the correctness of the returns made by the member institution on which its premium classification and premiums are based.[284] In addition to the report resulting from the annual examination, annual reports sent to the Minister of Finance by OSFI about each bank pursuant to the *Bank Act*[285] are also required to be sent to the CDIC.[286] When the CDIC concludes from the annual examination that a member institution is not following sound business practices, is in

---

272 *Ibid.*, s. 20.
273 *Ibid.*, s. 21(1).
274 *Ibid.*, s. 21(2).
275 For the rules concerning premium calculation, see *ibid.*, ss. 21(2), (4), (5), and 22–26.
276 *Ibid.*, s. 21(3).
277 *Ibid.*, s. 15.
278 *Ibid.*, ss. 17 & 18.
279 *Bank Act*, above note 32, s. 413(1)(a). For the narrow exception to this, see *ibid.*, ss. 413(1)(b), (3)–(6) and *CDIC Act*, above note 219, ss. 26.01–26.06.
280 *CDIC Act, ibid.*, s. 27(1). For costs, see ss. 27(2) and 28.1. For provincial institutions, see s. 28.
281 *Ibid.*, s. 29(1).
282 *Ibid.*, ss. 29(3) & (4). For duty to report in a timely manner, see s. 29(2).
283 *Ibid.*, s. 29(5).
284 *Ibid.*, s. 29.1.
285 Above note 32, s. 643.
286 *CDIC Act*, above note 219, s. 29.2.

breach of any CDIC by-laws, or is in breach of any of the conditions of its deposit insurance policy, then the CDIC shall send a copy of the report to the Minister of Finance and to the CEO or chair of the board of directors of the member institution,[287] who shall present the report to a meeting of the board and ensure that it is incorporated into the minutes of the meeting. A certified copy of that portion of the minutes shall also be sent to the CDIC.[288]

If the CDIC concludes that the member institution has not remedied reported problems in a satisfactory manner, it must inform the Minister of Finance and give at least thirty days' notice of termination of the insurance policy.[289] If, within sixty days, the CDIC is not satisfied that the member institution has taken remedial steps, the policy will terminate.[290] However, this notice of termination will be revoked if the CDIC is satisfied that the risk to depositors and the CDIC has been averted or substantially reduced.[291]

Once the deposit insurance is terminated or cancelled, the deposits in those institutions continue to be insured for a period of two years from the day of the termination or cancellation or for the term until maturity of a term deposit.[292] Exceptions to the two-year rule that continue to be insured are deposits assumed by another member institution or a former member institution with permission to receive deposits without being a member institution.[293] Termination or cancellation of a policy does not relieve a former member institution from obligations and liabilities that have previously accrued.[294]

In addition to cancelling deposit insurance for member institutions who are reported not to be following sound business practices, the CDIC has statutory authority in relation to a member institution that is, or is about to become, insolvent to be deemed to be a creditor and to take any actions under law to preserve the assets of the institution or to have it wound up or liquidated.[295] The CDIC requires the approval of the Minister of Finance to take action, and the Minister can deny approval if such action would not be in the public interest.[296] A member

---

287 *Ibid.*, s. 30(1).
288 *Ibid.*, s. 30(2).
289 *Ibid.*, ss. 31(1)–(4). For provincial institutions, see ss. 31(2) & (3), 31.1 & 32.
290 *Ibid.*, ss. 31(5) & (6).
291 *Ibid.*, s. 31(6).
292 *Ibid.*, ss. 34(1) and (3).
293 *Ibid.*, s. 34(2).
294 *Ibid.*, s. 34(4).
295 *Ibid.*, s. 35(1).
296 *Ibid.*, ss. 35(1.1) and (2).

institution must notify its depositors if deposit insurance is terminated or cancelled,[297] and the CDIC may give public notice if it deems that public interest requires notice to be given.[298]

While operating the deposit insurance scheme is the main statutory function of the CDIC, closely related is its role, also assigned by the legislation, in winding up insolvent financial institutions. The Superintendent of Financial Institutions is required to determine whether a federal member or institution is no longer viable, after giving the institution a reasonable opportunity to make representation.[299] The factors to be considered in coming to that conclusion are: (i) excessive dependency on loans, advances, guarantees, and other financial assistance to sustain its operations; (ii) loss of the confidence of depositors and the public; (iii) the regulatory capital is or is about to become substantially deficient; or (iv) failure to pay any liability that has become due and payable or that will be due or payable.[300]

Once the Superintendent has decided to take control, a report must be made to the CDIC,[301] and the CDIC may request that the Minister of Finance make one or more of the following orders in relation to restructuring:[302] (i) an order to vest the shares and subordinated debt in the CDIC, or (ii) an order to appoint the CDIC as the receiver.[303] The effect of a receivership order is set out in considerable detail in the *CDIC Act*,[304] but essentially, the CDIC enjoys all the powers, duties, and rights of any receiver to operate as if the member institution that is in receivership. Once the order is made, no criminal or other civil proceeding against the institution may be commenced or continued,[305] and any agreements to the contrary are deemed ineffective.[306] However, clearing arrangements between the institution and a member of the Canadian Payments Association are exempt, so that a clearing agent may continue to act as such during the receivership[307] and the various contractual arrangements for the supply of goods and services to the

---

297 *Ibid.*, s. 36(1).
298 *Ibid.*, s. 36(2).
299 *Ibid.*, s. 39.1(1).
300 *Ibid.*, s. 39.1(2).
301 *Ibid.*, ss. 39.1(1) and (3).
302 *Ibid.*, ss. 39.11, 39.12, & 39.13(1). Such orders extinguish adverse claims as indicated in s. 39.13(2).
303 *Ibid.*, s. 39.13(1). For exemption, see s. 39.16.
304 *Ibid.*, ss. 39.13(2)–(6) & 39.14. For the operation of the *Bank Act*, see s. 39.19.
305 *Ibid.*, ss. 39.15(1), (4), and (6). For exemption, see ss. 39.16 & 39.17.
306 *Ibid.*, s. 39.15(2). For exemption, see ss. 39.16 & 39.17.
307 *Ibid.*, s. 39.15(3).

institution while it is in receivership may be made and honoured.[308] But financial contracts such as swaps and derivatives may be terminated in accordance with their terms or set off in an amount payable under the agreement.[309] Any person may apply to a superior court for relief from these provisions, which may be granted if that person is likely to be materially prejudiced or if it is equitable on other grounds to grant leave; the CDIC must be joined as a defendant.[310]

Once the restructuring order for an insolvent member institution has been made and the CDIC is vested with its shares and subordinated debt, the Act permits the CDIC to engage in the following restructuring transactions: (i) the sale of all or part of the shares or subordinated debt; (ii) amalgamation; (iii) the sale of all or part of the institution's assets or the assumption of all or part of its liabilities or both; or (iv) any other transaction whose purpose is to restructure a substantial part of the member institution's business.[311] On the substantial completion of these transactions, a notice to that effect must be published in the *Canada Gazette*.[312] All transactions must be approved by the Minister of Finance[313] and the member institution.[314] If the restructuring transactions are not substantially completed within sixty days of the restructuring order or the expiration of any extension of that period, the CDIC must apply for a winding-up order under the *Winding-up and Restructuring Act*,[315] and the CDIC is deemed to be a creditor for the purposes of the winding-up.[316]

Within forty-five days of an order vesting shares and subordinated debt in the CDIC, of a winding-up order, or of a receivership order, the CDIC must give to each person who was a holder of shares or subordinated debt and to the member institution a notice of the offer of compensation or a notice that no compensation is being made.[317] The compensation may be wholly or partly in cash or such other form as the CDIC thinks appropriate.[318] The formal contents of the notice are

---

308 *Ibid.*, ss. 39.15(5) and (8)(a).
309 *Ibid.*, ss. 39.15(7) and (8)(b).
310 *Ibid.*, s. 39.17.
311 *Ibid.*, ss. 39.2(1), (2), and (4).
312 *Ibid.*, s. 39.2(3).
313 *Ibid.*, s. 39.2(5).
314 *Ibid.*, s. 39.2(6). Buyers of a special security hold for the life of the loan: see s. 39.21.
315 *Ibid.*, ss. 39.22(1) and (3).
316 *Ibid.*, s. 39.22(2).
317 *Ibid.*, ss. 39.24(1) & (2) and 39.27.
318 *Ibid.*, s. 39.24(3).

set out in detail in the Act,[319] and the notice should also be published in the *Canada Gazette* and a general-circulation newspaper at or near the head office of the member institution.[320] The offeree is entitled to receive compensation if the offeree notifies the CDIC within thirty days from the date of the notice of acceptance or does not notify an objection to the offer or notifies an objection to the offer but there are no dissenting offerees.[321] A member institution will receive compensation if it notifies the CDIC of its acceptance within ninety days after the date of the notice.[322]

Where offerees dissent, the Governor in Council shall appoint a federally appointed judge as an assessor,[323] and the CDIC shall notify each dissenting offeree of the appointment and their right to be heard and represented by counsel, and of the binding nature of the assessor's determination.[324] The assessor may take into account any matters considered relevant but must deduct the benefit derived from any special financial assistance provided directly or indirectly to the institution by the CDIC or the Bank of Canada.[325] Otherwise, the assessor shall award such compensation as considered just and reasonable, taking into consideration the costs of the proceeding and interest.[326] The determination of the assessor is final and conclusive and not subject to appeal except for judicial review under the *Federal Court Act*.[327] The assessor has considerable discretion about carrying out the determinations[328] and all the powers of a commissioner under Part II of the *Inquiries Act*.[329]

The CDIC must make payment or delivery to the person entitled within 60 days of the notice of the vesting order.[330] However, any creditor[331] or holder of shares or subordinated debt[332] may apply to a superior court for review of the allocation of the consideration for the sale or disposition of all or part of the assets of the member institution.[333] The

---

319 *Ibid.*, s. 39.25.
320 *Ibid.*, s. 39.26.
321 *Ibid.*, s. 39.28(1).
322 *Ibid.*, s. 39.28(2).
323 *Ibid.*, s. 39.29.
324 *Ibid.*, s. 39.3.
325 *Ibid.*, ss. 39.31(1) & (2).
326 *Ibid.*, ss. 39.31(3) & (4), 39.32 & 39.33.
327 *Ibid.*, s. 39.34(1). *Federal Court Act*, R.S.C. 1985, c. F-7.
328 *CDIC Act*, above note 219, ss. 39.34(2), 39.36(1), (3), & (4).
329 *Ibid.*, s. 39.36(2). *Inquiries Act*, above note 132.
330 *CDIC Act*, *ibid.*, s. 39.35.
331 *Ibid.*, s. 39.361(2)(a).
332 *Ibid.*, s. 39.361(2)(b).
333 *Ibid.*, s. 39.361(1).

court may make such order as it deems necessary to require the CDIC to rectify the allocation.[334]

Finally, the *CDIC Act* provides for a number of offences for various breaches of provisions of the Act: (i) preparing, signing, approving, or concurring in any false or deceptive or unfairly presented information submitted to the CDIC;[335] (ii) failure of the CEO or the directors to ensure the incorporation into the minutes of any report under section 30 concerning failure to follow sound business practices;[336] (iii) failure of a member institution to provide information as required to the CDIC;[337] and (iv) failure of a member institution to comply with the Act generally.[338] An offence under the Act carries, on summary conviction, a fine of up to $100,000, imprisonment of up to twelve months or both for an individual, and a fine of up to $500,000 for a member institution.[339] In addition, a court may order compliance with the Act or the by-laws,[340] along with an additional fine equal to any monetary benefit acquired by the individual or the institution.[341] Application may be made to a superior court for compliance with, or restraint from, acting in breach of the Act or by-laws,[342] and appeals are permitted to any higher court.[343] All fines are due to the Crown in right of Canada.[344]

G. THE FINANCIAL CONSUMER AGENCY OF CANADA

In 2001 Parliament enacted the *Financial Consumer Agency of Canada Act (FCAC Act)*,[345] which established the Financial Consumer Agency of Canada (FCAC) in sections 1–34 and amended the other four major pieces of financial institutions legislation, including the *Bank Act*, in

---

334 *Ibid.*, s. 39.361(3). For power of Governor in Council to make regulations, see s. 39.37. For power of CDIC to become involved in restructuring provincial institutions, see s. 39.38.
335 *Ibid.*, s. 47.
336 *Ibid.*, s. 48.
337 *Ibid.*, s. 49.
338 *Ibid.*, s. 50, other than ss. 47–49.
339 *Ibid.*, s. 50.1.
340 *Ibid.*, s. 51.
341 *Ibid.*, s. 52(1).
342 *Ibid.*, s. 52(2).
343 *Ibid.*, s. 53.
344 *Ibid.*, s. 54.
345 S.C. 1991, c. 9 [*FCAC Act*]. For current information, see online: www.fcac.gc.ca.

sections 35–592. The political symbolism of this approach is self-evident: consumer protection is now officially the main purpose of all financial institutions legislation. The FCAC was set up during the course of 2002 for the general purposes of ensuring that financial institutions comply with their statutory obligations to consumers and for providing information to consumers so as to assist them in understanding and enforcing their statutory rights against financial institutions. The FCAC operates pursuant to its own Act, as well as to provisions in other financial institutions legislation that relate to it, including the *Bank Act*.

The FCAC is an agency of the federal government whose head is the Minister of Finance.[346] The statutory objects of the FCAC are: (i) to supervise financial institutions in order to determine whether they are in compliance with their applicable consumer legislation; (ii) to promote the adoption of policies and procedures to implement applicable consumer legislation; (iii) to monitor voluntary codes of conduct designed to protect customers of financial institutions, provided that these have been adopted by the institutions and are publicly available; (iv) to monitor all other public commitments for the protection of customers made by financial institutions; (v) to promote consumer awareness about the legal obligations of financial institutions; and (vi) to foster an understanding of financial services and issues relating to financial services in cooperation with any other governmental or non-governmental organization.[347]

The day-to-day operation of the FCAC is conducted by its Commissioner, who is appointed by the Governor in Council and has the rank and power of a deputy head of department.[348] The Commissioner holds office during good behaviour for renewable five-year terms,[349] and in absence or incapacity, the Minister may appoint a qualified person to perform the duties for not more than ninety days without the approval of the Governor in Council.[350]

The duties of the Commissioner in relation to banks are set out in the *FCAC Act* and the *Bank Act*, and they mirror the statutory objects of the FCAC,[351] including entering into any agreements or arrangements with other federal or provincial government agencies in order to carry

---

346 *Ibid.*, s. 3(1).
347 *Ibid.*, s. 3(2).
348 *Ibid.*, s. 4(1). For regulations, see s. 32.
349 *Ibid.*, ss. 4(2) & (3). For remuneration, see s. 4(5); for expenses, see s. 4(6); for pension, see s. 4(7).
350 *Ibid.*, s. 4(4).
351 *Ibid.*, ss. 5 & 6. For the annual report to the Minister of Finance, see s. 34.

out its objects.[352] The Commissioner may appoint Deputy Commissioners[353] and staff,[354] to whom statutory duties may be delegated.[355] To ensure that the Commissioner is not in a conflict-of-interest position, the *FCAC Act* provides that: (i) the Commissioner may not hold any other position except another office under the Crown for no reward;[356] (ii) the Commissioner may not own any shares of any financial institution or similar business;[357] (iii) the Commissioner may borrow money from a financial institution only after first informing the Minister of Finance;[358] and (iv) the Commissioner may not receive any grant or annuity from a financial institution or any director, officer, or employee of a financial institution.[359]

The budget for the FCAC is financed by assessment against each financial institution, so as with the other supervisory bodies, the financial institutions pay for their own regulation.[360] The Minister of Finance may also advance funds from the Consolidated Revenue Fund,[361] but as the annual financial statements show, the budget is based almost entirely on assessment.

The *FCAC Act* provides further for the standards to be exercised by the FCAC in carrying out its statutory mandate, as well as for penalties for those institutions assessed to be in breach of any applicable legislation. The Act provides that all information regarding the business or affairs of a financial institution or of persons dealing with it obtained by the Commissioner in the course of carrying out statutory duties is confidential and is to be treated as confidential.[362] The Commissioner is entitled to disclose it, if satisfied that it will be treated as confidential, to any government or other agency or body that regulates financial institutions for regulatory purposes, to the CDIC for deposit insurance purposes, and to the Department of Finance and the Bank of Canada for purposes of policy analysis related to the regulation of financial institutions.[363]

---

352 *Ibid.*, s. 7.
353 *Ibid.*, s. 8.
354 *Ibid.*, ss. 10 & 11.
355 *Ibid.*, s. 9.
356 *Ibid.*, s. 6.
357 *Ibid.*, s. 14.
358 *Ibid.*, s. 15.
359 *Ibid.*, s. 16(1). For penalties, see s. 16(2).
360 *Ibid.*, s. 18.
361 *Ibid.*, s. 13.
362 *Ibid.*, s. 17(1).
363 *Ibid.*, s. 17(2).

Violations or failures to comply with an order bring penalties of up to $50,000 for a person and $200,000 for a financial institution.[364] In assessing the penalty, the following factors shall be considered: the degree of intention or negligence, the harm done by the violation, the previous five-year history of the person who committed the violation, and any other criteria that the Governor in Council may present.[365] If a person named in a notice of violation from the Commissioner pays the proposed penalty, that person is deemed to have committed the violation,[366] and a person who ignores the notice and does not pay is also deemed to have committed the violation.[367] Where a person makes representations, the Commissioner may decide on the balance of probabilities whether the person has committed the violation.[368] The Commissioner is required to give notice of any decision,[369] and the person to whom such notice is given may appeal the decision to the Federal Court.[370] The Federal Court is required to take reasonable caution to conduct its hearings in private so as to protect confidential information.[371] Any penalty is a debt due to the Crown in right of Canada,[372] and there is a five-year limitation period for recovery of that debt in the Federal Court.[373]

Violations under the *FCAC Act* are not subject to the *Criminal Code*,[374] due diligence is a permissible defence,[375] and all rules and principles of the common law apply.[376] But the Commissioner must commence proceedings in respect of a violation within two years after learning of the possible violation.[377] The Commissioner may make public the nature of the violation, the name of the person who committed it, and the amount of the penalty.[378]

---

364 *Ibid.*, ss. 19(2) and 22. For the power of the Governor in Council to make regulations regarding violations, see s. 19(1).
365 *Ibid.*, s. 20. For Commissioner's discretion to proceed as a violation or as an offence, see s. 21.
366 *Ibid.*, s. 23(1).
367 *Ibid.*, s. 23(3).
368 *Ibid.*, s. 23(2).
369 *Ibid.*, s. 23(4).
370 *Ibid.*, ss. 24(1) and (3).
371 *Ibid.*, s. 24(2).
372 *Ibid.*, ss. 25(1) and (3), 26, and 29.
373 *Ibid.*, s. 25(2).
374 *Ibid.*, s. 27.
375 *Ibid.*, s. 28(1).
376 *Ibid.*, s. 28(2).
377 *Ibid.*, s. 30.
378 *Ibid.*, s. 31.

Finally, the *FCAC Act* provides for statutory immunity from liability for the Crown, the Commissioner, and FCAC officers and employees for any acts or omissions in good faith while carrying out statutory duties.[379]

The *Bank Act* makes further provision for coordination with the FCAC in relation to several consumer-related matters. First, it requires that all banks establish customer complaints procedures and designate officers and employees responsible for their implementation.[380] Copies of these procedures must be filed with the FCAC,[381] and all banks are further required to inform customers concerning how to contact the FCAC for a complaint about a deposit account, loan interest disclosure,[382] payment, credit or charge card, or any other matter related to consumer law.[383] These procedures and the number and nature of complaints made to the FCAC are reported as part of the annual report of the Commissioner to the Minister of Finance.[384]

Secondly, when a bank decides to close a branch, notice must be given to the FCAC prior to closure so that the Commissioner may review the closure in accordance with the regulations[385] for branch closures.[386] The rules and regulations relating to branch closure do not forbid a bank to close any branch, which remains the bank's decision, but they require careful consideration and extensive notice to customers prior to any closure, once the review process is completed.

Thirdly, banks are required to provide the FCAC with the information it requires under the *FCAC Act*,[387] and that information is subject to the confidentiality and disclosure provisions stated above.[388] Fourthly, at least once annually, the FCAC makes such examination and inquiry as it thinks necessary to ensure that a bank is complying with all consumer-related statutory requirements and reports its conclusions to the Minister of Finance.[389] In carrying out this duty, the FCAC has a right

---

379 *Ibid.*, s. 33.
380 *Bank Act*, above note 32, ss. 455(1) and 573(1).
381 *Ibid.*, ss. 455(2) and 573(2).
382 Pursuant to s. 452(3), *ibid.*
383 *Ibid.*, ss. 456(1) and 574(1). Complaint Information (Banks) Regulations, SOR/2001-371; Complaint Information (Authorized Foreign Banks) Regulations, SOR/2001-370.
384 *Ibid.*, ss. 456(2) and 574(2).
385 Notice of Branch Closure (Banks) Regulations, SOR/2002-104; FCAC Bank Branch Closure Meeting Rules (31 October 2003).
386 *Bank Act*, above note 32, s. 459.2.
387 *Ibid.*, s. 658(1).
388 *Ibid.*, ss. 658(1) & (2).
389 *Ibid.*, s. 659(1).

of access to all bank records[390] and may require the directors and officers to provide information and explanations to the extent that they are reasonably able to do so.[391] The Commissioner has the powers of a commissioner under the *Inquiries Act*[392] to obtain evidence[393] and may enter into any "compliance agreement" to ensure compliance with consumer provisions.[394]

In its first few years of operation, the FCAC has placed emphasis on several aspects of its statutory mandate — in particular, consumer education through the publication of consumer guides to credit cards and the cost of banking; implementing consumer-complaint adjudication processes; obtaining approval of regulations about access to basic banking services for low-income consumers;[395] and implementing coordinate and outreach activities with various governmental and non-governmental organizations.[396] In light of the broad scope of the FCAC's statutory mandate, it may be anticipated that these and other activities will expand in variety and deepen in the near future.

H. THE OMBUDSMAN FOR BANKING SERVICES AND INVESTMENTS

Prior to the creation of the FCAC in 2001, customer-complaint processes and organizations existed within the financial services sector, but these were fragmented, industry-sponsored, and had a low public profile. The role assigned to the FCAC by the 2001 legislation was that of monitoring compliance by financial institutions with consumer-oriented banking legislation, but the broader role of resolving disputes between customers and banks over the numerous other aspects of the bank and customer relationship that fall under the common law was unassigned by the financial institutions legislation.

The *Bank Act, 1991*,[397] required, for the first time, that Canadian banks provide internal dispute-resolution mechanisms in relation to

---

390 *Ibid.*, s. 659(2)(a).
391 *Ibid.*, s. 659(2)(b).
392 Above note 132.
393 *Bank Act*, above note 32, s. 660.
394 *Ibid.*, s. 661.
395 Pursuant to *Bank Act*, *ibid.*, ss. 448.1 and 458.1; Access to Basic Banking Services Regulations, SOR/2003-184.
396 See FCAC Annual Reports for descriptions of these activities.
397 Above note 32.

such matters as bank charges for deposit accounts, payment, credit and charge cards, and the disclosure and calculation of the cost of borrowing. By 1994, the banks had implemented internal dispute-resolution procedures, but continuing complaints from small businesses that banks were insensitive to their financing requirements led in October 1994 to a Parliamentary report[398] proposing that a national ombudsman scheme for dispute resolution be introduced, modelled on the scheme first begun in the United Kingdom in 1986 and followed subsequently by Ireland (1990), Australia (1990), and New Zealand (1992). Customer dissatisfaction with internal bank dispute resolution was appealable under the 1991 Act to OSFI, but OSFI was not really designed to resolve such matters. In 1996, the banking industry established the Canadian Banking Ombudsman Inc. to hear appeals from individual banks' dispute resolutions in relation to both small business and individual customer disputes.

The Canadian Banking Ombudsman Inc. was a not-for-profit corporation that ran the Office of the Canadian Banking Ombudsman, and its members were the banks that joined the corporation. The member banks funded the corporation and were assessed on the basis of their assets. A two-tiered board system was implemented to ensure that the banks were kept at arms length from the day-to-day operations of the Office.[399] When the MacKay Task Force[400] reported in 1998, it recommended a single ombudsman system for the entire financial services sector, not just for banks, and further recommended that such a system be established by federal legislation and be state supervised.[401] This was in keeping with consumer empowerment as one of the strategic themes of the MacKay Report generally. The 2001 legislation empowered the Minister of Finance to set up a not-for-profit corporation whose purpose was to deal with complaints not resolved by dispute-resolution procedures within individual financial institutions.[402]

---

398 Canada, Parliament, House of Commons, House of Commons Standing Committee on Industry, *Taking Care of Small Business* (Ottawa: Publications Services, Parliamentary Publications Directorate, 1994) at 18–20.
399 For an analysis of how the earlier system operated, see M.H. Ogilvie, "Banking Ombudsmen: A Necessary Evil or Simply Not Necessary" (1996) 11 B.F.L.R. 167.
400 Task Force on the Future of the Canadian Financial Services Sector, *Change, Challenge, Opportunity: The Future of the Canadian Financial Services Sector* (Ottawa: Department of Finance, 1998) c. 2 at 4 ["the MacKay Task Force"].
401 *Ibid.* at 15.
402 *Bank Act*, above note 32, s. 455.1(1).

Faced with the prospect of a state-run scheme, banks and other financial institutions such as the insurance companies (property, health, and life insurance) united to propose an industry-run model, and the net outcome of discussions was that the government accepted that model and has not implemented the provisions in the 2001 legislation. The government was persuaded by the fact that all of the financial sector associations[403] supported this initiative.[404]

In November 2002, the Centre for Financial Services OmbudsNetwork (CFSON) was established, not as an ombudsman service, but as a national umbrella whose purpose is to direct consumers to industry-specific ombudsman's offices. There are three such services: the Canadian Life and Health Insurance OmbudService (CLHIO); the General Insurance OmbudService (GIO) for house, car, and business insurance; and the Ombudsman for Banking Services and Investments (OBSI) for banks, investment dealers, mutual fund dealers, and most federally regulated trust and loan companies.

CFSON is a not-for-profit corporation governed by an eleven-person board of directors drawn from the participating organizations, consumer and public interest constituencies. CFSON is structured to ensure independence through having board members from non-financial institutions; the absence of authority to intervene in the three ombudsmen services that are part of the CFSON; and funding from industry-level organizations such as the Canadian Bankers Association, rather than directly from individual financial institutions against whom redress is sought. There are no user fees for consumers who approach the CFSON for direction to the appropriate ombudsman service for their complaint. CFSON is a referral service,[405] and while part of its mandate is to establish industry-wide codes of conduct for dispute resolution, it cannot impose those standards and does not act as a final appeal body from industry-based ombudsmen services such as the Ombudsman for Banking Services and Investments (OBSI).

OBSI evolved from the Canadian Banking Ombudsman, first established in 1996, and merged with the IDA, MFDA, and IFIC in October 2002, to provide dispute resolution services for the customers of those

---

403 The Canadian Bankers Association (CBA), the Investment Dealers Association of Canada (IDA), the Mutual Fund Dealers Association of Canada (MFDA), the Investment Funds Institute of Canada (IFIC), the Insurance Bureau of Canada (IBC), and the Canadian Life and Health Insurance Association (CLHIA).
404 For a study of how this occurred, see Jacqueline J. Williams, "Canadian Financial Services Ombudsmen: The Role of Reputational Persuasion" (2004) 20 B.F.L.R. 41.
405 For current information, see online: www.cfson.ca.

financial services sectors, as well as the banks. OBSI is a not-for-profit corporation headed by the Ombudsman and a fourteen-member board of directors,[406] of whom eight are independent (insofar as they are not affiliated with any banks) and six are appointed by the four member associations, the Canadian Bankers Association (CBA), the Investment Dealers Association of Canada (IDA), the Mutual Fund Dealers Association of Canada (MFDA), and the Investment Funds Institute of Canada (IFIC). In addition to the board, OBSI is open to non-voting membership by any federally or provincially regulated financial services provider; there are approximately 750 members.

The eight independent board members act as a committee of the board and enjoy certain special powers to ensure the independence of the Ombudsman, including acting as the nominating committee for independent directors, reviewing and recommending the budget to the board, and acting as the audit committee. The independent directors' committee also recommends to the board an Ombudsman who enjoys renewable five-year terms and can be removed for cause by 75 percent of the board, including a majority of the independent directors. The Ombudsman has a dual role as both Ombudsman and CEO of OBSI but does not report to the board or solicit advice from the board with respect to specific complaints from consumers. To ensure the independence of the resolution process, the board is never involved in specific cases. Although the final decision about a complaint rests with the Ombudsman, the board does establish and review OBSI procedures and standards for complaint resolution, as well as customer complaints about the process generally.

Funding for OBSI is provided by board allocations to members of the CBA, IDA, MFDA, and IFIC. The board first approves its own budget and then requires members to pay their allocation. Member representation on the board has the potential to influence the budget process.

The mandate of OBSI is to receive, investigate, and resolve complaints from individual customers and small business clients of its member institutions after local resolution fails to satisfy the individual or small business customer. The dispute resolution process will be discussed later, within the larger context of dispute resolution for banking matters.[407] OBSI employs a staff of investigators and deputy ombudsmen to deal with each complaint, and while there is no evidence of absence of independence in individual complaint resolution, the independence

---

406 For what follows and for current information, see the "Terms of Reference" of OBSI, online: www.obsi.ca.
407 See Chapter 13.

of OBSI (or of the Canadian Life and Health Insurance OmbudService (CLHIO) or of the General Insurance OmbudService (GIO)) at the corporate or organizational level remains a matter for discussion. As an organization funded directly by the banking industry, with banking representatives on the board, OBSI has been criticized as not being perceived to be fair, notwithstanding the absence of empirical evidence.

The only likely alternative to OBSI would be a dispute resolution service established and managed by the state, which in turn might also be perceived to lack independence. In addition, it has been conceded that even when the government enjoys the legislative initiative of regulating various aspects of the provision of banking services, funding on the basis of banking industry assessments and representation on boards and committees are necessary to ensure that the regulatory mechanism works effectively for all stakeholders.

I. THE FINANCIAL TRANSACTIONS AND REPORTS ANALYSIS CENTRE OF CANADA

The Financial Transactions and Reports Analysis Centre of Canada (FINTRAC) was established on 5 July 2000[408] as an independent financial intelligence agency, whose objectives are the collection, analysis, and assessment of information in relation to money laundering. Although not directly involved in supervising or regulating banks and other financial institutions *qua* financial institutions, all financial institutions are required to report information to FINTRAC in relation to certain kinds of banking transactions. This requires disclosures about customers traditionally protected as confidential within the bank and customer relationship.

FINTRAC was established under the *Proceeds of Crime (Money Laundering) Act*[409] of 2000, which created a mandatory reporting system for certain prescribed transactions. That Act was the result of growing international attempts to track and sanction money launder-

---

[408] For banking law analysis of these developments, see Heather D. Lawson, "Bank Secrecy and Money Laundering" (2002) 17 B.F.L.R. 145; Heather D. Lawson, "Assessing the Divergent Obligation of Banks in the New Millennium: Preserving Customer Confidentiality While Complying with Money Laundering Initiatives" (2004) 19 B.F.L.R. 237; Alison Manzer, *A Guide to Canadian Money Laundering Legislation* (Toronto: Butterworths, 2004). For current information, see online: www.fintrac.gc.ca.

[409] S.C. 2000, c. 17 as am.

ing and criminal activities associated with money laundering, such as drug trafficking and terrorism.[410] In 1989, the G-7 leaders set up an intergovernmental body, the Financial Action Task Force on Money Laundering (FATF), to evaluate and develop recommendations for the enhancement and coordination of international efforts to combat money laundering. In 1990 FATF proposed forty recommendations, which were subsequently revised in 1996, and a number of countries, including Canada, considerably redrafted their pre-existing money laundering legislation[411] to incorporate these recommendations. In 1991, Parliament enacted the first *Proceeds of Crime (Money Laundering) Act*,[412] but FATF still considered Canadian legislation to be too soft, and a new Act was passed in 2000. This legislation is the basis for the detection of money laundering today. The 2000 legislation was further expanded in December 2001 after the events of 9/11, and the act was symbolically renamed the *Proceeds of Crime (Money Laundering) and Terrorist Financing Act*.[413]

Part 3 of this legislation establishes FINTRAC as an agency of the government of Canada for which the Minister of National Revenue is responsible.[414] The statutory objects are: (i) to act at arms length from law-enforcement agencies; (ii) to collect, analyze, assess, and disclose information in order to detect, prevent, and deter money laundering and the financing of terrorist activities; (iii) to protect personal information from unauthorized disclosure; (iv) to enhance public understanding of matters related to money laundering; and (v) to ensure compliance with the reporting requirements of the Act.[415]

FINTRAC is headed by a director who is appointed by the Governor in Council[416] and is assisted by a staff who are deemed to be employees of the Government of Canada.[417] FINTRAC has no direct enforcement role in relation to any conclusions it may draw from the information it receives and analyzes, rather its role is to analyze information received from banks and other mandated reporting organizations and then to

---

410 See above note 408 for details of the historical evolution of banking law related to money laundering.
411 The previous Act was *An Act to Amend the Criminal Code, the Food and Drug Act and the Narcotic Control Act*, R.S.C. 1985 (4th Supp.), c. 42.
412 S.C. 1991, c. 26.
413 S.C. 2001, c. 41, together with subsequent regulations reported regularly.
414 Above note 409, ss. 41 & 42.
415 *Ibid.*, s. 40.
416 *Ibid.*, ss. 43, 44, 45, 47, and 50.
417 *Ibid.*, ss. 46, 48, 49, 50, & 51. FINTRAC is funded from the Consolidated Revenue Fund.

disclose the information and analysis to the appropriate enforcement agencies, including the Minister of National Revenue,[418] the Canada Revenue Agency, the Canada Border Security Agency, the appropriate police force, the Department of Citizenship and Immigration,[419] the Canadian Security Intelligence Service (CSIS),[420] or the government or any government agency of a foreign state with which the Minister of National Revenue has an agreement or arrangement in writing for the exchange of information in relation to money laundering or terrorist financing or a substantially similar matter.[421] In addition to these activities, FINTRAC is mandated to conduct research into trends and developments in these activities and to inform the public and others engaged in this area about these activities, about their obligations under the Act, and about the nature and extent of these activities in Canada.[422]

The information that FINTRAC analyzes and discloses to law-enforcement authorities is required under the Act to be reported to it by various types of financial institutions, financial professionals, government agencies, and organizations such as casinos, where suspicious financial transactions occur.[423] The Act, together with the regulations, provides extensive detail about the types of transactions and information that banks are required to disclose.[424] Generally speaking, every transaction of a value in excess of $10,000, together with every other transaction of a reasonably suspicious nature, must be disclosed.[425]

Thus, while FINTRAC is not a bank or financial institution regulator in the sense of OSFI or CDIC, its statutory roles mean that it has an impact on how banks relate to their customers, insofar as they must know their customers and take greater care than in the past to know their customers' affairs. Banks are also required, in certain circumstances, to breach what was once the important contractual duty of secrecy in relation to their customers' affairs by disclosing some customer transactions to FINTRAC.[426]

---

418 Ibid., s. 52.
419 Ibid., s. 55(b). For details of disclosures, see ss. 53–55 and 57 generally.
420 Ibid., s.55.1.
421 Ibid., ss. 56 & 56.1.
422 Ibid., s. 58.
423 Ibid., s. 5.
424 Ibid., ss. 6–39.
425 For statutory protections for FINTRAC in use of information, see ibid., ss. 59–70.
426 See Chapter 8, Section F.

J. CONCLUSION

Modern states have many reasons for regulating banks and other financial institutions as demonstrated by the regulatory bodies discussed in this chapter. Central banks such as the Bank of Canada were originally established to give advice on national economic policy and to conduct one aspect of that policy: monetary policy. A central bank is at the heart of any country's economy and its banking system because it is both the government's bank and the banks' bank. As the government's bank, it gives advice; ensures monetary stability through supporting the currency, maintaining price stability, controlling the amount of money and credit provided through the banking system, and providing for adequate reserve requirements; and it is the lender of last resort to the commercial banks. In addition to managing monetary policy, however, the activities of a central bank also point to other reasons for regulation.

A second reason is to control systemic risk, that is, the possibility that the entire banking system might collapse as a result of one significant incident, and with it, a national economy. Systemic risk is derived from the linkages that necessarily exist among financial institutions through the clearing and settlement systems, so that if one member has a liquidity problem and cannot make payments, the entire payment system has the potential to collapse. Related is another type of systemic risk, where one institution becomes known to have solvency problems and the public responds by making a run on other banks, which are perfectly stable and solvent. As a lender of last resort, the central bank can guard against such risks by ensuring the efficiency and security of the clearing and payments system and being a last resort lender to a financial institution in difficulty, in order to keep the entire system operating. Systemic risk is the main reason for regulation of and by a central bank and of any organization, such as the Canadian Payments Association, which operates national payment and settlement systems or the Office of the Superintendent of Financial Institutions, which works to ensure that no financial institution reaches a solvency situation that could put the entire system at risk.

A third reason for state regulation of the banking sector is to minimize fraud through money laundering and terrorism. Markets require honesty and trust if they are to operate smoothly; fraud must be kept to a minimum and be known to be an exceptional event whose occurrence will be severely punished. Both FINTRAC and OSFI play their respective parts in this regard: OSFI through its day-to-day oversight and frequent examination of the daily operations of financial institutions and FINTRAC through its investigation of suspected problems and reference to police, revenue, and intelligence services for prosecution and sanction.

A fourth reason is consumer protection. The funds for banking operations are provided by depositors and shareholders whose confidence in the banking system must be maintained if it is to exist and operate smoothly. Historically, consumer protection rested on the ability and willingness of the common law to provide private law redress for individual complaints, primarily through the laws of contract and tort. Over the course of the twentieth century, however, consumer protection became a topic for legislation, which in the banking context, has had very specific foci. The *Bank Act* itself focuses largely on the corporate governance of banks, thereby ensuring their efficient operation, and generally speaking, all the regulatory bodies discussed in this chapter also operate in the interests of customers and shareholders by ensuring the solvency of financial institutions and minimizing fraud. However, in addition to the law of banking generally discussed in the remaining chapters of this book, Parliament has created specific regulatory agencies in relation to particular consumer concerns. The Canada Deposit Insurance Corporation operates the deposit insurance scheme to insure all or part of customers' deposits; the Financial Consumer Agency of Canada supervises compliance with consumer protection provisions; and the Ombudsman for Banking Services and Investments provides a dispute-resolution mechanism for all other individual disputes between banker and customer. Without the confidence of those who entrust their funds to the banks, financial intermediation and economic exchange would simply collapse, and social, economic, and political chaos would result.

CHAPTER 4

BANKS AS BUSINESS CORPORATIONS

A. INTRODUCTION

Banks are business corporations, albeit of a specialized nature and regulated to a far greater extent than any other business corporations in Canada. Doubt about their legal nature as business corporations is quelled immediately by perusal of the *Bank Act*, which is largely devoted to the corporate governance of banks and which is modelled on the *Canada Business Corporations Act* (*CBCA*).[1] Section 91(15), "Banking and the Incorporation of Banks," of the *Constitution Act, 1867*,[2] clearly identifies Parliament as having exclusive jurisdiction to incorporate and regulate banks, and there is no provincial legislation applicable to banks as business corporations. Perusal of the *Bank Act* also shows, however, that a "bank" can be one company or a family of interrelated companies involved in financial intermediation; a bank can be owned by a bank holding company; and a bank is permitted to own or control other financial institutions offering financial services beyond the narrow scope of deposit taking, such as trust and loan companies, mutual fund corporations, or brokerages. The evolution of banks into groups of financial institutions has occurred since the 1991 *Bank Act*, which

---

1   R.S.C. 1985, c. C-44 as am [*CBCA*].
2   Enacted as the *British North America Act, 1867* (U.K.) 1867, 30 & 31 Vict., c. 3, reprinted in R.S.C. 1985, App. II, No. 5.

authorized banks to purchase other financial institutions as they move toward universal, or "one-stop," banking. The MacKay Task Force[3] approved the trend, which was continued in the 2001 and 2007 amendments to the Act.

The purpose of this chapter is to describe and analyze the legal nature of banks as business corporations, while the next chapter (Chapter 5) will discuss the types of businesses in which banks are permitted to engage either directly or indirectly pursuant to the *Bank Act*.[4]

B. INCORPORATION

Since 1997, banks have been required to be incorporated by letters patent only,[5] that is, the decision is to be made by the Minister of Finance, which means, effectively, that it is a decision within the Cabinet. Prior to the 1980 *Bank Act*, the only means of incorporating a new bank was by a private act of Parliament, a more public process, but in 1980 incorporation by letters patent was added to facilitate an anticipated rush to incorporate Schedule II foreign banks once foreign banks were permitted to do business legally by the 1980 Act. The 1991 Act continued to permit incorporation by private act or by letters patent, but the 1997 Act restricted incorporation to letters patent. This appears to be part of the increasingly centralized control of the banking sector in the government through the Minister of Finance.[6]

The application for incorporation is filed with the Superintendent and should contain all the information the Superintendent requires, including the names of the first directors.[7] For at least four consecutive weeks prior to the application, public notice of an intention to apply is to be published in the *Canada Gazette* and in a general circulation newspaper at or near the place of the head office,[8] so that any person

---

3   Task Force on the Future of the Canadian Financial Services Sector, *Change, Challenge, Opportunity: The Future of the Canadian Financial Services Sector* (Ottawa: Department of Finance, 1998).
4   These two chapters will offer an overview of the *Bank Act* provisions. For a detailed discussion of the provisions, see M.H. Ogilvie, *Canadian Banking Law*, 2d ed. (Toronto: Carswell, 1998) cc. 3–27.
5   *Bank Act*, S.C. 1991, c. 46, s. 22.
6   For a larger discussion of this trend in the 2001 legislation, see M.H. Ogilvie, "Change, Challenge, Opportunity: Canadian Banking Sector Restructured Again" (2003) J. Bus. L. 487.
7   Above note 5, s. 25(1).
8   *Ibid.*, s. 25(2).

may object in writing to the Superintendent.[9] The Minister is to be informed of any objection, and if the Superintendent thinks it in the public interest, should hold a public inquiry,[10] the findings of which are to be reported to the Minister[11] and the public.[12] Prior to issuing letters patent, the Minister is required to consider the financial resources, business record, character and integrity, and competence of the applicant, as well as the feasibility of the plans and the best interests of the financial system in Canada.[13] If the applicant is a subsidiary of a foreign bank, the Minister must be satisfied that its home country will provide favourable reciprocal conditions for domestic Canadian banks.[14] Applications from governments and from government agencies or entities, whether Canadian or foreign, must be rejected.[15] Once the Minister has satisfied these requirements, the letters patent may be issued, in the discretion of the Minister. There is no *prima facie* entitlement to incorporation on application as permitted by business corporations legislation.[16]

In addition to incorporation by letters patent of a new body corporate, the *Bank Act* provides for existing corporations to continue as a bank, including trust and loan companies, insurance companies,[17] and any other federally incorporated corporation,[18] provided certain requirements are met. At least two-thirds of the shareholders of these corporations must approve the conversion to a bank,[19] and once the bank comes into existence,[20] shares are to be transferred to the existing shareholders on a share-for-share basis with the same rights, privileges, and restrictions as the shares of the corporation.[21] The Act protects existing shareholder rights into the newly incorporated bank for a period of ten years from the issuance of the letters patent.[22]

---

9   Ibid., s. 26(1).
10 Ibid., ss. 26(2), (3), and (5); Rules Governing Proceedings at Public Inquiries into Objections (Banks), SOR/92-308.
11 *Bank Act*, ibid., s. 26(3).
12 Ibid., s. 26(4).
13 Ibid., s. 27.
14 Ibid., s. 24.
15 Ibid., s. 23.
16 *CBCA*, above note 1, ss. 5, 7, and 8.
17 *Bank Act*, above note 5, s. 29(1).
18 Ibid., ss. 33(1) & (2) and 34(1).
19 Ibid., ss. 29(5) and 34(2) & (3).
20 Ibid., ss. 32 and 36.
21 Ibid., ss. 29(2), (3), (6), (7), & (8), and 38.
22 Ibid., s. 29(4).

Once incorporated,[23] the name and place of the head office of the bank is added to Schedule I of the Act if the bank is not a subsidiary of a foreign bank,[24] to Schedule II if the bank is a subsidiary of a foreign bank,[25] or to Schedule III if the bank is an authorized foreign bank.[26] Once any bank is incorporated, the *Bank Act* applies to that bank and is the charter of that bank.[27] This means that the *Bank Act* is effectively the constitution for every bank permitted to operate in Canada, so that all banks have a common constitution.[28]

Finally, the *Bank Act* also permits a bank to apply for a certificate of continuation as a business corporation or a cooperative or a cooperative association or for letters patent to continue as a trust or loan company or to amalgamate with a trust or loan company,[29] after which the *Bank Act* ceases to apply to it.[30]

A bank may choose any name, provided it is not prohibited by Parliament, deceptively misdescriptive, confusingly similar to an existing name, or reserved for another bank.[31] One exception is made for the use by a bank affiliated with another entity of substantially the same name with the consent of that entity.[32] The name may be in English or in French or some combination,[33] but outside Canada, a bank may use its name in any language.[34] Within Canada a bank may carry on business or identify itself by a name other than its corporate name, provided the Superintendent is satisfied it is not prohibited within the Act.[35] The Superintendent may order a change of name that does not comply with the Act.[36]

A bank is permitted to change its name by application to the Minister of Finance to amend its letters patent once a by-law effecting a

---

23 *Ibid.*, ss. 28, 30, 31, 35, 37, and 39 for notice, content of letters patent, etc.
24 *Ibid.*, ss. 14(1)(a), (2), & (3).
25 *Ibid.*, ss. 14(1)(b), (2), & (3).
26 *Ibid.*, s. 14.1.
27 *Ibid.*, s. 13.
28 *Ibid.*, s. 14.2 contains the only exception, in that the Governor in Council is permitted to exempt a foreign bank from any statutory provision by regulation. For changes to the incorporation instrument, see ss. 215 & 216, which provide for new letters patent after approval by a special shareholder resolution and Ministerial approval.
29 *Ibid.*, s. 39.1.
30 *Ibid.*, s. 39.2.
31 *Ibid.*, ss. 40 and 43.
32 *Ibid.*, s. 41.
33 *Ibid.*, s. 42(1).
34 *Ibid.*, s. 42(2).
35 *Ibid.*, ss. 42(3) & (4).
36 *Ibid.*, s. 4.

name change has been approved by two-thirds of the shareholders and approved by the Superintendent.[37] The name change takes effect on the day stated in the letters patent.[38] The bank is required to set out its legal name on all legal documents.[39] Other names under which a bank carries on business are insufficient for the validity of any transaction but can be used in addition to the formal legal name.

The *Bank Act* does not expressly require that a bank use the word "bank" in its name nor that it register any name used outside Canada, but the privileges bestowed by the Act in using the word "bank" and the sanctions for those who use the word but are not incorporated as banks strongly suggest the wisdom of using the word "bank" in a legal name. Unauthorized use of the words "bank," "banking," and "banker" attract for individuals a fine of up to $500,000 and/or up to five years imprisonment and for entities a fine of up to $5 million.[40]

C. STATUS AND POWERS

The *Bank Act* is the complete source for the legal status of all banks in Canada and for their powers to operate within and outside of the country. Every bank has an identical legal status and corporate powers derived from their shared constitution, the *Bank Act*.

Following the pattern of the *CBCA*, the *Bank Act* bestows on each bank the capacity of a natural person and all the rights, powers, and privileges of a natural person in law, subject to the Act,[41] in relation to its operations in Canada.[42] Outside Canada, its capacity to operate is determined by the Act and by the laws of the jurisdiction within which it is operating.[43] The purpose of conferring natural capacity on corporate persons in the *CBCA* was to abolish the *ultra vires* doctrine in the common law, which operated in an unpredictable manner.[44] The common law once assumed that corporations were created with lim-

---

37   *Ibid.*, ss. 215, 217(1)(i.1), (2), & (3).
38   *Ibid.*, s. 216.
39   *Ibid.*, s. 255. On corporate seal: s. 256.
40   *Ibid.*, ss. 938 and 985(1).
41   *Ibid.*, ss. 15(1) & (2).
42   *Ibid.*, s. 15(3). This status is for a period of five years only, after which Parliament must renew the charter after the five-year review: s. 21.
43   *Ibid.*, s. 15(4).
44   See any textbook on business corporations such as Bruce Welling, *Corporate Law in Canada: The Governing Principles*, 2d ed. (Toronto: Butterworths, 1991); Tom Hadden, Robert G. Forbes, & Ralph L. Simmons, *Canadian Business Organiza-*

ited powers, so that any activity expressly or implicitly *ultra vires* was invalid and unenforceable. The doctrine of *ultra vires* was intended to reassure shareholders and creditors that the activities in which they were investing or financing, respectively, would be the activities to which the company was restricted and that corporate assets would not be dissipated in unauthorized activities. *Ultra vires* became a defence that frustrated third party contractors with the company, but over the course of the late nineteenth and early twentieth centuries, the courts adopted various compromises by which third party contracts were sometimes enforced and sometimes not. Statutory elimination of the doctrine of *ultra vires* by bestowing the powers of a natural person on corporate bodies theoretically meant that like a natural person, corporations could engage in any activity, provided it was not illegal, such as criminal or tortious activities, and shareholders and creditors were forewarned, while third parties could enjoy greater security under contracts with the company.

While there is an ongoing debate in business corporations law generally as to whether the *CBCA* really abolished the doctrine of *ultra vires* completely,[45] in banking law it can be said that it did not. The *Bank Act* contains numerous provisions restricting the powers and activities of banks, so that it can be said that while in theory banks are endowed with the legal capacity of a natural person by the Act, the practical effect of that same Act is to restrict those powers considerably.

Nevertheless, third party contractors with a bank can be largely assured that their transactions are enforceable. The Act provides that no act, including property transfers, is invalid by reason only that the act or transfer is contrary to the Act or the bank's incorporating instrument.[46] Nor is it necessary for a bank to pass a by-law conferring any particular power on the bank or the directors[47] for an act of the bank to be legally enforceable.

The *Bank Act*, again following the *CBCA*,[48] also abolishes a doctrine from nineteenth-century company law related to *ultra vires*: the doctrine of constructive notice. The Act provides that no person is af-

---

tions Law (Toronto: Butterworths, 1984); and Christopher C. Nicholls, *Corporate Law* (Toronto: Emond Montgomery, 2005).

45 Nicholls, *ibid.* at 182–84. The Supreme Court of Canada appears to have erred in declaring the doctrine dead in *Communities Economic Development Fund v. Canadian Pickles Corp.* (1991), 85 D.L.R. (4th) 88 (S.C.C.) and *Continental Bank Leasing Corp. v. Canada* (1998), 163 D.L.R. (4th) 385 (S.C.C.).
46 *Bank Act*, above note 5, s. 16.
47 *Ibid.*, s. 17.
48 *CBCA*, above note 1, s. 17.

fected by, or is deemed to have notice or knowledge of, the contents of any document concerning a bank by reason only of the filing of the document with the Superintendent or the Minister or its availability at a branch of the bank.[49] The common law deemed all parties dealing with a company to have notice and knowledge of company documents because they were required to be registered in a public registry. A third party who learned that a company did not have the powers or capacity to enter a transaction was said to have constructive notice of the registered documents and was, therefore, deprived of lack of notice as a defence in relation to the enforceability of the transaction.

Strictly construed, section 19 of the *Bank Act* may not have completely abolished the constructive notice rule. First, some documents relating to banks are registered in other places than with the Superintendent, the Minister, or at a branch, for example, the special security registries. Secondly, the phrase "by reason only" suggests that constructive notice might still attach to other sources of information than those publicly registered. That the legislative intent was to retain the doctrine of constructive notice in certain unspecified circumstances may be further surmised from the following section, section 20, which partially codifies another nineteenth-century company law doctrine, the indoor management rule.[50]

Section 20 provides that a bank or a guarantor of a bank obligation may not assert against a person dealing with the bank or a person who has acquired rights from a bank that: (i) the bank's incorporating instrument or by-laws have not been complied with; (ii) the persons named as directors are not directors; (iii) the place named as the head office is not the head office; (iv) a person held out as a director, officer, or representative of the bank has not been appointed and has no such authority; or (v) a document issued by a director, officer, or representative with actual or usual authority is not valid or genuine. The sole exception is where the person has or ought to have such knowledge by virtue of that person's relationship with the bank.[51]

The indoor management rule meant that third parties were entitled to assume that the affairs of a company were being conducted within the terms of its corporate constitution, that is, directors, officers, and employees were acting within their authority when entering third-party transactions on behalf of the company . Therefore, except where the third party knew or ought to have known this was not the case,

---

49   *Bank Act*, above note 5, s. 19.
50   *Royal British Bank v. Turquand* (1856), 54 El. and Bl. 248, 119 E.R. 886 (Exch. Ct.).
51   *Bank Act*, above note 5, s. 20.

the company could not plead absence of authority against the enforceability of the transaction. Following the *CBCA*,[52] section 20 of the *Bank Act* is a codification of the indoor management rule; however, as with the *CBCA* provision, it does not deal with situations where a corporate officer or director lacking authority may bind the corporation.[53] Since none of these provisions in the *Bank Act* have been judicially considered, little further can be said about their scope and application.

The net outcome of the abolition of the *ultra vires* rule and the constructive notice rule in whole or in part and the codification of the indoor management rule in whole or in part is to assimilate the legal status of banks as bodies corporate with natural persons as far as possible. Generally speaking, a third party dealing with a bank is entitled to assume that the director or officer has authority to bind the bank to a transaction. While there are ambiguities in the law in relation to other business corporations in relation to third party transactions,[54] given the very public nature of banks and the very detailed regulation to which they are subject under the Act, third parties should generally have little concern about the enforceability of transactions by or against banks. Finally, Part II of the Act underlines that the bank as a body corporate may be liable by also providing that shareholders *qua* shareholders are not liable for any liability, act, or default of the Bank except as expressly provided by the Act.[55]

Once incorporated, banks are considered to have the legal capacity and status of natural persons in Canada. However, the Act itself reduces that capacity and status considerably as the rest of this text chronicles.

D. STARTING BUSINESS

After the letters patent are issued, a meeting of the first directors[56] must be held,[57] at which they are expected to make by-laws, adopt forms of share certificates and corporate records, authorize the issue of shares, appoint officers and auditors,[58] and make banking arrangements.[59]

---

52 *CBCA*, above note 1, s. 18.
53 Nicholls, above note 44 at 164–73.
54 *Ibid.*
55 *Bank Act*, above note 5, s. 19. See Section F, below in this chapter.
56 *Ibid.*, s. 45. As named in the letters patent: s. 31.
57 *Ibid.*, s. 45(2) for notice requirements.
58 *Ibid.*, s. 45(1)(e) until the first shareholders' meeting.
59 *Ibid.*, s. 45(1).

Once the bank has received $5 million from the issue of its shares, the directors shall also call the first shareholders' meeting to approve the by-laws, elect directors, and appoint auditors.[60]

However, the bank may not commence business until the Superintendent so orders,[61] and the bank must make an application for that order which contains a statement setting out the costs of incorporation and organization.[62] The Act restricts the right of the bank to engage in various financial transactions relating to the commencement of business prior to the order,[63] and the Superintendent shall not make the order until satisfied that the first shareholders' meeting has been held, there is $5 million in paid-in capital, the expenses of incorporation are reasonable, and there is compliance with the Act.[64] The order may be subject to conditions[65] and may be subsequently varied.[66] The Minister may revoke the order.[67] Once the order to commence business has been made, the bank shall publish a notice of the order in a general circulation newspaper at or near the place of the head office[68] and the Superintendent shall publish a notice in the *Canada Gazette*.[69] Starting up business is a closely regulated matter.[70]

E. DIRECTORS AND OFFICERS

1) Role

The *Bank Act* vests management and the supervision of the management of the business and affairs of a bank in the directors, subject to the Act.[71] As with other business corporations,[72] ultimate responsibility for the conduct of all of a bank's affairs rests with the board of directors. The day-to-day conduct of the bank's business is delegated to of-

---

60 *Ibid.*, ss. (46)(1) & (2). This meeting must confirm by election directors and auditors: ss. 45(2) and 47.
61 *Ibid.*, s. 48.
62 *Ibid.*, ss. 49(1) & (2).
63 *Ibid.*, ss. 50 & 51.
64 *Ibid.*, s. 52.
65 *Ibid.*, s. 53.
66 *Ibid.*, ss. 54, 54.1, and 55.
67 *Ibid.*, s. 54.1(2).
68 *Ibid.*, s. 56(1).
69 *Ibid.*, s. 56(2).
70 For use and return of funds should no order be given, see *ibid.*, ss. 57 & 58.
71 *Ibid.*, s. 157(1).
72 *CBCA*, above note 1, s. 102(1).

ficers and employees, and the *Bank Act* permits the directors to delegate certain functions to the senior officers of a bank. But it remains the case that final responsibility for the proper functioning of a bank rests with the board, not the shareholders or the officers and employees. Both the Act and recent changes in attitudes to directors demonstrate how awesome is this duty of directors.

2) Statutory Requirements for Directors

The *Bank Act* requires a bank to have at least seven directors[73] and sets no maximum number; domestic banks typically have twenty to thirty directors, and foreign banks typically have seven to fifteen directors. The formal qualifications are minimal: a director must not be under eighteen, be adjudged of unsound mind, be a bankrupt, be prohibited by the Act[74] from exercising voting rights attached to shares of the bank; be an officer, director, or employee of certain entities;[75] or be an employee or Minister of the federal or provincial governments or of a foreign government. Furthermore, a director must be a natural person, not another corporate body.[76] A director is not required to own shares of the bank.[77] One half of the directors of a foreign bank subsidiary must be resident Canadians, and a majority of the directors of domestic banks must be resident Canadians.[78] Not more than two-thirds of the directors may be affiliated with the bank as, for example, officers, employees, significant borrowers, or owners of a significant interest in a class of shares or substantial investment in the bank or an affiliate.[79] Not more than 15 percent of the directors may be employees, but up to four persons may be employees if they constitute less than one-half of the directors.[80]

Taken together, these requirements show that a board must be composed of directors who have legal capacity, are independent of governments, and resident Canadians and that a strong element of independence generally from conflicting interests should characterize the board as a whole. On the other hand, the fact that two-thirds can

---

73 *Bank Act*, above note 5, s. 159(1). The precise range is set out in by-laws: s. 165(1).
74 *Ibid.*, ss. 392, 401.3, and 156.09(9).
75 *Ibid.*
76 *Ibid.*, ss. 160 & 160.1.
77 *Ibid.*, s. 161.
78 *Ibid.*, s. 159(2).
79 *Ibid.*, ss. 163, 162 & 162.1; Affiliated Persons (Banks) Regulations, SOR/92-325.
80 *Bank Act, ibid.*, s. 164.

be drawn from the bank itself also means that considerable knowledge and expertise about the bank and banking generally is considered desirable in a bank board.[81]

Directors are elected by shareholders at the annual general meeting,[82] and the *Bank Act* provides that the minimum and maximum numbers to be elected[83] and their terms[84] should be set out in the by-laws. Although the Act provides for one-, two-, or three-year terms, the selection of length and the rollover of directors' terms is left to the by-laws for each bank to determine.[85] There is no statutory limit on the number of terms,[86] although as a practical matter, renewal on the board is a factor in decisions as to the number of terms served. Although election to a board is by majority,[87] the *Bank Act* makes provision for cumulative voting, where the by-laws so provide, to permit minority shareholders to cast all their votes in favour of a single candidate and have an increased chance of securing at least one director to represent them.[88]

Elections are void for all directors where the directors purportedly elected do not satisfy these statutory requirements unless the directors develop a plan within forty-five days approved by the Superintendent to rectify the situation.[89] Where the shareholders fail to elect the minimum number as set out in the Act (seven) or the by-laws, the directors elected may exercise the powers of directors if the number elected amounts to a quorum.[90] If the Superintendent does not approve the plan, the board shall consist of those who were incumbent directors prior to the meeting at which the purported election occurred,[91] and these directors shall call a special meeting of shareholders to elect new directors.[92] If they fail to do so, any shareholder may call the meeting.[93]

---

81 For more detailed analysis of board qualification policies, see Ogilvie, above note 4 at 49–51.
82 *Bank Act*, above note 5, ss. 165(2) and 167.
83 *Ibid.*, s. 165(1).
84 *Ibid.*, s. 166(1).
85 *Ibid.*, ss. 166(2)–(6). For filling vacancies, see ss. 176–77. For filling vacancies by class, see s. 178. For unexpired terms, see s. 179. For additional directives, see s. 179.1.
86 *Ibid.*, s. 169.
87 *Ibid.*, s. 167.
88 *Ibid.*, s. 168.
89 *Ibid.*, s. 170(1).
90 *Ibid.*, s. 170(2).
91 *Ibid.*, ss. 171(1) & (2).
92 *Ibid.*, s. 171(3).
93 *Ibid.*, s. 171(4).

Directors cease to hold office at the expiry of their term, upon resignation, upon death, upon becoming disqualified, or by removal[94] by the shareholders[95] or the Superintendent.[96] Shareholders may remove all the directors by a resolution at a special meeting[97] and may also fill any vacancies created by removal at the same meeting.[98]

Although the Act does not provide for additional grounds on which shareholders may remove a director beyond those stated (for example, standards of competence or inappropriate conduct), the Act does provide a mechanism for a director who resigns, is removed, or hears of a shareholder meeting called for the purpose of removing him, to comment on the removal. A director may submit to the bank a written statement giving the reasons for the resignation or why the director is opposed to any removal,[99] and where the resignation is a result of a disagreement with other directors or officers, the director is required to submit a written statement to the bank and to the Superintendent.[100] Copies of all statements are to be sent by the bank to each shareholder and to the Superintendent.[101] No legal liability is incurred by reason only of circulating a director's statement.[102]

By giving shareholders the power to remove bank directors, the Act serves as a reminder that they are the owners of the bank at the end of the day. Exercise of this power is unknown and it is difficult to assert, since incumbent directors typically select new directors for approval at annual meetings, which a tiny minority of shareholders attend or at which they vote by proxy.

3) Statutory Powers and Activities of Directors

The *Bank Act* permits directors to carry out their duties by meetings of the board or a committee or by resolutions outside board meetings. If decisions are made by resolution, all directors must sign the resolution,[103] which should be filed with the minutes of the proceedings of

---

94 *Ibid.*, ss. 172(1) & (2).
95 *Ibid.*, s. 173.
96 *Ibid.*, ss. 647 & 647.1.
97 *Ibid.*, s. 173(1). Directors elected by a class or series of shares can be removed only by those shareholders: s. 175(2).
98 *Ibid.*, s. 173(3).
99 *Ibid.*, s. 174(1).
100 *Ibid.*, s. 174(2).
101 *Ibid.*, s. 175(1).
102 *Ibid.*, s. 175(2).
103 *Ibid.*, s. 184.1(1).

the directors,[104] but resolutions of the audit committee and the conduct review committee cannot be approved by resolution, rather only by meetings.[105]

The board is required to meet at least four times each financial year at any place for which the by-laws provide.[106] Notice of meetings is required, although a director may waive notice.[107] A quorum may exercise all the powers of the directors, and for both board meetings and committee meetings, a quorum is a majority of the minimum number of directors required by the Act (seven) or any greater number established by the by-laws.[108] In addition, a majority of the directors present shall be resident Canadians, and for foreign bank subsidiaries, at least one-half shall be resident Canadians.[109] If the resident Canadian attendance requirement cannot be met for a meeting, the directors may still transact business if a resident Canadian director not present approves the business transacted and the addition of that director fulfills the resident Canadian statutory requirement.[110] Finally, at least one of the directors present must be a director who is not affiliated with the bank, although that number can also be made up if an unaffiliated director not present approves the business transacted at the meeting.[111] Meetings may take place by telephonic, electronic, or other communications facilities that permit all participants to communicate adequately with each other.[112]

Directors are deemed to have consented to any resolution unless they request that a dissent be entered in the minutes of the meeting or send a written dissent to the secretary of the meeting before the meeting is adjourned or by registered mail immediately after the meeting is adjourned.[113] An absent director is also deemed to have consented unless within seven days after that director becomes aware of the resolution, the director causes a dissent to be placed with the minutes or sends a dissent by registered mail or by delivery to the head office.[114]

---

104 *Ibid.*, s. 184.1(2).
105 *Ibid.*, ss. 184.1(3) & (4).
106 *Ibid.*, ss. 180(1) & (2).
107 *Ibid.*, ss. 180(3), 181(1) & (2). For adjourned meetings, see s. 181(3).
108 *Ibid.*, ss. 182(1), (2), & (3). Attendance is recorded and sent to shareholders: s. 186.
109 *Ibid.*, s. 183(1).
110 *Ibid.*, s. 183(2).
111 *Ibid.*, s. 183.1.
112 *Ibid.*, ss. 184(1) & (2).
113 *Ibid.*, ss. 185(1) & (2).
114 *Ibid.*, s. 185(3).

The Superintendent may also require a board to meet to consider the matters set out in any notice to the bank, and the Superintendent may attend and be heard at that meeting.[115]

While the *Bank Act* vests a general duty to manage on the board, it also expressly stipulates other specific duties of the directors: (i) establish an audit committee; (ii) establish a conduct review committee; (iii) establish procedures to resolve conflicts of interest; (iv) designate a committee to monitor the conflict procedures; (v) establish procedures for disclosing information to customers and dealing with customer complaints required by the Act to be disclosed; (vi) designate a committee to monitor the customer disclosure committee; (vii) establish investment and lending policies;[116] (viii) make, amend, or repeal by-laws subject to shareholder approval;[117] (ix) appoint other appropriate board committees;[118] (x) appoint the chief executive officer;[119] (xi) designate the offices of the bank and appoint officers;[120] (xii) establish the remuneration for directors, officers, and employees;[121] (xiii) propose persons to serve as director to the shareholders;[122] (xiv) fill an auditor vacancy between annual shareholder meetings;[123] (xv) notify the audit committee and the auditors of any error or misstatement in any annual or other statement;[124] (xvi) approve a related party transaction;[125] and (xvii) declare dividends.[126]

The audit committee should consist of at least three directors,[127] and the majority must be unaffiliated.[128] Officers and employees are not eligible to be members.[129] The statutory duties of the audit committee are to review the annual statement prior to director approval; review any returns required by the Superintendent; require appropriate internal control procedures; review transactions brought to its attention by the auditors that could adversely affect the well-being of the bank;

---

115 *Ibid.*, ss. 187(1) & (2).
116 *Ibid.*, ss. 157(2) & (3).
117 *Ibid.*, ss. 188–92.
118 *Ibid.*, s. 193.
119 *Ibid.*, s. 196(1).
120 *Ibid.*, ss. 197(1), (2), & (3).
121 *Ibid.*, s. 199(1). Directors' remuneration subject to approved by-law: s. 199(2).
122 *Ibid.*, ss. 159–87.
123 *Ibid.*, s. 319(1).
124 *Ibid.*, s. 332.
125 *Ibid.*, ss. 497, 486, and 506.
126 *Ibid.*, s. 79.
127 *Ibid.*, s. 194(1).
128 *Ibid.*, s. 194(2).
129 *Ibid.*

discuss the annual statement with the auditors; and discuss internal control procedures with the chief internal auditor.[130] The directors are required to approve the annual statement and all annual returns,[131] and the audit committee may call a board meeting to discuss a matter of concern.[132]

The membership of the conduct review committee must meet the same statutory requirements as the audit committee,[133] and its duties are to ensure that management establishes procedures for complying with the self-dealing provisions; to review the effectiveness of the procedures; to establish certain other procedures in relation to share transactions;[134] and to identify any related party transactions that may have a material effect on the stability or solvency of the bank.[135] The conduct review committee must report to the board after each of its meetings,[136] and the bank shall report to the Superintendent on its procedures[137] and not more than ninety days after the end of each financial year on its activities generally in that year.[138]

Although the board appoints the senior officers of a bank, the *Bank Act* forbids the directors to delegate certain duties to them: (i) submission to shareholders of any matter requiring shareholder approval;[139] (ii) filling board or auditor vacancies; (iii) issuing securities; (iv) declaring dividends; (v) authorizing share redemptions;[140] (vi) authorizing commissions on share issues; (vii) approving a management proxy circular; (viii) approving the annual and other financial statements; and (ix) adopting, amending, or repealing by-laws.[141]

In addition to the duties set out above, the *Bank Act* also provides for one right of a director, that is, to attend and be heard at every meeting of the shareholders.[142]

Finally, the Act makes provision for the validity of directors' decisions should there be a statutory defect in relation to them. An act of

---

130 *Ibid.*, s. 194(3).
131 *Ibid.*, s. 194(4).
132 *Ibid.*, s. 194(5).
133 *Ibid.*, ss. 195(1) & (2).
134 *Ibid.*, s. 495.1(1).
135 *Ibid.*, ss. 195(1) & (2).
136 *Ibid.*, s. 195(5).
137 *Ibid.*, s. 195(4).
138 *Ibid.*, s. 195(6).
139 For example, by-law approval, see *ibid.*, ss. 188–92.
140 Pursuant to s. 71, *ibid.*
141 *Ibid.*, s. 198.
142 *Ibid.*, s. 201.

a director or officer is valid, notwithstanding any defect in a qualification, selection, or appointment,[143] and an act of a board is valid, notwithstanding a defect in the composition of the board or an irregularity in its election or in the appointment of an individual member.[144] The purpose of these provisions is to protect third parties dealing with the board whose interests might be jeopardized if a director or board attempted to rely on a statutory breach to erode an obligation undertaken to a third party.[145]

4) Directors' Standards of Care

Again, following the lead of the *CBCA*,[146] the *Bank Act* sets the legal standard of care required of directors to be: (i) a duty to act honestly and in good faith, with a view to the best interests of the bank and (ii) to exercise the care, diligence, and skill that a reasonably prudent person would exercise in comparable circumstances.[147] A director, officer and employee is further required to comply with the Act, the regulations, and the bank's incorporating instrument and by-laws,[148] and no contract, resolution, or by-law can provide exemption from this duty.[149] The duty to act in good faith in the best interests of a bank is usually characterized as a codification of the fiduciary duty of directors, while the duty of care of a reasonably prudent person is usually characterized as a codification of the common law duties of directors. These provisions in the *Bank Act* have not been interpreted by the courts; however, identical provisions of business corporation statutes have been, so that statutory interpretation is likely to apply to the *Bank Act* provisions.[150]

At common law, company directors were not held to particularly high standards, provided they were honest. In the leading case, *Re City Equitable Fire Insurance Co.*,[151] Romer J. stated the standard of care in three propositions: (i) a director need only bring to that position the skill that may reasonably be expected from a person of the director's knowledge; (ii) a director need not give continuous attention to the

---

143 *Ibid.*, s. 200(1).
144 *Ibid.*, s. 200(2).
145 These provisions may not be entirely curative. See Ogilvie, above note 4 at 59–60.
146 *CBCA*, above note 1, s. 122.
147 *Bank Act*, above note 5, s. 158(1).
148 *Ibid.*, s. 158(2).
149 *Ibid.*, s. 158(3).
150 See generally Hadden, above note 44 at c. 5; Welling, above note 44 at c. 6; and Nicholls, above note 44 at 285–312.
151 [1925] 1 Ch. 407.

affairs of the company and need only attend board meetings when reasonably able to do so; and (iii) in the absence of grounds for suspicion, a director may trust officers to perform their duties honestly.[152]

While it seemed reasonably clear that the codification in both provincial and federal business corporations acts in the 1970s was intended to raise the common law standard of care from mere honesty to a standard of reasonableness, it was not clear whether the test was the reasonable person, the reasonable director, or the reasonable director with the skill and knowledge of the director in question.[153] However, in *Peoples Department Stores Inc. v. Wise*,[154] the Supreme Court of Canada decided that in the identical provision, section 122(1)(b) of the *CBCA*, there was no subjective element in the standard of care; rather, it meant the standard to be expected of a reasonable director, that is, a purely objective standard. The Court did not address whether there should be lower standards for outside or independent directors such as banks are required to have, so it is uncertain whether different standards are applicable to inside and outside directors, respectively.

Bank directors also have a duty to act in good faith with a view to the best interests of the bank, that is, they must place the bank's interests above their own in the event of a conflict. Section 158(1)(a) is a codification of the director's fiduciary duty, which courts have considered to include the following: to exercise powers honestly and in good faith; to exercise power for a proper purpose; to be loyal and avoid conflicts of interest; to disclose interests in corporate transactions; to avoid appropriation of corporate opportunities; and to account in takeovers. In all of these situations, there is a potential for conflict of interest. Acting in the best interests of the bank is the measure for whether or not the fiduciary duty has been breached, but it is not yet fully determined what that means. In *Peoples*, the Supreme Court of Canada stated that this was not restricted to the interests of shareholders or any other single group of stakeholders such as creditors, but rather, in relation to business corporations, the directors are required to act to create a better corporation or, in the case of a bank, a better bank.[155] But what is a better bank? Thus, there remains considerable ambiguity in relation to the fiduciary standard in the legislation, as well as in the common

---

152 *Ibid.* at 428.
153 See Nicholls, above note 44 at 289–97.
154 (2004), 244 D.L.R. (4th) 564 (S.C.C.) [*Peoples*]. See also "Symposium on the Supreme Court's Judgment in the Peoples Department Store Case" (2005) 41 Can. Bus. L.J. 167.
155 *Peoples, ibid.*

law standard as codified in the Act. In the absence of banking cases interpreting these provisions, it is uncertain whether judicial interpretation of similar provisions in business corporations acts are applicable, given certain peculiar features of banks as business corporations such as their unique role in the national economy or as the repositories for individuals' wealth. Whether such factors would attract considerably higher or different contents for both the common law and fiduciary duties is unknown.

The *Bank Act* makes further provision for directors' duties conceptually related to a fiduciary duty in relation to disclosure by directors, in that it provides for conflict of interest and for self-dealing by related parties. At common law, disclosure by directors and officers in "self-interested contracts" was required and conceptualized as a fiduciary obligation in which directors and officers were required to put the best interests of the company before their own. Although originally framed as an absolute prohibition on contracts between a company and its directors,[156] this position was unrealistic, given the preponderance of small companies in which directors might also be shareholders. A compromise position whereby company by-laws allowed for directors' contracts provided there was full disclosure and abstention from voting became the norm, and this was codified in business corporations legislation.[157]

A director or officer of a bank who is a party to a proposed material contract or material contract or is a director or officer of an entity or has a material interest in a party to a proposed material contract or material contract is required to disclose their interest in writing to the bank or request that such disclosure be entered in the directors' minutes.[158] This disclosure should be made when the proposed contract is first considered or when the director first becomes interested or when the director becomes a director.[159] The director is required to be absent at board meetings when the contract is considered and may not vote on the contract, with the exception of certain contracts, such as security arrangements by the director for the benefit of the bank or a subsidiary, contracts for directors' remuneration, indemnity[160] or insurance,[161] or

---

156 *Aberdeen Railway Co. v. Blaikie Brothers* (1854), 1 Macq. H.L. 461 at 471–72, Lord Cranworth L.C.
157 *CBCA*, above note 1, s. 120.
158 *Bank Act*, above note 5, s. 202(1).
159 *Ibid.*, s. 202(2). For officers, see ss. 202(3) & (4).
160 *Ibid.*, s. 212.
161 *Ibid.*, s. 213.

contracts with bank affiliates.¹⁶² One disclosure is deemed to be a sufficient declaration of an interest and a continuing disclosure.¹⁶³

A director who knowingly fails to make a disclosure ceases to hold office as a director and is ineligible to be a director of any federally incorporated financial institution for a period of five years from the date of the contravention.¹⁶⁴ However, a failure to disclose does not make an act by a board invalid,¹⁶⁵ nor is any resulting contract void or voidable if a director has made disclosure and the contract was approved by the directors or shareholders and was reasonable and fair to the bank at the time of approval.¹⁶⁶

The conflict provisions of the *Bank Act* are ambiguous. There is no definition of "material," and disclosure of all contracts would be prudent. There are no criteria for determining what is a fair and reasonable contract for the bank. Disclosure need only be made to other directors, rather than to shareholders, and no shareholder ratification of such contracts is required. Thus, once disclosure is made, the board is largely free to enter into most contracts in which a director may have an interest.¹⁶⁷

5) Directors' Liabilities and Indemnification

Directors of a bank are, of course, liable for breach of any statutory duty imposed upon them by the *Bank Act*,¹⁶⁸ any other applicable legislation,¹⁶⁹ and any applicable duty at common law. In addition, the Act makes express provision for liability for giving an undue preference to any creditor of a bank,¹⁷⁰ authorizing shares¹⁷¹ or subordinated indebtedness,¹⁷² redeeming shares,¹⁷³ reducing capital,¹⁷⁴ paying a dividend,¹⁷⁵

---

162 *Ibid.*, s. 203(1).
163 *Ibid.*, s. 204.
164 *Ibid.*, s. 203(2).
165 *Ibid.*, s. 203(3).
166 *Ibid.*, s. 205. Applications can be made for a court to set aside a contract: s. 206.
167 Self-dealing will be covered in Chapter 5, Section E.
168 *Ibid.*, ss. 980 and 986.
169 See Chapter 3.
170 *Ibid.*, s. 981.
171 *Ibid.*, ss. 65(1) and 207(1).
172 *Ibid.*, ss. 80 and 207(1).
173 *Ibid.*, ss. 71 and 207(2).
174 *Ibid.*, ss. 75 and 207(2).
175 *Ibid.*, ss. 79 and 207(2).

payment on indemnity,[176] or engaging in forbidden self-dealing,[177] contrary to the Act.[178] Directors are jointly and severally liable for such amounts paid or distributed and not recovered[179] and are entitled to contribution from all other directors.[180] The limitation period for actions against directors is two years from the date of the resolution authorizing the prohibited actions.[181]

Directors are also jointly and severally liable to each employee of a bank for up to six months' wages of services performed for the bank while they are directors,[182] provided the bank has been sued for the debt within six months after it has become due and not paid, liquidation proceedings have begun, or a winding-up order issued,[183] or any action against the director has been commenced within two years after the director has ceased to be such.[184] Any director who has paid a claim is entitled to subrogation[185] and to contribution from the other directors.[186]

The *Bank Act* alleviates the personal liability of potential directors in three ways. First, a director, officer, or employee is not liable pursuant to the Act[187] where there is reliance in good faith on financial statements or on a written report of the auditors said to fairly reflect the financial condition of the bank or on a report of an accountant, lawyer, notary, or other professional whose profession lends credibility to the report.[188] Secondly, a director or officer may be indemnified against all costs reasonably associated with a civil, criminal, or administrative proceeding, where the director or officer acted honestly and in good faith with a view to the best interests of the bank and had reasonable grounds for believing the impugned action was lawful.[189] Thirdly, a bank is permitted to purchase directors' and officers' insurance in order to make any permitted indemnification.[190] Should there be a dispute about indemnification, a bank or a director or officer may apply to a court, which may make any

---

176 *Ibid.*, ss. 212 and 207(2).
177 *Ibid.*, Part XI, s. 207(2).
178 *Ibid.*, ss. 207(1) & (2).
179 *Ibid.*, s. 207(2).
180 *Ibid.*, s. 208.
181 *Ibid.*, s. 209.
182 *Ibid.*, s. 210(1).
183 *Ibid.*, ss. 210(2) and (4).
184 *Ibid.*, s. 210(3).
185 *Ibid.*, s. 210(5).
186 *Ibid.*, s. 210(6).
187 *Ibid.*, ss. 158(1) & (2), 207, 210, and 506(1).
188 *Ibid.*, s. 211.
189 *Ibid.*, s. 212.
190 *Ibid.*, s. 213.

order it sees fit, and an applicant must give notice to the Superintendent, who is entitled to appear and be heard.[191]

F. SHAREHOLDERS

Banks derive their assets from customers, such as depositors and borrowers, and from shareholders.[192] But as with other business corporations, only shareholders enjoy legal rights and powers in relation to the corporate governance of banks, as a return on their investment in the working capital of the bank. Essentially, shareholders appoint the directors in whom the management of the bank is vested and have the power at annual or special business meetings to remove the directors and the management team they have employed. However, as with other large business corporations today, bank shareholders are largely passive investors, taking no active role beyond selling shares when unhappy with share performance. Nevertheless, the *Bank Act* makes substantial provision for shareholders, again modelled on the *CBCA*, to participate in the affairs of a bank.

1) Shareholders' Meetings

The shareholders' meeting is the main place where shareholders can express their views about the quality of management. Meetings must be held in Canada either at a place stipulated by the by-laws or at some other place chosen by the directors.[193] Meetings are normally called by the directors, who are required to call the first annual shareholders' meeting within six months after the end of the first financial year of the bank and to call the annual meeting within six months after the end of each financial year.[194] The directors may also call a special meeting at any time.[195]

If the directors fail to call a shareholders' meeting, shareholders who together hold not less than 5 percent of the issued and outstanding shares may requisition the directors to call a meeting for the purposes stated in the requisition.[196] On receipt of the requisition, the directors

---

191 *Ibid.*, s. 214.
192 See *ibid.*, s. 7 for extended definition.
193 *Ibid.*, s. 136.
194 *Ibid.*, s. 137(1)(a).
195 *Ibid.*, s. 137(1)(b).
196 *Ibid.*, s. 153(1). For form of requisition, see s. 153(2). For procedure, see s. 153(5).

are required to call the meeting and transact the stated business, but if they do not do so, any shareholder who signed the requisition may do so.[197] The bank shall reimburse the shareholders for reasonable expenses in relation to the requisition unless the meeting resolves otherwise.[198]

In addition, a court may call a shareholders' meeting either where it is impracticable to do so pursuant to the Act or by-laws or where the court thinks it fit to do so, on the application of a director or a shareholder.[199] The court may determine the quorum for such a meeting,[200] and the meeting is as valid as any other properly called shareholders' meeting.[201] For a court called meeting, notice must be given to the Superintendent by the applicant prior to the hearing, and the Superintendent may be heard at the application hearing.[202]

The Act permits the directors to set the record date for the determination of the shareholders entitled to receive notice, attend, and vote at the meeting.[203] Notice of the time and place of the meeting is required to be sent to each shareholder so entitled on the record date, director, and auditor, at least twenty-one days prior to the meeting and not more than fifty days prior.[204] Notice is also required to be published once a week for four consecutive weeks prior to the meeting, in a newspaper in general circulation in the place of the head office and in each place where the bank has a transfer agent or where a transfer of the bank's shares may be recorded.[205] Failure to receive notice does not deprive a shareholder of the right to vote at the meeting.[206] A shareholder may waive notice of a shareholders' meeting in any way,[207] and attendance constitutes waiver except where the express purpose of attending is to object to the transaction of business on the ground that the meeting is not lawfully called.[208] If a

---

197 *Ibid.*, ss. 153(3) & (4).
198 *Ibid.*, s. 153(6).
199 *Ibid.*, s. 154(1).
200 *Ibid.*, s. 154(2).
201 *Ibid.*, s. 153(3).
202 *Ibid.*, ss. 156(1) & (2).
203 *Ibid.*, ss. 137(2)–(5), 139(1), and 145. For discussions of whether shareholders of business corporations may requisition a meeting once the directors have set the record date under identical provisions in the *CBCA*, s. 134, see *RioCan Real Estate v. Realfund*, [1999] O.J. No. 1349 (S.C.J.) and *Airline Industry Revitalization Co. v. Air Canada* (1999), 45 O.R. (3d) 370 (S.C.J.).
204 *Bank Act*, above note 5, s. 138(1). For special requirement to set out number of eligible votes for banks with equity in excess of $5 billion, see s. 138(1.1).
205 *Ibid.*, s. 138(2).
206 *Ibid.*, s. 139(2).
207 *Ibid.*, s. 142(1).
208 *Ibid.*, s. 142(2).

meeting is adjourned, announcement of the adjournment at the meeting is notice if for less than thirty days; otherwise, notice of the continuation shall be given as for the original meeting.[209]

Turning from notice of meetings to the meetings themselves, the *Bank Act* deems all business at annual meetings and special meetings to be special business except for certain matters required to be considered at every annual meeting, that is, financial statements, auditors' reports, election and remuneration of directors, and auditors' appointments.[210] Notice of special business must be given, together with any special resolution[211] to be submitted to the meeting.[212]

The directors normally determine the agenda for a shareholders' meeting; however, shareholder proposals, first introduced in the 1980 *Bank Act* and modelled on the *CBCA*,[213] provide one vehicle for shareholders to consider possible matters of considerable concern. A single shareholder may submit to the bank notice of any matter which that shareholder proposes to raise at a meeting and may discuss at a meeting any matter in respect to which the shareholder is entitled to submit a proposal.[214] A copy of the proposal will be circulated with a management proxy circular,[215] together with any further statement of not more than two hundred words (including the shareholder's name and address) that the shareholder wishes to circulate.[216] The proposal may include nomination of directors if signed by one or more shareholders representing at least 5 percent of shareholders or of that class of shareholders.[217]

The Act sets out five conditions to be satisfied before a bank is required to circulate a proposal: (i) the proposal is submitted at least ninety days before the anniversary date of the previous annual meeting; (ii) the proposal is not for the purpose of enforcing a personal claim or redressing a personal grievance or for promoting economic, political, racial, religious, social, or similar causes; (iii) the proposal must not have been circulated within the two previous years and the shareholder have failed to present it, in person or by proxy, at the meeting; (iv) substantially the same proposal was defeated within the previ-

---

209 *Ibid.*, ss. 140(1) & (2).
210 *Ibid.*, s. 141(1).
211 *Ibid.*, s. 2 "special resolution."
212 *Ibid.*, S. 141(2).
213 *CBCA*, above note 1, s. 137.
214 *Bank Act*, above note 5, s. 143(1).
215 *Ibid.*, s. 143(2).
216 *Ibid.*, s. 143(3).
217 *Ibid.*, s. 143(4).

ous two years; and (v) the proposal is an attempt to secure publicity.[218] Only registered shareholders may submit a proposal, and banks are not required to circulate proposals from beneficial shareholders.[219] No liability is incurred by the bank or a person acting on behalf of the bank by reason only of circulating the proposal.[220]

When a bank exercises its statutory discretion to refuse to circulate a proposal, it must inform the shareholder of its reasons within ten days.[221] A shareholder may ask a court to restrain a meeting at which the proposal is sought to be presented and make such further order as it thinks fit.[222] Conversely, a bank or any person aggrieved by a proposal may apply for a court order to omit a proposal from a proxy circular.[223] Any applicant must inform the Superintendent in writing, and the Superintendent may appear and be heard at any hearing.[224]

Whether the shareholder proposals are effective mechanisms for redressing shareholder concerns is difficult to discuss. Two reported cases to date are insufficient empirical evidence; in one case[225] the court sustained a decision by a bank not to circulate a proposal because it related to the concerns of particular customers, but in the other case[226] the court ordered the bank to circulate several proposals which were designed to increase managerial accountability and reduce executive salaries and which were defeated at the annual meeting.[227]

Although highly unlikely, it is possible to have a one-shareholder meeting or a valid shareholder meeting with only one holder of a class or series of shares.[228] Otherwise, the *Bank Act* provides that in the absence of contrary by-laws, a majority of shareholders in person or by proxy constitute a quorum for a meeting.[229] The quorum need only be present at the start of the meeting,[230] and if there is no quorum then,

---

218 *Ibid.*, s. 143(5).
219 *Verdun v. Toronto-Dominion Bank* (1996), 139 D.L.R. (4th) 415 (S.C.C.).
220 *Bank Act*, above note 5, s. 143(6).
221 *Ibid.*, s. 144(1).
222 *Ibid.*, s. 144(2).
223 *Ibid.*, s. 144(3).
224 *Ibid.*, s. 144(4).
225 *Cappuccitti v. Bank of Montreal* (1989), 46 B.L.R. 255 (Ont. H.C.J.).
226 *Michaud v. National Bank of Canada*, [1997] R.J.Q. 547 (Que. C.S.). See also Brian R. Cheffins, "*Michaud v. National Bank of Canada* and Canadian Corporate Governance: A 'Victory' for Shareholder Rights?" (1998) 30 Can. Bus. L.J. 20.
227 See generally Janis Serra, "Shareholders as Winners and Losers under the Amended *Canada Business Corporations Act*" (2003) 39 Can. Bus. L.J. 52.
228 *Bank Act*, above note 5, s. 147.
229 *Ibid.*, s. 146(1).
230 *Ibid.*, s. 146(2).

the shareholders present may adjourn to a fixed time and place but may not transact other business.[231] With certain restrictions,[232] the voting rule is one share–one vote,[233] including situations of jointly owned shares[234] and of entities as shareholders who must designate a representative shareholder.[235] Voting is by show of hands unless a shareholder or proxy holder requests a ballot either before or after a vote by show of hands.[236]

While shareholders' meetings are the usual means by which annual and special business is transacted, the *Bank Act* also makes provision for a written resolution in lieu of a meeting if it is signed by all shareholders entitled to vote at a meeting, and a copy of the resolution is required to be kept with the minutes of meetings of shareholders.[237]

Shareholders' meetings may be the most important opportunity for shareholders to participate in the affairs of a bank, but in reality few attend because of the expense, the large number of shareholders, and the improbability of having much impact on day-to-day decision making by senior management. In any case, unlike other business corporations, banks in Canada are so closely regulated by the state and various state agencies that shareholders have very little influence over their direction.[238] However, shareholders who still wish to vote without incurring the expense and inconvenience of attending may do so by proxy.

At common law, shareholders were only permitted to vote their shares in person at a shareholders' meeting;[239] however, the practice developed of permitting shareholders to appoint representatives, or "proxies," to attend meetings and exercise their voting rights in accordance with the shareholders' instructions, by virtue of by-laws to that effect. The possibility of directors using by-laws to control the proxy system to procure desired outcomes ultimately resulted in the codification of proxy provisions in business corporations legislation and in the *Bank Act*, the provisions of which are modelled on those in the *CBCA*.[240]

---

231 *Ibid.*, s. 146(3).
232 *Ibid.*, s. 156.09 in relation to a 20 percent voting limit for banks with equity over $5 billion.
233 *Ibid.*, s. 148.
234 *Ibid.*, s. 150.
235 *Ibid.*, s. 149.
236 *Ibid.*, s. 151.
237 *Ibid.*, s. 152. The signature requirement makes this highly unrealistic!
238 See Chapter 3.
239 *Harben v. Phillips* (1883), 23 Ch. D. 14 (C.A.).
240 *CBCA*, above note 1, ss. 147–54.

Any shareholder entitled to vote may appoint a proxy holder, who need not be a shareholder, to attend and act at a shareholders' meeting to the extent authorized by the shareholder.[241] To do so, the shareholder must execute a form of proxy[242] containing very specific information as to the extent of the proxy's authority.[243] A proxy is valid only for the meeting for which it is executed[244] and may be revoked in writing or in any other way permitted by the by-laws.[245] Proxy solicitation is by the management of the bank, who are required to send a form of proxy to each shareholder with the notice of the meeting in a prescribed form.[246] Copies must also be sent to the auditors[247] and to the Superintendent.[248] The directors may also specify in the notice of meeting a time by which executed forms of proxy are to be deposited with the bank or its transfer agent.[249] This is to confirm rights to vote and to appoint proxies.

All appointed proxy holders are required to attend the shareholders' meeting in person, but may cause an alternate proxy holder to do so, and are required to comply with the directions of the shareholder.[250] Proxy holders have the same rights as shareholders to speak, to vote by ballot, and to vote by a show of hands.[251]

Where a form of proxy, management proxy circular, or dissident's proxy circular contains an untrue statement of a material fact or omits a material fact so as to mislead in the circumstances, an interested person or the Superintendent may apply to a court, which may make any order it thinks fit, including an order to restrain the solicitation or the meeting or the implementation of any resolution passed at the meeting, an order to correct the error, and an order to adjourn the meeting.[252] If the applicant is not the Superintendent, the Superintendent shall be notified and is entitled to appear and be heard at the meeting.[253]

---

241 *Bank Act*, above note 5, s. 156.02(1).
242 *Ibid.*, s. 156.02(2); Form of Proxy (Banks and Bank Holding Companies) Regulations, SOR/2001-390.
243 *Bank Act, ibid.*, ss. 156.02(3) & (4).
244 *Ibid.*, s. 156.02(5).
245 *Ibid.*, s. 156.02(6).
246 *Ibid.*, s. 156.04. See also s. 156.01 "solicit" and "solicitation." For shares registered with the registrant, see ss. 156.01 "registrant" and 156.07.
247 *Ibid.*, s. 156.05(1).
248 *Ibid.*, s. 156.05(2). For exemptions by the Superintendent, see ss. 156.05(3) & (4).
249 *Ibid.*, s. 156.03.
250 *Ibid.*, s. 156.06(1).
251 *Ibid.*, ss. 156.06(2) & (3).
252 *Ibid.*, s. 156.08(1).
253 *Ibid.*, s. 156.08(2).

The implementation of proxy voting was an evidence of the underlying fact that shareholders may "own" a bank but practically have little voice in its management. Nor does the *Bank Act* make provision for unanimous shareholder agreement, as does the *CBCA*,[254] whereby shareholders can unanimously agree to restrict in whole or in part the powers of directors to manage the affairs of the bank. Given how widely held bank shares are and how closely state-regulated banks are, there would be little point in such a provision in any case. One final statutory concession is the right of shareholders, as well as directors and the bank itself, to apply to a court to determine any controversy in respect to the election or appointment of a director or auditor,[255] by making any order it thinks fit,[256] but this does not significantly enhance shareholder voice in management.

2) Access to Records

Shareholder rights are better exercised with accurate information about a bank's affairs, and the *Bank Act*, again following the *CBCA* model,[257] makes statutory provision for disclosures required to be made to shareholders and for shareholder access to bank records. Although banks now keep records in many places and in both paper and electronic forms, the Act treats the head office as the central repository for the many records required to be kept. The Act stipulates that the head office must be within Canada,[258] and if the directors change the address of the head office, the bank is required to notify the Superintendent within fifteen days.[259]

The Act specifies a number of records a bank must keep: (i) its incorporating instrument and by-laws; (ii) the minutes and resolutions of shareholders' meetings; (iii) the names and other particulars of the directors and auditors required to be sent to the Superintendent;[260] (iv) any authorizations, conditions, and limitations set by the Superintendent;[261] (v) any exemptions granted by the Superintendent;[262] (vi) the particulars

---

254 *CBCA*, above note 1, s. 146.
255 *Bank Act*, above note 5, s. 155(1).
256 *Ibid.*, s. 155(2).
257 *CBCA*, above note 1, ss. 19–22.
258 *Bank Act*, above note 5, s. 237(1).
259 *Ibid.*, ss. 237(2) & (3).
260 *Ibid.*, ss. 632(1)(a), (c), and (e)–(h).
261 *Ibid.*, ss. 53 & 54(1).
262 *Ibid.*, ss. 39, 55, and 231.

from Schedules I or II;[263] (vii) corporate accounting records; (viii) the minutes and resolutions of directors' meetings; and (ix) the records for each customer showing all daily transactions with the bank and the balance owing to or by the customer.[264] These records must be kept at the head office or at any other place in Canada the directors think fit.[265]

A bank is also required to retain all signature cards and signing authorities relating to deposits or instruments paid over to the Bank of Canada until the Bank of Canada notifies the bank they are no longer needed.[266] Finally, the Act also requires a bank to maintain a central securities register for all securities issued in registered form.[267] Branches are also permitted to establish branch securities registers for the purpose of maintaining records of securities issued or transferred at that branch.[268]

The records may be kept in any paper or electronic form, provided they can be reproduced in an intelligible written form within a reasonable time.[269] A bank is under a statutory duty to prevent the loss, destruction, falsification, and unauthorized access to, or use of, information in the records required to be kept.[270] Banks may keep records outside Canada but are required to inform the Superintendent of them, but the Superintendent may forbid records to be kept outside Canada if this is incompatible with the performance of the Superintendent's duties or he is advised by the Minister that it is not in the national interest.[271]

Directors,[272] shareholders, and creditors of a bank may examine any of the nine categories of records listed above[273] during business hours, make extracts free of charge, or have copies made for a reasonable fee, and where the bank has publicly distributed shares, any other person may also have access and the right to make extracts for a reasonable fee.[274] Shareholders are entitled to one free paper copy of the by-laws annually.[275] A bank may also make these records available electronically.[276]

---

263 See Section B, above in this chapter.
264 Ibid., ss. 238(1) & (2).
265 Ibid., ss. 239(1) & (2). With the exception of branches outside Canada: s. 239(3).
266 Ibid., ss. 246(2), (3), & (4).
267 Ibid., ss. 248, 250, & 251(1).
268 Ibid., ss. 249, 251(2), & 252–54.
269 Ibid., ss. 243 and 239(5.1).
270 Ibid., s. 244.
271 Ibid., s. 245.
272 Ibid., s. 239(4).
273 Ibid., s. 238(1).
274 Ibid., s. 239(5).
275 Ibid., s. 239(6).
276 Ibid., s. 239(5.1).

Shareholders are also entitled to receive a basic list of shareholders within ten days after receipt by a bank of an affidavit so requesting, together with a reasonable fee.[277] A basic list is a list of shareholders compiled not more than ten days prior to receipt of the affidavit.[278] An applicant may also require the bank to list the name and address of every known holder of an option or right to acquire shares of the bank.[279] Shareholder lists may not be used to influence voting, to make an offer to buy shares, or on any other matter relating to the affairs of the bank.[280]

The Act requires banks to retain all these records without setting any limit, so it is assumed that they are to be kept indefinitely in either a paper or electronic form.[281] The Governor in Council may make regulations as to the records required to be retained by a bank and the length of time they are to be retained, but to date, no such regulations have been made.[282]

Shareholders have no common law rights to see any other records than those which the *Bank Act* statutorily mandates must be made available in accordance with the Act. As the provisions of the Act show, the records available are largely the formal public records of a bank and mostly available to any member of the public and not just to shareholders and directors. Shareholders have no access to confidential records, including those relating to the commercial activities of a bank; otherwise, any competitor could purchase a share and obtain such access.

3) Shareholders' Auditors

A bank's auditors are appointed by the shareholders at the annual meeting. When the practice of auditing financial records developed in the mid-nineteenth century, the right of shareholders to appoint the auditors was regarded as a significant means of overseeing management of a corporation: the auditors essentially reported to the shareholders about management's conduct of the financial aspects of a corporation. Today, however, the auditors are effectively chosen by senior management for approval at annual meetings, and the auditors interact so closely with senior management in performing audits that shareholders are largely

---

277 *Ibid.*, ss. 240(1)–(3) and (5)–(6).
278 *Ibid.*, s. 240(4).
279 *Ibid.*, s. 241.
280 *Ibid.*, s. 242.
281 *Ibid.*, s. 246.
282 *Ibid.*, s. 247.

passive observers with few opportunities to get behind the sophisticated accounting and reporting represented by an audit report. While the Supreme Court of Canada still maintains the fiction that auditors assist shareholders in overseeing management,[283] the facts of contemporary corporate life suggest otherwise.[284] The *Bank Act*, again following the *CBCA*,[285] emphasizes the independence of the auditors from senior management as its undergirding formal principle.

Shareholder annual meetings appoint auditors annually and fix their remuneration at the same time by ordinary resolution.[286] The qualifications to be an auditor of a bank for a firm of accountants are that two or more members of the firm must be in good standing as accountants, each with at least five years' experience in auditing financial institutions, be ordinarily resident in Canada, and be independent of the bank.[287] Independence is a question of fact, but an accountant will not be independent where any member of the firm is a director, officer, or employee of the bank or any bank affiliate; a partner of any such person; an owner of a material interest in the shares of the bank or any affiliate of that bank or has acted in relation to a bankruptcy of any affiliate of the within two years of the proposed appointment.[288]

Notice in writing of the appointment is required to be sent to the Superintendent,[289] who is also to be notified forthwith if an auditor ceases to conduct an audit.[290] An auditor who ceases to be qualified is required to resign immediately,[291] and any interested person may apply for a court order to have such an auditor removed.[292] The shareholders may revoke an appointment at any time by ordinary resolution at a special meeting, and the Superintendent may also do so at any time.[293]

---

283 *Hercules Management Ltd. v. Ernst & Young* (1997), 146 D.L.R. (4th) 577 (S.C.C.). See also *Turner v. Canadian Pacific Ltd.* (1979), 27 O.R. (2d) 549 (H.C.J.), where an auditor was found not liable for refusal to answer shareholders' questions.
284 Canada, Inquiry into the Collapse of the CCB and the Northland Report, *Report of the Inquiry into the Collapse of the CCB and the Northland Bank*, (Ottawa: Supply and Services, 1986) ["the Estey Report"].
285 *CBCA*, above note 1, ss. 161–72.
286 *Bank Act*, above note 5, s. 314. For subsidiaries, see s. 329.
287 *Ibid.*, ss. 313 and 315(1).
288 *Ibid.*, s. 315(2).
289 *Ibid.*, s. 315(3).
290 *Ibid.*, ss. 315(4) & (5).
291 *Ibid.*, s. 316(1).
292 *Ibid.*, s. 316(2).
293 *Ibid.*, s. 317.

In addition to revocation by the shareholders or the Superintendent, auditors may cease to hold office by resigning.[294]

The *Bank Act* codifies a number of rights auditors have to ensure they have as complete access as possible to bank financial records and to shareholders: (i) they are entitled to attend and be heard at shareholders' meetings;[295] (ii) if they resign or their appointment is revoked, they have a right to send a statement to the Superintendent with a copy to the shareholders;[296] (iii) they have a right of access to all such records as are in their opinion necessary to perform their duties as auditors;[297] and (iv) if replacing an auditor who has resigned or whose appointment is revoked, they have a duty to request from the previous auditor a written statement about the circumstances and containing the opinions of the previous auditor.[298]

The main duty placed on bank auditors in conducting the audit by the Act is to examine as necessary to report on the annual statement and other financial statements required by the Act to be placed before shareholders, and this examination shall be in accordance with generally accepted auditing standards, supplemented only by any specific requirements of the Superintendent.[299] The Superintendent may require the auditors to report on their procedures in conducting the examination; make any particular examination relating to the bank's safety for its creditors and shareholders or in the public interest; and may direct a special audit at any time,[300] with the expenses payable by the bank.[301] If required by the shareholders, the auditors shall also examine any financial statements made by the directors to the shareholders.[302]

The report to the shareholders shall be made in writing at least twenty-one days prior to the annual shareholders' meeting[303] and shall state whether the annual statement fairly presents the financial position of the bank.[304] Any additional examination required of the directors' fi-

---

294 *Ibid.*, s. 318. For filling vacancies, see s. 319.
295 *Ibid.*, s. 320. The Superintendent may also attend: s. 320(4). Auditors have similar rights in relation to attending and calling audit committee meetings: ss. 330 & 331.
296 *Ibid.*, s. 321.
297 *Ibid.*, s. 324. There is no civil liability attached to statements in good faith to auditors: s. 324(3).
298 *Ibid.*, s. 322.
299 *Ibid.*, s. 323.
300 *Ibid.*, ss. 325(1)–(3).
301 *Ibid.*, s. 325(4).
302 *Ibid.*, s. 327(1).
303 *Ibid.*, s. 326(1).
304 *Ibid.*, s. 326(2). Together with any unusual circumstances noted: s. 326(3).

nancial statements should be attached to that financial statement.[305] In addition, auditors are under a statutory duty to report in writing to the CEO and CFO any transactions or conditions affecting the well-being of the bank that are not satisfactory and require rectification, including *ultra vires* transactions and loans to any one person whose aggregate amount exceeds 0.5 percent of the regulatory capital and which may not be repaid.[306] If subsequent to the submission of an auditor's report, a director or officer of the bank discovers an error or misstatement in an annual statement or another financial statement, the auditors and the board's audit committee should be immediately informed.[307] If the auditors discover an erroneous statement, they shall inform each bank director, and the board should issue a revised financial statement or otherwise inform the shareholders and the Superintendent.[308] All oral or written reports pursuant to the Act by the auditors have qualified privilege.[309]

4) Pre-emptive Rights

One means for shareholders to retain their current level of control over management is to enjoy pre-emptive rights in new share offerings. A pre-emptive right is a right to require the bank to offer newly issued shares to existing shareholders on a *pro rata* basis in relation to their existing shareholdings prior to offering them to the general public. At common law, shareholders did not enjoy such a right, and company by-laws typically provided for a pre-emptive right where dilution of ownership was thought undesirable. Prior to the 1980 *Bank Act*, the legislation made provision for mandatory shareholder pre-emptive rights, but from 1980 this was no longer mandatory, again following the *CBCA*.[310]

Thus, the Act now states that there is no pre-emptive right except where the by-laws so provide.[311] Where there is a general pre-emptive right, a shareholder has no right in respect of shares issued under the following conditions: for a consideration other than money; as a share dividend; pursuant to the exercise of conversion privileges, options, or rights previously granted by the bank;[312] where the issue of shares to

---

305 *Ibid.*, s. 327(2).
306 *Ibid.*, s. 328.
307 *Ibid.*, s. 332(1).
308 *Ibid.*, s. 332(2) & (3).
309 *Ibid.*, s. 333.
310 *CBCA*, above note 1, s. 28.
311 *Bank Act*, above note 5, s. 68(1).
312 *Ibid.*, s. 68(2).

the shareholder is prohibited by the Act;[313] or where to the knowledge of the directors, the shareholder is not ordinarily resident in Canada and shares cannot be sold until the appropriate authority in the country of residence is notified.[314] The amount of shareholder control related to pre-emptive rights in relation to banks which are required to be widely held is probably negligible in contrast to the small companies of the nineteenth century for which this right was originally created.

5) Approval and Remedial Rights

Throughout the *Bank Act* there are various provisions granting rights of approval to shareholders in relation to various aspects of bank corporate governance, including granting approvals at annual and special meetings to ordinary resolutions relating to directors, by-laws, and auditors (as discussed elsewhere in this chapter) as well as in relation to sales,[315] amalgamations,[316] and winding-up.[317] However, the Act also makes provision for individual rights in relation to a bank, in addition to the rights each shareholder enjoys as a member of the collective shareholder group. In particular, it makes provision for the right to bring a derivative action against the bank and to have bank records rectified. The underlying purpose of these remedial rights for individual shareholders is to ensure fair treatment by the bank for each shareholder.

The derivative action permits a complainant,[318] who may be a shareholder, or the Superintendent to apply to a court for leave to bring an action in the name of, or on behalf of, a bank or any of its subsidiaries against the bank.[319] Prior to doing so, the applicant must give reasonable notice to the directors and prove that they are acting in good faith and that the action is in the best interests of the bank.[320] A court may make any order it thinks fit,[321] provided the order does not relate to any matter that requires the approval of the Minister of Finance or

---

313 *Ibid.*
314 *Ibid.*, s. 68(3).
315 *Ibid.*
316 *Ibid.*
317 *Ibid.*
318 *Ibid.*, s. 2 "complainant."
319 *Ibid.*, s. 334(1). See also *CBCA*, above note 1, ss. 239–40 and Nicholls, above note 44 at 399–419, for a fuller discussion of the derivative action in company law.
320 *Bank Act*, above note 5, s. 334(2). Notice must be given to the Superintendent as well: s. 334(3).
321 *Ibid.*, s. 335(1).

the Superintendent under the Act.[322] In making an order, a court is not constrained by the possibility that the shareholders have, or would approve, the conduct about which the action is brought.[323] Once a derivative action is commenced, court approval is required for any discontinuance or settlement.[324]

The nature and scope of the derivative action in banking law is contested, but it may be assumed that neither a complainant nor a court would permit one to proceed unless the bank was engaged in conduct that might do serious damage to the complainant or the bank's interests. In such circumstances, it seems more likely that the Superintendent would step in to oversee and direct an appropriate outcome than that such an action would continue. The same reason probably also explains why the *Bank Act* does not follow the *CBCA*[325] in providing an oppression remedy for shareholders: the state regulatory agencies are more likely to leap to action in the event of damaging illegal conduct, even to an individual or group of shareholders, because of the importance of banks to the national economy.

The other remedial right is that of rectifying bank records.[326] A security holder[327] or any other aggrieved person may apply for a court order to rectify the securities register of the bank or any other record of the bank.[328] An applicant must give notice of the application to the Superintendent,[329] and the court may make such order as it thinks fit.[330]

To facilitate shareholder derivative or rectification actions, the Act relieves a complainant of the normal requirement to give security for costs[331] and provides a discretion to the court to order at any time the bank or its subsidiaries to pay interim costs, including legal fees and disbursements, to the complainant, who remains accountable for these on the final disposition of the action.[332]

---

322 *Ibid.*, s. 335(2).
323 *Ibid.*, s. 336(1).
324 *Ibid.*, s. 336(2).
325 *CBCA*, above note 1, ss. 241–42 and Nicholls, above note 44 at 419–35 for a fuller discussion of the oppression remedy.
326 *CBCA, ibid.*, s. 243.
327 *Bank Act*, above note 5, s. 2 "security."
328 *Ibid.*, s. 338(1).
329 *Ibid.*, s. 338(2).
330 *Ibid.*, s. 338(3).
331 *Ibid.*, s. 337(1).
332 *Ibid.*, s. 337(2).

6) Shareholder Liability

Despite the foregoing provisions in the *Bank Act* bestowing various rights on bank shareholders, as large, widely held business corporations, banks are essentially run by their boards of directors and senior executives. Shareholder rights are largely fictions. Shareholders unhappy with the management of a bank are more likely to sell their shares than to become shareholder activists bent on enforcing particular sections of the Act. Nevertheless, shareholders do not entirely escape liability under the Act. Generally, shareholders *qua* shareholders are not liable for any act or default of the bank,[333] with two exceptions for which the *Bank Act* provides. A creditor may secure a court order compelling a shareholder to repay any money or property paid or distributed to the shareholder as a result of a reduction of capital contrary to the Act,[334] within two years from the payment or distribution.[335] Again, on the dissolution of the bank, a shareholder or incorporator to whom any of its property has been distributed may be liable in any legal action brought at the time of the dissolution for the amount distributed, for a period of two years from the date of the dissolution.[336] Such actions may be brought against shareholders as a class, and a court may refer the matter to a referee to determine individual shareholder liability.[337] Beyond these two provisions, the *Bank Act* imposes no further liability on shareholders and none in relation to the day-to-day operations of the bank.

G. CAPITAL STRUCTURE

Extensive provision for the capital structure of banks in Canada was made for the first time in the 1980 *Bank Act*, again following the lead of the *CBCA*. Comparison of the *Bank Act* and the *CBCA* demonstrates how closely the capital structure of banks is modelled on that of publicly distributed business corporations.[338] Banks, like any other business, require a pool of capital to finance their operations and likewise

---

333 *Ibid.*, s. 18.
334 *Ibid.*, ss. 76(1) and 75. Excluding holding shares as a personal representative: s. 76(2).
335 *Ibid.*, s. 76(3). Directors' liability is not affected by this: s. 76(4).
336 *Ibid.*, ss. 363(1) & (2) and 362(1).
337 *Ibid.*, ss. 363(3) & (4).
338 For extensive *CBCA* analysis, see the company law texts referred to above at note 44, as well as Christopher C. Nicholls, *Corporate Finance and Canadian Law* (Toronto: Carswell, 2000) and Jeffrey G. MacIntosh & Christopher C.

draw this capital from several sources, either by borrowing money with an obligation to repay or by selling shares to shareholders, for which there is no obligation to repay. Banks have several potential sources of debt financing, including customers' deposits, which are loans made by a customer to the bank,[339] as well as raising debt capital in the capital markets using a trust indenture, for which the *Bank Act* provides. The sale of shares to the public yields equity financing. Banks also derive operating capital from their banking operations, including earned interest on loans, service charges for the various services they provide to customers, and profits from the exploitation of research and development results in the computer service sector. Debt financing must be repaid first should a bank be liquidated, and equity financing can be repaid only from any assets left over after the creditors' claims are satisfied.

1) Equity Financing

Like any other business corporation, banks are authorized to solicit equity financing by issuing shares at such times, to such persons, and for such consideration as the directors may determine.[340] A bank share is not a proportionate fraction of the assets of the bank but represents a right to receive only a proportionate distribution of the value of the assets after another debt has been repaid in a liquidation. A share is a chose in action and not a chose in possession.

Although the *Bank Act* itself no longer sets minimum capital requirements for banks, banks in Canada are required to maintain adequate capital and adequate and appropriate forms of liquidity.[341] The requirements may be set by the Governor in Council through regulations and by guidelines issued by the Superintendent of Financial Institutions,[342] who may also direct a specific bank to increase its capital over the minimum set in the guidelines.[343] The Superintendent's valuation of any asset held by a bank or its subsidiaries will prevail over the bank's valuation.[344] Guidelines set by the Office of the Superintendent of Financial Institutions (OSFI) for capital adequacy are taken from the

---

Nicholls, *Securities Law* (Toronto: Irwin Law, 2002). The following discussion is deliberately very brief.
339 For the legal nature of the bank and customer relationship, see Chapter 6.
340 *Bank Act*, above note 5, s. 59(1). See also *CBCA*, above note 1, ss. 24–47 for correlative provisions.
341 *Bank Act*, ibid., s. 485(1).
342 Ibid., s. 485(2).
343 Ibid., ss. 485(3) & (4).
344 Ibid., s. 485(5).

new framework for regulatory capital known as "Basle II" because they were developed by the Basle Committee on Banking Supervision. These guidelines set out in very considerable detail the internationally agreed standards for regulatory capital and risk management.[345] The reason minimum capital requirements are set is to provide some protection for creditors, depositors, and shareholders in the event of a liquidation of a bank.

Bank shares shall be issued without nominal or par value,[346] that is, the value of a share shall be the market or sale value of that share on the day of issue. All shares shall be fully paid for in money or, if the Superintendent approves, in property[347] and may be in a currency other than Canadian dollars.[348] Again, following the *CBCA*, the current *Bank Act* eschews the earlier Acts, which permitted par value shares and partly paid shares, thereby simplifying the assessment of the actual market value of bank shares. Again, a bank is required to have at least one class of shares designated as common shares, which are non-redeemable and in which the rights of the holders are equal and include the rights to vote at shareholder meetings, to receive dividends, and to receive the remaining property of the bank on dissolution.[349] By by-law approved by the shareholders, a bank may issue more than one class of shares,[350] and all banks typically do so, setting out the specific attributes attached to these shares in relation to such matters as voting rights, restrictions on their alienation, dividend rights, and so on. For all classes of shares to which voting rights are attached, each share shall carry one vote only.[351] Finally, by by-law, a bank may also issue series of shares, that is, in any class of shares, it may issue one or more subdivisions of shares within that class, and each subdivision will have some features common to the class and some distinctive series features.[352] The reason for issuing series of shares with special features is to permit the directors to respond to market conditions by issuing shares attractive to a market at any given time so as to raise capital quickly. Since banks are subject to special adequacy and risk requirements not shared with other busi-

---

345 These may be seen online: www.osfi.gc.ca.
346 *Bank Act*, above note 5, s. 59(2). See also transitional provisions in ss. 59(3)–(5) for existing banks with par value shares and continuing bodies corporate.
347 *Ibid.*, s. 65(1).
348 *Ibid.*, s. 65(2).
349 *Ibid.*, ss. 60 and 64.
350 *Ibid.*, s. 61.
351 *Ibid.*, s. 63.
352 *Ibid.*, ss. 62(1)–(4).

ness corporations, a copy of the by-law proposing the issue of a series of shares must be sent to the Superintendent prior to issue.[353]

Once shares are issued, the consideration received for those shares is to be added to the stated capital account for each class and series of shares issued.[354] The stated capital account must precisely reflect the consideration received for issued shares,[355] although the consideration may take the form of property or shares of another body corporate exchanged for bank shares as set out in the Act.[356]

The *Bank Act* addresses several issues relating to rights, privileges, and restrictions in dealing with shares. First, existing shareholders enjoy pre-emptive rights in relation to new shares in their class of shares should the by-laws so provide.[357] Secondly, a bank may issue conversion privileges, options, or rights to acquire securities.[358] Thirdly, banks are permitted to purchase for cancellation and to redeem their own shares in certain circumstances designed to ensure that a bank will not thereby become insolvent.[359] The stated capital account shall be reduced to reflect these transactions[360] and may also be reduced generally by a special resolution of the shareholders, provided it is approved by the Superintendent.[361] Where money or property is paid or distributed to any person, including a shareholder, as a consequence of a reduction of capital contrary to the Act, a creditor may apply within two years for a court order for re-delivery of the money or property to the bank.[362] Conversely, when a "debt obligation" of a bank is converted into shares or a series of shares, a bank shall add the net value to the stated capital account.[363]

Finally, the Act provides that the directors may declare a dividend in money or property or by issuing fully paid shares or options or rights to acquire fully paid shares.[364] The directors must give the Superintend-

---

353 *Ibid.*, s. 62(5).
354 *Ibid.*, ss. 66(1) & (2).
355 *Ibid.*, ss. 66(4) & (5).
356 *Ibid.*, s. 66(3). For continuation situations, see s. 67.
357 *Ibid.*, s. 68, and see Section F(4), above in this chapter.
358 *Ibid.*, s. 69.
359 *Ibid.*, ss. 70–74.
360 *Ibid.*, s. 77.
361 *Ibid.*, s. 75. The approval of the Superintendent is not required if the reduction is the result of accounting changes under s. 308(4) and there is no return of capital to the shareholders: s. 75(4.1).
362 *Ibid.*, s. 76.
363 *Ibid.*, ss. 2 "debt obligation" and 78.
364 *Ibid.*, s. 79(1).

ent at least fifteen days' notice prior to the day fixed for payment.[365] If the dividend is paid by shares, the stated capital account should be amended accordingly.[366] Until 2007, the Act provided that the directors may not declare a dividend in two situations: (i) there are reasonable grounds for believing that the self-dealing provisions of the Act are being contravened[367] and (ii) the payment has not been approved by the Superintendent and the total of all dividends declared in that year would exceed the aggregate of the bank's net income up to the day in that year set for the payment and of its retained net income for the two preceding financial years.[368] The 2007 amendments no longer so provide, so presumably the Superintendent's approval is now sufficient.

Since the payment of a dividend, especially in money or property but not in a stock dividend, amounts to a reduction in the capital of a bank, the role of the Superintendent is to ensure that the solvency of the bank is protected in any distribution for the benefit of depositors and creditors. The *Bank Act*, therefore, does not follow the *CBCA*, section 42, which sets out the criteria that directors of business corporations must follow in deciding whether to declare a dividend. In addition, the jurisprudence on that provision and its predecessors, as well as the common law, does not apply. However, notwithstanding the supervisory role of OSFI, directors who vote for, or consent to, the payment of a dividend contrary to the Act are jointly and severally liable to restore to the bank any amounts paid not otherwise receivable by the bank.[369] Directors are equally liable for the redemption or purchase of shares or a reduction of capital contrary to the Act.[370]

Historically, purchasers of bank shares would have expected to receive paper certificates of considerable artistic merit evidencing their purchase. However, paper certificates have been overtaken by book-based registers in which share ownership is recorded, and share certificates have been assimilated into the general category of "investment securities." Paper share certificates were once regarded as mere evidence of what was recorded in the central securities register, which alone was regarded in law as the definitive record of the shareholder's investment. The paper certificates were not widely regarded at common

---

365 *Ibid.*, s. 79(2).
366 *Ibid.*, s. 79(3).
367 *Ibid.*, ss. 79(4) and 485(1)–(3). See also Chapter 5, Section E.
368 *Ibid.*, s. 79(5). Repealed Bill C-37, *An Act to amend the law governing financial institutions and to provide for related and consequential matters*, 1st Sess., 39th Parl., 2006, s. 11(2) (Royal Assent 29 March 2007).
369 *Ibid.*, ss. 207(1) and (2)(c). See also *Stavert v. Lovitt* (1908), 42 N.S.R. 449 (C.A.).
370 *Bank Act, ibid.*, ss. 207(1), (2)(a) & (b).

law as negotiable instruments, although they were often treated as such in commercial practice.[371] However, since the 1980 *Bank Act*, which followed the *CBCA* model again, paper certificates have been deemed to be negotiable instruments[372] and freely tradable as such. The Bank Act defines a "security" or a "security certificate" to include any instrument issued by a bank that is in bearer, order or registered form, of a type commonly dealt with on security exchanges, one of a class or a series of shares and evidence of a share in or obligation of a bank.[373]

The Act contains extensive and detailed provisions relating to the transfer of security certificates, which virtually replicate provisions in the *CBCA*.[374] These deal with such matters as the negotiable nature of security certificates, their contents, treatment of the registered holder, registration,[375] and transfer.[376] However, after the incorporation of the Canadian Depository for Securities Ltd. (CDS) in 1970,[377] a computer-based system for the issue, transfer, clearing, settlement, and safekeeping of securities has developed and largely replaced the older paper-based system contemplated by the *CBCA* and the *Bank Act*. The CDS is a private corporation owned by approximately 120 financial institutions and operates a single, national securities clearing and settlement system for all publicly traded equity and debt securities in Canada to serve the Toronto, Montreal, Vancouver, and Alberta Stock Exchanges. CDS maintains the records of all securities held and traded on behalf of all customers in Canada.[378]

2) Debt Financing

Should a bank wish to borrow money as a means of raising capital in addition to issuing shares, the *Bank Act* makes provision for it to do so by issuing debt securities such as bonds, debentures, or notes through the use of a "trust indenture," which is defined as any deed, indenture,

---

371 *Smith v. Rogers* (1899), 30 O.R. 256 (Div. Ct.).
372 *Bank Act*, above note 5, s. 83(1).
373 *Ibid.*, s. 81.
374 *CBCA*, above note 1, ss. 46–81. These were in turn modelled on Article 8 of the *Uniform Commercial Code*.
375 *Bank Act*, above note 5, ss. 248–54. See Section F(2), above in this chapter.
376 *Ibid.*, ss. 81–135. For an extensive analysis of these provisions, see Ogilvie, above note 4 at c. 8.
377 Under *Canada Corporations Act*, R.S.C. 1970, c. C-32, and continued in 1980 under *CBCA*, s. 181.
378 For an extensive discussion of CDS, see Bradley Crawford, *Payment, Clearing and Settlement in Canada* (Toronto: Canada Law Book, 2002) c. 14.

or other instrument made by a bank by which the bank issues subordinated indebtedness and in which a person is appointed as trustee for the holders of the subordinated indebtedness.[379]

In contrast to borrowing money from one or more large lenders, the issue of debt security is a means of borrowing from a large number of small lenders who purchase bonds or debentures. To facilitate collective action should such be necessary against the borrower, the trust indenture device is used. As the legal definition in the Act implies, a trust indenture is an agreement between the bank that issues the debt securities and a trustee, typically a trust company. The role of the trustee is to protect the security holders' interests in the event of a default in repayment by the bank. The trust indenture sets out such terms as the interest rate and the repayment terms, and because the terms are determined by the bank prior to entering the agreement with the trustee, who is chosen by the bank, there is a potential for conflict of interest on the part of the trustee. To ensure that the indenture trustee acts in the interests of the security holders, first the *CBCA*[380] and then the *Bank Act* provided rules to govern trust indentures.

The definition of what may be contained in a trust indenture as defined by the *Bank Act* is significant, that is, it is for the issue of "subordinated indebtedness," which term is defined as any indebtedness that will in the event of the insolvency and winding-up of the bank be subordinated to all deposit liabilities and to all other liabilities of the bank except those that expressly rank equally with the subordinated indebtedness.[381] This means that customer deposits rank above the interests of security holders under a trust indenture in an insolvency. Subordinated indebtedness must be fully paid for in money or, if the Superintendent approves, in property[382] and is deemed not to be a deposit.[383] Again, the protection of the prior rights of the depositors is evident.

The protections for security holders under a trust indenture include: (i) a prohibition on the appointment of a trustee that has a material conflict of interest;[384] (ii) the restriction of trustees to regulated trust companies;[385] (iii) the requirement that the issuing bank provide

---

379 *Bank Act*, above note 5, s. 294 "trust indenture." For more extensive discussion, see Ogilvie, above note 4 at c. 10.
380 *CBCA*, above note 1, ss. 82–93.
381 *Bank Act*, above note 5, s. 2 "subordinated indebtedness."
382 *Ibid.*, ss. 80(1) and (4).
383 *Ibid.*, s. 80(3). All documentary references must be to "subordinated indebtedness": s. 80(2).
384 *Ibid.*, ss. 297–99.
385 *Ibid.*, s. 300.

to the trustee evidence of compliance with the conditions in the trust indenture prior to issuing securities;[386] (iv) the requirement that the trustee notify security holders of default within thirty days;[387] and (v) the duty of care required of the trustee to act in the best interests of the security holders.[388]

3) Prospectus Requirements

Further confirmation of how regulated banks are when raising capital is found in the statutory requirements for the filing of a prospectus. A preliminary prospectus and a prospectus in a prescribed form must be filed with the Superintendent prior to the distribution of any of a bank's securities.[389] The Superintendent is required to issue a receipt for the preliminary prospectus once filed[390] but may withdraw that receipt if the preliminary prospectus is defective after giving a reasonable opportunity to make representations.[391] The Superintendent will go through the same process for a prospectus, ensuring that it complies with the Act and the regulations; does not contain any misrepresentation or any statement, promise, estimate, or forecast that is misleading, false, or deceptive; and that it is in the public interest to issue the receipt.[392] The Superintendent may require any changes to a preliminary prospectus and a prospectus.[393]

A prospectus is required to provide full, true, and plain disclosure of all material facts relating to the securities to be distributed and to contain or be accompanied by all required financial statements and other documents,[394] as well as certification by the CEO, CFO, or a promoter of the bank that all required disclosures have been made.[395] A similar certification is required from all underwriters associated in the

---

386 Ibid., ss. 301–3.
387 Ibid., s. 304.
388 Ibid., s. 305. No waiver of the statutory duties is permitted: s. 306. However, the Superintendent may waive the trust indenture provisions of the Act: ss. 295–96.
389 Ibid., s. 273. For filing requirements in other jurisdictions and the role of the Superintendent, see ss. 273(2) and 276. For regulations relating to form and content, see ss. 274 & 275; Prospectus (Banks and Bank Holding Companies) Regulations, SOR/2001-412; Prospectus Exemptions (Banks) Regulations, SOR/94-73.
390 Bank Act, ibid., ss. 277(1) & (2).
391 Ibid., ss. 277(3) & (4).
392 Ibid., s. 278.
393 Ibid., ss. 275(2), (3), & (4).
394 Ibid., s. 279(1).
395 Ibid., ss. 279(2) & (3) and 281.

distribution of the securities.[396] No prospectus shall be distributed until all the statutory requirements have been fulfilled.[397]

4) Insider Trading

Since 1980, the *Bank Act* has provided for the regulation of insider trading in bank securities, again modelled on the insider trading provisions of the *CBCA*.[398] The principle underlying these provisions is that insiders should be permitted to trade in a bank's securities but that it is improper for them to do so by making use of confidential information acquired by virtue of their position as insiders. Thus, all persons deemed to be insiders by the Act are required to report to the Superintendent all beneficial interests in bank securities and to compensate any person who suffers loss as a result of an insider transaction and restore any benefits received as a result of the transaction. The assumption is that disclosure will dissuade from insider trading.

An "insider" is a director, officer, distributing bank, or a person who controls more than 10 percent of the shares or the voting shares of a bank[399] or a director or officer of a subsidiary or a body corporate that is an insider of a distributing bank or a person who beneficially owns shares of such a body corporate affiliate.[400] An insider is required to report that fact to the Superintendent not more than ten days after the end of the month in which the person became an insider[401] and is required to make subsequent reports of any changes in security holding within the same period from which the change occurred.[402] The Superintendent may exempt any insider from the reporting requirements on whatever terms the Superintendent thinks fit[403] but will summarize in a publicly available periodical both the information contained in the reports and the particulars of any exemptions granted.[404]

---

396 *Ibid.*, ss. 280 & 281.
397 *Ibid.*, s. 282.
398 *CBCA*, above note 1, ss. 126–31. See also J.R. Kimber, *Report of the Attorney General's Committee on Securities Legislation in Ontario* (Toronto: Queen's Printer, 1965) and Welling, above note 44 at 356–61 for the common law.
399 *Bank Act*, above note 5, s. 265(1) "insider."
400 *Ibid.*, ss. 265(2), (3), & (4).
401 *Ibid.*, s. 266; Insider Reports Regulations, SOR/82-207.
402 *Bank Act, ibid.*, ss. 267 & 268.
403 *Ibid.*, s. 269(1); Insider Reports Exemptions (Banks) Regulations, SOR/2000-113.
404 *Bank Act, ibid.*, s. 269(2). This information is published in the *Canada Corporations Bulletin* by the Department of Industry and in the *OSC Bulletin*.

An insider is prohibited from knowingly selling, directly or indirectly, a share in a distributing bank or any of its affiliates if the insider does not own or has not fully paid for the share to be sold.[405] Nor is an insider permitted to buy or sell a call or put in respect of a share.[406] An exception is made for convertible shares.[407] The purpose of these provisions appears to be to prohibit profiting from leveraged transactions. Any insider who makes use of specific confidential information for the insider's own benefit is liable to compensate any person for any direct loss as a result of the transaction and is accountable to the bank for any direct benefit received as a result of the transaction.[408] Actions must be brought within two years of discovery of the facts or, if a reportable transaction, within two years from the time stipulated for reporting.[409]

The *Bank Act* provides two different kinds of sanctions for insider trading. For insiders who have contravened the reporting and prohibited trades sections, the general sanction provisions of the Act appear to apply, but for those who have used confidential information to profit, civil liability is imposed in the form of compensatory damages and restitution.[410] However, there are difficulties with the availability of these remedies set out in section 272 of the Act: (i) the difficulty in identifying persons to be compensated; (ii) ambiguity as to whether both those persons and the bank are to be compensated, that is, a double penalty; (iii) ambiguity as to what is "specific confidential information," which "might reasonably be expected" "to affect materially" the value of the security; and (iv) ambiguity as to the meaning of "direct loss" and "direct benefit." The absence of case law on these provisions may suggest either a very low incidence of such cases or their detection, or that the provisions in the Act are, indeed, difficult to litigate successfully because of their ambiguities.

H. FINANCIAL STATEMENTS

The *Bank Act* makes brief provision for the annual financial statements of a bank, which are required to reflect generally accepted accounting

---

405 *Ibid.*, s. 270(1).
406 *Ibid.*, ss. 265(1) "call," "put"; 270(3).
407 *Ibid.*, s. 270(2).
408 *Ibid.*, ss. 271 & 272(1).
409 *Ibid.*, ss. 271 & 272(2).
410 In addition, there may be common law remedies and statutory remedies available under provincial securities law.

principles. In addition to the usual corporate requirements for approval by both the board of directors and the annual shareholders' meeting, the annual statements are required to be sent to the Superintendent at least twenty-one days prior to the annual meeting of shareholders, to ensure appropriate oversight over a bank's affairs. In addition, the Superintendent is to be informed by a bank should it refuse any shareholder request to examine the current financial statements required to be kept at the head office, again to ensure that the Superintendent is present in any ensuing litigation concerning shareholder access.[411] Again, the additional step of informing the Superintendent over and above the usual business corporation practices is to ensure the external regulatory oversight thought necessary for the solvency of banks and the soundness of the financial sector and economy generally.

I. AMENDMENTS, AMALGAMATION, AND TRANSFERRING BUSINESS

Banks as corporate legal persons are dynamic and change over time, so the *Bank Act* contains provisions relating to several different kinds of changes banks are likely to make. Earlier in this chapter,[412] in the context of incorporation, two procedures were discussed whereby other business corporations could continue as banks, that is, trust and loan companies, insurance companies and business corporations to which the *CBCA* or any other federal statute applied. Reference was also made[413] to the statutory provisions for the continuation of a bank as a trust or loan company. In addition to continuation as another type of financial institution, the *Bank Act* provides for three other types of fundamental changes: (i) amendment to an incorporating instrument in relation to the capital structure of a bank; (ii) amalgamations of two or more bodies corporate, including banks to form a new bank; and (iii) sale of assets by a bank to another financial institution or to an authorized foreign bank.

The first process permits a bank to change its capital structure, name, or head office by special resolution of the shareholders and after approval of the Minister of Finance. Letters patent are required to effect the change. Subsequent changes to the by-laws to reflect the amended letters patent are to be approved by special shareholder resolution and the Superintendent. Any director or shareholder may initiate a proposal to change the let-

---

411 *Ibid.*, ss. 307–12.
412 See Section B, above in this chapter.
413 *Ibid.*

ters patent and no amendment affects any existing cause of action, claim, liability to prosecution or any civil, criminal, or administrative action or proceeding against the bank, its directors, or officers.[414]

The second process permits the amalgamation of two or more federally incorporated bodies corporate, including banks and bank holding companies, to amalgamate and continue as one bank by the issue of letters patent by the Minister of Finance. To effect amalgamation, each amalgamating party shall enter into an amalgamation agreement setting out such terms as name, head office, directors, capital structure, by-laws, and the proposed effective date of the amalgamation. The agreement must be approved by the shareholders of each body corporate and by the Superintendent. Public notice is required prior to the application to the Minister for letters patent, and the Minister is required to consider the same types of matters relating to the soundness, experience, and reputation of the applicants and the best interests of the financial system in Canada[415] as are considered in relation to an application for letters patent for any other new bank in Canada. The amalgamation takes effect on the day provided in the letters patent, and all legal claims and actions against one of the applicants can be continued against the amalgamated bank.[416]

The third process permits a bank to sell all or substantially all of its assets to a federally incorporated financial institution or to an authorized foreign bank for a consideration, which may be in cash or fully paid securities of the purchaser, or partially in cash and fully paid securities. The sale agreement must be submitted to the Superintendent prior to submission for shareholder approval by special resolution. Once approved by special resolution, the bank must secure the approval of the Minister within three months, although prior to such application for Ministerial approval must give public notice. The sale agreement is effective only after approval by the Minister. The Act contains no guidelines for the Minister in making the decision to approve.[417]

J. OWNERSHIP

The unique and foundational role of banks in any national economy means that issues relating to ownership, such as who may own banks

---

414 Ibid., ss. 215–22.
415 Ibid., s. 228(4).
416 Ibid., ss. 223–31.
417 Ibid., ss. 232–36.

and the maximum permitted size of the ownership of shares, are strictly and closely regulated to ensure that ownership is in what is regarded as the national interest. Thus, historically, banks in Canada have been required to be widely held and largely owned by Canadians resident in Canada. From the *Bank Act, 1980,* four different criteria have been used in successive Acts to regulate the ownership of shares in domestic Canadian banks: the issue, ownership, registration, and exercise of voting rights in shares. The current Act continues to use these criteria, although their particulars have changed over the past twenty-five years.

Prudential concerns[418] have dictated a general approach of prohibiting any person from owning more than 10 percent of the shares of any class of shares and of prohibiting foreign ownership in excess of 25 percent of all shares. Not only did these limits underscore domestic ownership without control; they also precluded the upstream commercial risks associated with self-dealing should a large shareholder with significant commercial interests gain a position to influence lending decisions contrary to the interests of the depositors and other shareholders. Wider-share ownership also tends to greater transparency in corporate governance.

The MacKay Task Force[419] sustained these reasons for the wide ownership rule but also proposed that the rule reflect additional policies, including fostering greater competition and the entry of new banks, which would be more likely if entrepreneurial individuals could be assured of enjoying the fruits of their risk taking by not being required to divest their holdings above 10 percent after the initial start-up period. The Task Force recommended a three-tier ownership regime based on asset size as the best way to balance traditional prudential concerns and the need to foster competition. The 10 percent rule could continue to apply to large banks with equity in excess of $5 billion, subject to the discretion of the Minister of Finance to authorize individual ownership up to 20 percent; medium-sized banks with an equity between $1 billion and $5 billion could be held or controlled up to 65 percent by a single person, subject to the discretion of the Minister to waive the other 35 percent public float; and small banks of less than $1 billion could be wholly owned by one person. The 2001 and 2007 amendments reflect these recommendations.[420]

---

418 See generally M.H. Ogilvie, above note 6.
419 See Chapter 2, Section D.
420 The ownership rules set out in Part VII of the Act are complex and beyond the scope of an introductory book of this sort. What follows is an overview of the central features, and interested readers are directed to Part VII for the details.

The Act provides that no person shall have a "significant interest" in any class of shares of a bank.[421] A significant interest means an interest in excess of 10 percent of the shares of any one class beneficially owned by a person or entities controlled by a person.[422] Ownership, rather than control, is the key test here. However, the Act also gives the Minister of Finance the discretion to approve the acquisition of a significant interest, including through amalgamation, merger, or reorganization.[423] Again, the role of the Minister in overall supervision of the banking sector and of individual banks is underlined by this provision. The remaining provisions of Part VII of the Act relating to ownership operate as exceptions to the 10 percent rule.

For large banks with an equity in excess of $8 billion, the Act provides that no person may be a "major shareholder,"[424] that is, no person may own more than 20 percent of the voting shares of any class or 30 percent of the shares of any class of non-voting shares.[425] This restriction does not apply to certain entities that control a large bank, including a widely held bank,[426] a widely held bank holding company,[427] a widely held insurance company,[428] another eligible Canadian financial institution,[429] an eligible foreign institution,[430] or an entity which controls one of these.[431] These exceptions reflect three other policies promoted by the 2001 amendments: the introduction of bank holding companies,[432] the further advancement of the assimilation of the four pillars of the financial services sector (banks, insurance companies, trust companies, and brokerages), and the encouragement of strategic alliances with foreign financial institutions.[433] This rule also applies in mergers;[434] in situations where a bank's equity increases to more than

---

421 *Bank Act*, above note 5, s. 372.
422 *Ibid.*, s. 8(1). An increased share ownership is an increased significant interest: s. 8(2). Also s. 2 "entity", s. 2 "person."
423 *Ibid.*, s. 373.
424 *Ibid.*, ss. 374(1) and 378 for definition. In 2007, the ceiling of $5 billion was raised to $8 billion: Bill C-37, above note 368, ss. 20 and 132.
425 *Ibid.*, s. 2.2. See also Equity of a Bank or a Bank Holding Company Regulations, SOR/2001-377.
426 *Bank Act, ibid.*, ss. 374(2) and 2.3 "widely held" entity.
427 *Ibid.*, s. 374(3).
428 *Ibid.*, ss. 374(4)(a) and s. 2 "insurance holding company."
429 *Ibid.*, ss. 374(4)(b) and s. 370(1) "eligible Canadian financial institution."
430 *Ibid.*, ss. 374(4)(c) and s. 370(1) "eligible foreign institution."
431 *Ibid.*, ss. 374(5) & (6).
432 See Section K, below in this chapter.
433 See Section L, below in this chapter.
434 *Bank Act*, above note 5, s. 374.1.

$8 billion; and to widely held banks that "control"[435] another bank.[436] To preclude a person from acquiring the voting power that comes with a significant interest, the Act prohibits a person with a significant interest in a widely held bank from having a significant interest in its subsidiary bank holding company[437] or in a bank holding company that controls the bank.[438] Finally, in respect to banks with equity in excess of $8 billion, the Act also prohibits any person from control of that bank, again except with the approval of the Minister.[439] "Control" means beneficial ownership of more than 50 percent of the shares that may be cast to elect directors.[440]

For medium-sized banks with an equity between $2 billion and $8 billion, at least 35 percent of the voting shares are required to be listed for public trading in Canada.[441] The Act contains transitional provisions in the event that such a bank acquires an equity in excess of $8 billion, to ensure that it complies with the holding requirements for large banks within the periods of time as specified by the Minister under the Act.[442] Again, the Minister may exempt a medium-sized bank from the ownership requirements set out in the Act.[443]

For small banks with equity of less than $2 billion, the *Bank Act* is silent, meaning, presumably, that there are no restrictions on ownership, so that any person may enjoy 100 percent ownership of all classes of shares whether voting or non-voting. The general oversight of the Minister of Finance, OSFI, and the other regulatory authorities must be assumed to be sufficient in the national interest.

The number of provisions in Part VII of the Act relating to ownership requiring the approval of the Minister of Finance demonstrates how closely ownership is regulated by the government of the day. The role of the Superintendent is to ensure that the paperwork is in order prior to the Ministerial decision. The Act contains a number of provi-

---

435 *Ibid.*, s. 3.
436 *Ibid.*, ss. 376 & 376.01.
437 *Ibid.*, s. 376.1.
438 *Ibid.*, s. 376.2.
439 *Ibid.*, ss. 377 & 377.1. See also Guidelines Respecting Control in Fact for the Purpose of Subsection 377(1) of the *Bank Act*, SOR/2002-163.
440 *Bank Act*, *ibid.*, s. 3.
441 *Ibid.*, s. 385. In 2007, the ceiling of $1 billion was raised to $2 billion: Bill C-37, above note 368, s. 133.
442 *Bank Act*, *ibid.*, ss. 385.1–87 and 389–94. See also Total Assets for Public Holding Requirements (Banks and Bank Holding Companies) Regulations, SOR/2001-436.
443 *Bank Act*, *ibid.*, s. 388. See also ss. 378.1–84 for prohibitions on ownership on both large and medium-sized banks by personal property leasing entities.

sions relating to the procedural aspects of an application for Ministerial approval[444] but also clearly provides that the Minister may impose any terms and conditions considered necessary for compliance with the Act.[445] The Minister may take into account all matters considered relevant to any application, including the financial resources of the applicant; the soundness of the plan; the business record and experience of the applicant; character and integrity; and the best interests of the financial system in Canada.[446]

Breach of the ownership provisions or of any order of the Minister may result in the Minister directing any person to dispose of any number of shares in the public interest,[447] with a right of appeal to the Federal Court.[448] Failure to comply with the Minister's direction may also result in a court order to do so.[449] Even in the absence of an order from the Minister, persons in breach of the share ownership ceilings are prohibited from exercising their voting rights[450] unless permitted expressly by the Minister.[451] Should a person prefer not to dispose of their shares, the Minister may permit the bank to continue as any federally incorporated body corporate and therefore not be subject to the widely held rules.[452]

Since the 2001 amendments to the *Bank Act*, several small banks have been incorporated in Canada, usually to serve particular or regional interests. It remains to be seen whether these institutions will expand beyond their immediate constituencies to become competitors with the large and medium-sized banks and therefore fulfil the MacKay Task Force's aim of enhancing competition in the banking sector.

K. BANK HOLDING COMPANIES

The MacKay Task Force recommended that a new, regulated holding company regime be implemented in relation to the financial services sector in Canada, and the 2001 Act introduced a regulated, non-operating bank holding company regime permitting bank holding companies

---

444 *Ibid.*, ss. 395–408.
445 *Ibid.*, s. 397.
446 *Ibid.*, s. 396.
447 *Ibid.*, ss. 402(1) & (2).
448 *Ibid.*, ss. 402(3) and 977.
449 *Ibid.*, s. 403.
450 *Ibid.*, s. 392.
451 *Ibid.*, s. 392(3).
452 *Ibid.*, s. 402.1.

to hold banks and other corporations in the same financial institutions group. Before 2001, financial institutions could be organized in two ways: a parent-subsidiary model and an unregulated holding company model. The latter was prohibited for banks and mutual insurance companies because both were required to be widely held, but the former was permitted by the 1991 Act, which for the first time, authorized Canadian banks to own insurance and trust companies and investment dealers as subsidiaries, provided the parent bank was widely held. The parent bank was essentially the holding company.

The MacKay Task Force suggested four reasons for a new holding company regime: (i) to provide greater flexibility to banks to set up separate entities devoted to a particular activity and to enter strategic partnerships to pursue that activity; (ii) to provide more nuanced regulation for each specific entity; (iii) to permit entities operating in foreign countries to establish local partnerships without being subject to significant regulatory burdens in both countries; and (iv) to provide a vehicle for creating economies of scale and scope in an assimilating financial institutions sector. The Task Force also recommended that the ownership requirements for bank holding companies be identical to those for banks, so that they would be widely held, although they could wholly own a regulated financial institution.

Comparison of Part XV of the *Bank Act*, which relates to bank holding companies, with Parts III to VI demonstrates how closely the corporate structure of a holding company reflects that of a bank. The 302 sections in Part XV largely replicate the earlier provisions in the Act relating to incorporation,[453] capital structure,[454] corporate governance,[455] capital adequacy,[456] ownership,[457] and supervision.[458] However, the provisions relating to the business and powers of bank holding companies are entirely new and reflect the new policy of the Act in permitting a holding company regime.

Section 922(1) emphasizes the non-operating status of bank holding companies by providing that they may not engage in any business other than: (i) acquiring, holding, and administering investments permitted by Part XV; and (ii) providing management, advisory, financial,

---

453 *Ibid.*, ss. 662–702.
454 *Ibid.*, ss. 703–24.
455 *Ibid.*, ss. 725–872.
456 *Ibid.*, s. 949. See also Regulatory Capital (Bank Holding Companies) Regulations, SOR/ 2001-420.
457 *Bank Act, ibid.*, ss. 873–921.
458 *Ibid.*, ss. 950–64. See also Supervisory Information (Bank Holding Companies) Regulations, SOR/2001-480.

accounting, information processing, and other permitted services to entities in which it has a substantial interest. The entities in which a bank may have a substantial investment,[459] that is, entities they may wholly own, include a bank, a bank holding company, a trust and loan company, an insurance company, a co-operative, a securities dealer, or a foreign financial institution engaged in these businesses.[460] In addition to holding these more traditional financial institutions, a bank holding company may also have a substantial investment in entities engaged in related financial services such as data processing, computerized information management services, credit cards, mutual funds, and so on.[461] On the other hand, a bank holding company is prohibited from holding entities engaged in financial services prohibited to banks under the Act, including personal property leasing or dealing in insurance, securities, or real property except as permitted by the Act.[462]

The *Bank Act* sets several general standards for investments by bank holding companies. Directors are required to establish investment and lending policies, standards, and procedures that a reasonable and prudent person would apply to avoid undue risk of loss and obtain a reasonable return.[463] Moreover, subject to the prohibitions and other requirements of the Act, a bank holding company is permitted to invest in any shares or ownership interests in any entity the directors consider necessary to manage liquidity.[464] In addition, bank holding companies are subject to various permissions from the Minister of Finance or Superintendent prior to acquiring control or a substantial interest in the various entities,[465] or prior to acquiring indirect investments in them,[466] and may be required to give such undertakings to the Superintendent as are required.[467] The Act also contains various provisions

---

459 *Bank Act, ibid.,* s. 10.
460 *Ibid.,* ss. 928(1) and 930(1). For uncontrolled event exception, see s. 928(4). Subsidiaries are also included: s. 925 and Specialized Financing (Bank Holding Companies) Regulations, SOR/2001-477.
461 *Bank Act, ibid.,* ss. 930(2) and 409–11. See also Information Technology Activities (Bank Holding Companies) Regulations, SOR/2003-62.
462 *Bank Act, ibid.,* ss. 930(3), 409, 412, and 416–18.
463 *Ibid.,* s. 927.
464 *Ibid.,* s. 926.
465 *Ibid.,* ss. 930(4)–(7) and (9)–(12). With the exception of foreign financial institutions: see s. 930(8) and see also Minority Investment (Bank Holding Companies) Regulations, SOR/2001-401.
466 *Bank Act, ibid.,* ss. 931 and 928(2).
467 *Ibid.,* s. 932.

relating to temporary permitted acquisitions;[468] loan workouts;[469] and realizations of security interests held by a subsidiary.[470]

Finally, the Act prohibits certain activities to bank holding companies and their subsidiaries: (i) acting as guarantors except on behalf of a subsidiary that has given an unqualified obligation to reimburse;[471] (ii) entering partnerships except with the approval of the Superintendent;[472] (iii) holding real property interests that exceed in aggregate value a prescribed percentage of their regulatory capital;[473] (iv) acquiring shares or ownership interests that exceed the aggregate value of their regulatory capital;[474] (v) holding real property and share interests that together exceed in aggregate value a prescribed percentage of the regulatory capital;[475] (vi) acquiring or transferring assets to a person within a twelve-month period greater than 10 percent of the total assets except with the Superintendent's approval;[476] and (vii) accepting deposits through a subsidiary that is not a bank for CDIC purposes.[477]

The bank holding company regime established in 2001 is undergirded by the same principles as the previous parent-subsidiary regime, including close regulation by the Minister of Finance and OSFI, widely held ownership, detailed regulation of permitted and prohibited activities and protection of depositors. The regulations[478] relating to the establishment of bank holding companies by banks demonstrate the same principles of approvals by all stakeholders to the Minister of Finance, and the largest domestic banks in Canada have now reorganized to take advantage of the opportunities for a broader range of activities contemplated by the introduction of the bank holding company regime in the 2001 Act.

---

468 *Ibid.*, ss. 928(3)(a) and 933.
469 *Ibid.*, ss. 928(3)(b) and 934.
470 *Ibid.*, ss. 928(3)(c) and 935.
471 *Ibid.*, s. 923.
472 *Ibid.*, s. 924.
473 *Ibid.*, ss. 937, 938, and 941. See also Investment Limits (Bank Holding Companies) Regulations, SOR/2001-392.
474 *Bank Act, ibid.*, s. 939.
475 *Ibid.*, s. 940. For divestments, see ss. 942–43.
476 *Ibid.*, s. 944.
477 *Ibid.*, ss. 947–48. See also transitional provisions: ss. 945–46.
478 Bank Holding Company Proposal Regulations, SOR/2004-199. It should be noted that the Act makes no provision for a public inquiry or objection procedure when a bank applies to incorporate a bank holding corporation: *Bank Act, ibid.*, ss. 674 and 678.

L. FOREIGN BANKS

Prior to the 1980 *Bank Act*, there were no statutory provisions permitting foreign banks to operate in Canada, although provided foreign banks did not call themselves "banks," there was no legal prohibition against carrying on business in Canada, and some "suitcase banking" was carried on in the commercial, but not the retail, sector.[479] The 1980 Act permitted foreign banks to provide banking services through incorporated "Schedule I" banks and to provide other financial services through a "non-bank affiliate of a foreign bank" with the approval of the Minister of Finance and subject to a very strict regulatory regime. The parent foreign bank was prohibited from acquiring a substantial investment in a Canadian financial institution but could do so in Canadian entities that did not have as their principal activity a financial service. The 1997 amendments permitted foreign banks to own regulated financial institutions directly, but not through the acquisition of a domestic financial institution, and also permitted non-bank foreign financial institutions to acquire Canadian non-bank financial entities and provide financial services other than deposit taking.

In late 1997, the federal government produced a policy paper[480] on the future of foreign banks, and many of the ideas in that paper were taken up by the MacKay Task Force. These included enhancing competition by permitting foreign banks to open branches directly in Canada without incorporation, although subject to home jurisdiction regulation and with a prohibition on retail deposit taking; increasing the range of models for doing business in Canada using regulated and unregulated models; reducing regulation significantly, especially where there were few prudential concerns; and relying on home jurisdiction regulation to some extent, a practice allowed under European Union banking policy but not before contemplated by Canadian banking policy. The resulting provisions in Parts XII and XII.1 of the 2001 Act are so extraordinarily complex and labyrinthine that it is difficult to assess how effective they are at enhancing competition while at the same time regulating it. However, a number of foreign banks have taken advan-

---

479 See M.H. Ogilvie, "The Foreign Bank Entry Regime and the Search for a 21st Century Banking Policy for Canada" (1998) J. Bus. L. 397 and M.H. Ogilvie, above note 6 at 498–501.
480 Canada, Department of Finance, *Foreign Bank Entry Policy: Consultation Paper* (Ottawa: Department of Finance, 1997).

tage of the 2001 regime, so it remains to be seen whether the Canadian customer will have greater banking choices.[481]

Foreign banks may operate in Canada in two ways: as "foreign banks" and as "authorized foreign banks." A "foreign bank" is, essentially, a bank according to the laws of the country other than Canada where it is incorporated and is engaged in banking business such as accepting deposits and lending money in that foreign country.[482] Part XII of the Act applies to a foreign bank, although the Minister of Finance has a statutory discretion to exempt a foreign bank from any provision of the Act.[483] An "authorized foreign bank"[484] is a foreign bank permitted by the Minister of Finance to establish a branch in Canada, and Part XII.1 applies to such entities. The Act is the charter for, and applies to, all banks in each category as much as to domestic Canadian banks.[485] However, neither category is required to separately incorporate a foreign bank subsidiary in Canada as was the case prior to 2001. Home-country incorporation is sufficient, although compliance with the Canadian banking regulatory regime is required to carry on business in Canada.[486]

Part XII of the Act begins with a general prohibition on foreign banks operating in Canada except as expressly permitted by the Act. Prohibited activities include carrying on business as described generally by the Act, maintaining branches, providing automated banking machines (ABMs) or similar automated services, and acquiring or holding control of a Canadian entity.[487] However, foreign banks are expressly permitted to carry on certain other activities, including arranging with Canadian financial institutions to permit Canadian non-residents to access accounts outside Canada from ABMs in Canada;[488] giving quotes on entering verbal agreements using a private telephone service in relation to foreign exchange, deposit, or loan rates;[489] operating as a foreign securities dealer;[490] holding and managing real property;[491]

---

481 The discussion that follows is not comprehensive but, in keeping with the domestic and consumer focuses of this text, is simply an overview. Readers interested in the complexities of Parts XII and XII.1 should consult the Act directly.
482 *Bank Act,* above note 5, s. 2 "foreign bank." Listed in Sch. II, s. 14(1)(b).
483 *Ibid.,* s. 12. The Governor in Council may make regulations accordingly: s. 14.2.
484 *Ibid.,* s. 2 "authorized foreign bank." Listed in Sch. III: s. 14.1.
485 *Ibid.,* s. 13.
486 Compare *ibid.,* s. 2 "foreign institution."
487 *Ibid.,* s. 510.
488 *Ibid.,* s. 511.
489 *Ibid.,* s. 512.
490 *Ibid.,* s. 513.
491 *Ibid.,* s. 514.

guaranteeing or accepting securities, bills of exchange, and depository bills issued by certain entities;[492] and maintaining representative offices and a head office in Canada from which to conduct banking business outside Canada.[493] The Minister of Finance may exempt a foreign bank from any of these provisions.[494]

Part XII further contains various provisions designed to ensure that foreign banks are engaged only in expressly permitted activities by defining and prohibiting any of their related entities from engaging indirectly in expressly prohibited activities.[495] Part XII also directs foreign banks to become authorized foreign banks if they wish to maintain branches and carry on the business of banking in Canada,[496] thereby ensuring that they will be regulated under Part XII.1 of the Act, which largely mirrors the regulatory regime for domestic Canadian banks. However, Part XII also contains detailed rules whereby foreign banks are permitted to acquire substantial investments in Canadian financial institutions, subject to the approval of the Minister of Finance.[497] By doing so, they will again be closely regulated by the Minister and OSFI.[498]

A foreign bank that wishes to engage in the business of banking in Canada may do so, provided it is approved by the Minister of Finance as an authorized foreign bank under Part XII.1 of the Act. Although there is no statutory requirement to incorporate a Canadian subsidiary, as an authorized foreign bank, the foreign bank is subject to virtually the same regulatory regime as a domestic bank once it receives Ministerial approval. Part XII.1 largely mirrors the earlier provisions, especially in Parts III and VIII of the Act relating to the provisions regarding bank corporate governance and the business of banking that are applicable to domestic banks. It is also in Part XII.1 that the policy of enhancing competition in the banking sector is most evident. The object of these provisions is clearly to permit authorized foreign banks to compete with domestic banks on the same regulatory playing field.

Consumer customers of authorized foreign banks should notice few, if any, differences in the conduct of their everyday banking affairs and should expect to enjoy the same regulatory protections as enjoyed

---

492 *Ibid.*, s. 518.
493 *Ibid.*, ss. 522, 522.01–.03; Foreign Bank Representative Office Regulations, SOR/92-299.
494 *Bank Act, ibid.*, s. 509.
495 *Ibid.*, ss. 515 and 519–20.
496 *Ibid.*, ss. 516–17 and 522.16–.19.
497 *Ibid.*, ss. 522.04–.15.
498 The *Investment Canada Act*, R.S.C. 1985, c. 28 (1st Supp.) as am. does not apply. See *ibid.*, Part XII.1.

in relation to Canadian domestic banks. Many foreign banks operating in the retail market have chosen to provide niche banking services such as credit cards only or electronic banking only, thereby avoiding the large capital investments required for "bricks and mortar" banks. Enhancing competition and consumer choice while ensuring close regulatory supervision remain the hallmarks of Parts XII and XII.1 of the 2001 *Bank Act* amendments continued in 2007.

M. LIQUIDATION AND DISSOLUTION

Over the past century, bank failures have been rare in Canada, and the few banks that have failed have been smaller institutions, such as the Home Bank in 1923, the Bank of Western Canada in 1967, and the Canadian Commercial Bank and the Northland Bank in 1985. However, the failure of a number of trust and loan companies in the 1980s was a reminder of the necessity for constant vigilance in the financial institutions sector generally. The continual assessment of the powers and operations of OSFI reflects that requirement. OSFI's role of day-to-day monitoring, providing prudential advice as required, and stepping in, should the need arise, to secure the solvency of financial institutions should ensure that no bank will fail. However, should a bank or any other financial institution experience solvency difficulties, the necessary statutory framework for their resolution is found in the *Bank Act*, as well as in the *Winding-Up and Restructuring Act (WURA)*.[499]

The *Bank Act* makes provision for the orderly winding-up of a solvent bank, and *WURA* provides for a bank that is insolvent within the meaning of *WURA*.[500] The *Bank Act* provides for the voluntary liquidation of a bank without assets; simple voluntary liquidations of banks; court supervised liquidations; and taking control by the Superintendent.

First, a bank that has no property and no liabilities may be dissolved by letters patent by the Minister of Finance if the application has been approved by a shareholder special resolution or a resolution of all the directors if there are no shareholders.[501] The bank ceases to exist on the day stated in the letters patent.[502] This type of liquidation would likely be sought where a bank had never carried on business after incorpora-

---

499 R.S.C. 1985, c. W-11 as am. [*WURA*]
500 *Bank Act*, above note 5, s. 340, and *ibid*.
501 *Ibid*., ss. 342(1) & (2).
502 *Ibid*., s. 342(3).

tion,[503] but it could also be sought by any bank that had disposed of all its assets and honoured all of its commitments prior to the application, so that the statutory requirements had been satisfied.[504]

Secondly, any bank with assets may apply for a voluntary dissolution under the *Bank Act* either at the proposal of its directors or by a shareholder proposal.[505] Once the shareholders have approved by special resolution that a solvent bank be dissolved, the bank may apply to the Minister for letters patent, and once approved, the bank shall cease to carry on business except everything necessary to complete the voluntary liquidation,[506] including notifying each known claimant and creditor of the bank, placing public notices in the *Canada Gazette* and various general circulation newspapers, collecting property, disposing of property, discharging its obligations, and distributing its remaining property to shareholders according to their respective rights.[507] Once these steps are completed, the Minister shall issue the letters patent dissolving the bank, which ceases to exist on the day stated in the letters patent.[508] A voluntary liquidation of a solvent bank does not require any form of oversight or supervision; rather, the directors and officers are entrusted with the orderly dissolution subject only to Ministerial approval.[509]

The third type of dissolution provided by the *Bank Act* is a court-supervised dissolution.[510] During the voluntary liquidation of a solvent bank, the Superintendent or any interested person may apply to a court for the continuance of the voluntary liquidation under court supervision.[511] Where the applicant is not the Superintendent, the Superintendent is to be notified of the application and may appear at the hearing of the application.[512] A court is empowered to make any order it thinks fit in connection with the liquidation and dissolution of the bank once it is satisfied that the bank is able to provide for the

---

503 *Ibid.*, s. 57.
504 *Kay v. Posluns* (1989), 60 D.L.R. (4th) 426 (Ont. H.C.J.), additional reasons at (18 September 1990) Doc. No. Toronto 26686/68 (Ont. H.C.J.); *Continental Bank of Canada v. Arthur Andersen & Co.* (1987), 39 D.L.R. (4th) 261 (Ont. H.C.J.).
505 *Bank Act*, above note 5, s. 343.
506 *Ibid.*, ss. 344–45.
507 *Ibid.*, s. 345(4).
508 *Ibid.*, s. 346.
509 However, it would appear that the bank may apply to a court to resolve any distribution issues: *Re B.C. Bancorp* (1990), 79 C.B.R. (N.S.) 281 (B.C.S.C.).
510 "Court" means the court in the jurisdiction of the head office: *Bank Act*, above note 5, s. 339.
511 *Ibid.*, ss. 346(1), 347(1) & (2).
512 *Ibid.*, s. 347(3).

discharge of all its obligations.[513] Once a court makes the liquidation order, the bank shall cease to carry on business except for the business required for the orderly liquidation.[514] The court shall appoint the liquidator at the time of making the order or thereafter, and the court may appoint a director, officer, or shareholder of the bank or of any other bank as the liquidator.[515] The liquidator may delegate any of the statutory powers of a liquidator to the directors or shareholders,[516] and the duties and powers of the liquidator as set out in the *Bank Act*[517] are essentially the standard duties and powers of any liquidator to do all things necessary to execute the liquidation. Once the court has made the order to liquidate and appointed the liquidator, the powers of the directors and shareholders are vested in the liquidator subject to any specific authorization by the court.[518]

The costs of the liquidation are to be paid out of the property of the bank.[519] The liquidator is entitled to rely in good faith on the financial statements of the bank; written auditor's reports; and opinions, reports, and statements of any professional advisor, such as a lawyer or accountant, retained by the liquidator.[520] The liquidator must apply to the court within one year of appointment for approval of the final accounts and the order to distribute the remaining property, if any, to the shareholders, or else to apply for an extension of time.[521] Prior to this application, the liquidator must notify the Superintendent, each shareholder or incorporator, and any person who provided a security or fidelity bond for the liquidation,[522] and the liquidator must publish notice in the *Canada Gazette* and in general circulation newspapers in each province in which the bank has transacted business in the previous twelve months.[523] Should the liquidator fail to make application to the court, a shareholder or incorporator may apply to a court to order

---

513 *Ibid.*, ss. 348 & 349.
514 *Ibid.*, s. 350(1)(a). A branch may receive deposits until it learns of the liquidation: *Re Home Bank* (1928), 10 C.B.R. 255 (Ont. S.C. in Bankruptcy).
515 *Bank Act, ibid.*, s. 351.
516 *Ibid.*, s. 350(2). For vacancy in liquidator's officer, see s. 352.
517 *Ibid.*, ss. 353(1) & (2) and 355. The liquidator represents the creditors, as well as the bank: *Re Central Bank* (1889), 17 O.R. 110 (H.C.J.).
518 *Bank Act, ibid.*, s. 350(1)(b).
519 *Ibid.*, s. 356.
520 *Ibid.*, s. 354.
521 *Ibid.*, s. 357(1).
522 *Ibid.*, s. 357(3).
523 *Ibid.*, s. 357(4).

the liquidator to show cause why a final accounting and distribution should not be made.[524]

Once the court has approved the final accounts, the court shall order the bank to apply to the Minister for letters patent dissolving the bank; give directions about the custody and disposal of the bank's records; and discharge the liquidator but for a duty to deliver a certified copy of the Minister's order to the Superintendent.[525] On application, the Minister may issue letters patent dissolving the bank, which shall cease to exist on the date of the issuance of the letters patent.[526] Throughout the liquidation process, the liquidator is under a statutory duty to provide all information to the Superintendent as the Superintendent requires.[527]

Certain statutory liabilities continue after the dissolved bank has ceased to exist as a legal entity. First, any civil, criminal, or administrative action commenced prior to dissolution or within two years after the date of the dissolution may be continued, and any property of the bank is available to satisfy an order or judgment.[528] Secondly, any shareholder or incorporator to whom property has been distributed is liable in such actions to the extent of the amount received in the distribution for a period of two years after the date of dissolution.[529] Thirdly, a court may order a class action against shareholders or incorporators as a class.[530]

Any property of a dissolved bank which has not been disposed of at dissolution rests in the Crown in right of Canada,[531] and any unclaimed money payable to a creditor, shareholder, or incorporator of a bank shall be paid to the Minister,[532] who shall forward these to the Bank of Canada,[533] together with all documentation relating to the entitlement of these payees.[534] Once payment is made to the Bank of Canada, the

---

524 *Ibid.*, s. 357(2). Shareholder applications in relation to proposals for distribution: s. 359.
525 *Ibid.*, ss. 358(1) & (2). Records must be available for inspection for six years: s. 368.
526 *Ibid.*, s. 360.
527 *Ibid.*, s. 341.
528 *Ibid.*, s. 362.
529 *Ibid.*, ss. 363(1) & (2).
530 *Ibid.*, ss. 363(3) & (4).
531 *Ibid.*, s. 365. For conversion of property to money where claimant cannot be found, see s. 364.
532 *Ibid.*, s. 366(1). The Minister must assert any such claim at the time of the winding-up and not later: *Re Ontario Bank* (1916), 38 O.L.R. 242 (H.C.J.).
533 *Bank Act, ibid.*, s. 366(3).
534 *Ibid.*, ss. 366(2) & (3).

liquidator, the bank, and the Minister are discharged from liability, and the Bank of Canada becomes solely liable to any claimant.[535]

The fourth process for which the *Bank Act* makes provision for a solvent bank in difficulties is for the Superintendent to take control.[536] The Superintendent may take control in various states of affairs where it appears that the interests of the creditors, depositors, and shareholders are materially prejudiced[537] and may have control of the assets for a period of up to sixteen days with a view either to correct the situation and return control to the directors or to request a winding-up of the bank under *WURA*.[538] During the Superintendent's control, the legal role of the directors is suspended,[539] and when the period of control expires, that role is resumed unless a winding-up is requested.[540]

The Superintendent would normally request that the Attorney General commence the winding-up of a bank when it is insolvent, and so the question becomes that of defining insolvency. While earlier *Bank Acts* contained definitions of insolvency in relation to banks, the present Act does not. Rather, the insolvency law for banks as for other business corporations is found in *WURA*.[541] Pursuant to section 3 of *WURA*, a bank is deemed to be insolvent in the following circumstances: (i) inability to pay debts as they become due; (ii) meeting with creditors for the purpose of compounding debts; (iii) admits an inability to meet liabilities; (iv) deals with any of its property with intent to defraud, delay, or defeat creditors; (v) acts in such manner that any of its property is seized by any process of execution; (vi) sells or conveys property without the consent of creditors or satisfying their claims; (vii) engages in transactions in breach of obligations under the *CDIC Act*. Inability to pay debts is defined as an inability to pay a sum exceeding $200 and the creditor has served legal process for payment and not been paid after sixty days.[542]

---

535 *Ibid.*, ss. 366(4) and 367. Claimant's heirs can also sue for claim: s. 361.
536 See Chapter 3, Section C for an extended discussion.
537 *Ibid.*, ss. 648(1), (1.1) & (1.2).
538 *Ibid.*, ss. 648(2) & (3), 650 & 651.
539 *Ibid.*, s. 649.
540 *Ibid.*, ss. 649(1), 650, and 652. For assistance by an advisory committee, see s. 653. For compensation for the costs of taking control, see ss. 654–56.
541 *WURA*, above note 499, s. 6. *WURA* as forum for all issues: *Re Northland Bank* (1988), 53 Man. R. (2d) 249 (Q.B.). *WURA* is a lengthy and detailed Act, and readers should refer to specialized texts on insolvency law. The present discussion is deliberately limited to an overview of the insolvency process regarding banks.
542 *WURA*, *ibid.*, s. 4.

A winding-up commences when the petition for winding-up is served,[543] and that petition may be made to the court in the province of the head office or the chief place of business in Canada.[544] The court can make such order as it thinks fit[545] and may order a winding-up when the Superintendent has taken control and asked the Attorney General to commence winding-up proceedings;[546] when the charter has expired; when a special shareholder resolution so requests; when the bank is insolvent; when the capital is impaired; or for any other just and equitable reason in the opinion of the court.[547]

From the time of the making of the winding-up order, the bank ceases to carry on business except that required for a beneficial winding-up in the opinion of the liquidator.[548] The liquidator is usually appointed when the winding-up order is made, but the Superintendent cannot be appointed as the liquidator of a bank.[549] On appointment, the liquidator assumes all the legal powers of the directors.[550] WURA sets out the statutory duties of the liquidator, including taking control of all property,[551] preparing a statement of assets and liabilities,[552] carrying on such business as is beneficial in the winding-up,[553] selling property, repaying indebtedness and bringing or defending any legal proceedings,[554] settling lists of contributories[555] and claimants[556] and distributing assets.[557] These duties are performed under court supervision and

---

543 *Ibid.*, s. 5.
544 *Ibid.*, s. 12. *WURA* applies only to the Canadian business of authorized foreign banks: *ibid.*, ss. 6(2), 8, and 150–58.3.
545 *Ibid.*, ss. 13, 14, and 16.
546 *Ibid.*, ss. 10.1 and 6(1).
547 *Ibid.*, ss. 10, 17 & 18. For stay of proceedings process, see *Re Commonwealth Trust Co.*, 2004 CarswellBC 478 (S.C.).
548 *WURA, ibid.*, ss. 19–22.1.
549 *Ibid.*, ss. 23–28 and 32. For the nature of the liquidator's authority, see *Canadian Commercial Bank (Liquidator) v. Parlee* (1988), 86 A.R. 167 (Q.B.); *Scarth v. Northland Bank (Liquidator of)* (1996), 43 C.B.R. (3d) 254 (Man. Q.B.).
550 *WURA, ibid.*, ss. 31, 36, and 41.
551 *Ibid.*, s. 33.
552 *Ibid.*, s. 34.
553 *Ibid.*, s. 35(1).
554 *Ibid.*, ss. 35(1) and 37–38. For valuation date for real property, see *Northland Bank v. Kuperman*, [1989] 4 W.W.R. 701 (Man. C.A.).
555 *WURA, ibid.*, ss. 50–62. For fraudulent preferences, see ss. 96–102.1.
556 *Ibid.*, ss. 63–95. Further classification of a participation agreement as a loan or capital investment: *Canada Deposit Insurance Corp. v. Canadian Commercial Bank (No. 3)* (1992), 97 D.L.R. (4th) 385 (S.C.C.).
557 *WURA, ibid.*, ss. 93–95. For an interim distribution without court approval, see *Canada Deposit Insurance Corp. v. Columbia Trust Co.* (1987), 37 D.L.R. (4th) 378 (B.C.S.C.).

any person dissatisfied with the conduct of the winding-up may appeal any decision to the courts.[558] The remuneration of the liquidator is determined by a court,[559] and a court will discharge the liquidator once the winding-up is completed.[560]

When a bank is wound up, one of the more challenging aspects of the process is the determination of the order in which claims against the bank shall be paid. The *Bank Act* makes provision for the following order: (i) all amounts due to the Crown in right of Canada except indebtedness evidenced by subordinated indebtedness; (ii) all amounts due to the Crown in right of a province except indebtedness evidenced by subordinated indebtedness; (iii) deposit liabilities; (iv) subordinated indebtedness and all other liabilities that rank equally with subordinated indebtedness; and (v) all fines and penalties for which the bank is liable.[561] Priorities within each category are to be determined in accordance with the laws governing priorities and the terms of the indebtednesses themselves,[562] but nothing in these orders of claims should prejudice or affect the priority of any security interest in any property of a bank.[563]

These provisions are challenging to apply in relation to the four categories of claims insofar as within each there are potentially multiple statutory claimants claiming pursuant to legislation that is incompatible, with the result that establishing a simple list in descending order of claimant is difficult. These difficulties are compounded by provisions in both *WURA* and the *Canadian Payments Act* (*CPA*), which also address issues of priority in insolvencies.

WURA provides for the termination of "eligible financial contracts,"[564] such as swaps and derivatives, and their set-off as between a bank being wound up and the counterparty in accordance with the contractual provisions. If the "net termination value"[565] results in an indebtedness to the counterparty, that party is deemed to be a creditor for that value.[566] *WURA* does not provide for the ranking of either the

---

558 *WURA*, ibid., ss. 39, 103–49 and *Re Northland Bank*, above note 541. For reopening accounts, see *Surrey Credit Union Ltd. v. Northland Bank* (1989), 77 C.B.R. (N.S.) 272 (Man. C.A.), leave to appeal to S.C.C. refused (1990), 113 N.R. 80n (S.C.C.).
559 *WURA*, ibid., s. 42.
560 *Bank Act*, above note 5, s. 49.
561 *Ibid.*, s. 369(1).
562 *Ibid.*, s. 369(3).
563 *Ibid.*, s. 369(2).
564 *WURA*, above note 499, s. 22.1(2) "eligible financial contract."
565 *Ibid.*, s. 22.1(2) "net termination value."
566 *Ibid.*, s. 22.1(1).

set-off or the remaining claim, so it is unknown when and where this *WURA* provision is to be placed in the claims order in a winding-up.

Even more problematical is section 31 of the *CPA*. Section 31(2) provides that in a winding-up, priority will be given to unpaid cheques or orders drawn on the insolvent bank and certified prior to the winding-up order and then to unpaid "priority payment instruments"[567] issued prior to the winding-up order.[568] These priorities are said to override all others for which statutory authority is given,[569] subject to the availability of depositors' insurance;[570] the claim being made within sixty days of the winding-up order;[571] no payment being made which gives the payee "preference"[572] over other creditors;[573] and subject to the rights of secured creditors generally.[574] Again it is not clear how this priority relates to the others set out in the *Bank Act*. Moreover, the requirements for payment, such as the availability of insurance, suggest that the payment process could be protracted even when the claim is made within the limitation period.

The net result of the failure of the three statutes to mesh together when creditors' claims are being established in the winding-up of an insolvent bank is that the precise order in which claims against the assets of an insolvent bank are to be paid is uncertain. On the other hand, the bewildering variety of claims which can be made by creditors, depositors, all levels of government, and shareholders means that a complete and coherent code is not likely to be established in the foreseeable future.

N. CONCLUSION

Like any other corporate person in law, banks are created by law, regulated by law, and cease to exist by operation of law. The basic model for banks as business corporations is the *CBCA* corporations model modified to account for the special nature of banks as the repositories of individuals' wealth and as the most significant corporate decision

---

567 *Canadian Payments Act*, R.S.C. 1985, c. C-21, s. 31(1) .
568 *Ibid.*, s. 31(2).
569 *Ibid.*
570 *Ibid.*, s. 31(3).
571 *Ibid.*, s. 31(4).
572 *Ibid.*, s. 31(6).
573 *Ibid.*, s. 31(5).
574 *Ibid.*, s. 31(2).

makers in the nation's economy. This chapter has demonstrated how closely the banking sector is regulated and supervised to ensure as far as possible the security and soundness of that sector. It has also shown how complex each "bank" actually is, not only *qua* bank, but also as a network of related corporate entities engaged, as the next chapter will show, in a great variety of financial services in Canada and beyond.

CHAPTER 5

BANKING BUSINESS

A. INTRODUCTION

Although banks are incorporated with the capacity of a natural person in law, they are not theoretically permitted to engage in any activities they wish; rather, like natural persons, banks are subject to restrictions on their activities, in particular, are permitted to engage only in the activities for which there is express provision in the *Bank Act*.[1] Historically, Bank Acts have prescribed the business in which banks may engage, as well as the business in which they may not engage, that is, banking business has been prescribed both positively and negatively. Over time, the two lists have lengthened and become more complex but also less specific insofar as some activities originally listed, such as opening branches or lending money or dealing in foreign exchange, are no longer expressly listed because they are self-evidently banking business and have long been so recognized at common law. In the current *Bank Act*, considerable care is taken in the definitions of what banks may do to distinguish banks from other financial institutions, especially trust companies and insurance companies, to ensure that the respective roles of institutions providing fiduciary and insurance services are protected in law.

However, at the same time as the *Bank Act* restricts the capacity of banks as natural persons to the activities expressly set out in the Act, in setting out those activities, the Act introduces ambiguity into the nature and scope of banking business. Section 409(1) provides: "Subject

---

1   S.C. 1991, c. 46, s. 15; see Chapter 4, Section C.

to this Act a bank shall not engage in or carry on any business other than the business of banking and such business generally as appertains thereto." This ambiguity is further reflected in section 409(2), which states what "the business of banking includes." The phrase "and such business generally as appertains thereto" has appeared in this or in similar formulations in earlier Bank Acts and appears to suggest that there may be scope for banks to engage in business not expressly permitted by the Act, provided it generally appertains to banking, even if restricted to banking as defined by the Act. Courts have consistently interpreted the phrase in this way, to mean activities reasonably incidental to banking[2] and activities that the business community would generally regard as being within the legitimate business of a banker.[3] This construction means that banks can expand the scope of the Act when they engage in activities reasonably close to those expressly permitted by the Act and accepted within the business community as appropriate extensions of existing activities.

The *Bank Act* further distinguishes between "the business of banking"[4] and "additional activities"[5] in which a bank may engage, thereby suggesting that the latter category should not be characterized as "banking" or, in some sense, as part of the core of banking. Selling lottery tickets or urban transit tickets[6] would not be characterized as banking in any common law sense of that concept, although expressly listed as an activity.

Finally, in addition to difficulties in defining precisely what banking is as a legal activity resulting from the express provisions in the Act, there are also difficulties resulting from what has been omitted from the Act. Previous acts listed such activities as opening branches, dealing in foreign currency and bullion, and dealing in negotiable instruments as permitted business for banks, but the current *Bank Act* does

---

2 *Jones v. Imperial Bank* (1876), 23 Gr. 262; *Provincial Treasurer of Alberta v. Long* (1973), 49 D.L.R. (3d) 695 (Alta. S.C.).

3 *Tennant v. Union Bank of Canada*, [1894] A.C. 31 (P.C.); *Central Computer Services Ltd. v. T.D. Bank* (1980), 107 D.L.R. (3d) 88 (Man. C.A.) (computerization of banking services); *Canada Deposit Insurance Corp. v. Canadian Commercial Bank* (1986), 27 D.L.R. (4th) 229 (Alta. Q.B.).

4 *Bank Act*, above note 1, s. 409.

5 *Ibid.*, s. 410.

6 *Ibid.*, s. 410(1)(e). Especially since these would include tickets offered by provincial and municipal governments and properly construed under s. 92(13) of the *Constitution Act, 1867* (U.K.), 30 & 31 Vict., c. 3, reprinted in R.S.C. 1985, App. II, No. 5: *Quirt v. Canada* (1891), 19 S.C.R. 510; *Canadian Western Bank v. Alberta*, [2005] 6 W.W.R. 226 at 252 (Alta. C.A.), Hunt J.A..

not. Since these services are universally regarded as banking services, it may be assumed that it is no longer necessary to list them expressly as permitted banking business, but rather to assume that either they are included within the phrase "the business of banking" in section 409(1) or "any financial service" in section 409(2)(a) or to be permitted at common law.

The net result of any analysis of the way in which the business of banking is defined for legal purposes within the Act is that while most of the provisions are specific and detailed, there is still some ambiguity in relation to what may or may not be included, and resort to the case law is still occasionally required to resolve that ambiguity. Section 409(2) provides that the business of banking includes providing any financial service; acting as a financial agent; providing investment counselling and portfolio management services; and issuing and operating payment, credit, and charge cards, including in cooperation with others. These are expressed in general terms, contemplating expansion by reference to either other provisions of the Act or the common law. The same observation applies to section 410(1), which lists other "activities" in which banks may engage, including dealing with real property; providing bank-related data processing services; developing and marketing information management systems and computer hardware and software and dealing generally in financial or economic information; promoting merchandise and services to credit card or charge card holders; selling lottery and urban transit tickets; acting as a custodian of property; and acting as a receiver, liquidator, or sequestrator.

In defining expressly those businesses or activities permitted to banks, the *Bank Act* does so positively and negatively, that is, it prescribes activities expressly permitted, as well as those expressly prohibited. This chapter will be organized on this basis and will assume that certain businesses are permitted by virtue of the common law or by virtue of section 409(2)(a) of the Act, although no longer expressly stated as such in the Act.

B. PERMITTED BUSINESS

1) Operating Branches

Although no longer expressly empowered to operate from branches, there can be no doubt that banks are permitted to do so, since the Act contains a definition of a branch and also makes frequent reference to branches. "Branch" is defined as an agency, a head office, or any other office of a bank.[7] There are approximately 12,000 branches in Canada, as well as 16,160 automated banking machines.[8] A branch has no legal identity separate from the bank; it is simply a part of the body corporate of the bank.[9] This means that customer accounts kept at separate branches may be consolidated to determine the net balance between bank and customer, subject to any contractual agreement to the contrary.[10] Secondly, a bank may be deemed to be resident for legal purposes in every jurisdiction where it has a branch regardless of the jurisdiction of the head office.[11] Thirdly, a bank may pay out funds from an account at one branch at another branch of the bank, although the *situs* of the indebtedness to the customer is at the branch of the account.[12]

On the other hand, branches have been treated as separate entities by the courts for certain practical purposes. First, each endorsing branch of a bank is entitled to separate notice of dishonour of a cheque so that it may reverse its accounts.[13] Secondly, a bank is entitled to pay out funds from an account only at the branch of that account and not at any other branch.[14] Thirdly, a customer is required to place a stop-payment order on a cheque only at the branch of the account and not at any other branch.[15] Fourthly, branches are deemed to be separate for the purposes of a writ or process originating a legal proceeding or in pursuance of a legal proceeding; an order or injunction; an instrument purporting to assign, perfect, or otherwise dispose of an interest in any property or deposit account; or an enforcement notice for a support or-

---

7   *Bank Act*, above note 1, s. 2 "branch." For restrictions on branches by banks from non-WHO countries, see ss. 422.1 & 422.2.
8   Canadian Bankers Association, *The Banking Industry in Canada* (Toronto: Canadian Bankers Association, 2005) at 36. There are also approximately twice that number operated by other non-bank financial institutions or private companies.
9   *Prince v. Oriental Bank Corp.* (1878), 3 App. Cas. 325 (P.C.); *Re Agra and Masterman's Bank* (1866), 36 L.J. Ch. 151.
10 *Garnett v. McKewan* (1872), L.R. 8 Exch. 10. For a further discussion of set-off, see Chapter 7, Section J.
11 *Canada Life Assurance Co. v. Canadian Imperial Bank of Commerce* (1976), 14 O.R. (2d) 777 (C.A.), aff'd (1979), 98 D.L.R. (3d) 670 (S.C.C.); *Bank of Montreal v. Perry* (1981), 31 O.R. (2d) 700 (H.C.J.).
12 *Bank Act*, above note 1, ss. 461(2)–(4). *Irwin v. Bank of Montreal* (1876), 38 U.C.Q.B. 375 (C.A.); *Bain v. Torrance* (1884), 1 Man. R. 32 (Q.B.).
13 *Clode v. Bayley* (1843), 12 M. & W. 51, 152 E.R. 1107 (Ex. Ch.); *R. v. Lovitt*, [1912] A.C. 212 (H.L.); *Bills of Exchange Act*, R.S.C. 1985, c. B-4, s. 50.
14 *Woodland v. Fear* (1857), 7 El. & Bl. 519, 119 E.R. 1339 (Ex. Ch.); *Clare & Co. v. Dresdner Bank* (1915), 2 K.B. 576; *Joachimson v. Swiss Bank Corp.*, [1921] 3 K.B. 110 (C.A.).
15 *Royal Bank of Canada v. Boyce; Royal Bank of Canada v. Wildman* (1966), 57 D.L.R. (2d) 683 (Ont. Co. Ct.); *Bank of Nova Scotia v. Gould* (1977), 17 O.R. (2d) 96 (Co. Ct.).

der.[16] Fifthly, branches are deemed to be separate for the purpose of determining the *situs*, or the locality, of the indebtedness represented by a deposit in a deposit account.[17] Sixthly, branches are treated as separate entities for the purpose of knowledge of customer business carried on at a particular branch, so that another branch is not deemed to have constructive notice of that business.[18] In none of these cases have the courts doubted the principle that a branch is a part of the whole bank; rather, branches have been treated as if they were separate entities for specific, purely commonsense reasons.

2) Borrowing and Dealing in Money

Previous Bank Acts expressly listed borrowing money and dealing in bills, notes, coins, bullion, and securities as parts of the business of banking, but since 1991, this is no longer the case. It is self-evident that banks engage in, and have long engaged in, these activities, since they are at the heart of banking. Deposit taking is the most obvious example of borrowing money, and the economic value in which banks deal may come in the form of bills, coins, bullion, or securities. Borrowing need not be secured, but both the *Bank Act* and the Office of the Superintendent of Financial Institutions (OSFI) place numerous restrictions on bank borrowing in its many manifestations.[19]

3) Lending

As with borrowing money, lending money has long been a core part of banking business at common law before the Bank Acts and since the beginning of banking in the West. Loans may be unsecured or secured and, generally speaking, may be on such terms as the bank negotiates with the borrower. The *Bank Act* places certain restrictions on the lending powers of banks in relation to certain categories of loans, for example, in relation to self-dealing by related parties[20] or property-value ceilings in residential mortgage lending[21] or cost-of-borrowing disclosure requirements.[22] Otherwise, the core terms of any loan, such as the

---

16 *Bank Act*, above note 1, s. 462.
17 Ibid., s. 461(4); *R. v. Lovitt*, above note 13.
18 *Royal Bank of Canada v. Hein Real Estate Corp.*, [1977] 3 W.W.R. 298 (Alta. C.A.).
19 For a more detailed discussion, see M.H. Ogilvie, *Canadian Banking Law*, 2d ed. (Toronto: Carswell, 1998) at 308–11.
20 *Bank Act*, above note 1, Part XI. See Section E, below in this chapter.
21 *Bank Act*, ibid., s. 418(1). See Section B(3), below in this chapter.
22 *Bank Act*, ibid., ss. 440–54. See Chapter 6, Section D.

amount, the nature of the security taken, and the repayment terms, are subject to negotiation. A lending bank's duties to the borrower are restricted to providing loans within the parameters of sound banking practice, complying with the lending agreement, and enforcing that agreement in accordance with its terms.[23]

In addition to enforcing a lending agreement according to its terms, the common law also requires lenders, including banks, to give a borrower notice of any contractual requirement to repay and a reasonable time within which to repay, prior to taking legal steps to enforce repayment including the seizure of any property for which the contract provides.[24] Reasonable notice must be given even where the loan is payable on demand.[25] What is reasonable notice depends on the circumstances of the case and may vary from a few hours to several weeks.[26] The goal is to permit the borrower sufficient time to repay or to persuade the bank that the borrower has access to other funds with which to repay shortly. An exception to the reasonable notice requirement is the loan represented by a line of credit extended to a customer for which a bank need not give notice of an intention to terminate in the absence of a contractual term to the contrary because a line of credit is typically extended "at the pleasure" of a bank.[27]

The *Bank Act* contains specific provisions relating to securing loans on both personal and real property. Earlier Bank Acts had placed restrictions on bank lending secured by interests in real property, but since 1980, have provided broad powers to take security on real property. A bank is permitted to hold, manage, and otherwise deal in real

---

23 The case law is legion. For a relatively recent survey, see M.H. Ogilvie, "Canadian Bank Lender Liability: Semper Caveat Lender" in William Blair, ed., *Banks, Liability and Risk*, 3d ed. (London: Lloyds of London Press, 2001) at 259–307.

24 *Atlantic Sporting Goods Distributors Ltd. v. Bank of Montreal* (1988), 87 N.S.R. (2d) 376 (T.D.), supplementary reasons at (1989), 91 N.S.R. (2d) 181 (T.D.); *Bank of Nova Scotia v. Dunphy Leasing Enterprises Ltd.* (1994), 18 Alta L.R. (3d) 2 (S.C.C.); *Royal Bank of Canada v. W. Got & Associates Electric Ltd.* (1999), 178 D.L.R. (4th) 385 (S.C.C.).

25 *Murano v. Bank of Montreal* (1998), 163 D.L.R. (4th) 21 (Ont. C.A.); *Canadian Engineering and Surveys (Yukon) Ltd. v. Banque Nationale de Paris* (Canada) (1999), 242 A.R.61 (Q.B.). Compare *Haggart Construction Ltd. v. Canadian Imperial Bank of Commerce*, [1998] 5 W.W.R. 586 (Alta. Q.B.), aff'd [2000] 2 W.W.R. 722 (Alta. C.A.).

26 *Ibid.*; *Vicply v. Royal Bank of Canada* (1996), 48 C.B.R. (3d) 129 (Que. C.A.).

27 *Inter-City Express Ltd. v. Toronto-Dominion Bank* (1976), 66 D.L.R. (3d) 754 (B.C.S.C.); *Yakiv v. March Films B.C. Ltd.* (1980), 109 D.L.R. (3d) 218 (B.C.S.C.); *CIP Inc. v. Toronto-Dominion Bank* (1988), 55 D.L.R. (4th) 308 (B.C.C.A.). Compare *Toronto-Dominion Bank v. Pritchard* (1997), 154 D.L.R. (4th) 141 (Ont. Div. Ct.).

property,[28] but in respect to residential mortgages, the Act continues to place some restrictions on banks' lending powers. The Act prohibits a bank from making a loan on the security of residential property if the amount of the loan, together with the amount of an outstanding mortgage of equal or prior claim against the property, exceeds 80 percent of the value of the property at the time of the loan.[29]

There are four statutory exceptions to this maximum value requirement: (i) loans guaranteed under any federal legislation, which provide for a different limit on the value of the property; (ii) loans for which repayment of an amount in excess of 75 percent is guaranteed or insured by a government agency or an OSFI-approved private insurer; (iii) loans for which the bank acquires from an entity other securities against any residential property; and (iv) loans secured by a mortgage taken back by the bank on a property disposed of by the bank when the mortgage secures the payment of an amount payable to the bank for the property.[30] This fourth exception permits banks to take any interest in property in order to secure a previous loan for which it may subsequently require additional security.

The *Bank Act* also places a limitation on the total value of a bank's interests in real property that have an indirect effect on the legal power of a bank to make secured loans on real property on an individual basis. Thus, a bank and its subsidiaries are prohibited from acquiring interests in real property if the aggregate value of all those real property interests exceeds a percentage of the regulatory capital as prescribed by OSFI.[31] When a bank exceeds the statutory ceilings in relation to loans secured on real property, the mortgage is valid as between bank and mortgagee,[32] but the bank would be subject to the provisions in the *Bank Act* sanctioning breaches of the Act.[33]

The Act also makes provision for banks to secure loans on personal property by stating that the rights, powers, and privileges that a bank

---

28 *Bank Act*, above note 1, s. 418(1).
29 *Ibid*.
30 *Ibid*., s. 418(2). The federal government guarantees mortgages through the Canada Mortgage and Housing Corporation (CMHC), as well as to various specific groups such as veterans, farmers, Aboriginals, etc., pursuant to relevant legislation. For a definition of "residential property," see s. 2 "residential property."
31 *Ibid*., ss. 476 and 478. See also Regulatory Capital (Banks) Regulations, SOR/92-531.
32 *Royal Bank of Canda v. Grobman* (1977), 83 D.L.R. (3d) 415 (Ont. H.C.J.).
33 *Bank Act*, above note 1, Part XVII. It should also be noted that the Act permits banks to acquire absolute title in real property, including real property against which a loan was secured, see ss. 433–34.

has pursuant to the Act in respect of real property on which it has taken security are also enjoyed in respect of any personal property on which it has taken security.³⁴ Clearly, the restrictions relating to residential mortgages do not apply, so banks are essentially empowered to take any type of security known to the law on personal property to secure a loan.

Whether a bank secures a loan on real property or on personal property, it would normally comply with local lending practices and register that security in local personal and real property security registries as provided in provincial legislation.

4) Providing Guarantees

Another aspect of banking business probably covered by the rubric in section 409(2)(a) "providing any financial service" is that of providing guarantees. Banks have long done so, but express permission to do so was not incorporated into the Act until 1980. The power to provide guarantees is subject to three restrictions: (i) the sum of money guaranteed must be a fixed sum with or without interest; (ii) the person guaranteed must have an unqualified obligation to reimburse the bank for the full amount; and (iii) where the person guaranteed is a subsidiary of the bank, the sum need not be fixed.³⁵ There are no further requirements³⁶ for guarantees in relation to such issues as the repayment obligations, taking security, or ceilings on the sum guaranteed.

5) Acting as a Financial Agent

Section 409(2)(b) permits banks to act as "financial agents" but provides no definition or further indication of what may be covered by that phrase. However, banks have long acted as agents of their customers in a variety of ways, including presenting and collecting negotiable instruments for payment; representing indirect clearers in the clearing and settlement system; arranging currency and interest-rate swaps; and coordinating a syndicated loan among a number of financial institutions. The content of "financial agency" is indefinite, but there is no statutory reason why it cannot encompass agency services that banks have traditionally provided, as well as any they may provide in the future that do not otherwise contravene the Act.

---

34   *Ibid.*, s. 432.
35   *Ibid.*, ss. 414(1) & (2).
36   *Ibid.*, s. 414(3) provides for regulations, but none have appeared.

6) Selling Tax Deferral Plans

The 1980 *Bank Act* first permitted banks to sell registered retirement savings plans (RRSPs), registered home ownership savings plans (RHOSPs), registered education savings plans (RESPs), and registered retirement income funds (RRIFs).[37] However, the current Act contains no express permission for them to do so. Since banks continue to sell tax deferral plans either directly or through subsidiaries, it must be assumed that they are now universally regarded as part of the business of banking or as encompassed by "financial service" in section 409(2)(a) of the Act.

7) Providing Investment Counselling and Portfolio Management

Section 409(2)(c) further provides that investment counselling and portfolio management are part of the business of banking and notwithstanding the absence of definitions for these activities, the fact that they are included in the business of banking means that banks may offer these services directly, rather than through subsidiaries. In fact, however, they are usually offered through brokerages owned by the banks as subsidiaries after the 1991 *Bank Act* permitted banks to purchase interests in brokerages.[38]

8) Providing Payment, Credit, and Charge Cards

Although Canadian banks have administered several international credit cards, such as Visa and Mastercard since 1967, the first *Bank Act* that expressly permitted them to do so was the 1980 Act. Since dealing in credit has long been regarded by the common law as a core function of banks, it was assumed, prior to 1980, that banks could deal in credit cards. The current Act not only expressly permits them to deal in credit but also allows them to do so in cooperation with other financial institutions.[39]

9) Dealing with Real Property

The *Bank Act* describes dealing with real property as one of the additional activities in which banks may engage.[40] Banks are permitted to pur-

---

37 *Banks and Banking Law Revision Act, 1980*, S.C. 1980–81–82–83, c. 40, ss. 173(1)(l)–(n) [*Bank Act, 1980*].
38 See Chapter 4, Section K.
39 *Bank Act*, above note 1, s. 409(2)(d). See Chapter 11, Section B.
40 *Ibid.*, s. 410(1)(a). Real property includes leasehold interests: see s. 2 "real property."

chase real property in the same circumstances as an individual would do so[41] and to acquire absolute title in real property.[42] While previous Acts had limited banks to holding real property only for actual use and occupation, the current Act allows real property holdings either directly or through subsidiaries to an aggregate of not more than 70 percent of the bank's regulatory capital[43] and aggregated with other interests of the bank to not more than 100 percent of the regulatory capital.[44]

10) Providing Information Processing Services

Banks are also expressly permitted to engage in providing data and information processing services, including collecting and transmitting primarily financial or economic information; advising on the design and implementation of information management systems and computer hardware and software; and engaging in specialized business management and advisory services.[45] As with the other activities, banks may engage in these directly as banks or through permitted entities pursuant to Part XI of the Act.

11) Promoting Merchandise and Services

Banks are permitted to promote merchandise and services to the holders of any payment, credit or charge card issued by the bank as an additional activity.[46]

12) Keeping Property

Banks are permitted to act as custodians of property as an additional activity.[47]

13) Acting as Receiver or Liquidator

Banks are permitted to act as a receiver, liquidator or sequestrator as an additional activity.[48]

---

41 Ibid., s. 433.
42 Ibid., s. 434.
43 Ibid., s. 476.
44 Ibid., s. 477.
45 Ibid., ss. 410(1)(b)–(c.2). See also Information Processing Activities (Banks and Authorized Foreign Banks) Regulations, SOR/2001-391.
46 Bank Act, ibid., s. 410(1)(d).
47 Ibid., s. 410(1)(f). See Chapter 12
48 Ibid., s. 410(1)(g).

14) Networking

The business of banking includes statutory permission to engage in networking the provision of services by acting as an agent for any person in respect of the provision of any service provided by a financial institution or entity, or by referring any person to a financial institution or entity,[49] with the exception of networking insurance.[50] Examples of networking activities include supplying credit cards and Interac services for electronic funds transfers at point of sales.

15) Lending to Receivers or Liquidators

Banks are permitted to lend money to a receiver, liquidator, custodian, or trustee under any winding-up act if that person has been duly authorized to borrow funds, and the bank may take security from that person as authorized by a court.[51]

16) Selling Securities

Banks are permitted to sell any securities taken in respect of a loan in the event of a default in payment in the same way as any person and may waive or vary any security agreement

17) Lending on Hydrocarbons and Minerals

The *Bank Act* empowers banks to make loans or advances on certain specific types of property in addition to real property, in particular, it permits a "special security" to be taken in respect of loans made to harvest natural resources,[52] as well as loans made in relation to hydrocarbons and minerals. Until the 1954 Act, no distinction was made between hydrocarbons and minerals on the one hand and other natural resources on the other, but the distinction has been retained in every *Bank Act* since. However, as there have been no cases on these provisions since 1954, there is some ambiguity about their meaning, scope, and relationship to the special security provisions.[53]

---

49 *Ibid.*, s. 411.
50 *Ibid.*, s. 416.
51 *Ibid.*, s. 430.
52 See Section C, below in this chapter.
53 A brief overview, therefore, is sufficient here.

The Act provides that a bank may make advances secured on "hydrocarbons"[54] and "minerals"[55] wherever found; on any rights to obtain and remove these; on the estate or interest of any person in these; and on the equipment used to obtain them.[56] The security is to be given by signature and delivery to the bank of an instrument in the prescribed form,[57] and the person giving the security must be the owner at the time of delivery of the instrument or at any time thereafter.[58] A bank may also take further security[59] or a substitute security subsequently.[60]

In addition to the rights and powers for which the security agreement provides expressly, the security vests in the bank the rights to take possession, seize, care for, maintain, use, operate, and sell property covered by the security in whole or in part in the event of non-payment of the loan or failure to care for the property covered by the security.[61] When a bank exercises any right conferred on it in relation to the security, it must account for any surplus in excess of the loan, interest, and expenses, to the person entitled to such surplus.[62] Any sale of property is to be by public auction duly advertised,[63] and the effect of a sale is to vest in the purchaser all the right and title in the property that the person giving the security had when the security was given or thereafter acquired.[64]

The rights and powers of a bank in respect of property covered by a security take priority over all rights subsequently acquired in the property, mechanics' lien holders and unpaid vendors of equipment but not over the rights of an unpaid vendor with a lien on equipment at the time the bank acquired the security unless the bank had no knowledge of that lien.[65] The bank's rights and powers have no priority over any other interest or right in a property unless registered or filed in the proper land registry or land titles office.[66]

---

54 *Bank Act*, ibid., s. 425(1) "hydrocarbons" defined.
55 Ibid., s. 425(1) "minerals" defined.
56 Ibid., s. 426(1).
57 Ibid., s. 426(2); Registration of Bank Special Security Regulations, SOR/92-301.
58 *Bank Act*, ibid.
59 Ibid., s. 426(11). By accepting a bill of exchange, a bank is also deemed to have made a loan: see s. 463. This also applies to the special security.
60 Ibid., s. 426(12).
61 Ibid., s. 426(3).
62 Ibid., s. 426(4).
63 Ibid., s. 426(6).
64 Ibid., s. 426(5).
65 Ibid., s. 426(7).
66 Ibid., ss. 426(8)–(10).

C. "SPECIAL SECURITY"

First introduced in the 1890 *Bank Act*,[67] the "special security"[68] is a form of taking security in Canada unique to banks and for which provision is made uniquely in the *Bank Act*. This security has enjoyed a significant role in facilitating the exploitation of Canada's natural resources and economic growth generally over the past 120 years or so. This is because by means of this security, banks have provided the capital necessary to recover and manufacture natural resources for domestic and international trade.[69]

The law relating to the special security is especially complex not only in itself but also because there have been historically and continue to be significant problems in relation to priorities in securities between those taken pursuant to the *Bank Act* and those taken pursuant to the myriad and similarly complex provincial legislation relating to secured transactions. Harmonization of the *Bank Act* and provincial personal property legislation continues to elude the law in Canada. The Law Commission of Canada had recommended that after a three-year transition period, the special security be abolished and that banks take securities for loans pursuant to provincial legislation.[70] However, the 2007 amendments to the *Bank Act* contain the special security provisions with a few minor changes, so the special security is likely to be a part of the business of banking for another few years. Since banks increasingly take security pursuant to provincial legislation for loans because that legislation is easier to understand and enforce, a brief overview of the special security provisions is sufficient.[71]

The *Bank Act* permits banks to lend money to any wholesale or retail dealer in various natural products, including agriculture, aquaculture, forestry, mining and fishing, and to borrowers engaged in those busi-

---

67 S.C. 1890, c. 31.
68 This name is taken from the title in the *Bank Act* containing the sections about the special security. It was previously known as a "section 88" and "section 173" security after the sections in which it was found in previous Acts.
69 For broader statements of its economic function, see *Bank of Montreal v. Guaranty Silk Dyeing and Finishing Co.*, [1935] 4 D.L.R. 483 (Ont. C.A.), Martin J.A.; *Landry Pulpwood Co. v. Banque Canadienne Nationale*, [1928] 1 D.L.R. 493 (S.C.C.), Mignault J.; and *Bank of Montreal v. Hall* (1990), 65 D.L.R. (4th) 361 (S.C.C.), LaForest J.
70 Law Commission of Canada, *Modernizing Canada's Secured Transactions Law: The Bank Act Security Provision* (Ottawa: Law Commission of Canada, 2004). See this study for the problems relating to the special security.
71 For a detailed analysis, including the case law, see Ogilvie, above note 19 at c. 22.

nesses, for the purpose of carrying out those businesses, including the purchase of equipment and materials and the purchase and care of animals, fish, seeds, pesticides, fertilizers, feed, and so on.[72] The security may be taken on these, as well as on the finished or marketable products, and must be in writing and signed by or on behalf of the party giving the security.[73] The prescribed forms are set out in the regulations,[74] and descriptions of the property need not be given in any great detail.

The Act sets out certain conditions which must be met before a bank may take a special security: (i) the person giving the security must be the owner of the security document at the time of delivery of the security document or at any time thereafter prior to the release of the security by the bank;[75] (ii) the bank loan must be made at the time the security is taken, that is, the exchange must be contemporaneous;[76] and (iii) when one type of security is exchanged for another, the bank must receive in exchange another security document in relation to the loan.[77] A special security cannot be taken for past indebtedness, only for present indebtedness and for after-acquired property. Third parties are alerted to security for after-acquired indebtedness by virtue of the registration which expressly refers to such.

The legal nature of the security taken by the bank is unclear from the Act, which provides for the nature of the security taken in two convoluted provisions that distinguish the nature of the security taken on the basis of the type of property on which it is taken. For some property, the legal nature of the security is similar to that under a warehouse receipt or bill of lading,[78] but for other property, the security gives a first and preferential lien on the property for the sum secured and the interest thereon.[79] Some courts have likened the special security to a pledge, but others think it is like a chattel mortgage.[80] Essentially, the bank acquires legal title in all present and after-acquired property covered by the security, while the borrower is left in possession and may deal with the property on a day-to-day basis, as if it were a floating charge.

---

72 *Bank Act*, above note 1, s. 427(1) and ss. 425(1) & (2) for definitions. The special security provisions also apply to warehouse receipts and bills of lading: see ss. 435–36. See Ogilvie, *ibid*. at 389–93.
73 *Bank Act*, *ibid*., s. 427(1).
74 Above note 57.
75 *Bank Act*, above note 1, s. 427(2)(a) & (b).
76 *Ibid*., s. 429(1).
77 *Ibid*., s. 429(2).
78 *Ibid*., ss. 427(2)(c); 427(1)(a), (b), (g), (h), (i), (j), and (o).
79 *Ibid*., ss. 427(2)(d); 427(1)(c), (d), (e), (f), (k), (l), (m), (n), nad (p).
80 Ogilvie, above note 19 at 367–70 for the legal authorities.

Thus, a special security appears to have some of the characteristics of a floating charge and of a chattel mortgage, so that it seems best to describe it as a unique type of security whose legal justification is found in the *Bank Act*.

Although the special security is assigned to the bank, it is not the assignment itself that is registered but a notice of intention as prescribed by the regulations, which simply records the borrower's intention to give a special security to the bank.[81] Registration is a prerequisite for the validity of the security.[82] The notice must be provided to the bank by the person giving the security and registered not more than three years prior to the date the security is given.[83] Registration, which constitutes constructive notice of the bank's interest, takes place at a provincial office of the Bank of Canada or its authorized representative,[84] and on payment of a prescribed fee, any person is entitled to have access through an agent to the register to see if the bank has a secured interest on any property.[85] Security taken against certain types of property (for example, aquacultural equipment, agricultural equipment, or forestry equipment affixed to real property) must also be registered in the appropriate land registry or land titles office.[86] Registration of the notice of intention must be made prior to giving the security; otherwise, the bank's interest will be void.[87] Registration may be cancelled by subsequent registration of a certificate of release stating either that the security has been released or that no security was ever taken.[88]

The notice of intention is uninformative; it does not contain the amount borrowed or details of the security taken by the bank, only the name of the person giving the security and the date on which the notice was filed. A searcher learns almost nothing from this document and must rely on the borrower to provide other details voluntarily.

Under the *Bank Act*, a bank that has taken a special security has power to enforce it in the event of non-payment of the loan, failure to care for the property given as the security, any attempt without the bank's consent to dispose of the property, or the seizure of the property covered by

---

81 *Bank Act*, above note 1, ss. 427(4) & (5) for definition of "notice of intention."
82 *Bank of Montreal v. Elgin Co-op. Services* (1983), 3 D.L.R. (4th) 115 at 119–20 (Ont. C.A.), Blair J.A.
83 *Bank Act*, above note 1, s. 427(4)(a).
84 *Ibid.*, ss. 427(4) & (5).
85 *Ibid.*, ss. 427(4)(c) & (d).
86 *Ibid.*, ss. 428(3) & (4) and for fishing vessels, ss. 428(5) & (6).
87 *Ibid.*, s. 427(4)(a).
88 *Ibid.*, ss. 427(4)(b) & (c). The Governor in Council may make regulations concerning the notice system: *ibid.*, s. 427(9).

the security.[89] No prior judicial authorization is required,[90] and the bank may do so using its own officers, employees, or agents.[91] The Act makes no provision for the procedures to be employed prior to and at the time of seizure, but the Supreme Court of Canada has held that reasonable notice of seizure pursuant to provincial legislation need not be given,[92] so it must be concluded that the *Bank Act*'s silence about the seizure process means that a bank is free to take possession by any means short of engaging in criminal conduct under the *Criminal Code*.[93]

Once the bank has seized property covered by a special security, it is permitted to sell all or part of the property, apply the proceeds to the outstanding debt, and return any surplus to the person by whom the security was given.[94] Where the property is perishable a quick sale is permitted; otherwise, sales should be by public auction duly advertised in accordance with the Act.[95] A sale of property vests in the purchaser all the rights and title to the property enjoyed by the person who gave the security at the time the security was given or acquired thereafter.[96] A bank is required to act expeditiously to sell the property after it takes possession[97] and to act honestly and in good faith and to deal with the property in a timely and appropriate manner having regard to the nature of the property in arranging the sale so as to ensure a reasonable price, including giving reasonable notice to the person who gave the security.[98]

Where the property covered by the special security has been manufactured into goods, wares, or merchandise, the bank has the same rights to the manufactured property as it had to the property covered by the special security, including when it is in the manufacturing process.[99] Where a guarantor has satisfied any debt associated with the spe-

---

89   *Ibid.*, s. 427(3).
90   *Banque Nationale du Canada v. Atomic Slipper Co.* (1991), 80 D.L.R. (4th) 134 (S.C.C.).
91   *Canadian Imperial Bank of Commerce v. Sledz*, [1991] 1 W.W.R. 42 (Alta. Master).
92   *Bank of Montreal v. Hall*, above note 69.
93   R.S.C. 1985, c. C-46 as am.
94   *Bank Act*, above note 1, s. 428(7). Courts have enforced independent contracts providing for deficiencies to be made up by the borrower: *Canadian Imperial Bank of Commerce v. Doucette* (1968), 70 D.L.R. (2d) 657 (P.E.I.S.C.); *Canadian Imperial Bank of Commerce v. Roisin* (1971), 17 D.L.R. (3d) 379 (Ont. Dist. Ct.); *Royal Bank of Canada v. Disco Sound Distributors Ltd.* (1986), 73 A.R. 13 (Master).
95   *Bank Act*, *ibid.*, ss. 428(8) and (10).
96   *Ibid.*, s. 428(9).
97   *Ibid.*, s. 428(11).
98   *Ibid.*, s. 428(10).
99   *Ibid.*, s. 428(12). It also has rights to property purchased from insurance proceeds after the original was destroyed: *De Vries v. Royal Bank of Canada* (1975), 58 D.L.R.

cial security, the guarantor is subrogated to all the powers, rights, and authority of the bank under the special security.[100] A bank may assign to any person all or any of its rights in respect of certain categories of property taken, including aquacultural and agricultural equipment.[101]

The *Bank Act* provides for four specific offences in relation to special securities, in addition to the general offence for contravening the Act:[102] (i) making a false statement in a document relating to a special security;[103] (ii) wilfully withholding or disposing of the property covered by the security;[104] (iii) non-compliance with the statutory provisions relating to sale of the property;[105] and (iv) acquiring a special security without giving the loan or advance concurrently.[106]

When there are competing claimants, in addition to the bank, to property covered by a special security, the apparently simple rules about priority break down in practice. The Act vests all the described property in the bank at the time the security is taken or after-acquired and provided the notice of intention is filed in compliance with the Act. The Act further provides that the special security takes priority over all rights subsequently acquired in the property and also over any claims of any unpaid vendors.[107] But the priority does not extend over the claims of an unpaid vendor who had a lien on the property at the time of the acquisition of the special security unless the bank had no knowledge of that lien.[108] A bank is under a general legal duty to search for any charges on property prior to taking a security, but the purpose of the priority for unpaid vendors of the borrower was originally to give a pledgee of documents of title priority over a prior unpaid seller's lien except where the pledgee had notice of the lien. The case law also restricts this provision to a non-consensual unpaid seller's lien for which provision is made in provincial sale of goods law.[109] The overall purpose of the *Bank Act* is to protect the priority of the bank's special security.[110]

(3d) 43 (Ont. H.C.J.), aff'd (1975), 11 O.R. (2d) 583 (C.A.); *Canadian Commercial Bank v. Canadian Imperial Bank of Commerce*, [1988] 3 W.W.R. 607 (B.C.C.A.).
100 *Bank Act*, ibid., s. 428(13).
101 *Ibid.*, ss. 428(14) and 427(1)(i), (j), (k), (l), (m), (n), (o), & (p).
102 *Ibid.*, ss. 980 & 980.1.
103 *Ibid.*, s. 984(1).
104 *Ibid.*, s. 984(2).
105 *Ibid.*, s. 984(3).
106 *Ibid.*, s. 984(4).
107 *Ibid.*, s. 428(1).
108 *Ibid.*, s. 428(2).
109 For expanded discussion and authorities, see Ogilvie, above note 19 at 384–86.
110 *Bank Act*, above note 1, s. 428(2). See also *Royal Bank of Canada v. Sparrow Electric Corp.* (1997), 143 D.L.R. (4th) 385 (S.C.C.).

The Act creates two exceptions to this priority scheme which privileges the special security over other claimants. These exceptions occur in a situation where a bankruptcy order has been made under the *Bankruptcy and Insolvency Act*:[111] (i) claims for employee salaries or other remuneration for a period of three months immediately preceding the making of a bankruptcy order against a business or a farm which has given a special security; and (ii) claims of a producer of agricultural products grown on land leased or owned for the products that were grown on the land and delivered to a manufacturer during the six-month period immediately preceding the making of a bankruptcy order or assignment.[112]

Each province has enacted personal property security legislation, which also makes provision for priorities in the event of a default in repayment of a loan or advance with the result that conflicts between creditors' rights occur when claims are made under both federal and provincial legislation which create different priority schemes. There are hundreds of cases dealing with conflicting claims, and the resulting law is extremely complex and uncertain.[113] If there is any underlying principle, it is for the courts to favour the bank's special security by virtue of the paramountcy of section 91(15) over section 92(13), but even that has been increasingly cast into doubt. The intractability of these problems suggests that the proposal of the Law Commission of Canada to abolish the special security and require banks to register securities under provincial legislation should be reconsidered in the future.

D. PERMITTED INVESTMENTS

Historically, banks have been prohibited from engaging in financial services offered by other financial institutions in the financial services sector and have also been prohibited from owning shares in other corporations in excess of 10 percent of the voting shares of any class of shares. The policy reason was to ensure that excessive economic power was not concentrated in the banking sector. However, in 1991, the *Bank Act* was amended to permit banks to have substantial investments in certain specific entities, which in turn offer various financial services to the public that banks are prohibited from offering directly

---

111 R.S.C. 1985, c. B-3 as am.
112 *Bank Act*, above note 1, ss. 428(7)(a) & (b).
113 Ogilvie, above note 19 at 382–89 and any standard personal property security text.

themselves. After these amendments, the largest banks in Canada acquired substantial investments in trust companies and stock brokerages, as well as in other companies as permitted by the Act. After the 2001 amendments to the Act permitting bank holding companies to own substantial investments in various financial institutions, including banks, the corporate structures of the major banks were reorganized again into the financial groups that presently exist. Thus, it may be said that banks are also engaged indirectly in, or are closely associated with, various other types of financial services historically prohibited to them. The statutory provisions regulating these activities, set out in Part IX of the Act, are complex and beyond the scope of this text. However, a brief overview of the main provisions should suffice here.

Banks are permitted to acquire control in a substantial investment only in certain expressly permitted entities, including a bank, a bank holding company, a trust and loan company, an insurance company, an insurance holding company, a securities company, or a cooperative credit society,[114] as well as certain other entities such as those involved in providing services exclusively to the bank or any member of the bank's group.[115] The Act makes provision for a number of restrictions on such acquisitions, of which the most important is the restriction on purchasing entities that engage in accepting deposit liabilities if their other activities include activities in which banks are not permitted to engage in directly such as fiduciary or insurance activities.[116] Banks require approvals from both the Minister of Finance and the Superintendent of Financial Institutions for certain acquisitions such as trust, loan or insurance companies,[117] but are permitted to acquire a substantial investment for brief periods of time in situations where they temporarily acquire control while engaging in otherwise legal business, for example, indirectly through acquiring another entity, in loan workouts, or in security interest realizations.[118] In addition, the *Bank Act* places limits on the value of all investments and interests acquired by a bank in relation to its total portfolio,[119] real property holdings,[120] shareholdings,[121]

---

114 *Bank Act*, above note 1, ss. 466(1), 468(1), and 464 for definitions and Entity Member of Group Regulations, SOR/2002-132.
115 *Bank Act*, ibid., s. 468(2).
116 *Ibid.*, ss. 468(3), (3.1), & (4).
117 *Ibid.*, ss. 468(5), (6), (10), & (11), and 469–70. See also SOR/2003-242; SOR/2001-383.
118 *Bank Act*, ibid., ss. 466(2)–(7), 468(7)–(9) and (12), and 471–74.
119 *Ibid.*, s. 475.
120 *Ibid.*, s. 476.
121 *Ibid.*, s. 477.

and aggregate value in relation to its regulatory capital,[122] in order to ensure that the solvency of a bank and the security of its depositors' interests are not jeopardized. Finally, the Act permits the Superintendent to order the divestment of any interests acquired by a bank which, in the opinion of the Superintendent, would jeopardize the solvency of the bank.[123]

The policy undergirding the complex and delicately balanced provisions relating to the investment powers of banks is that of protecting banks from insolvency through unwise direct corporate expansion into areas that might either jeopardize depositors' deposits or might result in what is widely regarded as excessive economic power vested in a handful of large financial institutions. Prudence and competition remain the underlying principles of the financial institutions sector generally.

E. PERMITTED SELF-DEALING

Since 1991, the *Bank Act* has provided that banks may engage only in certain types of transactions with related parties such as directors and officers. The purpose of these provisions is to ensure that a bank does not enter into any transactions with persons who may exercise influence over the bank's affairs. The general approach of Part XI of the Act is to prohibit self-dealing transactions entirely except for specific exceptions. Responsibility for ensuring compliance with Part XI is posited with a bank's conduct review committee of the board that must review all such transactions and report them annually to the Office of the Superintendent of Financial Institutions (OSFI).[124]

Section 489(1) of the Act provides that a bank shall not enter into any transaction with a related party of the bank either directly or indirectly. The definition of a "related party" is extensive but includes a shareholder with a significant interest in any class of shares; a director or "senior officer"[125] of a bank or a body corporate that controls a bank; a spouse or partner or child of a director or senior officer below eighteen years of age; or an entity controlled by any of these persons.[126] The Superintendent may also designate any person as a related party.[127] Pro-

---

122 *Ibid.*, s. 478.
123 *Ibid.*, ss. 479–84.
124 *Ibid.*, s. 195.
125 *Ibid.*, s. 485.1.
126 *Ibid.*, ss. 486(1), (2), (5), (7), & (8).
127 *Ibid.*, ss. 486(3), (4), and (6).

hibited transactions include guarantees; investments in any securities of a related party; or taking a security interest in the securities of the related parties.[128] Loans include deposits, financial leases, conditional sales contracts, repurchase agreements, or any other similar arrangement for obtaining funds on credit.[129]

However, certain related party transactions are permitted: (i) transactions of a nominal or immaterial value as measured by criteria established by the conduct review committee and approved in writing by the Superintendent;[130] (ii) loans, guarantees, and assignments if fully secured by securities of, or guaranteed by, the federal or provincial governments;[131] (iii) deposits by the bank for clearing purposes with a Canadian Payments Association (CPA) direct clearer or clearing group;[132] (iv) loans from the related party;[133] (v) acquisitions of securities guaranteed by the federal or provincial governments;[134] (vi) acquisition of goods for use in the ordinary course of business;[135] (vii) sales of any assets if fully paid for in money and there is an active market for those assets;[136] (viii) leases from and to a related party for use in the ordinary course of business;[137] (ix) any assets from or to a related party of the bank under a sale agreement approved by the minister;[138] (x) written contracts for services provided and used in the ordinary course of business;[139] and (xi) any transactions with the bank holding company or any other related company in the bank group, subject to any order made by the Superintendent.[140]

Loans to related parties are subject to further provisions in the Act. Loans to full-time senior officers should not exceed the greater of twice their annual salary plus $100,000.[141] Loans and other financial services can also be made to senior officers, spouses, partners, and children, on terms more favourable than those offered to the public if approved

---

128 See *ibid.*, ss. 488(1) & (2), and s. 487 for transactions not covered.
129 *Ibid.*, s. 488(3).
130 *Ibid.*, s. 490.
131 *Ibid.*, s. 491.
132 *Ibid.*, s. 492.
133 *Ibid.*, s. 493.
134 *Ibid.*, ss. 494(1)(a) & (b).
135 *Ibid.*, s. 494(1)(c).
136 *Ibid.*, ss. 494(2)–(4).
137 *Ibid.*, s. 494(5).
138 *Ibid.*, ss. 236 and 494(6).
139 *Ibid.*, s. 495.
140 *Ibid.*, ss. 495.1, 495.2, & 495.3.
141 *Ibid.*, ss. 496(1), (2), & (3), and 498.

by the conduct review committee of the bank.[142] Such loans, as well as guarantees or investments in the securities of the related party must be approved by at least two-thirds of the directors present at a meeting of the board of directors.[143] Such loans are subject to various statutory limits, and the aggregate must not exceed 50 percent of the regulatory capital of the bank.[144] The Superintendent of Financial Institutions may exempt a transaction from the legislative requirements.[145]

When deciding whether to enter into a permitted related party transaction, a bank shall take all reasonable steps to obtain full disclosure of the relationship of the party to the bank[146] and may rely on that disclosure in good faith to avoid liability.[147] When a bank enters into a prohibited transaction or another transaction for which the approval of the Superintendent is required without having obtained that approval, the bank shall immediately inform the Superintendent,[148] who may apply for a court order to set aside the transaction or for any other appropriate remedy, and the Superintendent may also make any other order.[149]

F. PROHIBITED BUSINESS

In addition to defining the business and activities in which banks may legally engage in Canada, the *Bank Act* defines the business and activities in which banks may not engage in Canada, again in Part VIII of the Act. This approach of setting out both positively and negatively the business of banking has been employed since the 1871 Act and may have been done to ensure that the discrete activities of other financial institutions such as trust and loan companies or securities or insurance companies were expressly prohibited to banks, to prevent them from entering those other businesses. Prior to the 1980 Act, any engagement in a prohibited activity would have resulted in a finding of *ultra vires*, rendering any contract null and void. However, the 1980 Act has provided for sanctions for banks engaged in such activities, while third parties contracting with such a bank are entitled to rely on the contract

---

142 *Ibid.*, ss. 496(4), (5), & (6), and 501.
143 *Ibid.*, s. 497(1).
144 *Ibid.*, s. 497(2).
145 *Ibid.*, ss. 499–500.
146 *Ibid.*, s. 504(1).
147 *Ibid.*, s. 504(2).
148 *Ibid.*, s. 505.
149 *Ibid.*, s. 506.

or pursue remedies in restitution. The following business and activities are expressly prohibited in banks in Canada.

1) Dealing in Goods, Wares, and Merchandise

Since the nineteenth century, banks have been expressly prohibited from dealing in goods, wares, and merchandise.[150] Although the Act does not define these words, it has been widely assumed that the purpose of this prohibition is to prevent banks in Canada from becoming involved in various commercial and retail enterprises either directly or indirectly through subsidiaries or substantial investments in such enterprises. Courts have consistently made this assumption in cases relating to this provision.[151] The only exception would occur when carrying on a business is related to a permitted banking business, that is, in a receivership or insolvency situation.[152] This prohibition serves to distinguish Canadian banking from banking in a number of other countries, particularly in the European Union, where banks are permitted to own and engage in various commercial and retail activities in addition to banking *per se*.

2) Fiduciary Activities

No bank in Canada may act as an executor, administrator, official guardian, tutor, curator, judicial advisor, or committee of a mentally incompetent person. Nor may a bank act as a trustee for a trust.[153] In short, banks are prohibited from engaging in fiduciary activities. In some senses, banks have always engaged in some fiduciary activities, such as giving financial advice, as the courts have acknowledged,[154] but the main concern of this provision is to ensure that they do not directly engage in the fiduciary activities associated with trust companies. Moreover, the Act does permit banks to be involved in fiduciary activities in various indirect ways,[155] including offering certain services in the fiduciary component that are expressly permitted, such as RRSPs and RRIFs,[156] and presumably also offering advice in relation to

---

150 *Ibid.*, s. 410(2).
151 *Ontario Bank v. McAllister* (1910), 43 S.C.R. 338; *Ball v. Royal Bank of Canada* (1915), 26 D.L.R. 385 (S.C.C.). See Ogilvie, above note 19 at 340–42 for authorities.
152 See Chapter 4, Section M.
153 *Bank Act*, above note 1, s. 412.
154 See Chapter 6, Section H.
155 *Bank Act*, above note 1, s. 409(2)(c); see Section D, above in this chapter.
156 *Bank Act*, *ibid.*, Part IX; see Section D, above in this chapter.

the various businesses and activities in which banks are permitted to engage by the Act.[157] Thus, the prohibition on fiduciary activities may be relatively narrow, to prohibit those activities expressly enumerated above and directly competing *qua* bank with trust companies.

3) Taking Deposits

Deposit taking has been a core business of banks for as long as banks have existed. However, the *Bank Act* restricts this business in certain ways for the purpose of ensuring that depositors' interests are as secure as Parliament has legislated them to be. Thus, banks are permitted to accept deposits in Canada only if they are members of the Canada Deposit Insurance Corporation or if they have otherwise been authorized pursuant to the *CDIC Act* to accept deposits[158] without being a CDIC member.[159] A non-CDIC-member deposit taker is required to ensure that the ratio of the total sum of all deposits of less than $150,000 to the total amount of all deposits on each day shall not be more than 1 percent, so as to ensure the security of small depositors' deposits.[160] Such a deposit taker is also required to give a prospective depositor notice in writing that its deposits are not CDIC insured prior to an account being opened[161] and to post notices in all branches to the public to that effect,[162] as well as in any advertisements.[163] Such a deposit taker is prohibited from sharing premises with a CDIC-insured institution,[164] and if it carries on business on premises adjacent to a CDIC-insured institution, it must clearly indicate to customers that its business and premises are separate.[165]

4) Dealing in Securities

Banks are prohibited from dealing in securities except to the extent permitted by the regulations.[166] The regulations prohibit banks from se-

---

157 As set out above in this chapter.
158 *Canada Deposit Insurance Corporation Act*, R.S.C. 1985, c. C-3, ss. 2 and 26.03(1) [*CDIC Act*].
159 *Bank Act*, above note 1, ss. 413(1), (4), & (5).
160 *Ibid.*, ss. 413(3) and s. 413(2) for deposits less than $150,000.
161 *Ibid.*, s. 413.1(1) and Notices of Uninsured Deposits Regulations, SOR/99-388.
162 *Bank Act*, *ibid.*, s. 413.1(2)(a).
163 *Ibid.*, s. 413.1(2)(b).
164 *Ibid.*, ss. 413.3(1) & (2).
165 *Ibid.*, s. 413.3(3).
166 *Ibid.*, s. 415.

curities dealings consisting of primary distributions of shares; secondary market trading; primary distributions of debt obligations of bodies corporate; and acting as a selling agent in the distribution of mutual funds.[167] They are, however, permitted to deal in securities on their own behalf; distribute debt obligations on behalf of a government, a public utility, or an international agency of which Canada is a member or which are money market securities; distribute shares of the bank; and act as selling agent for mutual funds, where the dealings relate to corporate sponsored accounts for pension plans, retirement plans, or other similar capital accumulation plans.[168] In addition, they are permitted to have a substantial investment in securities companies pursuant to Part IX of the Act.[169]

5) Dealing in Insurance

Banks are prohibited from engaging in insurance except to the extent permitted by the *Bank Act* or the regulations.[170] The Act permits banks to deal in insurance in two situations: (i) requiring insurance as a security for a loan; and (ii) obtaining group insurance for its employees or the employees of any body corporate in which it is permitted to have a substantial interest under Part IX.[171] However, the Act clearly prohibits banks from acting as an agent in placing insurance and from leasing or providing space in any branch in Canada to any person engaged in placing insurance.[172] This underlines the statutory policy of prohibiting banks from becoming involved in any direct competition with the insurance companies. The regulations concerning permitted insurance activities are extensive and detailed, providing for certain types of insurance that may be administered by a bank (credit card, mortgage, travel); how banks may promote permitted insurance businesses; and additional provisions defining the scope of permitted and prohibited activities.[173] They are also permitted to have a substantial investment in insurance companies pursuant to Part IX of the Act.[174]

---

167 Securities Dealing Restrictions (Banks) Regulations, SOR/92-279, s. 2.
168 *Ibid.*, ss. 3(1) & (2). For a complete list, see the regulation.
169 See Section D, above in this chapter.
170 *Bank Act*, above note 1, ss. 416(1) and (3).
171 *Ibid.*, s. 412(4).
172 *Ibid.*, s.416(2).
173 Insurance Business (Banks and Bank Holding Companies) Regulations, SOR/92-330 as am. See these regulations for the full details.
174 See Section D, above in this chapter.

6) Leasing

Banks are prohibited from engaging in Canada in any personal property leasing activity in which a financial leasing entity is not permitted to engage.[175] The activities of such entities are restricted to the actual leasing of certain types of personal property. These entities are precluded from directing customers or potential customers to particular dealers in leased property.[176] The regulations are detailed, but their underlying purpose is clearly to prohibit banks or financial leasing entities in which they have a substantial interest from engaging in motor vehicle leasing or personal household property leasing, thereby competing with those industries.[177]

7) Creating Security Interests

Until the 2001 Act, banks were permitted to create security interests on bank property only in restricted circumstances, for example, for obligations to the Bank of Canada or CIDC, or with the approval of the Superintendent of Financial Institutions.[178] However, since 2001, the directors of a bank have been permitted to establish policies in relation to the creation of security interests in property of the bank to secure obligations of the bank and the acquisition by the bank of beneficial interests in property that is subject to security interests.[179] The Superintendent may direct a bank to amend its policies,[180] and the Governor in Council may make regulations.[181] In the absence of regulations to date, it is impossible to say what types of security interests might be given over bank property, but it is very likely that these would be as limited as in the past, given the continuing requirement to ensure solvency and the protection of deposits. The fact that the *Bank Act* since 2001 expressly continues to permit security interests to be created in favour of the Bank of Canada and CDIC may confirm that view.[182]

---

175 *Bank Act*, above note 1, s. 417.
176 *Ibid.*, s. 464(1) "financial leasing entity."
177 Financial Leasing Entity Regulations, SOR/2001-389.
178 Previous version of s. 419 of *Bank Act*, which was in force until 1 January 2004.
179 *Bank Act*, above note 1, s. 419(1).
180 *Ibid.*, ss. 419(2) & (3).
181 *Ibid.*, s. 419.1.
182 *Ibid.*, s. 419.2.

8) Receivers

Banks may not grant to any person the right to appoint a receiver or a receiver and manager of the property or business of the bank.[183] The reason is that when banks are in financial difficulty, OSFI, CDIC, and other regulators are statutorily responsible for such banks.[184]

9) Entering Partnerships

Banks are not permitted to be a general partner in a limited partnership or a partner in a general partnership,[185] that is, they may not enter into any partnership in which they will be subject to unlimited joint and several liability.[186] The purpose of this prohibition is, again, to protect assets, especially deposits, against possible insolvency. Banks frequently enter various agreements with other financial institutions in relation to large loans, but these do not entail taking on unlimited liability, as prohibited by the Act.

G. CONCLUSION

As this chapter has shown, the banks continue to be closely regulated pursuant to the *Bank Act* in relation to the types of businesses and activities in which they may engage and the extent to which they may do so. The *Bank Act* defines banking business both positively and negatively and grants considerable discretion to the Governor in Council and the Office of the Superintendent of Financial Institutions (OSFI) to regulate through regulations and supervision. Banking has always been inherently a dynamic enterprise driven by the needs of the economy, the business community, and the ingenuity of bankers themselves to serve those needs. The *Bank Act* recognizes this fact and strives to strike a balance between the risks involved in a dynamic enterprise and the equally important need to protect depositors' and shareholders' interests, in the best interests overall of Canada.

---

183 *Ibid.*, s. 420.
184 Chapter 3, Sections C and F, and Chapter 4, Section M.
185 *Bank Act*, above note 1, s. 421(1).
186 *Ibid.*, s. 421(2).

CHAPTER 6

BANK AND CUSTOMER RELATIONSHIPS

A. INTRODUCTION

The legal relationship of bank and customer comes into being when a customer opens a bank account, that is, enters a legally binding contract with a bank. The account agreement is typically only the starting point, however, for a long-term relationship during which the bank will provide various services for the customer either encompassed by the account agreement or subject to additional contracts for those specific services, such as loans, safety deposit boxes, mortgages, foreign exchange transactions, or credit cards. Thus, there are really many relationships in law between a single customer and a bank regulated by the many contracts into which they might enter during the duration of their dealings with one another. In addition, and in common with other relationships based on contract, tortious and fiduciary obligations might also be implied into the relationship from time to time, such as when a bank is performing any contractual service for the customer, giving advice to the customer, or giving a reference to a third party in relation to the customer. The bank and customer relationship is multifaceted in law and in practice.

Until the late twentieth century, the contract opening a bank account was found as much in the common law as on paper. Historically, account agreements were simple and understood against the common law background of numerous implied terms. However, the account agreement is now a relatively sophisticated and lengthy standard form contract, in contrast to the earlier contracts consisting of eight or nine short terms replicated on the "signature card" or even on a chequebook cover. The terms of the contract today are drawn from three sources: the express terms contained in the agreement executed by bank and customer, the terms implied by the common law, and the terms implied by operation of the *Bank Act*, which increasingly over the past two decades has made provision for the regulation of the contract in relation to certain matters of a political origin.

This chapter and the next two chapters (Chapters 7 and 8) will focus on the account agreement and its operation, and subsequent chapters will address some of the other contractually based services provided to customers by banks but regulated by their own contracts, separate from the account agreement.[1]

B. THE "CUSTOMER"

Any person, including a corporate person in law, has the potential to be a "customer"[2] of a bank, and the absence of legal capacity to enter into contracts generally is not a bar to entering into an account contract with a bank. Section 437(1) of the *Bank Act* provides that a bank may without the intervention of any other person accept a deposit from any person whether or not qualified by law to enter into contracts. This provision is widely regarded as relating primarily to children below the age of legal majority, but the banking practice of requiring a parent to be a joint account holder with a child is contemplated within the permissive use of the word "may" in the section. In fact, it remains the case that banks are free in law to decide whether or not to enter into an account agreement with anyone so applying; to determine whether or not they will provide a particular service to anyone with whom they have an account agreement; and to provide a service only on the payment of some remuneration for that service.

The fundamental principle of the common law that parties are free to decide with whom they enter into contracts remains in the banking context, notwithstanding the 2001 amendments to the *Bank Act* requiring banks to open retail accounts for certain prescribed persons, since

---

1   See Chapters 9, 10, & 11.
2   The word "customer" continues to be used in legal literature, although increasingly bankers refer to "clients." For legal purposes, there appears to be no distinction between the two words, and I will continue to use "customer" here.

the regulations continue to permit banks to exercise their discretion in this regard. The *Bank Act* states that a bank shall open a retail deposit account for certain individuals[3] and shall not require either an initial minimum deposit or the maintenance of a minimum balance.[4] In addition, low fee retail deposit accounts are authorized for such persons.[5] These amendments were intended to ensure that low-income individuals would have access to banking services in Canada.

Although any person, regardless of age or financial value, may be permitted to enter into an account agreement with a bank, banks are also now required to know their customers for certain statutory purposes, in particular, pursuant to the *Proceeds of Crime (Money Laundering) and Terrorist Financing Act*.[6] The guidelines for implementing the provisions of this legislation place a duty on all financial institutions to ensure that they get and maintain accurate information records about their customers and, when required, to disclose such information to various state authorities on request.[7]

At common law, the definition of who may be a customer of a bank has also arisen in relation to other issues, in addition to legal and financial capacity to enter into a contract and identification for the purpose of detecting criminal activities. Any person with whom a bank has entered into an account agreement is clearly a "customer," and the contractual relationship comes into existence when the contract is executed, although there are as yet no transactions in the account.[8] An overdraft in the account is immaterial to the existence of the legal relationship.[9]

However, the definition of a customer at common law has been expanded beyond any person who has entered an account agreement to include other persons for whom a bank has provided some service, thereby entailing possible legal liability in relation to that service. In *Woods v. Martins Bank*,[10] the bank was found liable for breach of a duty

---

3   *Bank Act*, S.C. 1991, c. 46, s. 448.1(1).
4   *Ibid.*, ss. 448.1(2) & (3) and Access to Basic Banking Services Regulations, SOR/2003-184 for the details of what is required to open an account and the grounds on which a bank may refuse to do so.
5   *Ibid.*, s. 448.2.
6   S.C. 2000, c. 17 as am.
7   See generally Alison Manzer, *A Guide to Canadian Money Laundering Legislation* (Markham: LexisNexis Canada, 2005).
8   *Lacave & Co. v. Credit Lyonnais*, [1897] 1 Q.B. 148; *Ladbroke & Co. v. Todd* (1914), 19 Com. Cas. 256; *Great Western Railway v. London & County Banking Co.*, [1901] A.C. 414 (H.L.).
9   *Clarke v. London & County Banking Co.*, [1897] 1 Q.B. 552.
10 [1959] 1 Q.B. 55 (Leeds Assizes) [*Woods*].

of care in giving poor investment advice prior to the time when an account agreement was opened, so it may be concluded that whenever a bank offers a banking service to any person with whom it has no account contract, the bank is still responsible for performing that service to a legally acceptable standard, and the recipient of the service is a "customer," although not a contracting party with the bank.[11]

The question of who is a customer becomes more complicated when the person opening an account is not doing so in their own name. In some situations, the actual customer is clear, for example, a parent opening an account for a child who is identified as the customer or a local bank opening an overseas account for a customer going abroad who is also identified as the customer.[12] Less clear, however, are situations where an agent opens an account in the agent's name for an undisclosed principal or where a person opens an account in a name other than their own, aided by stolen or forged identification. In the former case, the general law of principal and agent would suggest that the customer is the principal, but in the latter, it is most likely that the customer is the actual person who opened the account and not the person in whose name the account was opened.[13] *Consensus ad idem* is required for account contracts as for any other contract, and in both situations, the decision to open the account and agreement to the terms of the account is found in the principal and in the rogue, respectively.

The net result of these cases is that a "customer" may be defined as anyone who has entered into a contractual relationship with a bank but also may be anyone for whom a bank has performed a banking service either on a contractual basis or in situations where a tortious or fiduciary obligation may arise.

C. THE BANK AND CUSTOMER RELATIONSHIP

The characterization of the bank and customer relationship as one of contract and the special nature of that contract as a contract of loan

---

11   The *Bank Act*, above note 3, now clearly contemplates such occasional services, as shown by the 2001 amendment requiring banks to cash Government of Canada cheques for non-customers: s. 458.1.
12   *Rowlandson v. National Westminster Bank*, [1978] 1 W.L.R. 798 (Ch. D.).
13   *Stoney Stanton Supplies (Coventry) Ltd. v. Midland Bank Ltd.*, [1966] 2 Lloyds Rep. 373 (C.A.); *Marfani & Co. v. Midland Bank Ltd.*, [1968] 1 W.L.R. 956 (C.A.).

dates from the foundation case of *Foley v. Hill*[14] decided by the House of Lords in 1848. Once the contract was characterized as a loan, banks were able to treat funds deposited with them as their own to use for lending purposes, that is, modern banking was established. Prior to *Foley v. Hill*, the legal nature of the bank and customer relationship was unclear. If the deposit of funds was one of bailment, then the bank would have been obliged to return the very funds deposited; if the deposit constituted the bank an agent, it would have been obliged to follow the customer's instructions as to their use; if the deposit was a trust, then the uses to which a bank might put the funds would be restricted. But as a loan, property in the funds is transferred to the bank and it need only return an equivalent amount when repaying the loan and is free to use the funds as it likes.

In *Foley*, a customer deposited funds in an account at an interest rate of 3 percent per annum. When the bank did not credit interest to the account, the customer started an action in Chancery for an accounting and argued that he was either the beneficiary of a trust or the bank's principal in relation to the funds. The House of Lords found that the customer could not succeed because the relationship was neither fiduciary nor one of agency, and that his action should be recommenced in common law as an action for debt for the amount due to him from the bank. In *Foley*, the House of Lords also acknowledged that a bank can occasionally be a fiduciary but that contract was the proper characterization of the core relationship.

According to *Foley v. Hill*, the contract of loan is between the bank as debtor and the customer as creditor. When deposited, the property in the funds is transferred to the debtor and the bank can use them as its own. The only requirement is that an equivalent amount of money be returned to the creditor on demand, together with any interest promised to be paid on the loan. In contrast to an ordinary contract of loan, it is the creditor who must seek out the debtor to demand repayment of the loan.[15] Moreover, the loan is always unsecured, so that in an insolvency of a bank, the customer is unlikely to receive much, if any, return of their deposits, but for the deposit insurance scheme operated by CDIC.[16] The loan is further distinguished from other loans insofar

---

14 (1848), 2 H.L. Cas. 28, 9 E.R. 1002. See also *Space Investments Ltd. v. CIBC Trust Co. (Bahamas) Ltd.*, [1986] 3 All E.R. 75 (P.C.).
15 *Joachimson v. Swiss Bank Corp.*, [1921] 3 K.B. 110 (C.A.) [*Joachimson*]. See also *Walton v. Mascall* (1844), 13 M. & W. 72, 47 E.R 1144 (Ch.); *Bradford Old Bank Ltd. v. Sutcliffe*, [1918] 2 K.B. 833 (C.A.); *Isaacs v. Barclays Bank Ltd.*, [1943] 2 All E.R. 682 (K.B.).
16 See Chapter 3, Section F.

as the creditor neither determines the purposes to which the loan is put by the debtor,[17] nor is entitled to receive any share of the profits earned by the bank from the use of the funds deposited. Should the debtor bank decline to repay the loan, the customer's action is for debt.

In the mid-nineteenth century, when *Foley v. Hill* was decided, banks did not use written agreements to the extent that they now do to regulate their relationship with their customers, and this is likely reflected in the emphasis in the decision on loan as the essence of the relationship. Although contemporary bank and customer relations are largely now reduced to contract, they still build that contract on the debtor and creditor analysis in *Foley*.[18]

D. THE CONTRACT

The general legal background against which the standard-form account agreement operates is the large volume of Anglo-Canadian common law built up over the past two centuries, some of which is reflected in the express account agreements in daily use. However, much of the common law is not reflected in the account agreement, so it must be implied into the bank and customer contract. The contract, then, is partly express and partly implied from both the common law and the *Bank Act*. The account contracts used by Canadian banks, as well as other financial institutions that engage in deposit taking, are very similar and applicable not only to individuals but also to joint account holders, corporations, unincorporated associations, and partnerships with small variations. Like all standard-form contracts today, they favour the *proferens*, the bank, at the expense of the customer, and persons who wish to have access to banking services have little real choice in the marketplace generally. In contrast to the United Kingdom, where the bank and customer relationship is also governed by a voluntary industry code, the *Good Banking Code of Practice*,[19] there is no such code operating in Canada to supplement the express contracts.

---

17 *Re Agra and Masterman's Bank* (1866), 36 L.J. Ch. 151.
18 See generally *Bank of Ottawa v. Hood* (1908), 42 S.C.R. 231; *Everly v. Dunkley* (1912), 27 O.L.R. 414 (Div. Ct.); *Royal Trust Co. v. Molsons Bank* (1912), 27 O.L.R. 441 (H.C.J.); *Sheppard v. First International Bank of Sweetgrass*, [1924] 1 D.L.R. 582 (Alta. S.C.A.D.); *Corporation Agencies Ltd. v. Home Bank*, [1927] A.C. 318 (P.C.); *British Columbia (Attorney-General) v. Royal Bank of Canada*, [1937] S.C.R. 459; *Dassen Gold Resources Ltd. v. Royal Bank of Canada*, [1997] 9 W.W.R. 658 (Alta. C.A.).
19 4th ed. (London: British Bankers' Association, 2001). See also Denis Rosenthal, "The 'Good Banking Code of Practice' in the United Kingdom" (1995) 10 B.F.L.R. 239.

1) Statutory Requirements

The *Bank Act* provisions relating to the bank and customer relationship both establish part of the general background in law of the express contract and require certain matters to be incorporated into those express contracts. First, the Act permits banks to accept deposits from any person whether or not that person is qualified by law to enter contracts, provided there are no prior claimants to those funds.[20] Secondly, any bank charges for keeping accounts must be disclosed by the express agreement on the opening of the account, in advertisements about accounts, and whenever the charges are changed throughout the operation of the account.[21] This disclosure must include the interest rate, how the rate is calculated, and the amount of any other charges for services provided within the account. Thirdly, a bank is required to provide to a customer a copy of the account agreement when an account is opened.[22] Fourthly, banks are required to open low fee and no-minimum-balance accounts for low-income individuals who can satisfy certain identification requirements set out in the regulations.[23] Fifthly, banks are required to disclose all borrowing costs, including the interest or discount rate, method of calculation, and any other costs in relation to loans at the time of the loan and in any advertising.[24] Account overdrafts are characterized as loans in law,[25] as well, of course, as lines of credit granted on account opening. Such disclosure is also required in relation to credit cards.[26]

Sixthly, banks are required to establish internal customer complaints procedures and to provide information in writing to customers

---

20 *Bank Act*, above note 3, ss. 437(1) & (2).
21 *Ibid.*, ss. 349.1–448 and Disclosure of Charges (Banks) Regulations, SOR/92-324; Disclosure of Charges (Authorized Foreign Banks) Regulations, SOR/99-278; Disclosure of Interest (Banks) Regulations, SOR/92-321; and Disclosure of Interest (Authorized Foreign Bank) Regulations, SOR/99-272. For the statutory exceptions where existing account holders open an account by telephone, see *Bank Act, ibid.*, ss. 445(3), (4), (5), & (6) and Disclosure on Account Opening by Telephone Request (Banks) Regulations, SOR/2001-472 and Disclosure on Account Opening by Telephone Request (Authorized Foreign Banks) Regulations, SOR/2001-471.
22 *Bank Act, ibid.*, s. 445(1)(a). A bank is also obliged to make various disclosures when opening an account in relation to registered products (RRSP, RRIF) as well as to make ongoing disclosures about charges: *ibid.*, s. 448.3.
23 *Ibid.*, ss. 448.1 & 448.2 and for regulations, above note 4.
24 *Ibid.*, ss. 449–54 and Cost of Borrowing (Banks) Regulations, SOR/2001-101; Cost of Borrowing (Authorized Foreign Bank) Regulations, SOR/2002-262.
25 Chapter 7, Section C.
26 *Bank Act*, above note 3, ss. 452(1) & (2).

about those procedures and how to contact both the Ombudsman for Banking Services and Investments (OBSI) and the Financial Consumer Agency of Canada (FCAC). Banks typically include that information as a term of the account contract, but are also required to provide the information by brochures and on a website, and to send such to any person who so requests in a written form.[27] Seventhly, a bank may not charge or receive any sum for the provision of products or services unless made by an express agreement with the customer or by court order.[28] Eighthly, maintaining a minimum credit balance may not be a condition for a loan to a customer except by express agreement.[29] Ninthly, banks are required to cash Government of Canada cheques without making a charge for doing so, provided the individual can satisfy stipulated identification requirements.[30]

Ninthly, banks are prohibited from coercing a customer into obtaining a product or service from the bank or its affiliates or another person identified by the bank as a condition for obtaining any other product or service from the bank unless that product or service is offered on more favourable terms.[31] A bank may require that a product or service offered by another person meets with the bank's approval, which shall not be withheld unreasonably.[32] Banks are required to disclose this prohibition on tied selling to their customers in plain language by an express statement available at the branch, on all its websites, and any other points of service.[33] Although the provision does not make explicit reference to accounts, accounts appear to fall within it.[34]

Tenthly, the *Bank Act* requires banks to give customer and public notice of an intention to close any branch at which it opens retail accounts and disburses cash to customers.[35] Notice must also be given to the FCAC at least four months prior to the proposed closure date for

---

27   Ibid., ss. 455, 455.1, & 456 and Complaint Information (Banks) Regulations, SOR/2001-371; Complaint Information (Authorized Foreign Banks) Regulations, SOR/2001-370.
28   *Bank Act*, ibid., s. 457.
29   Ibid., ss. 458(1), (2), & (3).
30   Ibid., ss. 458(4) & (5), and 458.1. The Governor in Council may make regulations about cheque hold periods: ibid., s. 458.2
31   Ibid., ss. 459.1(1), (2), & (3), and 459.5.
32   Ibid., s. 459.1(4).
33   Ibid., ss. 459.1(4.1), (4.2), & 5.
34   At this stage, it should also be noted that the *Bank Act* permits the Governor in Council to make regulations relating to the protection of customer information, but none have been made to date: ibid., s. 459.
35   Ibid., s. 459.2.

an urban branch and six months for a rural branch.³⁶ The regulations concerning notice are detailed and designed to ensure maximum publicity not only to affected customers but also to the community in which the branch is located. The FCAC is permitted to require the bank to hold a public meeting to discuss the proposed closure, but whatever the outcome of that meeting, the bank remains legally entitled to close any branch it wishes to close. It would appear that the purpose of the meeting is to permit local pressure to be brought to bear on the question with possible outcomes of a reversal of the decision to close or the provision of alternative banking arrangements either through an ABM or a visiting banking facility or sale of the branch to another financial institution. The underlying goal is to ensure that every potential customer has access to a branch of any financial institution within a travelling distance of ten kilometres.³⁷

Eleventhly, when a customer dies, a bank is required to transmit any deposit or any property held as security or for safekeeping to the appropriate person as identified by an affidavit and either a will or other testamentary instrument or grant of probate or administration, and the bank may refuse to do so until it receives documentation it regards as appropriate.³⁸ Twelfthly, banks are required to make all disclosures of information regarding their products and services and any policies in that regard to the public as required by the regulations.³⁹ No such regulations have been made yet by the Governor in Council.

Thirteenthly, the Act makes provision for unclaimed balances in an account. Where no transaction has taken place and no statement of account has been requested or acknowledged by a customer for ten years from the day of the last transaction or communication or, in the case of a fixed term deposit from the day of termination, then the bank will pay to the Bank of Canada by 31 December in each year the amount of the deposit, together with any interest earned on it. The bank is thereby discharged from all liability.⁴⁰ The person entitled to receive payment may request it from the Bank of Canada, which is obliged to pay over the funds received, together with information to identify the customer and interest calculated in such manner as the Minister of Finance determines for a period not exceeding ten years from the day

---

36 Notice of Branch Closure (Banks) Regulations, SOR/2002-104.
37 Significant numbers of bank branches have been closed in recent years, mitigated somewhat in rural areas by the willingness of cooperatives and *caisses populaires* to provide alternatives in those affected areas.
38 *Bank Act*, above note 3, s. 460.
39 *Ibid.*, s. 459.4.
40 *Ibid.*, ss. 438(1), (2), and (2.1).

on which the amount was received by the Bank of Canada.[41] Prior to remitting the funds to the Bank of Canada, the bank is required to mail to the deposit holder at the last recorded address or electronic address if designated by the person, a notice that the amount is unpaid.[42] This notice is to be given during the month of January following the first two-year period and at the end of the first five-year period, and at the end of the first nine-year period, as well as at the time of termination for a fixed term deposit.[43]

Finally, banks with equity in excess of $1 billion are required to publish annually public accountability statements describing their contributions to the Canadian economy and society, and such statements are to be disclosed to the public through various media.[44] This requirement was first introduced in the 2001 amendments for the purpose of requiring banks to justify themselves to Canadian consumers as good corporate citizens.

2) Express Terms

The standard form contracts typically used by Canadian banks to open accounts have changed since the late 1990s from account agreements to financial service agreements, that is, they typically cover various other services provided to customers who open accounts. In the past, some of these services were regulated by separate contracts, and others were entered against the background of the common law. A typical agreement today is still primarily about account operation but may also provide for fixed term deposits and GICs, safety deposit box rentals, overdraft protection, and foreign currency transactions. It will also make provision for traditional paper based transactions, as well as electronic transactions.[45]

Agreements currently in use normally contain provisions relating to the following matters: (i) agreement to open various accounts and to permit funds to be deposited in those accounts; (ii) a hold funds

---

41 *Ibid.*, ss. 438(3), (4), & (5).
42 *Ibid.*, s. 439(1).
43 *Ibid.*, s. 439(2). The notice must also state that the funds will be transferred to the Bank of Canada and give contact information to the Bank: *ibid.*, s. 439(3).
44 *Ibid.*, s. 459.3 and Public Accountability Statements Regulations, SOR/2002-133.
45 For surveys of current agreement issues, see M.H. Ogilvie, "Banker and Customer Revisited" (1986) 65 Can. Bar Rev. 3; "Banker and Customer: The Five Year Review, 1985–1990" (1991) 7 B.F.L.R. 171; "Banker and Customer: The Five Year Review, 1990–1995" (1997) 13 B.F.L.R. 359; "Banker and Customer: The Five Year Review, 1995–2000" (2001) 16 B.F.L.R. 231.

policy in relation to cheques or other instruments deposited in an account;[46] (iii) permission to the customer to access funds in the account by cheques or withdrawals of cash in person or electronically, provided there are funds or an overdraft facility; (iv) sole responsibility of the customer for cheques, passbooks, statements, cards, and PINs and a requirement that customers immediately inform the bank of any loss, fraud, or forgery in relation to these; (v) a provision about how countermand or "stop-payment" orders are to be made and allocation of responsibility in fulfilling an order; (vi) a statement about the conclusive nature of bank records; (vii) provisions about bank errors or bank system malfunctions; (viii) interest calculation and payment; (ix) agreement to provide regular statements of account and an account verification clause binding on the customer; (x) overdraft facilities; (xi) provisions relating to safety deposit boxes; (xii) provisions specific to joint accounts such as authorizations, joint and several liability, and survivorship; (xiii) provisions relating to funds held in trust, relieving the bank from responsibility for the trust;[47] (xiv) set-off rights for the bank among accounts; (xv) provisions for dormant accounts; (xvi) permission from the customer for the bank to employ such agents as it chooses without liability; (xvii) waiver by the customer of presentment, protest, and notice of dishonour on all instruments received by the bank and customer liability for all instruments; (xviii) unilateral changes to the contract by the bank once notice has been sent or posted at a branch; (xix) a unilateral right for the bank to cancel the agreement or refuse to provide any service under it without notice; (xx) waiver by the customer of confidentiality about customer personal and financial information; (xxi) backdating of previously opened accounts to be covered by the most recent contract; (xxii) dispute resolution contact information; and (xxiii) customer liability for all loss and damage, including any resulting from bank acts or omissions.

The standard form contract provisions cover most ordinary transactions within an account and ensure that virtually the entire risk of loss from these transactions is shifted to the customer. However, the courts have a lively appreciation of the problems for consumers, who are obliged to enter standard form contracts of adhesion today on terms that are not negotiable in a marketplace where there is virtually no real choice. The courts act to protect consumers either by the implication of terms where possible or by the application of the contract interpreta-

---

46 This disclosure is required by the Cheque Holding Policy Disclosure (Banks) Regulations, SOR/2002-39.
47 The *Bank Act*, above note 3, relieves banks of this duty: ss. 437(3) & (4).

tion rules of strict construction and *contra proferentem* to the express terms of these contracts, as well as general contract principles such as unconscionability and unreasonableness. Strict construction and *contra proferentem* have been frequently invoked in relation to account verification clauses, which are assimilated with exclusion clauses generally in contract law,[48] and unconscionability and similar doctrines have been invoked to mitigate particularly harsh results of a standard form contract.[49] These will be discussed later in this text. The courts recognize that bank account agreements are classic examples of contracts of adhesion and apply the general principles of contract law to them to prevent any abusive use of superior bargaining power by the banks.[50]

3) Implied Terms

The four common law implied terms in relation to the bank and customer relationship are today self-evident. Yet each one is a convenient topic within which numerous principles of banking law still applicable may be grouped for analysis. First, a bank is obliged to honour cheques and other payment instructions from customers and repay deposits.[51] Secondly, a bank is obliged to collect cheques and other instruments on a customer's behalf.[52] Thirdly, a bank is obliged to render statements of account to a customer or on the demand of the customer.[53] Fourthly, a bank is obliged to maintain secrecy in relation to a customer's affairs.[54]

The common law also implied certain reciprocal duties owed by the customer to the bank. First, a customer is obliged to take reasonable care in giving instructions so as not to mislead the bank or facilitate forgery or fraud.[55] Secondly, a customer is obliged to inform a bank as soon as it knows that a forged or fraudulent instrument is to be or has been presented.[56] Thirdly, a customer may be obliged to verify the accuracy of an account within a reasonable period of time, subject to

---

48 See Chapter 8, Section E.
49 Chapter 6, Section H(3).
50 See any standard contract law textbook.
51 *Joachimson*, above note 15 and Chapter 8, Section C.
52 *Joachimson*, ibid. and Chapter 8, Section D.
53 *Devaynes v. Noble; Clayton's Case* (1816), 1 Mer. 572, 35 E.R. 781 (H.L.) and Chapter 8, Section E.
54 *Tournier v. National Provincial & Union Bank of England*, [1924] 1 K.B. 461 (C.A.) and Chapter 8, Section F.
55 Chapter 8, Section C(1).
56 *Ibid.*

an account verification clause.⁵⁷ Fourthly, a bank is relieved from its duty of secrecy where the customer's affairs are such that a bank may be obliged by operation of law to make disclosure to the appropriate state authorities.⁵⁸

In contrast to the standard form account contracts currently in use, the common law balanced the duties owed by the bank and customer to one another. The common law conceptualized the relationship as essentially reciprocal and mutual in nature, with duties that were complementary and correlative.⁵⁹ Indeed, as the recent reluctance of both the Supreme Court of Canada and the House of Lords to impose the duty on the customer of verifying statements of accounts in the absence of an account verification clause demonstrated,⁶⁰ the common law still aspires to balance the duties of the parties where the contract does not.⁶¹

Moreover, there is also some support in the common law for the position that the duties of care owed in contractual performance by bank and customer are subject to a duty to take reasonable care in their performance. In *Hilton v. Westminster Bank Ltd.*,⁶² Atkin L.J. stated that in addition to the common law implied terms which he had formulated in *Joachimson v. Swiss Bank Corp.*,⁶³ a bank should exercise reasonable skill and care in performing all banking services. Thus, in the absence of express terms to the contrary in an account agreement, express terms which simply describe a service or function can be made subject to a standard of reasonable care either implicitly in contract or in tort, and the express contract can be supplemented by a standard of reasonableness in contract and tort.⁶⁴ Since the duty of reasonable care in consumer law generally is increasingly approaching a standard of strict

---

57 Chapter 8, Section E.
58 Chapter 8, Section F.
59 *London Joint Stock Bank Ltd. v. MacMillan*, [1918] A.C. 777 at 814 (H.L.), Viscount Haldane and at 814 and 824, Lord Shaw; *Joachimson*, above note 15 at 125–26, Warrington L.J., and at 126–28, Atkin L.J.; *Greenwood v. Martins Bank Ltd.*, [1933] A.C. 51 at 381 (H.L.), Scrutton L.J..
60 *Tai Hing Cotton Mill Ltd. v. Liu Chong Hing Bank Ltd.*, [1985] 2 All E.R. 947 (P.C.) [*Tai Hing*] and *Canadian Pacific Hotels Ltd. v. Bank of Montreal Ltd.* (1987), 40 D.L.R. (4th) 385 (S.C.C.) [*CP Hotels*].
61 In *CP Hotels*, ibid. at 433–34, LaForest J. stated that if the banks want to have very stringent terms in their favour, they should do so expressly in the contract and that no court should otherwise assist them in that regard.
62 (1926), 135 L.T. 358 at 362 (C.A.).
63 *Joachimson*, above note 15.
64 *Tai Hing* and *CP Hotels*, above note 60.

liability,[65] at least in relation to account agreements with consumers, the standard of care in the performance of banking services is likely very high, although there is no explicit banking case law assimilating the standard with strict liability to date.

E. CONTRACT MODIFICATION

The bank and customer contract may be of considerable duration; therefore, the question of whether it may be modified by the bank over time arises. In the first case to consider this question, *Burnett v. Westminster Bank*,[66] the bank gave notice of a change to the original terms on a chequebook cover; the change related to the restriction in the use of those cheques for the account for which they were MICR[67] encoded. The customer attempted to draw the cheque on another account at another branch of the same bank and then countermanded that cheque. The cheque cleared despite the countermand because it was machine-sorted using the MICR code. The customer brought an action for breach of contract and for restoration of the amount of the cheque to the account. The issue was whether the bank had effectively modified the original contract, which permitted cheques to be hand-drawn for any account, by giving notice in this way.[68] Mocatta J. found that a bank can unilaterally change contractual terms by giving reasonable notice but that there was no reasonable notice here because it had never done so before on chequebook covers. The court did not state what would have been reasonable, so it is difficult to assess what would have amounted to reasonable notice. The court did apply the notice cases from the law of contract generally,[69] so it must be assumed that these provide the appropriate rules for assessing the reasonableness of any notice.

Notice is required pursuant to the *Bank Act* for changes in borrowing rates, interest, and service charges,[70] and the statutory require-

---

65 *McMorran v. Dominion Stores* (1977), 74 D.L.R. (3d) 186 at 191 (Ont. H.C.J.), Lerner J. and S.M. Waddams, *Products Liability*, 4th ed. (Toronto: Carswell, 2002) at 67.
66 [1966] 1 Q.B. 742.
67 MICR (Magnetic ink character recognition) refers to the number encoded on the bottom left of all cheques containing the cheque number, bank sorting number, branch number, and account number, which are used to machine-sort cheques for clearing.
68 It was assumed that the customer had no knowledge of the notice for the purposes of the case.
69 *Parker v. South Eastern Railway Co.* (1877), 2 C.P.D. 416 (C.A.).
70 Above notes 21 and 24.

ments include notice by brochures, by post, by posters at a branch, and online, so it must be assumed that these would constitute reasonable notice by operation of the legislation. Moreover, banks now typically include an express term in account agreements backdating the terms of the most recently executed agreement into previous account agreements, and the question becomes whether this amounts to reasonable notice of modification of those previous agreements. Typically, such clauses are not highlighted in any way, nor is it usual practice for bank employees to give express notice of the clauses when the most recent contract is executed.

In *Armstrong, Baum Plumbing & Heating v. Toronto-Dominion Bank*,[71] the customer had over a dozen accounts with the bank prior to opening the account at issue. In relation to the earlier accounts, the agreement permitted the customer to report forgeries without liability, but in the last contract, the customer was also required to have secure accounting procedures in place and report forgeries within the terms of the account reconciliation clause, while the bank was exonerated from virtually all liability and permitted to amend the earlier agreements by the last agreement signed. On learning that a bookkeeper responsible for account reconciliation had forged four cheques, the customer reported this, but the bank refused to accept liability and relied on the last agreement. The issue was which agreement applied, the agreement that opened the accounts on which the forged cheques were drawn or the last one. The customer's inquiry at the time of executing the last agreement about changes was answered negatively, and the bank knew he had relied on that statement and not read the contract prior to execution. The court found that the customer had no notice of the clause backdating the recent contract provisions into the earlier contracts, notwithstanding his signature. A bank must take reasonable steps to bring a contract modification clause to the customer's attention, especially where the customer queries changes. The earlier contract was found applicable, and the bank was in breach of contract and negligent in tort.

The result of this case is that banks cannot rely on a customer's signature alone to enforce a contract modification clause, but rather must take reasonable steps to draw this clause to the customer's attention if later contract terms are to be incorporated into earlier account contracts. The court did not offer suggestions as to what those steps might be. Banks are, therefore, permitted to modify account agreements uni-

---

71 (1994), 15 B.L.R. (2d) 84 (Ont. Gen. Div.), aff'd (1997), 32 B.L.R. (2d) 230 (Ont. C.A.) [*Armstrong, Baum*]. See also *Rancan Fertilizer Systems Inc. v. Lavergne*, [1999] 8 W.W.R. 323 (Man. C.A.) [*Rancan*].

laterally, provided they give the customer reasonable notice, but what is reasonable notice has yet to be established.

F. PROPER LAW OF THE CONTRACT

The *Bank Act* provides that the debt owed by a bank by reason of a deposit in an account is situated at the place where the branch of an account is located[72] and that the debt is repayable at the branch of the account.[73] The proper law applicable to the contract is the law of the jurisdiction of the place of the debt because that is the law with which the contract has the closest connection, although the contract may otherwise provide by an express term identifying the law by which it is to be governed. Where the contract provides for jurisdiction, the courts will enforce that provision.[74] This rule also applies where a customer has two or more accounts with the same bank in two or more jurisdictions. In *Libyan Arab Foreign Bank v. Bankers Trust Co.*,[75] a customer had accounts in London and New York, and the court found that there was one contract governed by English law and the law of New York, respectively, for each of the two accounts.[76] Whether there is one contract in such circumstances or two has been questioned,[77] but regardless of the result, the principle that an account contract is normally governed by the law of the jurisdiction in which the branch of the account is found would apply.

G. TERMINATION OF THE CONTRACT

Account agreements are typically entered into for an indefinite period of time and are often expected to be of considerable duration. Some

---

72 *Bank Act*, above note 3, s. 461(4).
73 *Ibid.*, s. 461(2).
74 *Continental Bank NA v. Aeakos Compania Navierra S.A.*, [1994] 1 Lloyd's Rep. 505 (C.A.).
75 [1988] 1 Lloyd's Rep. 259 (Comm. Ct.).
76 *Sierra Leone Communications Co. Ltd. v. Barclays Bank plc*, [1998] 2 All E.R. 821 (Ch. D.) supports this approach by permitting severance of a contract where part has a closer connection with one country than another.
77 *Libyan Arab Foreign Bank v. Manufacturers Hanover Trust Co. (No. 2)*, [1989] 1 Lloyd's Rep. 608 (Comm. Ct.). American case law also follows the principle that the jurisdiction is the place of the branch: *Vishipco Line v. Chase Manhattan Bank*, 66 F.2d 854 (2d Circ. 1981); *Garcia v. Chase Manhattan Bank, N.A.*, 735 F.2d 645 (2d Circ. 1984); *Wells Fargo Asia Ltd. v. Citibank, N.A.*, 936 F.2d 723 (2d Cir. 1991).

may expressly provide for a termination date, such as a fixed term deposit, but most do not. In the absence of an express agreement as to a termination date, termination may be at any time after the execution of the agreement at the instance of either party or as a result of certain events, such as death, insolvency, or illegality.

A customer may terminate the agreement at any time by demanding that any outstanding funds in the account be paid and by closing the account.[78] The contract may require that the customer give a short period of notice to ensure that outstanding cheques have been cleared, but once notice has been given, a bank is obliged to comply.[79] A customer is responsible for any overdraft in the account prior to closure, and a bank is not responsible for honoring cheques subsequently presented. Where a customer terminates an account and orders that any balance be transferred to another customer, the contract is deemed to be terminated prior to the completion of the transfer by notice to the other customer.[80]

A bank may terminate an account contract unilaterally without the consent of the customer by giving reasonable notice, so as to permit customers to arrange their affairs and avoid any embarrassment resulting from the return of cheques, including potential defamation of the customer's credit reputation.[81] In determining what is reasonable notice, factors to be considered include whether the account has been in persistent overdraft or is being operated fraudulently[82] and whether there is an established course of dealing in which the bank has permitted overdrafts over a long period.[83] Where there has been a persistent overdraft situation about which the bank has expressed concern to the

---

78 *Bank of Baroda v. ASAA Mahomed*, [1999] Lloyd's Rep. Bank 14 (C.A.). Banks should terminate only at the request of the other party to the account and not at the request of any third party, even a family member: *Sinha v. Sinha* (2002), 306 A.R. 250 (Alta. Q.B.).
79 *Bank of Baroda v. ASAA Mahomed*, ibid.
80 *Rekstin v. Severo Sibirsko Gosudarstvennoe Akcionernoe Obschestvo Komseverputj*, [1933] 1 K.B. 47 (C.A.).
81 *Agra & Masterman's Bank Ltd. v. Leightonn* (1864), L.R. 2 Ex. 56; *Thomas v. Howell* (1874), L.R. 18 Eq. 198; *Prosperity Ltd. v. Lloyd's Bank Ltd.* (1923), 39 T.L.R. 372 (K.B.); *Bank of Nova Scotia v. Raymond Contractors Ltd.* (1988), 25 B.C.L.R. (2d) 54 (S.C.).
82 *Sutcliffe & Sons Ltd., Ex parte Royal Bank of Canda, Re*, [1933] 1 D.L.R. 562 (Ont. C.A.); *Inter City Express Ltd. v. Toronto-Dominion Bank* (1976), 66 D.L.R. (3d) 754 (B.C.S.C.).
83 *Buckingham & Co. v. London & Midland Bank Ltd.* (1895), 12 T.L.R. 70 (Q.B.); *Thermo King Corp. v. Provincial Bank of Canada* (1981), 130 D.L.R. (3d) 256 (Ont. C.A.).

customer, the bank may unilaterally close the account immediately and demand immediate payment of the outstanding amount.[84]

In addition to situations in which either bank or customer voluntarily decide to terminate an account agreement, termination may occur on the occurrence of certain other events, including the death, mental incompetence, or bankruptcy of the customer or the insolvency of the bank.

Receipt of notice of the death of a customer effects the termination of the bank and customer relationship.[85] Prior to notice, the bank may continue to honour cheques and other payment instructions, although the payee may be required to reimburse the deceased's estate.[86] The *Bank Act* requires that a bank transmit any debt owed to the customer and any property held as a security or for safekeeping to the legal representatives of the deceased on receipt of appropriate documentary evidence.[87] Typically, funds in the deceased's account are transferred to an estate account. A similar situation prevails once a bank receives notice of the mental incapacity[88] or the bankruptcy of the customer.[89] Prior to notice, the bank may continue to honour payment instructions, but once notice has been received, the account agreement is terminated and the bank should transfer the funds to the legally authorized person on receipt of appropriate legal authorization, again usually by transferring the funds into a new account operated pursuant to an account agreement with a legal guardian or receiver or trustee, respectively.

The bank and customer relationship is also terminated by the insolvency of the bank because the bank no longer has legal capacity to enter or perform contracts. Where a bank is still acting as an agent for collection in relation to a cheque deposited by a customer prior to insolvency, the funds remain the property of the customer and do not become part of the insolvent bank's assets for distribution to secured creditors over the claim of the unsecured customer.[90]

---

84 *National Bank of Greece Ltd. v. Pinios Shipping Co. (No. 1)*, [1989] 1 All E.R. 213 (C.A.).
85 *Bailey v. Jellett* (1884), 9 O.A.R. 187 (C.A.); *Re Bernard* (1911), 2 O.W.N. 716 (Div. Ct.); *McLellan v. Sterling Bank* (1911), 2 O.W.N. 798 (H.C.J.); *Kendrick v. Dominion Bank* (1920), 48 O.L.R. 539 (S.C.A.D.); *Curley v. Briggs* (1920), 13 Sask. L.R. 346 (C.A.).
86 *McLellan v. McLellan* (1911), 25 O.L.R. 214 (Div. Ct.).
87 *Bank Act*, above note 3, s. 460.
88 *Bradford Old Bank Ltd. v. Sutcliffe*, [1918] 2 K.B. 833 (C.A.).
89 *Re D.A. Bamford (Marine) Ltd.* (1970), 14 C.B.R. (N.S.) 304 (Ont. S.C.); *Re Russian Commercial & Industrial Bank*, [1955] 1 Ch. 148; *Plant Estate (Public Trustee of) v. Royal Bank of Canada*, [1996] 10 W.W.R. 87 (Alta. Q.B.).
90 *Re Farrow's Bank Ltd.*, [1923] 1 Ch. 41 (C.A.).

Finally, the courts have considered the question of whether the outbreak of war puts an end to the account contract when the bank and the customer are resident, respectively, in jurisdictions at war with one another. In *Arab Bank Ltd. v. Barclays Bank*,[91] the House of Lords decided that the effect of war was to suspend, rather than to terminate, the agreement and that the customer could demand repayment on the cessation of hostilities, but have no access to the account in the meantime. The application of this case to situations in which a foreign state seizes control of an overseas branch means that a customer could not demand repayment at a branch in the customer's jurisdiction, since the *situs* of the debt is clearly assumed to be the overseas branch.[92]

H. THE FIDUCIARY AND TORTIOUS RELATIONSHIPS

In *Foley v. Hill*, the House of Lords stated that the bank and customer relationship could occasionally be fiduciary, in addition to being contractual in nature, but the evolution during the last quarter of the twentieth century of fiduciary obligation as an important branch of private law has impacted on banking law in ways the mid-nineteenth-century law lords might not have imagined.

The modern development of banking law in which the contract between bank and customer is subject to superadded or implied obligations drawn from fiduciary and tort law dates to the decision in 1959 of Salmon J. in *Woods v. Martins Bank*,[93] which stated in a tentative fashion that a bank owes a fiduciary duty, then characterized as a duty of care, to a customer. In 1963, in *Hedley Byrne & Co. Ltd. v. Heller and Partners Ltd.*,[94] the House of Lords further stated, in *obiter dicta*, that a bank may owe a duty of care not to make negligent misstatements about a customer, and in 1975, in *Lloyds Bank Ltd. v. Bundy*,[95] an influential English Court of Appeal found that banks could also be subject to the equitable doctrines of undue influence and the newly formulated unequal bargaining power, as well as fiduciary obligation, in relation to customers.

---

91 [1954] A.C. 495 (H.L.).
92 *Isaacs v. Barclays Bank Ltd.*, above note 15; *Leader, Plunkett and Leader v. Direction der Disconto-Gesellschaft* (1914), 31 T.L.R. 83 (K.B.).
93 Above note 10.
94 [1964] A.C. 465 (H.L.).
95 [1975] Q.B. 326 (C.A.).

Since these cases, which have been applied and extended in numerous cases in Canada and England, it has become settled law that the bank and customer relationship can also be fiduciary and tortious in nature. However, the precise scope and application of these principles remains contested for two reasons. First, the substantive doctrinal content of fiduciary obligation, undue influence, unequal bargaining power, and negligent misrepresentation, as well as the doctrine of unconscionability, which is also increasingly invoked, remains imprecise in the private law generally and in banking law specifically. Secondly, the courts frequently apply several of these doctrines concurrently to the same fact situation, thereby suggesting either that each is found in that fact situation or that the doctrines themselves are indistinguishable or nearly indistinguishable in either content and/or application.

Many of the leading cases in the private law generally in this area are banking law cases and deal typically with fact situations, including giving financial or investment advice to customers, giving credit references to third parties in relation to customers, taking security for loans to customers, and arranging life insurance as a security for loans to customers. Prior to discussing these specific fact situation categories, it is necessary to assess the current formulations of the legal principles applied in them.[96]

1) Fiduciary Obligation

In *Woods v. Martins Bank*, a plaintiff described by the judge as "the very prototype of the lamb waiting to be shorn. And he did not have long to wait,"[97] was persuaded by a local branch manager to invest his inheritance in a company known to be in significant difficulty and lost the en-

---

[96] The secondary literature on fiduciary obligation is enormous, but in the banking law context, see M.H. Ogilvie, "Banks, Advice-Giving and Fiduciary Obligations" (1985) 17 Ottawa L. Rev. 263; Donovan Watters, "Banks, Fiduciary Obligations and Unconscionable Transactions" (1986) 65 Can. Bar. Rev. 37; Bradley Crawford, "Bankers' Fiduciary Duties and Negligence" (1986) 12 Can. Bus. L.J. 145; R.P. Austin, "The Corporate Fiduciary: *Standard Investments v. CIBC*" (1986) 12 Can. Bus. L.J. 96; Jacob S. Ziegel, "Bankers' Fiduciary Obligations and Chinese Walls: A Further Comment on *Standard v. CIBC*" (1986) 12 Can. Bus. L.J. 211; K. Kalinowsky, "The Constructive Trustee: A Stranger's Knowing Participation in a Breach of Trust" (1991) 7 B.F.L.R. 383; E.P. Ellinger, "The Bank as Fiduciary and Constructive Trustee" (1994) 9 B.F.L.R. 111; M.H. Ogilvie, "Fiduciary Obligation in Canada: From Concept to Principle" [1995] J. Bus. L. 638; John M. McCamus, "Prometheus Unbound: Fiduciary Obligation in the Supreme Court of Canada" (1997) 28 Can. Bus. L.J. 107.

[97] Above note 10 at 59.

tire sum when the company failed. The manager failed to disclose the facts to the plaintiff or to advise him that the bank's regional office had expressed considerable concern about the company. To the young man's case against the bank for breach of a duty of care, the bank argued that it owed no duty because he was not an account-owning customer at the time the advice was given, although subsequently became one.

Salmon J. rejected this argument for two reasons: (i) the bank's own advertisements expressly stated that it offered investment advice; and (ii) the manager held the bank out as being in the business of giving investment advice. He further found the manager to be grossly negligent although not fraudulent, and that he ought to have disclosed the bank's conflict of interest to the young man. He characterized the bank's legal duty variously as fiduciary, a duty of care, a duty to avoid a conflict of interest, and gross negligence, without further precision or clarification, although this is to be expected in a case that preceded *Hedley Byrne*, in which the House of Lords clarified the negligence standard of care for banks. Nevertheless, *Woods* stated that a bank is responsible for advice giving to anyone, including customers, although whether the standard of care is fiduciary or one of reasonableness remained ambiguous.[98]

In *Standard Investments Ltd. v. CIBC*,[99] the Ontario Court of Appeal confirmed that a bank may owe fiduciary duties to a customer, relying on the earlier English Court of Appeal decision in *Lloyd's Bank Ltd. v. Bundy*.[100] In *Standard Investments*, the bank's president provided assistance to an investment company at the same time as its board chairman was assisting other parties in relation to an attempted takeover of a trust company. Neither apparently knew of the conflict until several years later when the president learned the facts on becoming chairman of the board. The takeover bid failed and the investment company sued the bank to recover the lost value in the shares they had purchased after the share value fell, arguing that the bank was in breach of a fiduciary duty. At trial, Griffiths J. decided that there was a fiduciary relationship which required the bank to disclose its conflict of interest as between

---

98 This same ambiguity is found in the two subsequent "exotic cow" cases: *McBean v. Bank of Nova Scotia* (1981), 15 B.L.R. 296 (Ont. H.C.J.), aff'd (1982), 17 A.C.W.S. (2d) 154 (Ont. C.A.) [*McBean*] and *Hayward v. Bank of Nova Scotia* (1984), 7 D.L.R. (4th) 135 (Ont. H.C.J.), aff'd (1985), 19 D.L.R. (4th) 758 (Ont. C.A.) [*Hayward*]. In *McBean*, the court opted for negligent misrepresentation, whereas in *Hayward*, on virtually identical facts, it opted for fiduciary obligation based on unequal bargaining power and a duty to disclose and give independent advice.
99 (1986), 22 D.L.R. (4th) 410 (Ont. C.A.), leave to appeal to S.C.C. refused (1986), 53 O.R. (2d) 663n [*Standard Investments*].
100 Above note 95.

its two customers but that there was no breach of duty because even with such disclosure, the investment company would have continued with its takeover bid. Although he found the bank's conduct to be legal, he expressed his personal view that the bank's policy was "morally offensive."[101] The Ontario Court of Appeal agreed that the relationship was fiduciary but found the bank to be in breach of its fiduciary duty by not disclosing its conflict. The court did not require disclosure of another customer's affairs, which would constitute breach of its duty of secrecy to the customer, but merely disclosure of the fact of conflict and the result that it could not further assist the investment company.[102] Goodman J.A. relied on the discussion of the nature of a fiduciary relationship of Sir Eric Sachs in *Bundy*, in which it was characterized as a relationship of trust and confidence, inducing reliance and loss on the part of a beneficiary.[103]

The Supreme Court of Canada has never considered the fiduciary nature of the bank and customer relationship, although it has considered fiduciary obligation in numerous other contexts, including commercial contexts.[104] In *Hodgkinson v. Simms*,[105] the court confirmed that the essential requirement for finding a fiduciary relationship in the factual context of giving financial or investment advice is a voluntary undertaking to act on behalf of another with the result that there is trust, vulnerability, reliance, and loss. Although the court found on the facts that there was a fiduciary relationship in *Hodgkinson*, it has emphasized on several other occasions that fiduciary relationships are the exception, rather than the rule, in commercial transactions,[106] and that position is borne out in the banking jurisprudence in relation to fiduciary obligation generally.

A model statement of the modern nature of fiduciary obligation in commercial contexts is that of Millett L.J.:

---

101 *Standard Investments Ltd. v. Canadian Imperial Bank of Commerce* (1984), 5 D.L.R. (4th) 452 at 488 (Ont. H.C.J.).
102 In *Commonwealth Trading Bank of Australia v. Smith* (1991), 102 A.L.R. 453 (Fed. Ct.), a bank was found to be in breach of a fiduciary duty when it disclosed a conflict but did not advise independent advice.
103 Above note 94 at 340–41.
104 Ogilvie, above note 96; McCamus, above note 96; *Hodgkinson v. Simms* (1994), 117 D.L.R. (4th) 161 (S.C.C.); *Cadbury Schweppes Inc. v. FBI Foods Ltd.* (1999), 167 D.L.R. (4th) 577 (S.C.C.).
105 *Ibid.*
106 *LAC Minerals Ltd. v. International Corona Resources Ltd.* (1989), 61 D.L.R. (4th) 14 (S.C.C.); *Cadbury Schweppes Inc. v. FBI Foods Ltd.*, above note 104; *Mantel Bldg. v. Canada* (2000), 193 D.L.R. (4th) 1 (S.C.C.).

A fiduciary is someone who has undertaken to act for or on behalf of another in a particular matter in circumstances which give rise to a relationship of trust and confidence. The distinguishing obligation of a fiduciary is the obligation of loyalty. The principal is entitled to the single-minded loyalty of the fiduciary. This core liability has several facets. A fiduciary must act in good faith; he must not make a profit out of his trust; he must not place himself in a position where his duty and his interest may conflict; he may not act for his own benefit or for the benefit of a third person without the informed consent of his principal. This is not intended to be an exhaustive list, but it is sufficient to indicate the nature of fiduciary obligations. They are the defining characteristics of a fiduciary.[107]

Once it is clear that a fiduciary relationship arises only when there is a voluntary undertaking to act on behalf of another, it is equally clear that a bank could expressly exclude or restrict such an obligation by contract,[108] so that the bank and customer relationship would be one strictly of contract without any superadded fiduciary obligation.[109] It would be open to a future court to treat such a clause strictly and to subject it to the requirements of unconscionability and *contra proferentem* as a potential abuse of superior bargaining power.

2) Undue Influence

An alternative approach to resolving disputes between bank and customer in which the customer alleges that the bank acted inequitably in the performance of its obligations is to characterize the bank's conduct as undue influence. Whereas fiduciary duty typically arises when banks give advice, undue influence typically occurs when a customer is obliged to give a security to a bank for a loan either to the customer or to a third party. The starting point for the modern law is *Lloyd's Bank Ltd. v. Bundy*, in which a bank took a series of charges over a family farm from a father to secure the indebtedness of his son's business in the form of a substantial overdraft. The charges amounted to £11,000, although the

---

107 *Bristol and West Building Society v. Mothew*, [1998] 1 Ch. 1 at 18 (C.A.). Applied in *Arklow Investments Ltd. v. Maclean*, [2000] 1 W.L.R. 594 (P.C.). See also *Klein v. First Edina National Bank*, 196 N.W.2d 619 at 623 (Minn. 1972), *per curiam*.
108 See also *Kelly v. Cooper*, [1993] A.C. 205 (P.C.); *Henderson v. Mereitt Syndicates Ltd.*, [1995] 2 A.C. 145 (H.L.); *White v. Jones*, [1995] 2 A.C. 207 (H.L.), especially the speeches of Lord Browne-Wilkinson.
109 See Section H(6), below in this chapter, for the applications in Canadian banking law.

market value of the farm was £10,000. When the son's business failed, the bank sought vacant possession of the property against the father who was old and had little business experience, although he had received independent legal advice to give charges for up to about one-half the value of the property.

The English Court of Appeal found unanimously that the bank had exercised undue influence on the father and set aside the order for vacant possession. However, the alternative grounds on which both Lord Denning M.R. and Sir Eric Sachs[110] decided the case were the most lengthily stated in their respective judgments and have attracted great interest. Sir Eric Sachs considered the bank to be in breach of a fiduciary duty to the father by virtue of the father's trusting reliance on it and its failure to make full disclosure of the son's financial affairs and of its own conflict of interest. As stated above, this part of his decision was the foundation for the finding in *Standard Investments* that banks can be fiduciaries for their customers. On the other hand, Lord Denning M.R. proposed a new equitable doctrine, unequal bargaining power, on the basis of which to void the charges given by the father to the bank. Lord Denning characterized unequal bargaining power as the single thread running through a number of equitable doctrines such as duress of goods, undue influence, unconscionability, undue pressure, and salvage agreements and proposed that it be adopted to replace these in order to do justice where superior bargaining power had been abused. He found that the bank had abused its superior position as evidenced by the grossly inadequate consideration, the alleged failure by the bank to advise independent legal advice, the father's natural affection for his son, and the father's trust and confidence in the bank.

Although *Bundy* was applied in several subsequent English cases,[111] it was effectively overruled by the House of Lords in *National Westminster Bank plc v. Morgan*,[112] which established undue influence as the appropriate legal test in place of unequal bargaining power, whose status in English banking law proved to be short-lived. In *Morgan*, the bank proposed a "rescue package" to a husband and wife, the goal of which was to permit them to remain in their matrimonial home and to finance the husband's failing business for a little longer. Without this refinan-

---

110 Cairns L.J. briefly agreed with Sir Eric Sachs.
111 *Clifford Davies Management Ltd. v. WEA Records Ltd.*, [1975] 1 W.L.R. 61 (C.A.); *Horry v. Tate & Lyle Refineries Ltd.*, [1982] 2 Lloyd's Rep. 416 (Q.B.D.). See also *Backhouse v. Backhouse*, [1978] 1 W.L.R. 243 (Fam. D.); *Alec Lobb (Garages) Ltd. v. Total Oil (Great Britain) Ltd.*, [1983] 1 W.L.R. 87 (Ch. D.).
112 [1985] A.C. 686 (H.L.).

cing proposal, they would have lost their house and the husband's business would have failed. The wife signed the security documents during a fifteen-to-twenty-minute visit to their home by the bank manager, during which she was erroneously but honestly told that she would only be securing their matrimonial home and not the business, which she was unwilling to do. When the husband died, he had no business debts, but the bank sued for vacant possession of the house to recover the outstanding indebtedness on the mortgage. The manager had not suggested independent legal advice and the trial judge found that the wife understood that if she had not signed, they would have lost their home earlier.

The House of Lords decided that the relationship between the Morgans and the bank was simply one of bank and customer and that no fiduciary relationship had arisen. The law lords further found that no undue influence had been exercised by the bank. Although the manager's statements were inaccurate, they were made in good faith and for the purpose of securing the rescue package, without which the Morgans would have lost their home, and Mrs. Morgan understood this. Lord Scarman approved Sir Eric Sachs' approach in *Bundy* to fiduciary obligation, emphasized that it should be assessed on a case-by-case basis, and thought it rare in banking relationships. He further doubted the utility of unequal bargaining power, since all contractual relationships are unequal and saw no reason for the doctrine in the common law. Finally, the House of Lords stated that undue influence, meaning "the victimisation of one party by the other"[113] was the appropriate principle to apply where a bank has acted inequitably in relation to a customer, although there was no undue influence on the facts in *Morgan*.

After *Morgan*, the English courts explored the nature of undue influence in a series of banking cases typically involving a bank taking security from a wife or a child to secure a loan to another family member customer.[114] As a result of the increasing complexity and possibly

---

113 *Ibid.* at 705, Lord Scarman approving *Allcard v. Skinner* (1887), 36 Ch. D. 145 at 182–83 (C.A.), Lindley L.J.
114 *Avon Finance Co. v. Bridger*, [1985] 2 All E.R. 281 (C.A.); *Cornish v. Midland Bank plc*, [1985] 3 All E.R. 513 (C.A.); *Kingsnorth Trust Ltd. v. Bell*, [1986] 1 All E.R. 423 (C.A.); *Coldunell Ltd. v. Gallon*, [1986] 1 All E.R. 429 (C.A.); *Midland Bank plc v. Shephard*, [1988] 3 All E.R. 17 (C.A.); *Bank of Baroda v. Shah*, [1988] 3 All E.R. 24 (C.A.); *BCCI v. Aboody*, [1992] 4 All E.R. 955 (C.A.) [*Aboody*]; *Barclays Bank plc v. Khaira*, [1992] 1 W.L.R. 623 (Ch. D.). See also M.H. Ogilvie, "No Special Tenderness for Sexually Contracted Debt? Undue Influence and the Lending Banker" (1996) 27 Can. Bus. L.J. 365, as well as various comments: David Tiplady, "The Limits of Undue Influence" (1985) 48 Mod. L. Rev. 579; Cretney (1992) 109 Law

confusion in these cases, the House of Lords heard two companion cases in 1993 to clarify undue influence in banking law.

In *Barclays Bank plc v. O'Brien*,[115] a wife was induced by her husband's misrepresentations to give a second mortgage over their joint matrimonial home to secure the indebtedness of her husband's company. She signed the documents without reading them and without being advised to obtain independent legal advice. The House of Lords relieved her from the transaction because the bank ought to have taken reasonable steps to explain it and advise her to obtain independent legal advice. The bank was fixed with constructive notice of the husband's misrepresentation and could not enforce the security. In *CIBC Mortgages plc v. Pitt*,[116] the wife signed a charge over the matrimonial home to secure a loan to her and her husband to discharge a first mortgage and to purchase a holiday home. She signed under considerable pressure from her husband without reading the documents or being advised to obtain independent legal advice. Her husband lost the funds in share speculation. The House of Lords declined to find undue influence by the husband which tainted the bank and permitted the bank to enforce the charge. The husband was not acting as agent for the bank, nor were there any facts to put the bank on constructive notice. The transaction was routine and benefited both parties.

In these cases, the House of Lords rejected any special equity theory that a vulnerable person, such as a wife or aging parent, had an *ipso facto* right to equitable relief in the absence of some wrongdoing by the bank or attributable to the bank. The aggrieved party must show undue influence by the bank. The law lords accepted the analysis of undue influence formulated by the Court of Appeal in *BCCI v. Aboody*,[117] in which two classes of undue influence were proposed: actual (or class 1) and presumed (or class 2). For actual undue influence, the surety must prove the actual exercise of undue influence, but in presumed undue influence, the surety need only establish the existence of a relationship of trust and confidence in which it is fair to presume its abuse in the

---

Q. Rev. 534; Dixon [1994] 53 Cambridge L.J. 21; Dixon [1994] 53 Cambridge L.J. 232; Lelane (1994) 110 Law Q. Rev. 173; Arora [1994] J. Bus. L. 242; Fehlberg (1994) 57 Mod. L. Rev. 467; Chandler (1995) 111 Law Q. Rev. 51; Mee [1995] 54 Cambridge L.J. 536; Goo (1995) 15 Oxford J. Legal Stud. 119; Fehlberg (1996) 59 Mod. L. Rev. 675; Chen-Wishart [1997] 56 Cambridge L.J. 60.

115 [1994] 1 A.C. 180 (H.L.).
116 [1994] 1 A.C. 200 (H.L.).
117 Above note 114. See generally M.H. Ogilvie, "The Fiduciary Nature of Spousal Security Agreements in Banking Law" (2005) 42 Can. Bus. L.J. 245 and John D. McCamus, *The Law of Contracts* (Toronto: Irwin Law, 2005) at 382–404.

absence of contrary evidence. Class 2 undue influence was further divided into class 2A relationships such as doctor and patient or solicitor and client (that is, long-established relationships in law, in which the presumption automatically arises) and class 2B relationships, which are *de facto* relationships, in which the presumption arises. Family and other personal relationships fall within class 2B, so that to raise the presumption of undue influence, the surety must establish the presence of trust in the spouse or bank, which has been abused. Lord Browne-Wilkinson, in *O'Brien*, accepted that risk to be greater in spousal relationships because of the emotional ties.

After *O'Brien*, the surety must establish first undue influence by the spouse and then that the bank had either the actual or constructive notice required for liability. Lord Browne-Wilkinson stated that the bank would have notice if the transaction is not on its face to the surety's financial advantage and there is a substantial risk in the transaction that a legal or equitable wrong was done. With notice, the bank must take reasonable steps to ensure that the surety's consent was voluntary, including advising that the surety obtain independent legal advice.[118] In *Pitt*, the law lords further clarified that any manifest disadvantage in the transaction was simply evidence raising a rebuttable presumption of undue influence and was sufficient evidence of wrongdoing for actual undue influence.[119]

O'Brien and *Pitt* reaffirmed that the proper approach for the English courts to fact situations in which a bank is alleged to have treated a customer in an unfair way is by application of the doctrine of undue influence, rather than by deeming the bank and customer relationship to be fiduciary in nature. They reconfirmed that undue influence meant the victimization of one party by another and also followed the *Aboody* subdivision into the two classes of actual and presumed undue influence and the further subdivision into classes 2A and 2B. However, these cases raised new questions, including how actual undue influence differed conceptually from fiduciary obligation and the role of independent legal advice as a means by which a bank could defend itself in undue influence cases.[120]

---

118 Above note 115 at 196–97.
119 Above note 116 at 208–9. This was in response to several cases after *Morgan* that assumed manifest disadvantage necessary for a finding of actual undue influence: *Coldunell Ltd. v. Gallon*, above note 114; *Midland Bank plc v. Shephard*, above note 114; *Bank of Baroda v. Shah*, above note 114.
120 For extensive analysis of these, see Ogilvie, above note 117; McCamus, above note 117; E.P. Ellinger, F. Lomnicka, & R.J.A. Hooley, *Modern Banking Law*, 3d

Subsequent cases demonstrated practical problems in relation to how a bank could protect itself from being tainted by spousal undue influence, especially as to whether the independent legal advice requirement could be satisfied by merely suggesting it[121] or by ensuring that the quality of advice resulted in a voluntary decision to execute the security to the bank.[122] The House of Lords reviewed the situation again in 2001 in *Royal Bank of Scotland v. Etridge (No. 2)*,[123] in which eight separate cases were heard together, all involving the same paradigm situation of alleged undue influence tainting the bank where a husband and/or the bank procured a wife's signature to securities over a matrimonial home.

In the main speech with which all five law lords agreed,[124] Lord Nicholls characterized undue influence as one of two equitable categories of unacceptable conduct: coercion by unlawful threats and misuse of a position of influence. While some relationships are prone to undue influence, the presence of trust and confidence reposed by one party in another is the primary indicium of undue influence, although there may be others, depending on the circumstances, including manifest disadvantage in the resulting transaction. The exercise of undue influence is a question of fact to be proven by the person so alleging, and two facts must be proven: trust and confidence and a resulting transaction that calls for an explanation. Once these are shown, the other party bears the burden of showing no abuse of influence.[125]

An abuse of confidence may be shown by an absence of independent legal advice and/or manifest disadvantage in the transaction, which

---

ed. (Oxford: Oxford University Press, 2002) at 110–23, as well as the references, above note 114.

121 *Midland Bank v. Serter*, [1995] 2 F.L.R. 367 (C.A.); *Massey v. Midland Bank plc*, [1995] 1 All E.R. 929 (C.A.); *Banco Exterior Internacional v. Mann*, [1995] 1 All E.R. 936 (C.A.); *Barclays Bank plc v. Thomson*, [1997] 4 All E.R. 816 (C.A.); *Banco Exterior Internacional v. Thomas*, [1997] 1 All E.R. 46 (C.A.).

122 *Crédit Lyonnais Bank Nederland v. Burch*, [1997] 1 All E.R. 144 (C.A.); *Royal Bank of Scotland v. Etridge (No. 1)*, [1997] 3 All E.R. 628 (C.A.). See also the following comments: Tjiu [1996] J. Bus. L. 266; Haley [1997] J. Bus. L. 220; Tjiu (1997) 113 Law Q. Rev. 10; Capper (1998) 114 Law Q. Rev. 479; Price (1999) 115 Law Q. Rev. 8; Bridge [1999] 58 Cambridge L.J. 28; Chandler (1999) 115 Law Q. Rev. 213; Giliken (1999) 62 Mod. L. Rev. 609.

123 [2001] 4 All E.R. 449 (H.L.) [*Etridge (No. 2)*]. See also the following comments: Bigwood (2002) 65 Mod. L. Rev. 435; Watts (2002) 118 Law Q. Rev. 337; Oldham [2002] 64 Cambridge L.J. 29; Wong [2002] J. Bus. L. 439.

124 Five speeches were delivered, but Lord Nicholls' speech focused most on undue influence and doctrinal issues.

125 *Etridge (No. 2)*, above note 123 at 457–59.

the House of Lords treated as an evidentiary matter, rather than as a necessary ingredient for undue influence. There may be undue influence when the transaction is not readily explicable by the relationship of trust and confidence between the parties.[126] When the security transaction involves spouses or close family members, the bank is automatically put on notice of possible undue influence, so that it should ensure that independent legal advice be obtained. Lord Nicholls conceded that requiring independent legal advice was the most a bank could do, since it could never be certain that the ramifications of the security were fully understood by the surety. Once that advice was given, the bank could enforce a security and the legal burden would be redistributed to the lawyer, who could discharge the legal burden by explaining the nature and practical consequences of the transaction and that signing is voluntary.[127] Once the bank has obtained a written confirmation from the lawyer that legal advice has been given, it is free to proceed with the transaction and enforce it, without fear that an undue influence action will subsequently ensue.[128]

Lord Clyde thought the classes of undue influence introduced in *Aboody* added mystery rather than illumination,[129] and while he did not overrule them, he preferred to open up the concept of undue influence by adding coercion, domination, victimization, and all invidious means of persuasion to abuse of trust and confidence, as indices of undue influence. He thought that all cases are really cases of actual undue influence and that in the end, a court must determine whether execution of the security was voluntary or not.[130] Lord Hobhouse also doubted the *Aboody* classes because whether undue influence was actual or presumed, it must still be proven by a surety.[131]

Etridge (No. 2) confirmed that a surety is only bound by a security agreement over property with a bank to which there is voluntary consent; otherwise, the bank will be tainted by any undue influence exercised by the borrower over the spouse. Actual or constructive notice of any undue influence has the potential to taint. But the House of Lords also clarified certain aspects of undue influence in *obiter dicta*. Undue influence will be presumed where there is a relationship of trust and confidence and a resulting transaction calling for an explanation,

---

126 *Ibid.* at 460–62.
127 *Ibid.* at 462–63.
128 *Ibid.* at 469–73.
129 *Ibid.* at 477.
130 *Ibid.* at 478–79.
131 *Ibid.* at 481–83. Lord Scott also doubted the *Aboody* classes at 501–4.

although it need not be manifestly disadvantageous. In addition to victimization, any type of abuse of a relationship of trust, such as coercion, domination, or misrepresentation, may amount to undue influence and be factually proven. However, other questions about the legal nature of undue influence remain after *Etridge (No. 2)*, including the status of the *Aboody* classes 2 and 2A and 2B; the distinction in legal principle between undue influence and fiduciary obligation once undue influence is said to pertain to relationships of trust and confidence; the failure to require a certificate of independent legal advice, rather than merely acquiescence, in the current banking practice of advising; and the nature and extent of the lawyer's liability.[132]

The Supreme Court of Canada has never considered the nature of undue influence in the banking law context, and the last case in which it considered the principle, *Geffen v. Goodman*,[133] concerned a trust agreement among siblings where the son of one unsuccessfully attempted to have it set aside against his three uncles on the ground that it was procured by undue influence. Wilson J. accepted the victimization test in *Allcard v. Skinner* and the *Aboody* division as the starting points for analysis and suggested that domination was the key to a presumption of undue influence. She proposed a two-step test to determine whether the presumption arose: the determination of whether the potential for domination is inherent in the relationship and the determination of whether the resulting transaction was so unfair as to be evidence of one party being "unduly"[134] disadvantaged or the other being unduly benefited. Once the presumption is triggered, the onus is on the dominant party to prove no actual undue influence or independent legal advice. LaForest J. disagreed that manifest disadvantage was required for a presumption of undue influence.[135]

Although frequently applied in various non-banking fact situations since, *Geffen* did not resolve a number of issues relating to undue influence, including the necessity for the *Aboody* classes, how undue influence is conceptually distinct from fiduciary obligation, the status of manifest disadvantage on the nature of and necessity for independent legal advice. In a subsequent non-banking case, *Gold v. Rosenberg*,[136] the Supreme Court opined that independent legal advice was not required

---

132 Ogilvie, above note 117, explores these.
133 (1991), 81 D.L.R. (4th) 211 (S.C.C.).
134 *Ibid.* at 228.
135 *Ibid.* at 239–40.
136 (1997), 152 D.L.R. (4th) 385 (S.C.C.).

in all situations but failed to specify those in which it was required.[137] In several subsequent appellate court banking decisions,[138] courts declined to find undue influence in paradigm fact situations because there was no evidence that the wives reposed trust and confidence in their husbands, but rather they understood the transactions and entered into them voluntarily. In such situations, banks are not obliged to advise or to ensure the receipt of independent legal advice in order to avoid being tainted by undue influence. These courts have not further considered the conceptual content of undue influence, and it must be concluded that the nature of a bank's duties in taking security remains uncertain in Canadian banking law.

Canadian banking practice has generally moved toward ensuring that independent legal advice is obtained when dealing with vulnerable parties,[139] although Canadian courts have not followed the House of Lords' trilogy of *O'Brien/Pitt/Etridge (No. 2)* by making advice mandatory. Canadian banking cases will continue to be considered on a case-by-case finding of whether, on the facts, undue influence has been exercised, and independent legal advice will be treated as one of several criteria for that determination. This contrasts with the English approach, where its procurement effectively protects a bank from a claim of undue influence so that it may enforce the security. The *Allcard/Aboody* formulation of Wilson J. in *Geffen* also remains the content of undue influence for Canadian banking law purposes, although how that may be conceptually distinguished from fraud, fiduciary obligation, unequal bargaining power, or unconscionability remains obscure.

3) Unconscionability

Like undue influence, unconscionability in the commercial law context has not been considered by the Supreme Court of Canada. However, lower courts have increasingly found unconscionability in banking cases and in Canada, unconscionability often appears to do the work done by undue influence in English banking jurisprudence. In *Mor-*

---

137 *Ibid.* at 409, Sopinka J.
138 *Bank of Montreal v. Duguid* (2000), 185 D.L.R. (4th) 458 (Ont. C.A.), leave to appeal to S.C.C. granted (2000), 51 O.R. (3d) xvii but case discontinued 2 August 2001 [*Duguid*]; *CIBC Mortgage Corp. v. Rowatt* (2002), 220 D.L.R. (4th) 139 (Ont. C.A.), leave to appeal to S.C.C. refused (2002), 64 O.R. (3d) xvii [*Rowatt*]; *Bank of Montreal v. Courtney* (2005), 261 D.L.R. (4th) 665 (N.S.C.A.) [*Courtney*].
139 See generally Ted Tjaden, *The Law of Independent Legal Advice* (Scarborough: Carswell, 2000).

rison v. Coast Finance Ltd.,[140] Davey J.A. distinguished undue influence as relating to contractual consent from unconscionability as relating to an unfair advantage taken by a stronger party over a weaker party. Unconscionability therefore requires both an inequality of bargaining power between the parties insofar as one of the parties is incapable of protecting his own interests and an unfair advantage derived from that situation by the stronger party, that is, an advantage that engages the conscience of the court.

In contract law generally, most cases of unconscionability are concerned with circumstances such as poverty, illness, age, ignorance, or ethnic origin, which impair the weaker party's ability to consent voluntarily to a transaction,[141] and the list of circumstances seems to be open ended. In the law of contract generally, there would appear to be no limits on the types of transactions in which unconscionability may be found or on the types of advantages taken by the stronger party. What is required is that the advantage shocks the conscience of the court; mere unfairness in the bargain is not enough. In *Harry v. Kreutziger*,[142] Lambert J.A. expressed the test as a single question: "That single question is whether the transaction, seen as a whole, is sufficiently divergent from community standards of commercial morality that it should be rescinded."[143]

In banking law, the question is whether unconscionable conduct has been exercised directly by the bank or whether a bank is tainted by notice, actual or constructive, of unconscionable conduct exercised by a stronger family member over a weaker one to procure the execution of a security. Although there are banking cases in which the doctrine of unconscionability is poorly articulated,[144] it has been applied in a number of cases with the result that a transaction has not been enforced by the court. In banking cases as in contract cases generally, unconscionability is difficult to define with precision and uncertain in its application, yet it satisfies the desire of courts to do justice in situations where there is found to be an injustice which other legal principles do not address. Unconscionability captures the intuitive human sense of

---

140 (1965), 55 D.L.R. (2d) 710 (B.C.C.A.). See also the earlier case: *Waters v. Donnelly* (1884), 9 O.R. 391 at 401 (H.C.J.), Boyd C.
141 *Morrison v. Coast Finance*, ibid.; *Krupp v. Bell* (1968), 67 D.L.R. (2d) 256 (Sask. C.A.); *Marshall v. Canada Permanent Trust Co.* (1968), 69 D.L.R. (2d) 260 (Alta. S.C.T.D.).
142 (1978), 95 D.L.R. (3d) 231 (B.C.C.A.).
143 *Ibid.* at 241.
144 *Canadian Imperial Bank of Commerce v. Ohlson* (1997), 154 D.L.R. (4th) 33 (Alta. C.A.).

injustice and expresses the historical equitable foundations of the common law.

4) Unequal Bargaining Power

In *Lloyd's Bank Ltd. v. Bundy*,[145] Lord Denning M.R. proposed that various equitable doctrines such as undue influence and unconscionability be synthesized into a single principle of unequal bargaining power, which in itself, is also at the heart of fiduciary obligation. Given the imprecise nature and scope of these and their apparently similar purpose of addressing issues where there has been unequal bargaining power exercised to result in a disadvantageous transaction, the argument for a single principle is strong. However, while unequal bargaining power is undoubtedly a feature of all cases in which these other principles have been found to apply, it does not assist in distinguishing cases from one another where there is trust or threats or prior personal circumstances or unjust bargains so as to define the relevant principle and ensure that it is applied in keeping with the doctrine of *stare decisis*. All human relationships, including legal relationships, are unequal in a variety of ways, but that in itself does not distinguish those in which the law ought to intervene from all others.

The House of Lords rejected unequal bargaining in *Morgan*; however, in Canada it has enjoyed a life of its own in contract law generally and in banking law in particular, both as an independent legal doctrine and as a requirement when courts have found breach of fiduciary obligation, undue influence, or unconscionability. While English courts have preferred undue influence in striking down banking transactions, Canadian courts have preferred a more ambiguous approach, melding elements of all these doctrines without clearly differentiating them to strike down banking transactions. As a result, there remains great uncertainty in Canadian banking law as to their respective doctrinal contents, scope of application, and relationships, resulting in uncertainty in this area generally.

5) Misrepresentation

In addition to fiduciary obligation and contract, including the duties to avoid undue influence and unconscionable or unequal transactions, the bank and customer contract may also be subject to superadded duties in tort, in particular, the torts of fraudulent and negligent misrepresen-

---

145 Above note 95. See Section H(1), above in this chapter.

tation. Misrepresentation may be made either directly to the customer in relation to a transaction with the customer or about the customer by giving credit reports or other advice to third parties about a customer.

Fraudulent misrepresentation, or the tort of deceit, requires an absence of honest belief in the truth of a statement made to another; in short, it is a lie.[146] To prove fraudulent misrepresentation, the plaintiff must prove that the representor subjectively knew that the statement was false when it was made. Since this is an onerous burden of proof to discharge, cases of fraudulent misrepresentation are rare.[147]

In contrast, negligent misrepresentation cases are much more common. Liability for careless or negligently made statements was first recognized by the House of Lords in *Hedley Byrne & Co. v. Heller & Partners*,[148] in which an advertising agency asked to place advertising for a company requested its bank to obtain a banker's reference for the company from the company's bank. The reference attested to a credit limit amount for the company but was said to be "without responsibility" and for the sole use of the agency's bank. When the company became insolvent, the agency looked to the company's bank for compensation because without that reference it would not have done the advertising work. The House of Lords found that the bank was not liable for the loss because it had expressly excluded liability for its reference; however, in *obiter dicta,* the law lords recognized that an action could lie in negligent misrepresentation for economic loss. This principle is analogous to the tort of negligence established in *Donoghue v. Stevenson*[149] for negligently manufactured products,[150] and *Hedley Byrne* has joined *Donoghue v. Stevenson* as one of the most important cases in the common law in the twentieth century, and as such has been applied since in thousands of cases.

Although there was initial reluctance to find pre-contractual misrepresentation where a contract resulted in favour of treating the con-

---

146 *Derry v. Peek* (1889), 14 A.C. 337 at 374 (H.L.), Lord Herschell.
147 The first such case involving a bank in either Canada or England appears to be *Sugar v. Peat Marwick Ltd.* (1989), 66 O.R. (2d) 766 (H.C.J.) [*Sugar*]. See also M.H. Ogilvie, "How Banks Engage in Fraudulent Misrepresentation: *Sugar v. Peat Marwick*" (1990) 4 B.F.L.R. 88. Compare an earlier case in which the allegation was not proven: *Bank of Nova Scotia v. Boehm*, [1973] 3 W.W.R. 757 (B.C.S.C.).
148 Above note 94.
149 [1932] A.C. 562 (H.L.).
150 See earlier cases for the evolution of this concept: *Nocton v. Lord Ashburton*, [1914] A.C. 932 (H.L.) and *Robinson v. National Bank of Scotland*, [1916] S.C. (H.L.) 154.

tract alone as the source of legal duties between the parties,[151] the courts came to accept these as alternative sources of legal duties.[152] Negligent misrepresentation today means that when a bank makes statements to or about a customer, it owes a duty to the customer and to the users of those statements to take reasonable care in making the statements. Where there is reliance on those statements by anyone who might be reasonably expected to rely on them, with resulting loss, then the requirements for an action in negligent misrepresentation will be satisfied.[153] In *V.K. Mason Construction Ltd. v. Bank of Nova Scotia*,[154] the Supreme Court of Canada confirmed that negligent misrepresentation is a part of banking law when it found that a bank which had assured a builder that financing would be available to a developer, was liable to the builder in negligent misrepresentation for losses suffered when the developer was unable to pay for the work done.

6) Fiduciary and Tortious Relationships in Banking Practice

There are three main paradigm fact situations in which the courts have superadded one or more of the foregoing fiduciary or tortious duties in law onto the fundamental contractual relationship between bank and customer: (i) giving financial or other investment advice to customers; (ii) taking security from a customer to secure a loan either to the customer or to another customer, especially where there are family or matrimonial ties between the surety and the borrower; and (iii) giving credit references about customers to third parties which may result in compensable loss either to the customer or to the third party who relies on it. There are numerous cases in each category, especially in the first and third paradigms.[155] In many cases, the courts find alternative causes, so that a single case may be found to be about breach of

---

151 *J. Nunes Diamonds Ltd. v. Dominion Electric Protection Co.* (1972), 26 D.L.R. (3d) 699 (S.C.C.); *Sodd Corporation Inc. v. Tessis* (1977), 79 D.L.R. (3d) 632 (Ont. C.A.). In England: *Esso Petroleum Co. v. Mardon*, [1976] Q.B. 801 (C.A.).
152 *Caparo Industries plc v. Dickman*, [1990] 2 A.C. 605 (H.L.) and *Queen v. Cognos Inc.* (1993), 99 D.L.R. (4th) 626 (S.C.C.).
153 Banking relationships would clearly satisfy the "special relationship" requirement: *Queen v. Cognos Inc.*, *ibid.* at 648, Iacobucci J.; *Hercules Management Ltd. v. Ernst & Young* (1997), 146 D.L.R. (4th) 577 (S.C.C.).
154 (1985), 16 D.L.R. (4th) 598 (S.C.C.) [*V.K. Mason*].
155 In what follows, reference will be made to some leading cases. For full lists of cases, see M.H. Ogilvie, *Canadian Banking Law*, 2d ed. (Toronto: Carswell, 1998) c. 29.

fiduciary obligation and/or undue influence and/or misrepresentation. Often judicial descriptions of the doctrine so applied will involve elements of one or more other doctrines; this area is quite muddy.

a) Giving Advice

In relation to the first category of cases, where banks give financial or other investment advice to customers, courts generally prefer not to impose a fiduciary obligation on banks, but rather to construe these as cases of misrepresentation. In a few cases, a bank has been found to owe a fiduciary obligation where a customer is commercially unsophisticated, and the bank has failed to disclose relevant facts about the recommended investment or failed to advise the customer to obtain independent legal advice prior to investing.[156] However, banks have also been found to owe a fiduciary duty to make disclosures to sophisticated commercial customers when the bank is likely the sole source of accurate information about the proposed investment.[157] These cases suggest that the most likely condition for finding a fiduciary obligation is that the bank has placed itself in a conflict of interest whereby it cannot act solely for the beneficiary of one of its customers as required in a fiduciary relationship.

However, courts have declined to impose a fiduciary obligation in a variety of circumstances: provision of a financial analysis of investment possibilities without recommendations;[158] ending financing for an investment project;[159] refusal to consider a borrower's proposal for less than full payment of a loan;[160] personal friendship between a borrower and the bank manager;[161] and an absence of reliance on the bank in making the investment.[162]

---

156 *Woods*, above note 10; *McBean*, above note 98; *Hayward*, above note 98; *Hongkong Bank of Canada v. Phillips*, [1998] 2 W.W.R. 606 (Man. Q.B.); *Seaboard Life Insurance Co. v. Bank of Montreal* (1999), 48 B.L.R. (2d) 77 (B.C.S.C.).
157 *Standard Investments*, above note 99.
158 *Heller v. Royal Bank of Canada* (1990), 76 Alta. L.R. (2d) 280 (C.A.) [*Heller*]; *Dartboard Holdings Ltd. v. Royal Bank of Canada* (1991), 12 C.B.R. (3d) 88 (B.C.S.C.) [*Dartboard*].
159 *Streamside Engineering v. Canadian Imperial Bank of Commerce* (1990), 85 Nfld. & P.E.I.R. 220, 226 A.P.R. 220 (Nfld. T.D.); *Bank of Nova Scotia v. Baird* (2001), 199 Nfld. & P.E.I.R. 154, 600 A.P.R. 154 (Nfld. T.D.).
160 *Dassen Gold Resources Ltd. v. Royal Bank of Canada*, [1997] 9 W.W.R. 658 (Alta. C.A.).
161 *Bank of Montreal v. McIntosh*, [1995] 10 W.W.R. 726 (Sask. Q.B.).
162 *Wildfong v. Royal Bank of Canada* (1989), 78 Sask. R. 250 (Q.B.); *Kirch v. Royal Bank of Canada*, [1994] 2 W.W.R. 194 (Sask. Q.B.); *Royal Bank of Canada v. White* (1992), 105 Sask. R. 201 (C.A.), leave to appeal to S.C.C. refused (1993), 116 Sask. R. 45n (S.C.C.); *Alnu Electric Ltd. v. CIBC Mortgage Corp.* (1995), 165 N.B.R. (2d) 149, 424 A.P.R. 149 (Q.B.) [*Alnu*]; *Accursi v. Hongkong Bank of*

A more successful approach for customers in light of the courts' reluctance to impose fiduciary obligation on a bank is to frame an action in misrepresentation. Thus, courts have applied *Hedley Byrne* in a wide variety of situations in which banks have not exercised reasonable care in negligent misrepresentation: giving assurances of financing but providing no financing;[163] providing inaccurate financial projections for an investment opportunity;[164] and failure to inform that a cheque would not be honoured after promising to do so.[165]

On the other hand, and in keeping with the requirements for negligent misrepresentation set out in *Hedley Byrne*, there is no liability on the part of a bank when a bank followed reasonable banking practices in refusing to honour an earlier undertaking to make a loan;[166] where there was no undertaking to make a loan in the first place;[167] where a bank did not undertake to give investment advice to a commercially sophisticated customer;[168] and where there was no reliance on the bank's advice.[169] However, where there is a negligent misrepresentation, a bank will not be protected by a disclaimer clause; rather, a court will find negligent misrepresentation — that is, it will treat the clause as it would treat any such clause in contract law generally by regarding the negligent misrepresentation as overriding the operation of the clause.[170]

The first reported case in either Canada or England in which a bank was found liable to a customer in fraudulent misrepresentation appears to be *Sugar v. Peat Marwick Ltd.*[171] in 1988, in which a court found on

---

Canada (1998), 49 C.B.R. (3d) 226 (Ont. Ct. Gen. Div.); *Royal Bank of Canada v. Woloszyn* (1998), 170 N.S.R. (2d) 122, 515 A.P.R. 122 (S.C.).

163 *V.K. Mason*, above note 154; *Atlas Cabinets v. National Trust Co.* (1990), 68 D.L.R. (4th) 161 (B.C.C.A.); *Dartboard*, above note 158; *Raypath Resources Ltd. v. Toronto Dominion Bank* (1996), 135 D.L.R. (4th) 261 (Alta. C.A.) [*Raypath*]; *Keith Plumbing & Heating Co. v. Newport City Club Ltd.*, [2000] 6 W.W.R. 65 (B.C.C.A.) [*Keith Plumbing*]; *Chapeskie v. Canadian Imperial Bank of Commerce* (2004), 43 B.L.R. (3d) 307 (B.C.C.A.); *Matrix Contractors Building Services Inc. v. National Bank of Canada* (2005), 200 O.A.C. 201 (C.A.).
164 *Bank of Nova Scotia v. Lienaux* (1982), 53 N.S.R. (2d) 541, 109 A.P.R. 541 (T.D.); *Heller*, above note 158; *Dartboard*, above note 158.
165 *Raypath*, above note 163.
166 *Pawlik v. Bank of Montreal* (1997), 196 A.R. 61 (C.A.).
167 *Pike v. CIBC Mortgage Corp.* (1995), 168 N.B.R. (2d) 321, 430 A.P.R. 321 (Q.B.).
168 *Doraldick Investments Ltd. v. Canadian Imperial Bank of Commerce* (2000), 5 B.L.R. (3d) 200 (Ont. C.A.); *Desharnais v. Toronto Dominion Bank* (2002), 9 B.C.L.R. (4th) 236 (C.A.).
169 *Alnu*, above note 162.
170 *Keith Plumbing*, above note 163.
171 Above note 147. A credit union had previously been found liable in fraudulent misrepresentation: *Fraser Valley Credit Union v. Canorama Development Corp*

the facts that a bank knew of substantial falsifications in the financial records of an insolvent company whose assets were sold to an investor without revealing its knowledge. Since 1988, courts have found banks liable for fraudulent misrepresentation more frequently and in various fact situations, including a failure to inform a customer of substantial changes to a bank contract;[172] a failure to inform a customer of falsified financial records;[173] inducing a customer to execute securities by false representations that a loan would be made available;[174] and inducement to guarantee an overdraft by false statements made by a branch manager.[175]

b) Taking Security

Whereas in cases of giving investment or financial advice, courts tend to prefer misrepresentation and, rarely, breach of fiduciary obligation, as the most appropriate legal principles, in the second category of cases, those in which banks take securities from a third party for a loan to a borrower, the preferred legal principles are unconscionability and unequal bargaining power. Cases framed in breach of fiduciary obligation and undue influence generally do not succeed.

However legally framed, the paradigm fact situation in these cases involves a wife or aged parent giving a security to a bank for a loan made to a husband or a child for the purposes of the husband or child's business which subsequently fails. Frequently the matrimonial home is involved in the secured transaction or is the only asset available with which to repay the loan after the business fails. The factual finding around which the resolution of these cases inevitably turns is whether or not the wife or parent voluntarily consented to the security transaction, and this depends on such matters as literacy, commercial sophistication, actual knowledge of the transaction, and potential for emotional manipulation within the surety's personal relationship with the borrower or as actually exercised by the bank in the context of taking the security.

In numerous cases, an absence of independent legal advice alone has been sufficient for a court to strike down the security agreement

---

(1984), 56 B.C.L.R. 145 (B.C.S.C.) [*Fraser Valley*]. See also *Maple Valley Acres Ltd. v. Canadian Imperial Bank of Commerce* (2001), 46 R.P.R. (3d) 32 (Ont. S.C.J.) and *Sinha v. Sinha*, above note 78.

172 *Armstrong*, *Baum*, above note 71; *Rancan*, above note 71.
173 *Sugar*, above note 147.
174 *Fraser Valley*, above note 171.
175 *Goad v. Canadian Imperial Bank of Commerce* (1968), 67 D.L.R. (2d) 189 (Ont. H.C.J.) [*Goad*].

where a failure by the bank to disclose fully the nature of the transaction or any conflict resulted in a breach of duty to the surety.[176] In a number of cases, unequal bargaining between the bank and the surety are sufficient for a court to find unconscionability in the transaction, although the terms of the security were standard market terms and not *per se* excessively harsh.[177] On the other hand, where the surety possessed commercial knowledge, experience, or sophistication, courts have treated the parties as of approximately equal power and stated that no independent legal advice need be recommended or obtained, whether the surety is a spouse[178] or another commercial party,[179] and enforced the security against that surety.

As stated earlier,[180] Canadian courts have largely eschewed the use of undue influence to adjudicate cases in which banks take security from a spouse or other family member, preferring unequal bargaining power, simple absence of independent legal advice, or unconscionability. Undue influence has been found where a husband and wife were threatened unnecessarily by a bank with foreclosure,[181] as well as where a husband pressured a wife into becoming a surety on the actual facts

---

176 See, for example, *McKenzie v. Bank of Montreal* (1975), 70 D.L.R. (3d) 113 (Ont. C.A.) [*McKenzie*]; *Buchanan v. Canadian Imperial Bank of Commerce* (1980), 125 D.L.R. (3d) 394 (B.C.C.A.) [*Buchanan*]; *E. & R. Distributors v. Atlas Drywall Ltd.* (1980), 118 D.L.R. (3d) 339 (B.C.C.A.); *Beaulieu v. National Bank* (1983), 47 N.B.R. (2d) 220, 124 A.P.R. 220 (Q.B.); *Hayward*, above note 98; *Bertolo v. Bank of Montreal* (1986), 33 D.L.R. (4th) 610 (Ont. C.A.); *Weitzman v. Hendin* (1989), 69 O.R. (2d) 678 (C.A.); *Canadian Imperial Bank of Commerce v. Ohlson*, above note 144; *Royal Bank of Canada v. Hussain* (1998), 37 O.R. (3d) 85 (Gen. Div.); *Canadian Imperial Bank of Commerce v. Brown* (1999), 2 B.L.R. (3d) 260 (Ont. S.C.J.); *National Bank of Greece (Canada) v. Mboutsiadis* (2002), 2 R.P.R. (4th) 98 (Ont. S.C.J.). See also M.H. Ogilvie, "To Be or Not to Be (A Fiduciary): *Bertolo v. Bank of Montreal*" (1988) 2 B.F.L.R. 256.
177 *McKenzie*, ibid.; *Buchanan*, ibid.; *Bomek v. Bomek* (1983), 21 B.L.R. 205 (Man. C.A.), leave to appeal to S.C.C. refused (1983), 27 Man. R. (2d) 239n.
178 *Murphy v. Tignish Credit Union Ltd.* (1993), 105 Nfld. & P.E.I.R. 193, 331 A.P.R. 193 (P.E.I.T.D.); *Royal Bank of Canada v. Domingues* (1995), 21 B.L.R. (2d) 79 (Ont. Ct. Gen. Div); *Orlando v. Toronto Dominion Bank* (2001), 13 B.L.R. (3d) 268 (Ont. S.C.J.); *Scaravelli v. Bank of Montreal* (2004), 69 O.R. (3d) 295 (S.C.J.). See also M.H. Ogilvie, "Judicial Intuition and Bank Fiduciary Obligation: *Scaravelli v. Bank of Montreal*" (2005) 21 B.F.L.R. 89.
179 *Bank of Montreal v. Minaki International Resort Corp.* (1998), 112 O.A.C. 291 (C.A.); *Toronto Dominion Bank v. Forsythe* (2000), 183 D.L.R. (4th) 616 (Ont. C.A.); *Royal Bank of Canada v. Aldridge*, [2005] 3 W.W.R. 599 (Sask C.A.).
180 See Section H(2), above in this chapter.
181 *Royal Bank of Canada v. Druhan* (1997), 157 N.S.R. (2d) 29, 462 A.P.R. 29 (S.C.).

of the case.[182] However, where the wife understood the transaction, a defence of undue influence has failed, although there was pressure on the wife to sign;[183] pressure alone is not enough where the wife understands the transaction into which she has entered.

Finally, in a few cases on their facts, the courts have found banks liable in negligent misrepresentation to customers from whom they have taken security for a loan.[184]

c) Giving References

The *locus classicus* for the third category of cases, those in which banks incur liability by giving credit references about customers is, of course, *Hedley Byrne*, in which the House of Lords opined that a bank may be liable for economic loss resulting from a negligent misrepresentation. When banks give credit references, both the customer about whom the reference is given and the recipient or user of the reference may potentially suffer loss. Although a bank still owes a duty of secrecy generally to a customer,[185] customers are typically required to waive that duty expressly on entering an account agreement, and banks as a matter of business practice give credit references on request about customers, so there can no longer be an issue of breach of contract at least in relation to the practice apart from exceptional circumstances where the customer has never waived the implied common law duty.[186] The legal issues, therefore, are about bank references containing inaccurate information resulting in loss to either the customer or the user.

Liability to a customer might sound in breach of contract or in the tort of defamation. The contract action might arise either from an implied duty to give the reference accurately, that is, with reasonable skill and care, or a duty found either expressly or implicitly in a contractual waiver of the duty of secrecy requiring references to be accurate. To date, there are no cases about liability in contract to the customer. On the other hand, a cause of action in defamation was acknowledged in

---

182 *Bank of Montreal v. Featherstone* (1987), 35 D.L.R. (4th) 626 (Ont. H.C.J.), rev'd in part (1989), 68 O.R. (2d) 541 (Ont. C.A.); *Del Grande v. Toronto-Dominion Bank* (1995), 21 B.L.R. (2d) 220 (Ont. Ct. Gen. Div.). See also M.H. Ogilvie, "Special Tenderness for Sexually Contracted Debt: A Feminist Banking Law in Embryo?" (1996) 11 B.F.L.R. 447.
183 *Duguid*, above note 138; *Rowatt*, above note 138; *Courtney*, above note 138.
184 *Goad*, above note 175; *Boehm v. Bank of Nova Scotia*, [1973] 3 W.W.R. 757 (B.C.S.C.); *McBean*, above note 98; *Toronto-Dominion Bank v. Paconiel Investments Inc.* (1992), 6 O.R. (3d) 547 (C.A.).
185 See Chapter 8, Section F.
186 *Turner v. Royal Bank of Scotland plc*, [1999] 2 All E.R. (Comm.) 664 (C.A.).

obiter dicta in an early case where the action failed on its facts because the information conveyed to a third party was found to be privileged.[187] Liability in tort would arise only if the information was inaccurate because the truth of any statement given would be a complete defence for a bank.[188]

Liability to the third party recipient or user of the credit report may sound in negligent misrepresentation as in *Hedley Byrne* or in breach of fiduciary obligation resulting from trust by the beneficiary that the bank is acting in its best interests. To date, there have been no reported cases of fraudulent misrepresentation, although this is also another possible cause where an honest belief in the contents of the report is not present. Negligent misrepresentation cases have failed on several grounds, including the presence of a waiver clause excluding liability for negligent advice about the customer's credit status[189] and an absence of reliance on the report by a recipient who chose to enter into a contract with the bank's customer on other grounds.[190] Typically, however, the few cases on this question have been framed as cases of breach of fiduciary obligation, presumably because trust in the accuracy of information to which only the bank has access is at the heart of giving credit reports about customers.

In *Vita Health Co. (1985) Ltd. v. Toronto Dominion Bank*,[191] the recipient of the good credit reports in relation to a company which the bank subsequently petitioned into bankruptcy succeeded in an action for breach of fiduciary duty by the bank on the ground that by undertaking to give advice, the bank had incorporated the requisites for fiduciary obligation into the relationship, including trust, conflict of interest, advice, reliance, and loss. Yet many more cases demonstrate that courts are reluctant to find fiduciary obligation or its breach frequently when banks give credit reports. Courts have declined to find

---

187 *Robshaw v. Smith* (1878), 38 L.T.N.S. 423 (C.P.D.).
188 Where a customer seeks to verify information the bank has about that customer, the bank must respond fully and accurately: *Midland Bank Ltd. v. Seymour*, [1955] 2 Lloyd's Rep. 147 (Q.B.D.).
189 *Cypress-Batt Enterprises Ltd. v. Bank of British Columbia*, [1994] 9 W.W.R. 438 (B.C.S.C.); *Totem Building Supplies Ltd. v. Toronto-Dominion Bank* (1999), 248 A.R. 241 (Q.B.). Compare *Les Fenêtres St-Jean Inc. v. BNC* (1990), 69 D.L.R. (4th) 384 (Que. C.A.) where gross negligence was found under the Code Civil.
190 *Vita Health Co. (1985) Ltd. v. Toronto-Dominion Bank* (1994), 118 D.L.R. (4th) 289 (Man. C.A.), leave to appeal to S.C.C. refused (1995), 122 D.L.R. (4th) vii [*Vita Health*]. See also M.H. Ogilvie, "What Can I Say? Bankers' References: Two Recent Cases" (1994) 10 B.F.L.R. 115.
191 *Vita Health, ibid.*

either the existence of the duty or its breach where a third party ought to have assumed or had constructive knowledge of a publicly registered security interest of the bank omitted from a credit report[192] or where there was failure by the recipient to inform the bank of its reliance on the report;[193] honesty by the bank in its report;[194] the absence of a close enough business relationship between the bank and the third party;[195] and the simple characterization of the relationship to the third party as a commercial relationship only.[196]

In *Accord Business Credit Inc. v. Bank of Nova Scotia*,[197] Cumming J. decided that there can be no fiduciary relationship in the first place when a bank gives a standard credit report because the recipient should realize the conflict-of-interest position of a bank giving information about a customer; the bank does not undertake to act in the best interests of the recipient; and the recipient could not expect more than honesty from the bank in relation only to what is contained in the report and nothing about what is not contained in that report or is about the bank's future intentions or actions. The giving of credit reports was within a purely commercial relationship and not a fiduciary relationship.

While *Vita Health* establishes the possibility of a fiduciary duty owed by banks to third parties in relation to credit reports, the preponderance of Canadian case law eschews this approach, preferring to see the relationship as commercial in nature and subject to the normal principles in contract and tort law employed in such relationships. This reflects the general bias in the commercial law against imposing fiduciary obligations on banks other than in exceptional circumstances where they have undertaken to put the interests of the other party above their own.

---

192 *Kuruyo Trading Ltd. v. Acme Garment Co. (1975) Ltd.* (1988), 51 D.L.R. (4th) 334 (Man. C.A.).
193 *Royal Bank of Canada v. Aleman*, [1988] 3 W.W.R. 461 (Alta. Q.B.).
194 *Ibid.*
195 *Canadian Imperial Bank of Commerce v. Derksen Brothers Holdings Ltd.*, [1995] 5 W.W.R. 1 (Man. C.A.), leave to appeal to S.C.C. refused, [1996] 2 W.W.R. lxxix (S.C.C.).
196 *Accord Business Credit Inc. v. Bank of Nova Scotia*, [1997] O.J. No. 2562 (Gen. Div.) [*Accord*]. See also M.H. Ogilvie, "Bank Credit Reports and Fiduciary Obligations: *Accord v. Bank of Nova Scotia*" (1998) 14 B.F.L.R. 183.
197 *Accord, ibid.*

I. CONSTRUCTIVE TRUSTEE

In addition to the primary duty owed by a bank to its customer pursuant to the banking contract and any superadded tortious fiduciary duties, banks may occasionally owe a duty in constructive trusteeship to a third party in relation to funds deposited in a customer's account. The *Bank Act* provides that a bank is not bound to see to the execution of any trust to which any deposit made is subject,[198] regardless of whether the trust is express or arises by operation of law or whether the bank has notice of the trust when acting on the order of the holder of the account into which the deposit is made.[199] Nor is a bank required by the common law under ordinary circumstances to inquire into the source, origin, or nature of a customer's deposits into a personal account,[200] although it may be so required pursuant to certain criminal law legislation in relation to money laundering.[201]

On the other hand, while a bank is not under an obligation to execute any trust, it is under an obligation not to interfere with funds that are held in trust in an account and so is placed under a duty of inquiry in suspicious circumstances as to the owner of funds in an account and deemed to be a constructive trustee of those funds for their owner. The paradigm fact situation occurs when a bank seizes funds in an account to set off against a customer's indebtedness to the bank pursuant to a security agreement and a third party asserts a prior legal right to those funds in the customer's account. The bank's liability is based on being a *trustee de son tort*—that is, a constructive trustee by virtue of one's own wrongdoing, although there is no fraud on that person's part nor actual knowledge of the trust. The trust is required to give an accounting of the loss and is subject to tracing of any money in that person's hands.[202]

The concept of constructive trusteeship imposed on a bank in relation to funds in an account was originally applied as between bank and customer and subsequently extended to third parties. In *Selangor United Rubber Estates Ltd. v. Cradock (No. 3)*,[203] a bank issued several drafts in relation to a company takeover, which involved illegalities of

---

198 *Bank Act*, above note 3, s. 437(3).
199 *Ibid.*, s. 437(4).
200 *Thomson v. Clydesdale Bank*, [1893] A.C. 282 (H.L.); *No. 10 Management Ltd. v. Royal Bank of Canada* (1976), 69 D.L.R. (3d) 99 (Man. C.A.).
201 *Proceeds of Crime (Money Laundering) and Terrorist Financing Act*, S.C. 2001, c. 41.
202 The principle was first formulated in *Barnes v. Addy*, [1874] L.R. 9 Ch. App. 244 at 251–52 (H.L.), Lord Selbourne L.C..
203 [1968] 2 All E.R. 1073 (Ch. D.).

which the bank was unaware, and when the company subsequently went into liquidation, the receiver sued for recovery of the sums on the basis that the bank was either a constructive trustee or negligent in the performance of its duties to the company, its customer. Ungoed-Thomas J. found that the bank ought to have known that the company's money was being used to purchase its own shares so that it was both negligent and a constructive trustee for the company in respect of the funds. The court stated that a bank owes a duty to exercise reasonable skill and care in relation to a customer and that the standard was an objective standard applicable to bankers.[204]

Although the outcome in *Selangor* has been questioned on the grounds that in the circumstances it was unrealistic for the bank to suspect the true nature of the transactions,[205] the principle has been supported in later cases[206] and formulated in England in *Lipkin Gorman v. Karpnale Ltd.*,[207] in which the Court of Appeal stated that the duty of inquiry should not arise when an account is being operated in a normal manner, only when there are unusual transactions or circumstances. This cautious approach is also reflected in relation to constructive trusteeship for a third party in the decision of the Privy Council in *Royal Brunei Airlines v. Tan*.[208]

Prior to *Tan*, the English courts had moved cautiously toward imposing liability on a constructive trustee such as a bank in relation to third party claims in customers' deposits. The *locus classicus* was *Barnes v. Addy*, in which Lord Selborne L.C. stated that liability as a constructive trustee could arise only where there is "knowing receipt" of the funds and "knowing assistance" in a dishonest and fraudulent design.[209] The former is receipt based and not fault based, and the cause of action is in restitution by the third party; the latter is fault based and the cause is for compensation.[210]

---

204 *Ibid.* at 1118–19.
205 Ellinger *et al.*, above note 120 at 125.
206 *Karak Rubber Co. Ltd. v. Burden*, [1972] 2 All E.R. 1210 (Ch. D.); *Rowlandson v. National Westminster Bank*, [1978] 1 W.L.R. 798 (Ch. D.).
207 [1989] 1 W.L.R. 1340 (C.A.). See also *Barclays Bank plc v. Quincecare Ltd.*, [1992] 4 All E.R. 363 (C.A.).
208 [1995] 2 A.C. 378 (P.C.) [*Tan*].
209 Above note 202. Compare the earlier cases to the opposite effect: *Gray v. Johnston* (1868), L.R. 3 H.L. 1 and *Tassell v. Cooper* (1850), 9 C.B. 509, 137 E.R. 990.
210 See generally M.H. Ogilvie, "(Un)Knowing Assistance by the Ontario Court of Appeal" (2004) 40 Can. Bus. L.J. 399 and the scholarly literature cited there.

Knowing assistance, sometimes also called accessory liability,[211] is based on dishonestly and fraudulently participating in a disposition of property in breach of trust. There are four requirements for liability: (i) the existence of a trust; (ii) a dishonest and fraudulent design on the part of the trustee; (iii) assistance by the bank in that design; and (iv) knowledge by the bank of the trust, the design, and its own assistance.[212] Although each of these attracted further clarification in subsequent cases,[213] the requisite degree of knowledge required for liability by a bank was the most difficult to define until the decision of Peter Gibson J. in *Baden v. Société Générale pour Favoriser le Développement du Commerce et de l'Industrie en France SA*,[214] in which five mental states were set out: (i) actual knowledge; (ii) wilfully shutting one's eyes to the obvious; (iii) wilfully and recklessly neglecting to make the inquiries an honest and reasonable person would make; (iv) knowledge of circumstances that would indicate the facts to an honest and reasonable person; and (v) knowledge of facts that would put an honest and reasonable person on inquiry. In *Baden*, the court was inclined to the view that knowledge in any of the five categories was sufficient for knowing assistance but in *Tan*, the Privy Council required dishonesty.

Tan was concerned with a director and shareholder in a travel agency who helped the agency to withhold money from its principal for application to improper purposes. On the insolvency of the agency, the principal sought to recover the funds from the director on the grounds of knowing assistance, and the Privy Council upheld its claim. Lord Nicholls stated that dishonesty was the state of mind required for knowing assistance and not knowledge, either actual or constructive. Although honesty has a strong subjective element, Lord Nicholls further stated that it could be assessed objectively, that is, the standard is that expected of an honest person in those circumstances.[215] Subsequently, the House of Lords by a majority for whom Lord Hutton spoke, opted in *Twinsectra Ltd. v. Yardley*[216] for a combined test for finding dishonesty: "it must be established that the defendant's conduct was dishon-

---

211 Since the *Tan* case, above note 208.
212 *Baden, Delvaux and Lecuit v. Société Générale pour Favoriser le Développement du Commerce et de l'Industrie en France SA*, [1983] B.C.L.C. 325 (Ch. D.) [*Baden*] and *Tan*, ibid.
213 See generally Ellinger *et al.*, above note 120 at 224–38.
214 *Baden*, above note 212 at 404.
215 Above note 208 at 389–91.
216 [2002] 2 A.C. 164 (H.L.). In *Barlow Clowes International Ltd. v. Eurotrust International Ltd.* (2005), [2006] 1 All E.R. 333 (P.C.), the Privy Council recommended this test but this case has yet to be received in Canada.

est by ordinary standards of reasonable and honest people and that he himself realized that by those standards his conduct was dishonest."[217] In dissent, Lord Millett preferred the largely objective test of the standard expected of an honest person in similar circumstances regardless of any subjective appreciation of dishonest conduct.[218] Although this test for knowing assistance is ambiguous, and each case will likely be decided on its own facts, the requirement of actual dishonesty, which is difficult to prove, means that banks are less likely to be found to be actually dishonest and therefore are likely to face few claims of constructive trusteeship in knowing assistance.

The underlying rationale for the other branch of liability set out in *Barnes v. Addy* of knowing receipt is quite different. Knowing receipt is more analogous to the common law action for money had and received, and the remedy is in restitution and is subject to defences, whereas knowing assistance is analogous to the tort of conversion and requires culpability. Three requirements must be met for liability: (i) funds have been disposed of in breach of a trust or of some fiduciary duty; (ii) funds are received by the defendant for its own benefit; and (iii) there is knowledge on the part of the defendant that funds are traceable to a breach of trust.[219] The paradigm fact situation for banks is echoed in these requirements when banks seize funds in an account to pay down a customer's indebtedness when it knows or ought to know there may be a third party claimant with a prior legal right to those funds, thereby constituting the bank as the constructive trustee of them.

Again, the most difficult requirement for the courts to define has been the degree of knowledge required for knowing receipt. If actual knowledge of a trust was the standard, then knowing receipt would be indistinguishable from knowing assistance because dishonesty in receipt would be present in either case; therefore, the English courts have moved toward constructive knowledge arising from sufficient notice of suspicious circumstances to put the bank on inquiry, although they have also conceded that such notice will be unusual in commercial cases because the ordinary conduct of an account or performance of contractual transactions will be insufficient to put a bank on notice.[220]

---

217 *Twinsectra Ltd. v. Yardley*, ibid. at 172.
218 *Ibid.* at 198.
219 *El Ajou v. Dollar Land Holdings*, [1994] 2 All E.R. 685 at 700 (C.A.), Hoffman L.J.
220 *Belmont Finance Corp. Ltd. v. Williams Furniture (No. 2)*, [1980] 1 All E.R. 393 (C.A.); *Polly Peck International plc v. Nadir (No. 2)*, [1992] 4 All E.R. 769 (C.A.); *Eagle Trust plc v. SBC Securities Ltd.*, [1992] 4 All E.R. 488 (Ch. D.); *Cowan de Groot Properties Ltd. v. Eagle Trust plc*, [1992] 4 All E.R. 700 (Ch. D.); *Eagle Trust plc v. SBC Securities (No. 2)*, [1996] 1 B.C.L.C. 121 (Ch. D.).

As Millett J. put the matter in *Macmillan Inc. v. Bishopsgate Investment Trust plc (No. 3)*,[221] "Account officers are not detectives."[222]

The Supreme Court of Canada has considered the constructive trusteeship of a stranger to a trust in several recent cases in which they carried on a dialogue with this evolving English law. In *Air Canada v. M. & L. Travel Ltd.*,[223] knowing assistance was considered where a travel agency selling tickets for Air Canada deposited ticket-sale funds into its general operating account, rather than into its trust account. When financial problems arose, countermanded cheques prompted the bank to refuse to honour any cheques, demand repayment of its operating loan, and seize funds from the account to satisfy the bank's indebtedness. In an action brought against the agency and its directors, the Supreme Court found the agency to be in breach of trust and that the directors were personally liable as constructive trustees. Iacobucci J. stated that two factors should be considered in knowing assistance: knowledge and the nature of the breach of trust. The court decided that actual knowledge and not constructive knowledge was required; constructive knowledge alone would not amount to a sufficient want of probity. The court further decided that the breach of trust must also be dishonest and fraudulent. It concluded that placing funds held in trust for Air Canada in a general operating account liable to seizure by the bank, rather than in a trust account, amounted to a breach of trust with actual knowledge on the part of the participating director who was liable as a constructive trustee. Whereas the English approach requires dishonesty for knowing assistance in the person, the Canadian approach requires that the dishonesty be in the actions of the person alleged to be the constructive trustee. What is clear, however, is that knowing assistance requires actual dishonesty, which remains difficult to prove for any plaintiff in law.

The Supreme Court considered the second branch of *Barnes v. Addy*, knowing receipt, in the other recent cases, *Gold v. Primary Developments Ltd.*[224] and *Citadel General Assurance Co. v. Lloyd's Bank Canada*.[225] In *Gold*, an uncle who was an equal beneficiary under an estate with a nephew entered a loan agreement with a bank secured by the

---

221 [1995] 1 W.L.R. 978 (Ch. D.).
222 *Ibid.* at 1014. For a similar cautious approach, see *BCCI v. Akindele*, [2001] 1 Ch. 437 (C.A.).
223 (1993), 108 D.L.R. (4th) 592 (S.C.C.). See generally: M.H. Ogilvie, "Deconstructing the Unconstructive Constructions of the Supreme Court of Canada" [2000] J. Bus. L. 36.
224 (1997), 152 D.L.R. (4th) 385 (S.C.C.).
225 (1997), 152 D.L.R. (4th) 411 (S.C.C.).

estate, which the uncle alone administered. The nephew approved this in writing but subsequently sued the uncle, the car firm, and the bank for breach of trust and indemnification for losses suffered. The Ontario Court of Appeal found that the nephew's agreement precluded an action for breach of trust against the uncle and that the bank did not knowingly assist in a breach because it had no actual knowledge but relied on the lawyer's opinion that the transaction was valid. The lawyer was also found to be partially liable. The Supreme Court, in a 4–3 decision, agreed that the bank had not breached a trust, but thought the case was better characterized as being about knowing receipt.

Again writing for the majority on the law, Iacobucci J. thought that sufficient knowledge to place on inquiry rather than actual knowledge was the appropriate test for knowing receipt, which was characterized as about unjust enrichment for which restitution ought to be made rather than about fault. Although on the facts, Iacobucci J. expressed the minority view that the bank had sufficient facts to place it on inquiry as a constructive trustee of the nephew's interests; the majority disagreed and found there were insufficient facts, particularly in light of opinions from both lawyers and accountants that the transaction was legal. In the view of Sopinka J., the bank was under a duty to act reasonably, and it would be a "counsel of perfection"[226] to impose a higher duty.

In *Citadel*, an insurance agent, who collected premiums on behalf of the underwriters of the policies, deposited these in its only bank account, which was usually in overdraft. The bank knew of this practice and subsequently received instructions to make daily transfers between the agent's account and an affiliated company's account to cover overdrafts in either account. Subsequently, the agent failed and the underwriter sued the bank for the outstanding premiums. Writing for the full court, LaForest J. set out two requirements for finding knowing receipt in relation to banks. The first is that the stranger to the trust receives trust property for its own use and benefit as happens when banks seize funds in an account to reduce a customer's indebtedness. The second is constructive knowledge when the stranger is put on inquiry by the circumstances but fails to do so. The court expressly rejected strict liability as the outcome without resort to constructive knowledge. In light of bank employee evidence that they knew insurance premiums were passing through the account and that the company was persistently in an overdraft position, the court concluded the bank was put on inquiry and was a constructive trustee for the funds for the underwriter.

---

226 Above note 224 at 409.

While there are details that must still be resolved in relation to deeming a bank to be a constructive trustee of funds in a customer's account for a third party,[227] the recent flurry of cases from the highest courts has confirmed the fundamental differences between knowing receipt and knowing assistance: the former is found where there are suspicious circumstances to put a bank on inquiry and to be constructive trustee for any beneficiary of those funds, while the latter requires actual knowledge, dishonesty, and fraud in the use of funds to which a beneficiary has a prior legal right. Yet, informally, Canadian courts have been following this approach in relation to banks for many years. There are numerous cases relating to mechanics' liens and construction liens in which courts have found banks to be on inquiry as to prior legal rights in funds in an account and imposed constructive trusteeship on them when they have seized those funds to discharge a customer's indebtedness to them.[228] Since the factual circumstances of each case determine the decision as to whether a duty of inquiry has arisen, each case is its own authority, and it is difficult to discern a more detailed set of principles for future guidance. However, the frequency of findings and the almost inevitable finding of constructive trusteeship whenever the customer is a company suggests that what is now called knowing receipt is more commonly found in Canada than in England. The duty of inquiry is more onerous for banks,[229] and the courts will award exemplary damages against them.[230]

---

227 See generally Ogilvie, above notes 210 and 223 and the scholarly literature cited there.

228 Ogilvie, above note 155 at 488–91 for the references to the mid-1990s and the following: *Royal Bank v. Roycom Realty Ltd.* (1996), 48 Alta L.R. (3d) 145 (Q.B.); *Canadian Imperial Bank of Commerce v. Melnitzer (trustee of)* (1998), 50 C.B.R. (3d) 79 (Ont. C.A.); *Con-Drain Co. (1983) Ltd v. 846539 Ontario Ltd.* (1997), 35 C.L.R. (2d) 230 (Ont. Ct. Gen. Div.); *Thomas v. Barnhardt* (1998), 114 O.A.C. 197 (C.A.); *Transamerica Occidental Life Insurance Co. v. Toronto-Dominion Bank* (1999), 173 D.L.R. (4th) 468 (Ont. C.A.); *Provincial Drywall Supply Ltd. v. Toronto-Dominion Bank* (1999), 47 C.L.R. (2d) 299 (Man Q.B.); *Peppiatt v. Nicol* (2001), 148 O.A.C. 106 (C.A.); *A. & A. Jewellers Ltd. v. Royal Bank of Canada* (2001), 53 O.R. (3d) 97 (C.A.). Compare *Progress Doors Ltd. v. Toronto-Dominion Bank* (2001), 6 C.L.R. (3d) 148 (Ont. C.A.).

229 Compare the approaches of the majority and minority in *Arthur Anderson Inc. v. Toronto-Dominion Bank* (1994), 17 O.R. (3d) 363 (C.A.), additional reasons at (1994), 14 B.L.R. (2d) 1 at 49 (Ont. C.A.), leave to appeal to S.C.C. refused (1994), 19 O.R. (3d) i (S.C.C.) and M.H. Ogilvie, "Banking-Contract—Mirror Accounts—Interpretation of Banking Accounts—Termination of Banking Accounts—Constructive Trusts" (1994) 73 Can. Bar Rev. 592.

230 *Claibourne Industries Ltd. v. National Bank of Canada* (1989), 59 D.L.R. (4th) 533 (Ont. C.A.).

J. DUTY TO LIFE INSURE MORTGAGES

For many customers, the banking arrangement most frequently entered into after the execution of an account agreement is a lending agreement, in particular, the loan secured by a mortgage with which to purchase a residence. Since mortgagees typically have no other assets beyond their equity in the property purchased, banks require, in most cases, that life insurance be purchased as security against the repayment of the mortgage where there are joint mortgagees in the event that one of them dies before the mortgage is retired. Typically, mortgage insurance ensures repayment of the loan so that the survivor is not obliged to lose a home. Since banks are prohibited from engaging in tied selling, the mortgagees may either buy life insurance on their own from an insurer of their choice that is satisfactory to the bank or the bank will arrange to make application on behalf of the mortgagee to an insurance company, which may be a related entity.[231]

Where the bank undertakes to make the application, it is under a duty of care to the applicants to procure insurance or to inform them of the rejection of the application.[232] Failure to do so constitutes negligent misrepresentation, although the bank will not be liable where the customers do not rely on the bank's failure to inform them that insurance is not in place.[233] Where a bank fails to make the application without informing the customers, yet collects the premiums but no insurance coverage would have been available for medical reasons, the bank is obliged to retire the mortgage on the death of a joint mortgagee.[234] An insurer is not bound when the application contains a material misrepresentation.[235] Where the customers waive life insurance, there is no liability on the part of the bank and the surviving customer remains

---

231 See generally M.H. Ogilvie, "Financial Institutions and the Duty to Life Insure Mortgages" (1997) 12 B.F.L.R. 301 and "Financial Institutions and the Duty to Life Insure Mortgages (No. 2)" (2003) 18 B.F.L.R. 409.
232 *Labreche Estate v. Harasymiw* (1992), 89 D.L.R. (4th) 95 (Ont. Ct. Gen. Div.) [*Labreche*]; *Green v. Royal Bank of Canada* (1996), 28 O.R. (3d) 706 (Gen. Div.) [*Green*]; *Newbury v. Prudential Insurance Co. of America* (1996), 35 C.C.L.I. (2d) 61 (B.C.S.C.), aff'd (1997), 46 C.C.L.I. (2d) 185 (B.C.C.A.) [*Newbury*].
233 *Toronto-Dominion Bank v. De Graauw* (1999), 122 O.A.C. 193 (C.A.). A bank may waive its duty to procure life insurance: *Bank of Montreal v. Bakheet Estate* (1995), 167 A.R. 101 (Q.B.).
234 *Gooderham v. Bank of Nova Scotia* (2000), 47 O.R. (3d) 554 (S.C.J.).
235 *Tanner Estate v. Toronto Dominion Bank* (2002), 212 Nfld & P.E.I.R. 211, 637 A.P.R. 211 (P.E.I.S.C.T.D.); *Menard v. Toronto-Dominion Bank* (2005), 191 Man. R. (2d) 109 (Q.B.).

bound to discharge the mortgage from their own assets in the absence of insurance.[236] When a bank negligently misrepresents the insurance coverage to customers, nominal damages may be awarded when insurance coverage is not available in the market at all[237] or substantial damages may be awarded when it is available.[238]

When life insurance is cancelled, the bank is obliged to give the customers reasonable notice so that they may make other arrangements.[239] On the other hand, when a bank overlooks mortgage insurance contrary to bank policies, no fiduciary obligation is owed to a customer whose husband dies without insurance, with the result that she will have to discharge the mortgage in the absence of insurance.[240]

K. CONCLUSION

The bank and customer relationship is in law no different from any other private law relationship today. Founded in contract, it is subject to contractual duties, both express and implied, but also to superadded duties in tort and in fiduciary obligation. The nature of these duties, that is, the legal requirements and standards of care associated with them, are those required by the law in other private legal relationships today. Although account contracts have become lengthier, more comprehensive, and skilfully drafted to transfer most of the risks to the customer, the courts' response has equally persistently been to maintain some balance in that relationship so that the overwhelming economic power of banks is not permitted full expression in the law.

---

236 *Burrows v. Bank of Nova Scotia* (2002), 36 C.C.L.I. (3d) 72 (Ont. S.C.J.).
237 *Green*, above note 232.
238 *Labreche*, above note 232; *Newbury*, above note 232.
239 *Noseworthy v. Newfoundland and Labrador Credit Union* (1999), 185 Nfld. & P.E.I.R. 341, 562 A.P.R. 341 (Nfld. S.C.T.D.). In *Toronto-Dominion Bank v. Valentine* (2002), 218 D.L.R. (4th) 225 (Ont. C.A.), which was about life insurance for a demand loan, the court found that where the effect of demanding repayment was to terminate the insurance, the bank was under a duty to give notice to that effect. In *Kimmel Estate v. Royal Bank of Canada* (1995), 177 A.R. 253 (Q.B.) a bank which did not tell the customer that an insurance was cancelled when the account from which the premiums were paid was closed by the customer, was not liable to the customer's estate in tort or contract. See also *Gowanlock v. Bank of Nova Scotia*, [2001] 9 W.W.R. 71 (Man. Q.B.).
240 *Jones-Ottaway v. Bank of Montreal* (2001), 275 A.R. 305 (Q.B.).

CHAPTER 7

BANK ACCOUNTS

A. INTRODUCTION

A bank is first and foremost a deposit-taking institution. Without the deposit of funds, banks would never have come into existence and would not be able to continue to provide the numerous financial intermediation services they offer in society and to the economy. The *Bank Act* acknowledges this when it provides that banks may receive deposits from any person without the intervention of any other person.[1] As deposit-taking institutions, banks are reservoirs of society's economic wealth as stated by Isaacs J. in the High Court of Australia: "[A bank] is, in effect, a financial reservoir receiving streams of currency in every direction, and from which there issues outflowing streams where and as required to sustain and fructify or assist commercial, industrial or other enterprises or adventures."[2]

Foley v. Hill[3] framed the two main economic functions of banks and deposit-taking institutions in legal terms as a contract of loan between bank and customer, but those two economic functions, of borrowing money from customers and lending money to customers, remain at the economic heart and significance of banking in any society, whether the borrowing or lending transactions are performed on paper or elec-

---

1   *Bank Act*, S.C. 1991, c. 46, s. 437(1).
2   *Commissioners of the State Savings Bank of Victoria v. Permewan, Wright & Co. Ltd.* (1914), 19 C.L.R. 457 at 471 (H.C.A.).
3   (1848), 2 H.L. Cas. 28, 9 E.R. 1002 (H.L.).

tronically. Without deposit taking, neither of these functions could be performed.

This chapter will discuss various aspects of deposit taking by banks, including the legal nature of a deposit, the various types of deposit, and the legal relationships among the various types of deposits that banks may take from a single customer. The next chapter will deal with transactions within deposits, that is, account operation as between bank and customer.

B. THE LEGAL NATURE OF A BANK DEPOSIT

The *Bank Act* does not define the term "deposit," but it has been defined by the courts as "an entry ... to the credit of a customer"[4] and as "something laid up in a place or committed to the charge of a person for safekeeping."[5] The word "deposit" in the Act assumes the common understanding of the word as a deposit of funds in an account, but the word is also used in banking practice to refer to the transfer of various items of property for safekeeping or as security for a loan. In this chapter, the term "deposit" refers to the deposit of funds in an account in both the legal and the common understanding of the word.

A deposit of funds in an account is characterized legally as a "loan" by the customer to the bank.[6] Thus, a deposit is also properly characterized as a debt, that is, a legal chose in action, and subject to the usual characterization of a debt in that it is capable of being passed from the owner to another party.[7] A deposit of funds with a bank means that the bank becomes the legal owner of property in those funds and is obligated to repay only an equivalent amount on demand. By contrast to other debtor and creditor relationships, it is the creditor, that is, the customer, who must make the demand for repayment, and if the bank refuses to repay, the customer must sue in debt for money had and received.[8] Only the customer or the customer's legal representative may demand repayment, and a provincial government has no legal right to substitute itself for the customer.[9]

---

4 *Reference re Alberta Legislation*, [1938] 2 D.L.R. 81 at 99 (S.C.C.), Duff J.
5 *Mercantile Bank & Trust Co. (Liquidators of) v. Credit Europeen S.A.* (1960), 32 N.B.R. (2d) 239 at para. 60 (Q.B.), Stratton J.; see also *Canadian Imperial Bank of Commerce v. Gardner Watson Ltd.* (1983), 25 Alta. L.R. (2d) 319 at 328 (Q.B.), Quigley J.
6 *Foley v. Hill*, above note 3 and Chapter 6, Section C.
7 For example see *Conveyancing and Law of Property Act*, R.S.O. 1990, c. C.34, s. 53.
8 Above note 6.
9 *Attorney General of Canada v. Attorney General of Quebec*, [1947] 1 D.L.R. 81 (P.C.).

Since an account into which a deposit is made is governed by one continuing contract, there is no new contract with every deposit, rather simply another deposit to that account.[10] Although there is no case law directly on point, it would appear that the deposit is only final in transferring property in the funds deposited to the bank once a provisional credit to an account is finalized through the clearing system. The deposit may be in any currency agreed by bank and customer and may be made into an account kept in that currency if foreign currency accounts are provided by the bank or transferred into the currency in which the account is kept. A bank is required to repay the customer in the same currency as that in which the funds were deposited unless there is an agreement to the contrary.[11] Foreign currency deposits have increased in the past two decades, especially in the form of swap deposits, in which the bank sells foreign currency to the customer to deposit with the bank for repurchase at a specific price in the future, thereby facilitating the maintenance of foreign currency in Canada.[12]

When an account contract is entered into and deposits are made into the account, the bank may promise to pay interest on that loan made by the customer to the bank. However, while *Foley v. Hill* established the right of the customer to demand repayment of the loan, no obligation to pay interest was mandated. Effectively, a bank may receive something which it never gives: an interest-free loan. Banks offer accounts on which interest may be paid and accounts on which no interest is paid, the latter typically being chequing accounts. There is no legal prohibition on customers making interest-free loans to banks!

However, when banks offer accounts in which they promise to pay interest on deposits, they become subject to legislative regulation of that interest. But customers are subject to statutory regulations in relation to that interest as well, of which the *Criminal Code* provision imposing an interest rate of 60 percent per annum is the most notable. The *Bank Act* makes no provision mandating interest or stipulating minimum or maximum amounts payable.

Section 347(1) of the *Criminal Code* provides that anyone entering into an agreement or arrangement to receive interest at a criminal rate is guilty of either an indictable offence and liable to up to five years' imprisonment or of an offence punishable on summary conviction and liable to a fine of not more than $25,000 or up to six months' imprison-

---

10 Hart (Inspector of Taxes) v. Sangster, [1957] 2 All E.R. 208 (C.A.).
11 Sheppard v. First International Bank of Sweetgrass, [1924] 1 D.L.R. 582 (Alta. C.A.).
12 Air Canada v. British Columbia (Minister of Finance), [1981] 2 W.W.R. 97 (B.C.C.A.).

ment or both.[13] A "criminal rate"[14] means an effective annual rate of interest calculated in accordance with generally accepted actuarial practices that exceeds 60 percent on the "credit advanced,"[15] that is, the aggregate of the money and monetary value of any goods, services, or benefits actually advanced or to be advanced under an agreement or arrangement minus the aggregate of any "required deposit balance"[16] and any fee, fine, penalty, commission, and other similar charge or expense directly or indirectly incurred under the original or any collateral agreement or arrangement.[17] "Interest"[18] means the aggregate of all charges and expenses for the credit granted but excludes any repayment of the credit advanced, any "insurance charge,"[19] "official fee,"[20] "overdraft charge,"[21] "required deposit balance,"[22] or any amount required to be paid for property taxes. When a person receives a payment or partial payment of interest at a criminal rate, in the absence of evidence to the contrary, that person is deemed to have knowledge of the payment and that it was at a criminal rate.[23] The consent of the Attorney General of Canada is required for proceedings under this section.[24]

The criminal interest-rate ceiling has never been, and is unlikely ever to be, considered in relation to the loan made to the bank by a customer who makes a deposit in a bank account because the bank, the borrower, actually sets the interest rate terms on which it will receive deposits and is unlikely ever to offer an interest rate on deposits of 60 percent! On the other hand, the criminal interest-rate ceiling does apply to loans made by a bank to a customer, and the banks are careful to ensure that such loans do not infringe the provisions of the *Criminal Code*, with the result that there is no case law on these sections involving banks.

The other statutory control on interest ceilings on loans is found in provincial unconscionability legislation.[25] However, it is uncertain

---

13 R.S.C. 1985, c. C-46, s. 347(1).
14 Ibid., s. 347(2). For proof, see ss. 347(4)–(6).
15 Ibid.
16 Ibid.
17 Ibid.
18 Ibid.
19 Ibid.
20 Ibid.
21 Ibid.
22 Ibid.
23 Ibid., s. 347(3).
24 Ibid., s. 347(7).
25 For example, *Unconscionable Transactions Relief Act*, R.S.O. 1990, c. U.2.

from a constitutional law perspective whether such provincial legislation would apply within the banking context, even considered from the customer's perspective, because of the overwhelming presumption in constitutional law that virtually all matters relating to banks should be federally regulated. On the other hand, a court could exercise its inherent equitable jurisdiction to control unconscionable lending transactions of either the customer or the bank.[26]

While there are no statutory ceilings on interest in the banking context with the exception of the criminal rate, the *Bank Act* does require that banks disclose the rates of interest payable on deposits with them. As discussed earlier,[27] these provisions require disclosure at the time of entering a banking account contract and throughout the duration of the contract by disclosures of interest and charges or fees, whenever these change. Contravention of these provisions results in liability for breach of the *Bank Act*.

C. OVERDRAFTS

When an account is in funds, the customer is the creditor of the bank, but when there is a negative balance in the account, or an overdraft, the customer becomes the debtor of the bank.[28] An overdraft is legally characterized as a loan granted to a customer by the bank, and as such, a privilege accorded to certain customers either from time to time or on an ongoing basis. An overdraft privilege may be granted by contract or by a course of dealing by which customers have been permitted overdrafts.[29] When granted by contract, the overdraft privilege is usually for a stipulated sum for a stipulated period of time at a stipulated rate of interest. Where a bank has permitted overdrafts in the absence of a contract, the course of dealing is established when the customer draws a cheque without sufficient funds in the account and the bank honours that cheque and thereby creates a debit in the account. This

---

26   *Canadian Imperial Bank of Commerce v. Ohlson* (1997), 154 D.L.R. (4th) 33 (Alta. C.A.).
27   Chapter 6, Section D(1).
28   *Alberta Treasury Branches v. McIntosh* (1993), 138 A.R. 303 (Q.B.).
29   *Cumming v. Shand* (1860), 5 H. & N. 95, 157 E.R. 1114 (Exch.); *Cunliffe Brooks & Co. v. Blackburn and District Benefit Building Society* (1884), 9 App. Cas. 857 (H.L.); *Bank of New South Wales v. Laing*, [1954] A.C. 135 (P.C.); *Thermo King Corp. v. Provincial Bank of Canada* (1981), 130 D.L.R. (3d) 256 (Ont. C.A.), leave to appeal to S.C.C. refused (1982), 42 N.R. 352 (S.C.C.) [*Thermo King Corp.*].

is characterized as a request for an overdraft which has been granted.[30] Repetition creates the course of dealing, and a bank is required to give reasonable notice of a decision to terminate the practice of permitting overdrafts.[31] In the absence of a contract, a bank is under no legal obligation to grant an overdraft by a course of dealing, although in one instance a bank was obliged to give the overdraft where a customer gave a security for a promised advance.[32]

When a bank honours a cheque and creates an overdraft, the bank is deemed to act as the customer's agent in making payment to the payee of that cheque. Thus, a decision to honour amounts to payment and is irrevocable because once the bank decides to pay, it effectively makes a loan to the customer in the overdraft, and the customer's decision about the disposition of those funds is the customer's, with the bank being merely the agent effecting the customer's instructions.[33] Effectively, a decision to grant an overdraft is a chose in action belonging to the customer and can be stolen from the customer by means of a forged cheque.[34]

While a bank is required to give reasonable notice of a decision to end the practice of permitting overdrafts, it is less clear whether a bank can demand repayment of an overdraft at any time in the absence of a contract governing demand for repayment. Although there is case law suggesting that banks should not demand repayment when they know about the transaction and its importance to the customer,[35] there can be no doubt that a bank can demand repayment of the overdraft in the same manner as for any other loan. Moreover, a bank is permitted to apply the proceeds of a term deposit when it becomes due to an overdraft without notice to the depositor.[36]

Since an overdraft is a loan, it is to be expected that interest may be charged on that loan, since it is highly improbable that a bank would ever make an interest-free loan. Agreed overdraft facilities provide for

---

30   *Cuthbert v. Robarts Lubbock & Co.*, [1909] 2 Ch. 226 (C.A.).
31   *Thermo King Corp.*, above note 29; *Cumming v. Shand*, above note 29.
32   *Fleming v. Bank of New Zealand*, [1900] A.C. 577 (P.C.). A bank is required to give notice of a reduction in an overdraft facility and is liable to the customer where it does not and refuses to honour a cheque within the original overdraft facility: *Raypath Resources Ltd. v. Toronto Dominion Bank* (1996), 135 D.L.R. (4th) 261 (Alta. C.A.).
33   *Re Hone*, [1951] Ch. 85. See also *Coutts & Co. v. Stock*, [2000] 1 W.L.R. 906 (Ch. D.).
34   *R. v. Kohn* (1979), 69 Cr. App. R. 395 (C.A.).
35   *Williams & Glyn's Bank Ltd. v. Barnes*, [1981] Comm. L.R. 205 (Ch. D.); *CIP Inc. v. Toronto-Dominion Bank* (1988), 55 D.L.R. (4th) 308 (B.C.C.A.).
36   *Deep v. Bank of Montreal* (1991), 47 O.A.C. 319 (Ont. C.A.).

the payment of interest, typically at the bank's variable lending rate, but in the absence of an agreement, a late-nineteenth-century Australian case[37] confirms that the appropriate rate is the bank's variable rate. Again, as with any other loan, interest is compounded until the entire amount is repaid,[38] with the exception of the outbreak-of-war situation, in which an account contract is suspended and the accrual of interest on that account when in overdraft is likewise suspended until the return of peace.[39]

D. LIMITATION OF ACTIONS

Whether either the bank or the customer is, respectively, a debtor depending on the balance in the account, any outstanding debt, as a contractual debt, is subject to the law relating to limitation of actions in relation to debt.[40] Actions in debt to enforce payment of the debt must be brought within a limited period of time from the day on which the debt is payable. At common law that period was six years, and statutory limitation periods in most Canadian jurisdictions have codified that six-year period.[41] When a customer has a credit balance in an account, the debt becomes due when demand for all or part of the balance is made and not paid over by the bank, that is, the limitation period of (typically) six years runs from that day for the amount in the account requested by the customer.[42] If the customer makes a series of specific demands for payment, then each will be subject to its own limitation period, so a series of limitation periods would result.[43] The sole exception to the usual limitation period is for unclaimed balances transferred

---

37 *Re City and County Property Bank* (1895), 21 V.L.R. 405 (Vict. S.C.).
38 *Yourell v. Hibernian Bank Ltd.*, [1918] A.C. 372 (H.L.); *National Bank of Greece S.A. v. Pinios Shipping Co. (No. 1)*, [1990] 1 A.C. 637 (H.L.).
39 *Deutsche Bank und Disconts Gesellschaft v. Banque des Marchands de Moscou* (1931), 4 L.D.A.B. 293 (C.A.); *Arab Bank Ltd. v. Barclays Bank*, [1954] A.C. 495 (H.L.).
40 *Joachimson v. Swiss Bank Corp.*, [1921] 3 K.B. 110 at 130 (C.A.), Atkin J.A. [*Joachimson*]; *National Bank of Commerce v. National Westminster Bank*, [1990] 2 Lloyd's Rep. 514.
41 *Ibid.* Some provinces have reduced that time to a shorter period: see, for example, *Limitation Act*, S.O. 2002, c. 24. There is also an unresolved constitutional issue as to whether the federal or provincial limitation period would apply, although this is not a practical issue in provinces that have not abandoned the traditional six-year period.
42 *Joachimson*, above note 40.
43 *Ibid.* Compare *Bank of Baroda v. ASAA Mahomed*, [1999] Lloyd's Rep. Bank 14 (C.A.).

to the Bank of Canada in relation to which a customer may sue for their payment within ten years from the last transaction or requested statement of account or the day on which a fixed term deposit terminated.[44]

When an account is in overdraft so that the customer is the debtor of the bank, the limitation period runs from the date of each advance, so that a series of limitation periods are created where there are multiple advances.[45] Although where an overdraft is contractually payable on demand, the limitation period runs from the time of the demand.[46]

E. DEPOSIT RECEIPTS AND PASSBOOKS

Even in this age of computerization, banks continue to issue passbooks and deposit receipts as evidence of the receipt of funds by a bank and of the current state of a customer's account. Many customers still regard the passbook as a valuable way to know the state of an account. The common law has long implied a duty into the bank and customer relationship that the bank must render statements of account to the customer on a regular basis and this has been codified in many account agreements today. The evidentiary value of the content of these statements and other related legal matters will be discussed later,[47] but issues relating to their status as legal documents *per se* will be discussed here. The ambiguous legal status of passbooks and deposit receipts appears to result from attempts by customers to treat them as negotiable instruments and to use their transfer from one person to another as a means of informally assigning balances in an account. Newer formats for rendering account by banks such as computer-produced monthly statements, ABM receipts, and online banking account statements have not been assimilated with the concept of negotiability, so that only traditional passbooks and deposit receipts have been the subject of litigation and therefore of this discussion.

In England, a deposit receipt has been clearly held not to be a negotiable instrument because it does not contain an express promise by the bank to pay the amount involved. Rather, its sole purpose is to be a record of the transaction with which it is concerned.[48] For this same reason, a passbook has also been found not to be a negotiable instru-

---

44 *Bank Act*, above note 1, s. 438. See Chapter 6, Section D(1).
45 *Parr's Banking Co. v. Yates*, [1898] 2 Q.B. 460 (C.A.).
46 *Bradford Old Bank Ltd. v. Sutcliffe*, [1918] 2 K.B. 833 (C.A.).
47 Chapter 8, Section E.
48 *Akbar Khan v. Attar Singh*, [1936] 2 All E.R. 545 (H.L.).

ment.[49] This means that the delivery and transfer of a deposit receipt or passbook does not confer rights on the transferee, who must show a valid assignment in some other document of the funds before a bank would be legally obliged to release those funds to a person other than the customer. Nor could passbooks or deposit receipts be considered as good security documents because their mere possession confers no legal rights on the person with possession.[50] While possession of a passbook is sometimes made a precondition by contract for a bank to repay funds in an account and enforceable by the courts,[51] a bank is not released from its legal duty to repay a customer who has lost a passbook or deposit receipt and who can prove good legal title even where the deposit has earlier been paid to an imposter.[52]

The legal position about passbooks and deposit receipts appears to be different in Australia and Canada. In Australia, where a bank issues deposit receipts expressly made negotiable, these are enforceable as negotiable instruments,[53] but Canadian courts have gone further and found deposit receipts generally to be negotiable instruments. Early Canadian cases followed English jurisprudence by declining to consider deposit receipts to be negotiable instruments, although they were being assigned as such in late-nineteenth-century commercial practice.[54] However, in some later cases on this matter, the courts found deposit receipts to be negotiable where the phrase "This receipt is negotiable" was found on its face, although it did not contain an express promise or any other characteristics for a negotiable instrument in law.[55] A deposit receipt made payable to order was found to prove good title to a *bona fide* purchaser for value,[56] as was a receipt that was endorsed and delivered considered to be evidence of a transfer of a title to a transferee.

---

49 *Birch v. Treasury Solicitor*, [1951] 1 Ch. 298 (C.A.).
50 *Hopkins v. Abbott* (1875), L.R. 19 Eq. 222 (V.C.).
51 *Clegg v. Baretta* (1887), 56 L.T.F.D. 775 (Q.B.); *Atkinson v. Bradford Third Equitable Benefit Building Society* (1890), 25 Q.B.D. 377 (C.A.); *Re Dillon* (1890), 44 Ch. D. 76 (C.A.); *Re Tidd*, [1893] 3 Ch. 154; *Re Griffin*, [1899] 1 Ch. 408; *Kauter v. Hilton* (1953), 90 C.L.R. 86 (H.C.A.).
52 *Wood v. Clydesdale Bank*, [1914] S.C. 397 (H.L.).
53 *National Bank of Australasia v. Scottish Union and National Insurance Co.* (1951), 84 C.L.R. 177 (H.C.A.).
54 *Bank of Montreal v. Little* (1870), 17 Gr. 313, 17 Gr. 685 (Ont. Ch.); *Richer v. Voyer* (1874), L.R. 5 P.C. 461; *Lee (Administrator of Lawlor) v. Bank of British North America* (1879), 30 U.C.C.P. 255; *Saderquist v. Ontario Bank* (1899), 15 O.A.R. 609 (C.A.); *Scott v. Bank of New Brunswick* (1892), 21 S.C.R. 30; *Ontario (Attorney General) v. Newman* (1901), 1 O.L.R. 511 (C.A.); *R. v. Lovitt*, [1912] A.C. 212 (P.C.).
55 *Provincial Treasurer of Manitoba v. Bennett*, [1937] S.C.R. 138.
56 *Richer v. Voyer*, above note 54; *Re Central Bank* (1889), 17 O.R. 574 (H.C.J.).

with the result that once the bank had paid the transferee, the original depositor could not succeed against the bank.[57] A certificate of deposit for a term deposit has also been enforced against the issuing bank by its assignee to whom it was assigned by a customer as security.[58] The cases considering whether a deposit receipt is a negotiable instrument may be assumed to apply also to passbooks because although there are no cases in relation to passbooks, the courts treat passbooks as equivalent to deposit receipts as evidence of an account.[59]

In addition to the question of whether the transfer of a passbook or deposit receipt effects the transfer of a legal interest in commercial practice, the question has also arisen when the owner has handed over either of these to another person shortly before dying with words to indicate an intention that the funds represented should also pass to the recipient. Can a passbook or a deposit receipt be the subject of a *donatio mortis causa*, that is, a gift to take effect on the donor's death? The answer to this question may be found in the will of the donor,[60] and there may be an intention on the donor's part to reduce any taxes payable on the donor's death.[61] But in other situations, the donor's intention to make a gift irrevocably of the funds in the account represented by a passbook or deposit receipt must be clear from the circumstances.[62] One evidence the courts require for an irrevocable intention is that the passbook or deposit receipt reaches the hands of the donee prior to the donor's death.[63] However, there are too few cases on the point to make much of it.

F. JOINT ACCOUNTS

Many different types of bank accounts are and have been available over the years, distinguished by the special features associated with them. These include accounts that are strictly for savings without chequing or other transactions access and that have higher interest rates, often varying with the minimum balance in the account; accounts that are

---

57 *Maunder v. Royal Canadian Bank* (1871), 20 U.C.C.P. 125.
58 *ITT Commercial Finance Ltd. v. Bank of Nova Scotia* (1989), 91 N.S.R. (2d) 247, 233 A.P.R. 247 (N.S.S.C.T.D.).
59 *Kendrick v. Dominion Bank* (1920), 48 O.L.R. 539 (S.C.A.D.).
60 See Section F, below in this chapter.
61 *McEvoy v. Belfast Banking Co.*, [1935] A.C. 24 (H.L.).
62 *O'Brien v. O'Brien* (1882), 4 O.R. 450 (H.C.J.); *McDonald Estate v. McDonald* (1903), 33 S.C.R. 145; *Adams v. Union Bank of Halifax* (1906), 1 E.L.R. 317 (N.S.S.C.); *Cusack v. Day* [1925] 3 D.L.R. 1028 (B.C.C.A.).
63 *Moore v. Ulster Banking Co.* (1877), 11 Ir. C.L. 512.

partly for savings and partly for chequing and other transactions, with lower interest rates; and accounts without interest for transactions only. The mix of savings or no savings, interest or no interest, transactions or no transactions, minimum balance or no minimum balance changes from bank to bank and from time to time as banks compete with one another for customers and assess what is profitable for them. With the exception of the provisions introduced in the 2001 *Bank Act* relating to low-fee and no-minimum-deposit or no-minimum-balance accounts for low-income customers,[64] the way in which banks structure accounts is a matter for each bank to decide within the context of the marketplace in which they operate.

Accounts are also available to a variety of potential customers individually or jointly, with one or more other persons in law, whether other individuals, corporate bodies, trusts, partnerships, or estates. Two of these categories of accounts have attracted a considerable volume of case law over the years: joint accounts and trust accounts.[65] Typically, joint account agreements are the same agreements as for any other account opened by an individual alone, with several clauses in the agreement making specific provision for the account where more than one customer are executing it in relation to a single account. These clauses typically provide for joint authorization to instruct the bank as to the funds in the account by one account holder only or more than one; joint and several liability for liabilities arising from the use of the account; designation for survivorship in the event that an account holder dies; and a prohibition on use of the account in the event that one of the account holders is declared bankrupt or insolvent.

These clauses reflect the older common law in relation to signature, joint liability, survivorship, and loss of legal capacity by operation of law, and the courts have extensively considered these clauses in turn. The law relating to joint accounts evolved by analogy to joint tenancies in real property law. Thus, they are distinguished by the right of survivorship, as well as by the four unities of a joint tenancy: possession, interest, title, and time. The real property analogy continues to be a useful guide to the legal nature of joint accounts.

Five specific issues have arisen in relation to joint accounts: (i) the nature of the legal rights enjoyed by joint account holders; (ii) the operation of the right of survivorship where the joint account is used as a means of estate planning; (iii) the nature of the legal liability among joint account holders and the bank; (iv) the application of rights of set-

---

64 Chapter 6, Section D.
65 See Sections F & G, below in this chapter.

off and appropriation to funds in the joint account; and (v) the garnishment of joint accounts.[66]

A joint account is a debt owed by the bank to the joint account holders jointly,[67] that is, each holder has the same right to possession, interest, and title for the same time in that debt as the other joint account holders. When the account is opened, each holder acquires the same right to draw on the funds in relation to the bank regardless of whether the bank is required to act on the signature of one account holder only or more than one.[68]

However, the legal nature of the relationship in the debt between the joint account holders on the one hand and the bank on the other is not necessarily conclusive of ownership of the debt as among the joint account holders. Thus, courts have looked beyond the formality of the account agreement to find that joint accounts have been opened for the convenience of the holder who deposited the funds in the account so as to deprive the other account holders of any interest in those funds where the circumstances showed this to be the intention of the depositor.[69] Even where the account agreement provided for survivorship, courts have found no necessary inference of an intention to convey the debt to the survivor.[70]

A joint account agreement defines the legal nature of the account in relation to the parties to the agreement but not necessarily the legal entitlement of the joint account holders among themselves to the debt

---

66 Older cases about joint accounts were based on different social assumptions about the relationship of husbands and wives, but the following discussion will pick through that jurisprudence from a contemporary perspective, assuming the legal equality of both opposite-sex joint account holders and same-sex joint account holders. There are numerous cases about joint accounts between spouses, and readers are directed to M.H. Ogilvie, *Canadian Banking Law*, 2d ed. (Toronto: Carswell, 1998) at 522–31 for extensive lists. The footnotes here will refer only to the leading cases and a selection of recent cases.
67 *Re Head (No. 2)*, [1894] 2 Ch. 236.
68 *Hirschhorn v. Evans*, [1938] 3 All E.R. 491 (C.A.).
69 *Marshal v. Crutwell* (1875), L.R. 20 Eq. 328; *Vanwart v. Diocesan Synod of Fredericton* (1912), 42 N.B.R. 1 (S.C.); *Southby v. Southby* (1917), 38 D.L.R. 700 (Ont. S.C.A.D.); *Stadder v. Canadian Bank of Commerce*, [1929] 3 D.L.R. 651 (Ont. S.C.A.D.); *Whitford v. Whitford Estate*, [1942] S.C.R. 166; *Niles v. Lake*, [1947] S.C.R. 291; *Frosch v. Dadd*, [1960] O.R. 435 (C.A.). Compare *Wandich v. Viele* (2002), 24 R.F.L. (5th) 427 (Ont. S.C.J.).
70 *Bourque v. Landry* (1936), 10 M.P.R. 108 (N.B.S.C.); *Larondeau Estate v. Larendeau*, [1954] O.W.N. 722 (H.C.J.). Compare *Taylor Estate v. Taylor* (1995), 9 E.T.R. (2d) 15 (B.C.S.C.); *Hammond v. Hammond*, [1995] 7 W.W.R. 345 (B.C.S.C.); *Berbaum Estate v. Silver* (2001), 193 N.S.R. (2d) 120, 602 A.P.R. 120 (N.S.S.C.); *Re Power Estate* (2001), 205 Nfld. & P.E.I.R. 163, 615 A.P.R. 163 (Nfld. S.C.T.D.).

represented in the account. A bank that deals with the funds in a joint account does so at its own risk when it has received notice that one holder claims those funds and may be liable to that holder if it deals with the funds so as to affect the claim.[71]

The legal nature of a joint account as between the parties to the agreement is further clarified by the bank's liability when it has honoured a mandate without the requisite signatures or a forged signature on a cheque; in such cases, the bank is in breach of contract in relation to all the other joint account holders because its duty is owed to each account holder in any joint account contract and liable in damages to each.[72] The purpose of requiring more than one signature was to prevent one joint account holder from acting to the detriment of the other.[73] Where the funds withdrawn by means of a forged signature were used for the benefit of the complainant, equity would preclude that person from succeeding in damages against the bank because they were used for the complainant's benefit.[74] Where the funds are withdrawn by one joint account holder to purchase property in that person's own name only, a court will not order the property to be held in the names of the other joint account holder or holders,[75] in the absence of evidence to the contrary.[76] It might be that a bank could be a constructive trustee in appropriate circumstances, but there would appear to be no cases on this point.

The second issue in relation to joint accounts, of survivorship, is resolved using the same general principles as ownership *inter vivos*. Account agreement clauses typically state that there is a right of survivorship in the account when one of the joint account holders dies, and this applies in relation to the bank. However, disputes may arise as between the remaining joint account holders and the estate of the deceased as to legal title in those funds where the beneficiary under the estate is not a joint account holder. There may also be an issue of taxation where the survivor is also a beneficiary under the estate, and the characterization of the legal means by which the funds reach that person may have tax consequences.

---

71 *Hill v. Bank of Hochelaga*, [1921] 3 W.W.R. 430 (Alta. S.C.).
72 *Jackson v. White and Midland Bank Ltd.*, [1967] 2 Lloyd's Rep. 68 (Q.B.D.) [*Jackson*]. See also *Twibell v. London Suburban Bank*, [1869] W.N. 127 (C.P.) [*Twibell*]; *Welch v. Bank of England*, [1955] Ch. 508 (C.A.).
73 *Caitlin v. Cyprus Finance Corp. (London) Ltd.*, [1983] Q.B. 759.
74 *Twibell*, above note 72; *Jackson*, above note 72. This is the principle in *B. Liggett (Liverpool) Ltd. v. Barclays Bank Ltd.*, [1928] 1 K.B. 48.
75 *Re Bishop*, [1965] Ch. 450; *Re Cameron* (1967), 62 D.L.R. (2d) 389 (N.S.S.C.); *Feaver v. Feaver*, [1977] 5 W.W.R. 271 (B.C.S.C.).
76 *Jones v. Maynard*, [1951] 1 Ch. 572.

Just as opening a joint account creates a rebuttable presumption of an intention to transfer legal title in all funds deposited to the other holders,[77] the same rebuttable presumption persists when a joint account holder dies; that is, there is a rebuttable presumption of an intention to transfer legal title to the remaining joint account holders, rather than to the deceased's estate.[78] There is a huge volume of case law in which the courts have presumed as between husband and wife,[79] parent and child,[80] and in other close family relationships,[81] that the deceased's intention was to make a gift to the survivor of the funds the deceased deposited in the account.[82] However, this presumption may be rebutted by the circumstances of the case, and then the survivor will hold the funds on resulting trust for their ultimate beneficiary under the deceased's estate.[83] Thus, the deceased may have established a joint account for practical household purposes when in declining health but still intended to leave the funds to a beneficiary under a will;[84] or in anticipation of marriage but died accidentally with the result that the funds form part of the estate, since the marriage might never have happened;[85] or died after cohabitation ended but before a joint account had been closed with the result that funds in the account passed to the estate.[86] When a joint account holder withdraws funds after the death of another holder, there will be accountability to the deceased's estate where the funds devolved to the estate.[87]

---

77   *Hill v. Hill* (1904), 8 O.L.R. 710 (H.C.J.); *Everly v. Dunkley* (1912), 27 O.L.R. 414 (Div. Ct.); *Smith v. Gosnell* (1918), 43 O.L.R. 123 (H.C.); *Sproule v. Murray* (1919), 45 O.L.R. 326 (S.C.A.D.); *Mathews v. National Trust Co.*, [1925] 4 D.L.R. 774 (Ont. S.C.).
78   *Ibid.*; *Russell v. Scott* (1936), 55 C.L.R. 440 (H.C.A.); *Kogler v. Schabernig Estate* (2004), 7 E.T.R. (3d) 31 (B.C.S.C.).
79   See the cases cited above in notes 69–70.
80   *Hill v. Hill*, above note 77; *Smith v. Gosnell*, above note 77; *Sproule v. Murray*, above note 77; *Whitford v. Whitford*, above note 69; *Edwards Estate v. Bradley*, [1957] S.C.R. 599.
81   *Re Reid* (1921), 64 D.L.R. 598 (Ont. C.A.); *McKenna Estate v. McKenna* (1986), 185 A.P.R. 51 (P.E.I.S.C.); *Shaw v. MacKenzie Estate* (1994), 131 N.S.R. (2d) 118, 371 A.P.R. 118 (S.C.).
82   *Re Doherty Estate* (1997), 190 N.B.R. (2d) 303, 484 A.P.R. 303 (C.A.).
83   *Re Mailman Estate*, [1941] S.C.R. 368; *Taylor Estate v. Taylor*, above note 70; *Hammond v. Hammond*, above note 70; *Berbaum Estate v. Silver*, above note 70; *Re Power Estate*, above note 70; *Saylor v. Madsen Estate* (2005), 261 D.L.R. (4th) 597 (Ont. C.A.).
84   *Marshal v. Crutwell*, above note 69; *Re Potter* (1926), 29 O.W.N. 327 (H.C.); *McLean v. Vessey*, [1935] 4 D.L.R. 170 (P.E.I.S.C.).
85   *Stefaniuk v. Toronto Dominion Bank*, [1979] 3 W.W.R. 382 (Man. Q.B.).
86   *Wandich v. Viele*, above note 69.
87   *Shortill v. Grannen* (1920), 47 N.B.R. 463 (S.C.); *Usher v. Barnes* (1921), 48 N.B.R. 358 (S.C.).

Many account agreements permit the survivor to continue to draw cheques on a joint account, and the assumption is that a bank is discharged from liability because it is meeting demands made by the survivor. The only case on this principle is uncertain as to the assumptions on which this outcome is based. In *McEvoy v. Belfast Banking Co.*,[88] a customer in failing health established a joint account with his son and ordered the funds in the account payable to either or to the survivor; this was done to avoid death duties. Subsequently, the father made a will leaving his assets in trust for his son until his twenty-fifth birthday, when he was to receive the estate unconditionally. When the father died, the executors transferred £10,000 to their own names to run the father's company, with the full knowledge of the son. Four years later, when the company was in liquidation, the son demanded the money, but the House of Lords upheld the bank's conduct with several different reasons given for that decision. Lord Thankerton thought the account contract to be between the father and the bank so that the son as a third party had no rights in relation to it. Lords Warrington and Macmillan thought the father had shown sufficient intention to give the money to his son, but Lord Atkin found sufficient intention on the father's part but no ratification by the son, so that he never became a party to it. Whatever the reason, the outcome is considered good law, that is, the bank was discharged from liability.

The third legal issue considered by the courts is the liability of joint account holders to one another and to the bank for overdrafts in the account. In England, liability issues seem to be related to signature — whether more than one joint account holder is required by contract to sign. Where one joint account holder forged the other's signature, the innocent holder's action against the bank failed on the ground that where both are to sign, then both must sue for recovery in breach of contract.[89] The bank apparently owed a single obligation. Subsequent English cases have either distinguished this earlier authority[90] or held that contractual obligations are owed to each joint account holder separately not to honour cheques unless both had signed as re-

---

88 [1935] A.C. 24 (H.L.). For the principle that the bank should only deal with the deceased's legal representative, see *Tymkow v. Rusnak* (1992), 6 Alta. L.R. (3d) 210 (Q.B.); *Ramsay v. Royal Bank of Canada* (1995), 32 Alta. L.R. (3d) 180 (Prov. Ct.).
89 *Brewer v. Westminster Bank Ltd.*, [1952] 2 All E.R. 650 (Q.B.D.).
90 *Hirschhorn v. Evans*, above note 68; *Baker v. Barclays Bank*, [1955] 1 W.L.R. 822 (Birmingham Assizes); *Welch v. Bank of England*, above note 72; *Jackson*, above note 72; *Caitlin v. Cyprus Finance Corp. (London) Ltd.*, above note 73.

quired.[91] But a broad principle has not yet emerged as to whether one account holder can sue for breach of contract alone.

In Canada, the few cases have dealt with the opposite situation, where the bank is suing one joint account holder in relation to an overdraft created by the other, thereby presuming that a bank can sue one holder alone. A single joint account holder cannot be held liable by a bank for an overdraft created by another holder where there is no knowledge of the actions of the other holder in relation to the account or where there is no express contractual undertaking to be liable.[92] In the only case where the innocent joint account holder was found liable, that holder had personally asked the bank to honour cheques drawn by the other, although unaware that the cheques related to a fraudulent scheme.[93] Although there is no case law, it seems likely that even where there is an express undertaking of joint and several liability as is usual in joint account contracts, the courts may be prepared to treat it like any other clause in a standard form contract in an equitable manner in appropriate circumstances.

A related issue is the treatment of joint account holders when a bank learns that one or more is bankrupt or incompetent. While there is no case law on the matter, it seems that a bank ought to decline to honour all payment instructions for funds in the account for two reasons. First, this is the usual practice in relation to bankrupt or incompetent customers until a trustee is appointed and a trust account is established; and secondly, it is established in banking law that when banks learn of disputes among joint account holders, they should stop all further transactions in relation to the account and resort, if necessary, to interpleader proceedings to resolve any ownership issues in relation to the joint account.[94]

Thirdly, although there is little case law on the matter, it seems clear that funds in a joint account can be set off against an overdraft in another account held in the name of one of the joint account holders (as account contracts typically provide) prior to acquiring knowledge

---

91 *Caitlin v. Cyprus Finance Corp. (London) Ltd.*, ibid.
92 *Bank of Montreal v. Hancock* (1982), 137 D.L.R. (3d) 648 (Ont. H.C.J.); *Edmonton Savings & Credit Union Ltd. v. Yarmuch* (1985), 60 A.R. 219 (Q.B.). See also M.H. Ogilvie, "Joint Accounts and Overdraft Liability" (1985) 23 U.W.A. L. Rev. 67. When a bank converts a wife's personal account into a joint account at the request of her husband and without her knowledge, the bank is liable to the wife for funds withdrawn from the accounts and any damages: *Vuckovich v. Royal Bank of Canada* (1998), 158 D.L.R. (4th) 37 (Ont. C.A.).
93 *Bank of Montreal v. Vaillancourt* (1983), 149 D.L.R. (3d) 560 (Ont. C.A.).
94 *Hill v. Bank of Hochelaga*, above note 71.

about the ownership of funds in the joint account should the presumption of ownership subsequently be successfully disputed.[95] Banks may assume, *prima facie*, that funds in a joint account are available for the use of any holder in the absence of evidence to the contrary. The converse also seems correct, that is, banks are permitted to set off an overdraft in a joint account from funds in an individual account because all debts in a joint account are joint and several and the bank has a right of action against any one holder for an overdraft in a joint account.

Fourthly, a joint account cannot be the subject of a garnishment order, even where the joint account holders are spouses, in respect of an indebtedness owed by only one of the holders.[96] Joint account agreements apply only to the legal duties as between joint account holders and the bank as to the disposition of funds, but not to third parties to those funds to whom one of the joint account holders may be indebted. In relation to garnishment, a joint account holder may be able to rebut the presumption of joint ownership of funds in the account by proving that they belong to the joint account holder who is not the subject of the garnishment order.[97] On the other hand, if all the joint account holders are also jointly and severally liable to the party initiating the garnishment order, then the joint account may be garnished.

G. TRUST ACCOUNTS

Trust accounts, in which funds are held in trust explicitly for a third party to the bank and customer account agreement, are opened for

---

95 *Ibid.*
96 *MacDonald v. Tacquah Gold Mines Co.* (1884), 13 Q.B.D. 535 (C.A.); *Beasley v. Roney*, [1891] 1 Q.B. 509; *Hirschhorn v. Evans*, above note 68; *Runk v. Jackson*, [1917] 1 W.W.R. 485 (Alta. Dist. Ct.); *Re Davis* (1958), 13 D.L.R. (2d) 411 (B.C.S.C.); *Hoon v. Maloff* (1964), 42 D.L.R. (2d) 770 (B.C.S.C.); *Royal Bank of Canada v. Tompkins*, [1976] W.W.D. 174 (B.C.S.C.); *J.R. Corneau Holdings Ltd. v. Pockett*, [1978] 5 W.W.R. 483 (Man. Co. Ct.); *Canuck Truck Rentals Ltd. v. Mountain Truck Service* (1980), 16 C.P.C. 126 (B.C. Co. Ct.); *Olympic Bank v. Wallace* (1982), 19 B.L.R. 145 (B.C.S.C.); *Bank of Montreal v. Big White Land Dev. Ltd.* (1982), 17 B.L.R. 257 (B.C.S.C.); *Westcoast Commodities Inc. v. Chen* (1987), 28 D.L.R. (4th) 635 (Ont. H.C.J.); *Director of Support & Custody Enforcement v. Jones* (1991), 85 D.L.R. (4th) 375 (Ont. Div. Ct.). Compare *Empire Fertilizer Ltd. v. Cioci*, [1934] 4 D.L.R. 804 (Ont. C.A.); *Galipeau Musique Ltd. v. Heckbert* (1979), 28 N.B.R. (2d) 163, 63 A.P.R. 163 (Co. Ct.). See also M.H. Ogilvie, "Why Joint Accounts Should Not Be Garnished" (1987) 1 B.F.L.R. 267.
97 Ontario Law Reform Commission, *Report on the Enforcement of Judgment Debts and Related Matters*, vol. 2 (Toronto: The Commission, 1981) at 142–46.

many purposes by various categories of trustees: insolvency or receivership; by legal guardians of infants or others who lack legal capacity; by trustees themselves; by estate trustees; or by one or more individuals holding funds on behalf of an unincorporated association or community group; a religious organization; or some other person pursuant to a private arrangement for which no formal legal documentation is available. By opening a trust account, the bank is told, *ipso facto,* that the customer is a trustee, but the bank does not otherwise become involved, and from the bank's perspective, the customer operates the account like any other account. The customer is the trustee, not the bank, and the bank assumes that there is compliance with the trust in the operation of the account.

The *Bank Act* expressly prohibits banks from engaging in fiduciary activities such as being trustees directly[98] and further provides that a bank is not bound to see to the execution of any trust, whether express or arising by operation of law, to which any deposit under the Act is subject.[99] Nor is a bank bound to see to the execution of any trust of which it has notice if it acts on the order of the holder of the account into which deposits are made.[100] *Primâ fâcie,* a bank is statutorily exempt from any liability for breach of trust by a trustee, whether the funds are held in trust in a trust account or in any other account and for trust funds. This exemption codifies the earlier common law, which held that a bank is not *prima facie* responsible for ensuring that funds are properly applied within the terms of a trust, when it knows that funds are held in trust or in a trust account.[101]

However, as discussed earlier,[102] while banks are not liable for breach of trust by a trustee, when they have notice of the existence of a trust or open a trust account, they may themselves become constructive trustees for a third party in relation to funds deposited in an account not designated as a trust account. As a constructive trustee, a bank is required to hold the funds for the third party and not allow them to be used for some other purpose, although they are not obliged to carry out the trust purposes. Suspicious circumstances may result in a duty of inquiry in respect to funds and liability to the true owner or beneficiary of those funds when they apply funds held in trust to

---

98 Chapter 5, Section F(2).
99 *Bank Act*, above note 1, s. 437(3).
100 *Ibid.*, s. 437(4).
101 *Gray v. Johnston* (1868), L.R. 3 H.L. 1; *Bailey v. Jellett* (1884), 9 O.A.R. 187 (C.A.); *Banque Romande v. Mercantile Bank of Canada*, [1971] 3 O.R. 433 (C.A.), aff'd (1973), 45 D.L.R. (3d) 480 (S.C.C.).
102 Chapter 6, Section I.

pay down an indebtedness owed to it by the customer[103] or set off funds from a trust account against an indebtedness in the customer's own account.[104] Where an account is mixed, to the knowledge of the bank, all funds in the account should be treated as trust funds.[105]

H. GARNISHMENT OF DEPOSITS

The *Bank Act* provides that court orders in relation to an interest in any deposit account binds only property in the possession of a bank belonging to a person at the branch where the order is served and affects only money owing to that person on deposit at that branch.[106] Since a garnishment is a court order, this requirement means that a garnishment order must be directed to a specific branch of a bank at which the debtor is believed to have funds on deposit, and that each branch must be separately garnisheed. The bank is required to comply with a garnishment order; otherwise it would be in contempt of court, but where an order is served at the same time as the presentment of cheques, a bank is entitled to reasonable time to consider the situation.[107] A bank has a duty to satisfy itself as to the identity of the garnishee, who may keep an account under a trade name, although sued in their own name.[108] Where the account garnisheed is a trust account, the bank should seek directions from the court as to payment.[109]

I. APPROPRIATION OF PAYMENTS

In the normal course of a bank and customer relationship, a customer may become indebted to a bank in various ways, for example, by an overdraft in one or more accounts or by virtue of a loan extended to the

---

103 *Ibid.*, especially note 227.
104 *Re Gross* (1871), 6 Ch. App. 632 (C.A.); *Imperial Bank v. Begley*, [1936] 3 D.L.R. 1 (P.C.); *Fonthill Lumber Ltd. v. Bank of Montreal*, [1959] O.R. 451 (C.A.); *Bank of Montreal v. R. & R. Entertainment Ltd.* (1984), 13 D.L.R. (4th) 726 (N.B.C.A.); *Bateman v. Toronto Dominion Bank* (1991), 86 D.L.R. (4th) 354 (B.C.S.C.).
105 *Stobart v. Axford* (1893), 9 Man. R. 18 (Q.B.).
106 *Bank Act*, above note 1, s. 462(1).
107 *Todd v. Union Bank of Canada* (1887), 4 Man. R. 204 (C.A.). A bank cannot act on a pre-judgment garnishee order: *Royal Bank of Canada v. G.L.B. Holdings Ltd.* (1998), 171 Sask. R. 139 (Q.B.).
108 *Smith v. Gautschi*, [1917] 2 W.W.R. 225 (B.C.C.A.).
109 *Garon Realty & Insurance Ltd. v. James*, [1978] 6 W.W.R. 694 (B.C.S.C.).

customer. Where the customer also has other assets deposited with the bank, for example, funds in other accounts or securities given to secure a loan, failure by a customer to discharge a loan raises the question of whether a bank may use those assets to pay down the loan either with or without the consent of the customer. Bank agreements typically provide that banks may do so, and such clauses reflect the common law in this regard.

There are three discrete situations in which banks may affect a customer's funds: (i) by appropriation of payments within an individual account; (ii) by set-off between accounts, account consolidation or combination; and (iii) by exercise of a banker's lien over other assets of the customer, in order to discharge in whole or in part a customer's indebtedness. Each of these will be considered in this and the two succeeding sections.

The normal rule in debtor and creditor relationships is that when a debtor pays funds to a creditor, the debtor may decide to which debt the payment may be appropriated and the creditor is entitled to do so only when the debtor fails to designate the appropriation; furthermore, the creditor's appropriation is completed only when communicated to the debtor.[110] Where the right of appropriation devolves to the creditor, it may be exercised "up to the very last minute,"[111] even during an examination of the debtor by the creditor in an action for debt.[112] But in the bank and customer relationship, this presumption is displaced; that is, in relation to appropriation of payments, there is a presumption that the credit entries in an account extinguish the debt entries in historical order: the earliest payments in are attributed to the earliest drawings out. This is the "first in, first out" principle, known as the rule in *Clayton's Case*.[113]

This rule is a presumption only as to the intention of the parties, but it has become the standard banking practice in the operation of bank accounts. Moreover, it is widely understood to apply only within a single account and not across accounts held by one customer at the same bank.[114] However, the courts have found this presumption to be rebutted in a number of situations: (i) where a contrary intention is

---

110 *Deeley v. Lloyds Bank*, [1912] A.C. 756 (H.L.). See also *Royal Bank of Canada v. Slack* (1958), 11 D.L.R. (2d) 737 (Ont. C.A.).
111 *Cory Bros. & Co. v. The "Mecca,"* [1897] A.C. 286 (H.L.).
112 *Seymour v. Pickett*, [1905] 1 K.B. 715 (C.A.); *Thomson v. Stikeman* (1913), 17 D.L.R. 205 (Ont. C.A.).
113 *Devaynes v. Noble; Clayton's Case* (1816), 1 Mer. 572; 35 E.R. 781 (H.L.). See also *Salter & Arnold Ltd. v. Dominion Bank*, [1926] S.C.R. 621 [*Salter & Arnold*].
114 *Royal Bank of Canada v. Bank of Montreal* (1976), 67 D.L.R. (3d) 755 (Sask. C.A.).

expressed by both parties;[115] (ii) where a contrary course of dealing indicates another appropriation;[116] (iii) where trust funds are mingled in a personal account and are to be privileged;[117] (iv) where a new account is opened;[118] (v) where there is a secured transaction and a second mortgagee agrees to fresh advances by the first mortgagee;[119] (vi) where fresh advances are made pursuant to an initial agreement between the debtor and the first mortgagee;[120] (vii) where there is both a secured and an unsecured debt;[121] (viii) where funds paid in are earmarked for a particular purpose, for example, to meet a particular bill or cheque;[122] and (ix) where there are several depositors or creditors with conflicting claims to the funds in the account or a single creditor with conflicting claims to funds in the account. In this last situation, a *pro rata* sharing of the remaining funds in the account is the proper resolution when there are insufficient funds to satisfy all claims.[123]

Whether an appropriation is made in accordance with the presumption or an exception to the presumption, it is irrevocable once it is made,[124] although freezing an account is not an irrevocable appropriation alone.[125]

---

115 *Deeley v. Lloyds Bank*, above note 110; *Gillies v. Commercial Bank of Manitoba* (1895), 10 Man. R. 460 (C.A.); *Bank of Nova Scotia v. Neil* (1968), 69 D.L.R. (2d) 357 (B.C.C.A.); *Fuller Brush Co. v. Hazell* (1975), 54 D.L.R. (3d) 22 (Ont. H.C.J.); *Royal Bank of Canada v. Bender* (1994), 159 A.R. 303 (Q.B.); *Royal Bank of Canada v. Executive Life Insurance Agency Ltd.* (1996), 138 Nfld. & P.E.I.R. 10, 431 A.P.R. 10 (Nfld. S.C.T.D.).
116 *Leeson v. Leeson*, [1936] 2 K.B. 156 (C.A.).
117 *Re Hallett's Estate* (1880), 13 Ch. D. 696; *Re Oatway*, [1903] 2 Ch. 356; *Bailey v. Jellett* (1884), 9 O.A.R. 187 (C.A.).
118 *Siebe Gorman & Co. v. Barclays Bank Ltd.*, [1979] 2 Lloyd's Rep. 142 (Ch. D.).
119 *Ibid.*
120 *Ibid.*
121 *Deeley v. Lloyds Bank*, above note 110; *Royal Bank of Canada v. Slack*, above note 110; *Bank of Nova Scotia v. Neil*, above note 115.
122 *Farley v. Turner* (1857), 26 L.J. Ch. 710.
123 *Re Ontario Securities Commission and Greymac Credit Corp.* (1986), 30 D.L.R. (4th) 1 (Ont. C.A.), aff'd (1988), 52 D.L.R. (4th) 767n. (S.C.C.); *British Columbia v. National Bank of Canada* (1994), 119 D.L.R. (4th) 669 (B.C.C.A.). Compare *Law Society of Upper Canada v. Toronto-Dominion Bank* (1998), 169 D.L.R. (4th) 353 (Ont. C.A.) and M.H. Ogilvie, "*Pari Passu* Distribution of Commingled Funds" (2000) 15 B.F.L.R. 545; Lionel Smith, "Tracing in Bank Accounts: The Lowest Intermediate Balance Rule on Trial" (2000) 33 Can Bus. L.J. 75.
124 *Slovchenko v. Toronto-Dominion Bank* (1964), 42 D.L.R. (2d) 484 (Ont. H.C.J.).
125 *Clarkson v. Smith & Goldberg*, [1926] 1 D.L.R. 509 (Ont. C.A.).

J. SET-OFF AND ACCOUNT COMBINATION

The rule in *Clayton's Case* applies only to appropriations within a single account. But customers typically have several accounts with a bank, as well as accounts at several branches of the same bank. Where a customer creates an overdraft in an account or draws a cheque that can be paid only by combining funds in more than one account, the question is raised of whether a bank may combine or consolidate funds or accounts to discharge the overdraft loan or honour the payment instruction. In the case of an overdraft, the bank wishes to set off other funds to discharge an indebtedness to it, that is, for its own purposes, but where it wishes to do so to comply with a customer's mandate, it is doing so for the customer's purposes, that is, to discharge the customer's indebtedness to a third party. Banks are expected to honour a customer's mandates generally both by contract and to protect the customer's reputation.[126] Bank and customer agreements typically provide that banks may exercise a right of set-off to discharge an indebtedness to the bank without notice to the customer, but they are less likely to make provision for set-off to ensure payment of any payment instruction from the customer. The exercise of set-off, then, requires consideration of the common law against which account agreements operate. Most of the case law is concerned with the situation where a bank combines accounts in its own interest, and this situation will be considered first.

A bank's right to combine accounts in order to discharge an overdraft is based on the fundamental bank and customer contractual relationship entered into when the first account is opened. In *Re European Bank, Agra Bank Claims*,[127] the customer bank maintained three accounts at another bank, but both banks failed. The indebtedness in two accounts was covered, but the question arose of whether securities originally given to cover acceptances of bills of exchange in relation to one of these accounts could be applied to discharge the indebtedness in the third account or were to be given to the liquidator. The English Court of Appeal found that the securities could be applied to the indebtedness in the third account on the ground that there was essentially one account(ing) between the bank and customer, although there may have been several accounts.[128] Although it is arguable that each account opened between bank and customer is a separate contractual agreement, *Re European Bank* has become widely accepted in

---

126 Chapter 8, Section C(1).
127 (1872), L.R. 8 Ch. 41 (C.A.).
128 *Ibid.* at 44, James L.J.

banking law[129] and enshrined in most bank and customer contracts in widespread use today.

The last time a final appellate court considered this issue was in 1972 in the House of Lords in *National Westminster Bank Ltd.* v. *Halesowen Presswork & Assemblies Ltd.*,[130] which clarified the distinction between set-off and the exercise of a banker's lien. In that case, it was agreed that a customer whose company accounts were in substantial overdraft would open another account as a working account and that the corporate accounts would be consolidated and frozen until the company's affairs improved. The customer subsequently resolved to wind down voluntarily, and the bank took the view that this decision constituted a material change of circumstances and set-off the balance in the working account against the overdraft in the frozen account. The House of Lords upheld the bank's right to do so.

The law lords used the terms "set-off," "combination" and "consolidation of accounts" interchangeably, thereby indicating that these are different ways of referring to the same concept. However, they also distinguished "combination" and "lien." Account combination or set-off cannot be an exercise of a right of lien because the funds set-off belong to the bank by virtue of the bank and customer contract as a debt owed to the customer, whereas a lien does not confer legal title. A person cannot have a lien over that person's own property, especially when it is in that person's possession. In *Halesowen*, the law lords also rejected an argument that account combination by the bank constituted a fraudulent preference and thereby distinguished fraudulent preference, which can be initiated only by the insolvent person.[131] Where account combination is the result of an express agreement between bank and customer, there is a possibility of fraudulent preference;[132] otherwise, the courts have consistently upheld the right of banks to set-off between accounts in the ordinary course of business, and they have denied a right of recovery to a liquidator or trustee in bankruptcy.[133] This right of set-off may also be exercised against

---

129 *Garnett* v. *McKewan* (1872), L.R. 8 Exch. 10; *Salter & Arnold*, above note 113; *Wallinder* v. *Imperial Bank of Canada* (1925), 36 B.C.R. 226 (C.A.); *Sutcliffe & Sons Ltd., Ex parte Royal Bank of Canada, Re*, [1933] O.R. 120 (Ont. C.A.) [*Re Sutcliffe*]; *O'Hearn* v. *Bank of Nova Scotia*, [1970] S.C.R. 341.
130 [1972] A.C. 785 (H.L.) [*National Westminster Bank* v. *Halesowen*].
131 *Bankruptcy and Insolvency Act*, R.S.C. 1985, c. B-3, s. 42.
132 *Re D.W. McIntosh Ltd.* (1940), 21 C.B.R. 469 (Ont. S.C.); *Re West Bay Sales Ltd.* (1979), 26 O.R. (2d) 562 (S.C.).
133 *Salter & Arnold*, above note 113; *Re Sutcliffe*, above note 129; *Ross* v. *Royal Bank of Canada* (1966), 52 D.L.R. (2d) 578 (Ont. H.C.J.); *Re T.C. Marines Ltd.*, [1973] 2 O.R. 537 (H.C.J.). This is also the case where the accounts combined reflect the proceeds of a sale of goods or accounts receivable: *Re Sutcliffe, ibid.*; *Canadian*

a note or negotiable instrument provided it has matured[134] and against foreign currency term deposits when they fall due.[135]

The right to initiate a set-off is explicitly enjoyed only by a bank, although the effect of netting accounts between bank and customer is a benefit to the customer, as well as to the bank, because it reduces the amount of interest accruing on any overdraft and clarifies the net position with the bank. A customer may only initiate a set-off implicitly by giving a payment order that creates an overdraft, thereby inviting the bank to set-off an account in balance. Moreover, the right of set-off can be exercised only within the context of dealings between a bank and its customer. Thus, there can be no set-off with an account known to be a trust account[136] or with a cheque given for presentment only but not deposit[137] or with a letter of credit unconnected to a contract with a third party[138] or where there is no clear connection between several agreements in relation to which a bank had insurance proceeds.[139] Finally, there can be no exercise of the right of set-off where it has been expressly excluded by agreement[140] or by a course of dealings between the bank and the customer.[141]

Imperial Bank of Commerce v. Sitarenios (1976), 73 D.L.R. (3d) 663 (Ont. C.A.); Hudson v. Toronto Dominion Bank (1976), 22 C.B.R. (N.S.) 55 (Alta S.C. in Bkcy.); Mercantile Bank of Canada v. Leon's Furniture Ltd. (1992), 98 D.L.R. (4th) 449 (Ont. C.A.); Marketing Products Inc. v. 1254719 Ontario Ltd. (2000), 13 B.L.R. (3d) 264 (Ont. S.C.J.); Belliveau v. Royal Bank of Canada (2000), 3 B.L.R. (3d) 43 (N.B.C.A.); Bank of Montreal v. Royal Bank of Canada (2000), 276 A.R. 380 (Q.B.); Progress Doors Ltd. v. Toronto Dominion Bank (2000), 6 C.L.R. (3d) 148 (Ont. S.C.J.).

134 McCready Co. v. Alberta Clothing Co. (1910), 3 Alta. L.R. 67 (S.C.); Royal Trust Co. v. Molsons Bank (1912), 27 O.L.R. 441 (H.C.J.); Daniels v. Imperial Bank of Canada (1914), 19 D.L.R. 166 (Alta. S.C.); Re Sutcliffe, ibid.

135 Deep v. Bank of Montreal, above note 36. See also other permitted set-offs: Re Stewart Estate (1997), 31 B.L.R. (2d) 124 (Alta. Surr. Ct.) (term deposit); Bank of Montreal v. Royal Bank of Canada, above note 133 (GICs); Bence v. Royal Trust Corp. of Canada (1997), 157 Sask. R. 61 (Q.B.) (GICs). Compare where there is no express contractual right in RRSP contract: Belliveau v. Royal Bank, above note 133, or in letter of credit: 69971 Manitoba Ltd. v. National Bank of Canada (1995), 122 D.L.R. (4th) 609 (Man. C.A.).

136 See Section G, above in this chapter.

137 Rouxel v. Royal Bank (1918), 11 Sask. L.R. 218 (K.B.).

138 Pan Pacific Specialties Ltd. v. Shandong Machinery & Equipment (2001), 85 B.C.L.R. (3d) 362 (S.C.).

139 Albert Estate v. Gionet (1992), 131 N.B.R. (2d) 226, 333 A.P.R. 226 (Q.B.).

140 Greenwood Teall v. William Williams Brown & Co. (1894), 11 T.L.R. 56 (C.A.); New Brunswick (Minister of Commerce and Development) v. Bank of Nova Scotia (1988), 95 N.B.R. (2d) 330, 241 A.P.R. 330 (Q.B.); W.P. Greenhalgh & Sons v. Union Bank of Manchester Ltd., [1924] 2 K.B. 153.

141 Buckingham & Co. v. London & Midland Bank Ltd. (1895), 12 T.L.R. 70 (Q.B.).

The existence of a bank's right to account combination or set-off is well established, but the further question arises of whether a bank is under a legal duty to do so to protect a customer's interests or reputation, for example, by honouring a cheque creating an overdraft in one account where there are sufficient funds in another account. Typically, account agreements give a bank the discretion to decide whether or not to honour cheques when an overdraft will be created and there is no overdraft agreement in place. The legal position is uncertain. On the one hand, the statutory provision that a bank is obliged to repay deposits only at the branch of the account[142] suggests that a bank is not under any binding duty to combine accounts; yet on the other hand, there are cases which conclude that by drawing such a cheque, the customer is effectively instructing the bank to do so,[143] although there is no case stating that the bank must therefore do so.

There is also uncertainty about a final legal issue in relation to set-off, that is, whether or not a bank is required to give notice to the customer prior to the exercise of the right. In the earliest case about set-off, *Garnett v. McKewan*,[144] Kelly C.B. stated that there was no obligation to give notice to the customer. However, in a subsequent late-nineteenth-century decision, *Buckingham & Co. v. London and Midland Bank*,[145] in which there was a course of dealing keeping accounts separate, the court decided that notice was required for account combination. The course of dealing was probably the distinguishing feature in this second case because subsequent final appellate decisions have followed the position taken in *Garnett*, where the customer was insolvent.[146] The position where the customer is not insolvent remains uncertain, and there is conflicting case law as to whether reasonable notice must be given.[147] Where the account agreement provides that no notice is required for account combination or set-off, then the position is clear. But in the absence of agreement when insolvency is not at issue, then the position is unclear, although *Garnett* remains the preferred solution from the perspective of the customer's reputation in relation to third parties.

---

142 *Bank Act*, above note 1, s. 461.
143 *Bank of New South Wales v. Goulburn Valley Butter Company Proprietary*, [1902] A.C. 543 (P.C.); *Houben v. Bank of Nova Scotia* (1970), 3 N.B.R. (2d) 366 (Co. Ct.).
144 Above note 129.
145 Above note 141.
146 *British Guiana Bank v. Official Receiver* (1911), 104 L.T. 754 (P.C.); *National Westminster Bank v. Halesowen*, above note 130.
147 For reasonable notice, see *Ronald Elwyn Lister Ltd. v. Dunlop* (1982), 135 D.L.R. (3d) 1 (S.C.C.). For against reasonable notice, see *Wallinder v. Imperial Bank of Canada*, above note 129; *Brantford Cordage Co. v. Milne*, [1925] 1 D.L.R. 862 (Man. C.A.); *CIP Inc. v. Toronto-Dominion Bank* (1988), 55 D.L.R. (4th) 308 (B.C.C.A.).

K. BANKERS' LIENS

Since the late eighteenth century, the common law has recognized the existence of a banker's lien over commercial paper deposited with the bank by a customer or a third party as security as part of the law merchant.[148] As such, there is no need for an express agreement to create a banker's lien. Rather, it comes into effect at the time of deposit except where there is an express or implied agreement to the contrary or the commercial paper fits into a recognized category of exceptions to the rule.[149] The existence of an implied agreement that no lien has arisen is a question of fact.[150]

In contrast to other liens or securities, a banker's lien gives a bank a right to sell the security as if it were a pledge,[151] and since it normally attaches to the whole indebtedness of the customer, in the absence of a contrary agreement to limit its application, the sale proceeds may be applied to reduce in whole or in part that indebtedness.[152]

In the early case *Brandao v. Barnett*,[153] a court suggested that all classes of securities may be subject to a banker's lien, and in subsequent decisions, the courts have confirmed that in addition to negotiable instruments, this lien may attach to deposit receipts,[154] share certificates,[155] share warrants,[156] money-transfer orders,[157] insurance policies,[158] securities deposited for collection,[159] and their sale proceeds.[160] Land title deeds are not

---

148 *Davis v. Bowsher* (1794), 5 Term. Rep. 488, 101 E.R. 275 (K.B.); *Brandao v. Barnett* (1846), 12 Cl. & F. 787, 136 E.R. 207 (H.L.); *Standard Bank of Canada v. Finucane* (1921), 62 S.C.R. 110; *Salter & Arnold*, above note 113.
149 *Brandao v. Barnett*, ibid.; *Commercial Bank of New Brunswick v. Page* (1870), 13 N.B.R. 326 (App. Div.); *Sterling Bank v. Zuber* (1914), 32 O.L.R. 123 (S.C.A.D.); *Salter & Arnold*, above note 113.
150 *Campbell v. Imperial Bank*, [1924] 4 D.L.R. 289 (Ont. S.C.A.D.).
151 *Brandao v. Barnett*, above note 148. Compare *Re Cosslett (Contractors) Ltd.*, [1998] Ch. 495 (C.A.).
152 *Rosenberg v. International Banking Corp.* (1923), 14 Lloyd's L.R. 344; *Re London & Globe Finance Corp.*, [1902] 2 Ch. 416.
153 Above note 148.
154 See Section E, above in this chapter.
155 *Re United Service Co.* (1871), L.R. 6 Ch. 212.
156 *Wylde v. Radford* (1863), 33 L.J. Ch. 51.
157 *Misa v. Currie* (1876), 1 App. Cas. 554 (H.L.).
158 *Re Bowes* (1886), 33 Ch. D. 586.
159 *Johnson v. Robarts* (1875), L.R. 10 Ch. App. 505; *Sutters v. Briggs*, [1922] 1 A.C. 1 (H.L.).
160 *Re Keever*, [1967] 1 Ch. 182.

regarded as subject to a banker's lien,[161] nor would money be either, since this can simply be appropriated to an account in overdraft.[162]

However, in certain contexts and in certain specific fact situations, commercial paper cannot become subject to a banker's lien. A lien does not attach to the following personal property: property deposited for safekeeping;[163] property known to belong to someone else;[164] property affected by a trust;[165] and property deposited for another specific purpose.[166] In addition, the courts have dealt with a number of individual cases in which no banker's lien was found on the facts including: (i) where a bank credits a negotiable instrument as cash because it receives legal title to that sum, not a lien;[167] (ii) where a bank merely cashes a cheque without deposit;[168] (iii) where a bank advances a sum because it has no lien on other funds of the borrower prior to the due date;[169] and (iv) where a bank has funds or security of a partnership for the debts due by a partner.[170] It is also clear that a bank cannot have a lien on funds on deposit because these are properly characterized as a debt owing to the customer under *Foley v. Hill*.[171]

L. CONCLUSION

The bank account is the centrepiece of the bank and customer relationship and, unsurprisingly, the rules regulating its use constitute most of the clauses in the customer contract. This chapter has focused on the account *qua* account, and the next chapter will focus on transactions whereby funds are deposited into an account and removed from an account in accordance with the mandate from the customer to the bank.

---

161 *Wylde v. Radford*, above note 156.
162 See Section I, above in this chapter.
163 *Brandao v. Barnett*, above note 148.
164 *Jeffryes v. Agra & Masterman's Bank* (1866), L.R. 2 Eq. 674.
165 *Riddell v. Bank of Upper Canada* (1859), 18 U.C.Q.B. 139 (C.A.); *Rouxel v. Royal Bank*, above note 137.
166 *Brandao v. Barnett*, above note 148; *Riddell v. Bank of Upper Canada*, ibid.; *Sterling Bank v. Zuber*, above note 149; *Rouxel v. Royal Bank*, ibid.
167 *Bank of British North America v. Warren & Co.* (1909), 19 O.L.R. 257 (C.A.).
168 *Kaufman v. Royal Bank of Canada* (1994), 34 C.P.C. (3d) 334 (Ont. Ct. Gen. Div.).
169 *Bower v. Foreign & Colonial Gas Co.* (1874), 22 W.R. 740; *Jeffryes v. Agra & Masterman's Bank*, above note 164.
170 *Richards v. Bank of British North America* (1901), 8 B.C.R. 209 (C.A.).
171 Chapter 6, Section C.

CHAPTER 8

BANK ACCOUNT OPERATION

A. INTRODUCTION

The account governed by contract is the central depository in relation to which the bank and customer agreement operates. Historically, the common law recognized this in the implied terms of that agreement, which defined their legal relationship prior to the use of express account agreements in the late twentieth century. Those four implied terms are: (i) the implied duty of the bank to honour cheques and repay deposits;[1] (ii) the implied duty of the bank to collect cheques and other payment instruments;[2] (iii) the implied duty of the bank to render statements of account periodically or on demand to inform the customer of the historical performance of the first two duties;[3] and (iv) the implied duty of secrecy in relation to the customer's affairs which the bank came to know as a result of transactions in the account.[4] These four terms continue to be appropriate organizing principles for the discussion of the legal rules relating to account operation that will be examined in this chapter.

These rules and the legal standards of care governing account operation were originally formulated when customer instructions to a bank

---

1 See Section C, below in this chapter.
2 See Section D, below in this chapter.
3 See Section E, below in this chapter.
4 See Section F, below in this chapter.

were given orally, often in person, or in writing and usually by cheque. Today such instructions are more likely to be given electronically. Some comparative statistics published by the Canadian Payments Association (CPA) demonstrate the transition from paper to electronic transactions.[5] Measured by volume, in 1985, 97.6 percent of transactions were by paper; in 1995, 61.8 percent were by paper; and in 2005, 22.5 percent were by paper. Measured by value, the transition is also evident but not so dramatic: in 1985, 99.6 percent of value was transmitted by paper; in 1995, 98.3 percent was by paper; and in 2005, 68.2 percent of value was transmitted by paper. Cheques continue to be used for larger transactions and transactions at a distance, so the transition in relation to the amount of value flowing through the clearing system is slower in relation to transition in relation to paper payment instructions.

Despite the significant movement to electronic banking in the past twenty years, the legal rules developed in the era of paper banking remain fundamental to the legal relationship between bank and customer. Whether given electronically, orally, or by paper, a customer's instructions require the bank to execute them on the customer's behalf; these are simply different communication methods that a customer may use to convey instructions about account operation to a bank. The legal standards of care relating to bank and customer remain the same in law notwithstanding the method of communication employed. There are, of course, specific legal rules that are applicable to specific methods of communication, but the fundamental principles of the common law continue to undergird the legal relationship between bank and customer.

The legal principles discussed in this chapter relate to paper-based banking and remain relevant for all such transactions; cheques continue to be used in vast numbers today and customers still bank in person at their branches. The legal principles discussed in the succeeding chapters relate to electronic banking, yet they were formulated in relation to and built upon the principles discussed here. To date, there is very little case law on electronic banking and no legislation, so the courts must begin with the historic common law relating to paper transactions when dealing with the very few disputes to date regarding electronic banking that have come before them.

---

5   Canadian Payments Association, *Annual Review 2005* (Ottawa: Canadian Payments Association, 2005) at 23. These statistics are for the Automated Clearing Settlement System (ACSS). The Large Value Transfer System began in 1999 and is restricted to electronic transactions, so historical statistics for LVTS are neither available nor relevant.

B. GENERAL BACKGROUND

In addition to being characterized in law as a debtor and creditor relationship, in account operation, the bank and customer relationship is also characterized as one of principal and agent. The bank as agent is obliged by contract to carry out the instructions to pay money into and out of the account of the customer as principal. The standard of care required by the bank in performing the mandate is reasonable care.[6] Since this is a common law standard, it may be varied by express agreement. The duty to execute the customer's instructions is owed only to the customer as the other party to the account contract; it is not owed to the payee in the absence of other circumstances because the payee is a third party to the contract.[7]

Those circumstances as found by the courts include the following situations, in which the courts have found an express or implied contract with the third party, as well as the account contract with the customer: (i) acceptance of a cheque for certification because the funds to pay have been removed from the customer's account on certification;[8] (ii) a promise by the bank to the payee that the cheque will be paid once certain conditions are met;[9] (iii) where an unendorsed cheque is deposited and cleared;[10] and (iv) where a branch approves payment of a cheque drawn on it in a telephone conversation with another branch at which the cheque is presented for payment.[11] The circumstances in which a bank may become liable to the payee may be various, but the legal requirement in each is the same, that is, the bank has given a contractual undertaking to the payee.

Whether a customer issues instructions electronically or by some other means, the basic elements of payment are similar, that is, three processes must be engaged to secure the transmission of funds into the customer's account or from the customer's account to a third party payee: (i) the payment message; (ii) the movements in accounts; and

---

6 *Joachimson v. Swiss Bank Corp.*, [1921] 3 K.B. 110 (C.A.); *Barclays Bank plc v. Quincecare Ltd.*, [1992] 4 All E.R. 363 (Q.B.D.).
7 *Schimnowski v. Schimnowski*, [1996] 6 W.W.R. 194 (Man. C.A.).
8 See Section C(3), below in this chapter.
9 *Simpson v. Dolan* (1908), 16 O.L.R. 459 (Div. Ct.); *Adams v. Craig* (1911), 24 O.L.R. 490 (C.A.).
10 *Slovchenko v. Toronto-Dominion Bank*, [1964] 1 O.R. 410 (H.C.J.).
11 *William Ciurluini Ltd. v. Royal Bank of Canada* (1972), 26 D.L.R. (3d) 552 (Ont. H.C.J.) [*Ciurluini*]. See also *Dumas v. Boivin* (1936), 75 Que. S.C. 1; *Steinbach Credit Union Ltd. v. Seitz* (1988), 50 D.L.R. (4th) 436 (Man. C.A.); *Edmonton Motors Ltd. v. Edmonton Savings & Credit Union Ltd.* (1988), 85 A.R. 29 (Q.B.).

(iii) settlement between accounts and banks through the clearing and settlement system.[12]

The first process (the payment message) requires the mandate or instruction from a customer to his bank to make a payment or receive a payment, either by giving a payment instruction, for example, by cheque, or by depositing a payment instruction received from another payer. Where a bank acts without the initiating instruction of its customer, the bank is in breach of contract and the customer may claim legal redress. That instruction may be given orally, in writing, or electronically and includes preauthorized debits for bill payment for the indefinite future. The bank must comply within the terms of the mandate, which may require funds or an overdraft facility, as well as reasonable care on the part of the customer in giving the bank instructions. Any customer instruction must be unconditional.

The second basic element (movement in accounts) is the movement of funds in accordance with the customer's instruction. The customer's account is debited, and ultimately the payee's account is credited. This is accomplished by the movement in accounts through electronic messaging and not by the actual transfer of funds. The final element is settlement, that is, payment among the banks themselves of their obligations arising from customers' instructions. In Canada, this is done by daily settlement among the accounts that each financial institution is obliged to keep with the Bank of Canada, again by means of electronic messaging.

The specific method of giving instruction considered in this chapter is by paper, that is, by negotiable instruments, and most especially by cheque. While a cheque can be used by a customer to withdraw funds from the customer's account, its usual use is to instruct the bank to pay funds from the account to a third party payee. It is an instruction to the bank, which takes the form of a negotiable instrument. Statutorily defined as a bill drawn on a bank, payable on demand,[13] the negotiable nature of a cheque is of less interest here than its role as a means of giving instructions to a bank within the context of the bank and customer relationship. Negotiability means that it confers a right of action on a person with its lawful possession who may be the original payee or any indorser or bearer to whom it has been lawfully negotiated. A cheque is personal property that confers legal rights on its "true owner."[14]

---

12 Ross Cranston, *Principles of Banking Law*, 2d ed. (Oxford: Oxford University Press, 2002) at 232–34.
13 *Bills of Exchange Act*, R.S.C. 1985, c. B-4, s. 165(1).
14 For the history of cheques, see James M. Holden, *The History of Negotiable Instruments in English Law* (London: University of London, 1955); James S. Rogers, *The Early History of the Law of Bills and Notes—A Study of the Origins of Anglo-*

When a customer draws a cheque instructing a bank to pay a fixed sum on a stated date to a specific payee, the customer engages the implied and express duties of the paying bank to repay deposits and honour cheques. When a customer is a payee of a cheque drawn by a payer and deposits that instrument into an account for clearing and final payment, the customer engages the second implied duty at common law of the collecting bank to collect cheques and other payment instructions. The legal duties relating to the paying bank are considered in Section C and the legal duties of the collecting bank are considered in Section D.

C. THE PAYING BANK

1) Requirements for Payment

The paying bank as agent of the customer is under a duty to use reasonable care in carrying out the customer's instructions to pay. Normally, such instructions are conveyed on cheques preprinted by the bank for the customer, but the common law has historically upheld the right of a customer to draw a cheque on any paper or other material.[15] Most customer account agreements provide that customers must use the preprinted cheques, thereby abrogating the common law right by express agreement. The reason is simply that cheques are now machine sorted in the clearing process and unusual individual items must be hand-cleared at very considerable expense to the bank, and this expense is passed on to any customer using paper other than the preprinted forms.

The customer must satisfy two conditions in instructing a bank before a bank is required to honour that instruction: (i) there must be sufficient funds in the account or an agreed overdraft facility; and (ii) the instruction must be clearly drawn and unambiguous so as to prevent fraud or forgery. In *Canadian Pacific Hotels Ltd. v. Bank of Montreal*,[16] the Supreme Court of Canada rejected a possible third condition that the customer take reasonable care in the management of the customer's affairs, to ensure that no unauthorized instructions are received by the bank.

The first condition of sufficient funds is assessed at the time of presentment of the cheque,[17] either by sufficient funds in the account

---

American Commercial Law (Cambridge: Cambridge University Press, 1995); Benjamin Geva, *Bank Collections and Payment Transactions. A Comparative Legal Analysis* (Oxford: Oxford University Press, 2001).
15 *Roberts & Co. v. Marsh*, [1915] 1 K.B. 42 (C.A.).
16 (1987), 40 D.L.R. (4th) 385 (S.C.C.). See Section E, below in this chapter.
17 *Bank of New South Wales v. Laing*, [1954] A.C. 135 (P.C.).

on which the cheque is drawn[18] or by an overdraft facility.[19] A bank is not obliged to effect a partial payment.[20] By so doing, the bank would be in breach of its duty of secrecy to the customer by disclosure to the payee of the state of the account through partial payment.[21] A bank may wait for about a day to see if sufficient funds will be deposited if that was the past practice of the customer[22] or it may combine accounts [23] or it may interpret the cheque as a request for an overdraft,[24] but it is not obliged to do so. Where funds are deposited with a bank sufficient to cover the cheque, the bank must ensure that those funds are credited to the account within a reasonable period of time.[25] Where an express overdraft facility is in place, the bank must give notice of a decision to reduce it, so that a subsequent dishonour of a cheque causing loss to the customer will result in liability for the bank.[26]

A determination of whether sufficient funds are irrevocably available in an account is made difficult because funds deposited to an account by cheque are credited provisionally until a final payment decision has been made by the payer's branch. Return of a cheque for dishonour will result in a reversal of the provisional credit, but since there is no limitation within which a cheque may be returned, a customer may be requested to cover any overdraft created through the honour of a cheque on a provisional account balance at any time after the cheque has been paid. Effectively, the paying bank may not know whether there are sufficient cleared funds at the time of presentment

---

18 *Marzetti v. Williams* (1830), 1 B. & Ad. 415, 109 E.R. 842 (K.B.); *Whitaker v. Bank of England* (1835), 1 Cr. M. & R. 744, 149 E.R. 1280 (K.B.); *Jones v. Bank of Montreal* (1869), 29 U.C.Q.B. 448 (Q.B.); *Joachimson v. Swiss Bank Corp.*, above note 6; *Bank of New South Wales v. Laing*, ibid. Where a bank causes the insufficiency of funds, it is liable for breach of contract: *Searles v. AT&T Canada* (1998), 200 N.B.R. (2d) 305, 512 A.P.R. 305 (Q.B.).
19 *Rouse v. Bradford Banking Co.*, [1894] A.C. 586 (H.L.); *Fleming v. Bank of New Zealand*, [1900] A.C. 577 (P.C.); *Thermo King Corp. v. Provincial Bank of Canada* (1981), 130 D.L.R. (3d) 256 (Ont. C.A.), leave to appeal to S.C.C. refused (1982), 42 N.R. 352 (S.C.C.) [*Thermo King Corp.*]; *Bank of Montreal v. Vaillancourt* (1983), 42 O.R. (2d) 545 (C.A.); *National Trust Co. v. Harold's Demolition Inc.* (2001), 43 R.P.R. (3d) 212 (Ont. S.C.J.).
20 *Whitaker v. Bank of England*, above note 18.
21 *A.L. Underwood Ltd. v. Bank of Liverpool*, [1924] 1 K.B. 775 (C.A.).
22 *Ubacol Investments Ltd. v. Royal Bank of Canada* (1995), 30 Alta L.R. (3d) 327 (Q.B.).
23 Chapter 7, Section J.
24 *Bank of Montreal v. Boudreau* (1974), 49 D.L.R. (3d) 249 (N.B.C.A.).
25 *Marzetti v. Williams*, above note 18.
26 *Raypath Resources Ltd. v. Toronto Dominion Bank* (1996), 135 D.L.R. (4th) 261 (Alta. C.A.) [*Raypath*].

for payment.[27] The decision to honour a customer's cheque remains a matter of discretion for a bank where there are provisionally credited funds in an account, and banks usually exercise that discretion by reference to its past course of dealings with the customer,[28] by its own past practices,[29] by the clearing rules,[30] and by contract.[31] Finally, the place for the honour of the customer's mandate is the branch at which the account is held.[32]

The second condition, that a customer's mandate must be clearly drawn and unambiguous, is required for the prevention of fraud or forgery.[33] A customer is required to draw a cheque so as to ensure that words or numbers cannot be interpolated onto the cheque.[34] A customer is also obliged to inform the bank immediately when he becomes aware that a forged note has been, or is about to be, presented to the bank.[35] For its part, a bank in doubt as to whether the mandate on a cheque is the customer's instruction may refuse to honour that cheque or to take unreasonable risks[36] and may reasonably be expected to contact the customer to clarify the situation.[37] A bank is liable to the customer if it honours an irregular cheque.[38]

Once these two conditions are met, the payer's branch is normally required to honour the cheque. Presentment of the cheque for payment may be made either in person by the payee at the branch for cash or certification or by presentment through the clearing system. When pre-

---

27 Bradley Crawford, "Late Return of a Dishonoured Cheque" (2001) 36 Can. Bus. L.J. 1. See also *Jones v. Bank of Montreal*, above note 18; *Henderson v. Bank of Hamilton* (1895), 22 O.A.R. 414 (C.A.); *Garon Realty & Insurance Ltd. v. James*, [1978] 6 W.W.R. 694 (B.C.S.C.).
28 *Rolin v. Steward* (1854), 14 C.B. 595, 139 E.R. 245; *Re Mills* (1893), 10 Morr. 193; *Capital and Counties Bank Ltd. v. Gordon*, [1903] A.C. 240 (H.L.).
29 *Forman v. Bank of England* (1902), 18 T.L.R. 339 (K.B.).
30 *Parr's Bank Ltd. v. Thomas Ashby & Co.* (1898), 14 T.L.R. 563 (Q.B.).
31 *Westminster Bank Ltd. v. Zang*, [1966] A.C. 182 (H.L.).
32 Chapter 6, Section C.
33 *Young v. Grote* (1827), 4 Bing. 253, 130 E.R. 764; *London Joint Stock Bank Ltd. v. MacMillan*, [1918] A.C. 777 (H.L.) [*MacMillan*]; *Joachimson v. Swiss Bank Corp.*, above note 6.
34 *Will v. Bank of Montreal*, [1931] 3 D.L.R. 526 (Alta. S.C.); *Rapid Discount Corp. v. Thomas G. Hiscott Ltd.* (1977), 76 D.L.R. (3d) 450 (Ont. H.C.J.).
35 *McKenzie v. British Linen Co.* (1881), 6 App. Cas. 82 (H.L.); *Ogilvie v. West Australian Mortgage & Agency Co.*, [1896] A.C. 257 (P.C.); *Ewing v. Dominion Bank* (1904), 35 S.C.R. 133, leave to appeal to P.C. refused, [1904] A.C. 806 (P.C.).
36 *MacMillan*, above note 33.
37 *European Asian Bank A.G. v. Punjab & Sind Bank*, [1983] 2 All E.R. 508 (C.A.).
38 *Slingsby v. District Bank Ltd.*, [1932] 1 K.B. 544 (C.A.); *Arab Bank Ltd. v. Ross*, [1952] 1 All E.R. 709 (C.A.).

sentment is made by the payee for cash, payment is irrevocable when the cashier or teller counts out the amount onto the counter, although the payee has not yet picked up the cash or counted it.[39] Property in the money has passed so that it can be attached as the payee's property even before the payee has picked it up,[40] or if thieves intervene, the loss falls on the payee, not the bank.[41] Where presentment is for certification, acceptance for payment is effected by certification, although the certified cheque must still go through the clearing system.[42] Since a cheque is payable on demand,[43] the bank is required to decide when presentment is in person on the date whether or not to pay once it has ascertained that there are sufficient funds and that there are no irregularities on the cheque.[44] When a bank wrongfully refuses to honour a cheque, it is liable to the customer, not the payee or the holder.[45]

Where presentment for payment is through the clearing system, other issues arise. The clearing and settlement system in use today is ultimately modelled on the system developed in England in the eighteenth century, when cheques came into common use and will be described more extensively in a later chapter.[46] The rules governing its operation are set by the CPA, and the courts have consistently recognized that they bind all financial institutions that participate directly or indirectly in the clearing system.[47] In Canada, all banks are required to be CPA members,[48] but the clearing rules do not directly bind customers of those banks. Banks are bound by virtue of the multipartite contractual arrangements associated with CPA membership, but cus-

---

39 *Carter v. Shepherd* (1698), 5 Mod. Rep. 398, 87 E.R. 728; *Chambers v. Miller* (1862), 13 C.B.N.S. 125, 143 E.R. 50; *Hall v. Hatch* (1901), 3 O.L.R. 147 (H.C.J.).
40 *Hall v. Hatch*, ibid.
41 *Balmoral Supermarket Ltd. v. Bank of New Zealand*, [1974] 2 Lloyd's Rep. 164 (N.Z.S.C.).
42 See Section C(3), below in this chapter.
43 *Bills of Exchange Act*, above note 13, s. 165(1).
44 *Cocks v. Masterman* (1829), 9 B. & C. 902, 109 E.R. 335; *Todd v. Union Bank of Canada* (1887), 4 Man. R. 204 (Q.B.); *Morison v. London County & Westminster Bank*, [1914] 3 K.B. 356 (C.A.).
45 See Section C(4), below in this chapter.
46 Chapter 9.
47 *Bank of British North America v. Standard Bank of Canada* (1917), 38 O.L.R. 570 (S.C.A.D.). See also *Parr's Bank Ltd. v. Thomas Ashby & Co.*, above note 30. In *Advance Bank v. Toronto Dominion Bank* (2003), 227 D.L.R. (4th) 755 (Ont. S.C.J.) [*Advance Bank*], the court ruled that the CPA rules do not bind non-members of the CPA. See also Benjamin Geva, "Presentment and Payment in Cheque Electronic Clearing: *Advance Bank v. TD Bank*" (2005) 20 B.F.L.R. 361.
48 Chapter 3, Section E.

tomers are not parties to those agreements; they are parties only to the account contract with their own banks. The legal question then becomes whether the clearing rules regulating bank-to-bank relationships in cheque clearing also indirectly impact on the bank and customer relationship when a bank pays or collects a cheque. One issue, in particular, has proven difficult for the courts, that is, if presentment for payment is made through the clearing system, when has payment of the cheque been made irrevocably?[49]

This is a question that has been considered by a number of courts in various permutations[50] and has also attracted considerable academic comment.[51] A clear answer has yet to appear, but it now seems that a partial answer may have been given in the context of a slightly different question, that is, what is the latest time at which a paying bank may return a dishonoured cheque without incurring legal liability to the collecting bank or to the payee of that cheque? In *National Bank of Greece (Canada) v. Bank of Montreal*,[52] the Federal Court of Appeal decided that the latest time for returning a dishonoured item through the clearing system was after the passage of the deadline provided in the ACSS[53] or clearing system rules. After that time, the collecting bank was entitled to full reimbursement of the settlement paid to the customer for the returned item, although if there is no loss, then no reimbursement is required. The amount of the claim is to be assessed as a claim for restitution.[54] This result accords with a decision in 1931 of the

---

49 For doubts that there can be presentment through the clearing system, see *Advance Bank*, above note 47 and Geva, above note 47, who argues that a late return constitutes payment.

50 *W.J. Lafave & Sons Ltd. v. Banque Canadienne Nationale*, [1977] C.S. 802; *Garon Realty & Insurance Ltd. v. James*, above note 27; *Duncan District Credit Union v. Greater Victoria Savings Credit Union*, [1978] 3 W.W.R. 570 (B.C.S.C.); *Stanley Works of Canada Ltd. v. Banque Canadienne Nationale* (1981), 20 B.L.R. 282, [1982] R.L. 433. (Que. C.A.); *National Slag v. Canadian Imperial Bank of Commerce* (1985), 19 D.L.R. (4th) 383 (Ont. C.A.); *Process Piping Specialties Inc. v. BCIC*, [1986] R.J.Q. 2429 (S.C.); *Midland Doherty Ltd. v. Royal Bank of Canada*, [1990] R.J.Q. 121 (Que. C.A.).

51 Jerome Choquette, "Comment" (1982) 60 Can. Bar Rev. 746; Bradley Crawford, "Letter" (1983) 62 Can. Bar Rev. 921; Claude Gingras, "Collection of Cheques—Issues in the Processing and Clearing System" in Richard B. Miner, ed., *Current Issues in Canadian Business Law* (Toronto: Carswell, 1986) 465 at 476–88; Crawford, above note 27; Bradley Crawford, *Payment, Clearing and Settlement in Canada*, vol. 1 (Aurora: Canada Law Book, 2002) at 235–55 and 270–78.

52 [2001] 2 F.C. 288 (C.A.).

53 Chapter 9.

54 *Banque Canadienne Nationale v. Caisse Centrale Desjardins du Québec*, [2001] R.J.Q. 846 (C.A.). Compare *Canadian Imperial Bank of Commerce v. Farrage*

Supreme Court of Victoria in *Riedell v. Commercial Bank of Australia*,[55] little known in Canada.

The significance of adopting the clearing rules as between paying and collecting bank as the standard for late return is that in relation to the question of when is a customer's cheque irrevocably paid by its bank as agent, the final time for setting the point of irrevocability must be the time beyond which late return is impossible without penalty. This still does not set a precise time at which payment is irrevocable, but it sets the outer limit of time within which the decision about irrevocability can be made. If the paying bank waits beyond that time to make the payment decision, the cheque must be deemed to be paid irrevocably and the paying bank must incur the legal responsibility associated with its delay. Thus, when presentment for payment is made through the clearing system, the paying bank's decision to pay as agent of the customer is either when that decision is actually made or when the deadline beyond which the decision can no longer be made has passed.

A corollary situation involves "on-us" items, that is, cheques in relation to which the payer and the payee have accounts at the same bank, perhaps the same branch, and which are cleared internally within the bank, rather than through the payments system. Whether the cases involve different branches[56] or the same branch,[57] the earliest time at which payment can be said to be irrevocable is when the payer's account is debited, although the payee's account has not yet been credited.[58] Yet it is apparently not too late to countermand a cheque prior to the crediting of the payee's account.[59] In short, in relation to "on-us" items, the law remains uncertain as to when payment becomes irrevocable.

Canadian courts have not considered precisely when effective presentment for payment has occurred when presentment is through the clearing system. However, in England, this has been found to be when the cheque reaches the branch on which it is drawn, rather than the time of delivery to the paying bank from the collecting bank,[60] that is,

---

(1997), 122 Man. R. (2d) 315 (Q.B.); *Land Bank of Nova Scotia v. Regent Enterprises Ltd.* (1997), 157 Nfld & P.E.I.R. 102, 486 A.P.R. 102 (Nfld. C.A.) where the banks were permitted to recover, although the returned cheque was out of time.

55 [1931] V.L.R. 382 (S.C.).
56 *White v. Royal Bank of Canada* (1923), 53 O.L.R. 543 (S.C.A.D.); *Slovchenko v. Toronto-Dominion Bank*, above note 10.
57 *Capital Associates Ltd. v. Royal Bank of Canada* (1976), 65 D.L.R. (3d) 384 (S.C.C); *Momm v. Barclays Bank International Ltd.*, [1973] 3 All E.R. 588 (Q.B.).
58 *White v. Royal Bank*, above note 56; *Momm v. Barclays Bank International Ltd.*, ibid.
59 *Capital Associates Ltd. v. Royal Bank of Canada*, above note 57.
60 *Barclays Bank plc v. Bank of England*, [1985] 1 All E.R. 385 (Arbitrator).

presentment is when the cheque is presented to the branch entitled to make the payment decision.[61] The paying bank is regarded as a sub-agent of the collecting bank, which is the agent of the payee[62] and is under a duty of reasonable care to the collecting bank.[63]

A further issue considered by the courts is that of the order of presentment for payment to the paying bank. The general rule is that a bank should honour cheques strictly in the order of presentment, whether they are presented in person or through the clearing system.[64] A bank must not honour a cheque previously dishonoured prior to a cheque presented subsequently when there are sufficient funds.[65] The difficult question arises when two or more cheques are presented for payment simultaneously or nearly simultaneously, as occurs in the clearing system, and there are insufficient funds to honour all of them. In *Villiers v. Bank of Montreal*,[66] the Ontario High Court decided that a bank is entitled to treat all such cheques alike and to refuse to pay all of them, rather than to select which cheques to pay.

Villiers is the only case on this question, and in England there is a difference of opinion between two banking authorities on how to resolve the dilemma. The Institute of Bankers[67] has advised that banks pay the largest cheques first, in descending order, but Paget[68] advised that the smallest cheques be paid first in ascending order because the dishonour of small cheques would have the most negative effect on a customer's reputation. Paget's suggestion would also more likely protect the bank from customer actions on the ground of defamation.

There is no easy resolution of this riddle, although in automated cheque clearing, cheques would be posted automatically to the account and a bank would only subsequently be faced with a decision to dishonour at the end of the clearing process if the last cheque or cheques posted resulted in an overdraft. Essentially, the clearing process identifies the cheque which puts the account into overdraft, and at that point, the dilemma arises. Canadian banking practice appears to be to

---

61 *Ibid.*
62 *Ibid.*
63 *Ibid.*
64 *Kilsby v. Williams* (1822), 5 B. & Ald. 815, 106 E.R. 1388 (K.B.); *Bank of British North America v. Standard Bank*, above note 47.
65 *Caldwell v. Merchants Bank* (1876), 26 U.C.C.P. 294.
66 [1933] O.W.N. 649 (H.C.J.).
67 Institute of Bankers, *Questions on Banking Practice*, 10th ed. (London: Institute of Bankers, 1985) at no. 358.
68 Mark Hapgood, ed., *Paget's Law of Banking*, 11th ed. (London: Butterworths, 1996) at 330. There is no reference to this issue in the 12th edition (2003).

honour as many cheques as possible, but the legal foundation for that practice is not clear.

Finally, where a bank becomes aware that cheques are to be presented shortly, it must not dishonour cheques already presented unless the customer has so instructed.[69]

2) Postdated Cheques

Postdated cheques are instruments payable at some future date, as indicated on their face, which differs from their date of issue. A cheque is an instrument payable on demand,[70] but a postdated cheque is payable on the date on its face. Such cheques pose specific problems in an automated cheque clearing system should they be cleared prior to the date on the face and the customer has insufficient funds in the account but anticipated doing so on the date of the cheque. Although widely used in Canada, they are discouraged in other jurisdictions, and in Canada are frequently being replaced by preauthorized debits as a means of paying regular future debts such as rent or utility bills.

Despite judicial doubts,[71] postdated cheques are cheques for the purposes of the *Bills of Exchange Act*, which provides that a cheque is not invalid by reason only that it is postdated.[72] As a valid negotiable instrument, a postdated cheque may be negotiated to a holder in due course prior to the date on its face, and it should be regarded as completely regular[73] unless there is obvious bad faith[74] or no actual value is given[75] or there is no negotiation by endorsement.[76]

---

69 *Sednaoni, Zareff, Nakes & Co. v. Anglo-Austrian Bank* (1909), 2 L.D.A.B. 208.
70 *Bills of Exchange Act*, above note 13, s. 165(1).
71 See M.H. Ogilvie, *Canadian Banking Law*, 2d ed. (Toronto: Carswell, 1995) at 573 for earlier cases.
72 *Bills of Exchange Act*, above note 13, s. 27(d); *Comtract Air Compressors Inc. v. A.W. Service Industries Inc.* (2000), 6 B.L.R. (3d) 136 (Ont. S.C.J.) [*Comtract*]. Compare *Bank of Nova Scotia v. Kelly Motors Danforth Ltd.*, [1961] O.W.N. 34 (Co. Ct.), which is simply wrong.
73 *Hitchcock v. Edwards* (1889), 60 L.T. (N.S.) 636 (Q.B.D.); *Royal Bank of Scotland v. Tottenham*, [1894] 2 Q.B. 715 (C.A.); *Union Bank v. Tattersall* (1920), 15 Alta. L.R. 350 (S.C.A.D.); *2203850 Nova Scotia Ltd. v. Sarkar* (1995), 23 B.L.R. (2d) 28 (N.S.S.C.). Compare *Money Mart Cheque Cashing Centre (WPG) Ltd. v. Reis Lighting Products & Services Ltd.* (1994), 16 B.L.R. (2d) 184 (Man. Q.B.), which is wrongly decided.
74 *Elmhurst Investment Co. v. Allard*, [1963] Que. Q.B. 236; *Jacobs v. Larose*, [1971] C.A. 281 (Que.); *Thorne Riddell Inc. v. Rural Municipality of Rudy No 283* (1985), 46 Sask. R. 319 (C.A.).
75 *Banque Provinciale du Canada v. Claude*, [1965] 2 O.R. 819 (C.A.).
76 *National Money Mart Inc. v. A. & B. Enterprises Ltd.* (1997), 215 A.R. 141 (Q.B.).

The effect of postdating a cheque is to instruct the paying bank to refuse payment prior to the date on its face; therefore, the customer drawer may countermand it at any time prior to that date.[77] This right is subject to the rights of any holder for value in due course.[78] Where the customer countermands a postdated cheque, the bank should dishonour that cheque.[79] A bank should also decline to pay where the drawer dies or becomes mentally incapacitated while the cheque is postdated.[80] In *Keyes v. Royal Bank of Canada*,[81] the Supreme Court of Canada found that since a bank should not honour a postdated cheque prior to its date, it is liable to the customer to restore the funds to the account when the customer countermands and the bank erroneously certifies over the countermand. The limitation period for action on postdated cheques extends under the relevant provincial legislation from the date on which funds are withdrawn from the drawer's account and not from the date of issue.[82]

3) Certified Cheques

The practice of "certifying" cheques is also more widespread in Canada than in other jurisdictions; indeed, the practice is virtually unknown in the United Kingdom. The practice originated in North American banking in the nineteenth century,[83] but with the exception of the private banks, is no longer done in the United Kingdom.[84] The *Bills of Exchange Act* makes no provision for cheque certification, so its legal nature and status are defined entirely by the common law.

Certification probably has its origins in the English banking practice of "marking" cheques as between banks. A collecting bank could mark a cheque to indicate that it would be paid and not returned dis-

---

77 *Union Bank v. Tattersall*, above note 73; *Keyes v. Royal Bank of Canada*, [1947] 3 D.L.R. 161 (S.C.C.).
78 See Section D(2), below in this chapter; *T.D. Trapp & Co. v. Prescott* (1912), 18 D.L.R. 794 (S.C.C.) [*Trapp*].
79 *Morley v. Culverwell* (1840), 7 M. & W. 174, 151 E.R. 727 (Exch.); *Keyes v. Royal Bank of Canada*, above note 77; *Comtract*, above note 72; *Advantage Credit Union v. Funk* (2003), 238 Sask. R. 198 (C.A.).
80 See Section C(5), below in this chapter.
81 Above note 77; *Michaud v. Caisse populaire Notre-Dame de Lourdes Ltée* (2001), 245 N.B.R. (2d) 63 (Q.B.).
82 *Markham School for Human Development v. Ghods* (2002), 60 O.R. (3d) 624 (S.C.J.). Compare *Hansen v. Randa*, [1996] B.C.W.L.D. 2194 (S.C.).
83 *Gaden v. Newfoundland Savings Bank*, [1899] A.C. 281 (P.C.) [*Gaden*].
84 Maurice H. Megrah, *Paget's Law of Banking*, 9th ed. (London: Butterworths, 1982) at 234.

honoured through the clearing, but a marked cheque was good for one day only and had to be cleared within that day; otherwise, it might be dishonoured. A marked cheque was not regarded as a proper instrument for acceptance under section 18 of the *Bills of Exchange Act*, and the courts have treated such cheques as a promise to pay as between banks for clearing purposes but as having no legal validity in relation to customers.[85] A cheque is not an assignment of funds, and even in relation to a certified cheque, the bank must still ascertain the validity of the drawer's signature and availability of funds prior to payment, so that a payee or holder of the cheque would have difficulty in framing a valid legal action against the bank on the basis of a marked cheque. In any case, the practice has virtually died out in the United Kingdom.

"Certification" is the procedure whereby the paying bank marks a cheque in some way to show that it is drawn by a person upon an existing account in which there are sufficient funds. The cheque itself will be stamped "accepted" or "certified" or with similar words, together with the name of the bank. It need not be signed by any bank employee on behalf of the bank. The MICR (Magnetic Ink Character Recognition)-encoded numbers will be marked by a sticker bearing the MICR number of the bank's outstanding item or reserve account or will be mutilated so that it cannot be machine read and must be hand-sorted. At the time of certification, funds will be withdrawn from the customer's account and transferred to the bank's outstanding items account. In everyday banking practice, it is expected that a certified cheque will be paid when presented because the funds have already been set aside at certification.

Certification has always required some marking of the cheque by the bank.[86] Thus, a telephone assurance of payment by the drawee to the holder is not certification,[87] although such an assurance between banks by telephone will require payment.[88] A bank may also be stopped from dishonouring the holder's cheque by detrimental reliance[89] or by

---

85 *Bank of Baroda Ltd.* v. *Punjab National Bank Ltd.*, [1944] A.C. 176 (P.C.). See also *Gaden*, above note 83 and *Southland Savings Bank* v. *Anderson*, [1974] 1 N.Z.L.R. 118.

86 *Gaden*, ibid. Compare *Commercial Bank of New Brunswick* v. *Fleming* (1872), 14 N.B.R. 36 (C.A.); *Scott* v. *Merchants Bank of Canada* (1911), 17 O.W.R. 849 (Div. Ct.); *Stevens* v. *Merchants Bank of Canada* (1920), 30 Man. R. 46 (C.A.), where circumstances showed that initials of a bank employee meant something other than certification.

87 *Bank of Nova Scotia* v. *Pittman* (1979), 22 Nfld. & P.E.I.R. 278, 58 A.P.R. 278 (Nfld. Dist. Ct.).

88 *Ciurluini*, above note 11.

89 *Adams* v. *Craig*, above note 9.

virtue of a new contract between the bank and the holder where the holder has paid a fee for certification (which is the usual practice).[90] A bank is not required to certify a cheque at the request of either drawer or holder,[91] but rather has discretion to make that decision where there are insufficient funds or doubts about the customer's signature.[92] A refusal to certify is not wrongful dishonour because a request for certification is not presentment for payment.[93] The payee or holder may have recourse against the drawer only after the cheque has been returned through the clearing system and has been dishonoured at that time.[94]

Obviously, a certification is valid only if done by an employee of the bank with actual or ostensible authority,[95] and the older cases suggest that the onus is on the holder or payee to prove that the certification was within the authority of the employee.[96] Disputes about the validity of certification may also be adjudicated by a CPA compliance panel, and courts will not normally intervene.[97] If there are proven irregularities in the certification, then the holder is not entitled to enforce payment where aware of these, including certification by a bank employee outside the scope of authority,[98] certification of a postdated cheque,[99] and postdated certification of a current cheque.[100] However, even if the holder is not aware of irregularities in the certification, it may still be that any action against the bank would be subject to the real defences of the bank or any prior party.[101] The fact that there are insufficient funds in the account when the decision to certify is made will not defeat the holder's right to payment.[102]

A certified cheque is treated in law much like any other cheque. It cannot be certified prior to its date — that is, a postdated cheque can-

---

90 *City Front Developments Inc. v. Bank of Nova Scotia* (1998), 41 O.R. (3d) 599 (Gen. Div.).
91 *Meteor Equipment Rentals Ltd. v. MacMillan* (1970), 75 W.W.R. 660 (B.C. Co. Ct.).
92 See Section C(1), above in this chapter.
93 *Meteor Equipment Rentals Ltd. v. MacMillan*, above note 91.
94 Ibid.; *Bills of Exchange Act*, above note 13, s. 127.
95 *Stevens v. Merchants Bank of Canada*, above note 86.
96 Ibid.
97 *Bank of Nova Scotia v. Canada Trust Co.* (1998), 39 O.R. (3d) 84 (Gen. Div.).
98 *McIntosh v. Bank of New Brunswick* (1913), 15 D.L.R. 375 (N.B.S.C. en banc).
99 *Bank of Baroda Ltd. v. Punjab National Bank Ltd.*, above note 85.
100 *Leduc v. Banque d'Hochelaga*, [1926] 1 D.L.R. 433 (S.C.C.).
101 *Gaden*, above note 83.
102 *Leduc v. Banque d'Hochelaga*, above note 100.

not be certified until the date on its face.[103] It must be delivered to transfer property to a holder.[104] It is subject to the same principles as any other cheque when it is fraudulently raised;[105] where there is a forgery of the payee's endorsement;[106] or where it is materially altered by the drawer after certification.[107] This means, generally speaking,[108] that any relevant provisions in the *Bills of Exchange Act* apply, such as sections 49 and 50 relating to forgery, and that the funds are recoverable from anyone acting pursuant to the irregular instrument and payable to the payee or *bona fide* holder of the cheque.[109]

The most contentious issue in relation to certified cheques is the proper legal characterization of certification as an acceptance by the bank for payment which is irrevocable,[110] as is commonly understood in the business community. The earlier ambiguity in the common law can now be said to be resolved by the decision of the Ontario Court of Appeal in *A.E. Lepage Real Estate Services Ltd. v. Rattray Publications Ltd.*,[111] in which the court unanimously concluded that certification was acceptance and a guarantee of payment to the *bona fide* holder, whether the certification was at the request of the drawer or the payee. The policy reason for this conclusion was that this reflected commercial understanding of certification as being the equivalent of the payment of cash.[112] This position has now been applied in subsequent cases[113]

---

103 *Keyes v. Royal Bank of Canada*, above note 77; *Northern Bank v. Yuen* (1909), 2 Alta. L.R. 310 (S.C.).
104 *Halwell v. Township of Wilmot* (1897), 24 O.A.R. 628 (C.A.).
105 *Imperial Bank of Canada v. Bank of Hamilton*, [1903] A.C. 49 (P.C.).
106 *Bank of Montreal v. Dominion Bank* (1921), 60 D.L.R. 403 (Ont. Co. Ct.); *Smith v. Trader's Bank* (1906), 7 O.W.R. 791 (Div. Ct.).
107 *Kilburn v. Co-op Centre Credit Union Ltd.* (1972), 33 D.L.R. (3d) 233 (Alta. S.C.).
108 See any textbook on negotiable instruments for a further discussion.
109 *Barclays Bank Ltd. v. W.J. Simms Son & Cooke (Southern) Ltd.*, [1979] 3 All E.R. 522 (Q.B.) [*Simms*].
110 Most of the heat in this scholarly interlude has been generated by Crawford, *Payment, Clearing and Settlement in Canada*, above note 51 at 1223–52, who regards all other scholars and the appellate courts as wrong. See the now predominant view in Benjamin Geva, "The Irrevocability of Bank Drafts, Certified Cheques and Money Orders" (1986) 65 Can Bar Rev. 107 and *A.E. Lepage Real Estate Services Ltd. v. Rattray Publications Ltd.* (1994), 120 D.L.R. (4th) 499 (Ont. C.A.) [*Lepage*], followed by many cases as set out below.
111 *Lepage*, ibid.
112 *Ibid.* at 505, Finlayson J.A.
113 See the earlier cases: *Citizens Trust Co. v. Hongkong Bank of Canada* (1991), 85 D.L.R. (4th) 762 (B.C.S.C.) and *Maubach v. Bank of Nova Scotia* (1987), 44 D.L.R. (4th) 575 (Ont. C.A.). See also subsequent cases: *Centrac Inc. v. Canadian Imperial Bank of Commerce* (1994), 120 D.L.R. (4th) 765 (Ont. C.A.); *Toronto-Dominion*

and renders irrelevant much of the convoluted learned commentary[114] on the matter.

Certification of a cheque does not amount to payment, which must still be made, so that certified cheques differ slightly from ordinary cheques, which do not require acceptance but are payable on demand when presented for payment.[115] However, there is nothing in the nature of a cheque precluding acceptance, and marking a cheque as certified can be said to amount to acceptance by the bank within section 35 of the *Bills of Exchange Act*, which defines acceptance as a signification by the drawee of assent to the order of the drawer.[116] Once marked by a bank employee with authority to do so, the certified cheque is as good as accepted, and the bank is obliged to make payment when the certified cheque is presented for payment.

Once certification is conceptualized as acceptance or as equivalent to acceptance of an ordinary cheque, it matters little whether the request for certification was made by the drawer or the payee or another holder. Typically, cheques are certified at the request of the drawer, the customer, prior to delivery to the payee, but they can be certified at the request of an agent of the drawer[117] or by the payee from the ostensible date on the face of the cheque, usually to ensure payment where a cheque is to be presented for payment through the clearing system or the amount is too large to be paid in cash at the drawer's branch.

Where certification is at the request of the drawer, the effect of certification is to add the credit of the bank to that of the drawer, so that the drawer is not discharged.[118] The drawer is still liable to the payee for the amount of the cheque, but the bank assumes the primary liability to the payee by virtue of the transfer of funds from the drawer's account to the bank's outstanding items account.[119] However, it would appear that if the payee or holder requests certification, the drawer is relieved

---

Bank v. Bank of Montreal (1995), 22 O.R. (3d) 362 (Gen. Div.); *Bank of Nova Scotia v. Canada Trust Co.* (1998), 39 O.R. (3d) 84 (Gen. Div.); *City Front Developments Inc. v. Bank of Nova Scotia* (1998), 41 O.R. (3d) 599 (Gen. Div.); *Repet Equipment Inc. v. Canadian Imperial Bank of Commerce* (1999), 43 O.R. (3d) 135 (Gen. Div.). Compare *Rapid Transit Mix Ltd. v. Herle*, [2002] 6 W.W.R. 732 (Alta. Q.B.).

114 Especially Crawford, *Payment, Clearing and Settlement in Canada*, above note 51.
115 *Macbeth v. North & South Wales Bank*, [1908] A.C. 137 (H.L.); *Rapid Transit Mix Ltd. v. Herle*, above note 113.
116 For doubts that marking requires a signature or initials, see *Bank of Nova Scotia v. Canada Trust Co.*, above note 113.
117 *Lee v. Blake* (1924), 55 O.L.R. 310 (S.C.A.D.).
118 *Boyd v. Nasmith* (1888), 17 O.R. 40 (C.P.); *Gaden*, above note 83; *Collings v. Calgary* (1917), 37 D.L.R. 804 (S.C.C.).
119 *Bank of Baroda Ltd. v. Punjab National Bank Ltd.*, above note 85.

from liability once the bank certifies the cheque because the bank has agreed to honour the cheque from funds in its account. Thus, where a bank erroneously certifies a cheque over a countermand, it is obliged to honour the certified cheque and to look to the customer in relation to any indebtedness.[120] Where the certified cheque pays a just debt of the customer to the payee or another third party, the bank cannot look to the payee for compensation because the payee is not unjustly enriched, but must look to its customer for any reimbursement.[121]

Where the drawer has requested certification and the cheque is lost prior to delivery to the payee, the payee has no cause of action against the bank because the bank is not regarded as the trustee of the funds and the funds should be returned to the drawer's account.[122] Where a certified cheque is lost by the payee, the payee's remedy is either against the person who lost it or against the bank for payment, provided security is given by the payee.[123]

Where the payee or a holder has requested certification and the payee or holder loses the cheque, the drawer has no liability.[124] Nor is there any liability should the bank fail.[125]

Once a cheque has been certified, the drawer cannot countermand it.[126] If the payee knows that, prior to certification, there was a countermand and that the cheque was erroneously certified, the bank may decline to honour the cheque on the ground that the payee is not a holder in due course.[127] When a bank erroneously certifies a cheque, it must otherwise honour that cheque, but it may look to the payee or to the customer who has been unjustly enriched as a result to recover the funds paid.[128] The principle that restitution may be appropriate when the bank pays in error is well established.[129]

---

120 *Lepage*, above note 110.
121 *RCL Operators Ltd. v. National Bank of Canada* (1995), 131 D.L.R. (4th) 86 (N.B.C.A.).
122 *Loaf 'N Jug Ltd. v. Canadian Imperial Bank of Commerce*, [1979] 5 W.W.R. 663 (Alta. Dist. Ct.).
123 *Walker v. Tanna* (1988), 65 O.R. (2d) 208 (Div. Ct.); *Honeywell Ltd. v. Sherwood Credit Union Ltd.* (1989), 58 D.L.R. (4th) 249 (Sask. Q.B.).
124 *Bank of Baroda Ltd. v. Punjab National Bank Ltd.*, above note 85.
125 *Johnson v. Christmas* (1924), 37 Que. K.B. 142 (C.A.).
126 *Centrac Inc. v. Canadian Imperial Bank of Commerce*, above note 113.
127 *Toronto Dominion Bank v. Sheppard*, [1999] 7 W.W.R. 675 (Sask. Q.B.).
128 *Repet Equipment Inc. v. Canadian Imperial Bank of Commerce*, above note 113; *RCL Operators Ltd. v. National Bank of Canada*, above note 121.
129 *Simms*, above note 109.

4) Wrongful Dishonour of Cheques

When a customer's mandate to pay is clearly drawn and there are sufficient cleared funds in the account or available through an overdraft facility and there is no other reason for refusing to honour the cheque, the bank may be liable to the customer for wrongful dishonour either in breach of contract or in the tort of defamation. It is not clear whether the bank must give notice of a decision to dishonour to the customer because there are cases both ways.[130]

The action for breach of contract is based on the implied contractual duty of the bank to carry out the customer's payment instructions once the conditions are satisfied of sufficient funds and clear mandate, and the only question remaining in law is the award of damages for breach of the bank and customer contract. The right to damages was established in *Marzetti v. Williams*,[131] where only nominal damages were awarded because substantial damages were not proven. The injury typically suffered when there is wrongful dishonour is to the customer's credit reputation, and this is typically proven by evidence that the payee will no longer deal with the customer or requires payment by a more certain means than a cheque.

At one time a distinction was drawn between "traders," that is persons in business, and ordinary customers who were not engaged in business. In cases where the claimant was a trader, the courts presumed damage to business reputation, but in cases involving private customers, the courts stated that only nominal damages for breach of contract could be awarded unless special loss could be proven.[132] However, in England, the Court of Appeal recently declined to continue that distinction on the ground that the credit rating of individuals may determine the availability of loans, mortgages, employment, accommodation, or the like, so that substantial damages should also be available where such damage is proven.[133] This decision means that the status of the claimant is no longer the determinant of whether or not substantial damages are available and renders obsolete earlier case law in which traders who could not prove substantial damages to a business repu-

---

130 For notice, see *Thermo King Corp.*, above note 19; *Raypath*, above note 26. Against notice, see *Barclay Construction Corp. v. Bank of Montreal* (1989), 65 D.L.R. (4th) 213 (B.C.C.A.).
131 Above note 18.
132 *Wilson v. United Counties Bank Ltd.*, [1920] A.C. 102 at 112, Lord Birkenhead L.C. (H.L.).; *Gibbons v. Westminster Bank Ltd.*, [1939] 2 K.B. 882; *Rae v. Yorkshire Bank plc*, [1988] F.L.R. 1 (C.A.).
133 *Kpohraror v. Woolwich Building Society*, [1996] 4 All E.R. 119 (C.A.).

tation were awarded nominal damages;[134] professional persons were awarded only nominal damages because they were not conceptualized to be in business;[135] and ordinary customers were also restricted to nominal damages even where there was provable substantial loss.[136] All customers are subject to the same rules in the assessment of damages, in line with the earlier cases in which substantial damages were awarded to business customers.[137]

These actions for breach of contract often merged into tort law insofar as the damage proven was usually to business reputation. However, there have also been actions in defamation proper brought as an alternative when a bank wrongfully dishonours a cheque. Mere dishonour without stating reasons has not been found to be defamation,[138] but the use of words such as "present again,"[139] "refer to drawer,"[140] or "insufficient funds"[141] have been said to convey an innuendo sufficient to defame the drawer. Where a claimant has proven damages in both contract and tort, the courts have awarded damages under one head only.[142] Given the sometimes low public esteem in which banks are held from time to time, it may be strategically wiser to sue in defamation than in contract for loss of reputation because defamation cases require a jury. Finally, a cheque payable to self which is wrongfully dishonoured will not found an action in defamation because an action in defamation requires loss of public reputation.[143]

When a cheque is wrongfully dishonoured, in addition to the customer's causes of action in contract and tort, a third party may occasion-

---

134 *Rolin v. Steward* (1854), 14 C.B. 595, 139 E.R. 245; *Summers v. City Bank* (1874), L.R. 9 C.P. 580; *Bank of New South Wales v. Milvain* (1884), 10 V.L.R. 3 (S.C.); *Fleming v. Bank of New Zealand*, [1900] A.C. 577 (P.C.); *Davis v. Bank of Montreal*, [1945] 1 W.W.R. 651 (B.C.S.C.); *Jayson v. Midland Bank Ltd.*, [1968] 1 Lloyd's Rep. 409 (C.A.); *Smith v. Commonwealth Trust Co.* (1969), 10 D.L.R. (3d) 181 (B.C.S.C.). Compare *Mougeot v. Bank of Nova Scotia*, [1959] C.S. 415.
135 *Davidson v. Barclays Bank Ltd.*, [1940] 1 All E.R. 316 (K.B.).
136 Above note 132.
137 Above note 134.
138 *Bank of New South Wales v. Milvain*, above note 134; *Kinlan v. Ulster Bank Ltd.*, [1928] I.R. 171 (S.C.).
139 *Baker v. Australia & New Zealand Bank Ltd.*, [1958] N.Z.L.R. 907 (S.C.).
140 *Pyke v. Hibernian Bank Ltd.*, [1950] I.R. 195 (H.C.); *Jayson v. Midland Bank Ltd.*, above note 134.
141 *Davidson v. Barclays Bank Ltd.*, above note 135.
142 *Szek v. Lloyds Bank Ltd.* (1908), 2 L.D.A.B. 159 (£250 for breach of contract and nothing for defamation); *Baker v. Australia & New Zealand Bank Ltd.*, above note 139 (£100 for defamation and nothing for breach of contract).
143 *Kinlan v. Ulster Bank Ltd.*, above note 138.

ally also have a cause of action against the bank, other than the obvious one where the cheque is certified, thereby creating a contractual relationship between the bank and the payee. In *Thermo King Corp. v. Provincial Bank of Canada*,[144] a bank was found liable for the tort of inducing breach of contract to a third party when the bank refused to honour payment instructions, in keeping with previous overdraft arrangements with the customer. In addition, the bank may owe duties of care to a third party in the tort of conversion of a cheque to someone who is not the true owner[145] and as a constructive trustee for a third party.[146]

Most claims for wrongful dishonour will be made by the customer, and many will be framed in contract and in tort, but if the claim for breach of contract fails because the refusal to pay is justified, then the action in tort will also fail.

5) Termination of the Duty to Pay and Countermand of Cheques

The paying bank's duty to honour a customer's instructions to pay may be terminated in a number of situations in addition to an insufficiency of funds available to make payment. These range from problems with the cheque itself, to prior legal orders with respect to the disposition of funds in the account, to issues relating to the customer/drawer, such as death or bankruptcy, as well as a countermand by the customer of the original instructions to pay.

The means by which the customer gave the instructions, that is, the cheque, will be problematical when that cheque becomes stale. In contemporary banking practice, an uncertified cheque becomes stale when its date is six months prior to the day on which it is presented for payment, although individual banks might adhere to slightly different periods of time. Returning a stale-dated cheque to a payee is not regarded as wrongful dishonour, and the practice of stale-dating cheques is well founded in the law of negotiable instruments, which requires negotiable instruments to be presented for payment within a reasonable time. Clearly, a drawer who issues cheques is under a duty to ensure that sufficient funds are available for all outstanding cheques. A certified cheque is not treated as stale because the funds have already been removed from the customer's account and are available for payment at any time upon presentment. The only limitation on their

---

144 Above note 19.
145 See Section D(2), below in this chapter.
146 Chapter 6, Section I.

availability is the statutory requirement in the *Bank Act* to transfer unclaimed balances to the Bank of Canada after ten years,[147] after which the claim must be made to the central bank.

A second situation in which a bank is released from its contractual duty to pay in accordance with the customer's mandate is where there is a prior court order in relation to the funds in the account. These include (i) a garnishment order at the instance of a judgment creditor of the customer and (ii) a *Mareva* injunction. A garnishment order may be issued by any superior court in Canada pursuant to the applicable court rules of procedure to secure payment of a judgment debt. The order will be for a period of time, frequency, and amount determined by the court but in accordance with any specific statutory provisions relating to the order, for example, for wages owing or for maintenance of partners or children.[148] A *Mareva*[149] injunction may be obtained by any person with a claim against another prior to judgment, to restrain that person from removing assets from the jurisdiction or otherwise dealing with them so as to frustrate any subsequent court order. It is a contempt of court for a bank to honour a customer's mandate after being served with the injunction, except in accordance with the terms of the injunction, which will identify the customer's assets frozen in whole or in part.

The *Bills of Exchange Act* provides for a third situation in section 167(b), which states that the duty and authority of a bank to pay a cheque drawn by a customer is determined by notice of the customer's death. Presumably notice of death must be to the branch of the account. The cheque is not itself invalidated by the customer's death,. Rather, the payee or holder may have recourse against the customer's estate, and liability to pay will be determined in accordance with the underlying issue in relation to the cheque. A certified cheque could presumably be paid, provided the funds were set aside prior to notice of death by virtue of the bank's contract with the payee represented in the certification.

A fourth situation is where the customer becomes known to the bank to lack legal capacity, that is, is mentally incompetent to conduct their own affairs. Section 46(1) of the *Bills of Exchange Act* provides

---

147 *Bank Act*, S.C. 1991, c. 46, ss. 438–39.
148 Readers should consult the applicable legislation in the province of interest.
149 The name derives from *Mareva Compania Naviera SA v. International Bulk Carriers SA (The 'Mareva')*, [1975] 2 Lloyd's Rep. 509 (C.A.), in which it was formulated. See also David A. Crerar, "*Mareva* Freezing Orders and Non-Party Financial Institutions: A Practical Guide" (2006) 21 B.F.L.R. 169.

that capacity to incur liability as a party to a bill, that is a cheque, is coextensive with the capacity to contract. Once a person is formally declared incompetent, under provincial legislation that person has no power to enter contracts or deal with property. With notice of a formal order, the bank will cease to honour cheques and deal only with the guardian of that person. Without notice, the bank will continue to honour cheques because there is no duty on banks to monitor continuously the mental competence of their customers!

A fifth situation in which a bank is relieved from its contractual duty to honour a customer's mandate is on the bankruptcy of the customer. When a bank is notified or otherwise learns that a customer is an undischarged bankrupt, the bank will deal only with the trustee or receiver, who will usually countermand all cheques and establish a separate trust account from which to manage the bankrupt's affairs.[150] Where the bank has no notice but suspects a customer to have committed an act of bankruptcy, the situation in law is unclear, but banks as a matter of practice will exercise caution and make inquiries prior to honouring a customer's cheque in such situations.

A final situation in which the bank's mandate under the bank and customer contract to honour a customer's cheque is terminated is where the customer terminates the mandate by issuing a countermand order in respect of a cheque.[151] Section 167(a) of the *Bills of Exchange Act* provides that the duty and authority of a bank to pay a cheque is determined by countermand of payment. Popularly referred to as a "stop-payment order," a countermand is simply an order by the customer countering a previous order to pay. Since the paying bank acts as an agent of the customer, it is normally required to honour the countermand.

In deciding whether or not to honour the countermand, a bank must be certain that the order is given by a person with authority to do so. When the order comes from an individual customer known at the branch, there are unlikely to be problems. But the authority to issue a countermand order may be more problematical in relation to corporations or partnerships. The rule would appear to be that the authority to countermand rests in those with authority to sign cheques in the first

---

150 *Bankruptcy and Insolvency Act*, R.S.C. 1985, c. B-3, s. 78.
151 For countermand generally, see Alan Whiteley, "The Demise of Countermand" (1978) 36 U.T. Fac. L. Rev. 240; Sanda Rodgers Magnet, "Inaccurate or Ambiguous Countermand and Payment Over Countermand" (1979–80) 4 Can. Bus. L.J. 297; J. Reynolds, "Countermand of Cheques" (1981) 15 U.B.C. L. Rev. 341; Andrew D. Chant, "Countermanding Payment on a Cheque," in Richard B. Miner, ed., *Current Issues in Canadian Business Law*, above note 51 at 489.

place.¹⁵² Thus, where only one signing officer need sign, any authorized signing officer can countermand, but where two or more are required to sign, then an identical number are required for a countermand, although they need not be the same officers who signed the cheque in question. Since a bank is permitted to inquire where there is an ambiguous order to pay, it should also enjoy time to inquire about the validity of a countermand when that order is ambiguous.

A countermand order may be given in any way in the absence of an agreement to the contrary. At common law, it may be oral, in person or by telephone,¹⁵³ or by telegram.¹⁵⁴ Most account contracts today now require that oral countermands be confirmed in writing on a form provided by the bank, which requests specific information concerning the amount, payee, date, cheque, and account numbers, failure to provide which will expressly relieve the bank of any liability should it honour the cheque over the countermand. Whatever form a countermand takes, it must be an actual countermand communicated to the branch and not a "constructive countermand."¹⁵⁵ A bank that has received a countermand order is liable in negligence if it overlooks the order and honours the cheque.¹⁵⁶ However, where there are suspicious circumstances in relation to countermands, a bank may be placed on inquiry and liable if a countermand is part of a fraudulent scheme such as countermanding cheques after the goods for which they are payment are shipped or received; a bank is not necessarily under a duty to the customer in such circumstances.¹⁵⁷

To be effective, a countermand order must be received prior to final payment of the cheque or of certification of the cheque.¹⁵⁸ Where the cheque has been presented through the clearing system, the bank is required to act upon the countermand order at any time prior to the point in time when a provisional credit becomes a final credit in the

---

152 *Gaunt v. Taylor* (1843), 2 Hare 413, 67 E.R. 170.
153 *Sparkle Wash v. Saskatoon Credit Union Ltd.*, [1979] 2 W.W.R. 320 (Sask. Dist. Ct.) [*Sparkle*].
154 *Curtice v. London City & Midland Bank Ltd.*, [1908] 1 K.B. 293 (C.A.) [*Curtice*]; *Reade v. Royal Bank of Ireland Ltd.*, [1922] 2 I.R. 22 (C.A.) [*Reade*].
155 *Curtice* and *Reade*, ibid.
156 *Reade*, ibid. Compare *Curtice*, ibid. and *Commonwealth Trading Bank v. Reno Auto Sales Pty Ltd.*, [1967] V.R. 790 (S.C.), which are likely wrong in finding a bank not liable for ignoring a countermand until after the cheque was honoured.
157 *Semac Industries Ltd. v. 1131426 Ontario Ltd. (c.o.b. Bancroft Lumber & Wood Flooring Products)* (2001), 16 B.L.R. (3d) 88 (Ont. S.C.J.).
158 *Commercial Automation Ltd. v. Banque provinciale du Canada* (1962), 39 D.L.R. (2d) 316 (Que. S.C.).

payee's account. This was the result in *Capital Associates Ltd. v. Royal Bank of Canada*,[159] in which an "on-us" item where drawer and payee were customers at the same bank was countermanded and the countermand order was received after the funds had been withdrawn from the drawer's account and provisionally credited to the payee's account but not finally credited. This could not happen where presentment for payment is made in person at the branch, and there are cases in which the courts have overlooked countermands on the facts of the case, for example, where the drawer's branch reassured another branch by telephone of payment, although the drawer countermanded orally a few minutes later[160] and where the bank applied cheque proceeds to a loan to another customer at the drawer's instructions and notified the drawer of that fact prior to the countermand.[161]

The degree of accuracy required for an effective countermand is somewhat uncertain. The older view was that the customer's description of the cheque had to be completely accurate in all details relating to amount, date, payee's name, cheque serial number, etc.[162] However, in *Remfor Industries Ltd. v. Bank of Montreal*,[163] the Ontario Court of Appeal stated that the description need only be reasonably accurate and upheld a countermand as valid when the cheque for $10,853 was misdescribed as for $10,800. The court further placed a duty on the bank to ensure that the customer is assisted in providing accurate information by, for example, contacting the customer to verify the information required to identify the cheque.

In light of the conflicting authorities, a correct position may be closer to *Remfor* than to the older cases because bank computers can be programmed to prompt sufficient identifying information. That is, there may be a duty on a bank in receipt of a countermand to request sufficient information and ensure that it is programmed, so that when the cheque is presented, it can be readily identified. Countermanded cheques are still processed by hand so that the cheque can be set apart in clearing. The current bank practice of requiring customers to com-

---

159 (1973), 36 D.L.R. (3d) 579 (Que. C.A.), aff'd (1976), 65 D.L.R. (3d) 384 (S.C.C.).
160 *Ciurluini*, above note 11.
161 *Royal Bank of Canada v. Slusar*, [1990] 2 W.W.R. 90 (Sask. Q.B.).
162 *Westminster Bank Ltd. v. Hilton* (1926), 136 L.T. 315 (H.L.); *Shapera v. Toronto-Dominion Bank* (1970), 17 D.L.R. (3d) 122 (Man. Q.B.) [*Shapera*]; *Giordano v. Royal Bank of Canada* (1972), 29 D.L.R. (3d) 38 (Ont. H.C.J.), rev'd (1973), 38 D.L.R. (3d) 191 (Ont. C.A.), rev'd (1974), 38 D.L.R. (3d) 191n (S.C.C.); *Sparkle*, above note 153; *Solomon v. Royal Bank of Canada*, [1983] 2 W.W.R. 543 (Man. Q.B.).
163 (1978), 90 D.L.R. (3d) 316 (Ont. C.A.), leave to appeal to S.C.C. refused (1978), 5 B.L.R. 22n (S.C.C.).

plete a standard form setting out the required information, developed in light of the *Remfor* decision, facilitates this identification, as well as protecting the bank. Duties of care in countermand are, therefore, placed on both bank and customer.

Notification of countermand must be to the branch of the account on which the cheque is drawn.[164] This statement was not always self-evident because some older cases[165] confused notice of dishonour with the drawer's countermand and suggested that countermand should be to every branch! But notice to the branch of the account is the only practical rule because that is where the drawer's signature is kept, and every cheque cleared through the clearing system is returned to the branch on which it is drawn for a final payment decision. In any case, since a branch is an agency of the bank, notice to the agent is notice to the whole bank.

A countermanded cheque is still regarded as a negotiable instrument prior to presentment for payment[166] and may be enforced against the drawer by a holder in due course,[167] unless that person knew that the cheque had been countermanded.[168] A bank may be a holder in due course by virtue of section 165(3) of the *Bills of Exchange Act* and would have the rights of a holder in respect of any cheque deposited in a payee's account.[169] A holder may enforce a cheque to the same extent as a payee.[170]

When a bank honours a cheque over a countermand, it is in breach of its contractual duty to the customer to obey only the customer's mandate and is required to reimburse the drawer's account for the amount

---

164 The *Bank Act*, above note 147, ss. 461 and 462, confirms that branch as *situs* of the account for all legal purposes, and the rule that notification of a countermand need only be to the branch of the account was confirmed in *Royal Bank of Canada v. Boyce*; *Royal Bank of Canada v. Wildman* (1966), 57 D.L.R. (2d) 683 (Ont. Co. Ct.). Compare *Bank of Nova Scotia v. Gould* (1977), 79 D.L.R. (3d) 473 (Ont. Co. Ct.) [*Gould*], which added an equitable rider to this rule.
165 *London Provincial & South-Western Bank Ltd. v. Buszard* (1918), 35 T.L.R. 142 (K.B.); *Garrioch v. Canadian Bank of Commerce*, [1919] 3 W.W.R. 185 (Alta. S.C.).
166 *Canadian Bank of Commerce v. Brash* (1957), 10 D.L.R. (2d) 555 (Ont. C.A.); *Gould*, above note 164; *Canadian Imperial Bank of Commerce v. May Trucking Ltd.* (1981), 122 D.L.R. (3d) 189 (B.C.S.C.).
167 *Trapp*, above note 78; *Kelly v. Canadian Pacific R. Co.* (1915), 25 D.L.R. 79 (B.C.C.A.); *Union Bank v. Tattersall*, above note 73; *Huron & Erie Mortgage Corp. v. Rumig* (1969), 10 D.L.R. (3d) 309 (Ont. C.A.).
168 *Banque Provinciale du Canada v. Beauchemin* (1959), 18 D.L.R. (2d) 584 (S.C.C.).
169 *Bank of Nova Scotia v. Archo Industries Ltd.* (1970), 11 D.L.R. (3d) 593 (Sask. Q.B.).
170 *Clavelle v. Russell* (1918), 11 Sask. L.R. 111 (C.A.); *McTavish v. Cotswold School District*, [1931] 3 W.W.R. 623 (Sask. C.A.).

of the cheque[171] unless the customer subsequently ratifies payment of the cheque.[172] If the bank's mistaken payment results in an unjust enrichment of the payee or the drawer, then the bank may have an action against either for the recovery of money paid under a mistake as discussed below.[173]

6) Wrongful Payment by a Paying Bank

Payment over a proper countermand is one example of wrongful payment by a bank. Others include payment where there is a forged signature or signature by an agent of the customer in excess of the agent's authority; payment where a third party raises the amount payable; and payment where a payee's endorsement is forged by a third party. A cheque is one means whereby a customer gives instructions for payment to the bank, and the bank is obliged to comply strictly with those instructions and bear the loss when a payment is unauthorized. Thus, the bank is the first party to which the customer may look for compensation when a wrongful payment has occurred. However, a bank enjoys some defences in wrongful payment situations, that is, there are certain situations in which a bank may be relieved from liability, including ambiguous mandate, ratification, estoppel, and the equitable defence that the payment actually benefited the customer by discharging an indebtedness to the payee or holder. The law in this area is very unsettled and complex and overlaps with the law relating to negotiable instruments.[174] The following discussion is a simplified introduction to this area and perhaps a prompt for further clarification by future courts.

Where a customer alleges that the bank has wrongfully paid a cheque bearing a forged signature or that is otherwise unauthorized by the customer, the first defence of the bank is estoppel, which is partially codified in the *Bills of Exchange Act*. Section 49(1) provides that a forged or unauthorized signature is wholly inoperative, so that no right to retain the cheque or give a discharge for it or enforce payment of it can be acquired unless the party against whom it is sought to retain or enforce payment is precluded from setting up the forgery or want of authority. Careless conduct by the customer in drawing a cheque has

---

171 *Simms*, above note 109.
172 *Ibid.*
173 See Section C(7), below in this chapter.
174 See any text on negotiable instruments, and for more extensive analysis from a banking law perspective, see E.P. Ellinger, Eva Lomnicka, & Richard J.S. Hooley, *Modern Banking Law*, 3d ed. (Oxford: Oxford University Press, 2002) at 386–90 and M.H. Ogilvie, above note 71 at 589–602.

given rise to a defence by the bank that the customer is precluded or estopped from having the bank bear the loss, including signing a blank cheque;[175] drawing a cheque with blanks or ambiguities which a rogue could fill in;[176] failure to inform the bank of information in relation to a forged or unauthorized cheque;[177] and reassuring the bank about suspicious circumstances without making an appropriate inquiry.[178] A bank is required to know its customer's signature,[179] but not its customer's handwriting,[180] when making decisions to pay. Moreover, a bank is also permitted to use account verification clauses in the account agreement, whereby a customer is required to report discrepancies in an account statement within a fixed period of time or be forever precluded from questioning discrepancies. Such a clause may protect a bank against the customer's carelessness in drawing a cheque in the first place.[181]

Historically, the customer's duty to avoid negligence in drawing a cheque so as to prevent wrongful payment by the bank was normally restricted to the cheque itself.[182] However, recent courts have occasionally considered the question of whether the customer should bear the loss in relation to other situations within the larger context of drawing cheques, for example, failure to examine bank statements and promptly report problems[183] or failure to supervise employees properly, with the result that employees or other agents forge cheques and cause loss. Both the Privy Council and the Supreme Court of Canada have rejected imposing such a duty on a customer, with the result that the bank will typically bear the loss when an agent of the customer forges cheques or acts in some unauthorized manner in relation to cheques, in the absence of express agreement to the contrary.

---

175 *Bills of Exchange Act*, above note 13, ss. 31–32; *Lloyds Bank Ltd. v. Cooke*, [1907] 1 K.B. 794 (C.A.); *MacMillan*, above note 33; *Ontario Woodsworth Memorial Foundation v. Grozbord* (1964), 48 D.L.R. (2d) 385 (Ont. C.A.).
176 *Young v. Grote* (1827), 4 Bing. 253, 130 E.R. 764.
177 *Greenwood v. Martins Bank Ltd.*, [1933] A.C. 51 (H.L.); *Ewing v. Dominion Bank* (1904), 35 S.C.R. 133, leave to appeal to P.C. refused, [1904] A.C. 806 (P.C.).
178 *Mutual Mortgage Corp. v. Bank of Montreal* (1965), 55 D.L.R. (2d) 164 (B.C.C.A.); *Brown v. Westminster Bank Ltd.*, [1964] 2 Lloyd's Rep. 187 (Q.B.D.).
179 *Bank of Montreal v. R.* (1906), 38 S.C.R. 258; *Ewing & Co. v. Dominion Bank*, above note 177.
180 *Ibid.*
181 See Section E, below in this chapter.
182 *MacMillan*, above note 33 at 795, Lord Finlay L.C.
183 See Section E, below in this chapter.

In *Tai Hing Cotton Mill Ltd. v. Liu Chong Hing Bank Ltd.*,[184] and in *Canadian Pacific Hotels Ltd. v. Bank of Montreal*,[185] employees who had responsibility for account reconciliation and signing authority forged cheques and defalcated with substantial funds. To avoid liability for honouring forged cheques, the banks argued that the customer owed a duty to take reasonable care to ensure that proper controls and supervision were in place to prevent employees from forging cheques. However, neither the Privy Council nor the Supreme Court of Canada, respectively, accepted this position, with the result that the banks were obliged to reimburse the customers' accounts with the amount withdrawn through the forged and unauthorized mandates. Both courts further declined to enforce either an implied term in contract or a duty of reasonable care in tort, thereby effectively making a bank the insurer of its customer when its customer failed to employ efficient internal control systems in their businesses.[186]

The Supreme Court of Canada sustained this position generally in *Boma Manufacturing Ltd. v. Canadian Imperial Bank of Commerce*,[187] which was primarily concerned with liability for cheque conversion under the *Bills of Exchange Act*[188] but ultimately left the bank liable for fraudulently drawn cheques. Again, an employee drew 146 cheques on her employer's accounts and fraudulently obtained her employer's signature on nine other cheques, and deposited these in her own bank account at a branch at which she was well known. Her employer's companies sued her bank, the collecting bank, for conversion of the cheques, and the Supreme Court majority decided that her bank was liable in conversion, thereby implicitly relieving the employer from liability. The two dissenting judges, La Forest and McLachlin JJ., thought that as between the employer and the bank, the employer was in a better position to detect the fraudulent activity and should not expect the bank to be an insurer for its failure to do so. The customer's bank was not liable for the loss, although it might have been expected to be a little suspicious about the cheques.[189]

---

184 [1986] A.C. 80 (P.C.).
185 Above note 16.
186 *Ibid.* at 434, La Forest J., citing *Kepitigalla Rubber Estates Ltd. v. National Bank of India Ltd.*, [1909] 2 K.B. 1010 at 1021, Bray J. [*Kepitigalla*].
187 (1996), 140 D.L.R. (4th) 463 (S.C.C.).
188 Above note 13, ss. 20(5), 38–39, and 165(3).
189 See Section D(2), below in this chapter, for a longer discussion of *Boma* and the collecting bank.

Further discussion of the liability of a collecting bank will follow,[190] but the importance of these cases for the paying bank is found in the firmness with which final appellate courts have consistently declined to impose liability for loss caused on the customer who is in the best position to prevent the loss and to divert it instead either to the paying bank or to the collecting bank in conversion. In England recently, there is some authority for the position that a customer may not be estopped if the customer has constructive notice of forgery and fails to make inquiry[191] and for the position that the customer may be vicariously liable for the employee's conduct,[192] but these possibilities have yet to be firmly established in England or to be considered by Canadian courts.

The second defence of a bank is that the customer subsequently ratified the agent's conduct, so that the bank was right to honour the cheque. Ratification would normally be required where the agent signs a cheque in excess of the authority granted by the principal, but it is also a valid defence where the agent forged a cheque on the ground that it is unfair to hold the bank liable for an agent's abuse of a position when the principal willingly ratifies the agent's conduct.[193]

To date, there are no cases dealing with other alterations to a cheque. However, the courts have considered the defence of ratification when a family member who is not an agent has done so. Thus, a court has permitted a bank to rely on the defence of ratification when a father ratified a son's forgery,[194] although another court did not do so on the ground that ratification amounted to stifling a prosecution when a husband ratified a wife's forgery. The agreement with the bank was found to be unenforceable as an illegal agreement and the bank was found to be liable to reimburse the husband's account with the amount of the cheque.[195] It would appear that had the bank not formulated the husband's ratification as a contract, it would have been able to use his ratification as a defence and escape liability for the forgery.

---

190 *Ibid.*
191 *Price Meats Ltd. v. Barclays Bank plc*, [2000] 2 All E.R. (Comm.) 346 (Q.B.); *Patel v. Standard Chartered Bank*, [2001] Lloyd's Rep. Bank 229 (Q.B.).
192 *Credit Lyonnais Bank Nederland NV v. Export Credits Guarantee Department*, [1999] 1 All E.R. 929 (H.L.).
193 *McKenzie v. British Linen Co.*, above note 35; *Scott v. Bank of New Brunswick* (1892), 21 S.C.R. 30.
194 *West v. Commercial Bank of Australia Ltd.* (1935), 55 C.L.R. 315 (H.C.A.).
195 *Newell v. Royal Bank of Canada* (1997), 147 D.L.R. (4th) 268 (N.S.C.A.). See also M.H. Ogilvie, "Ratification of Forged Cheques and Common Law Illegality" (1998) 13 B.F.L.R. 509.

The third defence available to a bank is that the customer's instructions are ambiguous, as discussed above.[196]

But in addition to these three common law defences, equity has recognized the defence of discharge of an indebtedness owed by the bank to a third party. This was established in *B. Liggett (Liverpool) Ltd. v. Barclays Bank Ltd.*,[197] in which a bank paid a company cheque bearing one signature, rather than the two required signatures, to discharge the company's indebtedness. Wright J. found that the company's account could not be re-credited because: "[T]he general principle of equity, that those who pay legitimate demands which they are found in some way or other to meet, and have had the benefit of other people's money advanced to them for that purpose, shall not retain that benefit so as, in substance, to make those other people pay their debts."[198]

This principle has been invoked where banks erroneously pay over countermand,[199] and in cases in which the onus of proof is placed on the bank to prove the discharge of a customer's debt.[200] This principle is said to rest on the subrogation of the paying bank to the payee's rights against the customer, so that the bank can rely on those rights if the customer disputes payment.[201] *Liggett* can also be explained as an independent equitable doctrine to prevent unjust enrichment of the customer by both paying the customer's third party debts and re-crediting the account with the amount of the cheque.[202] Where there is no customer debt to discharge and the payee is unjustly enriched by the bank's erroneous payment of the cheque, the bank may seek restitution from the payee.[203] Where the bank makes an erroneous payment in breach of a customer's instructions, it cannot rely on an exemption clause in the bank and customer account agreement to relieve it from liability to the customer.[204]

---

196 See Section C(1), above in this chapter.
197 [1928] 1 K.B. 48 [*Liggett*]. See also *Lloyds Bank v. Chartered Bank of India, Australia & China*, [1929] 1 K.B. 40 (C.A.).
198 *Liggett*, ibid. at 60–61.
199 See Section C(5), above in this chapter.
200 *Sparkle*, above note 153; *Royal Bank of Canada v. LVG Auctions Ltd.* (1984), 12 D.L.R. (4th) 768 (Ont. C.A.).
201 *Liggett*, above note 197.
202 The logic of unjust enrichment would so suggest.
203 *Toronto-Dominion Bank v. Pella/Hunt Corp.* (1992), 10 O.R. (3d) 634 (Gen. Div.) [*Pella/Hunt*].
204 *Clansmen Resources Ltd. v. Toronto Dominion Bank*, [1990] 4 W.W.R. 73 (B.C.C.A.).

7) Recovery of Money Paid by Mistake

As the foregoing discussion shows, banks make payments by mistake for a variety of reasons, including simple error, either personal or by computer, in making a payment more than once, payment over an effective countermand, payment where there are insufficient funds, or payment of a forged or unauthorized cheque. *Prima facie*, in these situations, with the exception of insufficient funds which is treated as an overdraft, the bank is liable to reimburse the customer's account because it is in breach of contract with the customer. But the bank is also permitted to look to the recipient of the mistaken payment for restitution of the sum paid under a mistake of fact. While the claim will normally be in restitution, a bank may also sue the recipient in knowing receipt or assistance, where the recipient knew of the mistake at the time of the receipt of the funds.[205]

The bank will typically sue directly on the ground that the funds paid by mistake were its own funds, rather than the customer's, but a customer may also sue the payee directly for recovery of funds paid by mistake on the basis of two different theories at common law: (i) the customer is the principal when the bank as agent pays a cheque and the principal can sue directly;[206] and (ii) because the funds in the account are a debt owed by the bank to the customer, that is, a chose in action, the customer owns at common law and may pursue.[207] In practice, however, most actions are brought by the bank because once the customer is reimbursed by the bank, the customer is unlikely to be interested in pursuing a legal remedy for the bank.

The juristic basis for permitting a bank to recover money paid by mistake is not entirely clear in the common law. There is wide agreement[208] that the action is in restitution and that the starting point for

---

205 Chapter 6, Section I.
206 *Agip (Africa) Ltd. v. Jackson*, [1991] Ch. 547 (C.A.).
207 *Lipkin Gorman v. Karpnale Ltd.*, [1991] 2 A.C. 548 (H.L.) [*Lipkin Gorman*].
208 See Harold Luntz, "The Bank's Right to Recover Cheques Paid By Mistake" (1968) 6 Melb. L. Rev. 308; Sanda Rodgers Magnet, above note 151; Benjamin Geva, "Reflections on the Need to Revise the Bills of Exchange Act: Some Doctrinal Aspects" (1981) 6 Can. Bus. L.J. 269 at 302–13; J. Reynolds, above note 151; R.M Goode, "The Bank's Right to Recover Money Paid on a Stopped Cheque" (1981) 97 Law Q. Rev. 254; M.H. Ogilvie, "Recovery of Money Paid under a Mistake of Fact" (1994) 1 B.F.L.R. 413, as well as the textbooks Ellinger *et al.*, above note 174 at c. 11; Cranston, above note 12 at 245–51; Peter D. Maddaugh and John D. McCamus, *The Law of Restitution*, 2d ed. (Aurora: Canada Law Book, 2004) at 325–40. See also my extended discussion in Ogilvie, above note 71 at 602–14.

analysis is the early-nineteenth-century case *Kelly v. Solari*.[209] In *Kelly v. Solari*, Parke B. stated that an insurance company which had overlooked the cancellation of an insurance policy and had paid out funds by mistake was entitled to recover because:

> ... where money is paid to another under the influence of a mistake, that is, upon the supposition that a specific fact is true, which would entitle the other to the money, but which fact is untrue, and the money would not have been paid if it had been known to the payer that the fact was untrue, an action will lie to recover it back, and it is against conscience to retain it; though a demand may be necessary in those cases in which the party receiving may have been ignorant of the mistake.[210]

Notwithstanding the ambiguities in this statement, it continues to capture the flavour of a bank's action for restitution of funds paid by mistake. In *Barclays Bank Ltd. v. W.J. Simms Son & Cooke (Southern) Ltd.*,[211] in which a bank paid over a countermand, Robert Goff J. emphasized that if the bank had paid over as a result of a mistake, the bank had a right to recover the money from the recipient. Subsequently, in *Kleinwort Benson Ltd. v. Lincoln City Council*,[212] Lord Hope set out the principle simply:

> Subject to any defences that may arise from the circumstances, a claim for restitution for money paid under a mistake raises three questions: (1) Was there a mistake? (2) Did the mistake cause the payment? And (3) did the payee have a right to receive the sum which was paid to him?[213]

Although an earlier Canadian case, *Royal Bank v. The King*,[214] had adopted a similar position,[215] since *Simms*, Canadian courts have relied on the English precedent to permit recovery in restitution by a bank from the payee. In *Simms*, Robert Goff J. characterized the mistake required of the bank as "fundamental," but this is now regarded as meaning simply that the mistake must be material, in the sense that it caused

---

209 (1841), 9 M. & W. 54, 152 E.R. 24 (Exch. Ch.). See also the earlier case: *Price v. Neal* (1762), 3 Burr. 1354, 97 E.R. 871 (K.B.) and J.B. Ames, "The Doctrine of *Price v. Neal*" (1891) 4 Harv. L. Rev. 297.
210 *Kelly v. Solari*, ibid. at 58 (M. & W.), 26 (E.R.), Parke B.
211 Above note 109.
212 [1998] 3 W.L.R. 1095 (H.L.).
213 *Ibid.* at 1145.
214 [1931] 2 D.L.R. 685 (Man. K.B.).
215 *Shapera*, above note 162, and *Toronto-Dominion Bank v. Anker* (1978), 93 D.L.R. (3d) 510 (Ont. Co. Ct.) [*Anker*] followed *Royal Bank v. The King*, ibid.

the bank to pay money to the payee and not that some extra character is required for the mistake to be operative in an action for restitution.

In *Simms*, Robert Goff J. further stated that the bank's right of recovery in mistaken payment cases may fail in three situations in which the payee may have a good defence to the bank's action: (i) where the drawer intends to pay the payee; (ii) where the payment is made for good consideration, that is, it discharges a debt owed to the payee; and (iii) where the payee has changed position in good faith by virtue of receipt of the payment.[216] Each of these will be considered. These are commonly reduced to good consideration, estoppel, and change of position by the payee.

Where the payee can claim good consideration, that is, the money received as a result of the mistaken payment discharges a debt owed by the drawer to the payee, then the bank will not succeed in recovering those funds from the payee, but rather must look to its customer. Although there is some difference of opinion in the English case law as to the doctrinal correctness of this defence on the part of the payee,[217] Canadian cases have adopted and applied it especially in cases of payment over countermand.[218] This is explained as an application of the *Liggett*[219] principle that one who pays the debts of another without authority may take advantage of the payment. The result is that when the mistaken payment by the bank results in the discharge of an indebtedness to the payee, the bank cannot recover from the payee. Since the bank is also obliged to re-credit the customer's account because in breach of contract by paying over a countermand, the customer may be unjustly enriched. The courts have yet to face the dilemma this conflict of principles creates.

The second defence of estoppel and the third of change of position by the payee are difficult to distinguish conceptually.[220] To prove estoppel as a defence, the payee must satisfy three conditions: (i) a representation by the paying bank entitling the payee to believe the payee can treat that

---

216 Above note 109 at 695.
217 For a new consensus that this is juristically wrong, see *Simms*, ibid.; *Lloyds Bank plc v. Independent Insurance Co. Ltd.*, [2000] Q.B. 110 (C.A.); Cranston, above note 12 at 250–51; Ellinger *et al.*, above note 174 at 436–40.
218 *Shapera*, above note 162; *Royal Bank of Canada v. Huber* (1971), 23 D.L.R. (3d) 209 (Sask. C.A.); *Bank of Nova Scotia v. Cheng* (1981), 33 Nfld. & P.E.I.R. 89 (S.C.T.D.); *Lepage*, above note 110. Compare *Pella/Hunt*, above note 203, where bank could recover against payee on the facts. See also *Anker*, above note 215, and *Royal Bank of Canada v. LVG Auctions Ltd.*, above note 200.
219 Above note 197.
220 Ellinger *et al.*, above note 174 at 440–41.

money as the payee's own money; (ii) the payee detrimentally relied; and (iii) there is no fault or bad faith on the payee's part.[221] Estoppel differs from change of position in two ways: (i) estoppel requires a representation and not merely payment; and (ii) estoppel is a complete defence against recovery, but change of position operates to the extent that the recipient has changed position so that partial recovery is possible.[222] It would appear that estoppel is giving way to change of position as the preferred defence because it permits more finely tuned, equitable results.[223]

The third defence of change of position simply means that it would be inequitable to require the payee to refund the bank where the payee has relied on the payment by incurring some liability or giving up an advantage, provided the payee acts in good faith in that reliance, that is, actually believes there was an entitlement to the payment and did not know of the bank's error in making the payment. Full recognition of this defence of change of position came in the House of Lords decision in *Lipkin Gorman*,[224] although that result was in line with earlier lower court decisions in England.[225] Subsequent cases in England have clarified the circumstances in which full or partial restitution must be made by a payee to the bank, so that there must be a causal link between the mistaken payment and the payee's change of position;[226] the payee need not be required to prove detailed accounts of how the funds were spent;[227] the change of position must make it inequitable for restitution of the funds;[228] and the payee must be in good faith and not a wrongdoer.[229] To date, there has been no consideration of this recent flurry of English case law developing this rule of the law in relation to recovery from a payee by the bank, but there is nothing in Canadian case law to suggest that the defence of change of position would not be available to a payee in appropriate circumstances should it be pleaded. The general equitable inclinations of Canadian courts in similar circumstances would suggest as much.[230]

---

221 *National Westminster Bank Ltd. v. Barclays Bank International Ltd.*, [1975] Q.B. 654.
222 *National Westminster Bank plc v. Somer International (U.K.) Ltd.*, [2001] EWCA Civ. 970 (C.A.).
223 Ellinger *et al.*, above note 174; Cranston, above note 12 at 247–50.
224 Above note 207.
225 *United Overseas Bank v. Jiwani*, [1977] 1 All E.R. 733 (Ch. D.).
226 *Scottish Equitable plc v. Derby*, [2001] 3 All E.R. 818 (C.A.).
227 *Ibid.*; *Phillip Collins Ltd. v. Davis*, [2000] 3 All E.R. 808 (Ch. D.).
228 *Lipkin Gorman*, above note 207.
229 *Ibid.*
230 The willingness to follow *Liggett*, above note 197, without close consideration of the difficulties in that decision suggest as much.

D. THE COLLECTING BANK

1) Requirements for Collection

When a customer, the payee of a cheque, deposits a cheque or other instrument in an account with the customer's bank, that bank takes on the role of collecting bank, which involves presenting the cheque for payment through the clearing system to the paying bank, that is, the bank of the drawer of the cheque from whose account at the paying bank it is expected that the cheque will be paid. As a collecting bank, a bank is under a general implied common law duty in contract to the customer with whom it has an account agreement to collect cheques and other instruments on its customer's behalf.[231]

Just as the paying bank acts as the agent of the customer in paying a cheque on the customer's behalf, so too is the collecting bank an agent of the customer when it collects cheques on the customer's behalf. As the collecting bank, the bank is expected to exercise reasonable care in collection on behalf of the customer and is liable to the customer for breach of that duty. Conversely, a customer who gives an ambiguous mandate to a bank in relation to collection may also be liable to indemnify the bank for any loss it may suffer as a result of the customer's breach of contract. A bank must present instruments for payment in accordance with the *Bills of Exchange Act* and give notice of dishonour to the customer.[232] A bank is also liable if it employs a subagent in collection for any fault or error of the subagent in collection.[233]

The collecting bank's duty in collection is owed to its customer and not to the drawer of the cheque.[234] That duty encompasses the following major steps in the collection process: selecting the method of collection, presentment for payment, receipt of payment, return of dishonoured instruments, giving notice of dishonour, and reversal of a provisional credit made in the customer's account at the time of deposit. In performing these steps, the collecting bank owes a duty to its customer, but as discussed earlier,[235] it may also owe a duty as a constructive trustee to a third party with a prior legal claim to the funds

---

231 *Joachimson v. Swiss Bank Corp.*, above note 6.
232 *Bank of Van Diemen's Land v. Bank of Victoria* (1871), 7 Moo. P.C. N.S. 401, 17 E.R. 152; *Bank of Scotland v. Dominion Bank*, [1891] A.C. 592 (P.C.).
233 *MacKersy v. Ramsays, Bonars & Co.* (1843), 9 Cl. & Fin. 818, 8 E.R. 628 (H.L.); *Prince v. Oriental Bank Corp.*, [1878] 3 App. Cas. 325 (P.C.).
234 *Toor v. Bank of Montreal* (1991), 3 B.L.R. (2d) 1 (B.C.S.C.).
235 Chapter 6, Section I.

in the cheque deposited for collection. The present discussion will be limited, however, to the collecting bank's duties to its own customer.

The first duty of a collecting bank when a customer has deposited a cheque in an account is to select the method of collecting payment. This duty is easily discharged by selecting the common and usual method of collection, and this is through the automated clearing and settlement systems run by the Canadian Payments Association (CPA).[236] The duty to present for payment through the clearing system must be performed within a reasonable period of time after deposit of the cheque, with or without endorsement. With automated clearing, this means in accordance with the CPA rules, and as a matter of course, cheques are sent for collection on the same day they are deposited by the payee/customer in the account. Some of the older cases regarded a reasonable period of time as determined by such instances as distance, the vagaries of presentment through the post, a largely discontinued practice, or some peculiarity associated with the cheque that required clarification, but these cases seem unlikely to be applicable with automated clearing and settlement.[237]

When the drawer and payee of a cheque have accounts at the same bank or at the same branch, these "on-us" instruments are not sent through the clearing system but are cleared internally within the branch or the bank, and they are not subject to the CPA clearing rules. Although there is some ambiguity in the case law as to the characterization of such cheques as being presented for payment or for collection,[238] the bank's duty to ensure that the payee's account is finally credited is subject to the reasonable time implied term. The courts seem to treat collection and payment within a branch as a local version of collection and payment generally because they have itemized the steps between deposit of the cheque and final crediting of the account within the branch *as if* sent through the clearing system.[239]

The customer's account is provisionally credited with the full value of the cheque at the time of deposit as a matter of banking practice. If the

---

236 *Forman v. Bank of England* (1902), 18 T.L.R. 339 (K.B.); *Lajambe v. Saint-Hilaire* (1924), 30 R.L. (N.S.) 447 (Que. Sup. Ct.); *National Bank of Greece (Canada) v. Bank of Montreal*, above note 52. However, the CPA rules do not override the Bills of Exchange Act: *Bank of Nova Scotia v. Toronto-Dominion Bank* (2001), 200 D.L.R. (4th) 549 (Ont. C.A.); *Advance Bank*, above note 47.

237 For these, see Ogilvie, above note 71 at 625; Crawford, *Payment, Clearing and Settlement in Canada*, above note 51 at 263–66.

238 *Grace Chu Chan Po Kee v. The Hong Kong Chinese Bank Ltd.*, unreported decision of the Hong Kong High Court (9 January 1979), cited in Mark Hapgood, ed., *Paget's Law of Banking*, 12th ed. (London: Butterworths, 2003) at 471.

239 *Capital Associates Ltd. v. Royal Bank of Canada*, above note 57; *Bank of Nova Scotia v. Pittman*, above note 87.

bank makes a credit decision to permit the customer to have access to that credit prior to final payment by the drawer's bank, then the customer is, strictly speaking, drawing on a credit from the bank's own funds. Canadian banks typically have a "cheque hold" policy[240] clause in the account agreement, giving the bank a discretion to decide whether the customer may access those funds, and the decision to permit access is a credit decision on the bank's part. Without such a clause, a bank may refuse to allow access to uncleared funds for the very reason that they are uncleared, that is, no final payment has yet been made by the drawer's bank.

At common law, a collecting bank that failed to present a cheque for payment within a reasonable period of time after deposit was liable to the customer for any loss resulting from the delay as a breach of the account agreement.[241] The damages awarded were typically the amount of the cheque, but where the customer's reputation was damaged because a cheque was dishonoured for insufficient funds because of an unreasonable delay in collecting a cheque, the collecting bank could be liable for damage to the customer's reputation.[242]

When a cheque sent for collection is returned by the paying bank as dishonoured, the collecting bank is under a duty pursuant to section 96(a) of the *Bills of Exchange Act* to give notice of dishonour to the customer not later than the next business day following the dishonour. However, this duty to inform the customer only arises once the collecting bank learns of the dishonour, and for cheques collected through the clearing system, the dishonour will be known by the collecting bank only when the cheque is returned through the clearing.

However, the collecting bank is also under a duty to its customer to ensure that the paying bank makes the decision to pay or to dishonour within a reasonable period of time, that is, it is not permitted to send a cheque for collection and wait indefinitely until it receives notice from the paying bank, but must ensure a timely decision by the paying bank. A paying bank is the agent of the collecting bank and under a duty to present the cheque promptly to itself.[243] The period of time within which notice of dishonour should occur is that provided in the CPA rules for the return of dishonoured items, that is, not later than the business day following receipt by the paying bank.[244] If the return is

---

240 Permitted by Cheque Holding Policy Disclosure (Banks) Regulations, SOR/2002-39.
241 *Lubbock v. Tribe* (1838), 3 M. & W. 607, 150 E.R. 1287; *Yeoman Credit Ltd. v. Gregory*, [1963] 1 All E.R. 245 (Q.B.).
242 *Kilsby v. Williams* (1822), 5 B. & Ald. 815, 106 E.R. 1388.
243 *Bank of British North America v. Standard Bank of Canada*, above note 47.
244 Canadian Payments Association, *ACSS Rules Manual* (Ottawa: Canadian Payments Association, 1984) Rule 4A.

after this day, then the paying bank must fully reimburse the collecting bank the amount of the cheque.[245]

The liability of the paying bank to the customer who sent the cheque for collection in the first place is more problematical. The customer has no contract with the paying bank unless the drawer and payee are customers of the same bank, and therefore no privity of contract exists on the basis of which to found a claim for breach of contract.[246] On the other hand, the payee is within the bounds of reasonable foreseeability as likely to suffer loss through a delay in dishonouring the cheque and can succeed in the tort of negligence.[247] Where the drawer and payee are customers of the same bank, the payee can sue directly in breach of contract, as well for a delay in collection.

Once a cheque has been returned dishonoured, the collecting bank will reverse the provisional credit[248] in the customer's account or exercise its right of "charge-back." Provision is made in account agreements for this practice, but it is long established as correct in the common law.[249] There would appear to be no limitation on the time period within which a charge-back can be made, but it should probably be within a reasonable period of time as a matter of equity to the customer in knowing the state of the account. Where there are insufficient funds in the account so that the charge-back creates an overdraft, the bank enjoys a right to sue the customer to repay the loan created by the overdraft[250] or to sue for same any other party liable on the cheque.[251] Any surplus recovered should be returned to the customer.[252] In these actions, the status of the bank appears to be that of a holder for value rather than a holder in due course because it has notice of the dishonour.[253]

---

245 *National Bank of Greece (Canada) v. Bank of Montreal*, above note 52.
246 *Stanley Works of Canada Ltd. v. Banque Canadienne Nationale*, above note 50; *National Slag v. Canadian Imperial Bank of Commerce*, above note 50.
247 *Midland Doherty Ltd. v. Royal Bank of Canada*, above note 50.
248 *Re Mills* (1893), 10 Morr. 193 (Ch. D.); *Capital and Counties Bank Ltd. v. Gordon*, above note 28. For the practice of provisional credits, see *Prideaux v. Criddle* (1869), L.R. 4 Q.B. 455; *Owens v. Quebec Bank* (1870), 30 U.C.R. 382 (C.A.); *Conn v. Merchants Bank* (1879), 3 C.P. 380; *Bank of Nova Scotia v. Sharp* (1975), 57 D.L.R. (3d) 260 (B.C.C.A.).
249 *Ibid.*
250 *Bank of Nova Scotia v. Taylor* (1979), 27 N.B.R. (2d) 14 (Co. Ct.); *Bank of Montreal v. Vaillancourt*, above note 19.
251 *Huron & Erie Mortgage Corp. v. Rumig*, above note 167.
252 *Bank of British North America v. Warren & Co.* (1909), 19 O.L.R. 257 (C.A.).
253 *Royal Bank of Scotland v. Tottenham*, [1894] 2 Q.B. 715 (C.A.); *Westminster Bank Ltd. v. Zang*, [1966] A.C. 182 (H.L.).

2) Statutory Protection of the Collecting Bank

While acting as an agent of its customer in collecting a cheque, the collecting bank risks dealing with an instrument to which another person has a prior legal title or right which is better in law than the claim of the customer. A bank that collects a cheque for a person, even a customer, with a defective title or no title may be sued in conversion, restitution, or constructive trust. So the question becomes whether the law affords any protection to a bank that acts innocently in collecting a cheque deposited by a customer in an account with the bank. The collecting banker's legal power to collect is derived from its contract with the customer, which designates the bank as the customer's agent for collection.

Historically, the common law was unclear as to the status of the bank against a "true owner," and in England, attempts to overcome the confusion resulted in legislation in 1882,[254] 1906,[255] and 1957,[256] which alleviated in part bank liability but which is still subject to problems as revealed by subsequent case law.[257] The Canadian *Bills of Exchange Act*[258] contained a provision very similar to one in the English Act, and Canadian case law[259] confirmed that very little protection for a collecting bank could be found in the legislation. In 1966, Parliament amended the *Bills of Exchange Act* to give banks greater protection by adding section 165(3):

> Where a cheque is delivered to a bank for deposit to the credit of a person and the bank credits him with the amount of the cheque, the bank acquires all the rights and powers of a holder in due course of the cheque.[260]

Section 165(3) is drafted in broad terms, with the obvious policy of protecting a bank from liability in relation to cheques deposited in a customer's account by permitting a bank to presume that it was the

---

254 *Bills of Exchange Act, 1882* (U.K.), 45 & 46 Vict, c. 61, s. 82.
255 *Bills of Exchange (Crossed Cheques) Act, 1906* (U.K.), c. 81.
256 *Cheques Act, 1957* (U.K.), c. 36.
257 See generally *Paget's Law of Banking*, 12th ed., above note 238 at c. 22 & 23; Ellinger *et al.*, above note 174 at c. 14; Cranston, above note 12 at 263–66.
258 *Bills of Exchange Act*, above note 13, s. 175. For a brief Canadian history, see Ogilvie, above note 71 at 632–36; Crawford, *Payment, Clearing and Settlement in Canada*, above note 51 at 281–84.
259 *Imperial Bank of Canada v. Hays & Earl Ltd.* (1962), 35 D.L.R. (2d) 136 (Alta. S.C.).
260 S.C. 1966-67, c. 12, s. 47. See also Stephen A. Scott, "The Bank Is Always Right: Section 165(3) of the *Bills of Exchange Act* and Its Curious Parliamentary History" (1973) 19 McGill L.J. 78 and Sheilah Martin, "Section 165(3) of the *Bills of Exchange Act*" (1985) 11 Can. Bus. L.J. 23.

drawer's intention that the payee receive the proceeds of the cheque,[261] in complete contrast to the earlier law, where a bank enjoyed no such presumption. However, the subsequent case law casts doubt on how expansively section 165(3) should be interpreted and has left considerable confusion in its wake, beginning with the first decision of the Supreme Court of Canada on section 165(3), *Boma Manufacturing Ltd. v. Canadian Imperial Bank of Commerce.*[262]

In *Boma*, a bookkeeper with signing authority fraudulently drew cheques on her employer's accounts. Some were made payable to existing persons and some to non-existent persons; some were signed by the bookkeeper and some by the president; some were fraudulently endorsed by the bookkeeper. The employer sued the bookkeeper's bank, the collecting bank, for the cheques that were deposited in her account, for conversion. The majority in the Supreme Court of Canada held that the bank was liable in conversion to the employer on a restrictive reading of section 165(3). Iacobucci J., speaking for the majority, decided that the bank did not become the holder in due course under that section because it only refers to a person entitled to the cheque, that is, a payee or legitimate endorsee of a cheque, and the bookkeeper was neither. The bank took the cheques subject to the equities and was liable in conversion. La Forest J., for the minority, agreed on that point and further stated that s.165(3) is limited in application to situations in which a cheque is restrictively endorsed or in which the payee fails to endorse it upon presentment to a bank for deposit.

In addition to stripping banks of much of the statutory protection from charges of conversion when they collect cheques deposited by customers, the Supreme Court considered further issues within the context of section 165(3). First, the meaning of "delivered" was simplified to mere delivery by any person whether or not authorized to have possession of the forged instrument, thereby overturning earlier case law which had required authority to deliver for the person making the deposit,[263] in keeping with other references to delivery in sections 38

---

261 For pre-*Boma* judicial appreciation of the policy underlying s. 165(3), see *Groves-Raffin Construction Ltd. v. Bank of Nova Scotia* (1975), 64 D.L.R. (3d) 78 at 99–100 (B.C.C.A.), Bull J.A. [*Groves-Raffin*] and *Canadian Imperial Bank of Commerce v. Gardiner Watson Ltd.* (1983), 25 Alta L.R. (2d) 319 at 327 (Q.B.), Quigley J.

262 Above note 187. See also the earlier critique of the trial decision that identified the core problem in this area: M.H. Ogilvie, "Should the Collecting Bank Be the Drawer's Insurer?" (1994) 9 B.F.L.R. 227.

263 *Groves-Raffin*, above note 261; *Gough Electric Ltd. v. Canadian Imperial Bank of Commerce* (1986), 31 D.L.R. (4th) 307 (B.C.C.A.); *Toronto-Dominion Bank v. Dauphin Plains Credit Union Ltd.* (1992), 98 D.L.R. (4th) 736 (Man. C.A.).

and 39 of the *Bills of Exchange Act*. Secondly, the meaning of "person" was narrowed to a person who has a right to transfer a cheque to their bank for collection and deposit.[264] Thirdly, the court decided that the bank had no fictitious payee defence under section 20(5) of the Act because the cheques were payable to actual persons and therefore payable to order. The minority disagreed and thought that most of the cheques were made out to a fictitious person on the basis of a policy decision that a bank should not be liable when the employer was in the best position to minimize the loss.

The net effect of the *Boma* decision was to make the collecting bank the insurer of an employer whose poor supervision of the fraudulent employee created the factual situation in which the cheques could be forged in the first place. Subsequent cases have largely followed this interpretation of section 165(3), which, as a result, affords less protection for the innocent bank than was originally contemplated when it was added to the *Bills of Exchange Act* and casts doubt on the whole concept of negotiability. Thus, in *Westboro Flooring and Décor Inc. v. Bank of Nova Scotia*,[265] the Ontario Court of Appeal applied *Boma* where the employee did not forge any signatures but simply deposited cheques into a bogus bank account. In *Metroland Printing, Publishing and Distribution Ltd. v. Canadian Imperial Bank of Commerce*,[266] the bank was found liable when an employee caused a computer system to draw cheques bearing legitimate signatures and then negotiated those cheques through various bank accounts. And in *J.C. Creations Ltd. v. Vancouver City Savings Credit Union*,[267] the financial institution was again liable when an employee wrongfully deposited cheques made out to the employer in her own account at the credit union, which had not required her to endorse the cheques so that it did not become a holder in due course under section 165(3).

However, the question of whether some ambiguity has crept into this approach to section 165(3) was raised in a recent decision from the Supreme Court of Canada, in *373409 Alberta Ltd. v. Bank of Montreal*.[268]

---

264 See also *Titan West Warehouse Club Inc. v. National Bank*, [1998] 2 W.W.R. 212 (Sask. C.A.).

265 (2004), 241 D.L.R. (4th) 257 (Ont. C.A.). See also the comments by Nicholas Rafferty & Jonnette Watson Hamilton, "The Collecting Bank's Liability for Conversion of Cheques" (2003) 19 B.F.L.R. 77 and "Is the Collecting Bank Now the Insurer of a Cheque's Drawer against Losses Caused by the Fraud of the Drawer's Own Employee?" (2005) 20 B.F.L.R. 427.

266 (2001), 14 B.L.R. (3d) 212 (Ont. S.C.J.).

267 (2004), 236 D.L.R. (4th) 602 (B.C.C.A.).

268 (2002), 220 D.L.R. (4th) 193 (S.C.C.). See also M.H. Ogilvie, "If *Boma* is Wrong, Is the Bank Always Right?" (2003) 39 Can. Bus. L.J. 138. For an analysis of the

In this case, the sole shareholder and directing mind of two corporations altered a cheque payable to one and deposited it to the account of the other. When the first corporation went into liquidation, the receiver sued the bank in conversion for having deposited an unendorsed cheque. The court found the bank not liable in conversion because the first corporation through its directing mind had validly authorized the deposit, and the bank dealt with the cheque in a manner consistent with that instruction. This case was likely dependent on the dual role of the directing mind for its outcome, and the court did not consider the section 165(3) defence, leaving *Boma* as the definitive decision from the Supreme Court of Canada to date.

The impact of *Boma* on previous case law under section 165(3) is difficult to assess. If *Boma* means that banks are virtual insurers whenever a cheque is forged or unauthorized, then section 165(3) has been rendered nugatory as a defence for a bank. Previous case law which sought to explore and clarify the section 165(3) defence may no longer be applicable, although not expressly overturned in *Boma*.[269]

If, on the other hand, a bank persuades a court that it is a holder in due course under the section, then it is free to deal with the cheque as it sees fit and to sue any prior holder, endorser, or payee to recover any losses suffered as a result of any defect in the cheque.

Should there be any party which can prove a better claim in respect of a cheque, that party has another cause of action against the bank in addition to conversion, that is, by waiving a tort action in conversion, the "true owner" may sue in restitution for money had and received. A restitution action is independent from a conversion action,[270] but it is not self-evident that this is a mere advantageous approach because the collecting bank acts as an agent and the better recourse would be against its principal, the customer, to whose account the funds have been credited. However, a few cases have upheld this approach so that it is part of banking law.[271] The third course of action is in constructive trust, by holding the bank to be the constructive trustee of funds on behalf of a third party proving a prior, superior title to those funds.[272]

Alta. C.A. decision, see Nicholas Rafferty & Jonnette Watson Hamilton, "The Liability in Conversion of a Collecting Bank to the Payee: Is An Endorsement Required to Pass Title to a Cheque?" (2002) 17 B.F.L.R. 395.
269 See Ogilvie, above note 71 at 637–43.
270 *Bavins Jr. and Sims v. London & South Western Bank*, [1900] 1 Q.B. 270 (C.A.).
271 *Ibid.*, *R.E. Jones Ltd. v. Waring & Gillow Ltd.*, [1926] A.C. 670 (H.L.).
272 Chapter 6, Section I.

E. RENDERING STATEMENTS OF ACCOUNT

The third general duty implied by the common law into the bank and customer relationship is to render accounts periodically or on request as to the state of the customer's account after the bank has honoured the customer's mandates to pay out and collect funds into the account. This duty dates from *Clayton's Case*[273] in 1816, although the practice of rendering regular accounts is, obviously, much older. The interval between accounts appears to have been at the bank's discretion and should a customer's demand for a statement of account not be met, the customer's recourse is to sue in debt for the balance in the account.[274]

Today, banks carry out their duty to render statements of account in various ways, by passbooks, by periodic (usually monthly) statements with or without cheque return, or by online computerized access to the account record. The method of reporting is entirely a matter for the bank, provided the duty to report is performed, and typically is part of the bundled services tied to the various types of accounts offered by banks in response to their perceived consumer market. The status in law of passbooks, deposit receipts, and printed statements was considered earlier,[275] but it may be briefly recalled that they are not regarded as negotiable instruments, and cannot, therefore, be given as a security: mere possession of a bank passbook does not give good title to the funds of an account.[276]

Where the account contract provides that production of the passbook is required for repayment of funds in the account, the courts will require production,[277] although mere production may not be sufficient if there is no legal title to the funds. Where a passbook is lost, a bank is required to repay the balance once the customer has proven good title, regardless of whether payment has already been made to an imposter.[278]

The information in a passbook or periodic statement is considered to be no more than *prima facie* evidence of the true state of account be-

---

273 *Devaynes v. Noble; Clayton's Case* (1816), 1 Mer. 572, 35 E.R. 781 (H.L.) [*Clayton's Case*].
274 *Ibid.*
275 Chapter 7, Section E.
276 *Hopkins v. Abbott* (1875), L.R. 19 Eq. 222.
277 *Atkinson v. Bradford Third Equitable Benefit Building Society* (1890), 25 Q.B.D. 377 (C.A.); *Re Dillon* (1890), 44 Ch. D. 76 (C.A.); *Re Tidd*, [1893] 3 Ch. 154; *Re Griffin*, [1899] 1 Ch. 408.
278 *Wood v. Clydesdale Bank*, [1914] S.C. 397 (H.L.).

tween bank and customer.²⁷⁹ Either bank²⁸⁰ or customer²⁸¹ may question its accuracy at common law, which does not regard a bank statement as an account stated, that is, as a final and accurate account.²⁸² Unless a customer is precluded by contract from questioning a statement as discussed below in this section, both bank and customer have a common law right to rectify errors in the accounting between them.

Errors by the bank in keeping accounts may include crediting an account in error, crediting an account with the same amount twice, or debiting an account with the same amount twice. A bank which catches these errors itself may make corrections within a reasonable time.²⁸³ The records of the bank in relation to an account are regarded as *prima facie* evidence and would require collaboration to be binding.²⁸⁴ Such evidence might include paying-in slips, which are regarded as the property of the bank, although they may be required to be produced in any litigation relating to error correction.²⁸⁵ A bank must prove that a different sum was actually deposited if alleging that the deposit is different from the sum on the slip.²⁸⁶ A customer is not estopped by inaccuracies on the paying-in slip from arguing that a different sum was paid in.²⁸⁷

When a bank discovers an error and attempts to correct it, the bank may be estopped from doing so if the customer has detrimentally relied on the original statement of the bank.²⁸⁸ In *Holland v. Manchester & Liverpool District Banking Co.*,²⁸⁹ a bank erroneously credited an account twice so that the balance shown on the passbook was £70, rather than £60. The customer relied on that account in good faith and drew a

---

279 *Agricultural Savings & Loan Association v. Federal Bank* (1881), 6 O.A.R. 192; *R. v. Bank of Montreal* (1906), 11 O.L.R. 595 (C.A.); *Abbott v. Bank of Toronto*, [1934] 3 D.L.R. 256 (Ont. C.A.).
280 *Holman v. Royal Bank of Canada* (1975), 58 D.L.R. (3d) 154 (B.C. Co. Ct.).
281 *Kepitigalla*, above note 186.
282 *Blackburn Building Society v. Cunliffe, Brooks & Co.* (1884), 9 App. Cas. 857 (H.L.) [*Blackburn*]; *Bank of England v. Vagliano Bros.*, [1891] A.C. 107 (H.L.) [*Vagliano*]; *Kepitigalla*, ibid. On the facts, however, it can be an account stated: *Bishun Chand Firm v. Seth Girdhari Lal* (1934), 50 T.L.R. 465 at 468–69 (P.C.), Lord Wright.
283 *Commercial Bank of Scotland v. Rhind* (1860), 3 Macq. 643 (H.L.); *British & North European Bank Ltd. v. Zalzstein*, [1927] 2 K.B. 92 [*Zalzstein*].
284 *British Linen Bank. v. Thomson* (1853), 2 Stuart 175 (S.C.).
285 *Paramount Film Service Ltd. v. Payeur*, [1961] Que. R.P. 288 (S.C.).
286 *Docherty v. Royal Bank of Scotland*, 1963 S.L.T. (Notes) 43 (S.C.).
287 *Universal Guarantee Pty. Ltd. v. National Bank of Australia Ltd.*, [1965] 2 All E.R. 98 (P.C.).
288 *Skyring v. Greenwood and Cox* (1825), 4 B. & C. 281, 107 E.R. 1064; *General Dairies v. Maritime Electric Co.*, [1935] 4 D.L.R. 196 (S.C.C.).
289 (1909), 25 T.L.R. 386 (Ch. D.).

cheque for £67, which was dishonoured. The court found that the bank could correct its error but was also liable for damages suffered by the customer resulting from the dishonour of the cheque in both contract and tort.

However, the customer must persuade a court that it was genuinely misled by the account statement and changed position as a result. If an inequity results for the customer by mere error correction, then the customer must assent.[290] In *United Overseas Bank v. Jiwani*,[291] a customer's argument that the bank was estopped from error correction failed where a bank erroneously credited his account twice with the same amount because the court found the customer to be dishonest. The court further found that merely spending the money was not sufficient detriment where the customer's mode of living had not changed, in this case, because the customer would still have made the purchase. Presumably, detrimental reliance on the inaccurate statement is required for the customer to escape liability from repaying the funds to the bank.

Customers, as well as banks, also enjoy a common law right to have errors in account statements corrected, and at common law, the limitation period runs from the date that demand for repayment is made and not from the date of an erroneous debit.[292] The precise period will depend on limitations legislation in the jurisdiction of the account. Where the sum is for a small amount, banks will, as a matter of practice, normally correct it as a matter of good customer relations, but where the error is larger or suggests some illegal activity, the error correction will not be automatic.

The right of a customer to have an error corrected in the account statement depends on the presence of an account verification clause in the contract. If such a clause exists and is found by the court to apply to the facts, then the customer's common law right to error rectification will be barred by the express waiver in the clause. Otherwise, the customer has a right to rectification at any time. This right flows from the position taken by the common law on the question of how customers should receive bank statements.

Although the common law has long implied a contractual duty into the bank and customer contract that the bank render accounts, historically, no correlative duty was ever imposed on the customer to read

---

290 *Colonial Bank v. Exchange Bank of Yarmouth* (1885), 11 App. Cas. 84 (P.C.); *Zalzstein*, above note 283.
291 [1977] 1 All E.R. 733 (Ch. D.).
292 *National Bank of Commerce v. National Westminster Bank*, [1990] 2 Lloyd's Rep. 514 (Ch. D.).

and verify the accuracy of those accounts and report discrepancies at all. The common law did not require mutual obligations of both parties in relation to account statements.[293] Moreover, in the absence of an account verification clause in the account contract, this remains the case after two final appellate decisions in the mid-1980s.

In *Tai Hing Cotton Mill Ltd. v. Liu Chong Hing Bank Ltd.*,[294] a company sued three banks with which it had accounts from which a company clerk stole a large sum through about three hundred forged cheques over a six-year period. The Privy Council found that the customer owed no duty to the banks either to check bank statements or to operate the accounts with responsible care by utilizing reasonable internal accounting procedures so as to prevent forgeries. The Privy Council further found that the account verification clauses, known elsewhere as conclusive evidence clauses, were not drafted clearly enough to protect the banks and that the banks were liable to the company on the forged cheques. Lord Scarman thought that the common law should not imply duties of care on the customer's part so as to render the account contract inefficacious[295] and that if the banks sought such protection, they should draft such clauses better.[296]

The Supreme Court of Canada subsequently followed that decision in *Canadian Pacific Hotels Ltd. v. Bank of Montreal*,[297] involving similar facts. A large, commercially sophisticated company sued its bank for recovery of funds stolen as a result of the forgery of twenty-three cheques by an unsupervised clerk responsible for account reconciliation. Notwithstanding decisions by the trial judge and the majority of the Ontario Court of Appeal affixing responsibility on the customer for failing to ensure reasonable internal accounting practices and account statement verification, the Supreme Court followed *Tai Hing*, resulting in the liability of the bank to compensate the company for the losses resulting from the employee's forgeries. A customer owes no correlative duty at common law to a bank either to read and verify account statements at any time or, if a corporation, to ensure reasonable accounting procedures are in place to prevent loss caused by dishonest employees. The court took the same position as the Privy Council in *Tai Hing* that

---

293 *Chatterton v. London & County Bank, The Times*, (21 January 1891); *Lewes Sanitary Steam Laundry Co. v. Barclay & Co.* (1906), 95 L.T. 444 (Ch. D.); *Kepitigalla*, above note 186; *R. v. Bank of Montreal*, above note 279; *Abbott v. Bank of Toronto*, above note 279; *Holman v. Royal Bank of Canada*, above note 280.
294 Above note 184.
295 *Ibid.* at 107.
296 *Ibid.* at 110.
297 Above note 16.

banks which wish to reverse the long-standing approach of the common law should do so by revising their account agreements. The court further declined to impose a greater liability in tort on the customer than the non-liability for which the contract provided and opined that banks were rich enough to act effectively as insurers of their customers in such circumstances.[298]

This approach to customer loss as a result of dishonest employees hired and improperly supervised by the customer was confirmed in *Boma Manufacturing Ltd. v. Canadian Imperial Bank of Commerce*,[299] where the court stripped banks of much of the protection originally contemplated by section 165(3) of the *Bills of Exchange Act*, thereby reducing the ability of banks to transfer losses back to the customer with whom the loss originated.[300]

Despite the preponderance of binding authority in this area, it is salutary to note that several English cases had broached the possibility of imposing a duty to verify account statements on customers in the nineteenth century[301] and that the American courts did so.[302] Moreover, section 4-406 of the *Uniform Commercial Code* provides that a customer exercise reasonable promptness in examining a statement and promptly notify the bank of an error. The customer's right to dispute a statement is barred one year from the date when the statement was made available to the customer.

In Canada, however, the banks took the initiative, as suggested by the courts, and added account verification clauses to all of their account agreements. Although such clauses had been in use for much of the twentieth century, the banks in the past two decades have now ensured that all customer account agreements contain such clauses and that they are so well drafted as to protect them from liability in virtually any conceivable fact situation.[303]

---

298 *Ibid.*
299 Above note 187.
300 Earlier Canadian *obiter dicta* had supported affixing a customer with a duty to verify account statements: *Arrow Transfer Co. v. Royal Bank of Canada* (1972), 27 D.L.R. (3d) 81 at 101 (S.C.C.), Laskin J.; *No. 10 Management Ltd. v. Royal Bank of Canada* (1976), 69 D.L.R. (3d) 99 at 103–4 (Man. C.A.), Monnin J.A.
301 *Clayton's Case*, above note 273; *Blackburn*, above note 282; *Vagliano*, above note 282.
302 *Leather Mfrs. Bank v. Morgan*, 117 U.S. 96 (1886); *Critten v. Chemical National Bank of New York*, 171 N.Y. 219 (1902); *Morgan v. U.S. Mortgage & Trust*, 208 N.Y. 218 (1913) were the first cases in a long line of cases.
303 For a brief history of this evolution, see Keith W. Perrett, "Account Verification Clauses: Should Bank Customers Be Forced to Mind Their Own Business?" (1999) 14 B.F.L.R. 245.

A typical account verification clause requires customers to examine their periodic bank statements promptly and to notify the bank, within usually thirty days of the statement date, of any discrepancies. Failure to do so within the stipulated time period will release the bank from any liability or claim, including those arising from negligence, conversion, breach of trust, and breach of fiduciary duty. Since bank statements are normally sent through the post, a customer may typically have two or three weeks within which to query a statement. Effectively, the purpose of such clauses is to require the customer to waive the common law right to do nothing on receipt of an account statement yet be able to have it corrected at any time, and to impose a duty to examine and report on the customer by contract. The issue, then, becomes a matter of contract construction as to whether any specific clause protects the bank from liability on the facts.

The use of such clauses by banks has been consistently upheld by the courts, which treat them as a species of exemption clause in a standard form or adhesion contract. This means that they can be overridden when a bank engages in some other illegal conduct. In *Claiborne Industries Ltd. v. National Bank of Canada*,[304] for example, a bank which was found liable in the tort of civil conspiracy by assisting a customer in illegal fund transfers, was not permitted to rely on an account verification clause against a company whose accounts had been wrongfully debited. As a species of exemption clause, account verification clauses are subject to strict construction and then to the *contra proferentem* rule in cases of construction ambiguity.[305] However, the application of the rules of contract construction to account verification clauses has led to a divided approach to these clauses by Canadian courts.[306]

In one group of cases, the courts have applied the strict construction of the account verification clause to the facts and enforced the clause against the customer where it is drafted to cover clearly the circumstances in the case. This has included exempting banks from liability where they were negligent in the performance of their own duties under the account agreement where the account verification clause did not expressly provide for negligence but used general words of exemption which would include negligence.[307] In the other group of cases, the

---

304 (1989), 59 D.L.R. (4th) 533 (Ont. C.A.).
305 See any case listed below at notes 307–8.
306 Perrett, above note 303.
307 *Columbia Gramophone Co. v. Union Bank* (1916), 34 D.L.R. 743 (Ont. S.C.); *Union Bank of Canada v. Wood*, [1920] 3 W.W.R. 173 (Alta S.C.T.D.); *Stewart v. Royal Bank of Canada*, [1930] 4 D.L.R. 694 (S.C.C.); *Rutherford v. Royal Bank of Canada*, [1932] 2 D.L.R. 332 (S.C.C.); *Alberta v. Arnold* (1971), 14 D.L.R. (3d) 574

courts take a stricter view of these clauses and decline to enforce them against a customer where they do not expressly exclude the liability of the bank for its own negligence.[308] The former group of cases tend to result in decisions for the bank and the latter group result generally in decisions for the customer.

The latter group of cases is ultimately founded on an older line of English authorities[309] in contract law, which required that exemption clauses must expressly refer to negligence if a *proferens* wishes to use the clause successfully as a shield from liability in contract. Recent developments in the law of contract no longer require express mention of negligence. Rather, comprehensively drafted clauses, which on strict construction clearly include negligence are sufficient to shield the *proferens* from liability.[310] As a matter of contract construction alone, the first group of cases is in line with contract law generally but the second group is not.

However, there are other reasons why the approach of the first group of cases is to be preferred. They enforce the position that a customer should be responsible in law for implementing good accounting practices and for account reconciliation promptly on receipt of account statements, so as to protect the interests of both the customer and the bank. Most banks now provide computerized account reconciliation procedures so that corporate customers can identify problems quickly and report them within the period of time provided by account reconciliation clauses. Customers are in the best position to detect fraud perpetrated by their own employees and the narrow interpretation of the Supreme Court in *Boma* of section 165(3) of the *Bills of Exchange Act*

(S.C.C.); *Bad Boy Appliances & Furniture Ltd. v. Toronto-Dominion Bank* (1972), 25 D.L.R. (3d) 257 (Ont. C.A.) [*Bad Boy*]; *Canadian Imperial Bank of Commerce v. Haley* (1979), 100 D.L.R. (3d) 470 (N.B.C.A.); *Le Cercle Universitaire d'Ottawa v. National Bank of Canada* (1987), 61 O.R. (2d) 456 (H.C.J.); *Kelly Funeral Homes Ltd. v. Canadian Imperial Bank of Commerce* (1990), 72 D.L.R. (4th) 276 (Ont. H.C.J.); *Don Bodkin Leasing Ltd. v. Toronto-Dominion Bank* (1998), 40 O.R. (3d) 262 (Ont. C.A.). Banks are expected to point out an account verification clause when updating an account contract: *Armstrong, Baum Plumbing & Heating v. Toronto-Dominion Bank* (1994), 15 B.L.R. (2d) 84 (Ont. C.A.).

308 *Cavell Developments Ltd. v. Royal Bank of Canada* (1991), 78 D.L.R. (4th) 512 (B.C.C.A.); *239199 Alberta Ltd. v. Patel* (1993), 105 D.L.R. (4th) 739 (Alta. C.A.); *Mirtia Holdings Ltd. v. Toronto Dominion Bank* (1995), 30 Alta. L.R. (3d) 111 (Q.B.). Compare *Bank of Montreal v. H. & M. Chan Enterprises Ltd.* (1999), 183 Sask. R. 84 (Q.B.).

309 *Alderslade v. Hendon Laundry Ltd.*, [1945] 1 All E.R. 244 (C.A.); *Canada Steamship Lines v. The King*, [1952] A.C. 192 (P.C.).

310 See any current contract law text chapter on exemption clauses.

would suggest that permitting banks to limit liability by contract might be one way to redress the bargaining balance and the mutuality of obligation necessary to ensure the effective performance of the contract for the benefit of both parties.

The common law regards oral notice of account discrepancies as sufficient,[311] although banking practice normally involves giving details of the discrepancies in writing, especially where forgery or some other illegality might be at issue. An initial, oral notice should certainly be sufficient to put the bank on notice in dealing with the account until the full details are available. Finally, when a customer gives notice within the account verification clause time limits, that notice must be unambiguous, to ensure that the customer benefits from the provision for error correction within the account statement.

F. MAINTAINING CONFIDENTIALITY

1) General Considerations

In the course of a bank and customer relationship, banks learn a great deal about a customer, not only about their financial affairs but also about the customer's ways of life as revealed in their financial affairs. It is not difficult, then, to understand why the common law has long regarded the relationship as one in which the bank owes a duty of secrecy to the customer in relation to that information. Although several nineteenth-century courts treated that duty as a moral obligation,[312] it was not until the early twentieth-century case, *Tournier v. National Provincial & Union Bank of England*,[313] that the duty became a legal duty, and that case is the starting point for the discussion of the present law. Although the duty was described as "secrecy" in *Tournier* and a number of subsequent cases, recently the word "confidentiality" has come into widespread use, a somewhat unfortunate practice because that word is also used in relation to fiduciary obligation, so it is important to be aware of the context in which it is used. The recent practice of using "confidentiality" to describe the duty will be followed in this section.

---

311 *Campbell v. Imperial Bank*, [1924] 4 D.L.R. 289 (Ont. S.C.A.D.); *Bad Boy*, above note 307.
312 *Hardy v. Veasey* (1868), L.R. 3 Ex. 107; *Tassell v. Cooper* (1850), 9 C.B. 509, 137 E.R. 990 (C.P.).
313 [1924] 1 K.B. 461 (C.A.) [*Tournier*]

The confidential nature of the bank and customer relationship flows from the fact that it is an agency relationship with the usual characteristic that the agent owes a duty of loyalty and confidentiality to its principal in relation to the principal's affairs. A principal must feel confident that its agent will best promote its interests by holding them in confidence. This is particularly so when economic matters are at stake. But the duty of confidentiality is also founded on the value to an individual of protecting personal autonomy, which would be lost if a bank was free to publicize the customer's affairs to all and sundry. Public confidence in the bank and in the banking system generally would be lost if banks did not owe a duty of confidentiality to their customers.

However, confidentiality can also be a shield for significant wrongdoing, such as, especially today, the illicit movement of funds relating to terrorist financing, the illegal drug trade, and money laundering generally. The duty of confidentiality is not an absolute duty, like state privilege; rather, it is subject to legal restriction, both common law and statutory, in the public interest. Any consideration of the duty is subject to the delicate balancing of private interest on the one hand and public interest on the other. Moreover, even in the private sphere today, there are good reasons why the customers' financial records may be subject to disclosure when applications for credit are made to a bank. Overindebtedness is so endemic that all financial institutions need to have a high degree of certainty that loans will be repaid and therefore need to know about the credit record of a customer applying for a loan.

Although the duty of confidentiality originated in the common law, the evolution generally in the law of the protection of privacy has complemented and at times overtaken the traditional common law duty of confidentiality. Initially, this took the form in the banking law context of an industry code, the Privacy Model Code, of the Canadian Bankers Association,[314] which governed how all banks protected the confidentiality of customer information. However, in 2001, banks as federally regulated institutions became subject to the *Personal Information Protection and Electronic Documents Act*,[315] and this has superseded the Privacy Model Code. The ten principles enshrined in the Act are virtually identical to those in the Code and in such documents generally internationally: accountability for personal information; identifying valid purposes for collecting information; obtaining consent for information use; limitations on personal information collected; limitations on the use, disclosure, and retention of information; ensuring accuracy;

---

314 2d ed. (Toronto: Canadian Bankers Association, 1996).
315 S.C. 2000, c. 5.

safeguarding personal information; informing customers about policies and practices; providing customer access; and handling customer inquiries and complaints.[316]

Notwithstanding the comprehensive nature of this legislation, it contains no guarantees of absolute confidentiality on the part of the bank; rather, it directs how banks should manage the customer information they gather. Therefore, the case-by-case balance between private and public interests in the bank's duty of confidentiality remains the domain of the case law and any specific legislation modifying that law.

2) *Tournier*

In *Tournier*, a customer's employment contract was not renewed because his bank manager told his employer that he was involved in gambling. He sued the bank for slander and for breach of an implied duty of secrecy (or confidentiality) in the bank and customer relationship. The English Court of Appeal ordered a new trial on both issues but decided for the first time that the contractual relationship was subject to a duty of secrecy, in a decision which was explicitly conceptualized as the companion to *Joachimson v. Swiss Bank Corp.*,[317] which had defined the other common law implied terms. The court considered the nature and scope of the duty and further stated that it was subject to four qualifications or exceptions.

The court considered the duty to arise when the account agreement is executed but disagreed as to the duration and scope of the duty. Bankes and Atkin L.JJ. thought the duty covered all information learned by the bank during the relationship and that it continued in relation to that information after the end of the legal relationship, even to the customer's death. Scrutton L.J. thought it covered only information relating to account operation and ended when the bank and customer agreement ended. All agreed that it did not cover information learned after the contract was over. Subsequent cases have not clarified the duration and scope of the duty but have applied *Tournier* to award damages for breach of contract when a court considered the information to be protected by the duty of confidentiality.

Banks may also acquire information today about persons with whom they do not have a bank and customer account agreement, that is, another entity in a banking group may deal with an individual and acquire

---

316 *Ibid.*, Schedule 1. For privacy law generally, see Barbara McIsaac, Rick Shields, & Kris Klein, *The Law of Privacy in Canada* (Toronto: Carswell, 2005).
317 Above note 6.

information about them. The extent to which the bank may learn that information will depend on the extent of information sharing among entities in the group, and the question of whether the bank owes a duty of confidentiality in the absence of an account agreement has not been considered by the courts. Typical consumer contracts require the customer to permit information sharing, so the matter is a real one.[318]

In *Tournier*, the Court of Appeal agreed that the duty was qualified and not absolute, and identified four exceptional situations in which a bank is relieved from the implied duty: (i) compulsion of law; (ii) a higher public duty to disclose; (iii) in the interests of the bank; and (iv) with the express or implied consent of the customer.[319] In *Tournier*, Bankes L.J. gave examples of each of these: (i) statutory disclosures required under Evidence Acts; (ii) a higher state duty; (iii) bank law suits for the repayment of overdrafts; and (iv) contractual consent of the customer. Since *Tournier*, these categories have been explored and expanded by courts and legislatures.

3) *Tournier* Qualifications

The first exception to the confidentiality requirement, compulsion of law, means that a bank may be compelled to disclose information in its possession during the course of legal proceedings or some other legally constituted process. The compulsion to disclose must be clear and valid; a bank should not respond to a fishing expedition or a casual inquiry[320] or an unissued court order.[321] Moreover, a bank is under a duty to use its best efforts to obtain customer consent when it receives a valid order to make disclosure, to inform the customer, and to disclose only the specific information requested.[322] Clearly, this duty does

---

318 In England, it would appear that general principles of confidentiality would bind the banks: *Attorney-General v. Guardian Newspapers Ltd. (No. 2)*, [1990] 1 A.C. 109 at 281–82, Lord Goff.
319 Above note 313 at 472–73, Bankes L.J.
320 *Parry-Jones v. Law Society*, [1969] 1 Ch. 1 (C.A.); *Sommers v. Sturdy* (1957), 10 D.L.R. (2d) 269 (B.C.C.A.), leave to appeal to S.C.C. refused, [1957] S.C.R. x; *I.T.L. Industries Ltd. v. Winterbottom* (1979), 97 D.L.R. (3d) 553 (Ont. H.C.J.), rev'd on other grounds (1980), 106 D.L.R. (3d) 577 (Ont. C.A.). See also *Royal Bank of Scotland plc v. Golden Trinity (The)* (2001), 220 F.T.R. 1 (T.D.) which forbade fishing expeditions in private party litigation.
321 *Houghton v. Houghton*, [1965] 1 O.R. 481 (S.C.); *Astral Films Ltd. v. Sherman* (1978), 19 O.R. (2d) 206 (H.C.J.).
322 *Robertson v. Canadian Imperial Bank of Commerce*, [1995] 1 All E.R. 824 (P.C.). See also E.K. Rowan-Legg, "New Developments in Bank's Duty of Confidentiality" (1996) 26 Can. Bus. L.J. 455.

not operate when the compulsion relates to a criminal rather than a civil matter.[323] Courts have the inherent discretion to make compulsion orders in civil matters, such as *Mareva* injunctions or orders to trace funds through bank accounts.

However, some doubt exists about the formality of the legal order required before disclosure can be made to the police in a criminal investigation. In *R. v. Lillico*,[324] a bank made disclosures after receiving an affidavit but without a search warrant, and a court upheld the appropriateness of the disclosures because they were of banking information that did not threaten the "biographical core" of personal information[325] of the customer. Therefore, there was no infringement of the customer's privacy or of his section 8 right under the *Canadian Charter of Rights and Freedoms*[326] to be secure against unreasonable search and seizure. In *R. v. Eddy*,[327] the court came to the opposite conclusion where a bank made disclosures without a search warrant. Moreover, in *Schreiber v. Canada*,[328] in which the police made a broad sweeping request for all banking information available, the Supreme Court of Canada agreed with the Federal Court of Appeal[329] that this was too intrusive because it encompassed personal details, although it overturned the decision on other grounds. The court was unanimous that financial records are personal and confidential and attract section 8 protection. It would appear, therefore, that there is considerable uncertainty in the law as to whether a bank should comply with a police request in the absence of a search warrant, but that if there is compliance, there is a presumption that only banking information should be disclosed in the absence of greater legal compulsion.

Compulsion to disclose may also be founded on legislation, as well as on a court's inherent jurisdiction to make a compulsion order. The oldest statutory provision is found in the English *Bankers' Books Evidence Act*,[330] which compelled banks to produce both records and employees to give evidence in relation to legal proceedings involving

---

323 *Park v. Bank of Montreal*, [1997] B.C.J. No. 787 (S.C.); *Bank of China v. Fan* (2003), 22 B.C.L.R. (4th) 152 (S.C.).
324 (1994), 92 C.C.C. (3d) 90 (Ont. Ct. Gen. Div.). See also the pre-Charter case *R. v. Mowat*, [1968] 1 O.R. 179 (H.C.J.).
325 *R. v. Lillico*, ibid. at 95.
326 Part I of the *Constitution Act, 1982*, being Schedule B to the *Canada Act 1982* (U.K.), 1982, c. 11.
327 (1994), 119 Nfld. & P.E.I.R. 91 (Nfld. T.D.).
328 [1998] 1 S.C.R. 841.
329 (1997), 144 D.L.R. (4th) 711 (Fed. C.A.).
330 1879 (U.K.), c. 11.

customers. These provisions were subsequently replicated, and over the years, amended in both federal and provincial Evidence Acts in Canada,[331] which continue to apply to banks today. To avoid the inconvenience to banks resulting from the relinquishment of records over a long period of time in litigation, the Acts permit copies of bank records and affidavits from employees to be substituted.[332] Although most requests for disclosure are likely to be made pursuant to the federal *Evidence Act*, the courts have held that banks are equally compellable pursuant to the provincial Acts.[333]

Compulsion of law is also enshrined in other legislation. Thus, secondly, the *Income Tax Act*[334] permits the Canada Revenue Agency to demand production notwithstanding that any information or documents might disclose the confidential banking affairs of a customer. Thirdly, the *Winding-Up and Restructuring Act*[335] gives a court jurisdiction to examine a bank manager in relation to transactions between a bank and an insolvent company. Finally, the most comprehensive legislation is, of course, the *Proceeds of Crime (Money Laundering) and Terrorist Financing Act*,[336] which requires banks to report customer information on a regular and ongoing basis if customer transactions are suspicious or match the criteria for reporting set out in the Act.

Until recently, compulsion of law under *Tournier* meant compulsion by domestic courts and legislation, but with the globalization of business through multinational corporations and the globalization of crime by terrorists and drug dealers, compulsion of law may also mean

---

331 See, for example, the *Canada Evidence Act*, R.S.C. 1985, c. C-5, as well as the various provincial acts.
332 *Sommers v. Sturdy*, above note 320; *Astral Films Ltd. v. Sherman*, above note 321; *I.T.L. Industries Ltd. v. Winterbottom*, above note 320.
333 *Ibid*. For an extended survey, see Ogilvie, above note 71 at 671–74.
334 R.S.C. 1985 (5th Supp.), c. 1, s. 231. See also *Canadian Bank of Commerce v. Canada* (1962), 35 D.L.R. (2d) 49 (S.C.C.).
335 R.S.C. 1985, c. W-11, Part I. See also *Christofi v. Barclays Bank plc*, [1999] 4 All E.R. 437 (C.A.) for disclosure in bankruptcy generally.
336 S.C. 2001, c. 41. See also Heather D. Lawson, "Bank Secrecy and Money Laundering" (2001) 17 B.F.L.R. 145 and "Assessing the Divergent Obligation of Banks in the New Millennium: Preserving Customer Confidentiality While Complying with Money Laundering Initiatives" (2004) 19 B.F.L.R. 237; David Vernon, "A Partnership with Evil: Money Laundering, Terrorist Financing and Canadian Financial Institutions" (2004) 20 B.F.L.R. 89. In addition, the English courts have considered what a bank should do when faced with a decision as to whether or not to report information: *C. v. S.*, [1999] 2 All E.R. 343 (C.A.) and *Bank of Scotland v. A. Ltd.*, [2001] 3 All E.R. 58 (C.A.). The helpful role of a court in this is emphasized: Henry Knox, "To Disclose or Not to Disclose" (2002) 17 B.F.L.R. 269.

a requirement to disclose at the request of a foreign court. Banks carry out business internationally with a worldwide network of branches to service their customers whether they are involved in legal or illegal affairs. Two situations typically arise: (i) whether a Canadian court may order the disclosure of confidential information possessed by an overseas branch of interest in Canadian litigation; and (ii) whether a foreign court may order disclosure in a foreign jurisdiction of information possessed by a Canadian bank. The general rule in conflict of laws is that a state and its courts may not make orders binding on foreigners in relation to their conduct outside the jurisdiction; the concept of state sovereignty restricts the application of state law to that state and prohibits its application beyond that state.[337] Globalization challenges that traditional understanding.

Judicial decisions concerning the extraterritoriality of judicial orders in banking law over the past decade or so in the United States and the United Kingdom suggest that the traditional understanding is breaking down, but a coherent picture has yet to develop. For present purposes, it is sufficient to observe that courts are not averse to making such orders or enforcing orders from foreign courts, especially where international crime is at issue.[338]

The second exception to the confidentiality duty stated in *Tournier* is where there is a duty to the public that supersedes the bank's duty of confidentiality to its customer. In *Tournier*, Bankes L.J. identified danger to the state as a higher public duty[339] but did not give further consideration to the category, so that it remains somewhat opaque both in relation to when it may arise and its scope. Bankes L.J. doubted that a bank should disclose possible customer criminal activities to the public,[340] but Lord Chorley thought it should disclose trading with the enemy in time of war.[341]

The distinction between compulsion of law and higher public duty is equally opaque, particularly because legislation limiting a bank's duty of confidentiality could easily fit into both categories. In England, the Jack Committee recommended that the second qualification be abolished,[342] but the courts still work with it and may over time give it sufficient content to be a distinct qualification to *Tournier*. In England,

---

337 *Ralli Brothers v. Compania Naviera Sota y Aznar*, [1920] 2 K.B. 287 (C.A.).
338 For greater discussion, see Ogilvie, above note 71 at 680–84; Ellinger *et al.*, above note 174 at 159–66.
339 Above note 313 at 473.
340 *Ibid.*
341 *Law of Banking*, 6th ed. (London: Sweet & Maxwell, 1974) at 23.
342 1989 Cm. 622, paras. 5.30 and 541.

there seems to be some ground for suggesting that the first qualification deals with situations in which a bank is required by law to report information and the second with situations where the bank enjoys a discretion to do so.

In *Libyan Arab Foreign Bank v. Bankers Trust Co.*,[343] in which the defendant had conversations with the U.S. Federal Reserve Board about the plaintiff's affairs, the trial judge tentatively concluded that any information disclosed fitted into the second qualification. Again, in *Price Waterhouse v. BCCI Holdings (Luxembourg) SA*,[344] in which Price Waterhouse voluntarily disclosed information about the bank to the Bingham Inquiry, a non-statutory inquiry set up by the Chancellor of the Exchequer and the Governor of the Bank of England, the court thought that public interest in the disclosures superseded any duty of confidentiality because the inquiry's task was of vital importance to the effective regulation and supervision of the banking sector. Finally, in a subsequent case resulting from the collapse of BCCI, *Pharaon v. BCCI*,[345] the public interest in upholding the duty of confidentiality between bank and customer was overridden by a higher public interest in making confidential documents relating to the alleged fraud of an international bank available to parties in private foreign proceedings for the purpose of uncovering that fraud. In none of these cases was the bank under a statutory duty to make disclosures. Rather, it volunteered in the greater public interest and was sustained in that by the courts under the public interest qualification in *Tournier*.

Several Canadian cases have explored the content of this qualification within civil rather than criminal law contexts. In *Canadian Imperial Bank of Commerce v. Sayani*,[346] the B.C. Court of Appeal found a higher public duty where a bank disclosed just enough information about a dishonourable customer to a potential lender to that customer that the original proposal failed. Had the court condoned silence by the bank, the bank would have been a party to a misrepresentation. *Sayani* extends the category of public interest beyond crime to tort and leads to the question of whether it can be opened further, that is, where should the line be drawn between the public and private interests?[347]

---

343 [1988] 1 Lloyd's Rep. 259 (Q.B.D.).
344 [1992] B.C.L.C. 583 (Ch. D.).
345 [1998] 4 All E.R. 455 (Ch. D.).
346 [1994] 2 W.W.R. 260 (B.C.C.A.), leave to appeal to S.C.C. refused, [1994] 3 W.W.R. lxvi (S.C.C.).
347 See M.H. Ogilvie, "What Can I Say? Banker's References: Two Recent Cases" (1994) 10 B.F.L.R. 117.

On the other hand, Canadian courts have enforced the bank's duty of confidentiality to a customer in the private sphere. In *Murano v. Bank of Montreal*,[348] a bank manager spoke indiscriminately to a number of interested parties about a business customer's affairs, leaving the impression the customer was dishonest, with the result that the business collapsed. The court declined to accept that the bank acted in some greater public interest and found the bank to be in breach of its duty of confidentiality to the customer. A bank may, however, give advice without necessarily breaching its duty of confidentiality. In *Polar Heating Ltd. v. Banque Nationale de Paris*,[349] a bank was not liable for advising against the purchase of a business customer when it was about to call a loan to that customer. While the distinction between these two cases includes the indiscriminate spread of wrongful allegations, even in the absence of that distinction, it still remains difficult to define when bank disclosures will be in some greater public interest than the duty owed to its customer.

The third exception to the duty of confidentiality is where the bank's own interests require disclosure. The example given in *Tournier* is where a bank is obliged to disclose the amount of a customer loan or overdraft when it sues for repayment. A second example is where a bank makes disclosures when collecting cheques returned for insufficient funds.[350] A third example is where a bank with a security interest in a customer's property advises a third party of that interest in order to protect its own interest.[351] Fourthly, a bank is permitted to make disclosures to protect its priority in relation to customer property and to prevent third parties from making investments that might be lost.[352] Fifthly, as suggested in *Sayani*, it is also in a bank's own interest to protect its reputation to make disclosures about tortious or other illegal conduct of its customer to a third party.

A possible sixth example was suggested in *Rodaro v. Royal Bank of Canada*,[353] in which the Ontario Court of Appeal confirmed that disclosures made in the course of confidential negotiations for the sale of a customer's debt fall within the third qualification to *Tournier* but declined to decide whether there was an appropriate disclosure on the

---

348 (1996), 163 D.L.R. (4th) 21 (Ont. C.A.).
349 (1991), 7 C.B.R. (3d) 45 (Alta. Q.B.).
350 *Sunderland v. Barclays Bank Ltd.* (1938), 5 L.D.A.B. 163 (C.A.).
351 *Royal Bank of Canada v. Brattberg*, [1993] 8 W.W.R. 139 (Alta. Q.B.).
352 This would seem to follow from *Murano v. Bank of Montreal*, above note 348 and *Polar Heating Ltd. v. BNP*, above note 349.
353 (2002), 59 O.R. (3d) 74 (Ont. C.A.).

facts of the case.[354] Finally, the English courts have found that the disclosure of customer information to liquidators[355] or a trustee in bankruptcy[356] could also fall under the third qualification.

The concept that a bank should be permitted to put its own interests above those of the customer to whom it owes a *prima facie* duty of confidentiality is clearly one that requires careful delineation in the law and an especial thoughtfulness of any court deciding where the balance of interest should lie in any case. Moreover, it may be difficult to distinguish between the second and the third qualifications because it is often concurrently in the best interests of the bank to act in the higher public interest. Clearly, careful case-by-case analysis is required in this area.

To date, the courts have not considered two other fact situations in which a bank's best interests must be assessed: disclosure within a banking group and disclosure to credit checks in relation to the customer. While many account agreements contain standard clauses by which a customer waives a right to confidentiality in both matters today, it still remains wise for a bank to secure the express written permission of a customer to make such disclosures where no such waiver clause exists. It is conceivable that in certain fact situations, a bank making disclosures without express permission will be found in breach of the duty of confidentiality.

The final qualification to the duty of confidentiality is where there is disclosure with the express or implied consent of the customer. Express consent to make disclosures about customer affairs might be given in the standard form account contract when an account is opened, or given subsequently when a customer authorizes a credit check in relation to a loan application. Such clauses usually also waive the customer's right to confidentiality in relation to disclosures to other entities in the banking group. To date, no court has decided whether such clauses in account agreements are enforceable by the banks. Since they amount to a complete or nearly complete relinquishment of the qualified right to confidentiality set out in the common law, any future decision to uphold them will constitute a significant policy decision. On the other hand, the statutory incursions discussed above in the context of higher public interest suggest there is so little left of the duty of confidentiality that it makes little difference what decision is made.

---

354 For fuller discussion, see M.H. Ogilvie, "From Secrecy to Confidence to the Demise of the Banker and Customer Relationship" (2003) 19 B.F.L.R. 103.
355 *El Jawhary v. BCCI*, [1993] B.C.L.C. 396 (Ch. D.).
356 *Christofi v. Barclays Bank plc*, above note 335.

In those few instances where no express consent has been given, the question of implied consent arises. In *Tournier*, Scrutton L.J. suggested that implied consent could rarely arise[357] and, more recently, in *Turner v. Royal Bank of Scotland plc*,[358] a court found that a consumer customer cannot be deemed to have waived the right to confidentiality by merely opening an account. Several courts have implied consent by the customer where a bank was required to make statutory disclosures,[359] but such a position seems a little artificial. Less artificial are those instances where the nature of the transaction lends itself to finding implied consent, such as where giving a secured interest to a bank implies consent to disclose this interest to third parties[360] or where taking a guarantee implies consent to disclose the nature of the loan to the guarantor[361] or where clients willing to invest in a customer's scheme receive disclosure of the fact relating to that scheme.[362] Again, as with the other three qualifications to the general *Tournier* duty, the content of the fourth qualification of implied customer consent to disclose is likely to be decided on a case-by-case basis on a careful balancing of public and private interests as presented in the facts.

It should be self-evident that a bank should never make disclosures of customer information to third parties for personal purposes. In *Guertin v. Royal Bank of Canada*,[363] the manager of a local branch rejected a loan application after having received the business plan of the customers and gave details of the business plan to his wife, who then proceeded to purchase the small business in question. The court found this egregious conduct to be a breach of the duty of confidentiality and a breach of fiduciary duty and awarded compensatory damages to the customer. The court declined to award punitive damages without reasons, although they might have seemed to be most appropriate in the circumstances.

Until the 1990s, *Tournier* was virtually a solitary case in the common law. Widely agreed to be correct in its assertion of an implied duty of confidentiality in the bank and customer agreement, the rule was assumed by both banks and customers in everyday banking practice. However, the computerization and globalization of banking, along with

---

357 Above note 313 at 481.
358 [1999] 2 All E.R. (Comm.) 664 (C.A.).
359 *Bank of Montreal v. Intracom Investments Ltd.* (1983), 47 N.B.R. (2d) 391 (C.A.); *Canadian Imperial Bank of Commerce v. Larsen*, [1983] 5 W.W.R. 179 (B.C.C.A.).
360 *Royal Bank of Canada v. Vincenzi*, [1994] B.C.W.L.D. 1221 (S.C.).
361 *Bank of Montreal v. Intracom Investments Ltd.*, above note 359.
362 *Hongkong Bank of Canada v. Phillips*, [1998] 2 W.W.R. 606 (Man. Q.B.).
363 (1984), 47 O.R. (2d) 799 (Ont. C.A.).

the rise of global terrorist and drug distribution networks in that decade, resulted in banks, states, and customers being much more aware of the need for disclosure to safeguard national and individual security. The result has been case law exploring the content of the *Tournier* exceptions and legislation entrenching significantly into the duty itself. It is increasingly unclear whether much of the duty really exists anymore, and future developments in this area of the law might well result in its eclipse in banking law.

G. CONCLUSION

To this point in this textbook, the focus has been on the bank and customer relationship, largely defined by the common law. Occasionally, it has been necessary to refer to the larger banking context within which that relationship operates, especially to the clearing and settlement system and the computerization of banking practice embodied in that system. Chapters 9, 10, and 11 will examine this larger context and the extent to which, if any, the common law has been superseded.

CHAPTER 9

ELECTRONIC FUNDS TRANSFER SYSTEMS

A. INTRODUCTION

The latest stage in the evolution of payment systems between humans from barter to precious metals to money to negotiable instruments is the development of payment by computerized electronic funds transfer. Indeed, Paget describes electronic funds transfer as the third of three great ages of payment, succeeding payment by cash and paper-based payment.[1] Just as banks have been central to cash and paper-based payment systems, so, too, have they been central to payment by electronic funds transfer (EFT). Yet, despite all the recent marketplace excitement around the computerization of banking services, it is important to state at the outset that EFT is simply another method of effecting payment, of transferring economic value, and while its implementation has resulted in some new legal rules resulting from changes in banking practice, it has little impact on the underlying concepts in the law about the legal relationship between bank and customer. Each party to the contract is bound by the same duties and standards of care in giving and implementing payment instructions electronically as in giving and receiving instructions by paper.

---

1   Mark Hapgood, ed., *Paget on Banking*, 12th ed. (London: Butterworths, 2003) at 284 [*Paget*].

In contrast to the United States, where the *Electronic Funds Transfer Act* was passed in 1978,[2] or the United Kingdom, where there is a growing body of common law, as well as various European Union directives,[3] in Canada there is neither legislation nor a substantial body of case law defining the law in this area. Rather, in Canada the rules governing EFT remain within the realm of banking industry practice. The relative absence of case law may suggest that those rules are working well and have led to few disputes in the courts. On the other hand, the cost of litigation may have deterred most potential litigants. It is difficult to judge. However, the absence of law means that a text such as this is largely limited to describing the various services offered, and these will be covered in this and the next two chapters (Chapters 9 to 11).

The focus of this chapter is the infrastructure of the electronic and paper payments system, to which some references were made from time to time in the previous chapter, which assumed but did not explicitly address its existence. Whether customer payment or collection instructions are delivered electronically or by paper to the customer's bank, the actual transmission of economic value between and among banks requires an industry-wide infrastructure to facilitate that transmission. These infrastructures in Canada are operated by the Canadian Payments Association (CPA),[4] of which all deposit-taking financial institutions are members, so as to have access to the networks which permit them to offer payment and collection services to their customers. The major networks operated by the CPA include the Automated Clearing and Settlement System (ACSS), the United States Bulk Exchange System (USBES) for funds denominated in U.S. dollars, and the Large Value Transfer System (LVTS) for transfers in excess of $25 million. In addition, this chapter will examine automated debit and credit transfers within those systems. Chapter 10 will examine customer card based payment instructions issued on a transaction-by-transaction basis and encompassing current established systems, as well as those recently introduced but whose permanence is still unknown. Chapter 11 will examine other payment mechanisms frequently used by customers, such as credit cards, travellers' cheques, and bankers' drafts. Prior to discussing these systems, it is first necessary to examine the regulatory framework for them, including relevant constitutional issues.

---

2 Title XX of the *Financial Institutions Regulatory and Interest Rate Control Act of 1978* [*FIRIRCA*], Pub. L. No. 95-630, 92 Stat. 3641, 3728 (1978), 15 U.S.C.S. 1693. At the state level, this is governed by Article 4A of the *Uniform Commercial Code*.
3 EC Directive 97/5 on Cross Border Credit Transfers, [1997] OJ L43/25, introduced through Cross Border Credit Transfer Regulations, 1999, S.I. 1999/1876.
4 Chapter 3, Section E.

B. THE REGULATION OF PAYMENT SYSTEMS

The question of who may regulate derives from the question of which level of government in Canada has constitutional jurisdiction to regulate electronic funds transfer. This jurisdiction is not expressly set out in the Constitution Acts, but the answer must be the federal government, for a number of reasons: (i) the paramount and exclusive authority of Parliament over banking pursuant to section 91(15); (ii) the other provisions in the *Constitution Act, 1867*, which suggest a strong federal jurisdiction over payment methods, through sections 91(14), (16), (18), and (20), relating to currency and coinage, the issue of paper money, bills of exchange, and promissory notes, and legal tender; (iii) the jurisdiction of Parliament over trade and commerce pursuant to section 91(12) because payment systems are the circulation system for commerce and must necessarily be national in nature; and (iv) the general authority of Parliament in relation to matters of national importance, whether framed under section 91(10)(a), "other works and undertakings," the "peace, order and good government" power under section 91 or the residual power under section 91. This is not to suggest that there may be some overlap or conflict with provincial powers, especially under section 92(13) "property and civil rights," in relation to consumer or contract issues, but the national interest in a single federal regulatory regime in a matter as important as the payments system would suggest the overwhelming importance of a single, national regulatory regime.

Until the 1990s, there was virtually no Parliamentary oversight of the payments system. The Canadian Bankers' Association and, after 1983, the Canadian Payments Association (CPA), were free to structure and run the payments system as they wished, although clearly with considerable input from their bank members and users. The CPA by-laws were subject to Governor in Council confirmation, OSFI conducted an annual examination, and the chair and vice-chair of the CPA board were drawn from the Bank of Canada, so it could be said that the payment system was conducted within a culture of suasion, although there was no formal statutory oversight.

However, in 1996, the *Payment Clearing and Settlement Act* (PCSA),[5] was enacted by Parliament, and in 2001, the *Canadian Payments Act* was significantly amended to provide for greater oversight of the CPA by the Bank of Canada, the Minister of Finance, and OSFI. The struc-

---

5   S.C. 1996, c. 6 [*PCSA*]. See also Bradley Crawford, "The Payment Clearing and Settlement Act, 1996" (1997) 28 Can. Bus. L.J. 1.

ture and governance of the CPA was considered in an earlier chapter.[6] The focus of the *PCSA* is more specifically on oversight of the payments system itself and will be considered here.

The main purpose of the *PCSA* is to empower the Governor of the Bank of Canada to designate clearing and settlement systems for direct supervision where the Bank is of the opinion that the system could be operated in a way that could pose a systemic risk to the financial system in Canada and the national interest.[7] The Governor must consult with the Minister of Finance prior to making the designation.[8] "Systemic risk" means the inability of a participant to meet its settlement obligations as they become due, with the result that other participants or financial institutions would not be able to do so, that is, there would be a domino effect throughout the financial system as one bank after another failed.[9] The definition[10] of a designated clearing and settlement system captures all the systems operated by the CPA, as well as those operated by the Canadian Depository for Securities (CDS). To date, the Bank has designated only the Large Value Transfer System (LVTS) and the CDS Debt Clearing System.

Although the *PCSA* does not deem the Bank of Canada to be the *de facto* regulator of the CPA or of the clearing and settlement systems which it operates, the possibility that it may deem any system at any time under the *PCSA* bestows considerable authority, actual or potential, over all systems. Other provisions in the Act confirm this, including: (i) power for the Bank of Canada to enter into various regulatory agreements with a clearing house or participant in the system;[11] (ii) power to act as a guardian of financial assets;[12] and (iii) extensive information-gathering powers, including initial filing of information, continuing disclosures, audits, and required reporting on request.[13] Once a system is designated, it is exempt from judicial intervention, although completely under Bank of Canada supervision.[14]

Additional evidence of increasing centralized regulation of the payments system is found in the 2001 amendments to the *Canadian Pay-*

---

6   Chapter 3, Section E.
7   *PSCA*, above note 5, s. 4(1).
8   *Ibid.*
9   *Ibid.*, s. 2.
10 *Ibid.*
11 *Ibid.*, s. 14(1).
12 *Ibid.*, s. 14(3).
13 *Ibid.*, ss. 10(1) and 14.
14 *Ibid.*, s. 8. For more extensive analysis, see Crawford, above note 5.

ments Act continued in the 2007 amendments.[15] The Act provides that, in carrying out its statutory mandates to operate national clearing and settlement systems, facilitate their interaction with other systems and the development of new payment methods and technologies,[16] the CPA must promote the efficiency, safety, and soundness of its systems and take into account the interests of their users.[17] This statutory overlay is supported by the powers given to the Minister of Finance under Part 2 of the Act to designate any payment system in the public interest for significant Ministerial control over that system and its participants.[18] How this power to designate relates to that of the Governor of the Bank of Canada is uncertain, since neither Act provides guidance on the matter. Equally uncertain is the nature of the public interest that would justify such a move, although it is not unreasonable to suggest that security and solvency would be key ingredients in any decision to designate. To date, the power has not been exercised nor has there been any hint that it will be in the immediate future. Should designation occur, the powers of the Minister of Finance are significant: (i) the power to require the provision of all information requested by the Minister initially and on an ongoing basis;[19] and (ii) subjection to all directives issued by the Minister,[20] enforceable through court orders and significant sanctions.[21]

Although neither the Bank of Canada nor the Minister of Finance has exercised its statutory powers to regulate the payments systems to anywhere near the full extent of those powers, their mere presence in the law serves as a prompt to the CPA to self-regulate to a very high standard. Since international studies consistently rank the clearing and settlement system in Canada as amongst the most efficient and secure in the world, although not necessarily the most technologically up to date, the CPA may be said to exercise its statutory powers in a most responsible manner. Looking to the future, the challenge is to define the scope of the CPA's statutory mandate in relation to the numerous payment systems growing up outside the Automated Clearing and Settlement System (ACSS) and the Large Value Transfer System (LVTS).[22]

---

15   R.S.C. 1985, c. C-21 as am.
16   *Ibid.*, s. 5(1).
17   *Ibid.*, s. 5(2).
18   *Ibid.*, s. 37(1).
19   *Ibid.*, s. 38.
20   *Ibid.*, ss. 40 and 42.
21   *Ibid.*, at ss. 40, 45, & 46.
22   See Sections C and E, below in this chapter.

C. THE AUTOMATED CLEARING AND SETTLEMENT SYSTEM (ACSS)

The Automated Clearing and Settlement System (ACSS) came into operation on 19 November 1984 to calculate the settlement balances of direct clearers in place of the earlier method, whereby clerks from the direct clearers met each morning to calculate manually the net balances of the previous day's clearing. Although now automated, the fundamental principles undergirding the ACSS, or any other automated settlement system, continue to reflect those developed in the eighteenth century in the City of London, where bank clerks met at coffee houses twice daily to exchange cheques and settle balances among themselves.[23]

"Clearing" is the process whereby banks collect cheques deposited by their customers and pay cheques drawn by their customers or whereby collection and payment are carried out electronically. More specifically, clearing refers to the netting of the mutual claims bank participants in the clearing system have against each other in a process similar to set-off. The ACSS is a multilateral net-net system, rather than a bilateral one, in that netting occurs among all the participants, that is, all the direct clearing banks in system, rather than between any two of them or all of them with a central counterparty. "Settlement" is the companion process, whereby participants exchange economic value with one another so as to extinguish the payment obligations among the participants. This is accomplished on a daily basis through the adjustment of the balances in the accounts each direct clearer is required to maintain at the Bank of Canada.

The rules[24] for the operation of the clearing and settlement systems are made by the board of directors of the CPA pursuant to the *Canadian Payments Act*[25] but are effective only after approval by the Governor in Council.[26] The CPA first approved the Clearing By-law, By-law No. 3, in 1985, and this together with the *ACSS Rules Manual* are revised from time to time as required.[27]

---

23 For a description of the historical evolution of this system, see E.P. Ellinger, Eva Lomnicka, & Richard J.A. Hooley, *Modern Banking Law*, 3d ed. (Oxford: Oxford University Press, 2002) at 331–39 and c. 12.
24 Canadian Payments Association, *ACSS Rules Manual* (Ottawa: Canadian Payments Association, 1984). The *ACSS Rules Manual* is available online: www.cdnpay.ca. What follows is based on this material, which should be consulted for its most current version.
25 Above note 15, s. 19(1).
26 *Ibid.*, s. 18(2).
27 Check the Canadian Payments Association website, above note 24, for currency whenever used.

There are two classes of participants in the ACSS: direct clearers and indirect clearers. Direct clearers are CPA members with the largest annual volume of payment items processed by the ACSS, and they have settlement accounts at the Bank of Canada, as well as being connected by computer to the ACSS. There are eleven direct clearers at present, as well as the Bank of Canada, and they act for the indirect clearers in the ACSS. There are 108 indirect clearers. The indirect clearers are also CPA members, but as much smaller financial institutions accepting deposits, they do not have direct access to the clearing system. Rather, they are represented by the direct clearers, who clear on their behalf. The relationship between direct and indirect clearers is regulated by private contract, and indirect clearers do not usually maintain accounts at the Bank of Canada and have no computer connection to the ACSS. Some indirect clearers have formed groups and are represented by one member of their group as a group clearer. Groups of cooperative credit societies access the ACSS in this way, and at present two credit union centrals are direct clearers, although many individual credit unions continue to access the ACSS through a bank direct clearer.

The direct clearers participate in the ACSS at two different levels: at six regional settlement points throughout the country (Halifax, Montreal, Toronto, Winnipeg, Calgary, and Vancouver) and at the Bank of Canada. The regional settlement points are places where there is a clearing and provisional settlement among the participants in that region. The results are transmitted through the ACSS to the Bank of Canada, which does the final netting of the regional results to determine the net obligations of the direct clearers to one another on a daily basis and then settles those obligations by a single debit or credit entry to the settlement account of the clearer. The entire system operates on a network of personal computers and is linked by a secure, dedicated communication link to a data centre in Toronto to which the Bank of Canada has access and to which the data summaries are communicated daily for the final netting. Data is available through each day to the participants so that they can manage their positions and to the Bank of Canada so that it can assess solvency throughout the day. The net position is assessed at about 12:00 noon daily EST by the Bank of Canada for the previous day.

The ACSS clears and settles both paper and electronic payment instructions, or "payment items," a term which covers both paper and electronic payments. The Clearing By-law permits only certain payment items through the system: (i) paper payment orders, including cheques and other negotiable instruments, bank drafts, money orders, travellers' cheques, and Receiver General's warrants; (ii) payment orders recorded on magnetic, computer-readable tape; and (iii) payment orders transmitted electronically. The clearing rules further provide specific technical requirements that all payment items must satisfy before they will be permitted into the ACSS, including rules relating to size, encoding, paper quality, designs and legal requirements, for example, so that paper items fulfill the legal requirements for a negotiable instrument. Since the payment items are machine read and/or sorted, very specific technical requirements are necessary, and it is not possible to clear and settle a payment item through the ACSS unless the specifications set out in By-law No. 3 and the *ACSS Rules Manual* are completely fulfilled. Electronic items are grouped into three categories: (i) debit and credit transfers on magnetic tape; (ii) payment items generated at electronic point-of-sale (POS) terminals; and (iii) electronic data interchange (EDI) items.

Against this structural background, it is now possible to trace the clearing and settlement of an individual paper payment item.[28] When a customer deposits a cheque for collection into the customer's account, that cheque will already be MICR encoded with information at the bottom left-hand corner, identifying the cheque number, bank branch transit number, and account number. The cheque will be further encoded either at the branch or at the regional settlement point with the amount payable and sorted from the branch. The cheque will also be microfilmed, front and back, to ensure a copy is available for any future inquiry. An "on-us" item, that is, a cheque drawn on an account at another branch of the same bank, will be sent for clearing within that bank's own internal clearing system by being sent to the branch on which it is drawn, accepted or rejected for payment, and returned to the payee's branch for final credit to the customer's account. An interbank collection through the ACSS means that the cheque will be sorted by the bank for delivery to the regional clearing point, there to join millions of other cheques also sent for clearing between banks. If not encoded with the amount payable at the branch, it will be encoded at the regional clearing point. Numerous bags of cheques are delivered to the local regional clearing point in the late afternoon and early evening each day.

Until very recently, cheque clearing involved exchanges between individual bank regional data centres; however, banks no longer oper-

---

28 The following descriptions are based on the summary on the CPA website, *ibid.*, for "A Cheque's Travels" and "Detailed Schedule of the Cheque Clearing and Settlement System," as well as "A Guide to Risk in Payment Systems Owned and Operated by the CPA."

ate their own regional data centres. Instead, two independent processing companies, Symcor[29] and Intria,[30] have been incorporated and are wholly owned by various banks, and these companies conduct integrated clearing operations on behalf of the direct clearers at the regional settlement points. The regional centres operate daily except for statutory holidays and "non-business days" as defined in the *Bills of Exchange Act*, including Sundays.[31] The cheques are physically exchanged among the direct clearing banks at the regional clearing centres, using very high-speed automated sorting machines, usually by midnight on the day the customer/payee deposited the cheque with their bank. The cheques are then bundled and delivered to the branch on which they are drawn overnight either by air or ground transportation as circumstances dictate. At the branch, the decision to honour the cheque will be made, although some financial institutions have now centralized this decision to the regional settlement centre. If the decision is to honour the cheque, the cheque will remain at the branch of the account and be returned to the payer with the monthly statement or stored if the payer does not receive back honoured cheques. But if the cheque is dishonoured, it will be returned to the branch where it was deposited by the next business day and routed through the same route by which it was sent to the branch of the account on which it was drawn. It will be recalled that physical presentment of cheques for payment is still required by section 84 of the *Bills of Exchange Act*. The return process might take several days, but the payee's branch will not know it has been dishonoured until it is returned. When it is returned, the customer's account will be debited by the amount of the cheque originally provisionally credited.

Concurrently with the exchange of paper items at the regional data centres, the data relating to the cheques are entered into the ACSS by the collecting direct-clearing bank at the regional settlement points throughout the day in order to track the volume and value of payment items in the system. A preliminary net clearing balance is calculated by the ACSS at 9:30 a.m. for the previous day, and a final balance is struck at 11:00 a.m. By 12:00 noon, the Bank of Canada adjusts the balances among the direct clearers by transferring funds among their accounts, and that settlement is deemed to be final. Indirect clearers also extinguish their obligations with their direct clearers the same day through

---

29 Owned and operated by all of the large banks except those in Intria, below note 30.
30 Owned and operated by the Canadian Imperial Bank of Commerce and National Bank of Canada..
31 *Bills of Exchange Act*, R.S.C. 1985, c. B-4, ss. 2 and 42.

accounts that they maintain with their direct clearers. For paper payment items, clearing and settlement typically takes twelve to twenty hours during the week and sixty to eighty hours over a long weekend.

Paper payment item clearing involves various risks: human processing errors, lost cheques, systems malfunctions, fraud, counterfeit, and providing credit to a customer prior to final payment by the paying bank, for example. These risks create potential liability for both the collecting and the paying banks, and various tactics are adopted in order to mitigate them: "cheque holds" until final payment is made, monitoring high-risk customers, limiting withdrawals when cheques are in transit, and knowing the customer, as well as various improvements in the clearing process to reduce lost cheques, systems malfunctions, and detecting fraud earlier.

The ACSS is also used for clearing and settling electronic payment items. There are eight different streams of electronic payment items cleared through ACSS: automated banking machines (ABM) adjustments; automated fund transfers (AFT) of credits, that is, direct deposits; AFT debits, that is, recurring withdrawals; point-of-sale (POS) payments such as debit card transactions; POS credits; shared network payments by cash from an ABM other than that of the cardholder's financial institution; electronic data interchange (EDI) corporate-to-corporate credit payments; and bill payment remittance processing, for example, telephone or personal computer banking.

There are separate rules governing the exchange of electronic items, depending on the category into which they fall, and there are three categories: AFT debits and credits; POS items; and EDI items.[32]

An AFT credit transaction is one in which the payer instructs its financial institution to "push" funds or credits from its account to the account of a specific payee at another or the same financial institution, for example, an employee salary or government pension or disability payment. An AFT debit transaction is one in which a payer provides a payee with a prior written authorization to withdraw or "pull" funds from the payer's account for the purpose of paying a contractual obligation, for example, a mortgage, a cable bill, or a utility bill. AFT items were originally transmitted by computer tapes exchanged at four of the settlement points (Montreal, Toronto, Calgary, and Vancouver) but are now more likely to be transmitted electronically through the Data Transmission Network (DTN) of the ACSS at two times during the day, 9:30 a.m. and 4:30 p.m., by the direct clearers for both credit and debit payment items. On receiving an AFT file, the processing direct clearer

---

32 Again see the *ACSS Rules Manual*, above note 24, for the current details.

performs a file edit to ensure there are no problems with the file and then posts the items to the customers' accounts according to their due dates. Settlement between the financial institutions is made by the direct clearers by 5:00 a.m. on the transaction value date.

POS items are governed by the *ACSS Rules Manual* but are also subject to rules relating to their operating procedures established by the network that offers this method of payment, Interac.[33] Wholly owned by the banks, Interac is the association that provides the computer network to facilitate POS transactions and this network consists of the ABMs operated by Interac members to permit their customers to access their accounts from any ABM in the Interac network. Another set of rules also applicable is the Canadian Code of Practice for Consumer Debit Card Services, 2004,[34] which outlines industry and consumer responsibilities and with which the financial institutions voluntarily comply. The Code[35] deals with such matters as responsibility for debit cards and PINs, unauthorized use, theft, liability, and dispute-resolution procedures.

In a POS transaction, the cardholder/payer initiates a payment transaction by presenting the card at a POS device (an "Interac" terminal) by "swiping" the card. The payer's bank then verifies the payer by the personal identification number (PIN) and sends that information to the POS device, which then sends the purchase data to the payee's financial institution, which is a direct clearer. The direct clearer has access to the network. The payment data is then sent to the payer's financial institution's direct clearer and then to the payer's financial institution. Once the transaction is authorized, the debit is posted to the payer's account and the authorization message is sent to the payee's financial institution and the payee's account is credited. With the completion of the transaction, the payer receives a paper record of the transaction. The payer and payee direct clearers keep an electronic log of all POS transactions, and these are sent to the ACSS by 5:00 a.m. of the next business day for calculation in the final balances of the direct clearers by 11:00 a.m. and final settlement at the Bank of Canada.

Electronic data interchange (EDI) payment items are also regulated by the *ACSS Rules Manual* and used largely for bill payment remittances between businesses, as well as by consumers through telephone and home computer banking. A corporate EDI payment begins with a company/payer creating an EDI payment item and sending this to its

---

33 Online: www.interac.org.
34 (Ottawa: Industry Canada, 2004).
35 Chapter 10, Section C.

financial institution by a deadline agreed to with the financial institution. The payer's financial institution debits the company's account and sends the payment via the Data Transmission Network (DTN) by 5:00 a.m. the next day to the payee's financial institution, where the payee's account is credited. Where the EDI payment item is initiated by a customer to pay a bill by telephone or the Internet, the customer's financial institution groups these payments by a Corporate Creditor Identification Number (CCIN) and sends the payments via the DTN to the corporate creditor's financial institution. The corporate payee's account is credited, and remittance information is sent to the corporate creditor. With both corporate and consumer EDI payments, after they have been exchanged between payer and payee financial institutions, the payee direct clearer must by 6:00 p.m. on the transaction date provide application advice to the payer direct clearer to accept EDI items. Settlement between the direct clearers occurs the following day, when the payee direct clearer initiates a debit entry against each other financial institution to which it has transmitted credits into the ACSS by 5:00 a.m. for final settlement that morning.

For a bank customer using these electronic payment methods, there are none of the risks associated with paper such as loss or counterfeit. For their banks, however, there are risks associated with unauthorized or fraudulent transactions, which means that banks must take various steps to mitigate them, including assessing and setting credit limits for customers, ensuring there are sufficient customer funds or security for payment transactions, ensuring proper authentication of transactions, ensuring security in the devices and software used to run the transactions, and ensuring the means to unwind a transaction when there is default. Risks involving customers are managed by contract with the customer and risks relating to the systems are managed by contracts among the systems users and with the CPA. However, the major risk in electronic payments systems is the possibility of default by either a direct or an indirect clearer because it cannot meet the final settlement of accounts daily at the Bank of Canada. Although such an event is highly unlikely because of the close monitoring daily by the Bank of Canada, financial institutions occasionally fail, as did the Northland Bank and Canadian Commercial Bank in 1985, and the cumulative effect of such an event on the entire financial network is significant, as other financial institutions may not be able to meet their obligations without the credits expected from the defaulting institution.

When a direct or indirect clearer defaults, the CPA by-laws and rules provide for the partial unwinding of net-settlement positions and the return of unsettled payment items. CPA By-law No. 3, "Payment

Items and ACSS," provides that payment items resulting in a net loss for the defaulting direct clearer are to be unwound, with the exception of POS items because these are online, real-time irrevocable payments. If there is still a shortfall after unwinding in the settlement account of the defaulting direct clearer, the CPA By-law No. 3 requires the other direct clearers and the Bank of Canada to advance funds to it to allow settlement to occur in accordance with a formula set out in the by-law, which allocates the shortfall on a pro-rata basis based on the value of the payment items they entered into the clearings that were drawn on, or payable by, the defaulter that day. Thus, losses that cannot be recovered from their own customers are passed on to other participants in the clearing system.

When the default is of the direct clearer, an indirect clearer can be at risk for the amount in its settlement account after unwinding payment items from the direct clearer and the direct clearer is required to return payment items received from their indirect clearers. When the default is of an indirect clearer, the payment items are treated in the same way as in direct clearer default, with the exception of EDI items, which are not unwound because the accounts with the direct clearer are required to be pre-funded. However, instead of all participants covering the losses, only the direct clearer is required to do so and is therefore expected to manage risks with the indirect clearers for which it acts.

Until the implementation of the LVTS in 1999, the ACSS was the clearing and settlement system in Canada for large- and small-payment items; it remains the system for everyday consumer transactions, now that transactions in excess of $25 million have migrated to the LVTS.[36] However, by 2005, the ACSS handled only about 11 percent of the total annual clearings in Canada, as the other 89 percent was handled by the LVTS, that is, approximately $4.53 trillion handled annually as opposed to $36.72 trillion handled annually by the LVTS.[37] Nevertheless, for consumers and small business customers, the ACSS is the clearing and settlement system. This system is also constantly being changed and improved by the CPA, and the most important improvement on the horizon in the next three to four years will be the introduction of truncation and electronic cheque presentment (TECP).

Although customers today have the option of receiving back all cleared cheques with their monthly bank statements, many choose not

---

36 See Section E, below in this chapter.
37 Canadian Payments Association, *Annual Review 2005* (Ottawa: Canadian Payments Association, 2005) at 2 and 22.

to incur the additional expense of doing so. This suggests that for many customers who have no business need for, or are not encumbered by, a statutory duty to retain cheques (for example, lawyers), little more is required than a monthly statement of the debits and credits in the account. Recent technological developments permitting cheque imaging and electronic transmission of those images has resulted in several foreign jurisdictions, including the United States, the United Kingdom, France, and New Zealand, introducing cheque transaction and electronic clearing into their clearing and settlement systems, and since 2002, the CPA has been engaged in a project to implement cheque truncation and clearing within the ACSS by 2009. TECP has been used locally by the Credit Union Central of British Columbia for several years.[38]

Cheque truncation means that when a cheque is received at the collecting branch by virtue of customer deposit into an account, the front and back of the cheque will be digitally imaged either at the branch or at the regional data centre and that image will be transmitted electronically to the branch of the account on which the cheque is drawn for the decision to pay or not. The paper cheque will no longer be moved through the clearing system but will be destroyed once it has been imaged. Special software will be able to detect whether the cheque is fraudulent at the time of image capture, so that not only will lost cheques no longer be a problem but most fraudulent paper payment items should be rejected before transmission for payment and settlement. Payment information will be electronically captured by the ACSS and routed into the daily settlement process. The customer will receive paper images of the cheques on the back of the monthly statement, or electronic images if they home-bank, and so will have a record of the information on the front and back of the original cheques for personal or business records. The introduction of TECP is expected to introduce considerable efficiencies into the clearing and settlement system because paper cheques will no longer be encoded, sorted, and transported around the country, thereby reducing courier and personnel costs; paper cheques will no longer be liable to loss and fraudulent cheques will be kept to a minimum; and by utilizing electronic transmission systems already proven to be secure, risks should be reduced and customer service improved.

Before TECP is fully implemented, several legal hurdles must be surmounted. First, the *Bills of Exchange Act*, section 84, requires that physical presentment of cheques must be made prior to the decision

---

38 Interested readers should consult the materials posted regularly on the CPA website (www.cdnpay.ca) to monitor the progress of implementation.

to pay. This is so that the paying bank can be sure that the mandate to pay is a mandate from its customer and signed with the customer's signature. Secondly, the definition of a cheque in the *Bills of Exchange Act*, section 165(1), is applicable only to paper cheques and must be changed to encompass digital images. Thirdly, both federal and provincial Evidence Acts require that the original paper cheque be presented as evidence in any court proceeding in which proof of cheques and of payment is required. Fourthly, a number of professional organizations, such as provincial law societies, require their members to retain cleared cheques as part of their professional files. All of these issues are currently being addressed. The first two will be addressed in the next financial sector review; the third is being addressed by changes made or to be made to the various Evidence Acts and the fourth is being considered by professional societies, which are currently reviewing their record-keeping requirements for their members.

D. THE UNITED STATES BULK EXCHANGE SYSTEM (USBES)

The United States Bulk Exchange System (USBES) is the automated settlement system that has been operated by the CPA since September 1989 for the clearing and settlement of payments in U.S. dollars in Canada, reflecting the fact that numerous Canadians and Canadian companies maintain U.S. dollar accounts in Canadian banks and make payments in U.S. dollars. The *ACSS Rules Manual* (Rule K1) contains the rules for the operation of this system, which are relatively similar to those for the ACSS generally. The USBES governs both paper and electronic payment items drawn only on U.S. dollar accounts in Canadian bank branches and not on U.S. dollar accounts held at a U.S. branch of a Canadian bank or U.S. dollar payment items drawn on any other bank accounts in the U.S. or outside Canada.

Paper items are exchanged by direct clearers at five regional settlement points (Montreal, Toronto, Winnipeg, Calgary, and Vancouver) in a separate process from the ACSS Canadian dollar clearing but operating in a similar manner. Paper items acceptable for clearing include cheques, drafts, and postal money orders, as well as certain remittance items sold by Canadian financial institutions and payable at their correspondents in the United States. Participating direct clearers encode payment items with their amount payable and microfilm them, and then they are machine-sorted for physical delivery to the branches on which they are drawn for the pay/no-pay decision. Concurrently, the data is entered into the USBES, which performs the same netting and settlement functions as the ACSS for Canadian dollar settlement. Although Rule K provides for electronic payment items, in particular, EDI and AFT items, the electronic procedures are not yet in operation.

In contrast to the ACSS, where final settlement is at the Bank of Canada, final settlement for U.S. dollar transactions in Canada is between direct clearers in New York and may be effected through Fedwire, the Clearing House Interbank Payments System (CHIPS), the Federal Reserve, or any agreed New York correspondent. The place of settlement is left by the CPA rules to the private agreement of the participants in the system. To settle in New York, Canadian direct clearers must use American correspondents to access CHIPS, and because CHIPS requires the direct clearers to hold sufficient funds or collateral, default and the possible unwinding of transactions for default is not possible.

E. THE LARGE VALUE TRANSFER SYSTEM (LVTS)

The Large Value Transfer System (LVTS) came into operation on 4 February 1999 as the system for clearing and settling large-value Canadian dollar transactions, currently defined as payments in excess of $25 million. It now processes about 90 percent of the economic value exchanged in Canada and is typically used by large corporations, governments, and large institutions such as investment dealers to transfer payments. Its systemic importance to the payments system is such that it has been designated by the Bank of Canada under the *Payment Clearing and Settlement Act* (PCSA) and so is subject to especial Bank of Canada scrutiny, although it is owned and operated by the CPA pursuant to the LVTS By-law No. 7 and the LVTS Rules.[39]

Before the introduction of the LVTS in 1999, large-value payments were processed through a dedicated system called Interbank International Payment System (IIPS), which used the facilities operated by the Society for Worldwide Interbank Financial Telecommunication (SWIFT), based in Belgium. IIPS operated on the basis of an end-of-day bilateral balance of netted debits and credits, but this was considered to create too much systemic risk in the Canadian payments system, so the CPA moved toward the LVTS, which is a real-time, multilateral netting system operated in Canada by the CPA using the SWIFT network.

---

39 See the CPA website, above note 24 for current versions.

The movement toward a discrete large value payment system followed international trends after the Bank for International Settlements (BIS) published a series of reports in the early 1990s[40] identifying credit and liquidity risks as major concerns in relation to systemic risk in the world's banking systems.

The BIS recommended that systemically important payment systems become real-time, multilateral systems so as to reduce these risks. The LVTS is that system in Canada. As a real-time system, payment messages are processed by the payee bank when received from the payer bank so that payments are immediate, final, and irrevocable, and the participants and the Bank of Canada can monitor the system throughout the day so as to act immediately should there be any possibility of default. The LVTS is also multilateral, so that there is a continual recalculation of the net position of each participant throughout the day with settlement at the Bank of Canada of one net amount by each participant at the end of the day. These characteristics of the LVTS mean that there is unlikely ever to be a default, but should there be one, the Bank of Canada guarantees that the LVTS will settle so that any default will not affect the other participants.

There are fourteen members in the LVTS, together with the Bank of Canada, and these are the largest banks and credit union groups in Canada, which have satisfied the entry requirements for the LVTS, including having a settlement account with the central bank, meeting the technical requirements, and paying the required fee. Since payment messages are transmitted over SWIFT, membership in SWIFT is also required, for which technical certification is a necessity. Other financial institutions must arrange LVTS payments through the fourteen participants. The LVTS operates on SWIFT terminals located in the offices of the participants, using CPA software, and offers two options, called "Tranches," for exchanging payments throughout the day. The Tranches are distinguished by the method by which they are supported by collateral and not by their operations features, which offer both real-time and multilateral finality of payment.

---

40 Bank for International Settlements, *Report on Netting Schemes* (Basel: Bank for International Settlements, 1989) ["the Angels Report"]; Bank for International Settlements, *The Report of the Committee on Interbank Netting Schemes of the Central Banks of the Group of Ten Countries* (Basel: Bank for International Settlements, 1990) ["the Lamfalussy Report"]; Bank for International Settlements, *Report of the Committee on Central Bank Payment and Settlement with Respect to Cross-Border and Multi-Currency Transactions* (Basel, Bank for International Settlements, 1993) ["the Noel Report"].

The LVTS opens for payment transactions at 6:00 a.m. EST, but in the previous six-hour period (from about midnight), various initial processes must be completed to set credit limits for that day and ensure that every technical aspect is ready for the day. Each participant will set its Tranche 1 net debit cap and pledge the required supporting collateral with the Bank of Canada and will also learn from the Bank of Canada what its Tranche 2 net debit cap will be for that day based on the aggregate of the bilateral credit limits the other participants have established for it. At about 12:30 a.m., the LVTS will also open for Continuous Linked Settlement (CLS), which is a global irrevocable settlement system among international financial institutions, and this will run until 6:00 a.m. Payments are sent and received through the Bank of Canada.

Once the LVTS opens at 6:00 a.m., participants will send and receive payments until 6:00 p.m. over the SWIFT system through Brussels, that is, Canadian bank branches that may be across the street from one another in Canada, will wire transfer funds via Brussels to one another. The payment messages are encrypted for security and copied by the CPA, which also authorizes the payment, so as to ensure that risks to the system are minimized. Each payment receives a unique number to identify it and to confirm that it has passed various risk-control tests. Payment messages are in Canadian dollars and paid immediately and irrevocably. Throughout the day, the participants track their Tranche 1 and 2 positions so that they can respond if they come near their net cap amounts.

At 6:00 p.m., the LVTS closes, and until 6:30 p.m. pre-settlement occurs, where participants may enter transactions with one another to even out their positions and avoid the need to borrow from the Bank of Canada overnight. From 6:30 to 7:30, settlement for the day occurs while the Bank of Canada finalizes the net position for each participant and makes the appropriate credit or debit adjustment to each participant's settlement account. The LVTS then shuts down until the next day.

Although designed to reduce risks as far as possible, there are some risks in the LVTS system, such as the obvious ones of technological failure or financial institution insolvency independent of LVTS participation, which would gridlock payments so that no other institutions would be able to transmit and settle payments. However, there are also a number of controls to minimize the impact of such risks, including real-time, multilateral, irrevocable payment through the daily cycle; the use of the Tranches to place ceilings on every participant's net debit position; the pre-pledge of securities by the participants to the Bank of Canada; and the Bank of Canada guarantee to settle were a participant to fail during the daily LVTS cycle. Should the unlikely event of a default occur, the collateral pledged for that day would be used by the Bank of Canada, and the other institutions, who would already have granted the defaulter a bilateral credit limit, would be required to make up the shortfall on a pro-rata share basis of the bilateral limits they had initially granted to the defaulter by all the other non-defaulting institutions.

F. LEGAL SIGNIFICANCE FOR CUSTOMERS

Whenever any bank customer gives an instruction to its bank to pay or collect payment on that customer's behalf, the bank will execute that mandate through the clearing and settlement systems described above and operated by the CPA, with the exception of "on-us" items which are cleared and settled internally within their own bank, although some financial institutions also send "on-us" items through the ACSS. The customer has no choice; indeed, most bank and customer account agreements contain a term authorizing the bank to clear and settle on the customer's behalf as the bank sees fit. The only alternatives for a customer are to opt out of the banking system entirely by making or receiving payments in cash or services or by barter.

The binding effect in contract of the CPA systems on the banks is self-evident. All banks in Canada are statutorily required to be CPA members, whether they are domestic or foreign, or direct or indirect clearers, and by virtue of membership, they are parties to a multilateral contract, including abiding by the rules of membership in clearing and settling through the CPA.[41] As between direct and indirect clearers, express contracts set out the terms on which direct clearers will act and include requirements for CPA compliance by the indirect clearer, enforceable not by the CPA, but as a matter of contract between direct and indirect clearers.[42] The rules governing the ACSS, the USBES, and the LVTS are binding on all banks, as well as on other financial institutions that voluntarily comply with the conditions for membership and become CPA members.

---

41 *Canadian Payments Act*, above note 15, s. 4(1) requires all banks to be members, and s. 4(2) permits other financial institutions to be members if they meet certain requirements. All deposit-taking institutions join as a matter of course to access the clearing and settlement system. See also By-law No. 3, s. 1.02(4), which states that rules are binding on all members.

42 *National Bank of Greece (Canada) v. Canada Permanent Trust Co.*, [1987] R.J.Q. 607 (S.C.); *National Bank of Greece (Canada) v. Bank of Montreal*, [2001] 2 F.C. 288 (C.A.).

The legal significance of the CPA rules and systems for customers has been less obvious to both courts and commentators in the past.[43] While it has always been clear that customers are not bound directly by contract to the rules because they are not members of the CPA and not parties to the multilateral contract constituted by membership, there has been some ambiguity as to whether those rules could be implied into the bank and customer agreement so as to bind the bank in its performance of its collection duties for the customer. This question has arisen in relation to failure to return dishonoured cheques within the ACSS deadlines and courts have implied the ACSS deadlines into the bank and customer contract by analogy to find banks liable for damages to customers when the rule is breached by the bank.[44] Thus, while it is clear as a matter of contract law that the clearing and settlement system rules do not directly bind a customer, by implied contract, in the bank and customer contract, those rules bind the bank in the performance of its contractual duties to the customer.

Although the courts have never considered the binding effect of the LVTS rules on banks and customers, there can be no doubt of that effect. The *PCSA*'s designation of the LVTS by the Bank of Canada gives statutory paramountcy of the LVTS rules over all other laws of Canada or of a province. This must mean that the LVTS rules govern the relationships among the CPA, the participants in the LVTS, the financial institutions represented by the participants, and the customers of the participants and other financial institutions, regardless of any other legislation, rules, or contractual provisions between and among these parties, as well as any future case law resolving disputes arising from LVTS use. It is a simple matter of Parliamentary sovereignty.[45]

G. INTERNATIONAL CLEARING AND SETTLEMENT

The ACSS and the LVTS are restricted to electronic funds transfers within Canada; however, many customers today also require access to an electronic fund transfer network that transmits funds across borders to other parts

---

43 Chapter. 8, Section C. See also the *National Bank of Greece* cases, ibid. and *Advance Bank v. Toronto Dominion Bank* (2003), 227 D.L.R. (4th) 755 (Ont. S.C.J.) for the position that the CPA rules apply only to members; and *Bank of Nova Scotia v. Toronto-Dominion Bank* (2001), 200 D.L.R. (4th) 549 (C.A.) for the overriding importance of the *Bills of Exchange Act*.
44 Ibid.
45 See Section B, above in this chapter.

of the world.[46] Most international funds transfers are credit transfers involving the push of funds from the originator's bank to the beneficiary's bank in another jurisdiction, usually through intermediary banks. Most also involve more than one law, including the law of the originator's jurisdiction, of the beneficiary's jurisdiction, and possibly of other jurisdictions through which the funds flow, especially where intermediary banks are used. Such transfers are transmitted on the communication network maintained by the Society for Worldwide Interbank Financial Telecommunication (SWIFT), to which customers have access through their own branches.

SWIFT is a non-profit cooperative society organized in 1973, with headquarters in Brussels, Belgium. It is wholly owned by its approximately eight thousand member banks and other financial institutions, including Canadian financial institutions, and the ownership share varies in relation to their use of the system. SWIFT operates in over 190 countries in the world, and the estimated average daily value of payment messages is over $6 trillion U.S. dollars. SWIFT operates an international financial message system for payment messages and other financial information sent between users worldwide. It does not settle accounts (which financial institutions must do independently); rather, it is purely a message system. The normal transmission time is less than two minutes. The original SWIFT was restructured in 1990 and renamed as SWIFT II, which remains currently in operation.

There are two main operating centres, in Amsterdam and Culpepper, Virginia, where slice processors supervise the network that receives, forwards, and stores messages. Each country whose financial institutions are members of SWIFT has a SWIFT Access Point (SAP), and the SAPs for Canada are located in Montreal and Toronto. To transmit funds internationally, a customer will first instruct its own branch to send funds, and this branch will then electronically transmit that instruction from the branch to the SAP, where it will enter the SWIFT system. The SAP encodes the message and sends it to Culpepper or Amsterdam; each can handle all international message traffic alone and are interchangeable, therefore, it does not matter which is used. The message will include the name of the customer's bank's correspondent bank used overseas, as well as the amount and the beneficiary of the transfer. The SAP will acknowledge receipt of the message to the customer's originating bank and then send it to the SAP in the beneficiary's country. There the message will be

---

46 The internationally recognized authoritative texts on international funds transfers are by Benjamin Geva, *The Law of Electronic Funds Transfers*, looseleaf (New York: Matthew Bender, 1992) and *Bank Collections and Payment Transactions—Comparative Study of Legal Aspects* (Oxford: Oxford University Press, 2001).

decoded and sent through the domestic electronic funds transfer system either to the beneficiary's bank directly or through another bank. When the beneficiary's bank receives the message, it acknowledges receipt through the SWIFT system, and the beneficiary's account is credited. All this will occur within two minutes.

SWIFT messages are sent the same day the customer requests the transmission of credit, although because of time-zone differences, receiving banks will store messages received after business hours and transmit them the next day. Since SWIFT does not settle, settlement is done by the originator bank authorizing the beneficiary's bank to reimburse itself by drawing either on the originator bank or a local correspondent.

SWIFT operates on the basis of its own rules, to which its members subscribe as a matter of contract. SWIFT disclaims liability for breach of its duties, which include undertakings as to speed of delivery, maintaining the security of the system that relates to international messaging (such as the slice processor), SAPs, and system-control processors, with certain exceptions, such as lost interest resulting from late payment due to its fault; negligence in transmission; fraud by SWIFT employees or contractors; and fraud by third parties perpetrated within the limits of SWIFT's duties.

Finally, it will be recalled that the SWIFT communications system in Canada is used for the LVTS, although not for the ACSS.

Close economic ties between Canada and the United States and with the United Kingdom and the European Union mean that many cross-border credit transfers by customers, both corporate and individual, go into domestic electronic fund networks operating in those countries once the transmission has been sent on from the SWIFT Access Point (SAP) in those countries. Canadian customers will again access these from their own branches, which will send the payment instruction via SWIFT to the appropriate foreign electronic transfer network. While an analysis of these is beyond the scope of this book, a brief introduction will be useful.

In the United States, there are two major large value payment transfer systems: Fedwire, a public system, operated by the Federal Reserve, and the Clearing House Interbank Payments System (CHIPS), a private system based in New York. CHIPS began in 1970 for commercial banking and is owned by the New York Clearing House Association, whose members are the major American banks and certain foreign agencies of foreign banks. Messages are sent multilaterally by CHIPS members throughout the day in U.S. dollars only and settled each night through reserve adjustment accounts at the New York Federal Reserve Bank. Fedwire began operations in 1918 as a telegraph-telephone wire transfer service, but in 1970 it also began to offer electronic funds transmission.

It is national in scope and handles most U.S. transfers, large and small. Each Fedwire participant maintains an account at one of the twelve reserve banks and has computer access to that reserve bank. When transmitting and receiving banks have accounts at the same reserve bank, funds transfers occur through that bank, but where the accounts are at different reserve banks, an additional step is added between the two reserve banks. Balances are constantly adjusted throughout the day, and settlement occurs at the end of each day. There are also several smaller regional funds transfer networks in the U.S., again accessed by Canadian customers by giving their bank branch payment instructions and leaving it to their branch to access the appropriate network.

There are four main electronic clearing systems within the United Kingdom, each run by an independent company which is a member of the Association for Payment Clearing Services (APACS): (i) the Cheque and Credit Clearing Co. Ltd.; (ii) the British Automated Clearing Service Ltd. (BACS), which deals with low-value credit and debit transfers; (iii) the Clearing House Automated Payments System (CHAPS), which is a real-time gross settlement system for large-value payments; and (iv) CHAPS euro which is the real-time gross settlement (RTGS) system for euro payments within the European Union and which runs on the Trans-European Automated Real-time Gross-settlement Express Transfer (TARGET), the network connecting the various RTGS systems in each E.U. member state. CHAPS and CHAPS euro are being consolidated into a single system: New CHAPS.

These systems operate in similar ways to the Canadian systems. There are direct clearers, which are the larger banks and building societies, and indirect clearers; there is a fixed clearing cycle, and the rules bind the direct clearers as a matter of multilateral contract; with the exception of BACS, which has a three-day clearing cycle, the others clear almost instantaneously; there is settlement through settlement accounts at the Bank of England; and payments are real-time and irrevocable.[47]

H. THE LEGAL NATURE OF ELECTRONIC FUNDS TRANSFER (EFT)

How the law in Canada views the legal nature of electronic funds transfer is unknown. There is no legislation, and there are only several brief

---

47   For an extended description see Geva, *ibid.*; Ellinger *et al.*, above note 23 at 476–85; and *Paget*, above note 1 at 307–20.

cases, dealing with single issues. This contrasts with the United States and the United Kingdom, which have both legislation and a burgeoning body of case law. A brief summary of the types of issues that have arisen and how foreign courts have dealt with them is all that is possible, because it is not known how Canadian courts will decide cases dealing with these issues.[48] Electronic funds transfer contrasts with the previous payment mechanisms known to banking law, money and negotiable instruments, and especially negotiable instruments, the legal nature of which is defined by substantial legislation and case law. The problem of definition is further confounded by the variety of payment transfer systems and their rapid evolution as technology and demand develop. However, certain propositions seem clear at the outset.

First, payment by electronic transfer is not payment by legal tender, that is, in coins and bank notes, not only because the physical coins and notes are not transferred but also because of the credit risk inherent in electronic transfer and the possibility that a creditor's claim can be set off against a bank's counterclaim either at the local bank level or in the settlement process between banks. Payment by funds transfer involves the adjustment of bank balances between payer and payee. Secondly, electronic transfers are not negotiable instruments because they are not "unconditional orders in writing," nor are they "payable on demand." Thirdly, they are not assignments of debt either, because assignments are normally of a transfer of the total debt, not part of it on a periodic basis; because there is no real intention as required to effect an assignment; and because there is not always a sum available in the payer's account to be assigned. Credit transfers are intended as payment mechanisms for paying debts and do not transfer rights of enforcement separate from the right to payment of the debt by the payee in the first place.

Some early English cases suggest that the courts are likely to treat an electronic funds transfer as a transfer of value from the payer to the payee. In *R. v. Preddy*,[49] the defendants were charged with obtaining mortgage advances from lending institutions by deception contrary to the criminal law by deliberately giving false information on applications for mortgage advances. When the advances were approved, they were paid electronically from the lending institution to the defendant's account, and the House of Lords had to determine for the purposes of the applicable law whether the defendants had obtained property belonging to another. The House of Lords held that there was no transfer

---

48 See above notes 46 and 47 for extended discussion.
49 [1996] A.C. 815 (H.L.).

of property. In the main speech, Lord Goff stated that the credit balance in the lender's account was a chose in action which was reduced when funds were transferred to the defendant's account, and the defendant's chose in action against its bank was increased thereby. The defendant's chose in action had never belonged to the lender but was a newly created proprietary right distinct from the lender's chose in action against its own bank. This means that it is a misnomer to speak of the transfer of funds, since coins and notes are not transferred between accounts and there is no assignment of a debt. Property rights are not transferred between accounts; rather, an electronic payment message leads to the adjustment of property rights of the payer and payee with their respective banks between which *value* is transferred.

The concept of an electronic transfer as a transfer of value to the payee on the instruction of the payer confirms that agency in the bank and customer contract is at the foundation of an electronic transfer. Whether the instruction is transmitted in person at the branch or by paper in a cheque or electronically, the transfer of value is at the customer's mandate and in fulfilling that instruction, the bank acts as the customer's agent and is subject to all the duties of care associated with the contract.[50]

The parties to an electronic transfer are the customer, who is the payer, or "originator," of the transaction; the originator's bank, which effects the originator's instruction; the beneficiary of the payment order, the payee; and the beneficiary's bank. In addition, where the originator does not have a correspondent or direct clearing relationship with the beneficiary's bank, it will use an intermediary or correspondent bank or banks.

The originator initiates the transfer by giving a payment order to its bank as agent, which is required to carry out that order with reasonable skill and care.[51] An early issue for the bank will be assurance that it is the customer who is giving the order electronically, rather than some unauthorized third party. Electronic access merely authenticates the instruction but not the identity of the person who gave the instruction. To protect itself, the bank usually requires the bank and customer agreement to contain terms that place liability for unauthorized access on the customer, who is required to hold both card and access code in confidence as a condition of the agreement. Thus, the bank's duty is one of reasonable care to prevent unauthorized transfers.

---

50   *Royal Products Ltd. v. Midland Bank Ltd.*, [1981] 2 Lloyd's Rep. 194 (Q.B.D.) [*Royal Products*].
51   *Ibid.*

The courts have found that the originator's bank is subject to certain duties once the originator has sent a funds transfer instruction. First, the transfer must be effected on time, which is usually, given the means of transmission of the instruction, the same day.[52] This same rule also applies to the countermand of an electronic order.[53] Secondly, in the absence of an express instruction by the originator, the bank is free to choose the method of transfer[54] and may even choose a faster method than any designated by the customer as long as it is as secure and speedy as that specified by the customer.[55] Thirdly, where an intermediary bank must be used, the originator's bank must use reasonable care in engaging a reliable intermediary.[56] The originator bank will be vicariously liable not only for the negligence or default of its own employees and agents but also for any intermediary bank it employs,[57] subject to the contract with the customer.

The originator bank's contractual duty is owed only to the originator, to its customer, or to any other transferor who provides consideration for the transfer but who may not be a regular customer of the bank. But where the originator's bank was an intermediary bank, the correspondent owes no duty in contract to the originator because there is no privity of contract with the originator.[58] However, there may be privity and liability where the originator expressly selected the intermediary bank,[59] and there may also be privity if all banks in the chain of payment are deemed to be agents of one another by analogy with Article 4-201 of the *Uniform Commercial Code* which so provides.[60] Again, the originator bank owes no duty in contract to the beneficiary because there is no privity of contract.

Once the beneficiary's bank receives the payment instruction, it becomes the beneficiary's agent to accept it or otherwise deal with it in accordance with any instructions from the beneficiary. On receipt, the beneficiary's bank immediately borrows the funds from the benefici-

---

52 *Central Coordinates, Inc. v. Morgan Guaranty Trust Co.*, 494 N.Y.S.2d 602 (Sup. Ct. 1985).
53 *Mellon Bank v. Securities Settlement Corp.*, 710 F. Supp. 991 (N.J. 1989).
54 *Royal Products*, above note 50.
55 *Dovey v. Bank of New Zealand*, [2000] 3 N.Z.L.R. 641 (C.A.).
56 *Royal Products*, above note 50.
57 *Ibid.*
58 *Calico Printers Association v. Barclays Bank Ltd.* (1931), 36 Com. Cas. 197 (C.A.); *Royal Products, ibid.*
59 *Evra Corporation v. Swiss Bank Corp.*, 522 F. Supp. 820 (1981), rev'd on another ground, 673 F.2d 951 (7th Cir. 1982).
60 *Ibid.*

ary, thereby restoring the debtor and creditor relationship. Authority to accept funds is deemed to have been given by the beneficiary when the beneficiary supplied the originator with the account details.[61] The beneficiary's bank owes the beneficiary contractual and tortious duties of skill and care in receiving the funds transferred but owes no legal duties to the originator, because it has no privity of contract with the originator. Although there is no case law, it may owe a duty in tort to the originator on the basis that its obligation to the beneficiary is intended to benefit the originator.[62]

The time when payment is final in an electronic funds transfer is as difficult to ascertain as it is with a paper payment transfer. The issue is complicated by virtue of the various different types of electronic transfers, the number of parties involved especially in international funds transfers, the provisions in clearing and settlement rules, and the variety of fact situations that are likely to occur. Most authorities[63] are agreed, however, that there are six possible points in time at which payment may be regarded as completed: (i) when the originator's instruction is transmitted by the originator's bank; (ii) when the instruction reaches the beneficiary's bank or its agent; (iii) when the beneficiary's bank starts its internal clearing procedures; (iv) when the beneficiary's account is credited; (v) when the beneficiary is notified that the account has been credited; or (vi) when the beneficiary agrees, expressly or impliedly, to receive the amount awarded. The cases are further agreed to fall into two broad categories: (i) cases where countermand of a payment order has been attempted and (ii) cases of payment completion prior to a specified deadline.

The general principles of countermand[64] require that the originator's bank act upon a countermand of a payment instruction by an originator as soon as possible, and the courts have followed that paper-based rule when dealing with countermand in an electronic environment. Thus, where an originator has countermanded a payment instruction, the courts have determined that the original payment instruction cannot be countermanded once the beneficiary's bank has accepted payment either by returning an acceptance message or by acting on the payment order in some way, for example, by debiting an account of the origin-

---

61 *Royal Products*, above note 50.
62 By analogy with *Henderson v. Merrett Syndicates Ltd.*, [1995] 2 A.C. 145 (H.L.); *White v. Jones*, [1995] 2 A.C. 207 (H.L.); *Williams v. Natural Life Health Foods Ltd.*, [1998] 2 All E.R. 577 (H.L.).
63 See, for example: Ellinger *et al.*, above note 23 at 514 and at 514–25 for the following analysis.
64 Chapter 8, Section C(5).

ator bank held at the beneficiary's bank or crediting the beneficiary's account.[65] Once the funds have been made available to the beneficiary, the payment is irrevocable and countermand is impossible.

In cases where payments are required to be made by a specified time, such as contracts where time is of the essence or where a forfeiture clause may be invalid if payment is not made by a stipulated time, the principle appears to be that a payment made beyond the contractual deadline is not on time if the payee does not have an unconditional right to use the funds, that is, to treat them as cash.[66] How that point in time is identified by the law is less certain, that is, the time when a payment may be treated as cash. In *The Laconia*,[67] where the beneficiary's bank was advised of a transfer of a late payment just before receiving instructions from the beneficiary to refuse it, the House of Lords found that no irrevocable payment had been made because the transfer was never completed, since the beneficiary's bank had not made a decision to accept payment. In *TSB Bank of Scotland plc v. Welwyn Hatfield District Council*,[68] the court decided that retention of the money for three weeks, use of the money, and eventual return without interest amounted to acceptance by the beneficiary and therefore to irrevocable payment. On the other hand, in *HMV Fields Properties Ltd. v. Bracken Self Selection Fabrics Ltd.*,[69] when a tenant continued to pay rent although given a notice to vacate, the court found that the landlord's return of the rent after several weeks was permissible because there had been no acceptance and no knowledge of the payment by the beneficiary. Finally, in *The Chikuma*,[70] the House of Lords suggested that the beneficiary had not received unconditional payment of the funds until interest had started to accrue on them in his account.

The net result of these cases seems to be that determining the precise time when payment is irrevocable in the sense of being cash at the free disposal of the beneficiary is dependent on the facts of the case, including such factors as the beneficiary's knowledge of receipt of the funds, the retention time period for the funds, the accrual of interest, and the beneficiary's response on learning of the transmission of pay-

---

65 *Momm v. Barclays Bank International Ltd.*, [1977] Q.B. 790; *Delbrueck & Co. v. Manufacturers Hanover Trust Co.*, 609 F.2d 1047 (2d Cir. 1979); *Royal Products*, above note 50; *Libyan Arab Foreign Bank v. Manufacturers' Hanover Trust Co. (No. 2)*, [1989] 1 Lloyd's Rep. 608 (Q.B.).
66 *The Brimnes*, [1975] Q.B. 929 (C.A.).
67 [1977] A.C. 850 (H.L.).
68 [1993] 2 Bank. L.R. 267 (Ch. D.).
69 1991 S.L.T. 31.
70 [1981] 1 W.L.R. 314 (H.L.).

ment after the stipulated time for payment. One point is clear insofar as the courts treat the two categories of cases, attempted countermand and late payment, differently. In the former, no countermand is possible once the beneficiary's bank has agreed to accept payment for the beneficiary, but in the latter, irrevocable payment is determined by the facts on a case-by-case basis. In neither situation, however, is it possible to state in law precisely when the point of irrevocability has been reached.

A final issue that has been considered by the courts in relation to electronic funds transfer is that of recovery of funds paid by mistake. There appears to be no reason why the ordinary principles relating to recovery of funds paid by mistake should not apply equally to electronic as to paper transfers.[71] Thus, the originator's bank is required to follow the originator's instruction precisely when transmitting funds to the beneficiary's account, and when an error occurs and there is no unjust enrichment because there was no indebtedness to be discharged, the originator's bank is required to direct payment to the beneficiary and may be liable to the originator, its customer, for any damage resulting from the mistaken payment.[72] The presence of an exemption clause in the bank and customer agreement will not exonerate the bank that transfers funds erroneously.[73]

It would appear that courts regard the tracing of funds paid electronically by mistake as difficult. In *Agip (Africa) Ltd. v. Jackson*,[74] an employee fraudulently altered the name of the beneficiary in a money-laundering scheme, with the result that the funds were electronically transmitted away to parties unknown by the time the fraud was discovered. The English Court of Appeal held that the employer's common law action for money had and received failed because it was impossible to trace into a mixed fund at common law. The court thought the fact that the payment medium was electronic rather than paper was irrelevant.

---

71 Chapter 8, Section C(6).
72 *Royal Bank of Canada v. Stangl*, [1992] O.J. No. 378, 32 A.C.W.S. (3d) 17 (Gen. Div.). See also Benjamin Geva, "Ambiguous Wire Transactions: *Royal Bank of Canada v. Stangl*" (1995) 24 Can Bus. L.J. 435.
73 *Clansmen Resources Ltd. v. Toronto-Dominion Bank* (1990), 47 B.L.R. 54 (B.C.C.A.).
74 [1991] Ch. 547 (C.A.).

I. CONCLUSION

This chapter has described the arterial systems by which funds are electronically transmitted within Canada and around the world. To date, the rules governing these systems are set out by their own organizations, and there has been very little case law. How much case law there will be in the future will depend on how willing financial institutions are to unwind electronic transactions that have gone wrong as well as providing customer support in initiating electronic transactions so that customers understand the rules by which they are to use these systems. The next chapter is concerned with describing the various means by which customers access the electronic clearing and settlement systems in their everyday banking transactions.

CHAPTER 10

ELECTRONIC PAYMENTS

A. INTRODUCTION

From a customer's perspective, the evolution of payment methods offered by banks over the past decade as a result of technological advances has been dramatic, especially in comparison to the slow evolution of paper payment methods over the previous three hundred years. Until the early 1990s most transactions were in cash, by cheque, or by other negotiable instrument. However, since the late 1990s, most transactions have been executed electronically by use of various plastic payment cards whose original differentiated functions have now been reduced to one card, the debit card, or in some instances, the credit card or the credit card with debit card characteristics. While customers still use cash, cheques, and credit cards where appropriate for their purposes, the debit card is now used for ordinary banking transactions at ABMs operated by their own bank or as part of a network to which their bank belongs, for retail purchases at point of sale (POS), and also sometimes for some third party payment provider transactions that may or may not clear through the ACSS.

Chapter 9 described the payment systems over which payment transactions are carried out, but this chapter will describe the mechanisms by which customers may access those payment systems in order to make payments to other parties. At the outset, it is important to remember that a plastic card serves the same purpose as an oral instruction or a written cheque, that is, it is a means by which a customer gives a mandate to its bank to pay funds from the customer's account to another person, the payee of those funds. The card, together with other means of identification, such as the personal identification number (PIN), serves to authenticate the customer much as a signature on a cheque, although unlike a cheque on which the particulars of the mandate are written, the particulars must still be provided by the customer on a device provided by the banking network once the customer is authenticated in an electronic transaction.

This chapter will briefly survey the evolution of plastic payment cards prior to the virtually all-purpose debit card in use today and then examine the practice and law of debit card transactions. Further consideration will also be given to the rapidly developing third party payment systems (3PPS), involving both the financial institutions and private 3PPS providers, some of which operate over ACSS in whole or in part and some of which operate openly over the Internet, completely outside ACSS.

Credit card transactions will be discussed in the next chapter (Chapter 11), together with other payment mechanisms offered by banks to their customers, such as travellers' cheques and money orders. Credit cards operate outside the CPA payment network, although the others clear within it as negotiable instruments. The payment methods discussed in this chapter are those used daily by customers, while those discussed in the next chapter are those used from time to time for special transactions by customers.

B. THE EVOLUTION OF PLASTIC CARDS

Although debit card transactions involve immediate payment, rather than the extension of credit for a limited period of time, the use of plastic tokens to initiate payment transactions began with tokens used in the context of credit, rather than immediate payment. The earliest such tokens, usually in the form of a coin, originated in American retail stores prior to World War I as a means of identifying customers to whom those stores extended credit. They could be used only in the stores that issued them and that anticipated repayment on a regular, normally monthly, revolving credit basis. Retail-issued cards[1] remain as one category of plastic card now in widespread use by retail stores and gas companies, and they continue to be distinguished from bank-

---

1   For example, the Bay card, Sears card, and the Esso card.

issued cards in two legally significant ways: (i) they are bipartite cards in that the cardissuer and merchant are identical, so that two parties only are involved, the customer and the issuer; and (ii) credit is extended on a revolving credit basis, sometimes with no credit limit, provided minimum monthly instalments are made.

The second type of card to emerge, in the 1950s, was the so-called travel and entertainment card,[2] which is a tripartite card system involving the cardissuer, a private company, the merchant, and the cardholder. Sometimes called a "charge card," this card operated like a credit card prior to the introduction of the credit card, since it involves three separate contractual relationships: cardissuer-cardholder, cardissuer-merchant, and cardholder-merchant. Originally these cards required the cardholder to repay the entire monthly balance or to lose the privilege of holding a card, but some charge cards are now indistinguishable from credit cards because they offer a line of credit that can be maintained, provided a minimum monthly payment is made. Today, these cards are distinguished from credit cards by virtue of being made available to higher-net-worth individuals than credit cards, and they are therefore associated with higher social status. They are no longer legally distinctive.

The third plastic card to develop was the cheque guarantee card. Introduced in the United Kingdom in the mid-1960s, it was briefly marketed by several Canadian banks in the mid-1970s but was discontinued and is not used in Canada today. Its use continues in the U.K., although this appears to be waning there as well. A cheque guarantee card is a plastic card issued by a bank for use in conjunction with cheques. In *Re Charge Card Services Ltd.*,[3] Millett J. described the card as creating an obligation by the bank to the payee of the cheque that the cheque would be honoured up to the value embossed on the cheque guarantee card. Typically used in a retail store by showing the merchant the card, the drawer is essentially representing to the payee that the drawer has actual authority from the bank to make a contract with the merchant on the bank's behalf as an agent of the bank.[4] The phrase "cheque guarantee card" is a misnomer because in law, by giving such a card to a customer to use, the bank is essentially making itself liable to the merchant directly for the value of the cheque up to the limit of the card.[5]

---

2   For example, American Express, Diners Club.
3   [1986] 3 All E.R. 289 at 301 (Ch. D.).
4   See also *Commissioner of Police for the Metropolis v. Charles*, [1977] A.C. 177 (H.L.) and *R. v. Kassim*, [1991] 3 All E.R. 713 (H.L.).
5   *First Sport Ltd. v. Barclays Bank plc*, [1993] 3 All E.R. 789 at 795 (C.A.), Evans L.J.

Essentially, four legal relationships are involved in the use of a cheque guarantee card: (i) the contract of sale between the retailer and the customer; (ii) the bill of exchange (cheque) between the drawer/customer and the retailer/payee; (iii) the bank and customer contract; and (iv) the contract between the customer's bank and the retailer that the cheque will be honoured.[6] In *First Sport Ltd. v. Barclays Bank plc*,[7] the English Court of Appeal found that fourth contract to be a unilateral contract, which was required to be honoured by the bank when both chequebook and cheque guarantee card were stolen and used by a rogue.

It seems unlikely that cheque guarantee cards will ever be reintroduced in Canada for two reasons. First, in Canadian banking practice, the certified cheque is regarded as the usual means of guaranteeing cheque payment by a bank, and secondly, the preponderance of debit and credit card use suggests the time is past for the cheque guarantee card. The comparative ease with which it has been possible for a customer in Canada to obtain a credit card in contrast to British bank customers has resulted in earlier widespread use of the credit card, where in the U.K. cheques would have been used.

The fourth distinctive card is the credit card,[8] which started to come into widespread use in the 1960s.[9] The distinctive feature is, of course, the line of credit offered by the card, which is maintained provided a minimum monthly amount is repaid. The credit card is a tripartite card involving three parties, the cardissuer, the cardholder, and the merchant, and three separate contracts: (i) between cardissuer and cardholder, (ii) between cardissuer and merchant; and (iii) between cardholder and merchant. This card quickly proved much more attractive than the predecessor cards for several reasons: the line of credit from which the card gets its name; the worldwide adoption of the card as most merchants, large and small, joined the proprietary card networks so that cardholders may use their cards to make purchases of goods and services almost everywhere; and the relative ease of obtaining a card and maintaining one by paying the minimum monthly amount required.

The credit card was the first plastic card to require computerized technology for its use, but the subsequent cards in widespread use today not only offer electronic access but also clear and settle within the CPAs settlement system, and so could be said to be the truest examples

---

6   *Ibid.* at 798, Sir Thomas Bingham M.R.
7   *Ibid.*
8   For example, Visa, MasterCard.
9   See Chapter 11.

of access cards to contemporary electronic funds transfer. The first of these was the ABM card, or "cash card," which was used to obtain access to the customer's bank account by means of an automated banking machine (ABM). Originally, ABM cards could be used only at ABMs of the customer's own bank, but subsequently they could be used at any ABM in the Interac network, as well as at some networks outside Canada, such as Cirrus or Plus. While the customer can engage in many of the usual banking transactions at the customer's own bank network, typically, only cash can be obtained at another financial institution's ABM in the Interac network. Access is normally obtained by presenting the card to the ABM and the customer typing in a PIN on the keyboard at the ABM terminal.

The single-purpose ABM card has now largely given way to the all-purpose debit card, which operates in the same manner: by presentation of the card to the ABM terminal, together with a PIN. The debit card may be used not only in the same networks as the ABM card for ordinary banking transactions or for cash, but also for POS transactions on retail premises for the purchase of goods or services. In contrast to the credit card, the debit card offers no line of credit; rather, it is a device by which access is gained to electronic transfer systems, whereby value can be transferred from the account of the cardholder to the account of the person to whom the cardholder wishes to make payment by the transmission of electronic messages. The debit card itself contains no value and is merely an access device; therefore, it is distinguishable from electronic money, which is economic value stored in a digital form in a microprocessor or microchip and loaded onto a "smart card," also known as an "electronic purse" or a "digital cash card."

The smart card is programmed with a stipulated value by the cardissuer from an account or purchased by cash, and the cardholder may present the card to a retailer for the purchase of goods or services when the retailer's smart card terminal reads the value of the purchase from the card and transfers that value to the retailer's account. The card may be reloaded with value infinitely. Despite successful trials of the smart card on limited bases in Canada, it has not yet been introduced, nor has it been so in the United States. By contrast, it has been used in the European Union since the 1980s.[10]

Each of these plastic cards and the banking services they access are governed by their own contract, separate and distinct from the account agreement, although some account agreements will also incorporate

---

10 For a more detailed discussion of electronic money, see Section D, below in this chapter.

terms relating to the debit card, which is typically issued as a matter of course when an account agreement is signed today. Like all other bank contracts, account agreements are standard form agreements, that is, contracts of adhesion, and not subject to negotiation. In the absence of case law to date, it is reasonable to assume that the courts will treat them like any other contract of adhesion and subject them to strict construction and the *contra proferentem* rule in favour of the customer.

Of these cards, only two are currently in use by customers in everyday banking in Canada: the credit card and the debit card. A third, the smart card, may still come into widespread use in Canada in the future. The others are no longer in use (the cheque guarantee card and the ABM card) or are not directly linked to financial institutions (the travel and entertainment cards), other than in the sense that funds deposited with financial institutions may be used to pay down any balance owing on such cards. The debit card will be discussed in the next section, and the smart card will be discussed later in this chapter, while the credit card will be discussed in the next chapter.

C. DEBIT CARDS

Debit card operation in Canada is subject to voluntary industry codes of practice and to contract, but it is completely unregulated by legislation and unsupervised by any government department, agency, or corporation. The larger framework is found in the operating procedures of Interac Association, ACSS Rule E1 of the CPA in relation to clearing and settlement, and the Canadian Code of Practice for Consumer Debit Card Services, a voluntary industry code drafted by the Canadian Bankers Association, to which all the banks subscribe.[11] While the ACSS Rules and the Debit Card Code are publicly available, the Interac operating rules are proprietary and secret.[12] The other component, of contract, is found in the bank and customer contract regulating debit card use, as well as in the multilateral contracts that the bank has in relation to the CPA and Interac.

The Interac Association was formed in November 1984 by the larger banks as a private corporation whose purpose is to own and oper-

---

11 For the Debit Card Code, see www.cba.ca.
12 See www.interac.ca. See also Muharem Kianieff, "Looking for Cover: A Public Choice Critique of the Canadian Debit Card Code" (2005–06) 37 Ottawa L. Rev. 101.

ate a national network of ABMs.[13] The charter members were the direct clearers, who were members of the CPA and who invested in Interac and were directly connected to the shared services network. The original restricted nature of access to Interac for other banks and financial institutions prompted the Director of Investigation and Research in the Competition Bureau to complain to the Competition Tribunal on the ground of abuse of a dominant position in the supply of consumer-initiated electronic financial transfers on behalf of other financial institutions. The matter was resolved by a Consent Order on 20 June 1996, whereby Interac agreed to open access to other financial institutions and non-financial institutions to participate in the Interac network by performing functions such as acquiring or providing network connection and related data processing services to members.[14]

Interac specifies the standards for the functions, operation, and security of its network, and member institutions are responsible for acquiring or developing interface software and equipment that meet these standards. Member communication networks are linked to Interac by a gateway device, and Interac provides an online system of verification and authorization and links to ACSS for clearing and settlement in accordance with standards set by the CPA in Rule E1.

When a customer pays for goods or services at a POS with a debit card, the merchant first ascertains the price and prepares a message with the transaction details, including price, date, and time of the transaction, along with identifying information about the merchant, the customer, and the transaction. To pay, the customer slides the debit card through an Interac payment terminal, adds his unique PIN, and approves the transaction, designating the bank account from which funds are to be withdrawn. The PIN does not appear on the keyboard screen nor on the paper transaction record, to ensure its complete confidentiality. The customer information is immediately encrypted and is not stored in the transaction terminal. The PIN pad offers an opportunity to correct a mistake or cancel a transaction at any time prior to the receipt of authorization of the transaction.

Once the transaction message is encrypted, it is transmitted over a dedicated network provided by Interac to the customer's bank, which must be a CPA member, where the card, PIN, and account are con-

---

13 For the history of Interac, see the articles by John C. Pattison, Alison R. Manzer, Shameela Chinoy, & Benjamin Geva in Queens Business Law Symposium, *The Regulation of Financial Institutions: Issues and Perspectives* (Scarborough, ON: Carswell, 1997).
14 Chinoy and Geva, *ibid.* at 426–30.

firmed, as well as the availability of funds in the account. The bank immediately either authorizes or refuses the transaction in real time by a return message over the same network and directs the transfer of funds from the customer's account to the retailer's account through the ACSS. The POS item is not a payment; rather, it authorizes the payment through the clearing and settlement system. If the transaction is authorized, the customer will receive a record of the transaction, which may be used to check the monthly statement of transactions in the account provided by the bank.

At the end of the day, the acquirer, that is, the person who owns and operates the Interac terminal, prepares a computer tape of all the claims against each account holder bank to aggregate all of the account holder's transactions that day and then delivers the tape to a regional exchange centre for the account holder, as well as entering it into the ACSS. The ACSS calculates the net settlement amounts as between direct clearers, and these are added to the other net settlement amounts for clearing and settlement in the ACSS by about 11:00 a.m. on the next settlement day.

The Debit Card Code, to which all the banks and other financial institutions voluntarily subscribe, has been in use since 1992 and amended since. Essentially, its purpose is to suggest the type, nature, and content of terms in the bank and customer agreement relating to debit card conditions, and most agreements also incorporate the Code by reference in a term in that agreement.[15] The Code prescribes terms about periodic statements, dispute resolution, fee and service charge costs disclosure, PIN and card security, responsibility for unauthorized use, plain language, termination, as well as prescribing that the customer be given a copy of the agreement.

The cardholder agreements in general use reflect the Debit Card Code suggestions and are similar across the financial institutions sector. They constitute one of the five contractual relationships that regulate a debit card transaction at POS: (i) the bank and customer/cardholder agreement; (ii) the bank and merchant agreement; (iii) the merchant and cardholder contract for the sale of goods and services; (iv) the Interac Association multilateral contract among all Interac members; and (v) the CPA multilateral contract among all members of the CPA.

A typical bank and cardholder agreement contains the following provisions: (i) a provision for a customer-selected PIN when the card is first used; (ii) a duty on the customer to protect the card and PIN

---

15 Benjamin Geva, "Canadian Code of Practice for Consumer Debit Card Services" (1993) 4 J.B.F.L.P. 78.

safely and personal liability for all transactions by use of the card and PIN; (iii) a duty on the customer to notify the bank immediately of theft or misuse of the card and PIN; (iv) possible monetary limits for the use of electronic banking services; (v) bank liability for unauthorized transactions after being notified of card theft or PIN security breach, transactions on forged, faulty, expired, or cancelled cards, losses from fraudulent or negligent conduct of employees, agents, merchants, or companies involved in networking arrangements; (vi) service charge disclosure by the bank; (vii) a duty on the customer to ensure the accuracy of electronic payment instructions and to know the different billers' payment requirements; (viii) an account verification clause; (ix) an undertaking by the bank to provide ABM and POS terminal transaction records; (x) the right of both bank and customer to terminate the agreement; (xi) the right of the bank to change the terms of the agreement by written or electronic notice or notices posted in the branch; (xii) the exclusion of liability by the bank for loss or damage resulting from any malfunction or failure of the electronic banking service; (xiii) privacy protection undertakings by the bank; and (xiv) dispute resolution information and contacts.

The bank and merchant contract is also a standard form contract containing clauses limiting or waiving bank liability for disputes with customers about the underlying sales transaction and about personnel or systems failures or malfunctions, as well as providing for merchant liability for aspects of the POS transaction that may fall under merchant control and requiring merchant account verification within a stipulated time period. In particular relation to customers at POS, the merchant expressly agrees not to discriminate as to price, service, or any other aspects of the sale of goods or services in accepting the card and to operate the POS transaction so as to enter the transaction details accurately into the terminal to create the message, assist cardholders to ensure they can validate the request for authorization, obey the instructions transmitted by the network to either honour or not honour the card as instructed, and provide a copy of the transaction record to the customer. The merchant is prohibited from asking the customer to reveal the PIN and from using the Interac terminals for anything other than POS transactions, and is required to report errors or losses and to take lost or forgotten cards into custody until they can be returned to the customer.

To date there has been virtually no jurisprudence on debit cards. As stated above, it is clear that the courts will resolve disputes by first considering any applicable contract terms against the background of the law of contract, including the probable application of the *contra proferentem* rule and of doctrines such as unconscionability, unreasonableness, unequal bargaining power, and misrepresentation.[16] Some legal principles relating to their use may be discussed, however, from the little emerging law there is to date.

Banks typically issue debit cards to any person who opens an account, and section 437(1) of the *Bank Act* probably permits that practice. Section 437(1) provides that a bank may without the intervention of any other person accept a deposit from any person whether or not the person is qualified by law to enter into contracts. Since deposit acceptance implies the right of a customer to instruct the bank to make payments from those deposited funds and since a debit card is simply a device used to initiate a payment instruction, it is self-evident that persons who may not have legal capacity, such as minors, have an implicit statutory right to a debit card on opening an account. This should be distinguished from right to a credit card on the ground that there is no extension of credit by virtue of opening an account, and there is no statutory right for a bank customer to be given a credit card and certainly no right in law where customer creditworthiness is not present.

The enforceability of a debit card agreement as a matter of contract was raised in *Royal Bank of Canada v. Holoboff*[17] but not resolved. In that case, a minor "sold" his debit card and PIN to another high school student, who used them to make several "empty envelope" deposits over a holiday weekend and to withdraw phantom funds of about $5,000.00. The purchaser was convicted of fraud, and the bank sued its customer for restitution of the funds, framing its argument in breach of the debit card contract, as well as in the tort of conspiracy. No finding was made on the contract issue, although it was clear that the minor was in breach of several significant clauses in the contract, but the bank succeeded in tort. Although it was argued that the contract was unenforceable against the minor, the court did not adjudicate on its contractual enforceability. Yet it is clear that it could have been enforced under section 437(1) once it is realized that a debit card, like a cheque or another written instrument, is simply a means for issuing instructions to the bank in the ordinary course of bank account operation.

The question of liability for unauthorized use has arisen in the context of a number of criminal law cases, especially involving theft of a card and PIN, which customers are required by contract to keep separate, a counsel of perfection given the number of pass codes the average person is obliged to use today. Although both the Debit Card Code and the bank-cardholder agreement posit liability on the cardholder,

---

16 Chapter 6, Section H.
17 [1998] 10 W.W.R. 755 (Alta. Q.B.).

the cases suggest that there may be no cardholder liability in certain circumstances, such as kidnapping the cardholder and using threats of violence to procure an ABM withdrawal;[18] tying up the cardholder and threatening her daughter with a knife to get the PIN;[19] murdering the cardholder and using the card and PIN to get funds;[20] and theft by a trusted nanny to withdraw funds.[21] In such extreme circumstances, it is difficult to characterize the cardholder's conduct as negligence within the cardholder liability clause of the contract, and the bank is expected to assume the loss.

On the other hand, where the cardholder's conduct contributes to the unauthorized use, the cardholder will be liable, for example, by lending the card and PIN (even to a family member), by leaving the card and PIN in an insecure place at work, or by keeping the card and pin in an easily accessible pocket in the cardholder's clothing. In *Royal Bank of Canada v. Devarenne*,[22] the cardholder was liable by strict enforecement of the contract, where a thief stole his card and PIN, together with his wallet, while on a fishing trip. In *Couture v. Caisse Populaire de Bathurst Ltée*,[23] a cardholder who took two months to report the loss of his wallet containing his card and PIN on a separate slip of paper was liable for the loss in his account,[24] and in *Toronto-Dominion Bank v. Charles*,[25] the cardholder was liable for a two-day delay in reporting for loss in his account. These cases were decided as a simple matter of contract construction.

Where there is a dispute between the cardholder and the merchant about the sales contract for goods or services for which payment was made by debit card, it is clear that that dispute is to be resolved independently of the payment mechanism. Thus, payment by debit card should be no different from payment by credit card or in cash: the payment is final, although damages may be available once the underlying contractual dispute is resolved. Indeed, it is likely the case that payment by debit card is final once authorization is given in the course of the POS payment transaction. An authorization cannot be revoked pursuant to the CPA rules, and there is no obvious reason why a court

---

18 *R. v. B.(K.S.)* (1996), 126 W.A.C. 316 (B.C.C.A.).
19 *R. v. Forsyth* (1995), 30 W.C.B. (2d) 76 (Ont. Ct. Gen. Div.); (1997), 35 W.C.B. (2d) 307 (Ont. Ct. Gen. Div.).
20 *R. v. Linhart* (1989), 9 W.C.B. (2d) 246 (Ont. H.C.J.).
21 *R. v. Lariviere* (1996), 31 W.C.B. (2d) 279 (Man. Prov. Ct.).
22 (1998), 205 N.B.R. (2d) 250 (Q.B.).
23 (1996), 181 N.B.R. (2d) 161 (Q.B.).
24 *Ibid.*
25 (1998), 82 A.C.W.S. (3d) 521 (Ont. Ct. Gen. Div.).

should not accept that rule by analogy between cardholder and merchant. The Clearing By-Law confirms that POS items are to be treated as far as applicable in the same way as paper items, and this would confirm their irreversability in the ordinary course. The only exception would be the insolvency of the paying bank when all transactions are unwound under the ACSS Rules.

One final question that has arisen in the case law is whether giving a debit card to another can be a good *donatio causa mortis*, as is the case where a bankbook has been given in the past. In *Lamb v. Smith Estate*,[26] the court found that handing over part of a debit card without the PIN was insufficient evidence of an intention to make an irrevocable gift. The court regarded the gift to be the funds in the account, a chose in action, not a piece of plastic that could not be used to access those funds.

D. ELECTRONIC MONEY

Electronic money (emoney) is transferrable economic value which is stored in a microprocessor (microchip) embedded in a smart or digital card, or in a digital format in a computer file.[27] When stored in a smart card, emoney is distinguishable from a credit card in that it carries no line of credit and from a debit card in that it is not an access device to a payment system but another means of payment in itself. The EC Directive 2000/46, recital 3, describes emoney as an electronic surrogate for cash stored in a card or computer memory to provide an alternative means of payment to cash.[28] Payment is made by transferring digital information from the payer to the payee, so that value is immediately transferred on delivery of the information.

Commonly accepted definitions of emoney distinguish the two variations stated above of value stored either in a plastic card or in a computer file, which can be transferred over the Internet.[29] The plastic smart card was marketed earlier than the computer-file variation, al-

---

26 (1995), 132 Nfld. & P.E.I.R. 316. 9 E.T.R. (2d) 127 (Nfld. S.C.).
27 Bradley Crawford, *Payment, Clearing and Settlement in Canada*, vol. 1 (Aurora, ON: Canada Law Book, 2002) at 35.
28 [2000] OJ L275 at 39.
29 Crawford, above note 27 and Mark Hapgood, ed., *Paget on Banking*, 12th ed. (London: Butterworths, 2003) at 326–27.

though in North America, it has not been implemented to date and may well be overtaken by third party payment systems over the Internet.[30]

A smart card[31] is a plastic card containing a microchip, rather than a magnetic stripe, that is capable of storing words or information, or a digital snapshot of a fingerprint, palm print, or retinal scan. The monetary value stored in the chip is the "electronic purse" or "wallet," and the customer fills or loads the purse with "electronic cash" at a bank, at an ABM, or via a computer link with their bank, including by cell phone. The card may be used to make a purchase by inserting it into a terminal at a POS or some other device such as a vending machine or parking meter, and the terminal reads the information stored on the chip to ensure that the card is genuine and then deducts the amount of the transaction from the value stored in the card. Security is ensured by cryptographic algorithms, which perform various security functions, and the private part of the digital signature key does not leave the card, while the public part of the digital signature key is used to authenticate and use the card. This is done on the card itself and is not seen by the host reader's memory, so it is secure and it is also impossible to tamper with the card or destroy the chip. It is also possible to detect attempts at physical or electronic tampering. The merchant transmits a full record of the daily transactions to the bank electronically or on tapes; the account is credited and the information passed on by the bank into the clearing and settlement system.

The attractions of the smart card are its security insofar as there are no communication links in its use once it is loaded with value; the availability to anyone who can purchase the stored value by cash or cleared funds in a bank account so that no creditworthiness issues arise; the absence of requirements to remember and manually enter passwords; the anonymity at POS for the cardholder; and the convenience of conducting countless small or large transactions with one simple plastic card. On the other hand, theft or loss of the card will deprive the cardholder of the stored value, which may be spent before the cardholder becomes aware of the theft or loss.

Internationally, there are two major smart card systems in operation, Visa Cash and Mondex, and numerous others which operate on

---

30 See Section F, below in this chapter.
31 See generally Shameela Chinoy, "Electronic Money in Electronic Purses and Wallets" (1996) 12 B.F.L.R. 15; Bradley Crawford, "Is Electronic Money Really Money?" (1997) 12 B.F.L.R. 399; Muharem Kianieff, "Show Me the Money! A Critical Evaluation of Laissez-Faire Internet Currencies" (2002) 17 B.F.L.R. 215; Bradley Crawford, "New Methods of Payment and New Forms of Money" (2005) 20 B.F.L.R. 393.

a national basis.[32] Visa Cash operates as an "open" electronic money system, which means that there are multiple card issuers, acquirers, and retailers, and funds clearing and settlement is required. By contrast, a closed system is one in which cards can only be used to buy goods and services offered by the card issuer and there is no transfer of funds between financial institutions. Good examples of closed systems are those operating within enclosed communities such as universities, where a community member purchases a card and loads it with value at a dispenser operated by the institution and uses it at that institution only. The cards issued by Visa Cash are either disposable or multifunctional, being combined with a credit and/or debit card and reloadable from an ABM or a special-purpose machine. Reloading by personal computer or cell phone is being implemented. Value can be transferred only to merchants and not to other cardholders. Visa clears and settles transactions through its own settlement system.

Mondex was developed in the United Kingdom in the mid-1990s by National Westminster Bank, Midland Bank, and British Telecom, but since 1997, it is 51 percent owned by MasterCard. It is also an open stored-value card, and value is loaded at an ABM or a special-purpose machine. Value can be transferred from card to card, so it is possible to transfer value from person to person, as well as to participating merchants. Merchants who receive value from a customer can transfer that to a third party, such as a supplier or creditor, without the intermediation of a bank and provided the transferees are participants in the Mondex network. Mondex was the first network to develop the transfer of economic value by telephone and it is also possible to store value in several different currencies in the same card.

Mondex is designed to operate within the banking system. Franchisee banks in each country are required to identify a single "originator," which may be the central bank or a commercial bank whose function is to fulfill the role of a central bank for electronic money. The electronic money issued by the originator is a claim on it for real value. The originator distributes electronic money to the participating banks, and they pay for this by transferring an equivalent amount of real funds to the originator, which holds it as a float of real value behind the electronic money issued. The participating banks then issue the electronic money in Mondex cards to customers, who use them at participating merchants to purchase goods and services. Merchants may either transfer that value to other Mondex participants or deposit it in their bank

---

32 See Chinoy, *ibid*, for a list of the many others at 28–30.

accounts, and the transfer of value is cleared through the usual clearing and settlement system used by the participating banks.

Although a Mondex cardholder enjoys anonymity and privacy in relation to the merchant to whom value is transferred, Mondex does keep a record of transactions, both successful and unsuccessful, and each Mondex transaction has a unique number. Thus, a full audit trail exists in respect of each Mondex card in use, and there is no absolute privacy for the cardholder. Reported lost or stolen cards can be "locked out" or retained by a terminal when there is an attempt made to use or reload them.

Although Mondex cards have been introduced on trial bases in a number of countries around the world, they have not been widely adopted, and in Canada, Mondex is no longer in use after a decision in 1999 by the Canadian franchise not to proceed beyond limited trials in several medium-sized Canadian cities.[33] Canadians travelling abroad may encounter the network; however, it seems unlikely that Mondex will become widespread because it is being overtaken by other technology and newer payment methods. There appears to be a lack of consumer interest in, and acceptance of, both forms of emoney, smart cards and computer-based value transfer over the Internet, as newer payment services are being offered.[34]

When it seemed in the late 1990s that the smart card would come into widespread use, there was a flurry of legal analyses of the smart card, expressing significant concerns about its legal nature, its regulation and impact on national economies, and the very future of banks. With the apparent demise of the smart card in the face of a rapidly changing payment environment, those concerns seem less urgent. However, it is useful to list them briefly because of their legal interest, as well as their potential application to other payment mechanisms recently introduced.[35]

The first concern is whether electronic money is really money.[36] This concern is based on some understanding of electronic money as "new" money, rather than as a new method of using "old" money as the real value behind the method of transferring that value. Since central banks continue to control the supply of money and to supervise the monetary policy of most countries, this concern seems wrongheaded. It would become a concern only if a smart card scheme purported to

---

33   Guelph, Kingston, and Sherbrooke.
34   See Section F, below in this chapter.
35   Above note 31.
36   Crawford, *ibid.* and above note 27 at c. 3 frets unnecessarily about this.

create "new" money on its own, and none has ever even contemplated doing so. If one did, it would likely be faced with the universal wrath and power of the world's central banks and the Bank for International Settlements (BIS). While electronic money may not satisfy the traditional legal definitions of money,[37] those definitions will likely change over time to reflect the new payment mechanisms while complying with the role of central banks in controlling the money supply. "Money" in "electronic money" is simply another means of saying that economic value as commonly understood is being transferred electronically, not created *de novo* electronically.

A second concern is the proper legal characterization of electronic money, since it is clearly not cash or a cheque.[38] It seems clear that the value stored in a card is not within the traditional understandings of a deposit or a security, although it could be if some small adjustments were made to those understandings. However, it is not as clear that good policy should support such adjustments. If the stored value was deemed to be equivalent to a bank account, then CDIC insurance might be required for cards, including lost or stolen cards, which might make supporting such an insurance scheme extremely expensive for the deposit-taking institutions. In any case, CDIC exists to insure against bank failure, not cardholder failure. Again, it is unlikely that electronic money is a security, since it appears to be money in a different payment format and there is no likelihood of earning a profit or return on the value stored.

The legal characterization question also arises in relation to the transfer of stored value.[39] The card cannot be a negotiable instrument because the card is not transferred. Moreover, the value transferred is transferred irrevocably from cardholder to merchant and is not subject to the uncertainties relating to payment associated with a negotiable instrument. Again, the transfer is not an assignment because it is not in writing, signed, or a transfer of the whole interest, nor is the cardholder required to give notice to anyone in relation to the transfer. All that is transferred is the value, so that the better analogy is with cash or money. In short, electronic money is from a legal perspective *sui generis* and should be so regulated.

A third area of concern is regulation in the consumer interest. Electronic money is completely unregulated, and the Debit Card Code applies only to debit cards and not to any other type of card. Regulatory

---

37 Crawford, above note 31 at 400–2 and above note 27 at 37–40.
38 Crawford, above note 31 at 413–17.
39 *Ibid.*, at 417–23.

issues are many: ensuring that electronic money either does not create new money or that the money supply thereby created is centrally regulated to protect the value of the currency; regulation of new, non-bank players in the electronic money field to the same degree that banks are regulated to ensure solvency and safety in the systems; enforceable international standards, since electronic money transfers are international, as well as domestic; provision of supervision and oversight of the possible structural changes to traditional banking and banks to ensure solvency and safety as the digital revolution proceeds; maintaining competition; enacting and enforcing laws against fraud, theft, money laundering, and counterfeiting; providing standards for consumer contracts relating to disclosure, privacy, fair terms, liabilities for misuse, loss or theft of a card, dispute resolution, fees or service charges, exchange rates, and fees for foreign currency transactions, and so on. The underlying question of whether the regulation of electronic money itself is of benefit to consumers or whether the market should be permitted to proceed unregulated is also a matter of dispute.[40]

Electronic money will operate safely and efficiently only if there is confidence that it can ultimately be exchanged for real money, and while other issues such as widespread use and ease of use are important, electronic money must, in the end, be money.[41]

E. PREPAID CARDS

Despite the apparent demise of the smart card in North America at the end of the twentieth century, somewhat similar payment products have appeared since in the form of prepaid cards, some of which connect with the banking system and are loaded with economic value. The earliest were prepaid telephone cards, which appeared in the 1980s, followed by retailer electronic gift cards purchased with the value of the gift in the mid-1990s. These are known as "closed-loop" cards because they can be used only at the retail outlets that sell them and are limited in use to the value of the card. These cards are processed internally, unlike the newer "open-loop" cards, which are branded by a payment card network, such as the prepaid Visa or MasterCard branded cards, which can be redeemed at any retailer that is part of the Visa or Master-

---

40 See Kianieff, above note 31 for an extensive analysis of opposing views.
41 For a more detailed discussion in jurisdictions where emoney is a fact, see Emily Read & Heather Rowe, *E-Finance: Law and Regulation* (London: LexisNexis, 2003) and A.B. Munir, *Internet Banking: Law and Practice* (London: LexisNexis, 2004).

Card network. Some of these cards also permit cash withdrawals from ABMs in those networks, so that the transactions enter the clearing and settlement system with bank involvement.

Most of these stored-value cards use chip technology to store the value and to permit it to be read and transferred at specialized merchant terminals; that value is funded by cash payment or credit card or debit card payment, and some cards are reusable once reloaded with value. In addition to the original gift card, a variety of other purposes are now filled by various card providers, which use neither banks nor other deposit-taking financial institutions as part of the payment process other than to clear and settle. Some examples include: (i) "Taxi Dollars,"[42] used to pay taxi fares; (ii) various transit system fare cards; (iii) "Dexit,"[43] used in Toronto and expected to be rolled out elsewhere to make small purchases or micropayments by means of a prepaid key tag that transfers value via a low-frequency radio signal when held near a merchant terminal followed by electronic transfer of funds from Dexit's account to the merchant's bank account; (iv) "speedpass" (Imperial Oil) and "easy PAY" (Shell Canada Ltd.),[44] used to purchase fuel by means of a card which also uses low-frequency radio signals to transfer value but which accesses the holder's credit card to pay for the purchase; (v) various passes to pay for travel on toll highways, for which low-frequency radio signals are picked up from a transponder in a car to facilitate payment of the toll from a credit card or a bank account; and (vi) payroll cards.

Although not in wide use in Canada at the present time, payroll cards are in widespread use in the United States, where about 60 million people do not have a bank. A payroll card is issued by an employer to an employee for the employee's salary. The employer deposits the funds in a specific bank account, and the employee uses the card to withdraw cash at an ABM or to purchase goods and services at a POS terminal until the account is zero. The account is restocked at the next pay day. There are two methods currently used in relation to these accounts: (i) funds are transferred to an individual bank account for each employee, so that it is deposit insured; or (ii) funds for all employees are commingled in a single employer account, and notional sub-accounts are set up to identify each employee's share, which may not be deposit insured.

---

42 Online: www.taxidollars.com.
43 Online: www.dexit.com.
44 Online: www.imperialoil.ca and www.shellcanada.ca and follow the links.

Payroll cards are under trial at the present time in Canada but may not be as likely to be implemented here for reasons that are largely sociological: (i) the unbanked in Canada probably number about one-half million people because Canadian financial institutions are more likely to provide banking services to lower-income Canadians, especially since the 2001 *Bank Act* amendments; (ii) Canada does not have a high migrant population of seasonal workers nor the highly mobile workforce generally experienced in the United States; and (iii) there are significant legal issues relating to such matters as deposit insurance, funds ownership, counterfeiting cards, and money laundering with these cards, to suggest that implementation will be slow, if it ever happens at all.

Prepaid card and smart card use appears to be likely to evolve in the immediate future as technological advances occur. All such products in present use do not constitute "new money" created outside the supervision of the Bank of Canada, but rather are paid for with real money. These products are simply newer methods of transferring economic value to the sellers of goods and services. Some operate outside the banking system, but most interface with the banking system insofar as bank accounts and credit cards are likely to be involved, so that clearing and settlement ultimately occurs through the ACSS. This is not necessarily the case in respect to the third party payment systems concurrently growing up outside the clearing and settlement systems run by the CPA.

F. THIRD PARTY PAYMENT SYSTEMS (3PPS)

The rapidly changing payments environment since the beginning of the twenty-first century suggests that payment by cards may be overtaken by direct electronic payment in business-to-business, person-to-business, and person-to-person transactions. Moreover, banks and other financial institutions will not necessarily play the intermediation role they have played in the payments chain for the last five to six hundred years. Not only have newer payment means come onto the market, but new, non-financial institutions have done so as well, some in direct competition with the banks; some in cooperation with the banks, which have outsourced their services; and some by piggy-backing onto the banking system as a means of access to the clearing and settlement system.

These new players and payment methods are completely unregulated: no legislation, no case law, no regulations, and no regulators. Regulatory bodies such as OSFI, CDIC and the CPA, as well as the

Department of Finance, and the financial institutions themselves, are aware of the dangers that third party payment systems potentially pose to the safety, security, and efficiency of the existing payment, clearing, and settlement systems in Canada, and they are currently studying and watching the situation closely. This is also true in other countries worldwide with mature banking systems, not only in relation to their own domestic networks, but also in relation to international payment transactions, which computerization facilitates.

Given how recent and fast changing the situation is, it is impossible to describe in other than a fragmentary and fleeting manner. Some broad observations will be made here and some better-known systems will be described, as will some of the legal and regulatory issues raised. There are no major studies of this burgeoning situation over the past two or three years, and an introductory text with a consumer focus can do little else than alert consumers of banking services of the rapid changes, their unregulated nature, and the need to exercise caution in their use.

The earliest of these new payment systems evolved in the business-to-business payment context with electronic data interchange (EDI), which has been in use for over a decade. EDI is the use of direct electronic communications systems between businesses to exchange information relating to their business operations. The best known use of EDI is for inventory control in the retail sector: bar code scanners at cash registers are used to reorder merchandise being sold and to submit invoices for goods being sold as between retailer and supplier. Another example is in the manufacturing sector, where component suppliers supply parts as ordered electronically by manufacturers shortly before manufacture. In both instances, no large amounts of inventory need be stored, and an accurate record of demand is kept and supplied. In addition, payment is automatically authorized and effected through credit transfers over the ACSS and carried out under ACSS Rule E3.

The payment is initiated by the customer sending an electronic message to its bank to make the payment from the customer's account. The message will include the payee's payment information and will be transmitted as a credit transfer to the payee's bank by no later than 5:00 p.m. on the day on which value is given to the payee. The payee's bank acknowledges receipt and makes a record of each EDI payment item received from each direct clearer and prepares a single debit entry for the sum of all the items it accepts the preceding day for entry into the ACSS electronic network. All EDI debits are netted with all the other credits and debits in the ACSS to calculate the net obligations among direct clearers for settlement at the Bank of Canada.

Person-to-business payments have been transformed by electronic payment changes in the past four or five years. While many customers continue to pay bills such as electricity, gas, water, telephone, cable, and other regular monthly or bi-monthly bills, by cheque or in person at the branch, electronic payment methods have increased both within the CPA systems and without. The CPA offers several bill payment systems, and some new financial institution third party payment services piggy-back on these.

The CPA's bill payment remittance service, regulated by ACSS Rule H6, is designed for large public organizations such as the Canada Revenue Agency or large public utilities, which issue bills to the public in large numbers. To facilitate this, a large biller enters an agreement with a financial institution, normally a direct clearer, to act for it in bill payment collection. The agreement sets out how the process will operate and in particular presents the format for the invoice sent to the customer, so that it may be processed as a payment item by the ACSS. Customers may pay at any financial institution by cash or cheque or at an ABM, and once payment is made, it will be cleared like any other item in the ACSS.[45] Electronic payments at an ABM are treated like EDI payment items in the ACSS.

The second bill payment process offered by the CPA is the preauthorized debit (PAD) system regulated by ACSS Rule H4. Through this process, customers authorize billers to which they make regular, usually monthly, payments of about the same amount, to debit funds from a specified bank account. The authorization must be in writing, and advice is sent either by paper or electronically to the customer prior to the payment date so that they can cancel the authorization. While many customers have made use of the PAD system, many more still prefer to retain the sense of control over bill payment afforded by more traditional systems of payment in person at the branch or by cheque.

The third service universally available, that is, the "on-us" bill payment service offered by financial institutions, does not require CPA involvement. Again, a bank enters an account agreement with a large biller that receives numerous regular payments from numerous customers to which they provide services such as water, gas, or cable, for the purpose of receiving payments from that bank's customer in response to invoices sent by post. Customers who do online banking may pay those bills using the bank's online site from their account to the biller's account at the same bank. This bill payment process does not

---

45 Chapter 9, Section C.

involve sending payments through the ACSS; rather, it is a purely internal electronic process within the bank.

Various new 3PPS's presuppose the existence of these partly paper/partly electronic payment systems, and several will be described here. It is important to recall that many 3PPS's, including the stored-value cards discussed above and credit cards, provide payment systems that do not access the ACSS to make payments. Stored-value cards are purchased or reloaded with cash, and credit cards settle on an aggregated basis, rather than on an individual basis.

However, some 3PPS's access the ACSS bill payment remittance service through accounts established with financial institutions. The 3PPS operates by requiring a customer to establish an online bill payment to the 3PPS from its bank account, and the 3PPS sends the funds on to the ultimate payee as identified by the customer.[46] The 3PPS may also initiate an online payment at the customer's financial institution's online banking site, using the password and account number of the customer as supplied to the 3PPS. Or the 3PPS may require the customer to prefund from their bank accounts an epurse, and the funds from all the 3PPS customers are aggregated in a single account with the 3PPS's bank. The 3PPS then makes bill payments on request of the customer.

"HyperWallet"[47] is a good example of a popular 3PPS that piggybacks onto the bill payment system. A customer of HyperWallet registers online and receives a wallet number and unique password and then deposits funds online from the customer's bank account, using the security of the bank's website for the online transfers. The funds are transferred to HyperWallet's own bank account, and all of its customer epurses are aggregated there. The customer, or "wallet holder," may then instruct HyperWallet to make payments from the account online to any merchant with an email address, but the merchants must be HyperWallet participants with accounts at HyperWallet's bank in order to receive those payments. Merchants are required to pay fees to belong. Essentially two "on-us" payments are made, through the funding of the wallet by the customer from the customer's bank account and through the payment of funds from HyperWallet's account to the merchant's account. A HyperWallet customer can also send funds to another HyperWallet customer electronically in the same way that bills are paid to businesses. This process requires the banking system in order to operate insofar as bank accounts are required, and the bank's security systems for online banking are exploited to ensure the security of the

---

46 For example, online: www.cybux.net; www.othentik.com; www.usebybank.com.
47 Online: www.hyperwallet.com.

transfers. The process also allows customers to pay the 3PPS a fee to pay their bills, rather than paying their bills directly themselves.

Other 3PPS's operate by submitting debits and credits to the ACSS through an account with a bank. Some 3PPS's that do so are payroll processors and bill payment services, but others are aimed at consumers. "PayPal"[48] is a good example. Founded in 1998 by the eBay Company, PayPal permits anyone with an email address to send and receive payments online, using the existing banking system. A customer creates an account online with PayPal by registering bank account and credit card numbers, and then transfers funds to the PayPal account from either bank account or credit card by means of an electronic transfer, using the bank's secure funds transfer system. Again, PayPal's account is with a bank and all PayPal account holders' funds are aggregated in that account. When a PayPal account holder wishes to transfer funds, the account holder does so electronically, to purchase an item on eBay or another online auction site or to transmit funds to another account. In the latter case, the customer enters the recipient's email address and payment details and sends the payment. If the payment is larger than the amount of funds in the account, the difference will be charged to the customer's credit card. The recipient receives an email on the recipient's PayPal account, and the payment is added to the recipient's PayPal account balance. If the recipient does not have a PayPal account, one must be created before the payment will be credited. A PayPal customer can also have funds sent to the customer's own bank account electronically or by cheque. Again, PayPal is predicated on the banking system and customers willing to pay to use its services to send person-to-business and person-to-person payments.

Finally, the banks themselves have created another online bill payment system, CertaPay,[49] which operates along the same lines as HyperWallet by permitting person-to-person payments to be made using email for notification. Called Interac Email Money Transfers, the service requires the customer to provide the customer's bank with an accurate email address for the recipient, as well as a security question whose answer is known only to the customer and recipient but is not communicated to the recipient, who must answer correctly to receive the transfer of funds into the recipient's bank account. The bank, however, effects the transfer through the ACSS.

---

48 Online: www.paypal.com. See also online: www.telpay.com for payments outside Canada.
49 Online: www.certapay.com.

For customers, these and the many other online 3PPS's can be attractive for a number of reasons: the "buzz" of using the latest computer services to perform money and bill payment transfers at "the click of a mouse" instead of going to the bank in person or writing and posting a cheque; real-time bill payment and funds transfer; where a PAD authorization is in place, the peace of mind in knowing that bills will be paid on time (provided funds are available either in the epurse or by credit card); and the illusion of security because the banks are "somehow" involved.

On the other hand, there are a number of risks in these systems for both banks and customers. They are completely unregulated, although where they intersect with the banking system, for example, in "on-us" payments, as well as in ultimate clearing and settlement between banks, they are subject to the security of the banks' own internal systems, as well as to the CPA. Nevertheless, there are risks for consumers, including the following: unsound 3PPS business practices resulting in misuse of personal customer information such as account numbers, credit card numbers, and personal codes to produce fraud or unauthorized transactions; failure to authenticate customers and customer instructions, leading again to fraud or unauthorized transactions; risks to customers' funds in epurses because of the absence of legal standards about aggregate accounts relating to accounting, trusts, identification of ownership of those funds, and access to those funds by unauthorized persons; or insecure computer networks leading to possible identity theft by third-party computer hackers, as well as to draining bank accounts or running up credit card bills. For the banking system, there are significant reputational risks. Customers may think that because banks are involved, these transactions are as secure as bank transactions, and while many are secure, fraud and theft in significant amounts may suggest that there is not the same degree of security as for traditional banking transactions. On the other hand, by permitting 3PPS's to use their services, banks are encumbered with duties to know their customers and limit potential problems.

A final challenge to the traditional payments system comes from the very recent introduction of mobile payments (mpayments) into Canada. Mpayments can be made from a mobile phone by permitting mobile phone users to make small purchases on their phone and pay for these later as part of their phone bill. TelusMobility[50] permits customers to purchase games and ring-tones online and pay for these

---

50   Online: www.telusmobility.com.

on their phone bills, and PayMint[51] offers a wireless parking network that allows users to dial a log-in number on their cell phone and enter a parking lot code to pay for parking in participating parking locations, with payment charged to a preselected credit card. Mpayments for small-value purchases are now common in several European and Asian countries and typically bypass the banking system completely by allowing payment on phone bills or by charges to credit cards. They have not been used much for large-value payments, and it is uncertain whether they will ever be used in that way.[52]

G. CONCLUSION

Much of the discussion in this chapter will likely be outdated during the marketplace life of this volume. However, it should alert customers to the need to be aware of the possibilities and perils of the new payment mechanisms they will be offered by banks and by non-financial institutions over the coming years. The role of the contract between bank or 3PPS and customer is more important than ever before because in the immediate future, that contract will be the only legal mechanism setting out the rights and duties of the parties until legislation, industry codes, regulatory bodies, and case law develop.

---

51 Online: www.paymint.com.
52 For an extended discussion of how banks are cut out of payment systems, see Richard Owens, "Evolving Issues in Online Banking" (2003) 19 B.F.L.R. 1.

CHAPTER 11

CREDIT CARDS AND OTHER PAYMENT MECHANISMS

A. INTRODUCTION

In the previous chapters, payment mechanisms that presuppose the existence of a bank account in funds have been discussed, including cheques, debit cards, and electronic funds transfers. These are simply different means by which a customer instructs his agent, his bank, to pay funds from an account and collect funds into an account. This chapter will consider payment mechanisms or services offered by banks for which it is not strictly necessary for the customer to maintain an account with the bank selling the service, provided that the customer is able to pay for the service, that is, the means of making payments or transferring funds to a third party. Payment mechanisms to be considered are credit cards, travellers' cheques, money orders, and bank drafts. These are all conceptually quite different from one another and are grouped together only on the basis that no bank account is required for them, in contrast to the payment orders discussed earlier. The odd payment mechanism out is, of course, the credit card, which could have been discussed in Chapter 10, along with other payment cards, especially in the context of debit and smart cards, since there is growing convergence of their distinct features in one card. However, it is also possible to discuss credit cards quite separately from other plastic cards because they do present unique legal questions, and possession of a bank account is not a prerequisite for their use.

B. CREDIT CARDS

1) Legal Nature

The historical precursor[1] of the modern credit card was the credit coin, originally issued by large American retail stores just before World War I to customers who were approved for purchases on credit at those stores. Although credit coin use disappeared in the 1930s, the concept of giving creditworthy customers credit tokens was taken up in the 1920s by the oil companies, which issued early credit cards as identification cards for use in purchasing gas at the chains of outlets forming at that time to service the newly widespread use of automobiles. American airlines and railways subsequently followed suit. In 1950, the first modern credit card, Diners Club, was introduced as an all-purpose card providing credit and collection services for participating merchants. Diners Club pioneered the tripartite contractual arrangement characteristic of credit cards today. In 1958 the American Express card appeared, and in 1959 the Hilton Credit Corporation introduced Carte Blanche. Both of these were designed for business rather than consumer use. Modelled on the Diners Club contractual arrangement, none of these three cards had a line of credit attached to them; rather, monthly payment of the full outstanding balance was required. They were "charge" cards, not "credit" cards.

In 1966, the Bank of America saw the possibilities of adding a line of credit to the charge card and marketing this card to consumers, and established Bank Americard Service Corp. The following year, a national association of regional bank card associations formed Interbank, to promote a rival card. The former promoted "Chargex" (changed to "Visa" in 1976), and the latter promoted "MasterCharge," changed to "MasterCard" in 1981. Since the late 1960s, these two credit card corporations have licensed financial institutions worldwide to issue and administer their respective cards with their distinctive logos and colour schemes patented internationally as intellectual property.

In Canada, the normal practice is for a financial institution to be licensed by only one of these two parent U.S. corporations to carry its card. No financial institution enjoys licences to carry both Visa and MasterCard, although in the United States this may be done as a result of litigation in which restrictions to one card only were found to

---

1 See generally (and the references therein) M.H. Ogilvie, *Canadian Banking Law*, 2d ed. (Scarborough, ON: Carswell, 1998) at 702–4.

be anti-competitive.[2] Canadian financial institutions manage their licence within their own corporate structures, having been permitted to offer credit cards since the 1980 *Bank Act*.[3] The Act further permits banks to promote other merchandise and services to the holders of any credit cards they issue.[4] In recent years both MasterCard and Visa have bundled other services beside a line of credit into their cards at the option of the customer, including travel insurance, the AIR MILES Reward program, cheques, cash advances, and identity-theft-prevention advice services. Both credit card networks have also offered branded cards, bearing the names and other identifying information of universities, schools, charities, and retailers. However, the fundamental legal contracts and legal operation of credit cards have not changed in these branded, or affinity, cards; rather, collecting small sums on every transaction in which these cards are used for the cause they represent is merely an additional bundled feature covered in a contract with the cardissuer and the institution. The focus of this discussion will be on the banking contract aspects of credit cards, as these other services are of marginal interest in a text about banking law.

The *Bank Act* does not define "credit card," although some provincial legislation concerned with credit card abuses in consumer law, such as interest rate disclosure or unsolicited cards, provide definitions. These definitions focus on a card by which credit may be obtained[5] or a card by which goods or services may be obtained on a deferred payment basis[6] or a card or device by which a borrower may obtain advances under a credit agreement.[7]

The most comprehensive definition is found in the *Criminal Code*:

> "credit card" means any card, plate, coupon book or other device issued or distributed for the purpose of being used
> (a) on presentation to obtain, on credit, money, goods, services or any other thing of value, or

---

2   *Worthen Bank & Trust Co. v. National Bank Americard Inc.*, 345 F. Supp. 1309 (E.D. Ark. 1972), rev'd 485 F.2d 119 (8th Circ. 1973); *National Bank of Canada v. Interbank Card Association and Bank of Montreal*, 666 F.2d 6 (2d Circ. 1981).
3   *Bank Act*, S.C. 1991, c. 46, s. 409(2)(d). See also *Master Charge v. Price* (1977), 42 N.S.R. (2d) 244 (Co. Ct.); *Bank of Montreal v. Price* (1979), 105 D.L.R. (3d) 62 (N.S.S.C.A.D.).
4   *Bank Act*, ibid., s. 410(1)(d).
5   *Cost of Credit Disclosure Act*, R.S.N.B. 1973, c. C-28, s. 1(d) as am.
6   *Credit and Loan Agreements Act*, R.S.A. 1980, c. C-30, s. 21(a) as am.
7   *Consumer Protection Statute Law Amendment Act, 2002*, S.O. 2002, c. 30, s. 1 "credit card." Readers should consult their own provincial legislation for current definitions.

(b) in an automated teller machine, a remote service unit or a similar automated banking device to obtain any of the services offered through the machine, unit or device.[8]

This definition captures the common understanding of a credit card, and the term is often used to cover the traditional charge card, such as American Express to which no line of credit was attached, so that repayment of the entire monthly balance was required, as well as covering retail cards, such as the Bay card, which is used only at certain designated shops and is therefore bilateral, rather than trilateral, in nature. These "private label" cards do not involve banks directly, and since their only function is to identify customers to whom the retailer has granted a revolving line of credit, they do not raise the legal issues associated with tripartite cards such as Visa and MasterCard.[9]

Credit cards operate on a tripartite contractual basis involving three separate contracts: (i) cardissuer and cardholder; (ii) cardissuer and participating merchant; and (iii) cardissuer/consumer and merchant. This contrasts with the bipartite arrangement of retailer private label cards to which there are two parties: the retailer and the customer to whom the retailer not only sells goods and services but also provides credit for that sale. In the tripartite scheme, the cardissuer determines the content of its respective contracts with cardholder and merchant, but the contract of sale between the cardholder and merchant is determined by those two parties. The cardissuer is not contractually associated with the sale contract at all.

The proper legal characterization of this tripartite arrangement continues to elude legal scholars.[10] Four analogies frequently canvassed are to argue that credit cards are similar to: (i) cheques; (ii) other negotiable instruments, such as bills of exchange; (iii) irrevocable letters of credit;[11] and (iv) assignments or factoring of accounts receivable. The cheque analogy fails because a cheque is a conditional payment revocable by countermand prior to final payment, whereas in the credit card arrangement, the cardissuer promises to pay the merchant whether or not the cardholder pays the cardissuer or there is an underlying problem in the contract of sale with the cardholder. The bills of exchange

---

8   R.S.C. 1985, c. C-46, s. 321.
9   The first judicial definitions seem overtaken now: *Re Charge Card Services Ltd.*, [1988] 3 All E.R. 702 (C.A.).
10 There are several hundred law review articles, books, and studies attempting to define the precise legal character of the credit card.
11 Mr. Crawford, Q.C., favours this: Bradley Crawford, *Payment, Clearing and Settlement in Canada*, vol. 1 (Aurora, ON: Canada Law Book, 2002) at 342–51.

analogy also fails not only because there is no negotiable instrument, but also because credit card transactions involve three parties, whereas an instrument can only be negotiated between two parties.

The letter of credit analogy is somewhat closer insofar as both letter of credit and credit card involve the substitution of the purchaser's credit with the credit of another: the cardissuer in a credit card transaction and the issuing bank in a letter of credit. However, as the English Court of Appeal observed in *Re Charge Card Services Ltd.*,[12] there are a number of differences: (i) the letter of credit is used for large-value transactions negotiated at a distance, usually in international trade; (ii) the buyer selects the bank in letters of credit, but in credit card transactions, the seller decides which credit card will be used by entering a contract with the cardissuer; and (iii) in a letter of credit, the buyer pays for the facility, but in credit card transactions, the seller pays for the facility. Other differences may also be suggested: (i) in letters of credit, the issuing bank is the agent of the buyer, not the seller; and (ii) in letters of credit, the buyer may specify the requirements the seller must meet prior to entitlement to payment, but a credit card holder may not do so because payment to the seller is dependent on the merchant agreement.

In *Re Charge Card Services Ltd.*, a credit card company went into liquidation, and ownership of funds already paid by cardholders to the card company was disputed by various garages who had supplied gas to cardholders and by a factoring company to which the accounts receivable had been assigned. The court found that customer payments by credit card were absolute, not conditional, so that the garages could be paid for the services supplied.

Credit card transactions are also said to be analogous to the assignment or factoring of accounts receivable insofar as the cardissuer resembles a factor in purchasing a merchant's accounts receivable for cash and foregoes recourse against the merchant should the buyer fail to pay. However, a factor normally purchases all accounts receivable, but the cardissuer purchases only those of the merchant's credit card sales. Moreover, the factor has no contractual relationship with the buyer unlike the cardissuer and cardholder contract, so there may not be a true assignment of the accounts receivable to the cardissuer, who can enforce the independent promise to pay of the cardholder in its contract with the cardissuer.

The failure to find an appropriate legal characterization for credit cards may not be so troubling if they are simply considered to be a novel

---

12   Above note 9 at 710–11, Browne-Williamson V.-C.

legal creation because however they may be characterized by analogy to existing legal concepts, the fact remains that they are governed entirely by the two contracts entered into by the cardissuer with the cardholder and merchant, respectively. To say that they are contractual is not to characterize them legally; it is only to say where the rules for their operation reside. Their precise legal nature may remain illusive, but there can be no doubt about their legal reality in everyday transactions.

2) The Cardissuer and Cardholder Agreement

An application for a credit card is an application for credit,[13] so that the applicant must waive privacy rights by giving required information and permission for the bank to do a credit check to ensure creditworthiness. Once approved and issued with a card, the applicant is provided with a copy of the cardholder agreement, which is a standard form contract and not negotiable.

This contract governs the cardholder and cardissuer relationship and typically contains the following terms: (i) an assertion of card ownership by the cardissuer, with permission to the cardholder to use the card only under the terms of the contract; (ii) permission to the cardholder to use the card to make a purchase or obtain a cash advance and to be charged for that use; (iii) a prohibition on exceeding the assigned credit limit, which the cardissuer may change at any time; (iv) provision for how exchange rates will be calculated on foreign exchange transactions; (v) cardholder liability for the total debt regardless of how it was incurred; (vi) a provision for interest charges from the date of the transaction, with the exception of new debit items the first time they appear on an account statement, provided they are paid in full by the payment due date; (vii) a provision detailing how interest rates are calculated; (viii) a provision detailing how payments are applied to an outstanding balance, usually, in order, to interest, fees, cash advances, and purchases; (ix) a requirement to pay the minimum balance; (x) an undertaking to send statements of account monthly; (xi) an account verification clause; (xii) permission to the cardissuer to send offers of other goods and services to the cardholder; (xiii) a requirement of PIN

---

13 Some courts characterize credit cards as simple loan agreements: *Bank of Nova Scotia v. Forsyth* (1985), 63 B.C.L.R. 60 (Co. Ct.); *Royal Bank of Canada v. Scarlato* (1986), 59 C.B.R. (N.S.) 211 (Ont. Dist. Ct.). Capacity to enter credit card contracts is treated similarly to capacity to enter bank account contracts: *Royal Bank of Canada v. Shaw* (1993), 104 Nfld. & P.E.I.R. 356 (P.E.I.S.C.) and *Royal Bank of Canada v. Unick* (1994), 19 Alta. L.R. (3d) 254, 154 A.R. 81 (Q.B.).

confidentiality and that the PIN will be kept separate from the card; (xiv) cardholder responsibility for the card, including notice within twenty-four hours of loss or theft or the compromise of the PIN; (xv) cardholder liability of $50.00 for unauthorized use of the card where there is no reasonable care of the card, another unauthorized use within the previous twelve months, and the account is not in good standing; (xvi) cardholder liability of $500.00 where the cardholder disclosed the PIN, did not keep the PIN and card separate, or did not give notice within twenty-four hours of loss or theft or PIN compromise; (xvii) cardissuer exemption from liability in relation to the cardholder and merchant sales transaction; (xviii) a provision for crediting merchant credit notes to the cardholder account; (xix) cardissuer rights to cancel the card; (xx) cardissuer rights to change the terms of the agreement; (xxi) cardissuer rights to assign the agreement; (xxii) cardissuer rights to use or share cardholder personal information; and (xxiii) a law of the contract provision.

The courts interpret credit card contracts using the usual rules of contract construction. Thus, a joint and several liability clause was enforced when one of the two cardholders had engaged in fraudulent activities with the card.[14] Again, where a credit card contract on construction distinguished the liability of the primary cardholder from an authorized user, the court declined to make the authorized user responsible for the indebtedness of the primary cardholder, who was her deceased husband. Rather, she was found liable only for the expenses that she had charged to the account, and the cardissuer was obliged to swallow the losses resulting from her deceased husband's use of the card.[15] On the other hand, there is also some evidence that the courts take seriously the standard form nature of credit card contracts. In *Royal Bank of Canada v. Budaveri*,[16] an applicant whose grasp of English was poor received a credit card on an existing account with an indebtedness of about $12,000.00, and the bank argued that she should be liable for that amount, although her own expenses came to about $750.00, and she was not aware of the outstanding balance or the effect of the joint and several liability clause in the contract. The trial judge found that there was a duty on the bank to ensure that she understood the obligation at the time she applied for the credit card if she was to be jointly and severally liable. Whether this duty extends to other onerous

---

14 *Bank of Montreal v. Demakos* (1996), 31 O.R. (3d) 757 (Gen. Div.). See also A. Duncan Grace, "Cardholder Agreements" (1995) 10 B.F.L.R. 261.
15 *Canadian Imperial Bank of Commerce v. Bell Estate* (2005), 74 O.R. (3d) 360 (S.C.J.).
16 (2003), 44 B.L.R. (3d) 147 (Ont. S.C.J.).

obligations in credit card contracts remains to be tested in future cases. The fact that legislatures acted early on after the introduction of credit cards into the marketplace to counter perceived problems suggests that courts will likely follow that lead in future cases in which their nature as contracts of adhesion is at issue.

The first problem addressed by legislation when credit cards were first introduced was their widespread unsolicited distribution. Despite significant losses incurred by American banks in the 1960s when credit cards were widely distributed without solicitation, Canadian banks imitated this practice, thereby increasing the likelihood of fraudulent use. Provincial legislatures enacted legislation, in response, either banning the practice outright[17] or providing that use of the card by the recipient would be deemed to be acceptance of it although unsolicited.[18] Although the constitutional status of this legislation is unknown, it is unlikely to be tested because banks and other financial institutions ceased the practice of sending real cards and replaced it with the practice of sending application packages, often together with dummy cards.

A second issue addressed by provincial legislation is liability for unauthorized use. The first credit card contracts typically deemed the cardholder to be responsible for unauthorized use of the card and considered any use not approved in writing by the cardholder to be unauthorized, so that the cardholder could be responsible for the entire balance. When lost or stolen cards were used to incur debts, sometimes in excess of the credit limit, with the result that cardholders were being held liable by cardissuers, legislatures, first in the United States[19] and then in Canada,[20] enacted legislation to limit the liability of the cardholder to $50.00 prior to notification of the loss or theft to the cardissuer. Not all Canadian provinces have such a provision in their consumer protection legislation;[21] moreover, in those provinces which do not, the question of what is unauthorized use arises, especially where card contracts attempt to define such use, sometimes using words such as "reasonable," which are notoriously difficult to assess. It also remains the case that where a cardholder deliberately facilitates unauthorized use by lending the card, by keeping card and PIN together, or failing to give notice of loss or theft as soon as possible, the liability is likely to be

---

17 Above note 6, s. 22.
18 Above note 7, s. 68.
19 *Fair Credit Billing Act*, 15 U.S.C., s. 1643(a)(1) and Reg. 7, 12 C.F.R., s. 116.13(a)(4).
20 *Fair Trading Act*, R.S.A. 2000, c. F-2, s. 89; *Consumer Protection Act*, C.C.S.M. c. C200.
21 A glaring example is Ontario, where over half of credit cards are distributed in Canada.

extensive, possibly up to the credit limit, after which card use ought to be refused by the cardissuer, but there is no case law to this effect.

The question of the role of the cardissuer in monitoring card use is also raised, since the cardissuer is in the best position through computerized monitoring to see unusual use of a credit card and to confirm with the cardholder whether or not an unusual expenditure pattern has been authorized by the cardholder. In *Imperial Oil Ltd. v. Hough*,[22] an oil company card in the name of the female defendant was stolen and used by a male to make fifty-three unauthorized purchases, including four tires and seventeen inner tubes in six days. The court found the defendant was not liable for the debts because the retailers had failed to perform their required duty of asking for identification, which would have disclosed the problem immediately, given the different genders of the cardholder and the thief. The court further found that the obligation of retailers to investigate card users was designed to protect the cardholder, and failure to do so amounted to a breach of condition by the cardissuer. It would appear that cardissuers now take the legal duty to monitor seriously, since it has become common practice to phone a cardholder to confirm unusual expenditures or to refuse authorization for card use without notice to the cardholder[23] until the cardholder has confirmed expenditures recored on the card.

A third issue is disclosure of the cost of borrowing in credit card use. Both federal and provincial governments have enacted legislation, but there is constitutional ambiguity as to which is paramount. The likely answer is that federal legislation is paramount by virtue of Parliament's authority over banking pursuant to section 91(15) and over interest pursuant to section 91(19), although provincial jurisdiction over the credit aspects and contractual aspects might also be claimed pursuant to section 92(13), property and civil rights, and section 92(16), matters of a local nature. Provincial legislation requiring disclosure of the cost of borrowing in credit card contracts[24] predated federal legislation in the *Bank Act*,[25] but all the cost-of-borrowing legislation is very similar as a result of federal and provincial agreement to eliminate divergences of approach. Thus, the legislation generally requires full disclosure at the time of entering into the contract and on an ongoing basis of the

---

22 (1957), 11 D.L.R. (2d) 440 (Alta. S.C.). See also *Ambico Ltd. v. Loeb Inc.* (1993), 103 D.L.R. (4th) 721 (Ont. C.A.).
23 The embarrassment caused could result in a defamation action in the right circumstances.
24 Above note 6, s. 23; *Consumer Credit Transactions Act*, S.A. 1985, c. C-22.5, s. 30; and *Consumer Protection Act*, R.S.B.C. 1996, c. 69, s. 42.
25 *Bank Act*, above note 3, ss. 449–54.

entire cost of borrowing and how it is calculated, including the maximum amount available; the interest rate and how it is computed; the period of time for which the statement of account is furnished; service or transaction fees; annual fees; minimum payments required; and all other costs relating to the grant of credit.[26] The only limit imposed by law on the cost of borrowing is the 60 percent ceiling imposed by the *Criminal Code*[27] on all loans generally.[28]

Related to interest-rate disclosure in credit card agreements is a fourth issue drawn from the *Competition Act*,[29] which prohibits banks from making arrangements with one another in respect to the rate of interest or the charges on a loan, the amount or kind of a loan, and the amount of any charge for a customer service. Where such arrangements have been found to occur, every director, officer, or employee who knowingly makes such an arrangement is guilty of an indictable offence and liable to a fine of not more than $5 million or imprisonment for up to five years or both.

Fifthly, some provincial consumer legislation provides recourse where consumers wish to request that the cardissuer cancel or reverse a credit card charge and all related charges and interest, in particular, where the agreement is a consumer agreement that can be cancelled under consumer legislation (for example, within cooling-off periods or where no copy of the agreement is provided as required); where the payment contravenes the legislation (for example, improper interest-rate disclosure); or where payment was collected for unsolicited goods or services. Such legislation typically requires that the request be in writing and gives a right of action if the cardissuer does not comply.[30]

Sixthly, credit card fraud is addressed by section 342 of the *Criminal Code*, which makes it an indictable offence to steal a credit card; forge or falsify a credit card; possess, use, or traffic in a forged or falsified credit

---

26 Readers should check current provincial legislation in their jurisdictions.
27 *Criminal Code*, above note 8, s. 347. See also *Markson v. MBNA Canada Bank* (2004), 71 O.R. (3d) 741 (S.C.J.) for a failed attempt at certification of a consumer class action concerning an illegal criminal rate of interest.
28 In *Dahl v. Royal Bank of Canada* (2004), 243 D.L.R. (4th) 74 (B.C.C.A.), the question of whether banks could charge interest between the transaction date and the posting date (i.e., the date the retailer was paid) was considered, but the court decided it could not be determined until the contracts were available to the court. If the contracts did not provide for "interest" to be charged from the transaction date, then that "interest" failed to be such under both the *Bank Act* and provincial legislation and could not be charged to the cardholder.
29 R.S.C. 1985, c. C-34, s. 49(1).
30 Above note 7, s. 99.

card; or use a credit card knowing it has been revoked or cancelled. The maximum sentence is ten years.[31] The *Criminal Code* also makes it an indictable offence to make, have, or deal in instruments for forging or falsifying credit cards,[32] as well as for unauthorized possession and use of credit card data.[33] There are several hundred reported cases pursuant to the *Criminal Code* provisions about illegal credit card use, reflecting the fact that there is a considerable volume of illicit use in Canada.[34]

Finally, pursuant to the complaints procedures provisions in the *Bank Act*,[35] credit card disputes are included as a category of dispute to be resolved within the financial institutions ombudsman processes and according to those processes.[36]

One further issue has arisen in the courts. In *Dominix v. Canadian Imperial Bank of Commerce*,[37] the question arose of cardissuer liability where credit card use included the accumulation of air miles points redeemable for free air travel. When the cardholder failed to obtain the desired flights, he sued the bank for breach of contract, although there was no express term in the contract obliging the bank to ensure desired flights. The court held for the bank on the ground that the bank was not responsible for providing the flights or managing the intricacies of the air miles program. Rather, it had fulfilled its contractual duty by providing the points, and the cardholder would have to negotiate the flights like any other holder of such points.

3) The Cardissuer and Merchant Agreement

To participants in a credit card system, the merchant is required to enter the second contract required for the operation of the system, the merchant agreement. Most merchants participate in both MasterCard and Visa, and may also participate in American Express as well. Participation is largely required to stay in business today. It is well known that at the point of sale, the cardholder may pay for the goods or services by presentation of a credit card to the merchant, who receives authorization from the cardissuer to accept payment in this way on the understanding that the merchant will be paid by the cardissuer whether or not the cardholder pays the cardissuer.

---

31 Above note 8, ss. 342(1) & (2).
32 *Ibid.*, s. 342.01.
33 *Ibid.*, ss. 342(3) & (4).
34 Readers interested in this should consult criminal law textbooks.
35 *Bank Act*, above note 3, ss. 455–56(1).
36 See Chapter 13.
37 (2000), 15 B.L.R. (3d) 87 (Nfld. Prov. Ct.).

The terms of merchant agreements differ from plan to plan, from cardissuer to cardissuer, and from merchant to merchant, but most contain at least the following or very similar terms: (i) the merchant undertakes to accept a credit card in payment for goods and services without charging prices in excess of the ordinary price or other fees or charges for using a credit card or requiring minimum values for purchases on the credit card; (ii) the merchant promises to invoice the customer for the sale in an approved fashion and give the customer one copy once authorization for the transaction is received from the cardissuer and where there is no customer signature because the order was placed by mail, by phone, or by Internet communication, to accept the risk of repudiation; (iii) the merchant's requirement to keep an account with the bank and to deposit transaction vouchers or data within a stipulated number of days of the transaction with the bank; (iv) the merchant's warrant that every claim is for a *bona fide* transaction conducted in accordance with the agreement and that the transaction details will be kept secret; (v) the bank's right to examine all transactions reported and to reject payment for those using an invalid or expired card or where the signature is forged or unauthorized if payment is being made in person or where the transaction was not authorized or where the merchandise or service was not given or where the sales draft exceeded the merchant's floor limit or was illegible, etc.; (vi) the bank's promise to credit the merchant's account immediately upon receipt of transaction data that are problem free; (vii) the merchant's promise to pay all fees, including the rental fee for any equipment that remains the property of the bank; (viii) the merchant's promise to display the credit card plan logo as required; and (ix) a termination provision on notice by either party, but automatically in the event of merchant bankruptcy.

There is no legislation, nor are there any reported, cases on the merchant and cardissuer agreement, which is clearly a contract of adhesion between two commercial parties and presumably works efficiently in everyday commercial life. It remains to note that the cardissuer's agreements with the cardholder and merchant, respectively, are kept entirely separate from one another: the cardissuer grants the cardholder credit and the cardissuer promises to pay the merchant regardless of whether it is ever paid by the cardholder.

4) The Cardholder and Merchant Agreement

The underlying transaction is simply that of a sale or supply of goods and services by the merchant to the consumer/cardholder, and the cardissuer plays no role in it whatsoever, even to the extent of incorporating an express term into the cardholder agreement to that effect. Disputes concerning the quality or quantity of the goods sold or services provided must be resolved between the parties to that contract, the merchant and the cardholder; the payment mechanism, the line of credit in the credit card, is completely irrelevant. The cardissuer is strictly the financier of the sales transaction and not a party to it.

This strict separation of sales contract and credit arrangement is not always to the consumer's advantage. In *Hawreliak v. Paul*,[38] a purchase by credit card was said to be an executed contract, whereas it would have been executory and rescindable if financed by a loan, with the result that the purchaser could not take advantage of provincial consumer protection legislation that extended the right to rescind an executory, but not an executed, contract. This was an early credit card case, and most provincial consumer protection legislation now treats credit card purchases like any other credit purchases for consumer protection purposes. But the case also indirectly raises another, more important issue of whether a purchase by credit card is an absolute discharge of the purchaser's obligation to pay the merchant. Common understanding of credit cards would say that it is; not only is that how cardholders understand their use, that is, a credit card purchase is like a cash purchase, but also the merchant agreement implies that it is when there are no other problems in the transaction such as the use of an invalid or stolen card. *Hawreliak* suggests that this understanding is correct if a credit card purchase is an executed contract, and this receives support from English cases,[39] which consider payment by credit card to be tantamount to payment by cash, and therefore an absolute and not a conditional payment. This always assumes that there are no other problems such as the use of counterfeit money in cash payments or expired cards in credit card payments. In those cases, payment must still be made by the purchaser.

5) Clearing and Settlement

Cardissuers have outsourced much of the clearing and settlement of credit card transactions to specialized companies. When a credit card transaction occurs, the data relating to that transaction, or the vouchers if done manually, are transmitted to the merchant's financial institution or the data processing company to which the clearing and

---

38 (1983), 20 A.C.W.S. (2d) 162 (Ont. Prov. Ct.).
39 *Richardson (Inspector of Taxes) v. Worrall* (1985), 58 T.C. 642; *Re Charge Card Services Ltd.*, above note 9.

settlement is outsourced, and there it is sorted according to the financial institution that is the cardholder's cardissuer. The data is automatically recorded on computer tapes for the various cardissuers, and these are exchanged between cardissuers. The information is entered into the CPA's national clearing and settlement system, and the net settlement obligations among the cardissuers are settled at the Bank of Canada. The cardissuer processes the tapes to post the charges to each cardholder's account.

C. TRAVELLERS' CHEQUES

The travellers' cheque is not, legally speaking, a cheque. It does not satisfy certain statutory criteria for negotiable instruments, although it is widely accepted as a negotiable instrument and has been since its first introduction in 1891 by the American Express Company. It was introduced to serve the needs of travellers as a response to the development of tourism in the late nineteenth century and to provide an alternative, more flexible means of transporting funds than the older traveller's letter of credit, which had been used by merchants since the fourteenth century. The traveller's letter of credit was directed to specific overseas correspondents of the traveller's home bank, from which alone cash advances could be obtained when travelling abroad. The modern travellers' cheque, by contrast, is accepted for cash by numerous financial institutions, as well as suppliers of goods and services, so that the traveller enjoys numerous sources of cash while travelling worldwide.[40]

In form, travellers' cheques appear to be cheques, and the way in which travellers "cash" them fortifies the common perception that they are cheques. Three parties are involved in their use: the issuing bank; the traveller, who purchases them from the issuing bank; and the third party, who provides money if a financial institution, or goods or services if a merchant, against the travellers' cheques. The traveller purchases the cheques in various denominations in either domestic or foreign currency from the issuer for cash and receives the cheques,

---

40 Very little has been written about travellers' cheques, and nothing has been written in Canada other than brief surveys in banking law texts—for example, M.H. Ogilvie, *Canadian Banking Law*, 2d ed. (Scarborough, ON: Carswell, 1998) at 721–28. The leading article is still by E.P. Ellinger, "Travellers' Cheques and the Law" (1969) 19 U.T.L.J. 132, and Professor Ellinger is the author of the paragraphs on travellers' cheques in *Chitty on Contracts*, 29th ed. (London: Sweet and Maxwell, 2004).

which contain the instruction to the payee that when countersigned with a signature identical to the signature on the cheques, the bearer should be paid. The signature on the cheques must be placed there by the traveller when purchasing them from the issuer, so that both signatures are inscribed under supervision, first of the issuer and then of the payee. The issuer undertakes to pay the specific amount of money represented by the cheque to the order of the traveller or a transferee, provided the countersignature matches the signature executed at the time of the use of the cheques.

The travellers' cheques themselves are supplied by specialized financial institutions, of which American Express and Thomas Cook are the best known, which license banks to issue them to the public. They are cleared and settled through the ACSS like other cheques; however, they are probably not negotiable instruments. Professor Ellinger states that travellers' cheques fall into three general patterns: (i) an order by the directors of an issuing bank to that bank to pay to the order of the payee, provided the signature and countersignature correspond; (ii) an order given by the traveller to the bank to pay the amount to his own order, provided the traveller has countersigned; and (iii) a promise by the issuing bank to pay a certain sum to the payee, provided the two signatures correspond.[41] American Express and Thomas Cook use the first form.

The first two forms resemble bills of exchange, but the third resembles a promissory note. However, both orders and promise are conditional on the correspondence of the signature and the countersignature and cannot, therefore, be negotiable instruments because they are not an unconditional order or a promise to pay. Notwithstanding this legal technicality, they are commonly regarded as such and so treated in commercial usage, so that they are arguably a new type of negotiable instrument by virtue of universal mercantile acceptance.[42] Several English cases assume that they are *sui generis* and look to their contracts to determine liability. There are no reported Canadian cases, so it is necessary to look to English and American cases to discuss their legal nature.

The first legal issue considered by the courts is that of liability when travellers' cheques are lost or stolen prior to countersignature and after countersignature. In both instances, the rights of the purchaser against the issuer are governed by the contract for the purchase of the travellers' cheques. Generally speaking, in the absence of a contrary stipulation in the contract, when travellers' cheques are stolen prior to countersigna-

---

41 *Chitty on Contracts*, ibid. at para. 34-174.
42 Ibid. at para. 34-175.

ture, the traveller is entitled to obtain their face value from the issuing bank, provided the traveller signs an indemnity.[43] It is this security that entices travellers to use travellers' cheques rather than cash in the first place, and it is to be expected that the issuer would honour its promise that they will be repaid. The purpose of the indemnity is to protect the issuer should the cheques have been countersigned before they were lost because the issuer would then be required to honour them when presented by a holder in due course and would then be able to recover an indemnity from the traveller,[44] provided the holder was entitled to payment.[45]

The question of timely report of the loss of uncountersigned travellers' cheques arose in *Sullivan v. Knauth*,[46] in which the traveller took a month to report the loss because he had also lost the issuer's contact information. The cheques, being signed with forged countersignatures, were subsequently paid to a third party. The court held that the issuer was required to reimburse the traveller. It is arguable that a requirement for reporting loss within a reasonable period of time might be implied into the contract, or where there is such an express term, it should be enforced by a court, so that *Sullivan* may be a weak authority.

Agreements governing travellers' cheques typically provide for a duty on the part of the traveller to safeguard the cheques against loss or theft, and the English courts have upheld these clauses. In *Fellus v. National Westminster Bank plc*,[47] the traveller who left the cheques for a few minutes in a department store dressing room while trying on a jacket was found not to be negligent. On the other hand, in *Braithwaite v. Thomas Cook Travellers Cheques Ltd.*,[48] a traveller who fell asleep on the London underground after spending the evening drinking with friends was found to be negligent when the cheques were stolen.

The question of whether or not the traveller will be refunded for non-countersigned cheques is largely a matter of contract construction as shown in *Elawadi v. Bank of Credit and Commerce International SA*.[49] The contract stated that any refund was subject to the bank's approval, and although the court found the traveller to be grossly negligent in leaving the cheques in his car overnight, from which they were stolen, the court awarded a refund on the basis that the clause did not have the effect of

---

43 See generally *Rubin v. American Express Co.*, 315 N.Y.S.2d 89 (1970).
44 Ibid.
45 *Sullivan v. Knauth*, 115 N.E. 460 (1915).
46 Ibid.
47 (1983), 133 New L.J. 766 (Q.B.).
48 [1989] 1 All E.R. 235 (Q.B.).
49 [1989] 1 All E.R. 242 (Q.B.).

conferring on the bank absolute discretion about refunds. The court noted that brochures promoting the sale of the travellers' cheques emphasized the provision for refunds in the event of loss. Moreover, since the cheques had not been countersigned, there was no obligation on the bank to pay on their presentment, so there was no real reason to deny a refund.

While the decision in *El Awadi* seems correct in the whole circumstances, the interpretation of the contract is doubtful, since it is arguable that the contract gave the bank the absolute discretion to determine the availability of the funds. Thus, travellers' cheques agreements may well be treated like any other standard form contracts when the traveller is a consumer. *Braithwaite*'s emphasis on mutual obligation by issuer and traveller to safeguard the cheques is preferable, given the fact that their theft is well known and the procedures for reporting theft are clearly explained in the agreement.

Where the travellers' cheques are stolen or lost after being countersigned, the issuer is not liable to refund the traveller. In *Emerson v. American Express Co.*,[50] the traveller, a lawyer, insisted on signing and countersigning the cheques immediately after their purchase at the bank. When they were stolen, the court refused to refund the traveller on the ground that the countersignature made them payable to bearer and the bank was required to honour them when presented by a holder in due course. When the traveller has countersigned prior to actually using the cheques, it is unlikely, therefore, that a refund will be available unless the traveller can prove that the cheques were destroyed.

The normal practice is to require that cheques be signed prior to leaving the issuing bank to ensure that a signature made under supervision is available for comparison when they are countersigned. In *Braithwaite*, this was not done, because the traveller was in a hurry to catch a flight and signed them subsequently. The case was decided on other points, but in *Rosenfeld v. First National City Bank*,[51] the court held that cheques that had been signed after leaving the bank and then stolen were refundable on the grounds that the bank failed to perform its duty to supervise signature and to bring to the traveller's attention a clause, which was in very small print, that placed the risk of loss on the customer. Most agreements provide that if the cheques are not signed prior to leaving the issuing bank, there is no refund coverage in the event of loss or theft. In *Braithwaite* and *Rosenfeld*, the travellers were reminded of this, but the courts in those cases did not consider the enforceability of that clause, so its legal status remains unknown.

---

50   90 A.2d 236 (Mun. App. D.C. 1952) [*Emerson*].
51   319 N.Y.S.2d 35 (1971).

Where travellers' cheques are accepted by merchants to pay for goods or services, the merchant becomes the holder in due course, provided the cheque is countersigned, complete and regular on its face, and taken for good value and in good faith, and the merchant can obtain payment from the issuing bank or its agent. Even when spaces such as the one for the payee's name are left blank, the merchant can still take as holder in due course.[52] If the cheques have been lost or stolen prior to countersignature, the merchant does not acquire a good title,[53] nor will any third party who takes travellers' cheques where the countersignature is forged.[54] A merchant or third party who takes a cheque stolen or lost after countersignature in good faith becomes a holder in due course because a countersigned cheque is payable to bearer and transferred by delivery.[55]

The legal position is uncertain, however, where travellers' cheques are stolen from the issuing bank and signed and countersigned by the thief. One case found that the holder could not enforce payment against the bank[56] and another held that it could as a holder in due course.[57] Professor Ellinger prefers the latter case because the issuer could not question the genuineness of the countersignature, and even if the signatures were regarded as a material alteration, the holder could still maintain that the amount had not changed and the purpose of a travellers' cheque is to create an instrument honoured when both signatures are attached.[58]

Finally, it remains to consider issues of liability in relation to the selling agent and the issuing bank and the selling agent and the traveller. When banks are licensed to sell travellers' cheques, such as American Express or Thomas Cook, they do so as agents of these companies and as such would not normally be liable to the traveller; rather, while the bank must honour the cheques, ultimately the transactions are on behalf of the companies. Banks are only themselves liable for their own acts or omissions such as fraudulent or negligent statements inducing a traveller to purchase worthless travellers' cheques.[59] Where blank

---

52 *Emerson*, above note 50.
53 *Samberg v. American Express Co.*, 99 N.W. 879 (1909).
54 *Sullivan v. Knauth*, above note 45.
55 *Emerson*, above note 50.
56 *City National Bank of Galveston v. American Express Co.*, 16 S.W.2d 278 (Tex. Com. App. 1929).
57 *American Express Co. v. Anadarko Bank and Trust Co.*, 67 P.2d 55 (Okla. 1937).
58 *Chitty on Contracts*, above note 40 at para. 34-185.
59 *Lesch v. Farmers' & Merchants' State Bank of New Salem*, 211 N.W. 687 (N.D. 1926); *Mellon National Bank v. Citizens' Bank and Trust Co.*, 88 F.2d 128 (1937).

cheques are stolen and honoured by the issuing bank, the agreement between the bank and the company will determine who is liable for the loss, and the courts have enforced such agreements.[60] Where the company goes bankrupt, the ownership of blank travellers' cheques not sold to a traveller is also governed by the agreement, and again, the courts will enforce those agreements.[61]

Travellers' cheques continue to be widely used by foreign travellers despite the growth of credit card use and international facilities for debit cards through Cirrus and similar networks. The main risk is that of theft and loss, but provided that travellers exercise reasonable care to safeguard their cheques in accordance with the agreement entered into at the time of purchase, they should be able to enforce repayment by the issuing bank in accordance with the widely publicized promise to do so.

D. MONEY ORDERS

While travellers' cheques are used by bank customers as a means of taking funds with them when travelling abroad, money orders and bankers' drafts are normally used by bank customers as a means of transmitting funds abroad or at a distance either to another party or occasionally to themselves for deposit with a bank elsewhere. Money orders and bankers' drafts are remittance instruments used to pay funds as a substitute for cash. There is very little law about either,[62] nor are there any authoritative definitions in the common law and, from a customer's perspective, they seem to be virtually identical because they appear to serve the same function. Although both have existed for a long time, there are no express provisions about them in the *Bills of Exchange Act (BEA)*, and it is not entirely clear in law whether they are negotiable instruments, although they are treated as such by commercial custom.

Of the two, bankers' drafts are most likely negotiable instruments; money orders are not, although in form they appear to be. The personal money order sold by banks is similar to, and has its origin in, the postal money order that was widely used from the early nineteenth century in the United Kingdom as a means whereby those who were too poor to be

---

60 *First National City Bank of New York v. Frederics-Helton Travel Service Inc.*, 209 N.Y.S.2d 704 (Sup. Ct. 1961).
61 Ellinger, above note 40 at 153–56 for the cases.
62 The only study of these is by Benjamin Geva, "Irrevocability of Bank Drafts, Certified Cheques and Money Orders" (1986) 65 Can. Bar Rev. 107, and this section and the next section are drawn from that study.

bank customers could remit funds at a distance in a form other than cash. Postal orders came into use in Canada in the mid-nineteenth century, but they are now in decline because of the widespread availability of other methods of transmitting funds, especially electronic means. From the mid-twentieth century, American banks made personal money orders available to non-customers on a prepaid basis, and Canadian banks followed. Personal money orders also continue to be available on a prepaid basis from post offices, as well as from private money-transmission companies such as Western Union and Money Mart.

Money orders are sold by banks over the counter to customers and to non–account holders at their face value plus a transaction fee, and the face value may be in a foreign currency. The face value is the value the customer wishes to transmit and within the ceiling set for money orders set by the bank and stated on the order to deter raising of the face value by a rogue. To transmit a larger sum, the customer may use a different means of transmitting funds, or if the recipient cannot receive funds in that way, by sending several money orders. The bank imprints the face value on the money order, but the rest will be in blank form so that the purchaser or "remitter" may fill in the name of the payee, the date, the remitter's name and address, and the remitter's signature. The customer prepays for the money order by any means, and the bank credits the amount to its reserve account in the same way as funds for certified cheques.

But money orders differ from postal money orders in three ways: by the bank having information about the sender; by being payable to the order of the payee, rather than only to the payee; and by requiring the sender's signature and a date in order to be honoured. Prior to the enactment of the money laundering legislation, the postal money order was a relatively anonymous way to transmit funds, but that is no longer the case unless the amount is below the thresholds required to be reported. Private remittance companies, like Western Union, require disclosures of both sender and payee's names, addresses and telephone numbers.

Bank money orders differ from bankers' drafts in three ways: a bankers' draft is issued in complete form and signed by authorized bank officers, and the bank has a complete record of the sender. The comparative informality of the bank money order and the absence of legislative reference to it results in significant ambiguity as to whether it is a negotiable instrument.[63] The only recent Canadian case to

---

63   Professor Geva thinks it is: *ibid.* at 133.

consider it, *Goberdhan v. Banque Canadienne Nationale*,[64] in 1978, does not address the issue directly. In that case, the court held that a blank money order could not be countermanded for two reasons: (i) section 167(a) of the *BEA* refers solely to the countermand of cheques; and (ii) there is a primary obligation on a bank to honour a money order once it is issued. The court equated a money order with a bank note of the Bank of Canada and also with a certified cheque, because the bank has already set aside funds to honour it.

While this case does not decide whether a bank money order is a negotiable instrument, it captures two of the reasons why money orders are treated as negotiable in commercial usage because they are thought of as if cash or a certified cheque, that is, as a guaranteed payment. They are normally paid on presentment and demand, and are probably like certified cheques in that they are enforceable between the payee and the issuing bank directly, especially since they cannot be countermanded. Yet they are not always treated like other negotiable instruments in commercial usage, because many merchants will not take money orders as payment in across-the-counter transactions as they would cash. Their status remains ambiguous, and they should probably be regarded, like travellers' cheques, as *sui generis*.

Notwithstanding this ambiguity, the certified cheque analogy might be briefly explored. If treated in law as if certified cheques, money orders must consist of three quite separate legal relationships, between sender and payee, sender and bank, and bank and payee. A payee may enforce a money order directly against the issuing bank, and any failure of consideration between sender and payee should not affect the enforceability of the money order against the bank. The payee's status is similar to that of a holder in due course. In the unlikely event that there was a failure of consideration between the sender and the bank, for example, in the payment for the money order, then an action by either sender or payee should fail for want of consideration. However, in the absence of legal authority, it is unwise to speculate further about the legal nature of a money order.

E. BANKERS' DRAFTS

Bankers' drafts are negotiable instruments cleared through the clearing and settlement system, by which payment is made between banks, in

---

64 [1978] C.P. 340. See also Geva, above note 62 at 137–43 for American authority.

contrast to a money order, where payment is made between two persons, the sender and the payee, through the issuing bank. Bankers' drafts tend to be used to transmit larger sums of money, often abroad, and there are no economic limits on the value that may be transmitted. They are much less expensive than travellers' cheques because they are sold for a flat fee on top of their face value, although like all other paper payment mechanisms, they are subject to loss or theft, so that electronic transmission of funds is likely safer. When used to transmit funds abroad, they may be drawn either on an overseas branch of the bank or on a correspondent bank.

A bankers' draft is an instrument to pay a specific sum to the payee or to the payer's order, and when it is purchased, the bank normally imprints all of the particulars, including the date, the amount, the payee's name, and the purchaser's name, on the instrument prior to delivery to the customer, who must prepay for it. The draft will be drawn on another specified bank and signed by two authorized officers, making it a statutory payment obligation by the bank on the instruments.[65] The payee may be the purchaser, as when funds are being transmitted abroad, or another party to whom the purchaser wishes to transmit funds. As with certified cheques and money orders, the purchase funds will be placed in the branch's reserve account.

Strictly speaking, a bankers' draft drawn on a branch of the same bank is neither a cheque nor a bill, because there is no distinct drawer or drawee.[66] However, it is equivalent to a promissory note, and the holder has a statutory option to treat the instrument as a promissory note or a bill.[67] Treated as a bill, the bank's liability is as the drawer, but treated as a note, the bank's liability is as the maker to pay according to its terms.[68] However, the distinctions imposed by the *BEA* amount to academic hairsplitting, because it seems unlikely that a bank would refuse to favour an instrument drawn on itself and for which it has been prepaid. The *bona fide* holder of a bankers' draft is in as good a position as the holder of any other negotiable instrument and entitled to enforce it against the bank.[69]

---

65 *Bills of Exchange Act*, R.S.C. 1985, c. B-4, ss. 16(1), 165(1), and 176(1) [*BEA*].
66 *Ibid.*
67 Geva, above note 62 at 117–18.
68 *BEA*, above note 65, ss. 16(1), 165(1), 176(1), and 185(a).
69 See generally *Willans v. Ayers* (1877), 3 App. Cas. 133 (P.C.); *Re Commercial Bank of South Australia* (1887), 36 Ch. D. 522; *Capital and Counties Bank Ltd. v. Gordon*, [1903] A.C. 240 (H.L.).

A bankers' draft drawn on a corresponding bank satisfies the *BEA* requirements for both bills and cheques[70] and can be enforced like any other negotiable instrument. A draft drawn on a foreign correspondent bank is a foreign bill, because it is not drawn and payable within Canada or drawn on a person resident in Canada.[71] If dishonoured, it must be protested; otherwise, the drawer is discharged.[72] The protest will be governed by the law of the foreign jurisdiction where the bill is dishonoured.[73] Whether the draft is drawn on an inland or a foreign bank, the drawee bank incurs no liability to the holder, since it has not signed the instrument[74] nor accepted it.[75] Thus, liability to the holder or payee is that of the drawer bank alone, because it signed the draft.[76]

Normally, bankers' drafts are honoured immediately upon presentment for payment or deposit once the holder or payee shows sufficient identification, subject to the clearing and settlement rules for final payment. Bankers' drafts drawn on foreign correspondents are normally subject to delays until cleared to the drawer bank or one of its overseas branches.

Finally, it would seem that if bankers' drafts are negotiable instruments, they should be subject to the *BEA* when forged, altered, or not genuine, but there is no case law to that effect.

F. LETTERS OF CREDIT

The final payment mechanism that will be briefly mentioned in this chapter is the letter of credit. This means of effecting payment at a distance is unlikely ever to be used by an ordinary consumer customer of a bank, because it evolved to facilitate payments in commercial transactions at a distance and is largely used today in international trade. A brief description will suffice here.[77]

---

70 *BEA*, above note 65 at ss. 16(1) and 176(1).
71 *Ibid.*, s. 26.
72 *Ibid.*, ss. 108–25.
73 *Ibid.*, s. 161.
74 *Ibid.*, s. 130.
75 *Ibid.*, s. 126.
76 The fact that the signatures are preprinted facsimiles is irrelevant: *Re London and Mediterranean Bank; ex parte Birmingham Banking Co.* (1868), L.R. 3 Ch. App. 651 (C.A.).
77 Some leading texts include: H.C. Gutteridge & Maurice Megrah, *The Law of Bankers' Commercial Credits*, 7th ed. (London: Europa, 1984); Lazar Sarna, *Letters of Credit: The Law and Current Practice*, 3d ed., looseleaf (Toronto: Carswell,

A letter of credit is a written undertaking by a bank to pay money to a designated person upon receipt of a demand accompanied by the delivery of documents specified in the letter or upon the occurrence of an event specified in the letter. A letter of credit consists of four interconnected contractual relationships: (i) an underlying contract for the sale of goods between buyer and seller; (ii) a contract between the buyer and the issuing bank, in which the bank agrees to issue the letter on terms dictated by the buyer, who promises to indemnify the bank for all payments made; (iii) a contract between the issuing bank and the confirming bank, in which the confirming bank agrees to honour the credit on presentment of conforming documents by or on behalf of the seller, the beneficiary, and the confirming bank also agrees to reimburse the seller, the beneficiary, for doing so; and (iv) a contract between the confirming bank and the seller, by which the confirming bank agrees to pay the seller up to the amount of the credit against presentation of the stipulated documents.[78] In short, the purpose is to facilitate payment for the sale of goods or services at a distance, using banks as the means for confirming both the availability of payment and payment, as well as the delivery of the goods and services being bought. This is effected because the issuing bank is contractually bound to honour a credit commitment when the documents conforming to the terms for credit are presented.[79]

Letters of credit law is a separate and highly specialized branch of banking law of especial importance to international trade law and is normally discussed in the context of international trade law, rather than domestic banking law.

G. CONCLUSION

This chapter, together with the four preceding chapters, demonstrates that banks may perform their duties as agents to pay and collect funds on behalf of customers in many different ways and by many different legal mechanisms, whether paper or electronic. The core duties as be-

---

1989–); Leo D'Arcy, Carole Murray, & Barbara Cleave, eds., *Schmitthoff's Export Trade: The Law and Practice of International Trade*, 10th ed. (London: Sweet & Maxwell, 2000).

78 *United City Merchants Investments Ltd. v. Royal Bank of Canada*, [1983] 1 A.C. 168 at 182–83 (H.L.), Lord Diplock.

79 *Bank of Nova Scotia v. Angelica-Whitewear Ltd.* (1987), 36 D.L.R. (4th) 161 at 173 (S.C.C.), LeDain J..

tween bank and customer and the legal standard of care with which those duties are to be performed have remained constant over the centuries, although the evolution of the legal mechanisms within which those duties are performed continues to unfold in ways unimagined in the recent past.

CHAPTER 12

SAFEKEEPING

A. INTRODUCTION

Banks have provided safekeeping for customer property of value since the beginning of modern banking in late mediaeval Europe and safekeeping remains a service used by most customers in addition to those related to accounts and loans. Safekeeping is normally available by three means: safety deposit boxes, safekeeping, and night safe depositories, each governed by contract. In addition to such voluntary contracts of bailment, banks may also become bailees of customer property such as collateral securities taken for loans[1] and other securities traded by their customers through an agency and temporarily in the possession of the bank.[2] They might also become involuntary bailees of personal property forgotten at a branch by the customer and owe a duty to the customer not to damage them.[3] When customers enter into a contract

---

1 *Carnegie v. Federal Bank of Canada* (1884), 5 O.R. 418 (Ch.); *Hochelaga Bank v. Larue* (1910), 13 W.L.R. 114 (Alta. C.A.); *Royal Bank v. Talbot*, [1928] 3 D.L.R. 157 (Alta. S.C.A.D.); *Sterling Bank v. McVety*, [1923] 3 D.L.R. 246 (Sask. C.A.) [*McVety*].
2 *TDF Investments Ltd. v. Canadian Bank of Commerce* (1961), 27 D.L.R. (2d) 609 (Ont. C.A.). This is less likely today, since securities in paper form (now rare) are stored with the Canadian Depository for Securities Ltd., a central depository and settlement system for securities in Canada. See D.M. Hanley, "Central Depository System for Securities" (1983) 7 Can. Bus. L.J. 306.
3 *Bell v. Capital and Counties Bank* (1887), 3 T.L.R. 540 (Q.B.D.); *Heddle v. Bank of Hamilton* (1912), 5 D.L.R. 11 (B.C.C.A.).

395

of bailment for safekeeping, the bank is only a bailee and does not acquire a banker's lien[4] over the items deposited.[5]

There is no express provision in the *Bank Act* permitting banks to offer safekeeping services; however, this may be treated like all the other lacuna in the Act, such as branches and accounts, for which the Act does not contain express permission, on the grounds that these are self-evidently what banks have done since the inception of banking and that there are provisions in the Act in which statutory permission is implicit. Thus, in respect to safekeeping, the provision for transmission of property on death in section 460 presumes property in the possession of the bank available for transmission to representatives of the deceased's estate.

Each of the three bailment services provided by the banks will be considered in turn: safekeeping, safety deposit boxes, and night safe depositories.

B. SAFEKEEPING

The word "safekeeping" may be used broadly to encompass any facility provided by a bank for the bailment of customer property, or it may be used narrowly to refer to a particular type of custodial service distinguishable from safety deposit boxes and night safe depositories. In Canada, safety deposit boxes are the usual means of offering safekeeping, but in England, safekeeping is normally provided in a bank's safe for sealed envelopes or small locked boxes provided by the customer. English law on safekeeping, then, refers to this practice, and may be of limited application in Canada where the safety deposit box is the norm. However, Canadian banks occasionally offer safekeeping facilities, usually for securities or bullion, so the English case law is potentially of persuasive importance in relation to these.

Safekeeping, narrowly defined, involves the deposit by the customer of a sealed envelope or small locked box with a bank, which places these in its vault system, together with any others received from other customers. The vault is accessible by any bank employee permitted access, and the customer may recover the deposit during normal business hours; customers do not have keys or any part of the vault set apart for their own deposits. This service is provided under a contract, which consists of a comprehensibly drafted clause excluding liability on the

---

4   Chapter 7, Section K.
5   *Leese v. Martin* (1873), L.R. 17 Eq. 224.

part of the bank for all loss or damage and paid for by a small fee or provided free of charge to regular customers.

Where no fee is paid for safekeeping, it has been suggested that the bank is a gratuitous bailee, who is bound to exercise reasonable care.[6] However, it is unlikely that the standard is low because a reasonable person would take great care of the type of valuables normally entrusted to a bank for safekeeping because of their secure safekeeping facilities, so the standard is probably the same as that of a bailee for reward.[7] It is also arguable that although no fee is paid specifically for safekeeping, there is good consideration in the account agreement generally.[8] But even if a bank is a gratuitous bailee, it remains liable, although it is ignorant of the nature of the property committed to it for safekeeping,[9] and an acknowledgement that goods are received "for safe custody" does not affect the liability.[10] There are also some legal grounds for arguing that where no fee is paid for safekeeping, the bank is still a bailee for reward because there is a hope that the person might also contract for other services provided by the bank.[11] In short, notwithstanding that a bank may charge no fee for providing safekeeping services, the courts treat the bailment as if one for reward and determine the standard of care to be a higher standard as a result.[12]

As a bailee, a bank is subject to the usual duties of a bailee, including exercising reasonable care in the employment of employees;[13] liability for dishonest employees;[14] liability for loss or theft of the property left for safekeeping;[15] liability for delivering the property to the wrong person, usually in conversion;[16] and liability for inadvertent sale of the property.[17] The usual measure of damages is the value of the property lost or stolen,[18] but it may be less in the circumstances.[19]

---

6 *Giblin v. McMullen* (1869), L.R. 2 P.C. 317.
7 *Houghland v. R.R. Low (Luxury Coaches) Ltd.*, [1962] 2 All E.R. 159 (C.A.).
8 *Port Swettenham Authority v. T.W. Wu & Co (M.) Sdn. Bhd.*, [1979] A.C. 580 (P.C.).
9 *Giblin v. McMullen*, above note 6.
10 *Ross v. Hill* (1846), 2 C.B. 877, 135 E.R. 1190.
11 *De la Bere v. Pearson Ltd.*, [1907] 1 K.B. 483 (C.A.).
12 Above note 8 for this position.
13 *Williams v. Curzon Syndicate Ltd.* (1919), 35 T.L.R. 475 (C.A.).
14 *Lloyd v. Grace, Smith & Co.*, [1912] A.C. 716 (H.L.); *Morris v. C.W. Martin & Sons Ltd.*, [1965] 2 All E.R. 725 (C.A.).
15 *Lilley v. Doubleday* (1881), 7 Q.B.D. 510.
16 *Stevenson v. Hart* (1828), 4 Bing. 476, 130 E.R. 851; *Glyns Mills, Currie & Co. v. East and West India Dock Co.* (1882), 7 App. Cas. 591 (H.L.).
17 *United States of America v. Dollfus Mieg et Cie SA*, [1952] A.C. 582 (H.L.).
18 *Royal Bank v. Talbot*, above note 1.
19 *Union Bank v. Farmer*, [1917] 1 W.W.R. 1361 (Alta. S.C.T.D.); *McVety*, above note 1.

C. SAFETY DEPOSIT BOXES

Safekeeping in Canada is almost invariably in the form of safety deposit boxes rented by banks to customers on an annual basis. These boxes come in various sizes and are stored in the bank's vault with a double lock. Customers have access during banking hours on production of their key and a signature and possibly other identification. A two-key system for each box, one for the bank and one for the customer, is required for access to the box. This service is provided pursuant to contract, and today the standard account agreement is normally used for the provisions for safety deposit box operation. These provisions typically include the following: (i) an annual lease of the box, provided the annual rental fee is paid in advance; (ii) a promise of reasonable care by the bank in ensuring that only the customer or the customer's representative is permitted access; (iii) a requirement for identification from the customer for access; (iv) no liability for the bank if access is prevented because of failure in the working of the vaults or any mechanisms or locks therein; (v) customer liability for loss of keys, including the expense of a new lock; (vi) rules for entry by the customer into the vault, including with a bank employee and when there are no other customers in the vault; (vii) rules about the contents of boxes; (viii) a prohibition on the customer assigning or subletting the box; (ix) customer indemnification of the bank for costs incurred by virtue of any legal proceeding relating to the contents of the box; (x) the right of the bank to terminate the lease; (xi) the rights of the bank on non-payment of the rent, including forcible opening of the box and removal of the contents for storage on special deposit, for which a fee is required until the customer receives them; and (xii) provision for rent prepayment, usually by a preauthorized debit (PAD) from an account. Clearly, these contracts are contracts of adhesion, the general function of which is to restrict the liability of the bank in most circumstances.

Once a lease for a safety deposit box is entered, the bank becomes a bailee for reward of the contents of the box and, at common law, subject to a duty of reasonable care for those contents unless the contract expressly restricts that duty in some way. In *Cuvelier v. Bank of Montreal*,[20]

---

20 (2000), 189 N.S.R. (2d) 26, 590 A.P.R. 26 (S.C.). Two Quebec cases based on the Code Civil also set the standard as reasonable care: *Banque Canadienne Nationale v. Mastracchio* (1961), 30 D.L.R. (2d) 510 (S.C.C.) and *Banque Canadienne Nationale v. Boston Insurance Co.*, [1963] Que. Q.B. 487 (C.A.). See also A.L. Stein, "The Safety Deposit Vault or Leased Metal Box: The Responsibility of the Bank to Its Customer" (1972) 18 McGill L.J. 45.

the Nova Scotia Supreme Court upheld this duty to take reasonable care where the bank mistakenly "drilled," that is, had a locksmith open a safety deposit box. On discovering the mistake, the bank informed the customer and requested that he pick up the contents of the box. He discovered that $29,150.00 stored in the box was missing and successfully sued the bank for its return on the basis of breach of the bank's duty as a bailee to take reasonable care. The onus to prove the loss was on the customer, who did so by virtue of his children's evidence that their father kept large sums of money in his box. The customer's action for aggravated and punitive damages failed on the ground that the bank's conduct was a mistake but not egregious.

Punitive damages were, however, awarded in another case in which the safety deposit box was drilled. In *Mohtadi v. Canada Trust Co.*,[21] the trust company's records erroneously showed that the customer had not paid the box rental fee, although at the time when she rented it, she agreed that the rental be debited from her account. The trust company's own records were problematical, but the trust company drilled the box and removed the contents. She learned of this when she could not access the box and sued for wrongful interference with the contents, including lost items. The court found that there was wrongful interference and restored the contents to her. Although the court made no award for the alleged loss of jewellery in the box, it awarded nominal damages of $500.00 for the tort of wrongful interference, as well as $5,000.00 for aggravated damages and $15,000.00 for punitive damages, on the grounds that she was very angry and upset by these events and that the bank's misconduct was sufficient to justify punitive damages. *Mohtadi* suggests that a customer will be more likely to get aggravated and punitive damages suing in tort, rather than in breach of contract.

Comparison of these two Canadian cases about responsibility for the contents of a safety deposit box with the only other case on the matter suggests that the question of responsibility is more subtle. In *Commissioner of Taxation v. The Australia and New Zealand Banking Group Ltd.*,[22] a decision of the Australian High Court, the fact that the bank retained a duplicate of the customer key was used by the court to conclude that the bank retained control and custody of the contents and that a statutory power to compel production of documents in the box enjoyed by the tax authority could be directed against the bank. The court did not consider whether the bank was a bailee of the contents, so it is not clear whether retention of a duplicate key is significant. Bail-

---

21   (2002), 6 B.C.L.R. (4th) 25 (B.C.C.A.).
22   (1979), 53 A.L.J.R. 336 (H.C.A.).

ment means entrusting personal property to the possession of another for safekeeping, and it is to be expected that the bailee would have a means of accessing the place of safekeeping. Conversely, if the bailee does not retain a duplicate key, it may be asked whether the relationship is a true bailment or a unique relationship in law by virtue of the requirement in the two-key system used by Canadian banks that both bank and customer coordination is required for access. This does not affect the standard of care expected of banks with custody of a customer's personal property; rather, it suggests that the standard is restricted to that part of the custody arrangement over which the bank has control. Control over safety deposit boxes appears to be a shared control.

D. NIGHT SAFE DEPOSITORIES

Night safe depositories are normally used by businesses, especially small businesses, at the end of each business day, to ensure the safekeeping of money and paper payment items received during the course of that business day, which the depositor wishes to have deposited into accounts with the bank on the next business day. The depository consists of a locked chute into which locked wallets or other sealed packages may be put from a letter-box-like aperture on the outside wall of a bank branch. The packets slide into a locked bin and are cleared by bank employees in the morning. This service is also regulated by a specific contract, which provides for such matters as access by keys or pass codes; the contents of the packages deposited; required lists of the property deposited; and the liabilities of the two parties in the operation of this service. American case law holds that a bank should be treated as a bailee for reward from the moment of deposit by the customer, even though the bank is unaware of any actual deposit until the locked bin is opened each morning.[23] This seems self-evident, because banks hold out this service for a fee and should anticipate that bailment of valuables will be made in accordance with the contract by a customer.

In *Royal Bank of Canada v. Reynolds*,[24] the Nova Scotia Court of Appeal held that a deposit was completed only when the contents of a package deposited were verified and accepted by the bank. Prior to that time, the bank was a bailee and liable for funds stolen between the

---

23 *Bernstein v. Northwestern National Bank in Philadelphia*, 41 A.2d 440 (Pa. Super. 1945).
24 (1975), 66 D.L.R. (3d) 88 (N.S.C.A.).

time a package was deposited and processed by the bank. On construction, the exclusion clause applied only to the period of time when the property was still in the locked bin and did not protect the bank from liability for theft between the time when the bin was opened and the package contents were deposited in accounts.

E. CONCLUSION

The case law on contracts relating to safekeeping, safety deposit boxes, and night safe depositories is sparse. However, each relationship is governed by contract, and the courts will enforce those contracts in accordance with the normal rules of contract construction. Each of these arrangements has been found to be bailments for reward, and the law of bailment is well developed. The paucity of case law suggests, however, that problems are rare and likely to remain so.

CHAPTER 13

BANK AND CUSTOMER DISPUTE RESOLUTION

A. INTRODUCTION

Banks are large, complex organizations, and banking involves complex services and legal relationships managed by fallible individuals for fallible individuals. Errors occur and must be corrected. In most instances, this can be done simply at the branch when either the bank or the customer notices the problem and secures an immediate resolution. Occasionally, there is a difference of opinion as to the correct solution, and third party intervention may be required to determine what that solution is. Alternative dispute resolution (ADR) for customers has been available in the Canadian banking context since 1994, when individual banks implemented internal dispute resolution procedures for their own customers, followed in 1996 by the establishment of the Canadian Banking Ombudsman (CBO) by the banking sector to hear appeals from individual bank processes. In this, Canada followed the implementation of banking ombudsman schemes in other common law countries, including the United Kingdom (1986), Ireland (1990), Australia (1990), and New Zealand (1992).[1]

---

1   See generally M.H. Ogilvie, "Banking Ombudsmen: A Necessary Evil or Simply Not Necessary?" (1996) 11 B.F.L.R. 167 and Jacqueline J. Williams, "Canadian Financial Services Ombudsmen: The Role of Reputational Persuasion" (2004) 20 B.F.L.R. 41.

Since the mid-1990s, the provision of ADR in relation to banks and other financial institutions has been in a constant flux, with new law, new organizations, and the restructuring of old organizations becoming almost yearly events. In this chapter, the evolution of ADR in the financial services sector will be traced, and then the present system will be described. The proliferation of ombudsman schemes and the involvement of various state agencies have resulted in a surprising degree of complexity for a service devised to assist consumers and supposedly designed to facilitate, rather than obfuscate, dispute resolution.

B. THE EVOLUTION OF ADR IN THE BANKING SECTOR

The 1991 *Bank Act* required that Canadian banks offer internal dispute resolution procedures for customer complaints about bank charges applicable to deposit accounts, payment, credit or charge cards, or the disclosure and calculation of the cost of borrowing in respect of loans made by a bank.[2] The Act provided further recourse to the Office of the Superintendent of Financial Institutions (OSFI) for a customer dissatisfied with the proposed internal resolution, and although it was not really designed to resolve consumer complaints, OSFI continued to serve that appeal function until the establishment of the CBO in 1996. The creation of the CBO in 1996 was a response to public and political pressure, especially from the small business community, which complained that banks were insensitive to their particular financing needs and which proposed in 1994 that one improvement would be a national ombudsman scheme similar to that in the United Kingdom.[3] The Canadian Bankers Association proposed, in response, not only a model code of conduct for dealing with small and medium-sized businesses but also a model ADR code for small business complaints,[4] and in 1996 it established the CBO as a nationwide service for both small businesses and individuals.

---

2   S.C. 1991, c. 46, ss. 455–56.
3   Canada, Parliament, House of Commons, Standing Committee on Industry, *Taking Care of Small Business* (Ottawa: Publications Services, Parliamentary Publications Directorate , 1994).
4   Canadian Bankers Association, *A Model Code of Conduct for Bank Relations with Small and Medium-Sized Businesses* and *Canadian Banking Industry Alternative Dispute Resolution (ADR) Model* (Toronto: Canadian Bankers Association, 1995).

The Office of the CBO was run by a not-for-profit corporation, the Canadian Banking Ombudsman Inc., whose members were all banks that chose to join the corporation. The CBO was funded by member banks assessed on the basis of their assets, and a two-tiered board system was implemented to ensure that the banks were kept at arms length from the day-to-day operations of the CBO.[5] In 1998, the MacKay Task Force recommended a single ombudsman system for the entire financial services sector, including the insurance sector, and that such a service be established by federal legislation and be state supervised.[6] The 2001 legislation empowered the Minister of Finance to establish a not-for-profit corporation the purpose of which was to deal with complaints not resolved at the individual financial institution level.[7] However, this power has not been implemented, because the banks and the insurance companies proposed instead an industry-run model and the government accepted this alternative.[8]

In November 2002, the Centre for Financial Services OmbudsNetwork (CFSON) was established as a national umbrella organization the purpose of which is to direct consumers to industry-specific ombudsman offices. CFSON is not an ombudsman service. Its membership includes members of the CBA, the Investment Dealers Association of Canada (IDA), the Mutual Fund Dealers Association of Canada (MFDA), the Investment Funds Institute of Canada (IFIC), the Insurance Bureau of Canada (IBC), and the Canadian Life and Health Insurance Association (CLHIA). Its function is to direct consumers to the appropriate dispute resolution service for the consumer's problem: the Ombudsman for Banking Services and Investments (OBSI), the Canadian Life and Health Insurance OmbudService (CLHIO), or the General Insurance OmbudService (GIO). OBSI deals with disputes from banks, investment dealers, mutual fund dealers, and most federally regulated trust and loan companies.

CFSON is a not-for-profit corporation governed by an eleven-member board of directors drawn from the participating organizations and the consumer and public-interest constituencies. To ensure independence, CFSON is structured to include five directors who are not financial institution members; to exclude authority to intervene in the OBSI, CLHIO, and GIO; and to secure funding from industry-level organizations such as the CBA, rather than directly from financial institutions

---

5   Ogilvie, above note 1.
6   See Chapter 2, Section D for MacKay Task Force recommendations.
7   *Bank Act*, above note 2, s. 455.1(1).
8   Williams, above note 1.

against whom redress is sought by consumer complainants. Consumers pay no user fees for CFSON assistance in identifying the appropriate ombudsman service for their complaint. CFSON offers a 1-800 number and a website[9] to assist complainants. It has also developed industry-wide standards for all ombudsman bodies, including accessibility, timelines, courtesy, clarity, accuracy, and consistency in outcomes and provides an annual report on the system as a whole.

Although in operation for a short period of time, it is possible to identify some problems with the model adopted in CFSON. First, from a consumer perspective, it is confusing to have both CFSON and the industry ombudsman; CFSON appears to be an unnecessary bureaucratic layer. Secondly, it is not clear why a bifurcated model of CFSON and the industry ombudsman was adopted in place of a single national officer as is now used in other countries. The insurance sector's longstanding fear of the banking sector may be the answer. Thirdly, CFSON is said to have too may ties to the federal government insofar as a majority of its board have past government ties and its policies seem more sympathetic to the state than to the private sector. Fourthly, the standards which it has established are so trite and self-evident that it seems unnecessary to state them.[10] Notwithstanding these criticisms, the CFSON is the overriding structure within which OBSI, GIO, and CLHIO operate to deal with complaints from the consumers of their services.

For bank customers, OBSI provides ADR in relation to disputes with their own banks about banking transactions. However, it should be recalled that in 2001, Parliament created another organization that also plays a role in consumer dispute issues, that is, the Financial Consumer Agency of Canada (FCAC).[11] In operation since 2002, the FCAC has the specific function of ensuring that financial institutions comply with consumer legislation relating to banking. In this capacity, it receives complaints from customers concerning matters for which there is statutory provision, such as disclosure of lending rates, credit card interest, and internal bank customer complaint procedures, and investigates these with the bank. It does not resolve individual customer disputes; rather, it penalizes any institution in breach of consumer legislation, requires compliance, and reports its findings annually to Parliament. The FCAC operates as a watchdog over the banks in relation to consumer-oriented banking legislation but does not provide investigation or redress for individual complaints. For these, bank cus-

---

9   Online: www.cfson-cresf.ca.
10 Williams, above note 1 at 64–67.
11 Chapter 3, Section G.

tomers must first attempt a solution with their bank and secondly appeal to the Ombudsman for Banking Services and Investments (OBSI).

C. THE OMBUDSMAN FOR BANKING SERVICES AND INVESTMENTS (OBSI)

OBSI evolved from the previous CBO office first established in 1996 under the direction of the CBO Ombudsman, who continued as OBSI Ombudsman. Its role expanded in 2002 to provide dispute resolution for customers of investment dealers, investment funds, and mutual funds, as well as banks, and the membership base expanded from thirteen banks to over five hundred other financial institutions, including domestic and foreign banks. OBSI is a not-for-profit corporation composed of its board of directors and members. Its constitution is set out in its Terms of Reference,[12] which are largely unchanged from the Terms of Reference for the CBO.

There are fourteen directors, of whom eight are independent directors who are not affiliated in any way with the financial services industry, although all are knowledgeable about the sector. The independent directors are chosen on the basis of reputation and diversity, and the six other board members come from the financial sector, two from each of the Canadian Bankers Association (CBA) and the Investment Dealers Association of Canada (IDA), and one from each of the Mutual Fund Dealers Association of Canada (MFDA) and the Investment Funds Institute of Canada (IFIC). The directors are elected for three-year, staggered terms, and the independent directors are paid an annual fee and additional amounts for each meeting attended. The independent directors are a specific committee of the board with special powers to act as a nominating committee, recommend candidates for Ombusdman, and review the budget, and they must form the majority in all board committees. The board approves the annual budget, determines the Terms of Reference, and evaluates the performance of the office itself. The Ombudsman acts independently of the board in resolving disputes but reports to the board on the operation of the office.

The board appoints the Ombudsman[13] for a term of up to five years, and the Ombudsman may be reappointed. The Ombudsman must never have been a government employee and must not have worked

---

12   Online: www.obsi.ca. The description of how OBSI operates that follows in the text is drawn from the Terms of Reference on its website.
13   The OBSI Terms of Reference, *ibid.*, ss. 2–9 set out the role of the Ombudsman.

with a participating financial services provider for five years prior to appointment. The Ombudsman may be removed for cause by 75 percent of the board, provided that the vote includes a majority of the independent directors. While the Ombudsman makes the final decision about complaints brought to the office, with no appeal to the board, the board establishes and monitors OBSI standards for complaint handling and deals with customer complaints about the process used by OBSI in complaint handling.

OBSI is funded by annual assessments to financial service providers that are members of the CBA, IDA, MFDA, and IFIC, and the board approves the budget annually. Although the board is responsible for ensuring that funding is in place, the Ombudsman is responsible for managing the office itself, with power to appoint and dismiss employees, enter contracts with independent contractors, and ensure the proper handling of customer complaints. The Ombudsman normally attends all board meetings, makes an annual report to the board and, in turn, receives annual reports from the internal ombudsman of the member financial institutions about the complaints their respective offices have received from customers.

The chief criticism directed at the corporate governance structure of OBSI is that it is perceived to lack independence because neither its funding nor a significant minority of the board are independent of the financial services sector. The only alternative would be a state-run office, but that, too, would suffer from the perception of lack of independence, this time from the state, so there is no easy solution. However, the greatest assurance of no interference with the dispute adjudication process is gained from the integrity and high professionalism of the Ombudsman himself and of the staff of the Office in its conduct of the hearing process, about which there have never been any serious complaints.

D. HOW OBSI WORKS

When a customer of a bank or any other financial institution has a problem with a banking transaction, the first step is to raise the issue with the local branch, first with a staff member designated to resolve issues and then with the local branch manager, who has authority to resolve issues commensurate with the authority of a branch manager in that bank. If the customer is not satisfied with the manager's proposed resolution, then the customer or the manager, at the customer's request, may take the matter to a designated higher officer of the bank, either through a 1-800 number or some other form of communication at the customer's discretion. If the customer is still unhappy, the third step within the bank is to contact the bank's own ombudsman, whose contact information is provided by a brochure required to be available at the branch, including address, fax, email, and 1-800 number. The bank ombudsman will attempt to provide a resolution within a week or two or will advise of the steps being taken to secure a resolution within the same time period. The bank ombudsman typically is part of the immediate office of the president and reports directly to the president of the bank, but otherwise is independent from the everyday operations of the bank. At all three steps, the process is characterized by informality: complaints may be made orally or in writing, and corrections may be made immediately; there is no need for legal or other third party representation; and the aim is to be consumer friendly. Bank staff attend staff training programs to facilitate the goal of an informal and speedy resolution.

If the complainant is a small business, neutral mediation is offered by the bank. Participation is voluntary, and the cost is designed to be attractive to a small business, but if no resolution results, then the small business, like the individual consumer, may take the final step outside the bank by filing a complaint with OBSI, whose contact information is also provided by the bank.

Before OBSI will consider a complaint, certain requirements must be satisfied: (i) the complaint is made by the complainant, or a personal representative of the complainant, to whom the banking service was supplied; (ii) all the persons entitled to make that claim are complainants; (iii) the complainants are individuals or small business customers; (iv) the internal bank processes have been exhausted; (v) the complaint is made within 180 days of the internal proposed solution; (vi) the complaint was not contained in a previous complaint unless new evidence is available in the opinion of the Ombudsman; (vii) neither the complaint nor any other complaints by the same complainant are subject to any other dispute resolution process, including in any court of law unless the bank consents in writing to the Ombudsman; (viii) the complainant has waived the duty of confidence owed to the complainant as a customer; and (ix) the complaint is not frivolous, vexatious, or being pursued in a threatening manner.[14]

The Terms of Reference exclude three categories of dispute over which the Ombudsman has no jurisdiction: (i) complaints about the bank's general interest rates, prices for products and services, general industry policies, and credit-granting policies or risk-management poli-

---

14   Ibid., s. 10.

cies;[15] (ii) complaints which the Ombudsman decides are more suitably adjudicated in a court of law or in some other dispute-resolution process;[16] and (iii) complaints relating to a practice or policy of a bank that does not give rise to a breach of any obligation or duty owed by the bank to the complainant.[17] To ensure that a complaint falls within OBSI's jurisdiction, OBSI may consult with both complainant and bank,[18] and once OBSI agrees to investigate a complaint, it shall determine the process within the general standards set by the board.[19]

The complainant is required to sign a plain language agreement with OBSI prior to the start of the investigation, which sets out the process and authorizes the complainant's bank to send its files relating to the complaint but also requires that the complainant agree that OBSI files will not be used in any subsequent court proceeding and OBSI staff will not be called to testify.[20] OBSI normally requires the bank to provide all non-privileged information relating to the complaint, and the bank is expected to use its best efforts to obtain any consents necessary for disclosure, although OBSI may itself seek such consent if the bank does not do so.[21] Information provided to OBSI on a confidential basis by the complainant will not be disclosed without consent; however, if the information is prejudicial to another party, OBSI is not entitled to reach a decision adverse to that party by use of information for which consent to disclose is refused.[22] The sole exception is where OBSI takes account of a bank's proprietary systems and security measures of which it has knowledge, although no disclosure of this information is made to the complainant.[23]

The complaint investigation process is informal and flexible, involving examination of the files by an OBSI investigator assigned to the complaint, meetings with the complainant and the bank separately or together, and making a recommendation. After the investigation, OBSI may reject or cease to consider the complaint if it decides the bank has acted correctly;[24] promote a settlement or withdrawal of the complaint;

---

15 *Ibid.*, s. 11.
16 *Ibid.*, s. 12.
17 *Ibid.*, s. 13.
18 *Ibid.*, s. 15.
19 *Ibid.*, s. 14.
20 Ombudsman for Banking Services and Investments, *Annual Report 2004* (Toronto: Ombudsman for Banking Services and Investments, 2004) at 9.
21 Above note 12, s. 17.
22 *Ibid.*, s. 18.
23 *Ibid.*, s. 19.
24 *Ibid.*, ss. 2(a) and 16.

or make a recommendation for settlement or withdrawal.[25] Throughout the investigation process, the complainant and the bank may continue to negotiate a resolution themselves. OBSI's recommendation must be in writing and must include a summary of the reasons,[26] but it is not binding on either the complainant or the bank.[27] OBSI tries to ensure that there is consistency in all its recommendations, although it is not bound by its previous recommendations.[28] A recommendation to compensate is restricted to direct loss, damage, or inconvenience suffered as a result of the acts or omissions of the bank.[29] No other criteria for recommendations are provided by the Terms of Reference.[30]

Throughout the process, OBSI is committed to privacy. Thus, there is no disclosure to any person (including the board members) of any information or document concerning a complainant or of the complainant or the bank's name.[31] OBSI is under a strict rule that no disclosures be made,[32] with certain exceptions: (i) disclosures acquired by competent authorities or required in connection with legal proceedings against OBSI or its officers;[33] (ii) disclosures about a complaint or a bank made to the chair of the board;[34] (iii) disclosures to OBSI employees in the course of performing their duties;[35] and (iv) disclosures by the Ombudsman to a bank, of any threat to bank staff or property learned in the course of performing the duties of OBSI.[36]

Legal representation of a complainant is not expressly excluded by the Terms of Reference; however, it seems clear that dispute resolution at OBSI is designed to be informal and resolution oriented and in the complainant's interests, so that the expense of hiring legal counsel is avoided. OBSI aims to complete the process as soon as possible and generally completes about 80 percent of its files within ninety days from the day the complaint was filed.[37] The current ceiling for compensation has been set by the board at $350,000.00.[38]

---

25 Ibid., s. 20.
26 Ibid., s. 21.
27 Ibid., s. 22.
28 Ibid., s. 23.
29 Ibid., s. 24.
30 Ibid., s. 25.
31 Ibid., s. 26.
32 Ibid., s. 26. See the OBSI website, above note 12, for the privacy policy.
33 Ibid., s. 26.
34 Ibid., s. 16.
35 Ibid.
36 Ibid.
37 Above note 20 at 9.
38 Ibid.

The final recommendation of the Ombudsman is non-binding on the complainant, who may still sue the bank in the civil courts, although it is binding on the bank, which must in the meantime provide the recommended redress regardless of the complainant's decision to seek a legal solution. Banks always comply with the ombudsman's recommendation. OBSI accepts about 200 banking complaints a year for investigation. Many potential complainants are directed back to the bank for internal processes prior to OBSI investigation or are simply informed about what OBSI is permitted to do and referred to other options. Of the complaints investigated, about 15 percent result in compensation for the complainant, and this figure is in keeping with the experience of other, similar services internationally.[39] The most frequent types of issues about which complaints are made include, in order of volume: mortgages, debit cards, credit cards, and bank accounts. The debit and credit card complaints were predominantly about fraudulent, unauthorized transactions.[40]

OBSI is subject to ongoing review of its practices and procedures and will undergo an external audit in 2007 to ensure that it is following best practices internationally in the interests of consumers.

E. CONCLUSION

Dispute resolution in the banking sector has undergone many changes in the first decade of its existence. To date, and despite state threats to the contrary, the financial institutions sector generally has been quick to adapt to the new ADR environment, providing highly professional services through OBSI in the banking sector in particular. It is doubtful that a national, state-run system is necessary; it is equally doubtful that a state-run system can do a better job than is already being done voluntarily by the banking community.

---

39 *Ibid.* at 17.
40 *Ibid.*

TABLE OF CASES

2203850 Nova Scotia Ltd. v. Sarkar (1995), 145 N.S.R. (2d) 101,
   23 B.L.R. (2d) 28, [1995] N.S.J. No. 342 (S.C.) 264
239199 Alberta Ltd. v. Patel (1993), 145 A.R. 10, 105 D.L.R. (4th) 739,
   [1993] A.J. No. 577 (C.A.) 301–2
373409 Alberta Ltd. v. Bank of Montreal, [2002] 4 S.C.R. 312,
   220 D.L.R. (4th) 193, [2002] S.C.J. No. 82 294–95
69971 Manitoba Ltd. v. National Bank of Canada (1995), 122 D.L.R.
   (4th) 609, 100 Man. R. (2d) 214, [1995] M.J. No. 132 (C.A.) 248–49

A. & A. Jewellers Ltd. v. Royal Bank of Canada (2001), 53 O.R.
   (3d) 97, 143 O.A.C. 375, [2001] O.J. No. 840 (C.A.) 223
A.E. Lepage Real Estate Services Ltd. v. Rattray Publications Ltd. (1994),
   21 O.R. (3d) 164, 120 D.L.R. (4th) 499, [1994] O.J. No. 2950
   (C.A.) 268, 270, 286
A.L. Underwood Ltd. v. Bank of Liverpool, [1924] 1 K.B. 775 (C.A.) 258
Abbott v. Bank of Toronto, [1934] 3 D.L.R. 256 (Ont. C.A.) 296–97, 298–99
Aberdeen Railway Co. v. Blaikie Brothers (1854), 1 Macq. H.L. 461 100
Accord Business Credit Inc. v. Bank of Nova Scotia (1997), 33 O.T.C. 362,
   [1997] O.J. No. 2562 (Gen. Div.) 216
Accursi v. Hongkong Bank of Canada (1998), 43 O.T.C. 90, 49 C.B.R.
   (3d) 226, [1997] O.J. No. 3524 (Gen. Div.) 210
Adams v. Craig (1911), 24 O.L.R. 490, [1911] O.J. No. 92 (C.A.) 255, 266–67
Adams v. Union Bank of Halifax (1906), 1 E.L.R. 317 (N.S.S.C.) 235
Advance Bank v. Toronto Dominion Bank (2003), 65 O.R. (3d) 46,
   227 D.L.R. (4th) 755, [2003] O.J. No. 2027 (S.C.J.) 260, 334

Advantage Credit Union v. Funk (2003), 238 Sask. R. 198, [2003]
S.J. No. 619, 2003 SKCA 98 265
Agip (Africa) Ltd. v. Jackson, [1991] Ch. 547 (C.A.) 284, 343
Agra & Masterman's Bank Ltd. v. Leighton (1864), L.R. 2 Ex. 56 191
Agra and Masterman's Bank (Re) (1866), 36 L.J. Ch. 151 .... 151, 179–80
Agricultural Savings & Loan Association v. Federal Bank (1881),
6 O.A.R. 192 296–97
Air Canada v. British Columbia (Minister of Finance) (1980),
23 B.C.L.R. 52, [1981] 2 W.W.R. 97, [1980] B.C.J. No. 1971 (C.A.) 228
Air Canada v. M. & L. Travel Ltd., [1993] 3 S.C.R. 787, 108 D.L.R.
(4th) 592, [1993] S.C.J. No. 118 221
Airline Industry Revitalization Co. v. Air Canada (1999), 45 O.R.
(3d) 370, 178 D.L.R. (4th) 740, [1999] O.J. No. 3581 (S.C.J.) 104
Akbar Khan v. Attar Singh, [1936] 2 All E.R. 545 (H.L.) 223
Albert Estate v. Gionet (1992), 131 N.B.R. (2d) 226, 333 A.P.R. 226,
[1993] N.B.J. No. 33 (Q.B.) 249
Alberta Bank Taxation Reference (sub nom. Attorney-General of
Alberta v. Attorney-General of Canada) (1938), [1939] A.C. 117,
[1938] 4 D.L.R. 433, [1938] 3 W.W.R. 337 (P.C.) 15, 20
Alberta Treasury Branches v. McIntosh (1993), 138 A.R. 303,
7 Alta. L.R. (3d) 364, [1993] A.J. No. 78 (Q.B.) 230
Alberta v. Arnold (1970), [1971] S.C.R. 209, 14 D.L.R. (3d) 574,
[1970] S.C.J. No. 76 301
Alderslade v. Hendon Laundry Ltd., [1945] 1 All E.R. 244 (C.A.) 302
Alec Lobb (Garages) Ltd. v. Total Oil (Great Britain) Ltd., [1983]
1 W.L.R. 87, [1983] 1 All E.R. 944 (Ch. D.) 198
Allcard v. Skinner (1887), 36 Ch. D. 145 (C.A.) 199, 204
Alnu Electric Ltd. v. CIBC Mortgage Corp. (1995), 165 N.B.R.
(2d) 149, 424 A.P.R. 149, [1995] N.B.J. No. 360 (Q.B.) 210, 211
Ambico Ltd. v. Loeb Inc. (1993), 13 O.R. (3d) 423, 103 D.L.R.
(4th) 721, [1993] O.J. No. 1079 (C.A.) 378
American Express Co. v. Anadarko Bank and Trust Co., 67 P.2d 55
(Okla. 1937) 387
Arab Bank Ltd. v. Barclays Bank, [1954] A.C. 495 (H.L.) 193, 232
Arab Bank Ltd. v. Ross, [1952] 1 All E.R. 709 (C.A.) 259
Arklow Investments Ltd. v. Maclean, [2000] 1 W.L.R. 594 (P.C.) 197
Armstrong, Baum Plumbing & Heating v. Toronto-Dominion Bank
(1994), 15 B.L.R. (2d) 84, [1994] O.J. No. 331 (Gen. Div.), aff'd
(1997), 32 B.L.R. (2d) 230, [1997] O.J. No. 2285 (C.A.) 189, 212, 302
Arrow Transfer Co. v. Royal Bank of Canada, [1972] S.C.R. 845,
27 D.L.R. (3d) 81, [1972] S.C.J. No. 64 300
Arthur Anderson Inc. v. Toronto-Dominion Bank (1994), 17 O.R.
(3d) 363, 14 B.L.R. (2d) 1, [1994] O.J. No. 427 (C.A.), additional
reasons at (1994), 14 B.L.R. (2d) 1 at 49 (Ont. C.A.), leave to appeal
to S.C.C. refused (1994), 19 O.R. (3d) i, [1994] S.C.C.A. No. 189 223

Astral Films Ltd. v. Sherman (1978), 19 O.R. (2d) 206, 3 B.L.R. 150,
 5 C.P.C. 317 (H.C.J.) 16, 306, 308
Atkinson v. Bradford Third Equitable Benefit Building Society (1890),
 25 Q.B.D. 377 (C.A.) 234, 296
Atlantic Sporting Goods Distributors Ltd. v. Bank of Montreal (1988),
 87 N.S.R. (2d) 376, [1988] N.S.J. No. 411, supplementary reasons
 at (1989), 91 N.S.R. (2d) 181, [1989] N.S.J. No. 81 (T.D.) 153
Atlas Cabinets v. National Trust Co. (1990), 68 D.L.R. (4th) 161,
 45 B.C.L.R. (2d) 99, [1990] B.C.J. No. 719 (C.A.) 211
Attorney-General of Alberta v. Attorney-General of Canada, [1947]
 A.C. 503, [1947] 4 D.L.R. 1, [1947] 2 W.W.R. 401 (P.C.) 9, 20
Attorney-General of Canada v. Attorney-General of Quebec (1946),
 [1947] A.C. 33, [1947] 1 D.L.R. 81, [1946] 3 W.W.R. 659 (P.C.) 227
Attorney-General v. Guardian Newspapers Ltd. (No. 2), [1990] 1 A.C. 109 306
Avon Finance Co. v. Bridger, [1985] 2 All E.R. 281 (C.A.) 199

B. Liggett (Liverpool) Ltd. v. Barclays Bank Ltd., [1928]
 1 K.B. 48 .... 238, 283, 286, 287
B.C. Bancorp (Re) (1990), 79 C.B.R. (N.S.) 281, [1990] B.C.J. No. 724 (S.C.) ... 140
Backhouse v. Backhouse [1978] 1 W.L.R. 243 (Fam. D.) 198
Bad Boy Appliances & Furniture Ltd. v. Toronto-Dominion Bank, [1972]
 2 O.R. 221, 25 D.L.R. (3d) 257, [1972] O.J. No. 1705 (C.A.) 301–2, 303
Baden, Delvaux and Lecuit v. Société Générale pour Favoriser le
 Développement du Commerce et de l'Industrie en France SA,
 [1983] B.C.L.C. 325 (Ch. D.) 219
Bailey v. Jellett (1884), 9 O.A.R. 187, [1884] O.J. No. 466 (C.A.) 192, 243, 246
Bain v. Bank of Canada, [1935] 4 D.L.R. 112 (B.C.C.A.) 39
Bain v. Torrance (1884), 1 Man. R. 32 (Q.B.) 151
Baker v. Australia & New Zealand Bank Ltd., [1958] N.Z.L.R. 907 (S.C.) 272
Baker v. Barclays Bank, [1955] 1 W.L.R. 822 (Birmingham Assizes) 240–1
Ball v. Royal Bank of Canada (1915), 52 S.C.R. 254, 26 D.L.R. 385,
 9 W.W.R. 776 170
Balmoral Supermarket Ltd. v. Bank of New Zealand, [1974]
 2 Lloyd's Rep. 164 (N.Z.S.C.) 260
Banco Exterior Internacional v. Mann, [1995] 1 All E.R. 936 (C.A.) 202
Banco Exterior Internacional v. Thomas, [1997] 1 All E.R. 46 (C.A.) 202
Bank of Baroda Ltd. v. Punjab National Bank Ltd., [1944] A.C. 176
 (P.C.) 266, 267, 269
Bank of Baroda v. ASAA Mahomed, [1999] Lloyd's Rep. Bank 14 (C.A.) 191, 232
Bank of Baroda v. Shah, [1988] 3 All E.R. 24 (C.A.) 199, 201
Bank of British North America v. Standard Bank of Canada (1917),
 38 O.L.R. 570, 35 D.L.R. 761, [1917] O.J. No. 161 (S.C.A.D.) 260, 290
Bank of British North America v. Warren & Co. (1909), 19 O.L.R. 257,
 [1909] O.J. No. 123 (C.A.) 252, 291
Bank of Canada v. Bank of Montreal (1977), [1978] 1 S.C.R. 1148,
 76 D.L.R. (3d) 385, [1977] S.C.J. No. 109 (S.C.C.) 39, 245

Bank of China v. Fan (2003), 22 B.C.L.R. (4th) 152, 112 C.R.R. (2d) 255,
2003 BCSC 1672 306–7
Bank of England v. Vagliano Bros., [1891] A.C. 107 (H.L.) 297, 300
Bank of Montreal v. Bakheet Estate (1995), 167 A.R. 101, [1995]
A.J. No. 3 (Q.B.) 224
Bank of Montreal v. Big White Land Dev. Ltd. (1982), 17 B.L.R. 257,
[1982] B.C.J. No. 2148 (S.C.) 242
Bank of Montreal v. Boudreau (1974), 8 N.B.R. (2d) 487, 49 D.L.R.
(3d) 249, [1974] N.B.J. No. 67 (C.A.) 258
Bank of Montreal v. Courtney (2005), 261 D.L.R. (4th) 665, 239 N.S.R.
(2d) 80, 2005 NSCA 153 ....206, 214
Bank of Montreal v. Demakos (1996), 31 O.R. (3d) 757, 17 O.T.C. 206,
[1996] O.J. No. 4667 (Gen. Div.) 376
Bank of Montreal v. Dominion Bank (1921), 60 D.L.R. 403 (Ont. Co. Ct.) 268
Bank of Montreal v. Duguid (2000), 47 O.R. (3d) 737, 185 D.L.R.
(4th) 458, [2000] O.J. No. 1356 (C.A.), leave to appeal to S.C.C.
granted (2000), 51 O.R. (3d) xvii, but case discontinued
2 August 2001, [2000] S.C.C.A. No. 298 ....205, 214
Bank of Montreal v. Elgin Co-op. Services (1983), 44 O.R. (2d) 19,
3 D.L.R. (4th) 115, [1983] O.J. No. 3227 (C.A.) 162
Bank of Montreal v. Featherstone (1987), 58 O.R. (2d) 353, 35 D.L.R.
(4th) 626, [1987] O.J. No. 62 (H.C.J.), rev'd in part (1989), 68 O.R.
(2d) 541, 58 D.L.R. (4th) 567, [1989] O.J. No. 613 (C.A.) 213–14
Bank of Montreal v. Guaranty Silk Dyeing and Finishing Co., [1935]
4 D.L.R. 483 (Ont. C.A.) 160
Bank of Montreal v. H. & M. Chan Enterprises Ltd. (1999),
183 Sask. R. 84, [1999] S.J. No. 471 (Q.B.) 302
Bank of Montreal v. Hall, [1990] 1 S.C.R. 121, 65 D.L.R. (4th) 361,
[1990] S.C.J. No. 9 .... 15, 160, 163
Bank of Montreal v. Hancock (1982), 39 O.R. (2d) 82, 137 D.L.R.
(3d) 648, [1982] O.J. No. 3491 (H.C.J.) 241
Bank of Montreal v. Intracom Investments Ltd. (1983), 47 N.B.R.
(2d) 391, [1983] N.B.J. No. 208 (C.A.) 313
Bank of Montreal v. Little (1870), 17 Gr. 313, [1870] O.J. No. 240,
17 G.R. 685, [1870] O.J. No. 306 (Ont. Ch.) 234
Bank of Montreal v. McIntosh, [1995] 10 W.W.R. 726, 136 Sask. R. 89,
[1995] S.J. No. 585 (Q.B.) 210
Bank of Montreal v. Minaki International Resort Corp. (1998),
112 O.A.C. 291, [1998] O.J. No. 3407 (C.A.) 213
Bank of Montreal v. Perry (1981), 31 O.R. (2d) 700, [1981] O.J. No. 2904
(H.C.J.) 151
Bank of Montreal v. Price (1979), 33 N.S.R. (2d) 293, 105 D.L.R.
(3d) 62, [1979] N.S.J. No. 599 (S.C.A.D.) 372
Bank of Montreal v. R. & R. Entertainment Ltd. (1984), 56 N.B.R.
(2d) 154, 13 D.L.R. (4th) 726, [1984] N.B.J. No. 238 (C.A.) 243–44

Bank of Montreal v. R. (1906), 38 S.C.R. 258...280
Bank of Montreal v. Royal Bank of Canada (2000), 276 A.R. 380,
    [2000] A.J. No. 1332, 2000 ABQB 789...249
Bank of Montreal v. Vaillancourt (1983), 42 O.R. (2d) 545,
    149 D.L.R. (3d) 560, [1983] O.J. No. 3115 (C.A.)..................... 241, 258, 291
Bank of New South Wales v. Goulburn Valley Butter Company Proprietary,
    [1902] A.C. 543 (P.C.)...250
Bank of New South Wales v. Laing, [1954] A.C. 135 (P.C.).................. 230, 257–58
Bank of New South Wales v. Milvain (1884), 10 V.L.R. 3 (S.C.).................. 271–72
Bank of Nova Scotia v. Angelica-Whitewear Ltd., [1987] 1 S.C.R. 59,
    36 D.L.R. (4th) 161, [1987] S.C.J. No. 5 393
Bank of Nova Scotia v. Archo Industries Ltd. (1970), 11 D.L.R. (3d) 593,
    [1970] S.J. No. 47 (Q.B.)..278
Bank of Nova Scotia v. Baird (2001), 199 Nfld. & P.E.I.R. 154,
    600 A.P.R. 154, [2001] N.J. No. 51 (Nfld. T.D.)...210
Bank of Nova Scotia v. Boehm, [1973] 3 W.W.R. 757 (B.C.S.C.)......................208
Bank of Nova Scotia v. British Columbia (Superintendent of Financial
    Institutions) (2003), 223 D.L.R. (4th) 126, 11 B.C.L.R. (4th) 206,
    [2003] B.C.J. No. 92 (C.A.)..16
Bank of Nova Scotia v. Canada Trust Co. (1998), 39 O.R. (3d) 84,
    59 O.T.C. 129, [1998] O.J. No. 1398 (Gen. Div.)..16
Bank of Nova Scotia v. Canada Trust Co. (1998), 39 O.R. (3d) 84,
    41 B.L.R. (2d) 109, [1998] O.J. No. 1398 (Gen. Div.).....................267, 268–69
Bank of Nova Scotia v. Cheng (1981), 33 Nfld. & P.E.I.R. 89,
    [1981] N.J. No. 146 (S.C.T.D.)...286
Bank of Nova Scotia v. Dunphy Leasing Enterprises Ltd., [1994]
    1 S.C.R. 552, 18 Alta L.R. (3d) 2, [1994] S.C.J. No. 25 153
Bank of Nova Scotia v. Forsyth (1985), 63 B.C.L.R. 60, 56 C.B.R.
    (N.S.) 112, [1985] B.C.J. No. 2721 (Co. Ct.)...375
Bank of Nova Scotia v. Gould (1977), 17 O.R. (2d) 96, 79 D.L.R.
    (3d) 473, [1977] O.J. No. 2365 (Co. Ct.) 151, 278
Bank of Nova Scotia v. Kelly Motors Danforth Ltd., [1961]
    O.W.N. 34 (Co. Ct.)..264
Bank of Nova Scotia v. Lienaux (1982), 53 N.S.R. (2d) 541,
    109 A.P.R. 541, [1982] N.S.J. No. 484 (T.D.)..211
Bank of Nova Scotia v. Neil (1968), 69 D.L.R. (2d) 357, 65 W.W.R. 215
    (B.C.C.A.)..246
Bank of Nova Scotia v. Pittman (1979), 22 Nfld. & P.E.I.R. 278,
    58 A.P.R. 278, [1979] N.J. No. 140 (Dist. Ct.) 266, 289
Bank of Nova Scotia v. Raymond Contractors Ltd. (1988),
    25 B.C.L.R. (2d) 54, [1988] B.C.J. No. 340 (S.C.) 191
Bank of Nova Scotia v. Sharp (1975), 57 D.L.R. (3d) 260, [1975]
    6 W.W.R. 97 (B.C.C.A.)...291
Bank of Nova Scotia v. Taylor (1979), 27 N.B.R. (2d) 14, [1979]
    N.B.J. No. 192 (Co. Ct.)...291

Bank of Nova Scotia v. Toronto-Dominion Bank (2001), 200 D.L.R.
(4th) 549, 145 O.A.C. 106, [2001] O.J. No. 1717 (C.A.) 289, 334
Bank of Ottawa v. Hood (1908), 42 S.C.R. 231, [1908] S.C.J. No. 75 180
Bank of Scotland v. A. Ltd., [2001] 1 W.L.R. 751, [2001] 3 All E.R. 58,
[2001] EWCA CIV 52 308
Bank of Scotland v. Dominion Bank, [1891] A.C. 592 (P.C.) 288
Bank of Toronto v. Lambe (1887), 12 App. Cas. 575, 9 C.R.A.C. 296,
4 Cart. 7 (P.C.) 14
Bank of Van Diemen's Land v. Bank of Victoria (1871), 7 Moo. P.C.
N.S. 401, 17 E.R. 152 288
Banque Canadienne Nationale v. Boston Insurance Co., [1963]
Que. Q.B. 487 (C.A.) 398–99
Banque Canadienne Nationale v. Caisse Centrale Desjardins du Québec,
[2001] R.J.Q. 846, [2001] R.R.A. 332, [2001] J.Q. no 1446 (C.A.) 261–62
Banque Canadienne Nationale v. Mastracchio (1961), [1962] S.C.R. 53,
30 D.L.R. (2d) 510, [1961] S.C.J. No. 62 398–99
Banque Nationale du Canada v. Atomic Slipper Co., [1991] 1 S.C.R. 1059,
80 D.L.R. (4th) 134, [1991] S.C.J. No. 38 163
Banque Provinciale du Canada v. Beauchemin (1959), 18 D.L.R.
(2d) 584 (S.C.C.) 278
Banque Provinciale du Canada v. Claude, [1965] 2 O.R. 819,
52 D.L.R. (2d) 211, [1965] O.J. No. 1058 (C.A.) 264
Banque Romande v. Mercantile Bank of Canada, [1971] 3 O.R. 433,
20 D.L.R. (3d) 633, [1971] O.J. No. 1652 (C.A.), aff'd (1973),
45 D.L.R. (3d) 480 (S.C.C.) 243
Barclay Construction Corp. v. Bank of Montreal (1989), 65 D.L.R.
(4th) 213, 45 B.L.R. 282, [1989] B.C.J. No. 2257 (C.A.) 271
Barclays Bank Ltd. v. W.J. Simms Son & Cooke (Southern) Ltd.,
[1979] 3 All E.R. 522 (Q.B.) 268, 270, 279, 285–86
Barclays Bank plc v. Bank of England, [1985] 1 All E.R. 385
(Arbitrator) 262–63
Barclays Bank plc v. Khaira, [1992] 1 W.L.R. 623 (Ch. D.) 199
Barclays Bank plc v. O'Brien, [1994] 1 A.C. 180 (H.L.) 200
Barclays Bank plc v. Quincecare Ltd., [1992] 4 All E.R. 363 (C.A.) 218, 255
Barclays Bank plc v. Thomson, [1997] 4 All E.R. 816 (C.A.) 202
Barlow Clowes International Ltd. v. Eurotrust International Ltd.
(2005), [2006] 1 All E.R. 333 (P.C.) 219–20
Barnes v. Addy, [1874] L.R. 9 Ch. App. 244 (H.L.) 217, 218, 220, 221
Bateman v. Toronto Dominion Bank (1991), 86 D.L.R. (4th) 354,
64 B.C.L.R. (2d) 27, [1991] B.C.J. No. 3737 (S.C.) 244
Bavins Jr. and Sims v. London & South Western Bank, [1900]
1 Q.B. 270 (C.A.) 295
BCCI v. Aboody, [1992] 4 All E.R. 955 (C.A.) 199, 200
BCCI v. Akindele, [2001] 1 Ch. 437 (C.A.) 221
Beasley v. Roney, [1891] 1 Q.B. 509 242

Beaulieu v. National Bank (1983), 47 N.B.R. (2d) 220, 124 A.P.R. 220,
[1983] N.B.J. No. 193 (Q.B.) 213
Bell v. Capital and Counties Bank (1887), 3 T.L.R. 540 (Q.B.D.) 395
Belliveau v. Royal Bank of Canada (2000), 224 N.B.R. (2d) 354,
3 B.L.R. (3d) 43, [2000] N.B.J. No. 70 (C.A.) 248–49
Belmont Finance Corp. Ltd. v. Williams Furniture (No. 2), [1980]
1 All E.R. 393 (C.A.) 220
Bence v. Royal Trust Corp. of Canada (1997), 157 Sask. R. 61, [1997]
S.J. No. 452 (Q.B.) 249
Berbaum Estate v. Silver (2001), 193 N.S.R. (2d) 120, 602 A.P.R. 120,
2001 NSSC 55 .... 237, 239
Bergethaler Waisenamt, Re (1947), [1948] 1 D.L.R. 761, [1948]
1 W.W.R. 305, 28 C.B.R. 238 (Man. K.B.), rev'd [1949]
1 D.L.R. 769, [1949] 1 W.W.R. 323, 57 Man. R. 66 (C.A.) 12
Bernard, Re (1911), 2 O.W.N. 716, 18 O.W.R. 525, [1911] O.J. No. 792
(Div. Ct.) 192
Bernstein v. Northwestern National Bank in Philadelphia, 41 A.2d 440
(Pa. Super. 1945) 400
Bertolo v. Bank of Montreal (1986), 57 O.R. (2d) 577, 33 D.L.R.
(4th) 610, [1986] O.J. No. 1377 (C.A.) 213
Birch v. Treasury Solicitor, [1951] 1 Ch. 298 (C.A.) 234
Bishop, Re, [1965] Ch. 450 238
Bishun Chand Firm v. Seth Girdhari Lal (1934), 50 T.L.R. 465 (P.C.) 297
Blackburn Building Society v. Cunliffe, Brooks & Co. (1884),
9 App. Cas. 857 (H.L.) 297, 300
Boehm v. Bank of Nova Scotia, [1973] 3 W.W.R. 757 (B.C.S.C.) 214
Boma Manufacturing Ltd. v. Canadian Imperial Bank of Commerce, [1996]
3 S.C.R. 727, 140 D.L.R. (4th) 463, [1996] S.C.J. No. 111 .... 281, 293, 300
Bomek v. Bomek (1983), 20 Man. R. (2d) 150, 21 B.L.R. 205, [1983]
M.J. No. 96 (C.A.), leave to appeal to S.C.C. refused (1983),
52 N.R. 234n, [1984] 1 W.W.R. liii, 27 Man. R. (2d) 239n (S.C.C.) 213
Bourque v. Landry (1936), 10 M.P.R. 108 (N.B.S.C.) 237
Bower v. Foreign & Colonial Gas Co. (1874), 22 W.R. 740 252
Bowes, Re (1886), 33 Ch. D. 586 251
Boyd v. Nasmith (1888), 17 O.R. 40, [1888] O.J. No. 73 (C.P.) 269
Bradford Old Bank Ltd. v. Sutcliffe, [1918] 2 K.B. 833 (C.A.) 179, 192, 233
Braithwaite v. Thomas Cook Travellers Cheques Ltd., [1989]
1 All E.R. 235 (Q.B.) 385
Brandao v. Barnett (1846), 12 Cl. & F. 787, 136 E.R. 207 (H.L.) 251, 252
Brantford Cordage Co. v. Milne, [1925] 1 D.L.R. 862 (Man. C.A.) 250
Brantford v. Imperial Bank of Canada, [1930] 4 D.L.R. 658 (Ont. S.C.A.D.) 16
Breckenridge Speedway Ltd. v. The Queen in Right of Alberta (1967),
64 D.L.R. (2d) 488, 61 W.W.R. 257 (Alta. S.C.A.D.) 14
Brewer v. Westminster Bank Ltd., [1952] 2 All E.R. 650 (Q.B.D.) 240
Brimnes, The, [1975] Q.B. 929 (C.A.) 342

Bristol and West Building Society v. Mothew, [1998] 1 Ch. 1 (C.A.) 197
British & North European Bank Ltd. v. Zalzstein, [1927] 2 K.B. 92 297–98
British Columbia (Attorney-General) v. Royal Bank of Canada,
  [1937] S.C.R. 459, [1937] 3 D.L.R. 393 180
British Columbia v. National Bank of Canada (1994), 119 D.L.R.
  (4th) 669, 99 B.C.L.R. (2d) 358, [1994] B.C.J. No. 2584 (C.A.) 246
British Guiana Bank v. Official Receiver (1911), 104 L.T. 754 (P.C.) 250
British Linen Bank. v. Thomson (1853), 2 Stuart 175 (S.C.) 297
Brown v. Westminster Bank Ltd., [1964] 2 Lloyd's Rep. 187 (Q.B.D.) 280
Buchanan v. Canadian Imperial Bank of Commerce (1980), 125 D.L.R.
  (3d) 394, 23 B.C.L.R. 324, [1980] B.C.J. No. 696 (C.A.) 213
Buckingham & Co. v. London & Midland Bank Ltd. (1895),
  12 T.L.R. 70 (Q.B.) 191, 249
Burnett v. Westminster Bank, [1966] 1 Q.B. 742 188
Burrows v. Bank of Nova Scotia, [2002] O.T.C. 20, 36 C.C.L.I.
  (3d) 72, [2002] O.J. No. 156 (S.C.J.) 225

C. v. S., [1999] 2 All E.R. 343 (C.A.) 308
Cadbury Schweppes Inc. v. FBI Foods Ltd., [1999] 1 S.C.R. 142,
  167 D.L.R. (4th) 577, [1999] S.C.J. No. 6 196
Caisse Populaire Notre Dame Ltée v. Moyen, [1967] 61 D.L.R. (2d) 118,
  59 W.W.R. 129, [1967] S.J. No. 9 (Q.B.) 13
Caitlin v. Cyprus Finance Corp. (London) Ltd., [1983] Q.B. 759 .... 238, 240–41
Caldwell v. Merchants Bank (1876), 26 U.C.C.P. 294, [1876]
  O.J. No. 194 263
Calico Printers Association v. Barclays Bank Ltd. (1931),
  36 Com. Cas. 197 (C.A.) 340
Cameron, Re (1967), 62 D.L.R. (2d) 389, 53 M.P.R. 214 (N.S.S.C.) 238
Campbell v. Imperial Bank, [1924] 4 D.L.R. 289 (Ont. S.C.A.D.) 251, 303
Canada (Attorney General) v. Security Home Mortgage Corp. (2003),
  231 D.L.R. (4th) 353, 18 Alta. L.R. (4th) 250, 2003 ABQB 588 63
Canada Deposit Insurance Corp. v. Canadian Commercial Bank (1986),
  72 A.R. 379, 27 D.L.R. (4th) 229, [1986] A.J. No. 328 (Q.B.) 149
Canada Deposit Insurance Corp. v. Canadian Commercial Bank (No. 3),
  [1992] 3 S.C.R. 558, 97 D.L.R. (4th) 385, [1992] S.C.J. No. 96 144
Canada Deposit Insurance Corp. v. Columbia Trust Co. (1987), 37 D.L.R.
  (4th) 378, 13 B.C.L.R. (2d) 79, [1987] B.C.J. No. 784 (S.C.) 144
Canada Life Assurance Co. v. Canadian Imperial Bank of Commerce (1976),
  14 O.R. (2d) 777, 74 D.L.R. (3d) 599, [1976] O.J. No. 2373 (C.A.),
  aff'd [1979] 2 S.C.R. 669, 98 D.L.R. (3d) 670, [1979] S.C.J. No. 63 151
Canada Steamship Lines v. The King, [1952] A.C. 192, [1952]
  2 D.L.R. 786, 5 W.W.R. (N.S.) 609 (P.C.) 302
Canadian Bank of Commerce v. Brash (1957), 10 D.L.R. (2d) 555,
  [1957] O.W.N. 322 (C.A.) 278
Canadian Bank of Commerce v. Canada, [1962] S.C.R. 729,
  35 D.L.R. (2d) 49, [1962] S.C.J. No. 58 308

Canadian Commercial Bank (Liquidator) v. Parlee (1988),
    86 A.R. 167, [1988] A.J. No. 229 (Q.B.) 144
Canadian Commercial Bank v. Canadian Imperial Bank of Commerce
    (1988), 47 D.L.R. (4th) 632, [1988] 3 W.W.R. 607, [1988]
    B.C.J. No. 220 (C.A.) 163–64
Canadian Engineering and Surveys (Yukon) Ltd. v. Banque Nationale
    de Paris (Canada) (1999), 242 A.R.61, [1999] A.J. No. 309,
    1999 ABQB 215 153
Canadian Imperial Bank of Commerce v. Bell Estate (2005), 74 O.R.
    (3d) 360, [2005] O.T.C. 2, [2005] O.J. No. 323 (S.C.J.) 376
Canadian Imperial Bank of Commerce v. Brown (1999), 2 B.L.R.
    (3d) 260, [1999] O.J. No. 4823 (S.C.J.) 213
Canadian Imperial Bank of Commerce v. Derksen Brothers Holdings Ltd.,
    [1995] 5 W.W.R. 1, 100 Man. R. (2d) 224, [1995] M.J. No. 128 (C.A.),
    leave to appeal to S.C.C. refused, [1996] 2 W.W.R. lxxix,
    [1995] S.C.C.A. No. 268 216
Canadian Imperial Bank of Commerce v. Doucette (1968), 70 D.L.R.
    (2d) 657 (P.E.I.S.C.) 163
Canadian Imperial Bank of Commerce v. Farrage (1997), 122 Man. R.
    (2d) 315, [1997] M.J. No. 596 (Q.B.) 261–62
Canadian Imperial Bank of Commerce v. Gardiner Watson Ltd. (1983),
    43 A.R. 39, 25 Alta L.R. (2d) 319, [1983] A.J. No. 847 (Q.B.) 227, 293
Canadian Imperial Bank of Commerce v. Haley (1979), 25 N.B.R.
    (2d) 304, 100 D.L.R. (3d) 470, [1979] N.B.J. No. 77 (C.A.) 302
Canadian Imperial Bank of Commerce v. Larsen, [1983] 5 W.W.R. 179,
    45 B.C.L.R. 212, [1983] B.C.J. No. 2353 (C.A.) 313
Canadian Imperial Bank of Commerce v. May Trucking Ltd. (1981),
    122 D.L.R. (3d) 189, [1981] B.C.J. No. 1754 (S.C.) 278
Canadian Imperial Bank of Commerce v. Melnitzer (trustee of) (1998),
    50 C.B.R. (3d) 79, [1997] O.J. No. 4634 (C.A.) 223
Canadian Imperial Bank of Commerce v. Ohlson (1997), 209 A.R. 140,
    154 D.L.R. (4th) 33, [1997] A.J. No. 1185 (C.A.) 206, 213, 230
Canadian Imperial Bank of Commerce v. Roisin, [1971] 2 O.R. 199,
    17 D.L.R. (3d) 379, [1971] O.J. No. 1519 (Dist. Ct.) 163
Canadian Imperial Bank of Commerce v. Sayani (1993), 83 B.C.L.R.
    (2d) 167, [1994] 2 W.W.R. 260, [1993] B.C.J. No. 1898 (C.A.),
    leave to appeal to S.C.C. refused (1994), [1994] 1 S.C.R. vi,
    [1994] 3 W.W.R. lxvi, [1993] S.C.C.A. No. 485 310
Canadian Imperial Bank of Commerce v. Sitarenios (1976), 14 O.R.
    (2d) 345, 73 D.L.R. (3d) 663, [1976] O.J. No. 2322 (C.A.) 248–49
Canadian Imperial Bank of Commerce v. Sledz (1990), 76 Alta. L.R.
    (2d) 187, [1991] 1 W.W.R. 42, [1990] A.J. No. 328 (Master) 163
Canadian Logging Co., Re, [1927] 1 W.W.R. 406 (B.C.S.C. in Bkcy.) 16
Canadian Pacific Hotels Ltd. v. Bank of Montreal Ltd., [1987]
    1 S.C.R. 711, 40 D.L.R. (4th) 385, [1987] S.C.J. No. 29 .... 187, 257, 281, 299

Canadian Pioneer Management Ltd. v. Saskatchewan Labour Relations
   Board, [1980] 1 S.C.R. 433, 107 D.L.R. (3d) 1, [1980] 3 W.W.R. 214 .... 8, 12
Canadian Western Bank v. Alberta (2003), 343 A.R. 89, 4 C.C.L.I.
   (4th) 59, 2003 ABQB 795, aff'd (2005), 361 A.R. 112,
   249 D.L.R. (4th) 523, 2005 ABCA 12 .... 17–18, 22, 26, 27, 33, 149
Canuck Truck Rentals Ltd. v. Mountain Truck Service (1980),
   16 C.P.C. 126, [1980] B.C.J. No. 1358 (Co. Ct.) 242
Caparo Industries plc v. Dickman, [1990] 2 A.C. 605 (H.L.) 209
Capital and Counties Bank Ltd. v. Gordon, [1903] A.C. 240 (H.L.)...259, 291, 391
Capital Associates Ltd. v. Royal Bank of Canada (1973), 36 D.L.R.
   (3d) 579, 17 N.R. 205 (Que. C.A.), aff'd (1976), 65 D.L.R.
   (3d) 384, 17 N.R. 204 (S.C.C.)...262, 266–77, 289
Cappuccitti v. Bank of Montreal (1989), 46 B.L.R. 255, [1989]
   O.J. No. 2153 (H.C.J.) 106
Carnegie v. Federal Bank of Canada (1884), 5 O.R. 418, [1884]
   O.J. No. 230 (Ch.) 395
Carter v. Shepherd (1698), 5 Mod. Rep. 398, 87 E.R. 728 260
Cavell Developments Ltd. v. Royal Bank of Canada (1991), 78 D.L.R.
   (4th) 512, 54 B.C.L.R. (2d) 1, [1991] B.C.J. No. 614 (B.C.C.A.) 302
Centrac Inc. v. Canadian Imperial Bank of Commerce (1994), 21 O.R.
   (3d) 161, 120 D.L.R. (4th) 765, [1994] O.J. No. 2951 (C.A.).........268–69, 270
Central Bank (Re) (1889), 17 O.R. 110, [1889] O.J. No. 155 (H.C.J.) 141, 234
Central Computer Services Ltd. v. Toronto-Dominion Bank (1979), 107
   D.L.R. (3d) 88, 1 Man. R. (2d) 402, [1979] M.J. No. 116 (C.A.) 19–20, 149
Central Coordinates, Inc. v. Morgan Guaranty Trust Co.,
   494 N.Y.S.2d 602 (Sup. Ct. 1985) 340
Chambers v. Miller (1862), 13 C.B.N.S. 125, 143 E.R. 50 260
Chapeskie v. Canadian Imperial Bank of Commerce (2004),
   197 B.C.A.C. 22, 43 B.L.R. (3d) 307, 2004 BCCA 154............................... 211
Charge Card Services Ltd., Re, [1986] 3 All E.R. 289 (Ch. D.)......................... 347
Charge Card Services Ltd., Re, [1988] 3 All E.R. 702 (C.A.) 373–74, 382
Chatterton v. London & County Bank, The Times (21 January 1891).............. 299
Chikuma, The, [1981] 1 W.L.R. 314 (H.L.) 342
Christofi v. Barclays Bank plc (1999), [2000] 1 W.L.R. 937, [1999]
   4 All E.R. 437, [1999] E.W.J. No. 4380 (C.A.) 308, 312
CIBC Mortgage Corp. v. Rowatt (2002), 61 O.R. (3d) 737, 220 D.L.R.
   (4th) 139, [2002] O.J. No. 4109 (C.A.), leave to appeal to S.C.C.
   refused (2002), 64 O.R. (3d) xvii, [2002] S.C.C.A. No. 526 .... 205, 214
CIBC Mortgages plc v. Pitt, [1994] 1 A.C. 200 (H.L.) 200
CIP Inc. v. Toronto-Dominion Bank (1988), 55 D.L.R. (4th) 308,
   [1988] B.C.J. No. 2576 (C.A.) 153, 231, 250
Citadel General Assurance Co. v. Lloyd's Bank Canada, [1997]
   3 S.C.R. 805, 152 D.L.R. (4th) 411, [1997] S.C.J. No. 92 221
Citizens Trust Co. v. Hongkong Bank of Canada (1991), 85 D.L.R.
   (4th) 762, [1992] 2 W.W.R. 348, [1991] B.C.J. No. 3575 (S.C.) 268–69

City and County Property Bank, Re (1895), 21 V.L.R. 405 (Vict. S.C.) 232
City Equitable Fire Insurance Co. (Re), [1925] 1 Ch. 407 98
City Front Developments Inc. v. Bank of Nova Scotia (1998), 41 O.R.
    (3d) 599, 43 B.L.R. (2d) 210, [1998] O.J. No. 3578 (Gen. Div.) 266–67, 269
City National Bank of Galveston v. American Express Co.,
    16 S.W.2d 278 (Tex. Com. App. 1929) 387
Claiborne Industries Ltd. v. National Bank of Canada (1989), 69 O.R.
    (2d) 65, 59 D.L.R. (4th) 533, [1989] O.J. No. 1048 (C.A.) 301
Clansmen Resources Ltd. v. Toronto-Dominion Bank, [1990]
    4 W.W.R. 73, 47 B.L.R. 54, [1990] B.C.J. No. 549 (C.A.) 283, 343
Clare & Co. v. Dresdner Bank (1915), 2 K.B. 576 151
Clarke v. London & County Banking Co., [1897] 1 Q.B. 552 177
Clarkson v. Smith & Goldberg, [1926] 1 D.L.R. 509 (Ont. C.A.) 246
Clavelle v. Russell (1918), 11 Sask. L.R. 111 (C.A.) 278
Clegg v. Baretta (1887), 56 L.T.F.D. 775 (Q.B.) 234
Clifford Davies Management Ltd. v. WEA Records Ltd., [1973]
    1 W.L.R. 61 (C.A.) 198
Clode v. Bayley (1843), 12 M. & W. 51, 152 E.R. 1107 (Ex. Ch.) 151
Cocks v. Masterman (1829), 9 B. & C. 902, 109 E.R. 335 260
Coldunell Ltd. v. Gallon, [1986] 1 All E.R. 429 (C.A.) 199
Collings v. Calgary (1917), 55 S.C.R. 406, 37 D.L.R. 804, [1917]
    2 W.W.R. 241 269
Colonial Bank v. Exchange Bank of Yarmouth (1885),
    11 App. Cas. 84 (P.C.) 298
Columbia Gramophone Co. v. Union Bank (1916), 34 D.L.R. 743
    (Ont. S.C.) 301–2
Commercial Automation Ltd. v. Banque provinciale du Canada (1962),
    [1963] C.S. 668, 39 D.L.R. (2d) 316 276–77
Commercial Bank of New Brunswick v. Fleming (1872), 14 N.B.R. 36 (C.A.) 266
Commercial Bank of New Brunswick v. Page (1870), 13 N.B.R. 326
    (App. Div.) 251
Commercial Bank of Scotland v. Rhind (1860), 3 Macq. 643 (H.L.) 297
Commercial Bank of South Australia, Re (1887), 36 Ch. D. 522 391
Commissioner of Police for the Metropolis v. Charles, [1977] A.C. 177
    (H.L.) 347
Commissioner of Taxation v. The Australia and New Zealand Banking
    Group Ltd. (1979), 53 A.L.J.R. 336 (H.C.A.) 399
Commissioners of the State Savings Bank of Victoria v. Permewan,
    Wright & Co. Ltd. (1914), 19 C.L.R. 457 (H.C.A.) 6–7, 226
Commonwealth of Australia v. Bank of New South Wales (1948),
    76 C.L.R. 1 (H.C.A.), aff'd [1950] A.C. 235 (P.C.) 8
Commonwealth Trading Bank of Australia v. Smith (1991), 102 A.L.R. 453
    (Fed. Ct.) 196
Commonwealth Trading Bank v. Reno Auto Sales Pty Ltd.,
    [1967] V.R. 790 (S.C.) 276

Commonwealth Trust Co. (Re), 2004 CarswellBC 478 (S.C.) 144
Communities Economic Development Fund v. Canadian Pickles Corp.,
  [1991] 3 S.C.R. 388, 85 D.L.R. (4th) 88, [1991] S.C.J. No. 89 88
Comtract Air Compressors Inc. v. A.W. Service Industries Inc., [2000]
  O.T.C. 387, 6 B.L.R. (3d) 136, [2000] O.J. No. 1867 (S.C.J.) 264, 265
Con-Drain Co. (1983) Ltd v. 846539 Ontario Ltd. (1997), 35 C.L.R.
  (2d) 230, [1997] O.J. No. 4397 (Gen. Div.).. 223
Conn v. Merchants Bank (1879), 30 C.P. 380.. 291
Continental Bank Leasing Corp. v. Canada, [1998] 2 S.C.R. 298,
  163 D.L.R. (4th) 385, [1998] S.C.J. No. 63 88
Continental Bank NA v. Aeakos Compania Navierra S.A., [1994]
  1 Lloyd's Rep. 505 (C.A.) 190
Continental Bank of Canada v. Arthur Andersen & Co. (1987), 59 O.R.
  (2d) 774, 39 D.L.R. (4th) 261, [1987] O.J. No. 401 (H.C.J.) 140
Cornish v. Midland Bank plc, [1985] 3 All E.R. 513 (C.A.) 199
Corporation Agencies Ltd. v. Home Bank, [1927] A.C. 318 (P.C.) 180
Cory Bros. & Co. v. The "Mecca," [1897] A.C. 286 (H.L.) 245
Cosslett (Contractors) Ltd., Re, [1998] Ch. 495 (C.A.) 251
Coutts & Co. v. Stock, [2000] 1 W.L.R. 906 (Ch. D.) 231
Couture v. Caisse Populaire de Bathurst Ltée (1996), 181 N.B.R.
  (2d) 161, [1996] N.B.J. No. 361 (Q.B.) 355
Cowan de Groot Properties Ltd. v. Eagle Trust plc, [1992] 4 All E.R. 700
  (Ch. D.) 220
Credit Lyonnais Bank Nederland NV v. Export Credits Guarantee
  Department (1999), [1999] UKHL 9, [2000] 1 AC 486, [1999]
  1 All E.R. 929... 282
Credit Lyonnais Bank Nederland v. Burch, [1997] 1 All E.R. 144 (C.A.) 202
Critten v. Chemical National Bank of New York, 171 N.Y. 219 (1902)............. 300
Cumming v. Shand (1860), 5 H. & N. 95, 157 E.R. 1114 (Exch.)................. 230–31
Cunliffe Brooks & Co. v. Blackburn and District Benefit Building
  Society (1884), 9 App. Cas. 857 (H.L.)... 230
Curley v. Briggs (1920), 53 D.L.R. 351, [1920] 2 W.W.R. 1025, 13 Sask. L.R. 346
  (C.A.) 192
Curtice v. London City & Midland Bank Ltd., [1908] 1 K.B. 293 (C.A.) 276
Cusack v. Day [1925] 3 D.L.R. 1028 (B.C.C.A.) 235
Cuthbert v. Robarts Lubbock & Co., [1909] 2 Ch. 226 (C.A.) 231
Cuvelier v. Bank of Montreal (2000), 189 N.S.R. (2d) 26,
  590 A.P.R. 26, [2000] N.S.J. No. 334 (S.C.) 398–99
Cypress-Batt Enterprises Ltd. v. Bank of British Columbia, [1994]
  9 W.W.R. 438, 94 B.C.L.R. (2d) 299, [1994] B.C.J. No. 1447 (S.C.) 215

D.A. Bamford (Marine) Ltd., Re (1970), 14 C.B.R. (N.S.) 304, [1970]
  O.J. No. 1051 (S.C.).. 192
D.W. McIntosh Ltd., Re (1940), 21 C.B.R. 469, [1940] O.J. No. 105 (S.C.) 248
Dahl v. Royal Bank of Canada (2004), 243 D.L.R. (4th) 74, 31 B.C.L.R.
  (4th) 132, 2004 BCCA 419 379

Daniels v. Imperial Bank of Canada (1914), 19 D.L.R. 166 (Alta. S.C.) 248–49
Dartboard Holdings Ltd. v. Royal Bank of Canada (1991), 12 C.B.R.
    (3d) 88, [1991] B.C.J. No. 3713 (S.C.) 210–11
Dassen Gold Resources Ltd. v. Royal Bank of Canada (1997),
    200 A.R. 241, [1997] 9 W.W.R. 658, [1997] A.J. No. 777 (C.A.) 181, 210
Davidson v. Barclays Bank Ltd., [1940] 1 All E.R. 316 (K.B.) 271–72
Davis v. Bank of Montreal, [1945] 1 W.W.R. 6, 61 B.C.R. 294, [1945]
    B.C.J. No. 64 (S.C.) 272
Davis v. Bowsher (1794), 5 Term. Rep. 488, 101 E.R. 275 (K.B.) 251
Davis, Re (1958), 13 D.L.R. (2d) 411, 25 W.W.R. 630 (B.C.S.C.) 242
De la Bere v. Pearson Ltd., [1907] 1 K.B. 483 (C.A.) 397
De Vries v. Royal Bank of Canada (1975), 8 O.R. (2d) 347, 58 D.L.R.
    (3d) 43, [1975] O.J. No. 2290 (H.C.J.), aff'd (1975), 11 O.R.
    (2d) 583, 66 D.L.R. (3d) 618, 21 C.B.R. (N.S.) 271 (C.A.) 163–64
Deeley v. Lloyds Bank, [1912] A.C. 756 (H.L.) 245–46
Deep v. Bank of Montreal (1991), 47 O.A.C. 319, [1991] O.J. No. 209
    (C.A.) 231, 249
Del Grande v. Toronto-Dominion Bank (1995), 21 B.L.R. (2d) 220,
    [1995] O.J. No. 2005 (Gen. Div.) 214
Delbrueck & Co. v. Manufacturers Hanover Trust Co., 609 F.2d 1047
    (2d Cir. 1979) 341–42
Derry v. Peek (1889), 14 A.C. 337 (H.L.) 208
Desharnais v. Toronto Dominion Bank (2002), 175 B.C.A.C. 32,
    9 B.C.L.R. (4th) 236, 2002 BCCA 640 211
Deutsche Bank und Disconts Gesellschaft v. Banque des Marchands
    de Moscou (1931), 4 L.D.A.B. 293 (C.A.) 232
Devaynes v. Noble; Clayton's Case (1816), 1 Mer. 572, 35 E.R. 781
    (H.L.) 186, 245, 247, 296, 300
Dillon, Re (1890), 44 Ch. D. 76 (C.A.) 234, 296
Director of Support & Custody Enforcement v. Jones (1991), 5 O.R.
    (3d) 499, 85 D.L.R. (4th) 375, [1991] O.J. No. 1838 (Div. Ct.) 242
Docherty v. Royal Bank of Scotland, 1963 S.L.T. (Notes) 43 (S.C.) 297
Doherty Estate, Re (1997), 190 N.B.R. (2d) 303, 484 A.P.R. 303,
    [1997] N.B.J. No. 319 (C.A.) 239
Dominion Trust Company and U.S. Fidelity Claim, Re, [1918]
    3 W.W.R. 1023, 26 B.C.R. 339, [1918] B.C.J. No. 43 (S.C.) 12
Dominix v. Canadian Imperial Bank of Commerce (2000), 196 Nfld. &
    P.E.I.R. 324, 15 B.L.R. (3d) 87, [2000] N.J. No. 271 (Prov. Ct.) 380
Don Bodkin Leasing Ltd. v. Toronto-Dominion Bank (1998), 40 O.R.
    (3d) 262, 40 B.L.R. (2d) 179, [1998] O.J. No. 2241 (C.A.) 301–2
Donoghue v. Stevenson, [1932] A.C. 562 (H.L.) 208
Doraldick Investments Ltd. v. Canadian Imperial Bank of Commerce
    (2000), 131 O.A.C. 392, 5 B.L.R. (3d) 200, [2000] O.J. No. 1403 (C.A.) 211
Dovey v. Bank of New Zealand, [2000] 3 N.Z.L.R. 641 (C.A.) 340
Dumas v. Boivin (1936), 75 Que. S.C. 1 255

Duncan District Credit Union v. Greater Victoria Savings Credit Union,
[1978] 3 W.W.R. 570 (B.C.S.C.) 261

E. & R. Distributors v. Atlas Drywall Ltd. (1980), 118 D.L.R. (3d) 339,
25 B.C.L.R. 394, [1980] B.C.J. No. 1213 (C.A.) 212–13
Eagle Trust plc v. SBC Securities (No. 2), [1996] 1 B.C.L.C. 121 (Ch. D.) 220
Eagle Trust plc v. SBC Securities Ltd., [1992] 4 All E.R. 488 (Ch. D.) 220
Edmonton Motors Ltd. v. Edmonton Savings & Credit Union Ltd. (1988),
85 A.R. 29, 58 Alta. L.R. (2d) 370, [1988] A.J. No. 140 (Q.B.) 255
Edmonton Savings & Credit Union Ltd. v. Yarmuch (1985), 60 A.R. 219,
[1985] A.J. No. 862 (Q.B.) 241
Edwards Estate v. Bradley, [1957] S.C.R. 599, 9 D.L.R. (2d) 673,
[1957] S.C.J. No. 37 239
EGALE Canada Inc. v. Canada (Attorney General), [2001] 11 W.W.R. 685,
95 B.C.L.R. (3d) 122, 2001 BCSC 1365 9
El Ajou v. Dollar Land Holdings, [1994] 2 All E.R. 685 (C.A.) 220
El Jawhary v. BCCI, [1993] B.C.L.C. 396 (Ch. D.) 312
Elawadi v. Bank of Credit and Commerce International SA, [1989]
1 All E.R. 242 (Q.B.) 385
Electrical Fittings and Foundry Co. Ltd., Re, [1926] 1 D.L.R. 752,
58 O.L.R. 364, [1926] O.J. No. 107 (S.C. in Bkcy.) 16
Elmhurst Investment Co. v. Allard, [1963] Que. Q.B. 236 264
Emerson v. American Express Co., 90 A.2d 236 (Mun. App.
D.C. 1952) 386–87
Empire Fertilizer Ltd. v. Cioci, [1934] 4 D.L.R. 804 (Ont. C.A.) 242
Esso Petroleum Co. v. Mardon, [1976] Q.B. 801 (C.A.) 209
European Asian Bank A.G. v. Punjab & Sind Bank, [1983]
2 All E.R. 508 (C.A.) 259
European Bank, Agra Bank Claims, Re (1872), L.R. 8 Ch. 41 (C.A.) 247
Everly v. Dunkley (1912), 27 O.L.R. 414, [1912] O.J. No. 50 (Div. Ct.) 180, 239
Evra Corporation v. Swiss Bank Corp., 522 F. Supp. 820 (1981),
rev'd on another ground, 673 F.2d 951 (7th Cir. 1982) 340
Ewing v. Dominion Bank (1904), 35 S.C.R. 133, leave to appeal to
P.C. refused, [1904] A.C. 806, 13 C.R.A.C. 321 (P.C.) 259, 280
Exchange Bank v. Fletcher (1891), 19 S.C.R. 278, 14 L.N. 289 26

Farley v. Turner (1857), 26 L.J. Ch. 710 246
Farrow's Bank Ltd., Re, [1923] 1 Ch. 41 (C.A.) 192
Feaver v. Feaver, [1977] 5 W.W.R. 271, 1 R.F.L. (2d) 108 (B.C.S.C.) 238
Fellus v. National Westminster Bank plc (1983), 133 New L.J. 766 (Q.B.) 385
First National City Bank of New York v. Frederics-Helton Travel Service
Inc., 209 N.Y.S.2d 704 (Sup. Ct. 1961) 388
First Sport Ltd. v. Barclays Bank plc, [1993] 3 All E.R. 789 (C.A.) 348
Fleming v. Bank of New Zealand, [1900] A.C. 577 (P.C.) 231, 258, 271–72
Foley v. Hill (1848), 2 H.L. Cas. 28, 9 E.R. 1002 (H.L.) 178–79, 180, 193,
226–28, 252

Fonthill Lumber Ltd. v. Bank of Montreal, [1959] O.R. 451, 16 D.L.R.
(2d) 746, 38 C.B.R. 68 (C.A.) 244
Forman v. Bank of England (1902), 18 T.L.R. 339 (K.B.) 259, 289
Fraser Valley Credit Union v. Canada. (Superintendent of Financial Institutions)
(1999), 65 B.C.L.R. (3d) 85, 118 B.C.A.C. 194, 1999 BCCA 48 45
Fraser Valley Credit Union v. Canorama Development Corp (1984),
56 B.C.L.R. 145 (B.C.S.C.) 211–12
Frosch v. Dadd [1960] O.R. 435 (C.A.) 237
Fuller Brush Co. v. Hazell (1975), 6 O.R. (2d) 727, 54 D.L.R. (3d) 22,
[1975] O.J. No. 2191 (H.C.J.) 245–46

Gaden v. Newfoundland Savings Bank, [1899] A.C. 281, 12 C.R.A.C. 128
(P.C.) 265, 266, 267, 269
Galipeau Musique Ltd. v. Heckbert (1979), 28 N.B.R. (2d) 163, 63 A.P.R. 163,
[1979] N.B.J. No. 287 (Co. Ct.) 242
Garcia v. Chase Manhattan Bank, N.A., 735 F.2d 645 (2d Circ. 1984) 190
Garnett v. McKewan (1872), L.R. 8 Exch. 10 .... 151, 248, 250
Garon Realty & Insurance Ltd. v. James, [1978] 6 W.W.R. 694,
8 C.P.C. 65, [1978] B.C.J. No. 802 (S.C.) 244, 259, 261
Garrioch v. Canadian Bank of Commerce, [1919] 3 W.W.R. 185,
[1919] A.J. No. 54 (S.C.) 278
Gaunt v. Taylor (1843), 2 Hare 413, 67 E.R. 170 276
Geffen v. Goodman, [1991] 2 S.C.R. 353, 81 D.L.R. (4th) 211, [1991]
S.C.J. No. 53 204
General Dairies v. Maritime Electric Co., [1935] S.C.R. 519, [1935]
4 D.L.R. 196, 44 C.R.C. 43 297
Gibbons v. Westminster Bank Ltd., [1939] 2 K.B. 882 271
Giblin v. McMullen (1869), L.R. 2 P.C. 317 397
Gillies v. Commercial Bank of Manitoba (1895), 10 Man. R. 460 (C.A.) 245–46
Giordano v. Royal Bank of Canada, [1972] 3 O.R. 576, 29 D.L.R. (3d) 38,
[1972] O.J. No. 1750, [1972] O.J. No. 1751 (H.C.J.), rev'd [1973]
3 O.R. 771, 38 D.L.R. (3d) 191, [1973] O.J. No. 2090 (C.A.),
rev'd (1974), 38 D.L.R. (3d) 191n (S.C.C.) 277
Glyns Mills, Currie & Co. v. East and West India Dock Co. (1882),
7 App. Cas. 591 (H.L.) 397
Goad v. Canadian Imperial Bank of Commerce, [1968] 1 O.R. 579,
67 D.L.R. (2d) 189, [1968] O.J. No. 1061 (H.C.J.) 212, 214
Goberdhan v. Banque Canadienne Nationale, [1978] C.P. 340 389–90
Gold v. Primary Developments Ltd., [1997] 3 S.C.R. 767, 152 D.L.R.
(4th) 385, [1997] S.C.J. No. 93 221–22
Gold v. Rosenberg, [1997] 3 S.C.R. 767, 152 D.L.R. (4th) 385, [1997]
S.C.J. No. 93 204
Gooderham v. Bank of Nova Scotia (2000), 47 O.R. (3d) 554,
[2000] O.T.C. 179, [2000] O.J. No. 890 (S.C.J.) 204–5
Gough Electric Ltd. v. Canadian Imperial Bank of Commerce (1986),
31 D.L.R. (4th) 307, 7 B.C.L.R. (2d) 39, [1986] B.C.J. No. 784 (C.A.) ..293–94

Gowanlock v. Bank of Nova Scotia, [2001] 9 W.W.R. 71, 157 Man.R.
(2d) 124, 2001 MBQB 160 225
Grace Chu Chan Po Kee v. The Hong Kong Chinese Bank Ltd., unreported
decision of the Hong Kong High Court (9 January 1979) 289
Gray v. Johnston (1868), L.R. 3 H.L. 1 .... 218, 243
Great Western Railway v. London & County Banking Co., [1901]
A.C. 414 (H.L.) 177
Green v. Royal Bank of Canada (1996), 28 O.R. (3d) 706, 135 D.L.R.
(4th) 337, [1996] O.J. No. 1454 (Gen. Div.) 224, 225
Greenwood Teall v. William Williams Brown & Co. (1894),
11 T.L.R. 56 (C.A.) 249
Greenwood v. Martins Bank Ltd., [1933] A.C. 51 (H.L.) 187, 280
Griffin, Re, [1899] 1 Ch. 408 .... 234, 296
Gross, Re (1871), 6 Ch. App. 632 (C.A.) 244
Groves-Raffin Construction Ltd. v. Bank of Nova Scotia (1975),
64 D.L.R. (3d) 78, [1976] 2 W.W.R. 673 (B.C.C.A.) 293–94
Guertin v. Royal Bank of Canada (1984), 47 O.R. (2d) 799, 12 D.L.R.
(4th) 640, [1984] O.J. No. 3049 (C.A.) 313

Haggart Construction Ltd. v. Canadian Imperial Bank of Commerce (1998),
213 A.R. 241, [1998] 5 W.W.R. 586, 1998 ABQB 5, aff'd (1999),
250 A.R. 164, [2000] 2 W.W.R. 722, [1999] A.J. No. 1439 (C.A.) 153
Hall v. Hatch (1901), 3 O.L.R. 147, [1901] O.J. No. 141 (H.C.J.) 259–60
Hallett's Estate, Re (1880), 13 Ch. D. 696 246
Halwell v. Township of Wilmot (1897), 24 O.A.R. 628, [1897]
O.J. No. 70 (C.A.) 268
Hammond v. Hammond, [1995] 7 W.W.R. 345, 7 B.C.L.R. (3d) 25,
[1995] B.C.J. No. 1153 (S.C.) 237, 239
Hansen v. Randa, [1996] B.C.W.L.D. 2194, [1996] B.C.J. No. 1654 (S.C.) 265
Harben v. Phillips (1883), 23 Ch. D. 14 (C.A.) 107
Hardy v. Veasey (1868), L.R. 3 Ex. 107 303
Harris; Ex parte Union Bank, Re (1925), [1926] 1 D.L.R. 55,
29 O.W.N. 307, [1925] O.J. No. 324 (S.C.) 22
Harry v. Kreutziger (1978), 95 D.L.R. (3d) 231, 9 B.C.L.R. 166 (C.A.) 242
Hart (Inspector of Taxes) v. Sangster, [1957] 2 All E.R. 208 (C.A.) 228
Hawreliak v. Paul, [1983] O.J. No. 914, 20 A.C.W.S. (2d) 162 (Prov. Ct.) 382
Hayward v. Bank of Nova Scotia (1984), 45 O.R. (2d) 542, 7 D.L.R.
(4th) 135, [1984] O.J. No. 3136 (H.C.J.), aff'd (1985), 51 O.R.
(2d) 193, 19 D.L.R. (4th) 758, [1985] O.J. No. 2567 (C.A.) 195, 210, 213
Head (No. 2), Re, [1894] 2 Ch. 236 237
Heddle v. Bank of Hamilton (1912), 5 D.L.R. 11 (B.C.C.A.) 395
Hedley Byrne & Co. Ltd. v. Heller and Partners Ltd., [1964] A.C. 465 (H.L.) 193
Heller v. Royal Bank of Canada (1990), 76 Alta. L.R. (2d) 280,
[1990] A.J. No. 918 (C.A.) 210, 211
Henderson v. Bank of Hamilton (1895), 22 O.A.R. 414, [1895]
O.J. No. 52 (C.A.) 258–59

Henderson v. Merrett Syndicates Ltd., [1995] 2 A.C. 145 (H.L.) 341
Hercules Management Ltd. v. Ernst & Young, [1997] 2 S.C.R. 165,
    146 D.L.R. (4th) 577, [1997] S.C.J. No. 51 .... 112, 209
Hill v. Bank of Hochelaga, [1921] 3 W.W.R. 430 (Alta. S.C.) 238, 241
Hill v. Hill (1904), 8 O.L.R. 710, [1904] O.J. No. 245 (H.C.J.) 239
Hilton v. Westminster Bank Ltd. (1926), 135 L.T. 358 (C.A.) 187
Hirschhorn v. Evans, [1938] 3 All E.R. 491 (C.A.) 237, 240–41, 242
Hitchcock v. Edwards (1889), 60 L.T. (N.S.) 636 (Q.B.D.) 264
HMV Fields Properties Ltd. v. Bracken Self Selection Fabrics Ltd.,
    1991 S.L.T. 31 342
Hochelaga Bank v. Larue (1910), 13 W.L.R. 114 (Alta. C.A.) 395
Hodgkinson v. Simms, [1994] 3 S.C.R. 377, 117 D.L.R. (4th) 161,
    [1994] S.C.J. No. 84 196
Holland v. Manchester & Liverpool District Banking Co. (1909),
    25 T.L.R. 386 (Ch. D.) 297
Holman v. Royal Bank of Canada (1975), 58 D.L.R. (3d) 154
    (B.C. Co. Ct.) 297, 299
Home Bank (Re) (1928), 10 C.B.R. 255, [1928] O.J. No. 357
    (S.C. in Bankruptcy) 141
Hone, Re, [1951] Ch. 85 231
Honeywell Ltd. v. Sherwood Credit Union Ltd. (1989), 58 D.L.R.
    (4th) 249, 76 Sask. R. 228, [1989] S.J. No. 245 (Q.B.) 270
Hongkong Bank of Canada v. Phillips, [1998] 2 W.W.R. 606,
    119 Man. R. (2d) 243, [1997] M.J. No. 134 (Q.B.) 210, 313
Hoon v. Maloff (1964), 42 D.L.R. (2d) 770, 46 W.W.R. 445 (B.C.S.C.) 242
Hopkins v. Abbott (1875), L.R. 19 Eq. 222 (V.-C.) 234, 296
Horry v. Tate & Lyle Refineries Ltd., [1982] 2 Lloyd's Rep. 416 (Q.B.D.) 198
Houben v. Bank of Nova Scotia (1970), 3 N.B.R. (2d) 366, [1970]
    N.B.J. No. 147 (Co. Ct.) 250
Houghland v. R.R. Low (Luxury Coaches) Ltd., [1962] 2 All E.R. 159 (C.A.) 397
Houghton v. Houghton (1964), [1965] 1 O.R. 481, [1964] O.J. No. 860 (S.C.) 306
Hudson v. Toronto Dominion Bank (1976), 22 C.B.R. (N.S.) 55
    (Alta S.C. in Bkcy.) 248–49
Huron & Erie Mortgage Corp. v. Rumig (1969), [1970] 2 O.R. 204,
    10 D.L.R. (3d) 309, [1969] O.J. No. 1577 (C.A.) 278, 291

I.T.L. Industries Ltd. v. Winterbottom (1979), 24 O.R. (2d) 161, 97 D.L.R.
    (3d) 553, [1979] O.J. No. 4169 (H.C.J.), rev'd on other grounds (1980),
    27 O.R. (2d) 496, 106 D.L.R. (3d) 577, [1980] O.J. No. 3076
    (C.A.) 16, 306, 308
Imperial Bank of Canada v. Bank of Hamilton (1902), 13 C.R.A.C. 41,
    [1903] A.C. 49 (P.C.) 268
Imperial Bank of Canada v. Hays & Earl Ltd. (1962), 35 D.L.R.
    (2d) 136, 38 W.W.R. 169 (Alta. S.C.) 292
Imperial Bank v. Begley, [1936] 2 All E.R. 367, [1936] 3 D.L.R. 1, [1936]
    2 W.W.R. 243 (P.C.) 244

Imperial Oil Ltd. v. Hough (1957), 11 D.L.R. (2d) 440, 23 W.W.R. 85
(Alta. S.C.) 378
Inter City Express Ltd. v. Toronto-Dominion Bank (1976), 66 D.L.R.
(3d) 754 (B.C.S.C.) 153, 191
Irwin v. Bank of Montreal (1876), 38 U.C.Q.B. 375 (C.A.)..................................151
Isaacs v. Barclays Bank Ltd., [1943] 2 All E.R. 682 (K.B.) 179, 193
ITT Commercial Finance Ltd. v. Bank of Nova Scotia (1989), 91 N.S.R.
(2d) 247, 233 A.P.R. 247, [1989] N.S.J. No. 173 (S.C.T.D.) 235

J. Nunes Diamonds Ltd. v. Dominion Electric Protection Co., [1972]
S.C.R. 769, 26 D.L.R. (3d) 699, [1972] S.C.J. No. 60............................... 208–9
J.C. Creations Ltd. v. Vancouver City Savings Credit Union (2004),
236 D.L.R. (4th) 602, 24 B.C.L.R. (4th) 280, 2004 BCCA 107 294
J.R. Corneau Holdings Ltd. v. Pockett, [1978] 5 W.W.R. 483, [1978]
M.J. No. 285 (Co. Ct.) 242
Jackson v. White and Midland Bank Ltd., [1967] 2 Lloyd's Rep. 68
(Q.B.D.) 238, 240
Jacobs v. Larose, [1971] C.A. 281 (Que.) 264
Jayson v. Midland Bank Ltd., [1968] 1 Lloyd's Rep. 409 (C.A.).................. 271–72
Jeffryes v. Agra & Masterman's Bank (1866), L.R. 2 Eq. 674 252
Joachimson v. Swiss Bank Corp., [1921] 3 K.B. 110
(C.A.) 151, 179, 186, 187, 232, 255, 257–58, 259, 288, 305
Johnson v. Christmas (1924), 37 Que. K.B. 142 (C.A.) 270
Johnson v. Robarts (1875), L.R. 10 Ch. App. 505... 251–52
Jones v. Bank of Montreal (1869), 29 U.C.Q.B. 448, [1869]
O.J. No. 56 (Q.B.) 257–59
Jones v. Imperial Bank (1876), 23 Gr. 262... 149
Jones v. Maynard, [1951] 1 Ch. 572.. 238
Jones-Ottaway v. Bank of Montreal (2001), 275 A.R. 305, [2000]
A.J. No. 1177 (Q.B.) 225

Karak Rubber Co. Ltd. v. Burden, [1972] 2 All E.R. 1210 (Ch. D.).................... 218
Kaufman v. Royal Bank of Canada (1994), 34 C.P.C. (3d) 334, [1994]
O.J. No. 4162 (Gen. Div.) 252
Kauter v. Hilton (1953), 90 C.L.R. 86 (H.C.A.) 234
Kawneer Co. of Canada Ltd. v. Bank of Canada (1975), 9 O.R.
(2d) 468, 60 D.L.R. (3d) 636, [1975] O.J. No. 2421 (H.C.J.) 39
Kay v. Posluns (1989), 69 O.R. (2d) 209, 60 D.L.R. (4th) 426, [1989]
O.J. No. 987 (H.C.J.), additional reasons at (18 September 1990)
Doc. No. Toronto 26686/68 (Ont. H.C.J.) 139–40
Keever, Re, [1967] 1 Ch. 182 251
Keith Plumbing & Heating Co. v. Newport City Club Ltd., [2000]
6 W.W.R. 65, 75 B.C.L.R (3d) 186, [2000] B.C.J. No. 390 (C.A.) 211
Kelly Funeral Homes Ltd. v. Canadian Imperial Bank of Commerce
(1990), 72 D.L.R. (4th) 276, [1990] O.J. No. 521 (H.C.J.) 301–2
Kelly v. Canadian Pacific R. Co. (1915), 25 D.L.R. 79 (B.C.C.A.) 278

Kelly v. Cooper, [1993] A.C. 205 (P.C.) 197
Kelly v. Solari (1841), 9 M. & W. 54, 152 E.R. 24 (Exch. Ch.) 284–85
Kendrick v. Dominion Bank (1920), 48 O.L.R. 539, [1920]
   O.J. No. 81 (S.C.A.D.) 192, 235
Kepitigalla Rubber Estates Ltd. v. National Bank of India Ltd.,
   [1909] 2 K.B. 1010 .... 281, 296–97, 299
Keyes v. Royal Bank of Canada, [1947] S.C.R. 377, [1947] 3 D.L.R. 161 ... 265, 268
Kilburn v. Co-op Centre Credit Union Ltd. (1972), 33 D.L.R.
   (3d) 233, [1973] 1 W.W.R. 757 (Alta. S.C.) 268
Kilsby v. Williams (1822), 5 B. & Ald. 815, 106 E.R. 1388 (K.B.) 263, 290
Kimmel Estate v. Royal Bank of Canada (1995), 177 A.R. 253,
   [1995] A.J. No. 1173 (Q.B.) 225
Kingsnorth Trust Ltd. v. Bell, [1986] 1 All E.R. 423 (C.A.) 199
Kinlan v. Ulster Bank Ltd., [1928] I.R. 171 (S.C.) 272
Kirch v. Royal Bank of Canada (1993), [1994] 2 W.W.R. 194,
   114 Sask. R. 205, [1993] S.J. No. 558 (Q.B.) 210–11
Klein v. First Edina National Bank, 196 N.W.2d 619 (Minn. 1972) 197
Kleinwort Benson Ltd. v. Lincoln City Council, [1998]
   3 W.L.R. 1095 (H.L.) 285
Kogler v. Schabernig Estate (2004), 7 E.T.R. (3d) 31, [2004]
   B.C.J. No. 785, 2004 BCSC 22 239
Kpohraror v. Woolwich Building Society, [1996] 4 All E.R. 119 (C.A.) 271
Krupp v. Bell (1968), 67 D.L.R. (2d) 256 (Sask. C.A.) 206
Kuruyo Trading Ltd. v. Acme Garment Co. (1975) Ltd. (1988), 51 D.L.R.
   (4th) 334, 53 Man. R. (2d) 41, [1988] M.J. No. 159 (C.A.) 215–16

Laarakker v. Royal Bank of Canada (1980), 31 O.R. (2d) 188, 118 D.L.R.
   (3d) 716, [1980] O.J. No. 3844 (H.C.J.) 22
Labreche Estate v. Harasymiw (1992), 89 D.L.R. (4th) 95, 11 C.C.L.I.
   (2d) 161, [1992] O.J. No. 321 (Gen. Div.) 224–25
LAC Minerals Ltd. v. International Corona Resources Ltd., [1989]
   2 S.C.R. 574, 61 D.L.R. (4th) 14, [1989] S.C.J. No. 83 196
Lacave & Co. v. Credit Lyonnais, [1897] 1 Q.B. 148 177
Laconia, The, [1977] A.C. 850 (H.L.) 342
Ladbroke & Co. v. Todd (1914), 19 Com. Cas. 256 177
Lajambe v. Saint-Hilaire (1924), 30 R.L. (N.S.) 447 (Que. Sup. Ct.) 289
Lamb v. Smith Estate (1995), 132 Nfld. & P.E.I.R. 316. 9 E.T.R.
   (2d) 127, [1995] N.J. No. 239 (S.C.) 356
Land Bank of Nova Scotia v. Regent Enterprises Ltd. (1997), 157 Nfld &
   P.E.I.R. 102, 486 A.P.R. 102, [1997] N.J. No. 152 (C.A.) 261–62
Landry Pulpwood Co. v. Banque Canadienne Nationale (1927),
   [1927] S.C.R. 605, [1928] 1 D.L.R. 493 160
Larondeau Estate v. Laurendeau, [1954] O.W.N. 722, [1954]
   O.J. No. 217 (H.C.J.) 237
Law Society of Upper Canada v. Toronto-Dominion Bank (1998),
   42 O.R. (3d) 257, 169 D.L.R. (4th) 353, [1998] O.J. No. 5115 (C.A.) 246

Le Cercle Universitaire d'Ottawa v. National Bank of Canada (1987),
   61 O.R. (2d) 456, 43 D.L.R. (4th) 147, [1987] O.J. No. 908 (H.C.J.) 301–2
Leader, Plunkett and Leader v. Direction der Disconto-Gesellschaft
   (1914), 31 T.L.R. 83 (K.B.) 193
Leather Mfrs. Bank v. Morgan, 117 U.S. 96 (1886) 300
Leduc v. Banque d'Hochelaga, [1926] S.C.R. 76, [1926] 1 D.L.R. 433 267
Lee (Administrator of Lawlor) v. Bank of British North America (1879),
   30 U.C.C.P. 255, [1879] O.J. No. 290 234
Lee v. Blake (1924), 55 O.L.R. 310, [1924] O.J. No. 28 (S.C.A.D.) 269
Leese v. Martin (1873), L.R. 17 Eq. 224 395–96
Leeson v. Leeson, [1936] 2 K.B. 156 (C.A.) 245–46
Les Fenêtres St-Jean Inc. v. BNC, [1990] R.J.Q. 632, 69 D.L.R.
   (4th) 384, [1990] A.Q. No 221 (C.A.) 215
Lesch v. Farmers' & Merchants' State Bank of New Salem,
   211 N.W. 687 (N.D. 1926) 387
Lewes Sanitary Steam Laundry Co. v. Barclay & Co. (1906),
   95 L.T. 444 (Ch. D.) 299
Libyan Arab Foreign Bank v. Bankers Trust Co., [1988]
   1 Lloyd's Rep. 259 (Q.B.D.) 190, 310
Libyan Arab Foreign Bank v. Manufacturers Hanover Trust Co.
   (No. 2), [1989] 1 Lloyd's Rep. 608 (Comm. Ct.) 190, 341–42
Lilley v. Doubleday (1881), 7 Q.B.D. 510 397
Lipkin Gorman v. Karpnale Ltd., [1989] 1 W.L.R. 1340 (C.A.) 218
Lipkin Gorman v. Karpnale Ltd., [1991] 2 A.C. 548 (H.L.) 284, 287
Lloyd v. Grace, Smith & Co., [1912] A.C. 716 (H.L.) 397
Lloyds Bank Ltd. v. Bundy, [1975] Q.B. 326 (C.A.) 193
Lloyds Bank Ltd. v. Cooke, [1907] 1 K.B. 794 (C.A.) 279–80
Lloyds Bank plc v. Independent Insurance Co. Ltd., [2000]
   Q.B. 110 (C.A.) 286
Lloyds Bank v. Chartered Bank of India, Australia & China, [1929]
   1 K.B. 40 (C.A.) 283
Loaf 'N Jug Ltd. v. Canadian Imperial Bank of Commerce, [1979]
   5 W.W.R. 663 (Alta. Dist. Ct.) 270
London & Globe Finance Corp., Re, [1902] 2 Ch. 416 251
London and Mediterranean Bank; ex parte Birmingham
   Banking Co., Re (1868), L.R. 3 Ch. App. 651 (C.A.) 392
London Joint Stock Bank Ltd. v. MacMillan, [1918] A.C. 777
   (H.L.) 187, 259, 279–80
London Provincial & South-Western Bank Ltd. v. Buszard (1918),
   35 T.L.R. 142 (K.B.) 278
Lubbock v. Tribe (1838), 3 M. & W. 607, 150 E.R. 1287 290

Macbeth v. North & South Wales Bank, [1908] A.C. 137 (H.L.) 269
MacDonald v. Tacquah Gold Mines Co. (1884), 13 Q.B.D. 535 (C.A.) 242
MacKersy v. Ramsays, Bonars & Co. (1843), 9 Cl. & Fin. 818,
   8 E.R. 628 (H.L.) 288

Macmillan Inc. v. Bishopsgate Investment Trust plc (No. 3),
  [1995] 1 W.L.R. 978 (Ch. D.) 221
Mailman Estate, Re, [1941] S.C.R. 368, [1941] 3 D.L.R. 449 239
Mantel Bldg. v. Canada, [2000] 2 S.C.R. 860, 193 D.L.R. (4th) 1,
  [2000] S.C.J. No. 60 196
Maple Valley Acres Ltd. v. Canadian Imperial Bank of Commerce
  (2001), 46 R.P.R. (3d) 32, [2001] O.J. No. 3636 (S.C.J.) 212
Mareva Compania Naviera SA v. International Bulk Carriers SA
  (The "Mareva"), [1975] 2 Lloyd's Rep. 509 (C.A.) 274
Marfani & Co. v. Midland Bank Ltd., [1968] 1 W.L.R. 956 (C.A.) 178
Marketing Products Inc. v. 1254719 Ontario Ltd. (2000), 13 B.L.R.
  (3d) 264, [2000] O.J. No. 1484 (S.C.J.) 249
Markham School for Human Development v. Ghods (2002), 60 O.R.
  (3d) 624, 216 D.L.R. (4th) 202, [2002] O.J. No. 3153 (S.C.J.) 265
Markson v. MBNA Canada Bank (2004), 71 O.R. (3d) 741, 48 B.L.R.
  (3d) 129, [2004] O.J. No. 3226 (S.C.J.) 379
Marshal v. Crutwell (1875), L.R. 20 Eq. 328 .... 237, 239
Marshall v. Canada Permanent Trust Co. (1968), 69 D.L.R. (2d) 260
  (Alta. S.C.T.D.) 206
Marzetti v. Williams (1830), 1 B. & Ad. 415, 109 E.R. 842 (K.B.) 258, 271
Massey v. Midland Bank plc, [1995] 1 All E.R. 929 (C.A.) 202
Master Charge v. Price (1977), 42 N.S.R. (2d) 244, [1977]
  N.S.J. No. 757 (Co. Ct.) 372
Mathews v. National Trust Co., [1925] 4 D.L.R. 774 (Ont. S.C.) 239
Matrix Contractors Building Services Inc. v. National Bank of
  Canada (2005), 200 O.A.C. 201, [2005] O.J. No. 2931 (C.A.) 211
Maubach v. Bank of Nova Scotia (1987), 62 O.R. (2d) 220, 44 D.L.R.
  (4th) 575, [1988] O.J. No. 4 (C.A.) 268
Maunder v. Royal Canadian Bank (1871), 20 U.C.C.P. 125, [1871]
  O.J. No. 188 235
McBean v. Bank of Nova Scotia (1981), 15 B.L.R. 296, [1981] O.J. No. 2444
  (H.C.J.), aff'd (1982), 17 A.C.W.S. (2d) 154 (Ont. C.A.) 195
McCready Co. v. Alberta Clothing Co. (1910), 3 Alta. L.R. 67 (S.C.) 249
McDonald Estate v. McDonald (1903), 33 S.C.R. 145 235
McEvoy v. Belfast Banking Co., [1935] A.C. 24 (H.L.) 235, 240
McIntosh v. Bank of New Brunswick (1913), 15 D.L.R. 375
  (N.B.S.C. en banc) 267
McKenna Estate v. McKenna (1986), 61 Nfld. & P.E.I.R. 51,
  185 A.P.R. 51, [1986] P.E.I.J. No. 78 (S.C.) 239
McKenzie v. Bank of Montreal (1975), 12 O.R. (2d) 719, 70 D.L.R.
  (3d) 113, [1976] O.J. No. 2162 (C.A.) 213
McKenzie v. British Linen Co. (1881), 6 App. Cas. 82 (H.L.) 259, 282
McLean v. Vessey, [1935] 4 D.L.R. 170 (P.E.I.S.C.) 239
McLellan v. McLellan (1911), 25 O.L.R. 214, [1911] O.J. No. 30, (Div. Ct.) 192

McLellan v. Sterling Bank (1911), 2 O.W.N. 798, 18 O.W.R. 641,
    [1911] O.J. No. 815 (H.C.J.) 192
McMorran v. Dominion Stores (1977), 14 O.R. (2d) 559, 74 D.L.R.
    (3d) 186, [1977] O.J. No. 2135 (H.C.J.) 188
McTavish v. Cotswold School District, [1931] 3 W.W.R. 623 (Sask. C.A.) 278
Mellon Bank v. Securities Settlement Corp., 710 F. Supp. 991 (N.J. 1989) 340
Mellon National Bank v. Citizens' Bank and Trust Co., 88 F.2d 128 (1937) 387
Menard v. Toronto-Dominion Bank (2005), 191 Man. R. (2d) 109,
    20 C.C.L.I. (4th) 115, 2005 MBQB 27 224
Mercantile Bank & Trust Co. (Liquidators of) v. Credit Europeen S.A.
    (1960), 32 N.B.R. (2d) 239, 9 E.T.R. 195, [1980] N.B.J. No. 17 (Q.B.) 227
Mercantile Bank of Canada v. Leon's Furniture Ltd. (1992), 11 O.R.
    (3d) 713, 98 D.L.R. (4th) 449, [1992] O.J. No. 2753 (C.A.) 249
Metal Studios Ltd.; Ex parte City of Hamilton, Re, [1934] O.W.N. 173,
    15 C.B.R. 305, [1934] O.J. No. 256 (S.C. in Bkcy.) 16
Meteor Equipment Rentals Ltd. v. MacMillan (1970), 75 W.W.R. 660
    (B.C. Co. Ct.) 267
Metroland Printing, Publishing and Distribution Ltd. v. Canadian Imperial
    Bank of Commerce, [2001] O.T.C. 330, 14 B.L.R. (3d) 212, [2001]
    O.J. No. 1695 (S.C.J.) 294
Michaud v. Caisse populaire Notre-Dame de Lourdes Ltée (2001),
    245 N.B.R. (2d) 63, [2001] N.B.J. No. 422, 2001 NBBR 214 265
Michaud v. National Bank of Canada, [1997] R.J.Q. 547, [1997]
    A.Q. no 1 (C.S.) 106
Midland Bank Ltd. v. Seymour, [1955] 2 Lloyd's Rep. 147 (Q.B.D.) 215
Midland Bank plc v. Shephard, [1988] 3 All E.R. 17 (C.A.) 199, 201
Midland Bank v. Serter, [1995] 2 F.L.R. 367 (C.A.) 202
Midland Doherty Ltd. v. Royal Bank of Canada, [1990] R.J.Q. 121,
    [1990] A.Q. no 10 (C.A.) 261, 291
Mirtia Holdings Ltd. v. Toronto Dominion Bank (1995), 171 A.R. 105,
    30 Alta. L.R. (3d) 111, [1995] A.J. No. 536 (Q.B.) 302
Misa v. Currie (1876), 1 App. Cas. 554 (H.L.) 251
Mohtadi v. Canada Trust Co. (2002), 6 B.C.L.R. (4th) 25, [2002]
    4 C.T.C. 122, 2002 BCCA 562 399
Momm v. Barclays Bank International Ltd., [1973] 3 All E.R. 588 (Q.B.) 262
Momm v. Barclays Bank International Ltd., [1977] Q.B. 790 342
Money Mart Cheque Cashing Centre (WPG) Ltd. v. Reis Lighting
    Products & Services Ltd. (1994), 94 Man. R. (2d) 276, 16 B.L.R.
    (2d) 184, [1994] M.J. No. 385 (Q.B.) 264
Moore v. Ulster Banking Co. (1877), 11 Ir. C.L. 512 235
Morgan v. U.S. Mortgage & Trust, 208 N.Y. 218 (1913) 300
Morison v. London County & Westminster Bank, [1914] 3 K.B. 356 (C.A.) 260
Morley v. Culverwell (1840), 7 M. & W. 174, 151 E.R. 727 (Exch.) 265
Morris v. C.W. Martin & Sons Ltd., [1965] 2 All E.R. 725 (C.A.) 397
Morrison v. Coast Finance Ltd. (1965), 55 D.L.R. (2d) 710, 54 W.W.R. 257
    (B.C.C.A.) 205–6

Mougeot v. Bank of Nova Scotia, [1959] C.S. 415 272
Murano v. Bank of Montreal (1998), 41 O.R. (3d) 222, 163 D.L.R.
(4th) 21, [1998] O.J. No. 2897 (C.A.) 153, 311
Murphy v. Tignish Credit Union Ltd Murano v. Bank of Montreal.
(1993), 105 Nfld. & P.E.I.R. 193, 331 A.P.R. 193, [1993] P.E.I.J.
No. 6 (T.D.) 213
Mutual Mortgage Corp. v. Bank of Montreal (1965), 55 D.L.R. (2d) 164,
53 W.W.R. 724 (B.C.C.A.) 280

National Bank of Australasia v. Scottish Union and National Insurance
Co. (1951), 84 C.L.R. 177 (H.C.A.) 234
National Bank of Canada v. Interbank Card Association and Bank
of Montreal, 666 F.2d 6 (2d Circ. 1981) 372
National Bank of Commerce v. National Westminster Bank, [1990]
2 Lloyd's Rep. 514 .... 232, 298
National Bank of Greece (Canada) v. Bank of Montreal (2000), [2001]
2 F.C. 288, 266 N.R. 361, [2000] F.C.J. No. 2105 (C.A.) 261, 289, 291, 333
National Bank of Greece (Canada) v. Canada Permanent Trust Co.,
[1987] R.J.Q. 607, [1987] J.Q. no 311 (S.C.) 333
National Bank of Greece (Canada) v. Mboutsiadis (2002), 2 R.P.R.
(4th) 98, [2002] O.J. No. 1788 (S.C.J.) 213
National Bank of Greece Ltd. v. Pinios Shipping Co. (No. 1), [1989]
1 All E.R. 213 (C.A.) 192
National Bank of Greece S.A. v. Pinios Shipping Co. (No. 1), [1990]
1 A.C. 637 (H.L.) 232
National Money Mart Inc. v. A. & B. Enterprises Ltd. (1997),
215 A.R. 141, [1997] A.J. No. 1150 (Q.B.) 264
National Slag v. Canadian Imperial Bank of Commerce (1985),
19 D.L.R. (4th) 383, [1985] O.J. No. 14 (C.A.) 261, 291
National Trust Co. v. Harold's Demolition Inc. (2001), 43 R.P.R.
(3d) 212, [2001] O.J. No. 3269 (S.C.J.) 258
National Westminster Bank Ltd. v. Barclays Bank International Ltd.,
[1975] Q.B. 654 287
National Westminster Bank Ltd. v. Halesowen Presswork & Assemblies
Ltd., [1972] A.C. 785 (H.L.) 248
National Westminster Bank plc v. Morgan, [1985] A.C. 686 (H.L.) 198
National Westminster Bank plc v. Somer International (U.K.) Ltd.,
[2001] EWCA Civ. 970 (C.A.) 287
New Brunswick (Minister of Commerce and Development) v. Bank of
Nova Scotia (1988), 95 N.B.R. (2d) 330, 241 A.P.R. 330, [1988]
N.B.J. No. 1135 (Q.B.) 249
Newbury v. Prudential Insurance Co. of America (1996), 35 C.C.L.I.
(2d) 61, [1996] B.C.J. No. 78 (S.C.), aff'd (1997), 148 D.L.R.
(4th) 765, 46 C.C.L.I. (2d) 185, [1997] B.C.J. No. 1521 (C.A.) 224
Newell v. Royal Bank of Canada (1997), 156 N.S.R. (2d) 347,
147 D.L.R. (4th) 268, [1997] N.S.J. No. 13 (C.A.) 282

Niles v. Lake, [1947] S.C.R. 291, [1947] 2 D.L.R. 248, [1947] S.C.J. No. 13....... 236
No. 10 Management Ltd. v. Royal Bank of Canada (1976), 69 D.L.R.
  (3d) 99, [1976] M.J. No. 172 (C.A.) 217, 300
Nocton v. Lord Ashburton, [1914] A.C. 932 (H.L.) 208
Northern Bank v. Yuen (1909), 2 Alta. L.R. 310, 11 W.L.R. 698 (S.C.) 268
Northland Bank (Re) (1988), 53 Man. R. (2d) 249, [1988] M.J. No. 4 (Q.B.) 143
Northland Bank v. Kuperman, [1989] 4 W.W.R. 701, 58 Man. R.
  (2d) 233, [1989] M.J. No. 205 (C.A.).. 144
Noseworthy v. Newfoundland and Labrador Credit Union (1999), 185
  Nfld. & P.E.I.R. 341, 562 A.P.R. 341, [1999] N.J. No. 342 (S.C.T.D.) 225

O'Brien v. O'Brien (1882), 4 O.R. 450, [1882] O.J. No. 215 (H.C.J.) 235
O'Hearn v. Bank of Nova Scotia, [1970] S.C.R. 341, 10 D.L.R. (3d) 1,
  [1970] S.C.J. No. 2..248
Oatway, Re, [1903] 2 Ch. 356 246
Ogilvie v. West Australian Mortgage & Agency Co., [1896] A.C. 257 (P.C.) 259
Olympic Bank v. Wallace (1982), 19 B.L.R. 145, [1982] B.C.J.
  No. 1035 (S.C.)...242
Ontario (Attorney General) v. Newman (1901), 1 O.L.R. 511, [1901]
  O.J. No. 98 (C.A.)..234
Ontario Bank (Re) (1916), 38 O.L.R. 242, [1916] O.J. No. 36 (H.C.) 142
Ontario Bank v. McAllister (1910), 43 S.C.R. 338... 22, 170
Ontario Securities Commission and Greymac Credit Corp, Re (1986),
  55 O.R. (2d) 673, 30 D.L.R. (4th) 1, [1986] O.J. No. 830 (C.A.),
  aff'd [1988] 2 S.C.R. 172, 52 D.L.R. (4th) 767, [1988] S.C.J. No. 77 246
Ontario Woodsworth Memorial Foundation v. Grozbord (1964),
  [1965] 1 O.R. 435, 48 D.L.R. (2d) 385, [1964] O.J. No. 857 (C.A.) 280
Orlando v. Toronto Dominion Bank, [2001] O.T.C. 80, 13 B.L.R.
  (3d) 268, [2001] O.J. No. 349 (S.C.J.)...213
Owens v. Quebec Bank (1870), 30 U.C.R. 382, [1870] O.J. No. 79 (C.A.) 291

P.W. Ellis Co. Ltd., Re (1929), 36 O.W.N. 202, [1929] O.J. No. 185 (H.C.J.) 16
Pan Pacific Specialties Ltd. v. Shandong Machinery & Equipment
  (2001), 85 B.C.L.R. (3d) 362, [2001] B.C.J. No. 48, 2001 BCSC 62 249
Paramount Film Service Ltd. v. Payeur, [1961] Que. R.P. 288 (S.C.)..................297
Park v. Bank of Montreal, [1997] B.C.J. No. 787 (S.C.) 307
Parker v. South Eastern Railway Co. (1877), 2 C.P.D. 416 (C.A.)....................... 188
Parr's Bank Ltd. v. Thomas Ashby & Co. (1898), 14 T.L.R. 563 (Q.B.) 259, 260
Parr's Banking Co. v. Yates, [1898] 2 Q.B. 460 (C.A.)...233
Parry-Jones v. Law Society, [1969] 1 Ch. 1 (C.A.)..306
Patel v. Standard Chartered Bank, [2001] Lloyd's Rep. Bank 229 (Q.B.)...........282
Pawlik v. Bank of Montreal (1997), 196 A.R. 61, [1997] A.J. No. 31 (C.A.) 211
Peoples Department Stores Inc. v. Wise, [2004] 3 S.C.R. 461, 244 D.L.R.
  (4th) 564, 2004 SCC 68..99
Peppiatt v. Nicol (2001), 148 O.A.C. 105, [2001] O.J. No. 2584 (C.A.) 223
Pharaon v. BCCI, [1998] 4 All E.R. 455 (Ch. D.) 310

Phillip Collins Ltd. v. Davis, [2000] 3 All E.R. 808 (Ch. D.) 287
Pike v. CIBC Mortgage Corp. (1995), 168 N.B.R. (2d) 321, 430 A.P.R. 321,
    [1995] N.B.J. No. 487 (Q.B.) 211
Plant Estate (Public Trustee of) v. Royal Bank of Canada (1996),
    189 A.R. 389, [1996] 10 W.W.R. 87, [1996] A.J. No. 691 (Q.B.) 192
Polar Heating Ltd. v. Banque Nationale de Paris (1991), 7 C.B.R. (3d) 45,
    114 A.R. 299, [1991] A.J. No. 248 (Q.B.) 311
Polly Peck International plc v. Nadir (No. 2), [1992] 4 All E.R. 769 (C.A.) 220
Port Swettenham Authority v. T.W. Wu & Co (M.) Sdn. Bbd., [1979]
    A.C. 580 (P.C.) 397
Potter, Re (1926), 29 O.W.N. 327, [1926] O.J. No. 282 (H.C.) 239
Power Estate, Re (2001), 205 Nfld. & P.E.I.R. 163, 615 A.P.R. 163,
    [2001] N.J. No. 280 (S.C.T.D.) 237, 239
Price Meats Ltd. v. Barclays Bank plc, [2000] 2 All E.R. (Comm.) 346 (Q.B.) 282
Price v. Neal (1762), 3 Burr. 1354, 97 E.R. 871 (K.B.) 285
Price Waterhouse v. BCCI Holdings (Luxembourg) SA, [1992] B.C.L.C. 583
    (Ch. D.) 310
Prideaux v. Criddle (1869), L.R. 4 Q.B. 455 291
Prince v. Oriental Bank Corp. (1878), 3 App. Cas. 325 (P.C.) 151, 288
Process Piping Specialties Inc. v. BCIC, [1986] R.J.Q. 2429 (S.C.) 261
Progress Doors Ltd. v. Toronto Dominion Bank (2000), 6 C.L.R.
    (3d) 148, [2000] O.J. No. 3791 (S.C.J.) 223, 249
Prosperity Ltd. v. Lloyd's Bank Ltd. (1923), 39 T.L.R. 372 (K.B.) 191
Provincial Drywall Supply Ltd. v. Toronto-Dominion Bank (1999),
    140 Man. R. (2d) 1, 47 C.L.R. (2d) 299, [1999] M.J. No. 321 (Q.B.) 223
Provincial Treasurer of Alberta v. Long (1973), 49 D.L.R. (3d) 695
    (Alta. S.C.) 149
Provincial Treasurer of Manitoba v. Bennett, [1937] S.C.R. 138,
    [1937] 2 D.L.R. 1 234
Pyke v. Hibernian Bank Ltd., [1950] I.R. 195 (H.C.) 272

Quebec Bank Deposits Case (sub nom. Attorney-General of Canada v.
    Attorney-General of Quebec) (1946), [1947] A.C. 33, [1947]
    1 D.L.R. 81, [1946] 3 W.W.R. 659 (P.C.) 15

Queen v. Cognos Inc., [1993] 1 S.C.R. 87, 99 D.L.R. (4th) 626,
    [1993] S.C.J. No. 3 209
Quirt v. Canada (1891), 19 S.C.R. 510 149

R. v. B.(K.S.) (1996), 126 W.A.C. 316, 77 B.C.A.C. 316, [1996]
    B.C.J. No. 1523 (C.A.) 355
R. v. Bank of Montreal (1906), 11 O.L.R. 595, [1906] O.J. No. 315
    (C.A.) 297, 299
R. v. Eddy (1994), 119 Nfld. & P.E.I.R. 91, [1994] N.J. No. 142 (T.D.) 307
R. v. Forsyth, [1995] O.J. No. 4173, 30 W.C.B. (2d) 76 (Gen. Div.);
    [1997] O.J. No. 2781, 35 W.C.B. (2d) 307 (Gen. Div.) 355

R. v. Kassim, [1991] 3 All E.R. 713 (H.L.) 347
R. v. Kohn (1979), 69 Cr. App. R. 395 (C.A.)...231
R. v. Lariviere, [1996] M.J. No. 312, 31 W.C.B. (2d) 279 (Prov. Ct.)...................355
R. v. Lillico (1994), 92 C.C.C. (3d) 90, [1994] O.J. No. 4521 (Gen. Div.) 307
R. v. Linhart (1989), 9 W.C.B. (2d) 246 (Ont. H.C.J.) 355
R. v. Lovitt (1911), [1912] A.C. 212 (P.C.).. 151, 152, 234
R. v. Mowat (1967), [1968] 1 O.R. 179, 68 D.L.R. (2d) 665, [1967]
   O.J. No. 1109 (H.C.J.)..307
R. v. Preddy, [1996] A.C. 815 (H.L.) 338
R.E. Jones Ltd. v. Waring & Gillow Ltd., [1926] A.C. 670 (H.L.) 295
Rae v. Yorkshire Bank plc, [1988] F.L.R. 1 (C.A.) 271
Ralli Brothers v. Compania Naviera Sota y Aznar, [1920] 2 K.B. 287 (C.A.) 309
Ramsay v. Royal Bank of Canada (1995), 32 Alta. L.R. (3d) 180,
   [1995] A.J. No. 647 (Prov. Ct.)..240
Rancan Fertilizer Systems Inc. v. Lavergne, [1999] 8 W.W.R. 323,
   134 Man. R. (2d) 73, [1999] M.J. No. 65 (C.A.) 189
Rapid Discount Corp. v. Thomas G. Hiscott Ltd. (1977), 15 O.R. (2d) 658,
   76 D.L.R. (3d) 450, [1977] O.J. No. 2208 (H.C.J.) 259
Rapid Transit Mix Ltd. v. Herle (2002), 313 A.R. 300, [2002]
   6 W.W.R. 732, 2002 ABQB 279 269
Raypath Resources Ltd. v. Toronto Dominion Bank (1996),
   184 A.R. 109, 135 D.L.R. (4th) 261, [1996] A.J. No. 398 (C.A.).....211, 231, 258
RCL Operators Ltd. v. National Bank of Canada (1995), 171 N.B.R.
   (2d) 41, 131 D.L.R. (4th) 86, [1995] N.B.J. No. 545 (C.A.) 270
Reade v. Royal Bank of Ireland Ltd., [1922] 2 I.R. 22 (C.A.) 276
Reference re Alberta Legislation, [1938] S.C.R. 100, [1938] 2 D.L.R. 81...........227
Reference re Same-Sex Marriage, [2004] 3 S.C.R. 698, 246 D.L.R.
   (4th) 193, 2004 SCC 79 9
Reid, Re (1921), 64 D.L.R. 598 (Ont. C.A.) 239
Rekstin v. Severo Sibirsko Gosudarstvennoe Akcionernoe Obschestvo
   Komseverputj, [1933] 1 K.B. 47 (C.A.) 191
Remfor Industries Ltd. v. Bank of Montreal (1978), 21 O.R. (2d) 225,
   90 D.L.R. (3d) 316, [1978] O.J. No. 3530 (C.A.), leave to appeal
   to S.C.C. refused (1978), 5 B.L.R. 22n (S.C.C.) 277
Repet Equipment Inc. v. Canadian Imperial Bank of Commerce (1999),
   43 O.R. (3d) 135, 46 B.L.R. (2d) 109, [1999] O.J. No. 844
   (Gen. Div.) 269, 270
Richards v. Bank of British North America (1901), 8 B.C.R. 209,
   [1901] B.C.J. No. 43 (C.A.)...252
Richardson (Inspector of Taxes) v. Worrall (1985), 58 T.C. 642......................382
Richer v. Voyer (1874), L.R. 5 P.C. 461 234
Riddell v. Bank of Upper Canada (1859), 18 U.C.Q.B. 139, 18 U.C.R. 139,
   [1859] O.J. No. 43 (C.A.) 252
Riedell v. Commercial Bank of Australia, [1931] V.L.R. 382 (S.C.) 262
RioCan Real Estate v. Realfund (1999), 95 O.T.C. 269, [1999] O.J.
   No. 1349 (S.C.J.) 104

Roberts & Co. v. Marsh, [1915] 1 K.B. 42 (C.A.) 257
Robertson v. Canadian Imperial Bank of Commerce, [1995]
    1 All E.R. 824 (P.C.) 306
Robinson v. National Bank of Scotland, [1916] S.C. (H.L.) 154 208
Robshaw v. Smith (1878), 38 L.T.N.S. 423 (C.P.D.) 215
Rodaro v. Royal Bank of Canada (2002), 59 O.R. (3d) 74, 22 B.L.R.
    (3d) 274, [2002] O.J. No. 1365 (C.A.) 311
Rogerson Lumber Co. v. Four Seasons Chalet Ltd. (1980), 29 O.R.
    (2d) 193, 113 D.L.R. (3d) 671, [1980] O.J. No. 3651 (C.A.) 27
Rolin v. Steward (1854), 14 C.B. 595, 139 E.R. 245 .... 259, 272
Ronald Elwyn Lister Ltd. v. Dunlop, [1982] 1 S.C.R. 726, 135 D.L.R.
    (3d) 1, [1982] S.C.J. No. 38 250
Rosenberg v. International Banking Corp. (1923), 14 Lloyd's L.R. 344 251
Rosenfeld v. First National City Bank, 319 N.Y.S.2d 35 (1971) 386
Ross v. Hill (1846), 2 C.B. 877, 135 E.R. 1190 397
Ross v. Royal Bank of Canada (1965), [1966] 1 O.R. 90, 52 D.L.R.
    (2d) 578, [1965] O.J. No. 1073 (H.C.J.) 248
Rouse v. Bradford Banking Co., [1894] A.C. 586 (H.L.) 258
Rouxel v. Royal Bank (1918), 11 Sask. L.R. 218 (K.B.) 249, 252
Rowlandson v. National Westminster Bank, [1978] 1 W.L.R. 798
    (Ch. D.) 178, 218
Royal Bank of Canada v. Aldridge, [2005] 3 W.W.R. 599,
    254 Sask. R. 195, 2004 SKCA 133 213
Royal Bank of Canada v. Aleman (1988), 86 A.R. 64, [1988]
    3 W.W.R. 461, [1988] A.J. No. 145 (Q.B.) 216
Royal Bank of Canada v. Bank of Montreal (1976), 67 D.L.R. (3d) 755,
    [1976] 4 W.W.R. 721 (Sask. C.A.) 245
Royal Bank of Canada v. Bender (1994), 159 A.R. 303, 22 Alta. L.R.
    (3d) 51, [1994] A.J. No. 589 (Q.B.) 246
Royal Bank of Canada v. Boyce; Royal Bank of Canada v. Wildman,
    [1966] 2 O.R. 607, 57 D.L.R. (2d) 683, [1966] O.J. No. 1025
    (Co. Ct.) 151, 278
Royal Bank of Canada v. Brattberg (1993), 143 A.R. 131, [1993]
    8 W.W.R. 139, [1993] A.J. No. 548 (Q.B.) 311
Royal Bank of Canada v. Budaveri (2003), 44 B.L.R. (3d) 147, [2003]
    O.J. No. 5793 (S.C.J.) 376
Royal Bank of Canada v. Devarenne (1998), 205 N.B.R. (2d) 250,
    [1998] N.B.J. No. 376 (Q.B.) 355
Royal Bank of Canada v. Disco Sound Distributors Ltd. (1986),
    73 A.R. 13, [1986] A.J. No. 41 (Master) 163
Royal Bank of Canada v. Domingues (1995), 21 B.L.R. (2d) 79,
    [1995] O.J. No. 34 (Gen. Div.) 213
Royal Bank of Canada v. Druhan (1997), 157 N.S.R. (2d) 29,
    462 A.P.R. 29, [1996] N.S.J. No. 563 (S.C.) 213
Royal Bank of Canada v. Executive Life Insurance Agency Ltd. (1996),
    138 Nfld. & P.E.I.R. 10, 431 A.P.R. 10, [1996] N.J. No. 18 (S.C.T.D.) 246

Royal Bank of Canada v. G.L.B. Holdings Ltd. (1998),
 171 Sask. R. 139, [1998] S.J. No. 665 (Q.B.) 244
Royal Bank of Canada v. Grobman (1977), 18 O.R. (2d) 636,
 83 D.L.R. (3d) 415, [1977] O.J. No. 2516 (H.C.J.) 154
Royal Bank of Canada v. Hein Real Estate Corp. (1977), 2 A.R. 575,
 [1977] 3 W.W.R. 298, [1977] A.J. No. 513 (C.A.) 152
Royal Bank of Canada v. Holoboff (1998), 221 A.R. 192, [1998]
 10 W.W.R. 755, [1998] A.J. No. 380 (Alta. Q.B.) 354
Royal Bank of Canada v. Huber (1971), 23 D.L.R. (3d) 209, [1972]
 2 W.W.R. 338 (Sask. C.A.) 286
Royal Bank of Canada v. Hussain (1998), 37 O.R. (3d) 85, 38 B.L.R.
 (2d) 92, [1997] O.J. No. 5233 (Gen. Div.) 213
Royal Bank of Canada v. LVG Auctions Ltd. (1984), 47 O.R. (2d) 800,
 12 D.L.R. (4th) 768, [1984] O.J. No. 3050 (C.A.) 283
Royal Bank of Canada v. Reynolds (1975), 14 N.S.R. (2d) 465,
 66 D.L.R. (3d) 88, [1975] N.S.J. No. 440 (C.A.) 400
Royal Bank of Canada v. Roycom Realty Ltd. (1996), 195 A.R. 310,
 48 Alta L.R. (3d) 145, [1996] A.J. No. 1228 (Q.B.) 223
Royal Bank of Canada v. Scarlato (1986), 57 O.R. (2d) 179,
 59 C.B.R. (N.S.) 211, [1986] O.J. No. 2971 (Dist. Ct.) 375
Royal Bank of Canada v. Shaw (1993), 104 Nfld. & P.E.I.R. 356,
 [1993] P.E.I.J. No. 26 (S.C.) 375
Royal Bank of Canada v. Slack (1958), [1958] O.R. 262, 11 D.L.R.
 (2d) 737, [1958] O.J. No. 591 (C.A.) 245, 246
Royal Bank of Canada v. Slusar, [1990] 2 W.W.R. 90, 46 B.L.R. 119,
 [1989] S.J. No. 614 (Q.B.) 277
Royal Bank of Canada v. Sparrow Electric Corp., [1997] 1 S.C.R. 411,
 143 D.L.R. (4th) 385, [1997] S.C.J. No. 25 164
Royal Bank of Canada v. Stangl, [1992] O.J. No. 378, 32 A.C.W.S.
 (3d) 17 (Gen. Div.) 343
Royal Bank of Canada v. The King, [1913] A.C. 283, 9 D.L.R. 337,
 3 W.W.R. 994 (P.C.) 15
Royal Bank of Canada v. Tompkins, [1976] W.W.D. 174 (B.C.S.C.) 242
Royal Bank of Canada v. Unick (1994), 154 A.R. 81, 19 Alta. L.R.
 (3d) 254, [1994] A.J. No. 362 (Q.B.) 375
Royal Bank of Canada v. Vincenzi, [1994] B.C.W.L.D. 1221,
 [1994] B.C.J. No. 772 (S.C.) 313
Royal Bank of Canada v. W. Got & Associates Electric Ltd., [1999]
 3 S.C.R. 408, 178 D.L.R. (4th) 385, [1999] S.C.J. No. 59 153
Royal Bank of Canada v. White (1992), 105 Sask. R. 201, [1992]
 S.J. No. 559 (C.A.), leave to appeal to S.C.C. refused, [1993]
 1 S.C.R. x, (1993) 150 N.R. 394n, 116 Sask. R. 45n 210
Royal Bank of Canada v. Woloszyn (1998), 170 N.S.R. (2d) 122,
 515 A.P.R. 122, [1998] N.S.J. No. 407 (S.C.) 211

Royal Bank of Canada v. Workmen's Compensation Board of Nova
  Scotia, [1936] S.C.R. 560, [1936] 4 D.L.R. 9 16
Royal Bank of Scotland plc v. Golden Trinity (The) (2001), 220 F.T.R. 1,
  [2001] F.C.J. No. 1230, 2001 FCT 427 306
Royal Bank of Scotland v. Etridge (No. 1), [1997] 3 All E.R. 628 (C.A.) 202
Royal Bank of Scotland v. Etridge (No. 2), [2001] 4 All E.R. 449 (H.L.) 202
Royal Bank of Scotland v. Tottenham, [1894] 2 Q.B. 715 (C.A.) 264, 291
Royal Bank v. Talbot, [1928] 3 D.L.R. 157, 23 Alta. L.R. 395 (S.C.A.D.) ... 395, 397
Royal Bank v. The King, [1931] 2 D.L.R. 685 (Man. K.B.) 285
Royal British Bank v. Turquand (1856), 54 El. and Bl. 248, 119 E.R. 886
  (Exch. Ct.) 89
Royal Brunei Airlines v. Tan, [1995] 2 A.C. 378 (P.C.) 218
Royal Products Ltd. v. Midland Bank Ltd., [1981] 2 Lloyd's Rep. 194
  (Q.B.D.) 339
Royal Trust Co. v. Molsons Bank (1912), 27 O.L.R. 441, [1912]
  O.J. No. 52 (H.C.J.) 180, 249
Rubin v. American Express Co., 315 N.Y.S.2d 89 (1970) 385
Runk v. Jackson, [1917] 1 W.W.R. 485 (Alta. Dist. Ct.) 242
Russell v. Scott (1936), 55 C.L.R. 440 (H.C.A.) 239
Russian Commercial & Industrial Bank, Re, [1955] 1 Ch. 148 192
Rutherford v. Royal Bank of Canada (1931), [1932] S.C.R. 131,
  [1932] 2 D.L.R. 332, 13 C.B.R. 372 301

Saderquist v. Ontario Bank (1899), 15 O.A.R. 609, [1889] O.J. No. 45 (C.A.) ... 234
Salter & Arnold Ltd. v. Dominion Bank, [1926] S.C.R. 621, [1926]
  3 D.L.R. 684, 7 C.B.R. 639 .... 245, 248
Samberg v. American Express Co., 99 N.W. 879 (Mich. 1909) 387
Saskatchewan Co-operative Credit Society Ltd. v. Wilson, [1990]
  2 F.C. 115, 65 D.L.R. (4th) 437, 47 B.L.R. 85 (T.D.), aff'd. (1991),
  77 D.L.R. (4th) 186, 131 N.R. 59, [1991] F.C.J. No. 37 (C.A.) 61
Saylor v. Madsen Estate (2005), 261 D.L.R. (4th) 597, 20 E.T.R.
  (3d) 171, [2005] O.J. No. 4662 (C.A.) 239
Scaravelli v. Bank of Montreal (2004), 69 O.R. (3d) 295, [2004]
  O.T.C. 36, [2004] O.J. No. 109 (S.C.J.) 213
Scarth v. Northland Bank (Liquidator of) (1996), 114 Man. R.
  (2d) 314, 43 C.B.R. (3d) 254, [1996] M.J. No. 576 (Q.B.) 144
Schimnowski v. Schimnowski, [1996] 6 W.W.R. 194, 110 Man. R.
  (2d) 146, [1996] M.J. No. 207 (C.A.) 255
Schreiber v. Canada, [1997] 2 F.C. 176, 144 D.L.R. (4th) 711,
  [1997] F.C.J. No. 277 (C.A.) 307
Schreiber v. Canada, [1998] 1 S.C.R. 841, 158 D.L.R. (4th) 577,
  [1998] S.C.J. No. 42 307
Scott v. Bank of New Brunswick (1892), 21 S.C.R. 30, [1892] S.C.J.
  No. 39 .... 234, 282
Scott v. Merchants Bank (1911), 17 O.W.R. 849, 2 O.W.N. 514, [1911]
  O.J. No. 704 (Div. Ct.) 266

Scottish Equitable plc v. Derby, [2001] 3 All E.R. 818 (C.A.) 287
Seaboard Life Insurance Co. v. Bank of Montreal (1999), 48 B.L.R.
 (2d) 77, [1999] B.C.J. No. 1598 (S.C.) 210
Searles v. AT&T Canada (1998), 200 N.B.R. (2d) 305, 512 A.P.R. 305,
 [1998] N.B.J. No. 179 (Q.B.) 258
Sednaoni, Zareff, Nakes & Co. v. Anglo-Austrian Bank (1909),
 2 L.D.A.B. 208 264
Selangor United Rubber Estates Ltd. v. Cradock (No. 3), [1968]
 2 All E.R. 1073 (Ch. D.) 217
Semac Industries Ltd. v. 1131426 Ontario Ltd. (c.o.b. Bancroft Lumber
 & Wood Flooring Products), [2001] O.T.C. 649, 16 B.L.R. (3d) 88,
 [2001] O.J. No. 3443 (S.C.J.) 276
Seymour v. Pickett, [1905] 1 K.B. 715 (C.A.) 245
Shapera v. Toronto-Dominion Bank (1970), 17 D.L.R. (3d) 122,
 [1971] 1 W.W.R. 442 (Man. Q.B.) 277, 285, 286
Shaw v. MacKenzie Estate (1994), 131 N.S.R. (2d) 118, 371 A.P.R. 118,
 [1994] N.S.J. No. 225 (S.C.) 239
Sheppard v. First International Bank of Sweetgrass, [1924] 1 D.L.R. 582,
 [1924] 1 W.W.R. 290 (Alta. S.C.A.D.) 180, 228
Shortill v. Grannen (1920), 47 N.B.R. 463 (S.C.) 239
Siebe Gorman & Co. v. Barclays Bank Ltd., [1979] 2 Lloyd's Rep. 142
 (Ch. D.) 246
Sierra Leone Communications Co. Ltd. v. Barclays Bank plc, [1998]
 2 All E.R. 821 (Ch. D.) 190
Simpson v. Dolan (1908), 16 O.L.R. 459, [1908] O.J. No. 140 (Div. Ct.) 255
Sinha v. Sinha (2002), 306 A.R. 250, [2002] A.J. No. 146,
 2002 ABQB 122 .... 191, 212
Skyring v. Greenwood and Cox (1825), 4 B. & C. 281, 107 E.R. 1064 297
Slingsby v. District Bank Ltd., [1932] 1 K.B. 544 (C.A.) 259
Slovchenko v. Toronto-Dominion Bank (1963), [1964] 1 O.R. 410,
 42 D.L.R. (2d) 484, [1963] O.J. No. 844 (H.C.J.) 246, 255, 262
Smith v. Commonwealth Trust Co. (1969), 10 D.L.R. (3d) 181,
 72 W.W.R. 201 (B.C.S.C.) 272
Smith v. Gautschi, [1917] 2 W.W.R. 225, 23 B.C.R. 455, [1916]
 B.C.J. No. 100 (C.A.) 244
Smith v. Gosnell (1918), 43 O.L.R. 123, [1918] O.J. No. 115 (H.C.) 239
Smith v. Rogers (1899), 30 O.R. 256, [1899] O.J. No. 141 (Div. Ct.) 122
Smith v. Trader's Bank (1906), 7 O.W.R. 791, [1906] O.J. No. 541 (Div. Ct.) 268
Sodd Corporation Inc. v. Tessis (1977), 17 O.R. (2d) 158, 79 D.L.R. (3d) 632,
 [1977] O.J. No. 2371 (C.A.) 209
Solomon v. Royal Bank of Canada, [1983] 2 W.W.R. 543, 20 Man. R.
 (2d) 371, [1982] M.J. No. 422 (Q.B.) 277
Sommers v. Sturdy (1957), 10 D.L.R. (2d) 269, 22 W.W.R. 49, 119 C.C.C. 264
 (B.C.C.A.), leave to appeal to S.C.C. refused, [1957] S.C.R. x 16, 306, 308
Southby v. Southby (1917), 38 D.L.R. 700 (Ont. S.C.A.D.) 237
Southland Savings Bank v. Anderson, [1974] 1 N.Z.L.R. 118 266

Space Investments Ltd. v. CIBC Trust Co. (Bahamas) Ltd., [1986]
3 All E.R. 75 (P.C.) 179
Sparkle Wash v. Saskatoon Credit Union Ltd., [1979] 2 W.W.R. 320
(Sask. Dist. Ct.) 276
Sproule v. Murray (1919), 45 O.L.R. 326, [1919] O.J. No. 145 (S.C.A.D.) 239
Stadder v. Canadian Bank of Commerce (1929), 64 O.L.R. 69, [1929]
3 D.L.R. 651, [1929] O.J. No. 20 (S.C.A.D.) 237
Standard Bank of Canada v. Finucane (1921), 62 S.C.R. 110,
59 D.L.R. 465, [1921] 3 W.W.R. 314 251
Standard Investments Ltd. v. Canadian Imperial Bank of Commerce
(1984), 45 O.R. (2d) 16, 5 D.L.R. (4th) 452, [1983] O.J. No. 3288
(H.C.J.), rev'd (1986), 52 O.R. (2d) 473, 22 D.L.R. (4th) 410, [1985]
O.J. No. 2668 (C.A.), leave to appeal to S.C.C. refused, [1986]
1 S.C.R. vi, 53 O.R. (2d) 663n, 65 N.R. 78n 196
Stanley Works of Canada Ltd. v. Banque Canadienne Nationale (1981),
20 B.L.R. 282, [1982] R.L. 433 (Que. C.A.) 261, 291
Stavert v. Lovitt (1908), 42 N.S.R. 449 (C.A.) 121
Stefaniuk v. Toronto Dominion Bank (1979), 100 D.L.R. (3d) 190, [1979]
3 W.W.R. 382, [1979] M.J. No. 285 (Q.B.) 239
Steinbach Credit Union Ltd. v. Seitz (1988), 50 D.L.R. (4th) 436, [1988]
3 W.W.R. 334, [1988] M.J. No. 80 (C.A.) 255
Sterling Bank v. McVety, [1923] 3 D.L.R. 246 (Sask. C.A.) 255
Sterling Bank v. Zuber (1914), 32 O.L.R. 123, [1914] O.J. No. 119
(S.C.A.D.) 251, 252
Stevens v. Merchants Bank of Canada (1920), 30 Man. R. 46 (C.A.) 266, 267
Stevenson v. Hart (1828), 4 Bing. 476, 130 E.R. 851 397
Stewart Estate, Re (1997), 203 A.R. 125, 31 B.L.R. (2d) 124, [1997]
A.J. No. 391 (Surr. Ct.) 249
Stewart v. Royal Bank of Canada, [1930] S.C.R. 544, [1930] 4 D.L.R. 694 301
Stobart v. Axford (1893), 9 Man. R. 18 (Q.B.) 244
Stoney Stanton Supplies (Coventry) Ltd. v. Midland Bank Ltd., [1966]
2 Lloyds Rep. 373 (C.A.) 178
Streamside Engineering v. Canadian Imperial Bank of Commerce (1990), 85
Nfld. & P.E.I.R. 220, 226 A.P.R. 220, [1990] N.J. No. 241 (Nfld. T.D.) 210
Sugar v. Peat Marwick Ltd. (1989), 66 O.R. (2d) 766, 55 D.L.R.
(4th) 230, [1988] O.J. No. 1959 (H.C.J.) 208, 211
Sullivan v. Knauth, 115 N.E. 460 (1915) 385, 387
Summers v. City Bank (1874), L.R. 9 C.P. 580 272
Sun Life Assurance Co. of Canada v. Canada (Human Rights Commission),
[1991] 3 S.C.R. 689, 131 N.R. 387, [1991] S.C.J. No. 102 16
Sunderland v. Barclays Bank Ltd. (1938), 5 L.D.A.B. 163 (C.A.) 311
Surrey Credit Union Ltd. v. Northland Bank (1989), 62 Man. R. (2d) 285,
77 C.B.R. (N.S.) 272, [1989] M.J. No. 648 (C.A.), leave to appeal to
S.C.C.refused (1990), 113 N.R. 80n, 69 Man. R. (2d) 133n, 39 C.P.C.
(2d) 63n (S.C.C.) 145

Sutcliffe & Sons Ltd., Ex parte Royal Bank of Canada, Re, [1933]
O.R. 120, [1933] 1 D.L.R. 562, [1933] O.J. No. 311 (C.A.) 191, 248, 249
Sutters v. Briggs, [1922] 1 A.C. 1 (H.L.) 251
Swaan, Re (1980), 37 C.B.R. (N.S.) 1, [1980] B.C.J. No. 1870 (S.C.) 16
Szek v. Lloyds Bank Ltd. (1908), 2 L.D.A.B. 159 272

T.C. Marines Ltd., Re, [1973] 2 O.R. 537, 34 D.L.R. (3d) 489, [1973]
O.J. No. 1935 (H.C.J.) 248
T.D. Trapp & Co. v. Prescott (1912), 50 S.C.R. 263, 18 D.L.R. 794,
[1912] S.C.J. No. 51 265
Tai Hing Cotton Mill Ltd. v. Liu Chong Hing Bank Ltd. (1985),
[1986] A.C. 80, [1985] 2 All E.R. 947 (P.C.) 187, 281, 299
Tanner Estate v. Toronto Dominion Bank (2002), 212 Nfld & P.E.I.R. 211,
637 A.P.R. 211, 2002 PESCTD 24 224
Tassell v. Cooper (1850), 9 C.B. 509, 137 E.R. 990 (C.P.) 218, 303
Taylor Estate v. Taylor (1995), 9 E.T.R. (2d) 15, [1995] B.C.J. No. 1717
(S.C.) 237, 239
TDF Investments Ltd. v. Canadian Bank of Commerce, [1961] O.R. 385,
27 D.L.R. (2d) 609, [1961] O.J. No. 547 (C.A.) 395
Tennant v. Union Bank of Canada (1893), [1894] A.C. 31,
10 C.R.A.C. 387, 5 Cart. 244 (P.C.) 10, 19, 149
Thermo King Corp. v. Provincial Bank of Canada (1981), 34 O.R.
(2d) 369, 130 D.L.R. (3d) 256, [1981] O.J. No. 3136 (C.A.),
leave to appeal to S.C.C. refused (1982), 130 D.L.R. (3d) 256n,
42 N.R. 352 (S.C.C.) 191, 230, 258, 273
Thomas v. Barnhardt (1998), 114 O.A.C. 197, [1998] O.J. No. 3657 (C.A.) 223
Thomas v. Howell (1874), L.R. 18 Eq. 198 191
Thomson v. Clydesdale Bank, [1893] A.C. 282 (H.L.) 217
Thomson v. Stikeman (1913), 17 D.L.R. 205 (Ont. C.A.) 245
Thorne Riddell Inc. v. Rural Municipality of Rudy No 283 (1985),
46 Sask. R. 319, 56 C.B.R. (N.S.) 209, [1985] S.J. No. 71 (C.A.) 264
Tidd, Re, [1893] 3 Ch. 154 .... 234, 296
Titan West Warehouse Club Inc. v. National Bank, [1998] 2 W.W.R. 212,
35 B.L.R. (2d) 322, [1997] S.J. No. 584 (C.A.) 294
Todd v. Union Bank of Canada (1887), 4 Man. R. 204 (C.A.) 244, 260
Toor v. Bank of Montreal (1991), 3 B.L.R. (2d) 1, [1991]
B.C.J. No. 2711 (S.C.) 288
Toronto Dominion Bank v. Forsythe (2000), 47 O.R. (3d) 321,
183 D.L.R. (4th) 616, [2000] O.J. No. 686 (C.A.) 213
Toronto Dominion Bank v. Sheppard (1998), [1999] 7 W.W.R. 675,
173 Sask. R. 8, [1998] S.J. No. 577 (Q.B.) 270
Toronto-Dominion Bank v. Anker (1978), 22 O.R. (2d) 369, 93 D.L.R.
(3d) 510, [1978] O.J. No. 3652 (Co. Ct.) 285
Toronto-Dominion Bank v. Bank of Montreal (1995), 22 O.R. (3d) 362,
18 B.L.R. (2d) 248, [1995] O.J. No. 176 (Gen. Div.) 268–69

Toronto-Dominion Bank v. Charles, [1998] O.J. No. 3710, 82 A.C.W.S.
  (3d) 521 (Gen. Div.) 355
Toronto-Dominion Bank v. Dauphin Plains Credit Union Ltd. (1992),
  98 D.L.R. (4th) 736, 83 Man. R. (2d) 132, [1992] M.J. No. 574 (C.A.) 293
Toronto-Dominion Bank v. De Graauw (1999), 122 O.A.C. 193,
  [1999] O.J. No. 1522 (C.A.) 224
Toronto-Dominion Bank v. Paconiel Investments Inc. (1992), 6 O.R.
  (3d) 547, [1992] O.J. No. 23 (C.A.) 214
Toronto-Dominion Bank v. Pella/Hunt Corp. (1992), 10 O.R. (3d) 634,
  7 B.L.R. (2d) 99, [1992] O.J. No. 1776 (Gen. Div.) 283
Toronto-Dominion Bank v. Pritchard (1997), 154 D.L.R. (4th) 141,
  104 O.A.C. 373, [1997] O.J. No. 4622 (Div. Ct.) 153
Toronto-Dominion Bank v. Valentine (2002), 61 O.R. (3d) 161,
  218 D.L.R. (4th) 225, [2002] O.J. No. 3487 (C.A.) 225
Totem Building Supplies Ltd. v. Toronto-Dominion Bank (1999),
  248 A.R. 241, [1999] A.J. No. 456, 1999 ABQB 305 215
Tournier v. National Provincial & Union Bank of England, [1924]
  1 K.B. 461 (C.A.) 186, 303
Transamerica Commercial Finance Corp., Canada v. Imperial T.V. &
  Stereo Ltd. (Receivership) (1993), 146 A.R. 31, [1994] 1 W.W.R. 506,
  [1993] A.J. No. 740 (Q.B.) 13
Transamerica Occidental Life Insurance Co. v. Toronto-Dominion Bank (1999),
  44 O.R. (3d) 97, 173 D.L.R. (4th) 468, [1999] O.J. No. 1195 (C.A.) 223
TSB Bank of Scotland plc v. Welwyn Hatfield District Council, [1993]
  2 Bank. L.R. 267 (Ch. D.) 342
Turner v. Canadian Pacific Ltd. (1979), 27 O.R. (2d) 549, 107 D.L.R.
  (3d) 142, [1979] O.J. No. 4517 (H.C.J.) 112
Turner v. Royal Bank of Scotland plc, [1999] 2 All E.R. (Comm.) 664
  (C.A.) 214, 313
Twibell v. London Suburban Bank, [1869] W.N. 127 (C.P.) 238
Twinsectra Ltd. v. Yardley, [2002] 2 A.C. 164 (H.L.) 219
Tymkow v. Rusnak (1992), 6 Alta. L.R. (3d) 210, [1992] A.J. No. 1055 (Q.B.) 240

Ubacol Investments Ltd. v. Royal Bank of Canada (1995), 171 A.R. 122,
  30 Alta L.R. (3d) 327, [1995] A.J. No. 518 (Q.B.) 258
Union Bank of Canada v. Wood, [1920] 3 W.W.R. 173, [1920] A.J. No. 40,
  (S.C.T.D.) 301
Union Bank v. Farmer, [1917] 1 W.W.R. 1361, [1917] A.J. No. 7 (S.C.T.D.) 397
Union Bank v. Tattersall (1920), 52 D.L.R. 409, [1920] 2 W.W.R. 497,
  15 Alta. L.R. 350, (S.C.A.D.) 264, 265, 278
United City Merchants Investments Ltd. v. Royal Bank of Canada,
  [1983] 1 A.C. 168 (H.L.) 393
United Dominions Trust Ltd. v. Kirkwood, [1966] 1 All E.R. 968 (C.A.) 6, 20
United Overseas Bank v. Jiwani, [1977] 1 All E.R. 733 (Ch. D.) 287, 298
United Service Co., Re (1871), L.R. 6 Ch. 212 251
United States of America v. Dollfus Mieg et Cie SA, [1952] A.C. 582 (H.L.) 397

Universal Guarantee Pty. Ltd. v. National Bank of Australia Ltd.,
  [1965] 2 All E.R. 98 (P.C.) 297
Usher v. Barnes (1921), 48 N.B.R. 358 (S.C.) 239

V.K. Mason Construction Ltd. v. Bank of Nova Scotia, [1985] 1 S.C.R. 271,
  16 D.L.R. (4th) 598, [1985] S.C.J. No. 12 209
Vanwart v. Diocesan Synod of Fredericton (1912), 42 N.B.R. 1 (S.C.) 237
Verdun v. Toronto-Dominion Bank, [1996] 3 S.C.R. 550, 139 D.L.R.
  (4th) 415, [1996] S.C.J. No. 50 106
Vicply v. Royal Bank of Canada (1996), 48 C.B.R. (3d) 129, [1996]
  A.Q. no 1538 (Que. C.A.) 153
Villiers v. Bank of Montreal, [1933] O.W.N. 649, [1933] O.J. No. 139
  (H.C.J.) 263
Vishipco Line v. Chase Manhattan Bank, 66 F.2d 854 (2d Circ. 1981) 190
Vita Health Co. (1985) Ltd. v. Toronto-Dominion Bank (1994), 118 D.L.R.
  (4th) 289, 95 Man.R. (2d) 255, [1994] M.J. No. 470 (C.A.), leave to
  appeal to S.C.C. refused (1995), 122 D.L.R. (4th) vii, [1994]
  S.C.C.A. No. 457 215
Vuckovich v. Royal Bank of Canada (1998), 158 D.L.R. (4th) 37,
  37 R.F.L. (4th) 153, [1998] O.J. No. 1483 (C.A.) 241

W.J. Lafave & Sons Ltd. v. Banque Canadienne Nationale, [1977] C.S. 802 261
W.P. Greenhalgh & Sons v. Union Bank of Manchester Ltd.,
  [1924] 2 K.B. 153 249
Walker v. Tanna (1988), 65 O.R. (2d) 208, 30 O.A.C. 180, [1988]
  O.J. No. 904 (Div. Ct.) 270
Wallinder v. Imperial Bank of Canada (1925), 36 B.C.R. 226, [1925]
  B.C.J. No. 129 (C.A.) 248, 250
Walsh Advertising Co. v. R., [1962] Ex. C.R. 115 39
Walton v. Mascall (1844), 13 M. & W. 72, 47 E.R 1144 (Ch.) 179
Wandich v. Viele, [2002] O.T.C. 2, 24 R.F.L. (5th) 427, [2002]
  O.J. No. 5 (S.C.J.) 237, 239
Waters v. Donnelly (1884), 9 O.R. 391, [1884] O.J. No. 294 (H.C.J.) 206
Weitzman v. Hendin (1989), 69 O.R. (2d) 678, 61 D.L.R. (4th) 525,
  [1989] O.J. No. 1419 (C.A.) 213
Welch v. Bank of England, [1955] Ch. 508 (C.A.) 238, 240
Wells Fargo Asia Ltd. v. Citibank, N.A., 936 F.2d 723 (2d Cir. 1991) 190
West Bay Sales Ltd., Re (1979), 26 O.R. (2d) 562, 103 D.L.R. (3d) 342,
  [1979] O.J. No. 4426 (S.C.) 248
West v. Commercial Bank of Australia Ltd. (1935), 55 C.L.R. 315 (H.C.A.) 282
Westboro Flooring and Décor Inc. v. Bank of Nova Scotia (2004),
  71 O.R. (3d) 723, 241 D.L.R. (4th) 257, [2004] O.J. No. 2464 (C.A.) 294
Westcoast Commodities Inc. v. Chen (1987), 55 O.R. (2d) 264,
  28 D.L.R. (4th) 635, [1986] O.J. No. 490 (H.C.J.) 242
Westminster Bank Ltd. v. Hilton (1926), 136 L.T. 315 (H.L.) 277
Westminster Bank Ltd. v. Zang, [1966] A.C. 182 (H.L.) 259, 291

Whitaker v. Bank of England (1835), 1 Cr. M. & R. 744, 149 E.R.
1280 (K.B.) 258
White v. Bank of Toronto, [1953] O.R. 479, [1953] 3 D.L.R. 118,
[1953] O.J. No. 667 (C.A.) 22
White v. Jones, [1995] 2 A.C. 207, [1995] 2 W.L.R. 187, [1995]
1 All E.R. 691 (H.L.) 197, 341
White v. Royal Bank of Canada (1923), 53 O.L.R. 543, [1923]
O.J. No. 91 (S.C.A.D.) 262
Whitford v. Whitford Estate, [1942] S.C.R. 166, [1942] 1 D.L.R. 721 237
Wildfong v. Royal Bank of Canada (1989), 78 Sask. R. 250, [1989]
S.J. No. 354 (Q.B.) 210
Will v. Bank of Montreal, [1931] 3 D.L.R. 526 (Alta. S.C.) 259
Willans v. Ayers (1877), 3 App. Cas. 133 (P.C.) 391
William Ciurluini Ltd. v. Royal Bank of Canada, [1972] 2 O.R. 748,
26 D.L.R. (3d) 552, [1972] O.J. No. 1788 (H.C.J.) 255
Williams & Glyn's Bank Ltd. v. Barnes, [1981] Comm. L.R. 205 (Ch. D.) 231
Williams v. Curzon Syndicate Ltd. (1919), 35 T.L.R. 475 (C.A.) 397
Williams v. Natural Life Health Foods Ltd., [1998] 2 All E.R. 577 (H.L.) 341
Wilson v. United Counties Bank Ltd., [1920] A.C. 102 (H.L.) 271
Wood v. Clydesdale Bank, [1914] S.C. 397 (H.L.) 234, 296
Woodland v. Fear (1857), 7 El. & Bl. 519, 119 E.R. 1339 (Ex. Ch.) 151
Woods v. Martins Bank (1958), [1959] 1 Q.B. 55, [1958] 3 All E.R. 166,
[1958] 1 W.L.R. 1018 (Leeds Assizes) 20, 177, 193, 194
Worthen Bank & Trust Co. v. National Bank Americard Inc., 345
F. Supp. 1309 (E.D. Ark. 1972), rev'd 485 F.2d 119 (8th Circ. 1973) 372
Wylde v. Radford (1863), 33 L.J. Ch. 51 .... 251, 252

Yakiv v. March Films B.C. Ltd. (1980), 109 D.L.R. (3d) 218,
19 B.C.L.R. 211, [1980] B.C.J. No. 1443 (S.C.) 153
Yeoman Credit Ltd. v. Gregory, [1963] 1 All E.R. 245 (Q.B.) 290
Young v. Grote (1827), 4 Bing. 253, 130 E.R. 764 .... 259, 280
Yourell v. Hibernian Bank Ltd., [1918] A.C. 372 (H.L.) 232

INDEX

2006 Financial Institutions Legislation Review: Proposals for an Effective and Efficient Finance Services Framework (White Paper), 31
2007 amendments to the Bank Act (Bill C-37, S.C. 2007, c. 6, Royal Assent 29 March 2007), 31–32, 84, 121, 129–31, 160, 319
3PPS. See Third party payment systems (3PPS)

ABMs (Automated Banking Machines)
  ABM cards, 349–50
  ABM receipts, 233, 324, 353
  ABM withdrawals, 355, 362
  bank ABMs, 345
  bill payments, 365
  Interac ABMs, 325, 349, 351
  PINs (Personal Identification Numbers)
    cardholder agreements, 353, 375–77
    customer responsibility, 185, 325, 353, 355, 375–77
    Debit Card Code, 352
    debit card transactions, 324–25, 351–52
    electronic payments, 346
    retail transactions, 324–25, 351–52
    unauthorized use, 354–55
Accounts. See Bank accounts
ACSS. See Automated Clearing and Settlement System (ACSS)
Activities of banks. See Banking business
ADR (Alternative Dispute Resolution). See Dispute resolution
AFT (Automated Fund Transfers), 324
Alternative dispute resolution (ADR). See Dispute resolution
American Express, 347, 371, 373, 380, 383–84, 387
Association des banquiers canadiens. See Canadian Bankers Association
Auditors of banks
  appointment, 112
  audit committee of bank, 77, 95–97, 114
  duties, 113
  history, 111–12
  "independence" defined, 112
  qualifications, 112
  removal or resignation, 112–13
  reports of auditors
    errors or misstatements, 114
    revisions, 114
    to CEO and CFO re unsound transactions, 114

to shareholders, 113
to Superintendent, 113
rights of auditors
  access to records, 113
  attendance at shareholders' meetings, 113
Superintendent, involvement by, 111–12
Automated banking machines. *See* ABMs (Automated Banking Machines)
Automated Clearing and Settlement System (ACSS)
  ABMs (Automated Banking Machines), 324–25
  ACSS Rules Manual, 290, 320, 322, 324–26, 329, 350, 356
  automated fund transfers (AFT)
    AFT credit transactions, 324
    AFT debit transactions, 324
    automatic deposits, 324
    preauthorized bill payments, 324
  Bank of Canada, role of, 44, 318, 321
  bill payments, 324–26
  Canadian Code of Practice for Consumer Debit Card Services, 325
  CCIN (Corporate Creditor Identification Number), 326
  cheque clearing, 322–23
  "cheque holds" policy, 324
  cheque imaging, 328
  cheque transaction and electronic clearing, 328
  "cheque truncation" defined, 328
  Clearing By-Law (1985), 320–21, 356
  "clearing" defined, 320
  computer banking, 324
  data entry from paper items, 323
  debit card transactions, 324–25
  default of clearer, procedures for, 326–27
  direct clearers, 320, 333
  dishonoured cheques, 151, 258, 261, 263–67, 271–73, 278, 288–91, 323, 334
  DTN (Data Transmission Network), 324–26
  EDI (Electronic Data Interchange), 324–25
  electronic payment items, 324
  indirect clearers, 320, 333
  infrastucture of system, 315–44
  Interac network, 29, 54, 158, 325, 349–53, 368
  international funds transfers, 334–37
  membership of ACSS, 320, 333
  online banking, 324–26
  paper items, requirements for, 322
  "payment items" defined, 321
  PINs (Personal Identification Numbers), 325
  POS (Point-Of-Sale) payments, 324–25
  preauthorized debits, 324
  regional settlement points, 321
  risks and risk management, 324, 326
  rules. *See* Automated Clearing and Settlement System (ACSS); *ACSS Rules Manual*
  "settlement" defined, 320
  TECP (truncation and electronic cheque presentment), 327–28
  telephone banking, 324–26
Automated fund transfers (AFT), 324

Bank account statements. *See also* Bank accounts; Deposit receipts and passbooks
  account verification clauses, 298–303
  at common law, 233, 296, 298–303
  cheques returned with statements, 327–28
    cheque imaging, 327–29
    statutory duty to retain cheques, 328–29
  duties of bank, 296–303
  duties of customer
    account verification clauses, 185, 298–303
    to check statements, 299–303
    to prevent fraud by employees, 299–303
  errors, 185
  forms of statements, 296
  generally, 233–35, 296–303
  liability of bank
    account verification clauses, 298–303
    for careless, fraudulent clients, 294–95, 299–303
  online account statements, 233
  passbooks, status of, 233, 296–97

right to rectify errors
    account verification clauses, 298–303
    bank's right, 297–98
    customer's right, 298–97
    limitation of actions, 298
    notice requirements, 303
status as legal documents, 233, 296–97
use as proof of gift, 235
use as security document, 234–35, 296
whether negotiable instruments, 233–34, 296

Bank accounts
    account agreement. See Contract between bank and customer
    account reconciliation, 302
    account verification clauses, 298–303
    appropriation of payments
        exceptions to presumption, 244–45
        presumption of "first in, first out," 244–45
        rights of appropriation, 244–45
    bank as constructive trustee, 217–23, 238, 243–44, 273, 288, 292, 295
    bankers' liens, 251
        at common law, 251
        banker's lien vs. account set-off, 248
        classes of securities subject to lien, 251
        exempt securities, 252
        right to sell security, 251
    certified cheques, 265–70
    confidentiality. See Confidentiality of customer information
    contract. See Contract between bank and customer
    countermand of cheques by paying bank, 273, 275–78
    deposit receipts and passbooks, 233–25
    dishonoured cheques, 151, 258, 261, 263–67, 271–73, 278, 288–91, 323, 334
    dormant accounts, 185
    duty of paying bank to pay, 273
    foreign currency, 228
    garnishment of deposits
        direction to specific branch, 244
        joint accounts, 242

trust accounts, 244
inactive accounts, 185
insufficient funds. See Bank accounts, dishonoured cheques
interest. See Interest
joint accounts, 185, 235
    bank duty to third parties, 242
    bank liabilities, 238, 241
    bankrupt or incompetent account holders, 241
    garnishment, 242, 244
    overdraft liabilities, 240–42
    ownership issues, 241–42
    rights of account holders, 237–38
    set-off of funds, 241–42
    signatures, 238
    survivorship rights, 185, 237–40
    tax consequences, 238
legal nature of bank deposit, 179, 227–30
liabilities, 185
limitation of actions, 232
lines of credit, 181
low-income customer accounts, 177, 181, 236
minimum balances, 177, 181
operation of accounts, 253–314
    bank's duty to customers, 253, 278
    bank's duty to third parties, 255
    bank's standard of care, 255
    cheques as negotiable instruments, 256
    customer's instructions, 254–57
    historically, 253–57
    paper vs. electronic, 254
    payment instructions, 256
    pre-authorized payments, 256, 264, 324
overdrafts, 181, 185, 191, 257–58
    interest, 231–32
    overdraft privileges, 230–31
    overdrafts as "loans," 181, 230
    repayments, 231
passbooks, 185, 233–35, 296
payment by paying bank, 257
postdated cheques, 264
privacy. See Confidentiality of customer information
recovery of money paid by mistake, 284

set-off and account combination, 247
  account combination vs. banker's
    lien, 248
  account set-off vs. banker's lien,
    248
  customer agreement, 247
  duty to set-off or combine ac-
    counts, 250
  notice requirements, 250
  right to set-off or combine ac-
    counts, 247–50
  set-off not permitted, 249
statements. *See* Bank account statements
termination of bank duty to pay, 273
termination of account
  bankruptcy of customer, 192
  death of customer, 192
  insolvency of bank, 192
  mental incapacity of customer, 192
  notice by customer, 191
  notice by bank, 191
  "reasonable notice," 191
  suspension in time of war, 193
  transfer of funds, 192
  unilateral termination by bank,
    191
trust accounts, 185, 242
  bank as constructive trustee, 217–23,
    238, 243–44, 273, 288, 292, 295
  bank not liable for trustee actions,
    243
  bank not "trustee," 243
  types of accounts, 235–36
  U.S. dollar accounts, 329–30
unclaimed account balances, 183–84,
  232–33
wrongful dishonour of cheques by
  paying bank, 271
wrongful payment by a paying bank,
  279
Bank Act (1871), 9
Bank Act (1923), 25
Bank Act (1980), 9, 27–28
  general provisions, 28
  White Paper on the Revision of
    Canadian Banking Legislation
    (1975), 27
Bank Act (1991)
  1997 amendments, 29

1998 MacKay Task Force, 29–30, 75,
  84, 129, 132–33, 136, 404
2001 amendments, 29–31, 129–30
2006 White Paper, 31
2007 amendments (Bill C-37, S.C.
  2007, c. 6, Royal Assent 29 March
  2007), 31–32, 84, 121, 129–31,
  160, 319
application to "chartered" banks, 25
consumer protection, 70, 73
dispute resolution mechanisms, 74–75
general provisions, 28–29
incorporation of banks, 84–87
interpretation, 26–27
reform of the *Bank Act*, 27–32
Bank and customer relationship. *See
  also* Contract between bank and
  customer; Customers; Fiduciary
  and tortious relationships
characterization of, 178
generally, 175–225
legal nature of, 179
  contract vs. fiduciary, 179
  debtor-creditor, 179
Bank branches. *See* Bank incorporation
  and powers, branch operations
Bank Circulation Redemption Fund, 52
Bank deposits. *See also* Deposit insurance; Deposit receipts and passbooks; Deposit taking
Canada Deposit Insurance Corporation (CDIC), 58–69, 171
currency, choice of, 228
deposit as "loan," 152, 227
"deposit" defined, 61–62, 227
deposit insurance. *See* Deposit insurance
deposit receipts. *See* Deposit receipts
  and passbooks
foreign currency, 228
garnishment of deposits
  direction to specific branch, 244
  joint accounts, 242
  trust accounts, 244
interest on deposits, 228–30
  "criminal rate" defined, 229
  disclosure requirements, 230
  "interest" defined, 229
  provincial legislation, 229–30
legal nature of deposit, 227–30

passbooks. *See* Deposit receipts and passbooks
priorities in bank winding-up, 123
provincial jurisdiction over, 15
receipts for deposits. *See* Deposit receipts and passbooks
repayments, 227
Bank for International Settlements (BIS), 34–36, 360
Bank holding companies. *See also* Ownership of banks; Permitted investments by banks
  approvals by Minister and Superintendent, 134–35
  business and powers, 133
  corporate structure, 133
  creation of holding company regime, 30, 34, 130, 132–35
  directors, duties of, 134
  history, 132–33
  insurance companies, 133, 166
  MacKay Task Force (1998), 132–33
  ownership requirements, 133
  permitted activities, 133–35
  prohibited activities, 133–35
  standards for investments, 134
  status as non-operating entities, 133
  stock brokerages, 133, 166
  trust and loan companies, 33, 133, 166
Bank incorporation and powers. *See also* Bank holding companies; Ownership of banks; Permitted investments by banks
  activities. *See* Banking business
  amalgamations, 127
  amendments to charter, 127
  annual inspections by Superintendent, 26, 50
  annual reports to Superintendent, 49
  application to Superintendent, 84–87
  auditors. *See* Auditors of banks
  authorized foreign banks. *See* Foreign banks
  Bank Act, 84–87
  Bank Act as bank "charter," 25, 86, 137
  "bank" defined, 7, 10–14
  bank records. *See* Bank records
  board of directors. *See* Board of directors

borrowing money. *See* Trust indentures
branch operations
  "branch" defined, 150–51
  branch closures, 31, 73, 182–83
  legal status, 151
  when deemed separate entities, 151–52
business. *See* Banking business
by-laws. *See* By-laws of banks
capital structure. *See* Capital structure of banks
changes to name, head office, 127
charter, 25, 86, 127
confidentiality. *See* Confidentiality of bank information
conversion from "bank," 86, 127
conversion to "bank," 85, 127
corporate governance. *See* Auditors of banks; Bank records; Board of directors; Directors; Insider trading of bank securities; Liquidation and dissolution of bank; Officers of the bank; Shareholders;
debt financing. *See* Trust indentures
directors. *See* Board of directors; Directors
disclosure of executive compensation, 50
dissolution. *See* Liquidation and dissolution of banks
equity financing. *See* Shares and securities of a bank
examinations by Superintendent, 26, 50
executive compensation, disclosure of, 50
financial statements, 126–27
  approval of, 127
  reports to Superintendent, 127
  shareholder access, 127
financing. *See* Capital structure of banks
foreign banks. *See* Foreign banks
head office, 109, 127
history, 5, 84
holding companies. *See* Bank holding companies
insider trading. *See* Insider trading of bank securities
insolvency. *See* Liquidation and dissolution of bank

investments. *See* Permitted investments by banks
letters patent, 84–87, 90, 127–28, 140, 142
liquidation. *See* Liquidation and dissolution of bank
mergers, 29–30
name, 86–87, 127
officers. See Officers of the bank
ownership. *See* Bank holding companies; Ownership of banks
ownership by banks
    cooperative credit societies, 134, 166
    insurance companies, 133, 166
    non-financial institutions, 29
    stock brokerages, 133, 166
    trust and loan companies, 33, 133, 166
prospectus requirements, 124
provincial jurisdiction, 15
public accountability statements, 184
records. *See* Bank records
register of bank securities, 110, 121
register of banks, 49
reorganizations, 166
sale of bank assets, 128
shareholders. *See* Shareholders
solvency, 49, 50, 121
starting business, 90–91
status and powers
    constructive notice doctrine, 88–89
    indoor management rule, 89–90
    natural person powers, 87–88, 90
    restrictions on powers, 88
    ultra vires doctrine, 87–88
subsidiaries, 28, 34, 133, 156, 165–67, 170
Superintendent. *See* Superintendent of Financial Institutions
transfer of business, 127
"universal banking," 28–29, 31, 34, 84
winding-up. *See* Liquidation and dissolution of bank
Bank money order. *See* Money orders
Bank of Canada
    bank records, 110
    clearing and settlement, role in, 43–44, 318, 321
    history, 2, 5, 38–39
    lender of last resort, 81
    limitation of actions, 232–33
    monetary policy, 42–43, 81
    prohibited activities, 42
    structure and powers, 39–42, 318
    systemic risks, control of, 43–44, 56, 81, 318, 330–31
    unclaimed account balances, 41, 183–84, 232–33
Bank of Canada Act, 38–44
Bank of Montreal, 4, 8, 38
Bank records
    access by auditors, 113
    access by Financial Consumer Agency of Canada, 74
    access by Superintendent, 50
    Bank of Canada transactions, 111
    by-laws, 110
    categories to be kept, 109–10
    confidential bank records, 111
    duty to prevent loss, destruction, fraud, theft, 110
    head office as repository, 109
    inspection and seizure, 16
    location of, 109–10
    paper or electronic form, 110
    provincial inspection and seizure, 16
    register of bank securities, 110, 121
    retention of records, 111
    search warrants, 16
    shareholder access to, 109
    shareholders, list of, 111
    who may access, 110
Bankers' drafts
    defined, 390–91
    distinguished from money orders, 389
    legal nature of, 391
Bankers' liens, 248, 251
Banking business
    "additional activities" defined, 149
    "any financial service" defined, 150, 155
    "banking" defined, 1, 6–7, 148–52
    at common law, 6–23, 150
    characterization by courts, 10–23
    from "activities" perspective, 14–23, 148–52
    from "institutional" perspective, 11–14, 21
    incremental approach to defining, 22, 149

"business of banking" defined, 149–50
constitutional issues. *See* Constitutional jurisdiction over banking
consumer protection. *See* Customers, consumer protection
core business, 1–2, 9, 16–18, 149, 152, 156, 171
customer complaints procedures, 31, 73, 181–82, 408
See also Dispute resolution
expansion of activities, 28
history, 3–6, 24
Interac network, 29, 54, 158, 325, 349–53, 368
legal nature, 179
permitted business
 account operation, 20
 acting as financial agent, 155
 acting as receiver or liquidator, 157, 170
 borrowing money, 152
 characterization by courts, 10–23
 charge cards, 156
 computerized payroll services, 19
 creating security interests, 173
 credit-card-balance insurance, 16–17
 credit cards. *See* Credit cards
 credit references and reporting, 18, 214–16
 data processing services, 157
 dealing in insurance. *See* Insurance activities of banks
 dealing in money, 152
 dealing in securities, 29, 156, 171–72
 dealing with real property, 156–57
 deposit taking. *See* Deposit taking
 expansion of activities, 28
 financial advice, 209–12
 generally, 19, 150–59
 indirect activities. *See* Permitted investments by banks
 information processing services, 157
 insurance activities. *See* Insurance activities of banks
 Interac network, 29, 54, 158, 325, 349–53, 368
 investment counselling, 29, 156, 210–12
 investments. *See* Permitted investments by banks
 keeping property. *See* Safekeeping of property by banks
 lending. *See* Loans
 mortgage insurance, 224
 networking, 29, 158
 operating branches, 150–51
 operating subsidiaries, 166
 partnerships with limited liability, 174
 payment cards, 156
 portfolio management, 29, 156
 promoting merchandise and services, 157
 providing guarantees, 155
 real property business, 156
 related party transactions. *See* Permitted self-dealing
 residential mortgages, 28
 security taking. *See* Loans; Special security
 self-dealing. *See* Permitted self-dealing
 selling lottery and transit tickets, 150
 selling securities on default of loan, 158
 selling tax deferral plans, 156
 small business services, 19
prohibited business
 acting as trustee, 243
 commercial and retail business, 170
 creating security interests, 173
 dealing in goods, wares, and merchandise, 170
 dealing in insurance, 172
 dealing in securities, 156, 171–72
 fiduciary activities, 170, 243
 generally, 14, 134, 169–74
 history, 169
 leasing activities, 173
 non-insured deposit taking, 171
 receivership of own property, 174
 unlimited liability partnerships, 174
 sanctions, 169

standard of care, 187–88
ultra vires, 169
Banknotes, 42
Bankruptcy receivership activities by banks, 157
Basle Committee on Banking Supervision, 35, 119
framework for regulatory capital, 119
"Basle II". See Basle Committee on Banking Supervision
Bill C-37 (2006), S.C. 2007, c. 6 (Royal Assent 29 March 2007), An act to amend the law governing financial institutions and to provide for related and consequential matters, 31–32, 84, 121, 129–31, 160, 319
Bill payments
preauthorized withdrawals from accounts, 256, 264, 324, 365, 398
Bills of exchange
Bills of Exchange Act
amendments for cheque imaging, 328–29
history, 3
BIS (Bank for International Settlements), 34–36, 360
Board of directors. See also Directors
committees
audit committee, 95–97
conduct review committee, 95, 97
meetings, 95
resolutions, 95
composition, 92
decisions and acts, validity of, 97–98, 101
dissolution of banks. See Liquidation and dissolution of banks
elections, 93
liquidation of banks. See Liquidation and dissolution of banks
meetings
annual, 93
by telecommunications, 95
notice of meeting, 95
number required, 95
quorum, 95
"resident Canadian" requirement, 95
shareholders' meetings. See Shareholders

Superintendent, involvement by, 96
minutes of proceedings, 94
powers and duties
appoint officers, 96
attend shareholders' meetings, 97
declare dividends, 96, 120–21
delegate powers, 97
establish committees, 96
establish policies and procedures, 96
generally, 94–98
prohibited powers
declarations of dividends, 121
delegations of power, 97
records, 109–10
resolutions, 94–95
deemed consent by director, 95
dissents, 95
validity of acts and decisions, 97–98, 101
Borrowing by banks. See also Trust indentures
deposit-taking, 152
restrictions on borrowing, 152
By-laws of banks
approval by Superintendent, 127
capital structure, 119–20, 127
changes to name, head office, 127
election of directors, 93
filing with Superintendent, 49
generally, 88–91, 95, 98, 100, 114–15
letters patent, changes by, 127–28
meetings, 103–06
records, 109–10
shareholders' right to copies of, 110
voting, 107–08

Caisses populaires, 25, 32–33
Canada Business Corporations Act (CBCA)
relationship to Bank Act, 27, 83
Canada Deposit Insurance Corporation (CDIC). See also Deposit insurance
amalgamated institutions, deposits of, 62
annual inspection of members, 64
auditors of CDIC, 60
compensation to shareholders on insolvency, 67–69
assessor's determinations, 68
review by court, 68

consumer protection. *See* Customers, consumer protection
corporate structure, 59–60
"deposit" defined, 61–62
Deposit Insurance Fund, 63
exempt deposits, 61–62
"insured deposits," 61–62
interventions in failed institutions, 59
liability of CDIC, 63
membership, 64
   required by deposit-takers, 171
objects, 58–61
offences and penalties, 69
powers
   access to records, 63
   application for winding-up order, 67
   appointment as receiver, 66
   assignment of rights in deposits, 63
   cancellation of insurance, 65
   initiation of creditor remedies, 65
   inspection of members, 64
   intervention in failed institutions, 59
   sale of information, 63
   termination of insurance, 65
premiums paid by members, 64
priority of claims, 63
receivership orders, 66
repayment of insured deposits, 62–63
   interest payable, 63
restructuring of insolvent institutions, 66–69
termination or continuance of insurance, 65
winding-up of Corporation, 60
winding-up of insolvent institutions, 66–69
Canada Deposit Insurance Corporation Act, 59–69
Canada Gazette, 43, 67, 68, 84, 91, 140, 141
Canadian Bankers Association
   Bank Circulation Redemption Fund, 52
   dispute resolution services, 77
   membership, 52
   national clearing and settlement system, 5, 52–53
   status and role, 52–53
Canadian Banking Ombudsman (CBO). *See* Dispute resolution
Canadian Banking Ombudsman Inc. *See* Dispute resolution
Canadian Code of Practice for Consumer Debit Card Services. *See* Debit cards
Canadian Depository for Securities Ltd. (CDS), 54, 122, 318
   Debt Clearing System, 54, 318
Canadian Life and Health Insurance OmbudService (CLHIO). *See* Dispute resolution
Canadian Payments Act, 54–58, 145, 317–19, 320
   2001 amendments, 318
   2007 amendments, 319
Canadian Payments Association (CPA)
   ACSS (Automated Clearing and Settlement System), 54, 320–28
   Canadian Payments Act, 54–58, 145, 317–19, 320
   CDS (Canadian Depository for Securities Ltd.), 54, 122, 318
   clearing and settlement. *See* Clearing and settlement systems
   confidentiality of information, 58
   designation of payment system by Minister, 57
   Interac network, 29, 54, 158, 325, 349–53, 368
   LVTS (Large Value Transfer System), 54, 330–33
   membership and governance, 54–55, 260, 316, 331, 333
   Payment Clearing and Settlement Act (PCSA), 317
   Stakeholder Advisory Council, 56
   status and role, 53–58
   supervision by government, 56
   USBES (United States Bulk Exchange System), 318, 329–30
   winding-up by Parliament, 57
Capital structure of banks. *See also* Shares and securities of a bank; Trust indentures
   adequate capital
      Basle Committee on Banking Supervision, 119

Basle II, 119
  guidelines, 118–19
  minimum requirements, 30, 119
  reserves, 2
adequate liquidity, 118
bank shares. *See* Shares and securities of a bank
borrowing. *See* Trust indentures
changes to, 127
debt financing. *See* Trust indentures
equity financing. *See* Shares and securities of a bank
insider trading. *See* Insider trading of bank securities
minimum capital requirements, 30, 118–19
prospectus requirements, 124
reserves, 2
securities. *See* Shares and securities of a bank
shares. *See* Shares and securities of a bank
stated capital account, 120
  adjustments to, 120
  dividends, affect on capital, 121
  reductions contrary to *Bank Act*, 120–21
  shareholders' resolutions re, 120
valuation of assets by Superintendent, 118
CBCA. See *Canada Business Corporations Act (CBCA)*
CBO (Canadian Banking Ombudsman). See Dispute resolution
CCIN (Corporate Creditor Identification Number), 326
CDIC. See Canada Deposit Insurance Corporation (CDIC)
CDS (Canadian Depository for Securities Ltd.), 54, 122, 318
Central banks. See Bank of Canada; Bank for International Settlements (BIS)
Central securities register, 110, 121
  Canadian Depository for Securities Ltd. (CDS), 122
Centre for Financial Services OmbudsNetwork (CFSON). *See* Dispute resolution
Certified cheques. *See* Cheques

CFSON (Centre for Financial Services OmbudsNetwork). *See* Dispute resolution
Charge cards provided by banks, 156
  distinguished from credit cards, 371
"Chartered" banks, 9, 25
Cheque clearing systems. *See* Cheques, cheque clearing systems
Cheques. *See also* Clearing and settlement systems
  as negotiable instruments, 256
  certified cheques, 265–70
  cheque clearing systems, 322–23, 328
  "cheque" defined, 329
  "cheque holds" policy, 290, 324
  cheque imaging, 31, 328–29
  "cheque transaction and electronic clearing," 328
  "cheque truncation" defined, 328
  cheques returned with statements, 327–28
  clarity and unambiguity, 257, 259
  countermand of cheques, 185, 275–79
  customer duty to report forgery, 259
  digital images, 31, 328–29
  dishonoured cheques, 151, 258, 261, 263–67, 271–73, 278, 288–91, 323, 334
  electronic images, 31, 328–29
  Evidence Acts requirements, 329
  fraudulent cheques, 281, 293
  Government of Canada cheques, cashing of, 182
  history, 3
  honouring of cheque where overdraft, 230–31
  MICR (Magnetic Ink Character Recognition), 188, 266, 322, 329
  microfilming of cheques, 322
  paper cheques, 328
  postdated cheques, 264-65
  restricted uses, 188
  retention of cleared cheques, statutory duty of, 328–29
  stale-dated cheques, 273
  stop-payment orders, 185, 275–79
  TECP (Truncation and Electronic Cheque Presentment), 327–28
Civil procedure and evidence, 16
Clearing and settlement systems

Index 459

Bank of Canada, role of, 44, 318, 321
defined, 318
history, 3–5, 38, 256, 260
regulation of payment systems
  Canadian Payments Act, 54–58,
    145, 317, 320
  Canadian Payments Association
    (CPA), 53–58, 316–33
  Payment Clearing and Settlement
    Act (PCSA) (1996), 317–18
  rules and procedures generally,
    260–64, 289–91, 316–43
  by collecting bank. See Collecting
    bank
  by electronic funds transfer.
    See Electronic funds transfer
    (EFT) systems
  by paying bank. See Paying bank
systemic risks, control of, 43–44, 56,
  81, 318, 330–31
systems operated by CPA
  ACSS (Automated Clearing and
    Settlement System), 54, 320–28
  LVTS (Large Value Transfer System), 54, 330–33
  USBES (United States Bulk Exchange System), 316, 329–30
CLS (Continuous Linked Settlement), 332
Collecting bank
  bank as constructive trustee, 217–23,
    238, 243–44, 273, 288, 292, 295
  clearing and settlement system,
    289–91
  dishonoured cheques
    bank right of "charge-back," 291
    duty to ensure prompt return, 290
    notice to payee customer, 290
    reimbursement where overdraft,
      291
    remedies of payee customer, 291
    reversal of provisional credit, 291
  duty to collect on behalf of customer,
    288–91
  liabilities of bank, 288
  no duty to cheque issuer, 288
  presentment of cheque for payment,
    288–91
    "cheque hold" policy of bank, 290
    clearing and settlement system,
      289–91
    damages for unreasonable delay,
      290
    internal "on-us" clearance, 289
    within "reasonable time," 289
  statutory protection of collecting bank
    bank as customer's agent for collection, 292
    bank as "holder in due course,"
      292–95
    bank as insurer of careless customers, 294–95
    defence of fictitious payee, 294
    "delivery" of forged cheque defined, 293
    history, 292
    liability of bank for "conversion,"
      292–93
    liability of bank for restitution,
      295–93
Computerized payroll services, 19
Confidentiality of bank information
  bank's information, 47–48, 50, 71, 78
  Canadian Payments Act information,
    58
  disclosure to FCAC, 71, 73
  disclosure to Ombudsman, 409
  disclosure to shareholders, 109
  exceptions, 73
  Superintendent disclosures, 47–50
Confidentiality of customer information
  bank duty of confidentiality, 177,
    303–14
    at common law, 304
    express permission from customer, 312
    information sharing within banking group, 305
    remedies for breaches, 313
  exception for bank's own interests
    bankruptcy proceedings, 312
    dishonoured cheques, 312
    priority of claims, 311
    protection of bank's reputation,
      311
    suits for repayment of overdrafts,
      311
  exception for credit reporting,
    214–16, 304, 312
  exception for customer consent
    express consent, 312

implied consent, 313
waiver of confidentiality, 185, 214–16
exception for higher public duty
commercial information, 310–11
dangers to the state, 309–10, 314
public inquiries, 310
public vs. private interests, 310–11
exception for statutory disclosures (civil matters)
Bankers' Books Evidence Act (UK, 1879), 307
Evidence Acts, 306, 308
FCAC disclosures, 71, 73
foreign court requests for disclosure, 309
generally, 306–7
Income Tax Act, 308
Mareva injunctions, 307
Superintendent disclosures, 48
Winding-up and Restructuring Act, 308
exception for statutory disclosures (criminal)
Canadian Charter of Rights and Freedoms, s. 8, 307
criminal investigations, 307
foreign court requests for disclosure, 309
illegal activities, 304
money laundering, 78–80, 177, 304, 308–9
Proceeds of Crime (Money Laundering) Act (2000), 78–80
Proceeds of Crime (Money Laundering) and Terrorist Financing Act (2001), 79, 308–9
search warrants, 307
unreasonable search and seizure, 307
generally, 29, 177
industry codes
Canadian Bankers Association, 304
Privacy Model Code, 304
money laundering, 78–80, 177, 304, 308–9
Personal Information and Protection of Privacy Act (2001), 304–5
"secrecy" vs. "confidentiality," 303
Tournier, 303–14

duration and scope of duty, 305
duty of secrecy, 305
waiver of confidentiality, 185
Constitutional jurisdiction over banking
Constitution Act, 1867, 7–21, 24, 32, 37, 83, 165, 317, 378
doctrine of interjurisdictional immunity, 16–18
doctrine of paramountcy, 17
generally, 6–10, 83
provincial jurisdiction. See also Provincial savings offices; Treasury Branches
bank records, inspection and seizure of, 16
deposit taking, 15
evidence and civil procedure, 16
historically, 9–10
insurance, 16–17, 25
search warrants, 16
security taking, 15
stock brokerages, 25
taxation, 15
trust and loan companies, 25
Constructive trusteeship, 217–23, 238, 243–44, 273, 288, 292, 295
Consumer education, 74
Consumer protection. See Customers, consumer protection
Continuous Linked Settlement (CLS), 332
Contract between bank and customer
bank obligations
collect cheques for customer, 186
honour cheques, 186
maintain customer privacy, 186
non-customers, to, 178
provide account statements, 186
repay deposits, 186
take reasonable care, 187–88
branch closures. See Bank incorporation and powers, branch operations, branch closures
common law provisions, 176, 180, 187
confidentiality. See Confidentiality of customer information
contract as "loan," 179
contract of adhesion, 186
customer complaint procedures, 181–82, 185

Index   461

customer obligations
  account reconciliation, 302
  account verification clauses, 298–303
  report fraud, 185–86
  take reasonable care, 185–87
death of customer, 183
disclosure of bank charges, 29, 181
disclosure of borrowing costs, 29, 181
dormant accounts, 185
express terms, 184–86
  backdating of changed terms, 189
history, 175–76
implied terms, 186–88
industry codes, 180
interest rates, 181, 185
legal capacity, 177, 181
low-income account provisions, 177, 181
modifications to contract
  notice requirements, 188–89
  "reasonable notice," 188–89
  reliance on customer signature, 189
  unilateral change by bank, 188
overdrafts, 181, 185
plain language requirements, 182, 352, 409
privacy. See Confidentiality of customer information
proper law of the contract
  jurisdiction of branch location, 190
  split jurisdictions, 190
public accountability statements, 184
standard-form provisions, 185
statutory requirements, 181
termination, 190
  bankruptcy of customer, 192
  death of customer, 192
  fixed date, 191
  insolvency of bank, 192
  mental incapacity of customer, 192
  notice by bank, 191
  notice by customer, 191
  "reasonable notice," 191
  reimbursement of estate, 192
  suspension in time of war, 193
  transfer of funds, 192
  unilateral termination by bank, 191

trust funds, 185. *See also* Trust accounts
unclaimed account balances, 183–84, 232–33
Cooperative credit associations, 2, 32, 55
  ownership by banks, 134, 166
Core banking business. *See* Banking business, core business
Corporate Creditor Identification Number (CCIN), 326
Corporate governance. *See* Auditors of banks; Bank records; Board of directors; Directors; Insider trading of bank securities; Liquidation and dissolution of bank; Officers of the bank; Shareholders
Cost-of-borrowing disclosure, 18
CPA. *See* Canadian Payments Association (CPA)
Credit cards
  absolute vs. conditional payments, 374, 382
  air miles programs, 380
  anti-competitive offences, 379
  bank credit cards, 372
  cancellation of charges, 379
  cardholder and merchant agreement, 381–82
  cardholder negligence, 377
  cardissuer and cardholder agreement, 375–80
    joint and several liability, 376
    liability for unauthorized use, 377
    terms, 375–76
    waiver of privacy for credit check, 375
  cardissuer and merchant agreement, 380–82
    terms, 381
  cardissuer duty to monitor usage, 378
  cardissuer liability for air miles programs, 380
  cardissuer liability for fraudulent use, 378, 381
  clearing and settlement, 382–83
  Competition Act offences, 379
  complaints procedures, 380
  constitutional issues, 378
  consumer protection, 377, 379, 382
  cost of borrowing, 378–79

credit-card-balance insurance, 16–17
"credit card" defined, 372
Criminal Code offences, 379–80
disclosure of interest rates, 181, 378–79
dispute resolution, 380
distinguished from charge cards, 371
history, 371
illegal credit card use, 379–80
insurance for credit card balances, 16–17
interest rate disclosure, 378–79
legal nature, 371–75
lost or stolen cards, 377
merchant's duties, 381
offences for anti-competitive behaviour, 379
permitted business of banks, 156
"private label" cards, 373
provincial legislation, 377, 378
retail cards, 373
retailer duty to ask for ID, 378
reversal of charges, 379
unsolicited distribution of cards, 377
Credit reporting by banks
bank liability for economic loss, 214
commercial vs. fiduciary relationship, 216
jurisdiction, 18
negligent misrepresentation, 214–15
waiver of duty of secrecy, 214
Credit unions, 2
activities of, 12–13
"banking" activities of, 13
constitutional validity of, 13
membership in Canadian Payments Association, 55
national structure, 30
provincial regulation of, 13, 25
Cross-border payments systems, 25
Customers. *See also* Contract between bank and customer; Fiduciary and tortious relationships
bank branch closures. *See* Bank incorporation and powers, branch operations, branch closures
bank-customer relationship, 178
debtor-creditor relationship, 179–80
history, 179
legal nature, 179

bankruptcy of customer, 192
bill payments, 324–26
computer banking, 324
confidentiality. *See* Confidentiality of customer information
constructive trusteeship, 217–23, 238, 243–44, 273, 288, 292, 295
consumer protection
Bank Act, 29, 73
by courts, 185–86
disclosure of bank charges, 29, 181
disclosure of borrowing costs, 29, 181
Financial Consumer Agency of Canada (FCAC), 47, 69–74
privacy of information, 29, 177
Superintendent of Financial Institutions, 41, 44–52
tied selling abuses, 29, 182
contract with bank. *See* Contract between bank and customer
costs of banking services, disclosure of, 29, 31, 181
countermand of cheques. *See* Cheques, countermand of cheques
credit limits, 326, 347, 375, 377
"customer" defined, 176–78
agent for undisclosed principal, 178
banking service where no contract, 178
fraudulent identification, 178
customer complaints procedures, 31, 73–75, 181–82, 185, 408
See also Dispute resolution
bank's duty to refer customers to FCAC, 73, 182
death of customer, 183, 192
debit card transactions, 324–25
deposits. *See* Bank deposits
disclosure of bank charges, 29, 31, 181
disclosure of borrowing costs, 29, 181
dishonoured cheques. *See* Cheques, dishonoured cheques
dispute resolution. *See* Dispute resolution
fiduciary relationship. *See* Fiduciary and tortious relationships
information about customers. *See* Confidentiality of customer information

Index 463

insolvency of bank, 192
liability for loss and damage, 185
low-income accounts, 177, 181
mental incapacity of customer, 192
minimum credit balance, 182
money laundering. *See* Money laundering
non-customers, 177–78
online banking, 324–26
ownership of funds in bank insolvency, 192
preauthorized debits, 324
privacy. *See* Confidentiality of customer information
public accountability statements, 184
reputation of customer, 191, 247, 250, 263, 271–72, 290
responsibilities
   cheques, passbooks, cards, PINs, 185
   inform bank of loss, fraud, forgery, 185, 259
   stop-payment orders. *See* Cheques, countermand of cheques
telephone banking, 324–26
tied selling abuses
   consumer protection, 29, 182
   defined, 182
   mortgage life insurance, 224
unclaimed account balances, 183–84

Debit cards
   ABM terminals, 349
   ACSS clearing of payments, 324–25, 351–56
   bank liability, 355
   bank-merchant contract, 353
   breach of agreement, 354–55
   Canadian Code of Practice for Consumer Debit Card Services. *See* Debit Card Code, Debit Cards
   cardholder agreements, 350, 352–53
   cardholder liability, 354–55
   contractual relationships, 350, 352–53
   debit card as immediate payment, 346, 350
   Debit Card Code, 325, 350, 352
   distinguished from credit card, 354
   distinguished from "smart card," 349
   finality of payment, 355–56
   gifting, 356
   industry codes, 350
   Interac Association, 350–51
      membership, 351
      role and procedures, 351–56
   introduction of, 349
   issuance of card, 354
   liability for unauthorized use, 354–55
   merchant duties and liabilities, 353
   PINs (Personal Identification Numbers), 349, 351–56
   POS (Point-Of-Sale) transactions, 349, 351–56
   regulation of, 350
   right to obtain and use card, 354
   theft of card and PIN, 354–55
   transactions and ACSS clearing, 324–25, 351–56
   unauthorized use, 354–55
Debt financing of banks, 122–24
Department of Insurance, 45
Deposit insurance. *See also* Canada Deposit Insurance Corporation (CDIC)
   history, 33, 58
   provincial schemes, 58, 60
Deposit Insurance Fund, 63
Deposit receipts and passbooks
   ABM receipts, 233
   certificates for term deposits, 235
   duties of bank to provide, 233
   online account statements, 233
   passbooks, 185, 233–35, 296
   status as legal documents, 233
   use as "negotiable instrument," 233–34
   use as proof of gift, 235
   use as security document, 234–35
Deposit taking. *See also* Bank deposits; Deposit insurance; Deposit receipts and passbooks
   as "borrowing," 152, 227
   as core banking business, 1–2, 9, 16–18, 149, 152, 156, 171, 226–27
   bank accounts. *See* Bank accounts
   deposit insurance. *See* Deposit insurance
   depositors, prior rights in winding-up, 123

foreign banks, by, 136
generally, 1–2, 9, 16–18, 149, 152, 156, 171, 226–27
loan companies, by, 33
membership in CDIC, 171
membership in CPA, 260
minimum deposit, 177
"near banks" and non-banks, by, 2, 33
prohibited activities, 171
provincial institutions, 59
Deposits. *See* Bank deposits; Deposit receipts and passbooks
Directors. *See also* Board of directors; Officers of the bank
conflict of interest, 99–101
delegation of powers, 97
disclosure of personal interests, 99–101
  absence from meetings, 100
  business corporations principles, 100
  "material" not defined, 101
  penalties for non-disclosure, 101
  permitted exceptions, 100
  shareholder ratification not required, 101
  timing of disclosure, 100
  validity of contracts, 101
disqualification, 94
duty of care
  best interests of the bank, 99
  business corporations principles, 98–100
  common law duties, 98
  conflict of interest, 99–101
  disclosure of interests, 99–101
  fiduciary duties, 98–99
  objective vs. subjective standard, 99
  proper purpose, 99
  standard of care, 98–101
elections
  by minority shareholders, 93
  by-laws, 93
  cumulative voting, 93
  procedures, 93
  void elections, 93
fiduciary obligations, 98–99
first directors, 90
indemnification, 101–02
  due diligence defence, 102
  good faith defence, 102
  indemnity from legal suits, 102
  liability insurance, 102
  reliance on professional reports, 102
indoor management rule, 89–90
liability of directors, 101–02
  breach of duty, 101
  employee wages, 102
  joint and several liability, 102, 121
  limitation of actions, 102
  restoration of bank losses, 121
  subrogation, 102
meetings. *See* Board of directors
number of directors, 92
powers and activities, 92–94
  See also Board of directors
presumption of authority, 89–90
qualifications, 92
removal from office, 94
resignations, 94
role, 91
shareholders' meetings, right to attend, 97
standard of care, 98–101
Superintendent, actions by, 93–94
term of office
  ceasing to hold office, 94
  failure to disclose interests, 101
  length of term, 94,
  removal from office, 94
under *Bank Act*, 101, 121
validity of acts and decisions, 97–98, 101
Dishonoured cheques, 151, 258, 261, 263–67, 271–73, 278, 288–91, 323, 334
Dispute resolution
ADR (alternative dispute resolution), 403
Bank Act (1991), 74, 403
Canadian Bankers Association, 403
Canadian Banking Ombudsman (CBO), 75–76, 402–3
Canadian Life and Health Insurance OmbudService (CLHIO), 76
Centre for Financial Services OmbudsNetwork (CFSON), 76, 404
codes of conduct, 76

membership, 76, 404
structure and operation, 76, 404–5
contract requirements, 181–82
customer complaints procedures, 31, 73, 181–82, 185, 408
Financial Consumer Agency of Canada (FCAC), 405
General Insurance OmbudService (GIO), 76
MacKay Task Force (1998), 404
model ADR code, 403
Office of the Canadian Banking Ombudsman, 75
Ombudsman for Banking Services and Investments (OBSI)
application requirements, 408
bank's duty to refer customers, 182
bank's own ombudsman, 408
board of directors, 77, 404, 406–7
confidential information, 409–11
excluded complaints, 408–9
history, 30, 74–76, 404, 406
jurisdiction, 408–9
mandate, 77, 405–7
membership, 77, 406
Ombudsman, 77, 406–7
privacy, 409–11
procedures, 407–11
recommendations, 410–11
structure and operation, 76–78, 405–11
Terms of Reference, 406, 408, 410
types of complaints, 411
small business, for, 75, 77, 403, 408
Dissolution of banks. *See* Liquidation and dissolution of banks
Dividends
declaration by board of directors, 120–21
prohibited declarations, 121
Superintendent's approval, 121
Doctrine of constructive notice, 89
Doctrine of interjurisdictional immunity, 16–17
Doctrine of paramountcy, 17
Doctrine of *ultra vires*, 87–88
DTN (Data Transmission Network), 324–26
EDI (Electronic Data Interchange), 324–25

EFT. *See* Electronic funds transfer (EFT)
Electronic funds transfer (EFT) systems. *See also* Automated Clearing and Settlement System (ACSS); International funds transfers; United States Bulk Exchange System (USBES)
Bank of Canada, role of, 44, 318, 321
Canadian Payments Act, 54–58, 145, 317, 320
Canadian Payments Association, 316
constitutional issues, 317
membership 331, 333
infrastructure of system, 315–44
Interac network, 29, 54, 158, 325, 349–53, 368
legal nature of Electronic Funds Transfer (EFT), 337
bank as customer's agent, 339
bank liability for transfer but not identity, 339
banks' duties, 340–41
customer liability for unauthorized access, 339
EFTs as transfer of value, 338–39
EFTs characterized, 338
recovery of funds paid in error, 343
time when payment irrevocable, 341–43
timing of countermane, 341–43
vicarious liability of bank, 340
legal significance for customers
ACSS rules implied in bank-customer contract, 333
LVTS rules implied in bank-customer contract, 333
Minister of Finance, role of, 317
Payment Clearing and Settlement Act (PCSA) (1996), 317–18
regulation of payment systems, 317–19
Electronic money. *See* Smart cards
Electronic payments, 345–69
3PPS (third party payment systems). *See* Third party payment systems
ABM (automated banking machine) card, 349
"cash card," 349
"charge card," 347
cheque guarantee card, 347–48

Cirrus network, 349
credit card. *See* Credit cards
debit cards. *See* Debit cards
"digital cash card," 349
electronic money. *See* Smart cards
"electronic purse," 349, 357
generally, 345–46, 350
Interac network, 29, 54, 158, 325, 349–53, 368
plastic cards, 346–56
  history, 346
Plus network, 349
prepaid cards, 361
retail-issued cards, 346
"smart card". *See* Smart cards
travel and entertainment card, 347
electronic purse, 349, 357
Email Money Transfers, 367
Emoney. *See* Smart cards
Equity financing of banks, 118–22
European Union (EU) banking directives, 28

FATF (Financial Action Task Force on Money Laundering), 79
FCAC. *See* Financial Consumer Agency of Canada (FCAC)
Fiduciary and tortious relationships
  characteristics of, 197
  concurrent applications of doctrines, 194–95
  constructive notice requirement, 200–01
  constructive trusteeship, 217–23, 238, 243–44, 273, 288, 292, 295
    actual vs. constructive knowledge, 221
    duty of bank as trustee, 217–23, 243–44
    duty to inquire into suspicious transactions, 218, 243–44
    "knowing assistance" in dishonest transactions, 218–23
    "knowing receipt" of funds in trust, 218–23
    third parties, prior rights and claims, 217
  defence of good faith, 199
  disclosure of conflict of interest, 195, 198
  duty of care, 193, 195
  duty to life insure mortgages applications by bank, 224
    negligent misrepresentation by bank, 224–25
    remedies for breach by bank, 224
  exception for commercial transactions, 196
  fiduciary obligation generally, 194–97
  giving advice
    commercial sophistication of client, 210–11
    fiduciary duty vs. misrepresentation, 210–11
    fraudulent misrepresentation, 211–12
    investment advice, 195
    negligent misrepresentation, 210–11
    no liability where reasonable practices, 211
  giving credit references, 214
    commercial vs. fiduciary relationship, 216
    liability for economic loss, 214
    negligent misrepresentation, 214–15
    waiver of duty of secrecy, 214
  history, 193
  independent legal advice, 199, 201–5
    liability of lawyer, 203–4
    written confirmation, 203
  misrepresentation
    actions for economic loss, 208–9
    fraudulent, 208, 211–12
    negligent, 193, 208, 210–11, 224–25
  "morally offensive" conduct, 196
  prohibited activities, 170–71
  taking security, 212
    commercial sophistication of client, 213
    independent legal advice, 212–13
    unconscionability, 213
    unequal bargaining powers, 213
    voluntary consent, 212
  trust and confidence, 196, 200–3
  unconscionability, 186, 205, 212–13
    applicable circumstances, 206

defined, 206
  distinguished from undue influence, 206
undue influence, 193, 197–205
  abuse of trust and confidence, 196, 200–3
  actual vs. presumed, 200–1
  by third party, 200
  constructive notice requirement, 200–3
  defined, 199, 201–2
  security for loans, 197–99
  unequal bargaining power, 193, 197, 198, 206, 207, 212–13
Financial Action Task Force on Money Laundering (FATF), 79
Financial Consumer Agency of Canada (FCAC), 47, 69–74
  annual report to Minister, 73
  bank branch closures, 73, 182–83
  bank's duty to refer customers, 73, 182
  Commissioner, 70–71
    appeals to Federal Court, 72
    decisions of Commissioner, 72
  confidentiality of information, 71
  consumer education, 74
  consumer protection, 69–74
  customer complaints procedures, 31, 73, 181–82, 408
  Financial Consumer Agency of Canada Act, 69–73
  history, 69–70
  limitation of actions, 72
  objects, 70
  powers
    access bank records, 74
    enter into compliance agreements with banks, 74
    obtain evidence under *Inquiries Act*, 74
    require information from banks, 73
    require public meeting re branch closure, 183
  structure and operation, 47, 70–71
  violations and penalties, 72
Financial institutions regulation. *See* Regulation of financial institutions

Financial statements, 126–27
Financial Transactions and Reports Analysis Centre of Canada (FINTRAC), 78
Financing of banks. *See* Capital structure of banks
FINTRAC (Financial Transactions and Reports Analysis Centre of Canada), 78, 79
Foreign Bank Entry Policy: Consultation Paper (1997), 136n
Foreign banks
  2001 *Bank Act* amendments, 136–39
  2007 *Bank Act* amendments, 31–32
  "authorized foreign bank" (Part XII.1, Sch. III bank)
    defined, 137
    branches in Canada, 138
    permitted activities, 137–39
    prohibited activities, 137–39
    purchase of domestic bank assets, 128
  Bank Act as charter of foreign banks, 137
  "foreign bank" (Part XII, Sch. II bank)
    defined, 137
    permitted activities, 137–39
    prohibited activities, 137–39
  Foreign Bank Entry Policy: Consultation Paper (1997), 136
  directors, qualifications of, 92
  history, 28–29
    1980 *Bank Act*, 136
    pre-1980 regime, 136
  incorporation, 85–86, 136–39
  MacKay Task Force (1998), 136
  meetings, 95
    quorum, 95
    "resident Canadian" requirement, 95
  status and powers. *See* Bank incorporation and powers, status and powers
  subsidiaries, 25, 30, 85–86, 92, 95, 137–38
Foreign currency, 228.
"four pillars," 9, 11, 28–29, 33–34, 130
Funds transfer networks. *See* Electronic funds transfer (EFT) systems

General Insurance OmbudService (GIO), 76
Globalization of business, 308–9
Globalization of crime, 308–9
Guaranteed Investment Certificates (GICs), 31

Holding companies. *See* Bank holding companies
Hydrocarbons and minerals, lending by banks. *See* Loans, loans on hydrocarbons and minerals

IIPS (Interbank International Payment System), 330
Identity theft, 368, 372
Independent legal advice, 199, 201–5
Indoor management rule, 89–90
Insider trading of bank securities
   civil liability
      ambiguities in *Bank Act*, 126
      compensation for losses, 125–26
      limitation periods, 126
   "insider" defined, 125–26
   prohibited trades, 125–26
      exception for convertible shares, 126
   reports to Superintendent, 125
   exemptions from reporting, 125
Insolvency. *See* Liquidation and dissolution of bank
Insurance activities of banks
   credit-card-balance insurance, 16–17
   dealing in insurance, 172
   insurance companies
      ownership by banks, 133-34, 166
      membership in Canadian Payments Association, 55
      regulation of, 16–17, 32-33
   mortgage insurance, 172, 224-25
   prohibited activities, 172
   travel insurance, 172
Interac network, 29, 54, 158, 325, 349–53, 368
Interac Email Money Transfers, 367
Interbank clearing and settlement. *See* Clearing and settlement systems
Interbank International Payment System (IIPS), 330
Interest
   Criminal Code, s. 347(1), 229–30
   "criminal rate" defined, 229
   disclosure of calculation method, 181
   disclosure of rates, 181, 230
   "interest" defined, 229
   interest on bank deposits, 228
   interest on overdrafts, 231–32
   interest-rate ceilings, 229
   provincial legislation, 229–30
Interjurisdictional immunity, 16
International funds transfers
   SAP (SWIFT Access Point), 335
   SWIFT (Society for Worldwide Interbank Financial Telecommunication), 53, 330–31
   liability for breaches, 336
   membership, 335
   procedures, 335–37
   rules, 336
   SWIFT II, 335
International Monetary Fund, 35–36
International regulation of banks, 25, 34–36
   Bank for International Settlements (BIS), 34–36, 360
   Basle Committee on Banking Supervision, 35, 119
      framework for regulatory capital, 119
   "Basle II". *See* Basle Committee on Banking Supervision
Investment counselling by banks. *See also* Securities dealers; Securities sales by banks
   commercial sophistication of client, 210–11
   fiduciary duty vs. misrepresentation, 210–11
   fraudulent misrepresentation, 211–12
   generally, 156, 195
   negligent misrepresentation, 210–11
   no liability where reasonable practices, 211
Investment Dealers Association of Canada (IDA), 77
Investment Funds Institute of Canada (IFIC), 77
Investment products
   Guaranteed Investment Certificates (GICs), 31
   term deposits, 31

Index 469

Joint accounts. See Bank accounts, joint accounts
Large Value Transfer System (LVTS)
BIS (Bank for International Settlements), 331
Bank of Canada, role of 330–31
CLS (Continuous Linked Settlement) system, 332
credit limits, 332
IIPS (Interbank International Payment System), 330–31
LVTS Rules, 330, 334
membership, 331
procedures, 331–33
real-time systems, 330–31
risks and risk management, 332–33
rules, 330, 334
SWIFT (Society for Worldwide Interbank Financial Telecommunication), 53, 330–31
"tranches" procedures, 331
Law Commission of Canada, 160, 165
Lending by banks. See Loans
Letters of credit, 392–93
Liquidation and dissolution of bank. See also Receivership of bank
approval of Minister, 67, 139–46
Canadian Payments Act, 145–46
CDIC (Canada Deposit Insurance Corporation)
application for restructuring, 66
application for winding-up, 67
approvals by Minister, 67
as deemed creditor, 63, 67
as receiver, 66
right to remaining assets, 63
role of, 62–63, 66–68
compensation to shareholders, 67–69
assessor's determinations, 68
review by court, 68costs, 60
court-supervised voluntary liquidation, 140–41
application to court, 140
Bank of Canada, role of, 142–43
costs, 141
final accounting, 142
letters patent dissolving bank, 142
liabilities of shareholders, 142
liquidator, role of, 141–42
notices required, 141
orders of the court, 140–41
property and money to Crown, 142
Superintendent, role of, 140
customer funds, ownership of, 62–63, 192
directors, role of, 140–46
dissolution by letters patent, 139, 142
"inability to pay debts" defined, 143
inactive bank, dissolution of, 139
"insolvency" defined, 143
insured deposits, 62–63
liquidator, role of, 144
payment of creditors' claims, 145–46
petition by CDIC for winding-up, 67
petition to court for winding-up, 144
priority of claims, 63, 123, 145–46
receivership orders, 66–67
repayment of insured deposits, 62–63
restructuring transactions by CDIC, 66–67
shareholders, role of, 139–46
Superintendent taking control of bank
determination of viability, 66
duration of control, 143
liquidator, role of, 144
petition to court for winding-up, 51, 144
request for winding-up, 143
suspension of director's legal role, 143
winding-up order by court, 144
suspension of director's legal role, 143
voluntary liquidation, 139–40
winding-up order by court, 144
Liquidator activities by banks, 157
Loans. See also Deposit taking; Interest; Security for loans; Special security; Trust and loan companies
bank account overdrafts, 181, 230–32
bank deposits. See Deposit taking
disclosure of borrowing costs, 29, 31, 152, 181
duties to borrower, 153
interest. See Interest
lines of credit, 181
loan companies, 33
loans on hydrocarbons and minerals, 158–59

loans on receivers or liquidators,
  158–59
loans to related parties (self dealing)
  approval by directors, 169
  full disclosure requirements, 169
  "related party" defined, 167
minimum credit balance, 177, 182
repayment
  exceptions for line of credit, 153
  "reasonable notice" requirements,
    153
restrictions on lending powers, 152
security for loans. *See* Security for
  loans; Special security
terms to be negotiated, 152–53
LVTS. *See* Large Value Transfer System
  (LVTS)

MacKay Task Force (1998), 30, 75, 84,
  129, 132–33, 136, 404
MICR (Magnetic Ink Character Recognition), 188, 266, 322
Minerals, lending by banks. *See* Loans,
  loans on hydrocarbons and minerals
Minister of Finance
  oversight role
    Bank of Canada, 39–40, 183
    Canada Deposit Insurance Corporation (CDIC), 59, 64–67
    Canadian Payments Association,
      54–58
    Financial Consumer Agency of
      Canada, 69, 71, 73
    Superintendent of Financial Institutions, 46–50
  supervision of banking sector, 37, 130
    amalgamation of banks, 128
    bank holding companies, 134–35
    bank investments, 166
    changes to banks, 127
    control of payment systems,
      317–19
    customer complaints, 75, 404
    foreign banks, 136–43
    incorporation of banks, 84–85, 91
    ownership and control of banks,
      129–32
    sale of bank assets, 128
    self-dealing, 168

Minister of National Revenue, 79–80
Money laundering
  drug trafficking, 79
  duties of bank
    disclose suspicious transactions,
      80
    monitor nature of deposits, 217
  Financial Transactions and Reports Analysis Centre of Canada
    (FINTRAC), 78
  Financial Action Task Force on
    Money Laundering (FATF), 79
  money order requirements, 389
  *Proceeds of Crime (Money Laundering)
    Act* (2000), 78–80
  Proceeds of Crime (Money Laundering) and Terrorist Financing Act
    (2001), 79
  terrorism financing, 79
Money Mart, 389
Money orders
  countermand not available, 389–90
  defined, 388
  distinguished from bankers' drafts,
    389
  distinguished from postal orders, 389
  legal nature of, 388–89
  Money Mart, 389
  postal money orders, 389–90
  Western Union, 389
Mortgages, residential
  generally, 28, 33, 152, 154
  mortgage insurance
    applications by bank, 224
    duties of bank, 224–25
    negligent misrepresentation by
      bank, 224–25
    remedies for breach by bank, 224
  preauthorized payments, 324
Mutual Fund Dealers Association of
  Canada (MFDA), 77

"Near banks." *See also* Credit unions;
  Provincial savings offices; Treasury branches; Trust and loan
  companies; Trust companies
  regulation of, 32–33
Negotiable instruments, 122
Night safe depositories, 400–1

Index 471

Non-banks. *See* Credit unions; Provincial savings offices; Treasury branches; Trust and loan companies; Trust companies
OBSI (Ombudsman for Banking Services and Investments). *See* Dispute resolution
Office of the Canadian Banking Ombudsman, 75
Office of the Inspector General of Banks, 45
Office of the Superintendent of Financial Institutions (OSFI). *See* Superintendent of Financial Institutions
Office of the Superintendent of Financial Institutions Act, 44–52
Officers of the bank
　disclosure of personal interests, 99–101
　　business corporations principles, 100
　　"material" not defined, 101
　　permitted exceptions, 100
　　shareholder ratification not required, 101
　　timing of disclosure, 100
　　validity of contracts, 101
　duty of care, 98
　　best interests of the bank, 99
　　business corporations principles, 98–100
　　common law duties, 98
　　conflict of interest, 99–101
　　disclosure of interests, 99–101
　　fiduciary duties, 98–99
　　objective vs. subjective standard, 99
　　proper purpose, 99
　　standard of care, 98–101
　indemnification, 101–2
　　due diligence defence, 102
　　good faith defence, 102
　　indemnity from legal suits, 102
　　liability insurance, 102
　　reliance on professional reports, 102
　liability of officers, 101–02
Ombudsman for Banking Services and Investments (OBSI). *See* Dispute resolution
Online banking account statements
"On-us" clearances, 262, 277, 289, 322, 333, 365–66, 368
OSFI (Office of the Superintendent of Financial Institutions). *See* Superintendent of Financial Institutions
Overdrafts. *See* Bank accounts, overdrafts
Ownership of banks. *See also* Bank holding companies; Permitted investments by banks
　2001 amendments to *Bank Act*, 30, 129–30
　2007 amendments to *Bank Act*, 32, 129–30
　assimilation of financial sector, 130
　breaches and enforcement, 132
　"control" defined, 131
　criteria for ownership, 128–32
　foreign alliances, 30, 130
　holding companies. *See* Bank holding companies
　Minister of Finance, role of, 129–32
　ownership vs. control, 130
　prohibited shareholdings, 129–30
　"significant interest" defined, 130
　Superintendent, role of, 131–32
　three-tier ownership regime, 32, 129–30
　　large banks, 129–31
　　medium-sized banks, 129–31
　　small banks, 129–31

Palm prints, 357
Passbooks, 185, 233–35, 296
Paying bank
　bank's duty of care, 257
　bank's exercise of discretion, 259
　cheques
　　clarity and unambiguity, 257, 259
　　customer duty to report forgery, 259
　　stale-dated cheques, 273
　certified cheques, 260
　　bank's discretion and liability, 267, 270
　　certification as "acceptance" for payment, 268–69
　　"certification" defined, 266
　　procedures, 265–70

remedies for lost cheques, 270
validity of certification, 267
clearing and settlement system, 260–64
countermand orders from customers
  accuracy requirements, 277
  duties of care, 278
  forms of countermand, 276
  liability of bank, 278
  timing, 276–77
  validity of countermand, 275–76
  who has authority to countermand, 275–76
customer's instructions, 257
  bank's duty to obey, 278
dishonoured cheques
  notice requirements, 271
  sufficiency of funds, 257–58
  wrongful dishonour, 271–73
overdraft policies, 257–58
postdated cheques
  customer right to countermand, 265
  generally, 264–65
  liabilities of bank, 265
presentment of cheque for payment, 259–60
  clearing and settlement system, 260–64
  internal "on-us" clearance, 262
  order of payments, 263
  when cheque "irrevocably paid," 261–63
recovery of money paid by mistake
  claims for restitution, 284
  defence of change of payee position, 287
  defence of estoppel, 286–87
  defence of good consideration, 286
  history, 284–85
  liability of bank to customer, 284
stop-payment orders. *See also* Paying bank, countermand orders from customers sufficiency of funds, 257–58
termination of bank duty to pay
  bankruptcy of customer, 275
  countermand by customer, 275–79
  garnishment order from court, 274
  Mareva injunction, 274

  mental incompetency of customer, 274–75
  notice of customer's death, 274
  stale-dated cheques, 273
  "stop-payment order," 275–79
wrongful dishonour of cheques
  assessment of damages, 271–73
  damage to reputation, 271–73
  duty of care to third party, 272–73
  tort of defamation, 271–73
wrongful payment by bank
  careless conduct by customer, 279–80
  defence of discharge of customer debt, 283
  defence of estoppel, 279–80
  defence of ratification by customer, 282
  fraudulent cheques, 281
  liability of banks, 279–83
  types of wrongful payment, 279
Payment cards provided by banks, 156
Payment Clearing and Settlement Act (PCSA), 44, 317–18
PCSA. *See Payment Clearing and Settlement Act (PCSA)*
Pension plans, regulation of, 32–33, 45, 172
Permitted business. *See* Banking business, permitted business
Permitted investments by banks
  approvals from Minister and Superintendent, 166
  cooperative credit societies, 133–34, 166
  divestment of unsafe investments, 167
  history, 165
  insurance companies, 133–34, 166
  limits on value of investments, 166–67
  restrictions on acquisitions, 166
  stock brokerages, 133–34, 166
  trust and loan companies, 33, 133–34, 166
Permitted self-dealing
  approvals by Superintendent, 169
  conduct review committee, role of, 97, 167
  full disclosure requirements, 169
  loans to related parties, 168–69

approval by directors, 169
permitted transactions, 168
prohibited transactions, 168
"related party" defined, 167
Personal identification numbers. *See* PINs (Personal identification numbers)
PINs (Personal Identification Numbers)
cardholder agreements, 353, 375–77
customer responsibility, 185, 325, 353, 355, 375–77
Debit Card Code, 352
debit card transactions, 324–25, 351–52
electronic payments, 346
retail transactions, 324–25, 351–52
unauthroized use, 354–55
Plain language requirements, 182, 352, 409
Plastic cards, 346
Point-Of-Sale (POS), 158, 322, 324, 345
Portfolio management by banks, 156
Postal money orders, 329, 389
Postdated cheques, 264
Preauthorized bill payments, 256, 264, 324
Preauthorized debit (PAD) system, 365, 398
Pre-emptive rights. *See* Shareholders, pre-emptive rights
Prepaid cards, 361
"closed loop cards," 361
"Dexit" cards, 362
"open loop" cards, 361
payroll cards, 362–63
deposit insurance, 362
use in Canada, 363
prepaid telephone cards, 361
retailer electronic gift cards, 361
"speedpass" fuel cards, 362
stored-value cards, 362
"Taxi Dollars," 362
toll highway transponders, 362
Privacy. *See* Confidentiality of bank information; Confidentiality of customer information
Proceeds of Crime (Money Laundering) Act (2000), 78–80
Proceeds of Crime (Money Laundering) and Terrorist Financing Act (2001), 79

Prohibited business. *See* Banking business, prohibited business
Promissory notes, 3, 8, 317, 384, 391
Prospectus requirements for bank financing, 124
Provincial jurisdiction. *See* Constitutional jurisdiction over banking
Provincial savings offices
"banking" activities of, 14
constitutional validity of, 13–14
provincial regulation of, 13–14
Provincial treasury branches. *See* Treasury Branches
Proxies. *See* Shareholders, proxies
Public Accountability Statements Regulations, 184n

Receivership of bank. *See also* Liquidation and dissolution of bank
application by CDIC for winding-up order, 67
approvals by Minister, 67
CDIC as creditor, 67
CDIC as receiver, 66–67
compensation to shareholders, 67–69
assessor's determinations, 68
review by court, 68
receivers and liquidators
loans from banks, 158
permitted activities of banks, 157
prohibited activities, 174
receivership orders, 66–67
restructuring transactions, 66–67
Records. *See* Bank records
Recovery of money paid by mistake, 284
Register of banks, 49
Register of securities, 110, 121–22, 318
Regulation of financial institutions. *See also* Minister of Finance; Superintendent of Financial Institutions
consumer protection. *See* Customers, consumer protection
control of fraud, 81
control of systemic risk, 43–44, 56, 81, 318, 330–31
generally, 5, 32
international regulation, 34
management of monetary policy, 81
Related party transactions. *See* Permitted self-dealing

Residential mortgages. *See* Mortgages, residential
RESP (Registered Education Savings Plan), 156
RHOSP (Registered Home Ownership savings Plan), 156
RRIF (Registered Retirement Income Fund), 156
RRSP (Registered Retirement Savings Plan), 156

Safekeeping of property by banks
  bailee duties of banks, 397–99
  death of customer, 183
  generally, 157, 395–401
  involuntary bailment, 395
  night safe depositories, 400–01
  remedies for breaches, 399–401
  "safekeeping" defined, 396
  safety deposit boxes, 398–99
  securities, 395
  standard of care, 397
Safety deposit box, 398–99
Sale of Tax Deferral Plans, 156
Schedule I bank. *See* Bank incorporation and powers
Schedule II bank. *See* Foreign banks
Schedule III bank. *See* Foreign banks
Search warrants, jurisdiction over, 16
Securities commissions, regulation of, 32
Securities dealers
  membership in Canadian Payments Association, 55
  ownership by banks, 134, 156, 166
Securities sales by banks
  commercial sophistication of client, 210–11
  fiduciary duty vs. misrepresentation, 210–11
  fraudulent misrepresentation, 211–12
  investment advice, 195
  investment counselling, 156, 210–12
  negligent misrepresentation, 210–11
  no liability where reasonable practices, 211
  ownership of stock brokerages, 134, 156, 166
  permitted activities, 156, 158
  portfolio management, 156
  prohibited activities, 171

Security for loans. *See also* Special security
  banker's liens, 251–52
  death of customer, 183
  duties of bank, 197–205
  fiduciary relationship with clients, 212–14
    commercial sophistication of client, 213
    independent legal advice, 212–13
    unconscionability, 213
    undue influence, 197–205
    unequal bargaining powers, 213
    voluntary consent, 212
  insurance for credit card balances, 16–17
  passbooks as valid security documents, 234
  priority of claims, 160, 164–65
  provincial legislation, 15–16, 160
  registration of security, 155
  sale of securities in default, 158
  special security for natural products. *See* Special security
  tortious actions by banks, 212–14
  types of security
    personal property, 154–55
    real property, 153–54
    residential mortgages, 154
Self-dealing. *See* Permitted self-dealing
Settlement of payments systems. *See* Clearing and settlement systems
Shareholders
  access to financial statements, 127
  access to records, 109–11
  approval and remedial rights, 115
    amalgamations, 128
    changes in capital structure, 127
    changes in name, head office, 127
    generally, 115–16
    sale of bank assets, 128
  auditors. *See* Auditors of banks
  election of directors, 93
  liability of, 117, 142
  list of shareholders
    access to, 111
    "basic list," 111
    preparation of, 111
    prohibited uses, 111
  meetings, 103

agenda, 105
attendance by directors, 97
attendance by proxy holders, 108
attendance by Superintendent, 104
called by court, 104
called by directors, 103
called by shareholders, 103–4
fixing of record date, 104
location, 103
notices, 104–5
required business, 105
shareholders' proposals, 105–6
"special business," 105
power to remove directors, 94
pre-emptive rights
common law rights, 114
new share offerings, right to, 114, 119
no right except by by-law, 114
restrictions on rights, 114–15
proposals from shareholders
board refusal to circulate, 106
board requirement to circulate, 105
content and requirements, 105–6
proxies
appointment of proxy holder, 107–8
attendance at meetings, 108
codification in *Bank Act*, 107
common law practices, 107
false or misleading proxies, 108
form of proxy, 108
management proxy circular, 105
solicitation by bank, 108
quorum requirements, 106
rights and remedies
court applications, 109
derivative actions, 115–16
oppression remedy, lack of, 116
rectifying bank records, 116
right to grant approvals, 115
right to copies of by-laws, 110
shareholder liability, 117, 142
shareholders' auditors. *See* Auditors of banks
special resolutions
changes to bank name, head office, 127
dissolution of inactive bank, 139

generally, 105
liquidation of solvent bank, 140
sale of assets, 128
stated capital account, 120
unanimous shareholder agreements, 109
voting
management proxy circular, 105
proxies, 107–09
quorum, 106
right to vote, 104
rules, 107
written resolutions in lieu of meeting, 107
Shares and securities of a bank. *See also* Capital structure of banks
bank holding own shares
redemption of shares, 120
stated capital account, adjustments to, 120
by-laws re shares, 119–20
Canadian Depository for Securities Ltd. (CDS), 122
central securities register, 110, 121–22
classes of shares, 119
consideration for acquiring, 119–20
conversion of "debt obligation" to shares, 120
conversion privileges, 120
distribution of securities
approval by Superintendent, 124
certifications by CEO, CFO, 124
prospecture requirements, 124
underwriters, 124
dividends paid in shares, 121
prohibited dividends, 121
Superintendent's approval, 121
insider trading. *See* Insider trading of bank securities
market value of, 119
options and rights to acquire, 120
paper share certificates, 121–22
as negotiable instruments, 122
pre-emptive rights of shareholders, 114–15, 119
"security," 122
"security certificate," 122
transfer of, 122
series of shares, 119

"share" defined, 118
stated capital account, adjustments to, 120
voting rights, 119
Small business services
accounting services, 19
dispute resolution, 75, 77, 403, 408
generally, 400
Smart cards
closed "institutional" systems, 358
digital fingerprints, 357
digital signature keys, 357
distinguished from credit card, 356
distinguished from debit card, 356
"electronic purse," 349, 357
emoney defined, 356
forms of, 356
legal nature of
characterization of, 360
transfer of stored value, 360
whether "money," 359–60
Mondex "open" system, 358
"originator" bank, 358
POS (Point-Of-Sale) payments, 357
privacy of information, 357, 359
regulation of, 360–61
reloading cards, 357–58
retinal scans, 357
security of information, 357, 359
"smart card" defined, 357
theft or loss of card, 357, 359
transactions and clearing, 357–59
Visa Cash "open" system, 358
Society for Worldwide Interbank Financial Telecommunication (SWIFT), 53, 330
Special security. *See also* Security for loans
administration, 31
assignment by bank, 165
conditions to be met, 161
eligible borrowers, 160–61
enforcement for non-payment, 162–63
seizure and sale of property, 163
exploitation of natural resources, 160
harmonization of *Bank Act* and provincial Acts, 160
legal nature of special security, 161
floating charge or chattel mortgage, 161–62

manufactured property, right to, 163
offences, 164
priority of claims
exceptions for bankruptcy orders, 165
federal vs. provincial legislation, 160, 165
generally, 164–65
provincial regulation of, 15–16, 160
registration of security
Bank of Canada, 162
cancellation, 162
land registry office, 162
"special security" defined, 160
Stock brokerages, 25, 33
membership in Canadian Payments Association, 55
ownership by banks, 134, 156, 166
Stop-payment orders. *See* Cheques, stop-payment orders
Subordinated indebtedness. *See* Trust indentures
Superintendent of Financial Institutions
administration of Office, 46–47
annual report to Minister, 48
Bank Act, 48–52
confidentiality of information
customer information, 48
industry information, 47
permitted disclosures, 47–48, 50
conflict of interest guarantees, 48–49
consultation committee, 47
duties and roles
actuarial advice to government, 45
annual report to Minister, 50
consumer complaints, 403
disclose confidential information, 47–50
ensure solvency of banks, 49, 121, 139
examine banks annually, 50
monitor related party transactions, 48
monitor risk management, 45
monitor securities activities of banks, 48
monitor self-dealing, 48
obtain annual reports from banks, 49
pension plan oversight, 45

protect confidential information, 47–50
provincial institutions, review of, 45
register of banks, 49
supervise financial institutions, 45
generally, 44–52
history, 44, 403
liability, exemption from, 48
OSFI Act, 44–52
penalties for non-compliance, 48
powers
    approve bank amalgamations, 128
    approve bank changes, 127
    approve bank dividends, 121
    approve bank requests, 49
    approve sale of bank assets, 128
    attend bank board meetings, 96
    direct bank to remedy unsound conduct, 50–51
    disqualify and remove bank officers, 51
    enforce bank compliance, 51
    examine bank records, 50
    intervene in unsound institutions, 45
    obtain evidence under *Inquiries Act* powers, 50
    prudential agreements with banks, 51
    request winding-up of banks, 51
    require bank board meetings, 96
    take control of banks, 51–52
    valuation of bank assets, 118
    status within government, 46
Superintendent, appointment of, 47
SWIFT (Society for Worldwide Interbank Financial Telecommunication). *See* International funds transfers, SWIFT

Task Force on the Future of the Canadian Financial Services Sector (1998). *See* MacKay Task Force
Tax Deferral Plans, 156
TECP (Truncation and Electronic Cheque Presentment), 327–29
Term deposits, 31, 65, 183–84, 191, 231, 233, 235, 249
Third party payment systems (3PPS)
    ACSS, role of, 365–69
    barcodes and scanners, 364
    bill payment systems, 365
    CertaPay service, 367
    contracts, 369
    eBay purchases, 367
    EDI (electronic data interchange), 364
    epurses, 366–69
    fraud or unauthorized transactions, 368
    HyperWallet system, 366
    identity theft, 368
    Interac Email Money Transfers, 367
    inventory systems, 364
    mobile phone payments, 368–69
    mpayments, 368–69
    "on us" bill payment services, 365–66
    online banking, 365
    PAD (preauthorized debit) system, 365
    PayMint parking payments, 369
    PayPal service, 367
    regulation of, 363–64
    risks for banks, 368
    risks for consumers, 369
    TelusMobility purchases, 368
    transactions and clearing, 364
    unauthorized transactions, 368
Thomas Cook travellers' cheques, 385
Tied selling. *See* Customers, tied selling abuses
Tortious relationships. *See* Fiduciary and tortious relationships
Tournier, 305–14
Tranches, 331–32
Travellers' cheques, 383–87
    bank as agent, 387
    bank liabilities, 387
    clearing and settlement, 384
    history, 383
    legal nature of, 384
    lost or stolen cheques, 384–85
    refunds, 385–86
    signature requirements, 384, 386
    thefts from issuing bank, 387
    traveller's duties, 385
    whether "cheques," 383
Treasury Branches
    "banking" activities of, 14
    constitutional validity of, 13–14

provincial regulation of, 13–14, 32
Truncation and electronic cheque presentment (TECP), 327–29
Trust accounts, 242
    bank as constructive trustee, 217–23, 238, 243–44, 273, 288, 292, 295
Trust and loan companies
    federal regulation of, 11
    history of, 32–33
    membership in Canadian Payments Association, 55
    ownership by banks, 33, 166
    provincial regulation of, 11, 25, 32
    status as "banks," 2
    Trust and Loan Companies Act (1991), 9
Trust companies
    activities of, 12
    "banking" activities of, 12–13
    constitutional validity of, 12
    history of, 32–33
    membership in Canadian Payments Association, 55
    provincial regulation of, 12, 25, 32
    trust indentures. *See* Trust indentures
Trust indentures
    defined, 122–23
    security holders, 123
    subordinated indebtedness, 123
    trustees
        conflict of interest, 123
        duties, 123
        trust companies, 123
Trusteeship, constructive, 217–23, 238, 243–44, 273, 288, 292, 295

Ultra vires doctrine, 87–88
Unconscionability in bank's dealings with customer, 205
Undue influence of bank on customer, 193, 197–205
United Kingdom electronic clearing systems, 337
United Nations Commission on International Trade Law (UNCITRAL), 53
United States Bulk Exchange System (USBES)
    ACSS Rules Manual (Rule K1), 329
    clearing and settlement procedures, 329
    purpose, 318
    U.S. dollar accounts, 329–30
United States payment transfer systems, 336–37
    CHIPS (Clearing House Interbank Payments System), 336
    Fedwire (Federal Reserve), 336–37
"Universal banking," 28–29, 31, 34, 84

White Paper (2006), 31
White Paper on the Revision of Canadian Banking Legislation (1975), 27
Winding-Up and Restructuring Act (WURA). *See* Liquidation and dissolution of bank
Winding-up of bank. *See* Liquidation and dissolution of bank
World Bank, 35–36
World Trade Organization, 35–36
Wrongful dishonour of cheques by paying bank, 271
Wrongful payment by paying bank, 279
WURA (*Winding-Up and Restructuring Act*). *See* Liquidation and dissolution of bank

ABOUT THE AUTHOR

M.H. Ogilvie is Professor of Law and Chancellor's Professor at Carleton University in Ottawa, and a member of the Bars of Ontario and Nova Scotia. Dr. Ogilvie is a graduate of Trinity College, Toronto, the University of Oxford, and Dalhousie University, and has been a Visiting Scholar at the Universities of Edinburgh, Emory, Princeton, Oxford, and Toronto. She was elected a Fellow of the Royal Society of Canada in 1993; awarded the David W. Mundell Medal in 1996, and the Law Society Medal in 2001; and was the first Chancellor's Professor appointed at Carleton University in 2002. Dr. Ogilvie is the author of numerous books and articles on Banking Law in Canadian and international law journals and is a member of the editorial board of the Banking and Finance Law Review and the Banking Law Specialist Editor of the Canadian Business Law Journal. She has been a director of the Canadian Payments Association since 2002.